India's Immortal Tale
Of Adventure, Love, and Wisdom

Ramayana

Retold by
KRISHNA DHARMA

TORCHLIGHT
PUBLISHING

First printing 1998
Second printing 2000
Third printing 2004
Fourth printing 2008
Fifth printing 2012

Cover design by Yamaraja Dasa
Illustrations by Bhaktisiddanta
Interior design by Christopher Glenn / Glenn Graphics
Printed in India

Published simultaneously in the United States of America
and Canada by Torchlight Publishing, Inc.

Library of Congress Cataloging-in-Publication Data

Krishna Dharma, 1955-
          Ramayana : India's immortal tale of adventure, love, and
      wisdom / Krishna Dharma.—Updated and revised ed.
                p. cm.
        Originally published: 1998
        ISBN 978-1-887089-22-7
        1. Rama (Hindu deity). I. Valmiki. Ramayana
      BL 1139.25 .K75 2000
      294.5'92204521—dc21   99-053808

**Attention Colleges, Universities, Corporations, Associations, and
Professional Organizations:** *Ramayana* is available at special discounts for bulk
purchases for fund-raising or educational use. Special books, booklets, or excerpts
can be created to suit your specific needs.

Torchlight Publishing, Inc.
For more information, contact the Publisher.
P. O. Box 52, Badger CA 93603
Email: torchlightpublishing@yahoo.com
www.torchlight.com

DEDICATED TO
HIS DIVINE GRACE A. C. BHAKTIVEDANTA
SWAMI PRABHUPADA,
BY WHOSE TEACHINGS
I HAVE LEARNED TO LOVE THE
RAMAYANA.

CONTENTS

Part One: Betrayed

Part Two: Exiled

Part Three: War

Line Illustrations

Prologue

Part One

Part Two

Part Three

INTRODUCTION

R*amayana* is the first of the great epics of ancient India. It is written in the tradition of the Vedas, following the wisdom of those timeless Sanskrit scriptures. Originally compiled by the sage Valmiki, it is famous as the *Adi Kavya*, or the original poem. Its origins are lost in distant antiquity, although followers of the Vedic tradition say it was first composed around 880,000 B.C. Of course, many modern scholars and scientists will undoubtedly take issue with that claim. It matters little, though, when it was written—*Ramayana* remains one of the most moving and beautiful stories of all time. It tells the history of Rama, a king who appeared in the solar dynasty, the line descending from the sun-god Surya. Rama and his wife Sita are said by the Vedas to be manifestations of Vishnu and Lakshmi, who are accepted as the Supreme Person and His eternal consort. Rama is described as the seventh of the ten avatars, or incarnations of Vishnu, who appear in the current cycle of ages.

The book can thus be read on different levels. On one level it is simply a wonderful story. For lovers of tales like *Lord of the Rings*, it is an account of fantastic happenings in a world of magic and mysticism, a world where humans lived alongside other, more powerful beings and where human society itself possessed knowledge of divine forces now unknown.

For those fascinated by different cultures, *Ramayana* graphically depicts the so-called Vedic age, a time when great warrior kings ruled the world, guided by spiritually aware mystics and saints. It was an age when men lived in the understanding that they were eternal souls, passing from life to life towards a state of final emancipation. Thus, the pursuit of virtue and truth was considered paramount, and human life was seen as an opportunity to attain spiritual liberation—freedom from the cycle of birth and death.

But for those who accept the divinity of Rama, *Ramayana* becomes a different affair. If Rama is accepted as God, then it may be questioned: Why does he appear? What is he doing as he moves about the earth, seeming to act exactly like an ordinary man?

Such questions are answered in the renowned spiritual treatise, *Bhagavad-gita*, The Song of God. Therein it is stated that God appears in this world for different reasons. He comes to establish religion and to destroy demonic elements in society when they become too powerful. But he also appears in order to reciprocate the love of his devotees. It is this last fact which is most significant and which is said to be the primary reason for the Lord's appearance. The *Bhagavad-gita* explains that the Lord has no material purpose to fulfill when he appears. He is not acting in the same way as ordinary men who are interested in material gains such as profit, fame, and adoration. Nor does the Lord have any political purpose. He is simply acting out of love.

If *Ramayana* is studied with this in mind, it becomes an immensely profound and deeply moving literature. The various interactions between Rama and the other characters are seen in a different light—a light of divine loving sentiments that can touch the very soul of the reader.

I shall leave you to judge for yourself. However you view *Ramayana*, I am confident you will find it enjoyable and uplifting. I have read it at least a dozen times and am still finding great pleasure in reading it again and again. I hope you will also experience the same joy from this book.

KRISHNA DHARMA DAS
SEPTEMBER 1999

PROLOGUE

Coursing through the sky in his celestial chariot, Ravana appeared like a blazing comet. His dark body shone with a brilliant aura. From his ten heads his reddish eyes darted about, scouring the mountains below. His twenty powerful arms hanging from his huge frame looked like five-hooded serpents. Seated on a throne of gems he directed his golden chariot by thought alone and it moved swiftly over the Himalayan range.

The demon was out on his conquests. All around him flew thousands of Rakshasas, clutching swords, barbed spears, spiked maces and iron bludgeons, all of those weapons smeared with blood. Some Rakshasas had the heads of tigers, some of donkeys and some of fierce fiends. Others appeared in their natural forms: large blackish bodies, fearful faces with tall pointed ears and rows of sharp fangs, with a mass of red hair on their heads. They wore iron breastplates studded with gems and were adorned with bright gold earrings and other shining ornaments. Surrounding Ravana they looked like dark clouds with lightning covering the sun.

Ravana wished to defeat in battle even the gods themselves. Wanting to establish his supreme power in the universe, he had gone to the higher planets and conquered hosts of Gandharvas and Yakshas, powerful celestial fighters. Now he was returning from his victorious fight with Kuvera, his own brother and the treasurer of the gods. That lordly deity had been made to retreat by Ravana, losing to the demon his wonderful chariot, known in all the worlds as the Pushpaka.

The fearless Ravana, overlord of all the demons, looked down from the Pushpaka at the forests below. It was a picture of tranquillity. Amongst the trees were many verdant clearings covered with varieties of wild shrubs and forest flowers. Crystal waterfalls cascaded onto many coloured rocks. Lakes filled with lotuses and swans shone from the mountain plateaus as the hordes of Rakshasas soared overhead.

Sometimes the demons would see groups of rishis, ascetic brahmins who dwelt in those high mountain ranges, practising austerities and worshipping the gods. They would see the columns of smoke rising up amongst the trees from the sacrificial fires tended by the sages. Using their powers of sorcery the Rakshasas dropped down volumes of blood, faeces and urine, defiling the sacrifices. They would then hurl huge boulders and blazing coals, crushing and burning the sages where they sat in meditation. Finally the demons would themselves descend, howling and roaring. They tore apart the bodies of the rishis, drinking their blood and devouring their flesh.

Ravana admired the Pushpaka as it proceeded according to his will. His brother Kuvera would be sorry to lose such a splendid vehicle. It looked more like a city of the gods floating in the air than a chariot. Numerous cat's-eye and crystal pillars ran along its sides, supporting golden mansions inlaid with coral. Large floors made entirely of gems stood upon gold statues of lions and tigers. Groves of artificial trees, shining with golden leaves and fruits, surrounded large ponds crowded with white lotuses. In those clear ponds stood ivory elephants and silver goddesses. Networks of pearls and wreaths of celestial flowers hung all over that car. It was encrusted with countless precious stones and emblazoned with gold carvings of wolves, sharks, and fierce bears. Sweeping through the skies it emitted the sounds of celestial music and the fragrance of the parijata flower, known only to the gods.

As Ravana sat idly aboard the chariot, gazing around at the magnificent scenery below, he suddenly noticed a lady sitting in meditation. This was most unusual. Women were rarely seen in those mountains. Sometimes the rishis would have their wives with them, but this woman seemed to be entirely alone. Ravana slowed the chariot and moved down to look more closely. Perhaps there were more ascetics nearby. The Rakshasas could use a little entertainment. And, if this woman was as beautiful as she seemed at first glance, so could he.

Ordering the Rakshasas to wait in the sky, Ravana himself rose up from the chariot and descended to the ground. He saw the young ascetic girl sitting on a flat piece of soft grassland surrounded by wild flowers. She glowed with a golden beauty. Her limbs were exquisitely formed and her full breasts were covered by a black deerskin. Ravana could see the contours of her tapering thighs through the thin cloth covering her crossed legs. Dark locks of thickly matted hair hung down to her waist, framing her white-complexioned face. Her red lips moved slightly as she intoned the sacred syllable Om. Her smooth golden arms were bared in front of her as she sat with folded palms, her long curling lashes covering half closed eyes.

Ravana's mind was overpowered by lust. Who was this youthful lady? What was she doing here in such a lonely place? Did she have a protector? Never mind. He would soon deal with that. The forest was no place for such a maiden. She would make an excellent addition to his other consorts.

By his mystic power Ravana assumed a human form and approached the girl. He spoke loudly, disturbing her reverie. "O most beautiful maiden,

The girl fully opened her black eyes and looked at Ravana.

who are you? Why are you practising asceticism in this lonely region? To whom do you belong? What fortunate man has you for his wife?"

The demon was unable to resist the charms of women. As he gazed upon the alluring form of the girl he was possessed by increasing desire. He laughed and waited for her to reply.

The girl fully opened her black eyes and looked at Ravana. Seeing him as a guest in her hermitage she spoke respectfully, telling him her name. She was Vedavati, the daughter of a powerful sage, who was himself a son of the gods' preceptor, Brihaspati. Looking down in shyness she said, "I was born as an incarnation of the holy Vedas. My father was sought by numerous gods and other celestial beings who wished to have my hand in marriage. However, none but Vishnu, the Lord of all the worlds, can be my spouse. Thus I am seated here, absorbed in thought of the Lord and awaiting his favour."

Vedavati had meditated for thousands of years. Her body, like that of the gods, neither aged nor required any sustenance. She could understand by her own inner vision who Ravana was and what was his intention. In gentle tones she said that only Vishnu could be her husband. That inconceivable Lord was all powerful and all seeing and she had chosen him alone. She could not belong to anyone else. Ravana should continue on his way as before.

Ravana laughed again. He was not going to leave behind this jewel of a woman. Hearing the name of Vishnu, his sworn enemy, only made him all the more determined. The demon's voice boomed like thunder. "Your resolution to practise austerity befits only old women, O lady of shapely limbs. Why do you waste your fleeting youth in this way? I am Ravana, lord of the Rakshasas, the very mighty race of demons. Become my wife and live with me in my capital, Lanka, the golden city I forcibly seized from the gods. Who is this Vishnu anyway?"

Ravana spoke derisively of Vishnu, whom he knew to be the Lord of all the gods. The arrogant demon cared nothing for any universal authority. He had been granted boons by Brahma, the creator of the universe, who had so blessed the Rakshasa that he could not be killed by practically any created being, neither god nor demon. Ravana could assume forms at will. Vedavati's mention of Vishnu did not bother him in the least. He stood smiling before the maiden, his eyes full of lust.

Hearing Ravana deride Vishnu, Vedavati flared up with anger and rebuked the demon. She told him to leave immediately for his own good, lest he incite the powerful anger of that supreme deity.

Ravana smiled. This high-spirited woman would make a perfect consort for him. He stepped forward and grabbed hold of her long locks.

Vedavati at once uttered a powerful Sanskrit mantra which momentarily checked the demon's advance. She lifted a hand and by her mystic power cut through her hair. The Rakshasa fell back in surprise as she spoke furiously.

"O evil one, I shall now quit this body defiled by your touch! As I have been insulted by you I shall take birth again only for your destruction. Appearing from the earth, I shall become the pious daughter of a virtuous man. You and your entire race will be destroyed as a result of that birth."

Vedavati closed her eyes and meditated on Vishnu, seeing him within her heart. Before Ravana's eyes she invoked fire from within herself. Her body was immediately consumed by flames and in a few moments Ravana stood looking at her ashes. Baffled by her words, the disappointed demon rose again to his chariot and continued on his way.

The demon and his Rakshasa followers spent some time in the Himalayan mountains, wreaking havoc amongst the many ascetics living there. Gradually they approached the far northern region where there lay Mount Kailash, the abode of Shiva. As the Pushpaka began crossing that mountain, it was suddenly brought to a halt. Ravana was surprised and he descended to the ground, surrounded by his ministers who accompanied him on the chariot. As he gazed around at the brilliant scenery on the mountainside, he saw a strange being with a monkey's head.

The creature appeared dreadful, with a dark yellowish complexion and misshapen features. Although his body was large, he had a dwarfish stature. He was clean shaven and muscular and he stood holding a large glowing pike. As he gazed at Ravana, the demon called out to him. "Who are you and where is this region? Why have I been impeded?"

"I am Nandi, the servant of Shiva," replied the unusual being. "You have arrived at Shiva's abode, which is inaccessible to all created beings. You will not be able to pass this mountain. Therefore turn back and go the way you have come."

Ravana looked at the strange body of Nandi and laughed out loud. He spoke in a derisory voice. "Why should I heed you, O monkey-faced one? Who is this Shiva anyway?"

Hearing his master insulted infuriated Nandi. Raising his pike, which shot forth tongues of fire, he exclaimed, "O Rakshasa, I should kill you at once but I will not do so, as you already stand killed by your own sins. But I say this, as you disregard me in my monkey form, there shall be born on earth many monkeys of terrible strength who will annihilate your race."

As Nandi spoke the sound of heavenly drums reverberated in the sky and a shower of flowers fell. Ravana's eyes flamed in anger. Disregarding the

curse, he roared, "I shall remove this hill from my path. What do I care for
you and your master?"

The Rakshasa immediately plunged his twenty massive arms deep into
the side of the hill. He began tearing it up and it slowly rose above the earth,
shaking violently. As the hill shook, Shiva's consort, Parvati, slipped from
her position and clung to her husband. Shiva reassured her, "Do not be
afraid. This is the action of the vain demon Ravana. I shall deal with him
shortly. He cannot harm you."

Parvati's eyes turned red as she replied to her powerful husband. "As
this wretch has frightened a woman by his violence, his death shall be
caused by a woman."

Shiva stood up and pressed down upon the hill with his toe. Ravana at
once felt an unbearable pressure. His arms, which resembled huge pillars
holding the hill, were crushed. He let out a tremendous cry that resounded
throughout the three worlds of heaven, earth and hell, terrifying all beings.
He was trapped by the weight of the mountain and could not move.

The Rakshasa's ministers at once surrounded him and advised him to
appease Shiva. "We have heard how that all-powerful one is easily pleased.
Offer him prayers and seek his compassion at once. Surely he will be gracious to you."

Ravana, who had made a study of all the scriptures, began reciting
hymns from the Samaveda in glorification of Shiva. But even after a hundred years had passed the Rakshasa still remained trapped. Although in
great pain, he continued offering prayers to Shiva. Finally Shiva relented
and relieved Ravana of the pressure. He appeared before the demon and
spoke kindly. "O ten-headed one, your prayers have pleased me. Do not be
so rash again. Leave now and go wherever you like."

Ravana bowed to the god, who stood holding his famous trident. The
crescent moon shone from his head and a large serpent was coiled around
his blue neck. He gazed at Ravana with his three eyes as the demon folded
his palms to address him. "My lord, if you are actually pleased with me then
please give me your weapon."

Shiva smiled. Ravana's lust for battle would prove to be his destruction
before long. Saying, "So be it", Shiva raised his palm in benediction and
immediately vanished from that spot. Ravana felt the mantras for invoking
Shiva's powerful Pashupata weapon appear within his mind. He smiled.
Who could resist such power? Even he had been unable to overcome Shiva.
The great deity was surely worthy of his worship.

Ravana mounted the Pushpaka, which had waited in the sky all the
time he was trapped. Being unable to proceed further to the north he turned
back southwards, still accompanied by his numerous Rakshasa forces. As he

moved across the Earth, seeking further martial engagements, he came upon the city of Ayodhya. This was the capital of the world of humans. The emperor of the earth dwelt there and Ravana considered him as fit for a fight. If he conquered this king then the whole earth would be subjugated.

Ravana had little interest in human affairs-the Rakshasas were a superior race of beings more on a level with the gods-but the demon wanted to establish his supremacy over all beings. His army of Rakshasas surrounded the city, challenging the emperor to battle.

A fierce fight ensued between the two armies of Ravana and the Ayodhya king, Anaranya. Tens of thousands of chariots and elephants came onto the battlefield, along with hundreds of thousands of foot soldiers. Showers of arrows, like swarms of black bees, fell upon the demons. Anaranya's army threw lances, darts, steel bullets and iron maces by the million. They swept towards the enemy, shouting courageously with their weapons raised.

Ravana's forces used sorcery to appear and disappear at will, flying in the sky and hurling down rocks and sharp weapons. The king's army replied with showers of swift and deadly arrows. Using powerful catapults the warriors threw at the Rakshasas large iron darts which whistled through the air. But Anaranya's fighters could not easily engage with the elusive demons. Although they rushed forward, slashing at the enemy with their blue steel swords, the soldiers found themselves cleaving the air as the Rakshasas rose into the sky. The Rakshasas, who towered over their human foes, would then suddenly descend behind the soldiers, cutting them down with razor-sharp scimitars.

Gradually the demons overpowered the king's army. The battlefield became strewn with the mangled bodies of Anaranya's troops. Blood flowed in waves upon the ground. Heads rolled on the earth with their golden earrings flashing and their teeth clenched in fury. Large and well-muscled arms, still clutching broad swords and lances, lay severed amidst the entrails of slain warriors. The demons sent up great shouts as they hacked down the king's army.

Anaranya himself exhibited great prowess. He knew the secrets of the celestial weapons and by invoking those divine missiles he killed innumerable Rakshasas. When the demons hid using their sorcery, he released the Shabda weapon of sound, which found them wherever they were. As hordes of Rakshasas rushed at the emperor, he let go the wind weapon which lifted the demons and hurled them far away. Anaranya was difficult to look upon as he stood in his chariot releasing his weapons. They fell upon the Rakshasa forces like blazing meteors. But the demons far outnumbered the humans. Although hard pressed by the king, the Rakshasas responded with more and more sorcery, vanishing into the sky and entering the earth. Eventually Ravana's hordes completely annihilated their enemies and Anaranya stood alone against the demons.

Seeing all his forces consumed like so many moths entering a fire, the emperor became infuriated. He went towards Ravana, who had stood by in a war chariot as his Rakshasas fought with the soldiers. Anaranya took up his great bow and let loose eight hundred fierce arrows, which sped like flames of fire towards Ravana. By the incantations of Anaranya those arrows were imbued with the power of thunderbolts. The king fired them so swiftly that they flew in a long line, almost end to end. They struck Ravana furiously on his heads and chest, sounding like claps of thunder. But the demon did not flinch in the least.

Angered by the king's sudden attack, Ravana took up a terrible looking mace. He whirled it above his head with such force that it glowed bright orange and threw off tongues of fire. He flew with the speed of a tempest towards the emperor and struck him a great blow on the forehead. The king fell from his chariot and lay bleeding on the ground. The Rakshasa began laughing and deriding the fallen monarch.

"What is the use of fighting with Ravana? There is none who can face me in battle and remain alive. Clearly you are a foolish man, too much addicted to wine and women. Thus you have not heard of my unassailable power."

Ravana continued insulting the dying king, mocking his ancestral line in which the earth's emperors had appeared for thousands of years. Anaranya looked up at the demon with eyes red from anger. Gasping for breath as his life slipped away, he spoke with difficulty. "I have not been killed by you, O vile Rakshasa. Death is certain and comes to all beings according to their destiny. None can be killed before their fate decrees, nor can any be saved when their time has arrived. I am thus killed by my own fate. Do not indulge in self-praise, Ravana, for your own death will soon come."

The emperor possessed mystic power, gained by his long practise of austerity. He was loath to waste that accumulated power on Ravana, but the demon had to be checked. The dying king could at least do something before he departed. Anaranya fixed his fading gaze on the lord of Rakshasas and, concentrating his mind, he uttered a curse. "In the very line you now deride, O Ravana, there will soon appear a king who will kill you and all your race!"

As Anaranya spoke the sound of kettledrums was heard resounding in the sky, and a shower of celestial flowers fell upon him. Heavenly voices were heard to say, "It shall be so." Having delivered his curse the emperor slumped to the ground, his life spent. Before the eyes of the demon, Anaranya left his body and rose upwards to the heavens, his ethereal form glowing like fire.

Ravana snorted derisively. Who cared for the curse of some puny being? What human could ever kill him? He only bothered fighting with them by way of idle sport. Anaranya's curse was simply the insane words of a dying man. It could never come to pass. If any kings dared challenge him they would meet the same end as this one here. As for the celestial voices, well, he would soon deal with those arrogant deities.

The demon again mounted the Pushpaka, which was stationed in the sky. Not being interested in pillaging the paltry wealth of a human city, he left and soared up into the heavens. Perhaps there were some gods around who could put up a better fight.

Ravana went up to the heavenly planets inhabited by the principal gods. But the gods swiftly ran away, unwilling to encounter him in battle. They knew of the inviolable boons of Brahma. It was pointless fighting the demon. The gods prayed to Vishnu, hiding themselves in fear.

Ravana decided to rest for a while in heaven. He went to Amaravati, the city of Indra, king of the gods. As the Rakshasa was seated in the celestial Nandana gardens, he saw an Apsara, a heavenly nymph, named Rambha. The face of that celestial girl shone with incomparable beauty and she was adorned with bright garlands and jewels. Her soul-captivating eyes glanced here and there and her fleshy hips swayed as she moved. Ravana gazed upon her large round breasts and shapely thighs. Her hands, soft like rose petals, pulled her shining blue dress tight around her body as she saw the demon staring at her.

Ravana assumed a godly form of great splendour, concealing his terrible ten-headed body. He sprang to his feet and quickly went over to Rambha, immediately taking her by the hand. Completely overcome by lust, he smiled at the celestial girl. "Where do you go and whose are you, lovely lady?" he asked. "Who will today enjoy the nectar of your soft, red lips? Who will be blessed by the touch of your tender breasts? Which fortunate man will lie tightly embraced by you, his mind completely captured by carnal delights?"

Ravana was not at all concerned whether she was married or not. He had stolen the wives of gods, Gandharvas and demons everywhere, taking them to Lanka to join his harem. The Rakshasa was accustomed to having his way and spoke only in an attempt to win over Rambha. He praised her divine beauty and told her of his own power and glory. What woman would refuse the opportunity to become the consort of the mighty Ravana?

But the beautiful girl did not reciprocate his advances. She pulled away from him, her bright bracelets falling to the ground as she wrested herself from Ravana's grasp. Folding her palms and looking down, she addressed the Rakshasa reproachfully. "Please do not speak in this way. I am as good as your daughter and I therefore deserve to be protected by you, O Ravana. Indeed I am the wedded wife of another."

Rambha told him she was married to a god, Nalakuvara, who was the son of Kuvera, Ravana's own brother. She was thus related to Ravana and he should not make amorous advances towards her.

Ravana laughed loudly. He had no regard whatsoever for any moral codes. He moved towards Rambha who ran behind a golden bush. Ravana pursued her, pulling off his red silk robes and revealing his immense, lustrous body. The maiden tried to evade him, dodging here and there with her garland and necklaces swinging, but it was useless. Taking hold of Rambha the Rakshasa forcibly laid her across a nearby rock. He snatched off her garments and began ravishing her, his eyes expanded in delight. Rambha cried out for help, but seeing the fierce Rakshasa no one dared intervene. The demon's powerful hands pinned the white arms of the maiden against the rock. Her dark hair fell in disarray, its golden clasps and flowers dislodged. Ravana violently molested her in front of his demon followers. Although she begged him to desist, the Rakshasa took that struggling heavenly girl against her desire.

After Ravana had sated his lust he stood up, fastening his waist cloth. Shedding tears, Rambha backed away from the demon and fled. Her clothes torn and her garlands crushed, she went before her husband. When he saw her in that condition Nalakuvara became infuriated. But when he heard it was Ravana who had raped her, he felt helpless. The demon had already defeated Nalakuvara's powerful father, who was supported by innumerable Yaksha warriors. There was no possibility of facing Ravana in a fight. Nalakuvara considered the situation carefully. Although he could not fight the demon, he could at least curse him as a result of his evil act. The righteous curses of the gods invoked the infallible power of Vishnu. Considering this the only means of punishing Ravana, Nalakuvara touched holy water and then uttered his imprecation.

"This evil Rakshasa has violated a celestial lady. If he ever again rapes another maiden he will immediately fall dead."

Ravana soon heard of that curse. He had seen such curses, made by gods and rishis, come to pass many times. Once uttered they could not be retracted. Although he did not like to accept it, Ravana could understand that some powerful force maintained the universal order and laws. Thinking it possible that Nakakuvera's words might just be effective, he decided not to again force himself upon another female. Better not to take any chances. After all, there were enough women who would willingly accept him.

Being disappointed that no gods would fight with him, Ravana left the heavenly planets. He began heading for the southern quarter of the universe, where lived the Danavas and Daityas, the most powerful celestial demons. Surely they would afford him battle. Who else was there left for him to conquer?

As Ravana flew in the Pushpaka he suddenly saw ahead of him the celestial seer, Narada, shining brightly and holding his tamboura. The seer plucked the strings gently, singing the praises of Vishnu. Ravana had met him many times before and was pleased to see him. The Rakshasa usually had little time for sages, especially devotees of Vishnu. He preferred to kill and eat them rather than speak with them. The rishis and seers generally favoured the gods, but Narada was different. He would often give Ravana good advice and seemed to be his well wisher. Ravana raised a hand in salute to the sage.

The seer came before Ravana and greeted him. Narada could travel freely anywhere in the universe. It was even said that he could leave the material worlds and journey to Vaikuntha, the spiritual abode of the Lord himself, which knows no decay and is free of all suffering. Narada smiled at Ravana. His large eyes were like two shining sapphires. On his head his coiled golden hair was held in place by a jeweled silver band. Clad in the soft skin of a black renku deer, Narada stood in the air in front of Ravana, who invited him onto the chariot. Sitting cross-legged on a golden seat next to the demon, the seer began to address him in gentle and pleasing tones.

"Why are you harassing this world of humans, O valiant one? It is already in the grip of death. These people do not deserve to be attacked by you, Ravana, who cannot be overcome by even the entire heavenly host united together. Who would destroy people who are wracked by numerous anxieties, surrounded by endless calamities, and are subject to old age and hundreds of diseases?"

Narada told Ravana that everyone in the material world would in time go to the abode of Yamaraja, the great lord of death. There was no need for Ravana to kill them. Death conquers all. Even the gods would eventually succumb to death. If Ravana should conquer Yamaraja the entire universe would be conquered.

The sage knew that Ravana could not overpower Yamaraja. But he wanted to distract the demon from his evil aim of killing more people and overthrowing the gods. He also wanted the Rakshasa to greatly increase his sinful actions by assailing the god of Death. Ravana would thus create for himself a karmic destiny which would soon result in his own destruction.

The demon pondered Narada's suggestion. This sounded interesting. He liked the idea of fighting with the immensely powerful Yamaraja. Perhaps this would be a battle worthy of him. And if Death himself were slain then the whole universal order would be cast into utter chaos! That appealed to Ravana, who wanted to assert himself over any and all powers in the universe. He nodded slowly at Narada, who sat smiling at him. Ravana told the sage he would leave immediately for Death's abode. As Narada rose up into the sky, playing upon his tamboura, Ravana began heading towards the domain of Yamaraja, the god of justice.

As Ravana approached the ethereal region known as Yamaloka, he saw everywhere living beings reaping the fruits of their actions. He also saw the millions of soldiers and servants of Yamaraja, known as the Yamadutas. They appeared fierce and unapproachable. Their bodies were powerful but hideously deformed, covered all over with black hairs that stood erect. In their hands they held nooses and terrible weapons. Their faces were contorted into frightful expressions and they yelled and shrieked in dissonant tones. Moving swiftly, they struck and tortured people who were running in all directions.

Fearful screams and cries resounded everywhere in that dark and desolate place. Ravana saw in hundreds and thousands people being eaten up by fierce dogs, consumed by fires, or being hurled into vats of boiling oil by the Yamadutas. Other unrighteous men and women were running here and there on burning sands, being pursued by Yamadutas holding lances and tridents. Some were being dragged through trees with leaves like steel razors that shredded their bodies. Howling in terrible pain they would fall to the ground, but their bodies would again become whole. They would then leap up and race off, only to be quickly caught by the Yamadutas and put through the same suffering again.

Ravana witnessed innumerable kinds of punishment being meted out to sinful souls. Searching for Yamaraja, he coursed on rapidly in the Pushpaka. In other parts of that mystical and indescribable region, Ravana saw people enjoying celestial delights by virtue of their own good deeds. It seemed as though they were situated in a separate dimension of space and time. Beautiful heavenly landscapes stretched out into the distance. Large shining mansions stood next to clear blue lakes. Young men and women with highly attractive forms were dressed in golden garments and ornaments, embracing one another and laughing. Excellent food and drink was laid out on gold and silver tables. Musicians played and young girls danced. Ravana saw countless people intoxicated with pleasure and entirely oblivious to the scenes of suffering elsewhere.

Leaving behind that glowing region of happiness, Ravana continued deeply into Yamaloka. He crossed over the broad Vaitarani river, which flowed with blood and excrement, and came to another dark terrain where countless Yamadutas were relentlessly pursuing wicked persons. The terrible cackles of the Yamadutas echoed there, along with the howls of jackals and wolves. Everywhere stood people who appeared emaciated and pale, seized with unbearable thirst and crying out for water.

Descending from his chariot, Ravana began to beat back the Yamadutas, freeing the people they were punishing. He felt no compassion for the pain of others, but he calculated that by oppressing the Yamadutas he would cause Yamaraja to appear. As the demon freed many thousands of wretched persons from their tormentors, he was suddenly attacked by a massed force of Yamadutas. They assailed Ravana with spears, iron bars, steel clubs, pikes, javelins and maces. They rose up and began demolishing the seats, daises, pillars and houses on the Pushpaka. But the indestructible chariot was immediately recreated by the power of Brahma, by whom it had first been fashioned.

Ravana's Rakshasa forces fought back against the Yamadutas. Millions upon millions of servants of Yamaraja advanced in great waves. They rained down an unlimited number of arrows and other fierce weapons upon Ravana and his followers. The Rakshasas engaged with the Yamadutas, sending up their terrible war cries. The clash of weapons and the shouts of the warriors sounded like the roaring ocean tossed by a storm.

Leaving off the other Rakshasas, the Yamadutas concentrated upon Ravana. Covered all over with their arrows and bleeding profusely, the demon king appeared like a great mountain giving forth streams of red lava. Using his knowledge of mystical weapons, the Rakshasa returned volleys of arrows, spears, maces, rocks and huge trees. This fearful and deadly shower fell upon the forces of Yamaraja who stood in front of Ravana.

By whirling their maces and lances the Yamadutas repelled all Ravana's missiles and surrounded him in thousands. They appeared like a mass of carnivorous ants around a large black beetle. Ravana became completely covered by darts and lances piercing every part of his body. He roared in anger and pain, quickly rising upwards from out of the midst of his assailants.

Descending to the ground he held his bow and placed upon it a blazing arrow. The demon invoked the power of Shiva, imbuing the arrow with the divine force of that immortal god. As the weapon was released a sheet of fire rushed across the ground, consuming Yamaraja's forces. Enormous orange and white flames leapt in all directions, burning the Yamadutas' bodies to ashes. The ground itself became molten and the forces of Yamaraja fell back in a confused mass.

In the flames'wake came innumerable ghostly followers of Shiva, filling the earth and sky with their terrifying forms. They rushed about the battle-field striking fear into the Yamadutas' hearts. By the power of Shiva's weapon, waves of fearsome carnivorous beasts sprang up from the ground, howling horribly and tearing at the Yamadutas.

Ravana sent up a victory cry, making the ground shake. Hearing that shout, Yamaraja, seated in his palace, could understand that Ravana was overpowering his forces. He ordered his chariot to be fetched and quickly mounted it. Yamaraja stood in his stupendous chariot with a lance and mace in his hands. Angered, the great god burned with a glaring radiance. By his side stood the personified form of Kaladanda, the infallible rod of Death, his body a brilliant black and his eyes blazing like two red fires. On the other side of Yamaraja stood the very Time Spirit himself, the destroyer of the worlds, fearful in appearance. Standing together those three deities could not be countenanced. On all four sides of the chariot, which looked like a dark mountain, hung the frightful nooses of Death.

Drawn by a thousand red and black steeds shining with a bright luster, and having a thousand great wheels, the celestial chariot advanced with a terrible noise. Seeing that god moving off in anger, all the denizens of heaven trembled.

In an instant Yamaraja 's chariot arrived at the spot where Ravana stood roaring. Ravana's followers immediately fled in all directions simply upon seeing that awful chariot. Some of them fell unconscious on the spot. But Ravana himself was not afraid. Seeing his awful adversary he felt over-joyed, anticipating the fight. The demon stood firm as Yamaraja hurled at him many blazing javelins and iron clubs. They struck Ravana with tremen-dous force, piercing him and causing streams of blood to flow from his body.

Ravana raised his bow to counter Yamaraja's attack. Using sorcery, he fired thousands of straight-flying arrows imbued with the force of a thun-derbolt. Those arrows struck Yamaraja all over his body, but the god remained unmoved. Again and again Ravana fired off his arrows and darts, charging them with celestial power. He struck all three deities with his fiery weapons, but they stood firm. Yamaraja sent back at the demon countless barbed lances which struck him violently on the breast. Stunned by those irresistible weapons, Ravana fell unconscious to the ground. Yamaraja, observing the rules of fair combat, did not further attack his overpowered enemy.

After some time Ravana came back to his senses and saw Yamaraja still stationed before him. He contemplated his next move. This was indeed a formidable opponent. Rarely was the demon extended in a fight. Ravana rallied himself and stretched his bow to full length, releasing celestial arrows which filled the sky. They fell upon Yamaraja like fiery serpents. Being assailed by those arrows, and bleeding profusely, Yamaraja roared in anger. As he opened his mouth, fire covered by billows of smoke issued forth. The whole region was brilliantly illuminated by that fire, as if the sun itself had risen in that ever-dark place.

Witnessing the astonishing battle between Yamaraja and the Rakshasa, the gods assembled above them. They feared that the dissolution of all the worlds was imminent. Yamaraja's anger would surely annihilate the entire universe.

Ravana continuously sent his furious weapons towards the three gods. Death personified, highly enraged by Ravana, then spoke to Yamaraja. "My lord, do not exert yourself further. Let me remain alone here with this Rakshasa. I shall make short work of him. None in the past, no matter how powerful, have been able to overcome me. Every god, rishi and demon has succumbed to my power. Indeed, all created beings must surely submit to me. There is no doubt about this, therefore you need not bother yourself with this wretch any longer. Leave him to me."

Yamaraja had become infuriated by Ravana's insolence. He felt insulted and he told Death to stand back, for he personally would destroy the demon. The god lifted up his mace and gazed upon Ravana. As it was raised, that mace threw off a halo of blazing fire. Yamaraja held it in his hand like the globe of the sun and he fixed his red eyes on the demon. Just as he was about to release the mace to destroy Ravana, Brahma appeared before him. He was seen and heard only by Yamaraja as he spoke to the angry god.

"O immeasurably powerful one, this Rakshasa is not to be killed by you at this time. Indeed I have conferred upon him a boon that he cannot be slain except by a human. This cannot be falsified, lest the order of the universe be cast into chaos. Therefore hold back your mace. Ravana is not yet destined to die. If you release your infallible mace upon this demon, it will result in the death of all other created beings."

Long ago Ravana had pleased Brahma by performing difficult asceticism and had won from the god a boon. Brahma had granted Ravana immunity from being slain by any beings, except for humans or animals, whom Ravana utterly disregarded.

Hearing that command of Brahma, the chief of the gods, Yamaraja lowered his mace. Realising that nothing could be accomplished by him in that battle, he then and there disappeared from Ravana's sight. When he saw Yamaraja depart, the Rakshasha considered himself victorious and roared in joy. Now he was surely the most powerful being in the universe. What was there left to prove? Even the great lord of death had run away from him.

Ravana looked around and saw that the slain Yamadutas had been brought back to life by Yamaraja's power. Ignoring Ravana they continued their grisly task of meting out punishment. Ravana felt he had no further purpose to achieve in Yamaloka. He had established his supremacy and that was all he desired. It was time to return to Lanka, his golden city. Getting aboard the Pushpaka he left that region, followed by his forces, and flew to the north, heading again for the earth planet where Lanka was situated.

PART ONE

BETRAYED

CHAPTER ONE

KING DASARATH'S LONGING

King Dasarath paced his palace balcony. His handsome brow was furrowed. In a pensive mood, he surveyed the scene around him. People thronged the inner courtyard below. Feudal kings and princes came with their retinues to pay tribute. From his seventh-story terrace Dasarath could see much of his city, which stretched to the horizon in all directions. Crowds of citizens moved along the well-planned roads, which were interspersed with mango groves and orchards. The broad central highway, built entirely of red stone, ran the full hundred-mile length of the city. Large white mansions lined that road, with many-colored pennants waving in the breeze on their roofs. The road was sprinkled with perfumed water and strewn with flowers. Above the city the king could see the golden airplanes of Apsaras, the consorts of the gods.

Looking out over his capital, Ayodhya, Dasarath was plunged in an ocean of anguish. He entered the palace and walked slowly towards his inner chambers. As he descended the wide marble stairways, he heard his priests chanting sacred Sanskrit texts. The sound of mantras mingled with that of drums and lutes being beautifully played by royal musicians. Even that sound, which normally gave him so much joy, could not placate him.

The king entered his rooms, leaving his personal guards at the door. Declining the food and drinks offered to him by his maidservants, he went over to the large latticed window. He moved aside the silk drapes and continued gazing out at his city. Ayodhya had been constructed by Manu, a son of Surya, the all-powerful sun-god. Manu had been the first of the kings in Dasarath's line, all of them emperors of the globe. As he thought of his long ancestry, the king only felt more pain. He sighed and turned back into his rooms.

Seeing the anxious king, his three queens tried gently to console him. They sat him on a large golden couch covered with silk pillows and studded with gems. His senior wife, Kaushalya, gently massaged his feet, while Sumitra and Kaikeyi fanned him with snow-white chamara whisks.

The king sat lost in thought. He looked at the exquisite carvings of the gods lining his walls. All his life he had done so much to please those deities. Once he had even gone into battle against the celestial demons on their behalf. Surely they would help him now. Dasarath silently prayed to them.

While the king sat absorbed in his thoughts and prayers, a messenger came telling him that his chief priest Vasishtha was now present in the assembly hall. Dasarath had been waiting for this news. He rose up, and with the gait of a powerful lion went along the wide palace passageways, his large sword swinging at his side and his gold ornaments jangling as he walked.

Near to the hall he was joined by his chief ministers. All of them were heroes who had been tried in battle, and all were learned and wise. The state ran smoothly under their expert administration. There were no citizens without employment and no criminals left unchecked. The ministers were devoted to Dasarath's service, and as they walked they considered the problem facing the king.

Flanked by his bodyguards and ministers, Dasarath entered his great hall. It vied in splendor with the assembly hall of Indra, the king of the gods. Massive marble pillars rose up to a roof which seemed to reach the sky. Balconies of alabaster and coral, worked with gold filigree, were gradually tiered all around the hall. Along the balconies were gold seats spread with white cushions. Large silk tapestries depicting the pastimes of the gods hung from the walls, which were lined with lapis lazuli and encrusted with jewels. The air was filled with the scent of incense. In the center of the hall sat numerous priests who continuously chanted prayers from the ancient scriptures, invoking the presence of deities. The great megha drum resounded deeply as Dasarath strode towards his seat. Everyone stood and there was a cry of "Victory! All glories to Emperor Dasarath!" The king, appearing like a god, took his seat on a large throne of refined gold bedecked with brilliant celestial gems.

A hush descended on the assembly as Dasarath prepared to speak. Everyone sat in expectation. The citizens knew of the king's worry; they loved him like a father and shared his anxiety. They were grouped in the hall according to their class. At the front were the brahmins, wearing simple cloth and holding their waterpots and prayer beads. On one side sat the warriors, their powerful bodies clad in silks and gold ornaments, with long swords hanging from their belts. Near to them were the tradespeople in their colorful dress, and behind them were the servants and workers, also beautifully adorned. All social classes were represented in that assembly.

Dasarath looked around the hall, smiling affectionately at everyone. Although the king was preoccupied with his worry, no one could detect in him any negligence or laxity in his duties. Seeing him smiling at them, the people felt reassured that Dasarath would find a solution to his problem. They sat awaiting his speech.

Placing his hand on his golden scepter, the king turned to his chief priest Vasishtha, who sat on a raised seat near the throne. With a powerful voice that boomed around the hall, Dasarath addressed the priest. "I have called this assembly to settle a great worry of mine. As you know, this wide earth has for a long time been held under the sway of victorious kings in my line. O jewel among sages, is that glorious history about to end? What can I do to ensure that our proud lineage will continue?"

Dasarath was perturbed that he had no son. Having ruled as the undisputed emperor of the earth for thousands of years, his retirement was now approaching; but there was no one to succeed him. Somehow, none of his wives had given birth to a son. The king had called for a full assembly to propose an idea he was considering. He needed the approval of the brahmins and he wanted the consent of his people. Dasarath looked anxiously at Vasishtha, who was both his priest and preceptor. "O learned one, you know well the perils that attend a kingdom bereft of a monarch. How can I retire to the forest leaving this world without a protector?"

Vasishtha sat surrounded by many other brahmin sages. His hand rested upon his staff as he listened to Dasarath. The sun shone through the carved lattice windows of the hall, covering the king with golden light. Vasishtha, shining with his own mystic power, appeared like a second sun as he replied to the king. "O emperor, I have no doubt that you will soon be blessed with a powerful son who can succeed you. Not long ago I heard this told by Sanat Kumar, the immortal sage who roams the universe. A divine arrangement is being worked by the gods for your everlasting benefit."

Vasishtha lived in a hermitage outside the city. He was frequently visited by wandering sages and mystics. Some days previously the famous seer Sanat Kumar, who always appeared like a young boy, had spoken with Vasishtha. He told him that soon four powerful sons would be born to the emperor. These sons would be divine incarnations, appearing to fulfill the purpose of the gods. Vasishtha continued, "The brahmins have all been praying to the Lord for your sake, O monarch. We have seen auspicious signs in the heavens. It is clear that some great plan of the Supreme will be achieved through you."

The king felt joy to hear his priest's words. Like his forebears before him, Dasarath had religiously pursued his duties as emperor. Under his benevolent rule, the world enjoyed prosperity and peace. The king desired not only the immediate material enjoyment of his people but their spiritual well-being as well. He kept everyone on the path of piety and truth, leading them towards freedom from the cycle of birth and death. Seeing all the people as his own children, he was concerned that their happiness would continue after his retirement. He spoke again. "I have been considering the performance of a horse sacrifice for the pleasure of the gods and Vishnu. O noble sages, will this be successful? Can I satisfy the Lord in this way and thereby attain my desired end?"

Dasarath knew that nothing could be achieved unless Vishnu, the Supreme Lord, was pleased. Although they controlled the universe, the other gods were but Vishnu's agents. Many times in the past the king's ancestors had performed great sacrifices for satisfying the Lord and achieving their purposes. The king now considered this to be his only means of deliverance. He looked hopefully at Vasishtha, who had been speaking with the other sages at his side. Turning towards the king Vasishtha said, "We are in agreement, O tiger among men. Let the sacrifice proceed! We shall immediately prepare a ground on the banks of the Sarayu. You will certainly get a son by this method."

The assembly erupted with joyful shouts. Everywhere were cries of "Let it be so! Let the sacrifice proceed!"

The king, his eyes grown wide with delight as he anticipated the fulfillment of his desire, said to Vasishtha, "Let the preparations begin today. Protected by four hundred of my best warriors, the sacrificial horse will roam the globe before returning for the sacrifice."

After Dasarath had issued all necessary instructions the assembly was dismissed and the king retired to his inner chambers. Together with his wives, he worshipped Vishnu and the gods, praying that his sacrifice would succeed.

*   *   *

The whole city of Ayodhya was filled with excitement as the news of the king's sacrifice spread. In the large public squares minstrels sang songs recounting the exploits of heroes in Dasarath's line, while troupes of female dancers depicted the tales with precise and beautiful gestures. The temples became crowded with joyful people praying for the success of Dasarath's sacrifice. From the balconies of houses lining the wide avenues, wealthy people threw down gems for the brahmins and the jewels sparkled brightly on the clean, paved roads. The city resonated with the sound of lutes, trumpets and kettledrums. Augmenting the music was the chanting of brahmins reciting the holy scriptures. With flags and pennants flying, festoons hanging between the houses and flowers strewn everywhere, Ayodhya had the appearance of a festival held by the gods in heaven.

The priests of Ayodhya set about preparing for the sacrifice. Selecting and consecrating a purebred horse which was free from any blemish, they released it to range freely across the country. As it traveled, it was followed and protected by four hundred powerful generals from the king's army. According to the ritual, wherever the horse went, the residing rulers were called upon to attend the sacrifice and pay homage to Dasarath. Anyone refusing would be immediately challenged to a fight. If they were not subjugated, then the sacrifice could not proceed. None, however, wished the emperor any ill. The horse came back to Ayodhya without incident at the end of one year.

Seeing the horse returned, Dasarath called Vasishtha. He touched his guru's feet and asked him with all humility, "O holy one, if you deem it fit, please now commence the sacrifice. You are my dearest friend as well as my guru. Indeed, you are a highly exalted soul. Fully depending on you, I am confident of the sacrifice's outcome."

After assuring the king, Vasishtha spoke with the priests, instructing them to have the sacrificial arena built. Chief among them was Rishwashringa, a powerful brahmin who had come from the kingdom of Anga. It had long ago been prophesied that Rishwashringa would help Dasarath obtain progeny. Along with Vasishta, he took charge of the arrangements for the sacrifice.

Vasishta ordered that many white marble palaces be constructed for the monarchs who would attend. The very best food and drink was made available, and actors and dancers came to entertain the guests. Horse stables, elephant stalls and vast dormitories to accomodate thousands of people were built. Vasishtha instructed the king's ministers, "Everyone should have whatever they desire. Take care that no one is disrespected at any time, even under the impulse of passion or anger."

Vasishtha spoke to the king's charioteer and minister, Sumantra, who was especially close to Dasarath. "We have invited kings from all over the globe. On behalf of the emperor you should personally ensure that they are all properly received. Take particular care of the celebrated king Janaka, the heroic and truthful ruler of Mithila. With my inner vision I can see that he will in the future become intimately related to our house."

Soon many kings came to Ayodhya bearing valuable gifts of jewels, pearls, clothing and golden ornaments. Upon their arrival they in turn were offered gifts at Vasishtha's command, who had instructed his assistants, "Give freely to all. No gift should ever be made with disrespect or irreverence, for such begrudging gifts will doubtlessly bring ruin to the giver."

The royal astrologers ascertained the most favorable day for the com-
mencement of the sacrifice. Dasarath, headed by Vasishtha and
Rishwashringa, and accompanied by his three wives, then came to the sacrificial compound, which resembled an assembly of the gods. Many fires
blazed, each dedicated to a different deity and attended by numerous brahmins. The great compound was crowded with sages absorbed in prayer and
meditation. On all sides stood warriors equipped with every kind of weapon,
fully alert to any danger. The king sat surrounded by brahmins, who consecrated him for the sacrifice. He and his wives made offerings into the fires
and joined in the chanting of prayers.

After some days the horse was brought before the sacrificial fire dedicated to Vishnu. Learned priests constantly poured into it oblations of clar-
ified butter along with handfuls of grains. Taking the horse by its reins,
Vasishta uttered a powerful mantra and the animal fell unconscious. It was
immediately placed upon the fire. As the horse was consumed by the blazing fire, those with divine vision saw the soul of the creature rise from the
fire, glowing brilliantly, and ascend towards heaven.

As the sacrifice concluded, Dasarath was delighted. He said to the
priests, "According to the ordinance it is fitting that I now bestow upon you
proper charity. Therefore, O holy ones, take this entire earth as a gift. This
is the only appropriate offering for great souls like yourselves."

The priests replied, "You alone are able to protect this earth with its
countless people. As ascetics we having nothing to do with the world, nor
are we able to maintain it; therefore we leave it with you, O monarch."

The brahmins had no interest in wealth but wished only to live simply,
unencumbered by material possessions. However, Dasarath understood that
unless charity were given to the priests the sacrifice was not complete.
Falling at the brahmins' feet, he implored, "If you refuse my gift, then the
success of my endeavor is most uncertain."

The priests quickly raised up the king. They understood the scriptural
injunction to which the king alluded. "If it so pleases you, then you may give
to us a little wealth. We have no use for the earth."

The king distributed to the brahmins hundreds of millions of gold and
silver coins, as well as millions of milk-bearing cows. He supplied tens of
thousands of brahmins present at that sacrifice with enough wealth to last
their entire lives.

Vasishtha and Rishwashringa then arranged for one final ritual to be
performed. They called the gods by name to come and accept the sacrificial
offerings made to them. The celestial smoke from the offerings, sanctified by
Vedic mantras, rose upwards to the skies and was received by the gods. With
the universal creator Brahma at their head, they personally assembled in sky

above Dasarath's sacrificial compound. Unseen by everyone, the gods began to address Brahma:

"Because of a boon granted by you, O lord, the king of the Rakshasas Ravana is constantly harassing us and is extremely difficult to overpower. Having begged from you that he be made invincible to us as well as to practically all other created beings, that evil-minded one now seeks to overthrow us. He profanes even great saints and has no regard for anyone at all."

Brahma, was concerned that his boon to Ravana had created such problems, listened as Indra, on behalf of the gods, continued: "Ravana sought invincibility but did not ask for immunity against humans, whom he considered of no consequence. Thus his death must come at the hands of a human. Please, therefore, beseech the Lord to appear as Dasarath's son."

Although Ravana could still be killed by a human, the gods knew that no ordinary man could slay him. It could only be done by the all-powerful Vishnu himself, if he came to the earth as a man. And here was the ideal opportunity. The emperor of the earth was praying to Vishnu for a powerful son. Surely the Lord would consent to appear in Dasarath's family, especially if Brahma, Vishnu's devoted servant, also prayed to him to appear.

Brahma assented to the gods' request. He knew that the time for the Lord's appearance had come. Seated in meditation, Brahma thought of the Lord within his heart. At that moment Vishnu appeared in the sky. Only the gods saw him as he descended upon the back of his eagle carrier, Garuda. His beautiful body was blackish and he shone with a brilliant luster. He was dressed in yellow silk with a garland of blue lotuses. A necklace of bright celestial gems hung around his neck. Adorned with numerous gold ornaments and jewels, he held in his four hands a conch shell, a mace, a discus weapon and a lotus flower. Gracefully descending, he sat amid the gods as they worshipped him with hymns and prayers.

Brahma addressed Vishnu in a reverential tone. "O Lord, here is the worthy Dasarath praying for a son. All the worlds are sorely afflicted by the evil Rakshasa Ravana, who must be slain by a man. Be pleased, therefore, to take birth as Dasarath's son. Appearing in a human form, please dispatch Ravana in an encounter and save the worlds from their suffering."

Vishnu smiled at the gods. He spoke reassuringly in a voice deep like the rumbling of thunderclouds. "O gods, give up all fear. Along with my own expansions I shall soon be born as four sons of Dasarath. I myself shall appear as his eldest son, and my personal weapons will incarnate as my brothers. After annihilating Ravana and his demon hordes, I will remain on the mortal plane, ruling the globe for eleven thousand years."

The inconceivable Vishnu then disappeared even as he was being worshipped. The gods felt their purpose was accomplished and, after accepting Dasarath's offerings, they returned to the heavens.

In the sacrificial compound the rituals were almost over. Dasarath sat expectantly, hoping for some sign of success. He was apprehensive. If he could not obtain a son by this method, then he would surely be lost. He looked at the blazing fire as the last offerings were being made.

Suddenly there arose from the sacrificial fire a shining and beautiful personality form. Everyone watched in wonder as he descended near the king, remaining slightly above the ground. In his hands he held a golden bowl filled with celestial ambrosia. He spoke to Dasarath in a voice resounding like a kettledrum. "O king, know me to be a messenger of the Lord of all created beings, Vishnu."

"Please accept my heartfelt welcome, O divine one," replied the king with his palms joined. "What shall I do for you?"

"By worshipping the gods in sacrifice you have received this reward," said the messenger. "Take now this ambrosia prepared by the gods which will bestow upon you the offspring you desire. Give it to your wives and through them you will soon secure four celebrated sons."

Accepting the ambrosia with his head bent low and saying, "So be it," the king felt a surge of joy as he took the golden vessel, even as a pauper would feel happiness upon suddenly gaining great wealth.

As a mark of respect, the king walked with folded hands around the messenger, who, having discharged his duty, immediately vanished into the fire from which he had appeared. The king stood in amazement holding the bowl. All around him the brahmins cried out, "Victory! Victory!" After offering his prostrate obeisances to Vasishtha, Dasarath left the sacrifice along with his wives and returned to his palace.

The king gave half of the ambrosia to Kaushalya. He gave the other half to Kaikeyi, the youngest wife, who was especially dear to him. Both of these wives each gave a part of their share to the king's third wife, Sumitra.

All those noble wives of the emperor felt honored and immediately ate the ambrosia. In a short time they felt within themselves the presence of powerful offspring. Their minds were enlivened by the divine energy of the children inside their wombs, and they felt elated. Dasarath, who had at last attained his desired object, felt as delighted as Indra, the king of the gods in heaven.

*   *   *

Having decided to incarnate in Dasarath's family, Vishnu summoned the gods and commanded them, "Soon my advent upon earth will occur. Assisted by all of you, I will crush the despicable Ravana. Foolishly, that evil one did not ask immunity from humans or animals, considering both to be entirely powerless in the face of his strength. As promised, I will descend as a human. O gods, without leaving your posts as universal controllers, you are capable of expanding yourselves onto earth. You should therefore appear in the world as powerful monkeys."

Vishnu's plan for the protection of the worlds was unfolding. The gods took birth as monkeys who had strength equal to their godly power. They could assume various forms at will, they were gallant, as swift as the wind, highly intelligent and practically invulnerable in battle.

The earth became populated with millions of huge monkeys who, in the way of the gods, grew up as soon as they were born. As haughty and strong as lions and tigers, they roared loudly and sprang about fearlessly. They were headed by Vali, the expansion of Indra, and by Sugriva, the expansion of Surya. Fearful in appearance, they thronged the peaks of mountains and resided in great forests. When they came together they appeared like masses of clouds moving about on the surface of the globe.

CHAPTER TWO

THE BIRTH OF RAMA

Dasarath, his desire fulfilled, dwelt happily in Ayodhya awaiting the birth of his sons. The brahmins and kings who had assembled for the sacrifice left for their various abodes, sent on their way with kind words and gifts by the emperor. Four seasons passed. Then, at a time when favorable stars were visible in the heavens, Kaushalya gave birth to a son named Rama.

Though Rama was the Lord of creation, Kaushalya saw him simply as her own dear child. She held him tight to her bosom, overwhelmed with motherly affection and unable to recognize his divinity. Coming out of the delivery room, Kaushalya shone brilliantly with that baby boy, who had eyes like lotus petals.

Next, a son named Bharat was born from Kaikeyi; and from Sumitra, who had received two portions of ambrosia, were born twin sons, Lakshmana and Shatrughna. All three boys resembled celestials and they seemed to blaze with their splendor.

In the heavens Gandharvas, heavenly musicians, began to sing melodiously while bevies of Apsaras danced. Kettledrums resounded in the sky and showers of flowers fell upon the earth. In Ayodhya, the streets quickly became crowded with rejoicing citizens. Minstrels, bards and chanters of sacred hymns gathered in every quarter, glorifying the birth of Rama and his brothers. The city, decorated all over with colorful flags and garlands, looked beautiful.

King Dasarath, overwhelmed with happiness, gave a large heap of shining jewels to the brahmins and arranged for a feast to be distributed to his entire kingdom. Vasishtha joyfully performed the name-giving ceremony and all the other rites of passage for the brothers.

Of all the brothers Rama was especially glorious. His attractive body had the hue of a celestial emerald. Dressed in the finest silk and adorned with golden ornaments, he captured the mind of all who saw him. Rama was devoted to his father's service. He took delight in the science of archery and quickly mastered the arts of horseback and elephant riding, as well as the various methods of driving a chariot.

Lakshmana was deeply attached to his elder brother Rama from his infancy. He was like a second self to Rama, and he pleased him in every way. Unless Lakshmana was present, Rama would neither sleep nor eat. Whenever Rama went out to the forest to hunt, Lakshmana would follow at his heels, guarding him on all sides.

Shatrughna was just as dear to Bharata, and these two brothers were also inseparable.

Dasarath felt as pleased with his four sons as Brahma feels with the four gods presiding over the four quarters of the universe. Those princes were tigers among men yet they were modest, wise, far-sighted and glorious in every way. They were attached to their studies and soon became well versed in all aspects of kingship.

As the princes' studies neared completion the king began to think about their marriages. One day, while lost in such thoughts, the powerful mystic Vishvamitra arrived at his palace. The sage instructed the gatekeepers, "Tell the king that Vishvamitra, the son of Gadhi, is at his door."

Upon seeing the lustrous rishi, the gatekeepers were struck with awe. They ran to Dasarath's quarters to inform him.

Dasarath quickly went with his ministers to greet the sage, even as Indra might greet Brahma. As soon as he saw Vishvamitra standing at his door, the king respectfully brought him in, sat him down and personally washed his feet. Standing with folded palms before the sage, Dasarath was thrilled with joy as he spoke. "I consider your arrival here to be as welcome as the obtaining of celestial nectar in one's own hands, as rainfall arrived in a desert, as the birth of a child to a childless couple or as the recovery of a lost treasure. What can I do for you today?"

Dasarath was aware of Vishvamitra's glory. The sage was famous all over the world for his performance of difficult austerities and his virtuous behavior. He was also well known for his almost limitless powers. Once, by his own ascetic power, he had created an entire constellation of planets which still shone in the southern sky. The king felt honored to see him and wondered what had brought him to Ayodhya. Sitting at Vishvamitra's feet, Dasarath continued to address him.

"You are worthy of my service in every way and it is by great good fortune that you have called at my door. My night has ended in a splendid sunrise as I see here before me the best of the brahmin sages. Simply by seeing you I have received a blessing equal to the results of visiting every place of pilgrimage. I wish now to perform some pleasing work for you, O noble sage, and you may consider it already completed. As a guest, you are as good as God to me, and I shall not hesitate to do anything you desire."

Addressed in such a delightful way Vishvamitra felt joy as he replied to Dasarath. "Your speech has pleased me in every way, O tiger among kings. You are descended from proud ancestry and have been instructed by the god-like sage Vasishtha. Make a firm resolve to satisfy my desire and prove true to your promise, O virtuous one."

Vishvamitra had walked for three days without eating or sleeping, his mind fixed on his purpose. His body was lean and powerful, golden colored and covered by a black deerskin. He held in his hands a staff and a water-pot, his only possessions. He had come to ask something from Dasarath which he knew would be hard for the king to grant. The sage gazed stead-fastly into Dasarath's eyes as he spoke.

"I stand here this very day consecrated for a sacrifice. However, two powerful Rakshasa demons named Maricha and Subahu constantly impede its performance. These demons are avowed enemies of both gods and humans. They are capable of ranging the skies and assuming any form they like. Every time my sacrifice is close to completion, these Rakshasas appear overhead and drop down volumes of flesh and blood, ruining it entirely. Thwarted in my attempts, I have left that sacrifice feeling dispirited, having accomplished nothing other than exertion."

Dasarath listened intently as the sage spoke. He knew that Vishvamitra would not have come to him, the emperor of the earth, unless there was some difficult task at hand. The Rakshasas were dangerous beings who hated sages. The king knew they had been increasingly disruptive, and this was now confirmed by Vishvamitra.

"Although capable of destroying those Rakshasas with a curse, O king, I will not do so, as a condition of my sacrifice is that I do not give way to anger. My mind must remain steady and controlled. Nor is it the sacred duty of brahmins to attack an enemy. This is always the duty of kings and warriors. Please, therefore, give to me your eldest and most heroic son, Rama. Although a youth, Rama is possessed of true prowess and is more than a match for any Rakshasa."

The king's mouth fell open. He gazed in horror at Vishvamitra. Was he serious? Send Rama? The prince was just a boy! He had never seen action on the battlefield. Of course, there was no doubting his bravery and prowess, but how could he face the Rakshasas? Those vicious beings knew every kind of sorcery. They could contend with even the gods. What chance would a youth like Rama stand against them?

Seeing the king's reaction, Vishvamitra tried to reassure him. "You need entertain no fear on Rama's account. Accompanied by me he will proceed safely to the sacrificial arena. Immediately upon encountering those Rakshasas, who are overly proud of their strength, I am sure he will quickly dispatch them. Therefore, release Rama and let him remain with me for a period of but ten days. Do not allow your parental affection to prevail. I shall confer upon Rama boons by which he will attain fame in all the worlds. I will then return him unharmed. O king, you should not have any doubt."

Vishvamitra fell silent. He was aware of Rama's true identity. By his meditations the sage could see in his heart the Supreme Lord, and he knew Rama to be that same person. Vishvamitra understood that the annihilation of the demons was a part of Rama's plan on earth. The sage was acting only as an instrument of the Lord's desire.

Dasarath stood mortified, oblivious to the divinity of his young son, overpowered by grief at the prospect of losing his young son Rama. Trembling all over, the king felt pained at heart and fell unconscious to the ground. Remaining senseless for some time, Dasarath finally came round and said to the sage, "My lotus-eyed son is less than sixteen years old. How then can he fight with the Rakshasas? I myself, marching at the head of hundreds of thousands of highly trained soldiers, shall personally come to wage war on the demons. Do not take Rama!"

Dasarath sought desperately to change Vishvamitra's mind. For as long as he breathed, he said, he would stand with bow in hand and beat back any Rakshasas who came to attack Vishvamitra's sacrifice. The sage need have no doubt. Dasarath wailed piteously, "The Rakshasas are given to treacherous fighting. The inexperienced Rama is still not fully trained. He is yet unable to estimate the strength or weakness of the enemy, nor is he familiar with the use of the celestial weapons necessary for dispatching such powerful enemies as Rakshasas."

Dasarath knelt before the sage. He looked up at him with tears in his eyes. Seeing Vishvamitra's resolute expression he took hold of his feet and implored him to relent. He tried to think of life without Rama. It was unimaginable. After such a long time and so much prayer he had finally obtained a son worthy to succeed him. And such a son! It seemed that with each passing day Rama endeared himself more to his elders with his virtuous behavior. Now he was just attaining maturity and could soon be installed as Prince Regent. How could he lose Rama now? He continued his plea, "Separated from Rama I doubt I shall survive for even an hour. Please do not take him or, if you really must, then please also allow me to go with him. Taking my entire army I shall station myself on the battlefield and ward off the demons. Tell me all that you know about those Rakshasas, O sage, and I shall make every preparation."

Vishvamitra replied, "There is a Rakshasa named Ravana to whom Brahma has granted a boon of invulnerability. Possessed of extraordinary strength and followed by numerous other Rakshasas, he has oppressed both heaven and earth to the utmost degree. When this mighty demon cannot himself be bothered to assail the sacrifices of sages, he sends out his two lieutenants, Maricha and Subahu."

Hearing Ravana's name, the king became alarmed. He stood up suddenly. "Even the gods and Gandharvas united with the entire heavenly host cannot defeat that demon. How then shall I, a mere mortal, stand before him? What then of Rama? Brahma has made Ravana unslayable. I with all my troops will prove incapable of overcoming Ravana, who deprives even the most powerful fighters of their prowess on the battlefield."

The king had heard numerous accounts of Ravana's exploits. Many years ago the demon had slain Anaranya, his ancestor. The demon had defeated the gods and had even once fought and overcome the mighty Yamaraja. To confront him in battle was more or less suicide. The king clasped his hands together. "How can I permit my gentle son to go out? Under no circumstances can I allow Rama to risk his life against Ravana. Rather, I shall go out myself with my army to protect your sacrifice, even if it means my death. Rama shall remain here."

Hearing Dasarath's faltering speech, Vishvamitra blazed up with anger. Did Dasarath have no faith in him? How dare he refuse his request! Kings and warriors must always respect and obey brahmins, for this was the sacred law. And Dasarath had already promised to satisfy him. The sage's eyes opened wide with fury as he spoke.

"After giving your solemn pledge to fulfill my desire, you now decline! This refusal shames your royal lineage and will bring ruin to your race. If you care not about this infamy, then I shall return the way I came. With your promise falsified you may remain peacefully among your relatives."

Seeing Vishvamitra seized with fury, the gods themselves became fearful and the earth shook. The wise Vasishtha, perceiving the imminent danger from Vishvamitra's curse, spoke to the king. "Born in the line of the sun-god, you are like virtue personified. It does not befit you to abandon righteousness. You always remain firm in your vows and are famed as being fixed in truth. Summon strength from within yourself now. If you fail to redeem your promise, you will lose all the merit that has accrued to you from the performance of pious acts. Send Rama with Vishvamitra. Whether or not Rama has mastered archery is of no consequence, as he will be protected by the sage."

Vasishtha, who also knew Rama's divine plan, looked at the agonized king. He told him how Vishvamitra had inconceivable power and great learning. Formerly, while ruling over a kingdom, he had received from Shiva the knowledge of every celestial weapon. He would undoubtedly give this knowledge to Rama. Although quite able to punish the Rakshasas himself, Vishvamitra had asked for Rama only to do good to the prince.

Dasarath still appeared doubtful. His hands shook as he folded them, imploring Vishvamitra to relent. Tears streamed from his eyes.

Vasishtha then took the king aside and spoke in confidence. He told him of Rama's identity. He also said that the arrival of Vishvamitra had been arranged by Providence for the good of the world. The king should therefore have no fear in sending Rama with the sage.

Dasarath was astonished. To him, Rama was his beloved child in need of protection. How could he possibly be the Supreme Lord? Dasarath looked at Vasishtha, who stood silently gazing into the king's eyes. The sage could not possibly tell a lie. Accepting the words of his preceptor and feeling somewhat reassured, Dasarath agreed to send his son with Vishvamitra, who permitted the king to send Lakshmana as well, for Dasarath knew that Lakshmana would never let Rama go out alone for a fight. Dasarath personally called for his two sons and embraced them both. As his tearful wives watched, the king committed the boys to Vishvamitra's care. "Render service to this sage as you would to myself. My dear sons, I shall pray for your safe return. Go now with my blessings."

As they parted at the city gates, Vasishtha uttered benedictory hymns and prayers. Flowers rained from the skies. Loud blasts of conches and the beating of kettledrums resounded everywhere. Led by the smiling Vishvamitra, Rama and Lakshmana went out from the kingdom, watched by their parents and the citizens until they disappeared into the distance.

CHAPTER THREE

WITH THE SAGE VISHVAMITRA

Vishvamitra walked ahead of the two princes, who each carried a bow in hand and had swords strapped to their waists. Wearing on their shoulders two large quivers of arrows, the princes looked like a pair of three-headed serpents following behind the sage. Their brilliant jewels set off their dark complexions. The two resplendent boys added luster even to the shining sage Vishvamitra, as the two gods Skanda and Ganapati adorn the immortal Shiva.

After covering about twelve miles along the beautiful southern bank of the Sarayu, they arrived at a stretch of soft grass, sheltered by trees. Vishvamitra stopped and turned towards Rama and Lakshmana. "Sit here comfortably and sip a little sanctified water for purification. I will now tell you the mystical mantras known as Bala and Atibala. These hymns will confer upon you freedom from all fatigue and fever. Indeed they will release you from hunger and thirst and will even prevent decrepitude. While you mutter these sacred spells, none on earth will be your equal in either battle, intellectual judgment or argument. Bala and Atibala are the sources of all wisdom, being the daughters of the self-born creator, Brahma."

Vishvamitra looked upon the brothers' faces and he felt a deep affection for them. Although he knew they were not ordinary men, out of love he wanted to serve them, acting as their teacher and guide. For their part the princes felt an equal affection for the sage, and they gladly reciprocated his love, accepting him as their guru. The sage positioned himself near the seated princes and, after sipping holy water for purification, held up his right palm and began chanting the mantras.

With a cheerful expression Rama and Lakshmana received the two hymns from the sage. When the instruction was complete, they rested for the night on the bank of the river, enjoying the cool breeze that wafted gently across the water.

Shortly before dawn Vishvamitra, who had remained awake in meditation all night, awoke the two princes, calling out to them. "O Rama and

Lakshmana, O tigers among men, the sun approaches the eastern horizon! Rise up now and perform your ablutions. We must proceed."

The brothers immediately rose and bathed in the river. After their prayers and meditations they approached Vishvamitra and bowed at his feet. The sage, having bestowed blessings upon the boys, again led the way as the sun rose upon another cloudless day.

Soon they saw the river Ganges where it met the Sarayu. On the bank of the Ganges were many simple dwellings made from leaves and mud, in which there lived a community of ascetics. The princes asked Vishvamitra about the hermitage. The sage, remembering the history of the site, laughed heartily and told them the story of how Cupid had once come to assail Shiva here.

A very long time ago the god of love had a human form. On one occasion he had been bold enough to fire his arrows of love at the inconquerable Shiva. The powerful Shiva, who had been absorbed in deep meditation at the hermitage, became infuriated and gazed at Cupid with his third eye. A searing flame shot out, reducing Cupid's body to ashes. From then on Cupid became known as Ananga, the bodiless one, and the land there became known as Anga.

Finishing the tale Vishvamitra said, "All these sages are disciples of the glorious Shiva. Let us halt for the night here and converse with these mystics, O princes."

While Vishvamitra spoke, the ascetics dwelling in the hermitage sensed from a distance the approach of the sage and the princes. Realizing who they were, those worshippers of Shiva, who himself always worships Vishnu, felt happy in heart and came out quickly to greet their exalted guests.

Having been graciously received, the three travelers performed their evening rituals and took a simple meal of forest fare. Vishvamitra entertained the assembly with ancient tales of heroes and sages of the past.

The following morning, after crossing the Ganges in a boat provided by the ascetics, Vishvamitra and the princes came to a vast, desolate region. On all sides were huge trees stripped of their foliage. The ground was laid waste and a wind gusted, carrying sand and debris which lashed their faces. The cries of wild animals and vultures resounded there and even the sky above was dark and overcast.

Rama and Lakshmana looked around. What had happened? The land so far had been beautiful and verdant. Rama asked Vishvamitra, "This forest ahead appears inaccessible and foreboding. What is this land inhabited with fierce beasts of prey and presenting such a terrible aspect?"

Smiling even in the face of that fearful scene, Vishvamitra replied, "My dearest Rama, a long time ago this was the site of two prosperous kingdoms built by the gods. It came to pass one day that Indra became afflicted with the sin of killing a brahmin. Overcome with impurity, Indra sought the powerful rishis, the most exalted of the brahmins, as his refuge. They performed rituals of purification and bathed his body with Ganges water which fell here on this tract of land. Pleased with this land for receiving his impurities, Indra blessed it saying, 'Here will rise two great kingdoms which will flourish for many years and will be known as Malada and Karusa.'"

The party had stopped at the edge of a forest of bare trees as Vishvamitra spoke. The way ahead was virtually enveloped by darkness. Terrible sounds emanated from the forest. The sage continued telling the brothers about the land. Some time after Indra had founded the cities, there came to that region a Yaksha woman named Tataka, as powerful as a thousand elephants and able to assume any form she desired. She was the mother of Maricha, who now assailed Vishvamitra's hermitage. Fearsome and filled with malice towards all beings, Tataka constantly ravaged that land and thus no one lived there. Although it was once the site of flourishing cities, it was now almost impossible to even approach.

Turning towards the princes, Vishvamitra said, "The time has now come for the demise of the evil Tataka. You two princes should follow me to the place where she resides. Search her out and end her life immediately."

Rama replied with a smile, "Being a woman, O sage, how can Tataka have such power?"

Vishvamitra knew that the virtuous Rama was hesitant to attack a woman, but Tataka was no ordinary woman. The sage described her background. She had been born as the beautiful daughter of a great and powerful Yaksha named Suketu. As a youth she was given a boon by Brahma that she would possess the strength of a thousand elephants. She married the famous Yaksha, Sunda, who was eventually killed as a result of a curse made by the sage Agastya. When Tataka learned of her husband's death, she became infuriated with Agastya and, along with her son Maricha, she rushed towards the sage desiring to kill him. The sage stood his ground. He said to the two advancing Yakshas, "As you act so wickedly may you both become demons! O Tataka, you shall lose your attractive form and instead become an ugly man-eating Rakshasi!" Agastya then vanished from the spot.

Vishvamitra raised his hand and indicated the path ahead of them. Tataka had turned the entire region into a desolate forest by her malevolent presence. She was always angry and would attack anyone who approached the area.

Having told the brothers Tataka's history, the sage reassured them: "Although the scriptures state that a woman should always be protected and never attacked, in this case you need not fear any sin. The killing of Tataka is necessary for the good of society. One wishing to protect the afflicted must sometimes perform even a seemingly sinful act. This is the eternal duty of kings. O Rama, you should not hesitate."

Citing other historical examples of kings and gods who had killed evil women, Vishvamitra urged Rama to quickly kill Tataka.

Rama accepted the sage's order and grasped his golden bow. Standing ready for combat, he said to Vishvamitra, "My father instructed me on leaving Ayodhya that your order should be followed without hesitation. In obedience then to both his and your command I shall now face the fierce Rakshasi. I wish to do good to the brahmins and cows in this region, as well as to satisfy your holy self. Please point out to me the whereabouts of that wicked demon."

Vishvamitra led them a little further into the wilderness. Rama twanged his bowstring, which produced a terrific sound, filling the four quarters. All the forest animals were terrified by the noise.

Tataka herself was stunned and overcome with anger. Who had dared to challenge her? Whoever it was, they would soon regret their foolishness. She came out from her cave and ran towards the source of the sound, screaming horribly.

Seeing her at a distance emerging from the forest in a terrible fury, monstrous in size and awful in appearance, Rama said to Lakshmana. "Behold, my dear brother, this formidable and fearful Yaksha woman. The very sight of this sinful wretch would break the hearts of the timid. Watch me put her to flight with my sharp arrows. In truth, I do not really want to kill her, as she is a woman. I shall put an end to her strength by rendering her immobile and powerless, cutting from her body her hands and feet."

As Rama spoke, Tataka rushed towards him roaring, with her arms upraised. Uttering a powerful mantra, Vishvamitra checked her progress, calling out, "May victory attend the Ayodhya princes!"

Creating a swirling cloud of dust, Tataka confounded the princes and disappeared. With her mystic powers of illusion she employed numerous conjuring tricks. She assumed many forms, one after another. Sometimes she appeared in front of the brothers. Then she would be above them. Then again she would suddenly appear behind them. One moment she appeared as a furious horned animal. In the next moment she became a terrible looking fiend. Then she swooped down upon them as a great clawed bird. Hurling upon the brothers huge rocks and boulders, she screamed fearfully.

Rama flew into a rage. He parried the rocks with a shower of shafts from his bow. He shot arrows with blinding speed. His bow appeared to be always bent into a circle. Taking razor-headed arrows he severed Tataka's two arms, even as she came running towards him. Lakshmana also became furious. He released sharp arrows with deadly accuracy and sliced off her nose and ears.

The Yaksha woman disappeared and rose up to the sky. Even though deprived of her arms, she used her sorcery to throw down more massive trees and boulders. Remaining invisible, she moved hither and thither, screaming all the while. Vishvamitra saw the boys mystified by the Rakshasi's illusory powers. He realized they were holding back because Tataka was a woman. The sage called to the brothers. "Have done with your tenderness! This woman should not be spared! Sinful and wicked, she thoroughly deserves death at your hands. Act swiftly to end her life before nightfall, as the demons are always more powerful after sunset!"

Rama then showed his skill at archery. He released arrows capable of striking an invisible target by seeking out sound. Reciting mantras as he let them go, Rama covered Tataka in a network of arrows. Those arrows reduced the falling stones to powder. They pierced the Rakshasi and she screamed in pain. She quickly came down to earth again. Tataka then assumed a vast form and rushed with the force of a tempest towards the two brothers. Rama decided that she should be killed. He quickly fired an arrow imbued with the energy of a thunderbolt. It hit the Rakshasi full in the chest. Tataka's heart was ripped apart and with a hideous cry she fell down dead.

Having watched Rama slay the demoness, the gods, headed by Indra, assembled in the skies and applauded. Celestial flowers rained down on the two princes. Acknowledging the gods' pleasure, Rama and Lakshmana modestly bowed their heads. The thousand-eyed Indra said to Vishvamitra, "All the gods are gratified with Rama's feat. O holy brahmin, show Rama your affection by giving to him your knowledge of the celestial missiles. A great objective of the gods will soon be accomplished by Rama with the use of these weapons."

Indra was considering Vishnu's desire that Ravana and his Rakshasa hordes be annihilated. As he looked upon the mighty Rama he knew that the time for the destruction of the Rakshasas was imminent.

After Indra had spoken, the gods returned to the heavens and twilight fell. Embracing Rama and Lakshmana, Vishvamitra said, "Let us remain for the night in this forest. Freed from the curse of Tataka, it is now rendered so very peaceful and attractive. In the morning we shall continue on to my hermitage."

The three of them rested for the night, praised by heavenly bards and singers who had assembled in the canopy of the sky.

The next morning Vishvamitra remembered Indra's words. He sat the two princes down and faced them. "Steady your minds, O heroes, for I shall now tell you the knowledge of the gods' mystic weapons, including even those presided over by the invincible Brahma, Shiva and Vishnu. Equipped with this knowledge you will be able to forcibly bring under your control even the hosts of gods and demons, including the Gandharvas and Nagas, the powerful celestial serpents."

Vishvamitra sat facing the rising sun and, after purifying himself by sipping water and intoning sacred hymns, he began to repeat to Rama a string of mantras capable of invoking the celestial weapons. Calling each weapon by the name of its presiding deity, Vishvamitra delivered to Rama all those divine missiles, thousands in number and difficult for even the gods to remember in their entirety. As they were called they came before Rama in their shining ethereal forms. Some appeared like glowing coal, others were smoky while others were brilliant like the sun or moon. Filled with joy at being called to Rama's service, they stood before him with folded hands and asked for his command.

Rama accepted them with affection and asked them to personally appear within his mind whenever he thought of them. The personified missiles replied, "It shall be as you say." Taking leave of Rama, the weapons circumambulated him with respect and returned to their own heavenly abodes.

After teaching the brothers the full knowledge of firing and recalling the weapons, Vishvamitra finally said, "The instruction is complete. O glorious princes, we should now continue towards our destination."

They moved on from that spot and soon saw in the distance a great cluster of trees, appearing like a mass of dark clouds on the horizon. As they came closer they saw it was a beautiful copse containing varieties of flowering and fruit-bearing trees. Sweetly singing birds filled the air and graceful deer moved about next to rivulets of clear water. Looking at Vishvamitra, Rama inquired, "What is the name of this place so pleasing to the mind? It seems we have arrived at the site of some holy hermitage. Can it be that we have now reached your own abode, O learned brahmin?"

Although possessed of infinite knowledge, Rama had fully assumed the role of Vishvamitra's student. He listened attentively as the sage smiled and told him the ancient story of Bali and Indra. Once the immensely powerful King Bali, lord of the demons and enemy of the gods, seized the seat of Indra and began to rule over the universe. Becoming famous throughout all the three worlds of heaven, earth and hell, he remained in that position for a long time.

The gods had become perturbed and with Indra at their head they sought out Vishnu. The Lord then appeared as Vamana, accepting the form of a brahmin boy. On the plea of charity, he took from Bali the three worlds, restoring them again to the gods. Vamana then remained for some time at this hermitage, known as the Siddha-ashrama, sanctifying it by his presence. Vishvamitra concluded, "It is here that I have my dwelling, O Rama. Let us go there now."

Taking the two princes by the hand, the sage entered his hermitage. As he walked into the large compound he resembled a full and cloudless moon accompanied by two brilliant stars. There were numerous hermits moving about in that grassy enclosure. Some tended sacred fires, while some of the younger ones chopped wood or worked on constructing the large central altar meant for the main sacrifice. In some places groups of sages sat reciting the Sanskrit hymns of the Vedas, while elsewhere other sages cleaned and prepared sacrificial paraphernalia. Rama and Lakshmana looked with interest upon the busy scene that greeted them. Despite the bustle, an atmosphere of tranquility prevailed and the hermits glowed with ascetic power.

Seeing that Vishvamitra and the princes had arrived, the hermits sprang up and paid their respects. They offered water and forest fruits to the two princes. It was late in the evening and long shadows stretched across the ground. The sacrifice would begin the next day. On Vishvamitra's order the hermits showed the two boys to a secluded cottage. One of the sages said, "Rest now for the night, and tomorrow, led by Vishvamitra, we will go through the ceremony to consecrate our sacrifice. Surely our success is now certain because we see you two princes before us, equipped with every weapon and shining like the sun."

The sages gazed with gratitude at Rama and Lakshmana. They had been afflicted by the Rakshasas for a long time and had prayed for deliverance. In his prayers and meditations, Vishvamitra had understood the Lord's plan. The sage had thus gone to Ayodhya, looking for Rama. Now the divine prince had actually come to personally deliver the ascetics from their suffering. As they watched the two boys lie down to sleep, the sages were struck with wonder. In their hearts they offered worship and praise to Vishnu.

Before dawn the next morning the princes rose and went through their daily rituals. After offering obeisances to Vishvamitra, they sat down by the side of the sacrificial altar. Facing the sage with folded hands, Rama asked,

"O venerable sir, please tell us when and where we can expect the evil Rakshasas to appear?"

Vishvamitra remained impassive, but the other hermits applauded the boys, seeing their readiness to tackle the demons. One of them replied, "Vishvamitra is now observing a vow of silence, which he will keep for the next six days and nights, remaining awake throughout. At the end of that period, close to the completion of the sacrifice, the two demons will assail this area with all their force. But be ready, for the treacherous Rakshasas could appear at any time!"

The princes were eager for a fight. They stood vigilantly by Vishvamitra's side as he sat silently meditating upon the sacrificial hymns. Rama leaned on his great bow, which stood almost as tall as him. Lakshmana held in his hand a shining blue sword, its golden handle impressed with bright gems.

As the sixth night approached and the final rituals were being performed, the sacrificial fire suddenly blazed forth furiously. A loud clamor came from the sky, which was covered over by clouds. Swooping down upon that sacrifice, the two Rakshasa demons Maricha and Subahu, appeared from the sky. They were accompanied by their fierce and terrible looking followers. As they spread their sorcery, torrents of blood and pus, as well as large pieces of flesh, fell upon the altar. Blazing fires sprang from the earth and hot coals flew everywhere.

Shrieking horribly, the Rakshasas danced about, wreaking havoc. The hermits fell back, but this time they were not fearful. Vishvamitra quickly stood up. It was time for these evil beings to receive their just deserts. They had defiled his sacrifice once too often. They would not do so again. Gathering the other ascetics, Vishvamitra moved aside and ordered Rama to attack the Rakshasas.

Rama became infuriated upon seeing the scene of devastation. He rushed forward toward the Rakshasas, calling to his brother, "Watch now as I scatter these wicked demons who feed on raw flesh."

Even as he spoke, Rama continuously worked his bow. He sent swift arrows in all directions. The Rakshasas were stunned; they had not expected any resistance. Some of them closed quickly on Rama, covering him on all sides. Rama released arrows with deadly accuracy and speed. The Rakshasas were cut to pieces. Rama looked for Maricha. Seeing his huge form nearby, tearing at the sacrificial altar, Rama invoked a celestial weapon. He placed it on his bow and, although still feeling furious, he calmly said to Lakshmana. "I shall release the Manava weapon, presided over by the father of the gods, Manu."

Rama angrily fired his weapon at the fearsome, roaring Maricha. The demon was struck by the mighty missile and he was lifted and flung a distance of eight hundred miles, landing in the ocean. Although reeling and struck senseless by Rama's arrow, Maricha was not killed. Rama looked at Lakshmana. "See the force of that weapon, my brother. It easily hurled the demon to a vast distance."

Rama and Lakshmana continuously discharged flaming arrows at the other Rakshasas. Imbued with mystic power one arrow expanded into thousands. It appeared as if a continuous line of shafts was leaving Rama's bow, so fast was his movement. The Rakshasas screamed in pain. Some of them vanished and others fell dead on the ground. Some entered the earth while others flew into the sky.

Regrouping, a large number of the demons rushed down from the sky towards the princes. They hurled lances, iron maces, massive rocks and blazing coals. Rama and Lakshmana stood firm, parrying that shower of weapons with their arrows. Tightly grasping his golden bow, Rama said to his brother, "Fear not Lakshmana, for I shall now swiftly deal with these blood-sucking demons. They are wicked and merciless and always given to sinful acts. This indeed shall be the last sacrifice they defile."

Having said this to his brother, Rama moved with agility, evading the rocks thrown by the demons. He invoked the weapon presided over by the god of fire, Agni. Fired from from Rama's fully extended bow, the weapon hit the Rakshasha Subahu full upon the chest. His heart torn apart, he fell dead on the ground like an uprooted tree. Rama then invoked the Vayu-astra, the powerful wind weapon. He fired it and a roaring gale went towards the Rakshasas. They were blown away like so many pieces of dust and debris. Those who were not killed by that weapon fled for their lives.

As the clamor of the battle died down, Rama and Lakshmana felt their anger subside. They stood holding their bows and looking at Vishvamitra. The sage was delighted. He approached the princes. "I have accomplished my purpose, O mighty-armed heroes. You have perfectly followed your preceptor's order. We can now continue the sacrifice for the good of the people."

With tears in his eyes Vishvamitra gazed for some time at the two handsome brothers. He thought of Vishnu's cosmic arrangement. The Lord always protected his worshippers and, for the well-being of the world, ensured that sacrifices could proceed. Overwhelmed with love the sage finally said to the boys, "Rest peacefully now, for tomorrow we shall leave this place."

The many ascetics in the hermitage gathered around to congratulate the brothers. They led them to a spacious cottage near the river. After showing the princes their accommodation, the hermits offered them forest fruits and cooked wild vegetables. Rama and Lakshmana graciously accepted their offerings and then laid down for sleep, exhausted by the day's events.

The next morning the princes came before Vishvamitra and respectfully asked, "What other order of yours should we now carry out, O best among the brahmins?"

The sage told them of a sacrifice about to be performed by Janaka, the king of Mithila. He wanted to take the princes there, where they would see a magnificent bow owned by Janaka. The strength of that bow was inestimable. It was formerly held by Shiva himself and it could not be bent by either gods, Gandharvas or demons-what to speak of humans. Janaka kept it enshrined in a hall where it was worshipped daily by his priests.

"Indeed," said the sage, "the bow can hardly even be gazed upon except by the mighty. The king has declared that any man who bends this bow will win the hand of his daughter Sita, a veritable jewel among women who was born from the earth itself. Let us leave for that place immediately."

Vishvamitra gave orders to the sages to make ready for the journey. A hundred carts were filled, largely with sacrificial paraphernalia, and yoked to strong asses. At the head of a thousand rishis, who were all reciting auspicious texts from the scriptures, Vishvamitra and the two princes set off towards Mithila, traveling in a northerly direction along the bank of the Ganges.

As they left, herds of beasts and flocks of birds dwelling around the hermitage began to follow them out of affection. Vishvamitra and other sages addressed the creatures in their own speech and persuaded them to return.

They walked for some days. Having covered a long distance and arriving at the bank of the Sone river, the sages stopped to rest just before nightfall. The lowing of cattle and the cries of cowherds could be heard all around. As they settled down the travelers looked across the smooth waters of the river, which glowed orange under the setting sun. During the day they had passed many flourishing villages and settlements and seen that the land was farmed and well managed. Rama, seated comfortably among the ascetics, asked Vishvamitra where they were.

Vishvamitra, who had lived thousands of years and knew the history of the entire earth, smilingly began to narrate the story of that land. It was called Kushanabha after an ancient king of the same name who was a son of a rishi named Kusha. Kushanabha was Vishvamitra's grandfather. Having descended in the line of Kusha, Vishvamitra was also known as Kaushika and he had an elder sister named Kaushiki. After unfailingly serving her rishi husband, she had ascended bodily to heaven and later become the holy river Koshi. Vishvamitra had for a long time led a life of asceticism on the

bank of that river, by the side of the Himalayas. Because of his desire to perform a sacrifice, he came down to the plains and it was soon after that he
had secured Rama's assistance.

The evening passed as Vishvamitra told this and other tales. Seeing the
onset of night the sage at last said, "The beasts and birds are buried in sleep
and all the quarters stand enveloped in darkness. The firmament shines
brightly with stars as though covered with innumerable eyes. Here rises the
moon, dispelling the darkness of the world and spreading his soothing rays
all around. Fearful hosts of nocturnal fiends are freely roaming here and
there. Let us rest, ready for our renewed journey tomorrow."

Glorifying Vishvamitra, the brothers lay down and courted sleep, awed
at the sage's stories.

CHAPTER FOUR

THE TRIAL OF STRENGTH

A beautiful sunrise over the Sone heralded the dawn. The sounds of birds and forest animals filled the air as the sages and the princes bathed in the river. After performing their morning rituals and prayers, the boys came before Vishvamitra. The sage pointed to the river and said, "Here we should cross this river and make our way northwards to the Ganges."

The boys looked around and saw nearby a line of sages, holding their waterpots and staffs, wading through the water at some shallow point. Rama and Lakshmana fastened their silk garments up around their waists and placed their bows across their shoulders. Then, with Vishvamitra going immediately before them, they followed the sages through the clear, cool waters of the Sone.

After some time they sighted the Ganges shining in the late afternoon sun, appearing in the distance like a line of gold running across the landscape. Upon reaching the riverbank, they broke their journey and prepared to rest for the night. After worshipping the river with libations of water and lighting the sacred fire, the boys sat before Vishvamitra and inquired, "O holy sage, we wish to hear of the origin of this great river, which arrives at the Himalayas from the heavens, flows across the earth and, it is heard, courses even through hell itself. How has this river become so holy and why does she spread her influence through all the three worlds?"

Moved by this question Vishvamitra called to mind the glories of the Ganges and began to speak. [See Appendix One, The Story of the River Ganges.] In flowing and beautiful Sanskrit verse, Vishvamitra narrated at length the history of the sacred river. When he was finished, the princes were wonderstruck. Asking the sage again and again to continue speaking, the brothers listened all night as Vishvamitra recounted various other stories of the gods and demons.

The following morning they went towards the northeast, heading for Mithila. Gradually the forest paths gave way to roads laid with stone that led to the city. The forest opened to fields of crops. As they came closer to Mithila they saw well-planned gardens and groves with seats and fountains. The sounds of wild animals were replaced with the clamor of people in the city.

Shouts of children and the rumbling of horse-drawn chariots greeted them as they entered the gates of Mithila. Huge elephants swayed along majestically, with smiling people waving from the howdahs on their backs. Gazing about them, the travelers saw the golden domes of innumerable temples along with many mansions of brilliant white stone. Along the roadside were shops displaying countless varieties of fruits, vegetables and all kinds of sweetmeats. Other vendors displayed rows of shining gems looking like numbers of rainbows. Everyone called out respectful greetings as the party moved slowly past. As they went along the wide, smooth road they were met by the king's ministers, who had already been informed of their arrival.

Headed by Vishvamitra and the princes, the party was led along the main highway to Janaka's palace. People thronged the sides of the road to gaze upon the famous sage and his two illustrious charges. As they looked upon the powerful princes, some of them guessed that they might be the sons of Emperor Dasarath. The people wondered what had brought the princes to Mithila. Were they going to attempt to string the king's great bow? As Rama smiled at the people they were filled with a desire to see this handsome, powerful prince win Sita's hand.

Janaka personally came out to greet them, accompanied by his priests and counselors. He immediately fell at Vishvamitra's feet and had him brought into the palace, where he offered him and the two princes golden seats. The king had water fetched for washing their feet and personally performed the ceremony.

Once the formalities were complete, a meal was offered to the sage and the princes. As they sat on the floor on silk rugs, ivory tables were placed in front of them. Gold and silver dishes were fetched containing choice foods of every description. They ate heartily and when they were finished, Janaka said to Vishvamitra, "Great indeed is my good fortune today for I see before me your holy self. I am blessed by your presence. Tell me who are these two boys accompanying you? They appear like two powerful tigers and they rival the gods in beauty and grace. What brings you here to my house, along with these boys equipped with weapons?"

The king had waited until the travelers were rested and refreshed before making his inquiries. Vishvamitra told him all about the boys and how they had disposed of the Rakshasas in the forest. They had come now to see the famous bow. Janaka was thrilled to hear that they were princes from Ayodhya. Nothing could be better than an alliance with Dasarath's line. If only Rama could pass the test of the bow.

At that point Satananda, Janaka's head priest, spoke to the princes. After welcoming them he began to narrate the history of Vishvamitra. Satananda was himself a great ascetic. He knew Vishvamitra well, having previously spent time with him in his hermitage. Seeing the famous sage again, Satananda felt inspired by affection to speak of his glories. Looking upon the beautiful faces of Rama and Lakshmana, who sat enraptured by his speech, the priest told the story of Vishvamitra, who had performed difficult asceticism for thousands of years. [See Appendix Two, The History of Vishvamitra.]

He told them how the sage had once been a great king and, after practicing tremendous austerities, had been blessed by Brahma to become a powerful rishi. When Satananda finished his astonishing tale, everyone gazed with awe at Vishvamitra, who sat flanked by the princes, his mind absorbed in thoughts of the Supreme Lord. Janaka approached the effulgent rishi and spoke to him with joined palms. "I stand blessed by your appearance, O holy sage. This account of your many glories has filled my mind with wonder. Indeed, I could go on hearing it again and again. But dusk has now fallen and I beg your leave. Let us meet again in the morning and it will be my very great delight to satisfy your every desire."

Janaka, along with his ministers and priest, circumambulated Vishvamitra in respect and then departed. After performing their evening rituals and prayers, Vishvamitra and the princes rested for the night in the king's palace.

The following morning Janaka again came before Vishvamitra. He bowed low before the sage and touched his feet, asking in a pleasing voice, "Please instruct me what I should do for you today, O sinless one. You are worthy in every way of receiving my service."

Hearing these words from the virtuous and gentle king, Vishvamitra asked that they now be shown the bow. Janaka assented, but before taking them to see the bow he described its history.

Long past, in a former age the bow had belonged to Shiva. That deity had become angry with the other gods when they had denied him a share of the sacrificial offerings made by the sages. Shiva had threatened them with the bow saying, "I shall now sever your worshipable heads from your bodies. Stand ready on the battlefield if you have any valor."

But the gods relented and quickly worshiped the infuriated Shiva. They had managed to appease him, whereupon he gave the bow to them. The famous bow was then given by the gods to Janaka's ancestor, Devarata, after he had fought for them in a battle against the demons. It had since been kept in the king's family, being worshipped as if it were Shiva himself.

Janaka continued speaking to the sage and the princes, who listened with great curiosity. "Once I was performing a sacrifice to please the gods in order to get a worthy successor in my line. As the sacrificial ground was being prepared with a golden ploughshare, a wonderful child appeared from out of the earth itself. This female child, who became known by the name of Sita, grew up in my palace as my daughter. Her beauty is matchless. I have raised her with love and will give her in marriage to whoever can show exceptional prowess. Various rulers and princes have approached me and sued for her hand. Seeing these kings, I set a standard for winning Sita, saying, 'Whosoever can hold and string the mighty bow of Shiva will win this princess.'

"Many proud kings thought they would easily bend the bow. However, coming before that bow they were soon shorn of their valor and pride. They were hardly able to move the bow even slightly, far less lift and string it. Angry at their failure, numerous kings together beseiged Mithila for one full year. When my resources were exhausted I prayed to the gods for support. I then received from them a vast army equipped with every kind of weapon. That celestial army quickly dispersed those bellicose kings in all directions. Thus this bow remains here, unconquered and awaiting some truly powerful king."

Janaka looked at the two royal brothers. Rama's fame had reached him and he felt sure that the prince would win his daughter's hand. As the king beheld Rama's beautiful features, his powerful physique and noble bearing, he longed for the prince to pass the test and become his son-in-law. He stood before Vishvamitra with folded palms. "Come now, O sage, and bring these boys with you. If any can string the bow, then the hand of the divinely born Sita will be won."

Janaka led them to the part of his great palace where the bow was kept. It was stored in an iron chest which was adorned with gold engravings and covered over with numerous flower garlands. Three hundred powerfully built men somehow managed to move the chest to the center of the hall where it lay. Janaka turned towards Rama. "Here is the wonderful celestial bow. It has been kept and worshipped by the Janakas for many generations. Not even the gods, demons, Yakshas, Gandharvas or Kinnaras can string it; how then could any ordinary man? Gaze now upon this bow, O Rama."

Janaka ordered that the chest be opened. As the lid was lifted the brilliant bow was revealed. It spread a golden glow all around. Constructed of pure horn, it was skillfully worked with gold and silver images of the pastimes of the gods. Hundreds of golden bells and ornaments hung from the bow, which was studded with diamonds and other gems.

Seeing the bow the two princes gasped in appreciation. Rama bowed down in respect and then walked slowly around it. He looked towards Vishvamitra who nodded slightly. Understanding Vishvamitra's indication, Rama stood with joined palms at the bow's center. He turned to Janaka. "I wish to attempt your test. I shall now try to lift this heavenly bow to gauge its weight and strength."

While being extolled by Vishvamitra and other sages, who uttered "Victory! Victory!" Rama placed his hand upon the bow. There was complete silence in the hall. Janaka held his breath as Rama stood motionless. Vishvamitra, knowing the extent of Rama's power, smiled slightly.

In the balcony of the hall stood Sita. She looked at Rama, feeling a natural attraction for the prince. Until then she had never been interested in any of her suitors, although the most powerful kings from all around the world had come there. To the gentle Sita they were all arrogant and overly proud of themselves. Sita was deeply religious. All her life she had prayed that Vishnu might become her husband. As she watched Rama approach the bow she felt her love for the Lord being awakened. Was this Vishnu himself? Becoming absorbed in her loving sentiment, Sita felt anxiety. Would Rama string the bow and become her husband? She held the matrimonial garland with trembling hands.

Suddenly Rama seized the bow by its middle part and raised it high above his head. A gasp of astonishment filled the hall. It was inconceivable. Rama tossed the bow slightly to gauge its weight. Placing one end of the colossal bow on the ground, Rama then moved to the other end and strung it. He pulled the string and bent the bow round into a semi-circle. It broke suddenly and a sound like the crash of thunder reverberated around the hall. The earth shook as if there were an earthquake. Everyone was stunned and rendered senseless for some moments.

Janaka was amazed. He turned to Vishvamitra. "I have now witnessed Rama's strength. His achievement is incredible. Having secured Rama as her husband, Sita will bring undying fame to my family."

Janaka's eyes were filled with tears. Surely Rama was a divine personality. There could be no doubt. Till then no king had been able to move the bow even slightly; some could hardly even look upon it. But Rama had handled it as if it were a piece of bamboo. The king looked up to Sita in the balcony. She was filled with delight upon seeing Rama's feat and her breast heaved with excitement. Awaiting her father's indication to come down, she stood surrounded by her many female attendants. Janaka turned to speak to Rama, who stood peacefully, having replaced the broken bow in its chest. "I shall now fulfill my pledge to give Sita's hand to whoever could string this bow. Sita is dearer to me than my own life, but I gladly offer her to you."

Sita came down from the balcony with a garland of golden flowers in her hands and stood by her father. She was resplendent in a silk sari of deep maroon, a necklace of pearls shining on her breast. As she walked her golden anklets tinkled and her diamond earrings swung to and fro. Smiling gently, she shyly lifted her eyes a little and looked at Rama, who caught her glance. Both felt their hearts moved by love. In that moment their union was forged. Sita's father signaled and she went before Rama. She placed the garland around his neck, indicating her acceptance of him as her husband. She blushed slightly and kept her eyes down. Walking slowly, she went back to her father, who felt as if his heart might burst with happiness.

The king wanted to perform the marriage ceremony as soon as possible. He asked for Vishvamitra's permission, and when the sage agreed, the king arranged for swift messengers to go to Ayodhya to inform Dasarath.

The ministers of Janaka left immediately and arrived at Ayodhya after three days. They quickly went to the palace and were ushered into the presence of Dasarath, who appeared to them like a powerful god. Put at ease by the emperor's benign expression and gentle words of welcome, the ministers politely told him of the events in Mithila. The emperor was delighted to hear the submission of Janaka's envoys. Rama and Lakshmana were well! They had conquered over the demons, and more than that, Rama had now won the beautiful Sita for his bride.

Dasarath recalled how he had been contemplating the marriage of his son even as Vishvamitra had arrived at his palace. The sage must have been sent by Providence, by whose arrangement this union had surely been made. After consulting with his counselors, Dasarath made up his mind to leave the next day for Mithila.

Taking with him his ministers and preceded by a party of priests, Dasarath went the next morning towards Mithila, with his army marching close behind. They arrived after five days. Dasarath approached Janaka, who graciously received the abundant riches brought as gifts. Janaka embraced the emperor, and the two old friends sat together discussing the wedding. Janaka told Dasarath how Sita had appeared from the earth. He also told him of a prophesy he had heard.

"Once the celestial seer Narada informed me that Sita is Vishnu's eternal consort and that he would one day become her husband in this world. I thus devised a test which would only be possible for Vishnu to pass. Your son has now passed that difficult test and must therefore be Sita's eternal husband."

She shyly lifted her eyes a little and looked at Rama, who caught her glance.

Dasarath was again astonished to hear of Rama's divinity. He still found it hard to believe, having raised Rama as his child. He looked at the son who stood before him modestly with bowed head and folded palms. Dasarath was overpowered by love. His loving sentiments overcame any thoughts of Rama's divinity. The emperor looked again at Janaka and said, "I approve this marriage in every way. Perform the ceremony under the guidance of learned brahmins. O king, the success of a gift depends upon the way it is given. Therefore be sure that all the necessary rites are properly observed without loss of time."

Dasarath wanted to ensure that the marriage ceremony was performed carefully according to scriptural codes. He did not want any ill fortune created by neglect of sacred rituals. Such errors would blight the marriage and create future difficulties for the couple.

Janaka issued instructions to his ministers and then sat with Dasarath in his great palace hall. Both of them listened as Vasishtha recited Rama's family lineage. After hearing of Rama's ancestry, beginning with the sun-god, Janaka recited Sita's genealogy, describing his own ancestry, which began with Brahma.

When Janaka finished, Vishvamitra spoke. He suggested that Sita's sister, Urmila, wed Rama's brother Lakshmana. The sage also advised that Janaka's brother Kushadhvaja allow his two daughters to marry Bharata and Shatrughna. Then there could be one ceremony for all four marriages.

Rising from his seat with joy, Janaka said, "Let it be so!" again and again. He fell prostrate before Vishvamitra and said, "I am ever your servant. Your words are worthy of my worship and I stand commanded by you. Let the wedding take place tomorrow, a day marked by favorable stars."

As the two kings sat talking together, the sun gradually set. Janaka took his leave from Dasarath and departed for his personal quarters, flanked by his ministers and a hundred warriors. Thousands of golden oil lamps lit up the hall as the crowds of brahmins made their way out, all of them constantly uttering auspicious Vedic hymns.

*   *   *

The following morning Dasarath rose early and performed the first ritual for invoking good fortune. He had his four sons brought before him and then gave to the brahmin priests a hundred thousand cows on behalf of each of them. The emperor also distributed gold and gems to the thousands of rishis assembled in Mithila to witness the wedding. The four princes shaved their heads and dressed in silk robes, putting on brilliant jeweled ornaments.

Living peacefully in the forest, Rama, Lakshmana, and Sita were happy. (p.52)

The bow broke suddenly and a great noise like a crash of thunder
reverberated around the hall. (p. 62)

With a shout of "Victory to Rama," Hanuman sprang into the air. (p. 272)

Samudra assured Rama that Rama would be able to cross the ocean. (p. 294)

The bridge was completed in only five days and reached
right across the ocean to the shores of Lanka. (p. 295)

Rama released the weapon and it flew at Ravana, lighting up the earth and sky. (p. 377)

Rama quickly approached His mother, fell before her and clasped her feet. (p. 390)

As Rama ruled over Ayodhya everything became auspicious. (p. 422)

Surrounded by the four handsome and effulgent youths, Dasarath shone like Brahma surrounded by the celestial guardians of the four quarters.

A great pavilion had been erected for the ceremony. Its walls were constructed of marble and it was supported on numerous pillars studded with sparkling gems. Fragrant and brightly colored flower garlands were draped everywhere and the air was filled with the scent of black aloe incense. Large stands constructed of mahogany inlaid with coral and pearl, holding rows of golden seats, surrounded the sacrificial area. Kings from all around the world along with their ministers filled the stands, eager to see the wedding.

The entire pavilion was crowded with jubilant people who cried out, "All glories to Rama and Sita!" Hundreds of elderly brahmins wearing simple loin cloths, with clean white threads hanging from their left shoulders, were seated around the sacrificial arena. They recited Vedic hymns continuously and the melodic rise and fall of their metrical chanting filled the pavilion. Musical instruments played while expert singers sang the praises of Rama and Sita. The whole assembly appeared like an exuberant festival held in the heavens by the gods.

Dasarath and his four sons approached the sacrificial fire, which was tended by Vasishtha. When they were seated, the princes saw Sita and the other three princesses enter the arena. The princes' minds were captivated by the beauty of their wives-to-be. Adorned with shining silk garments, jewels and gold ornaments, the princesses appeared like four goddesses descended from the celestial realm. They sat down opposite their intended spouses, glancing down shyly, and Vasishtha immediately began the wedding ceremony.

Janaka stepped forward, speaking in a voice choked with emotion. "My dear Rama, I now give to you Sita, my own beloved daughter, to be your assistant in all your religious duties. She will always remain exclusively devoted to you and will follow you like your own shadow. Take her hand in yours and accept her. I bless you both."

Janaka took Rama's hand and placed it over Sita's. Vasishtha sprinkled sanctified water over their clasped hands, signifying the confirmation of the gift of Sita. Holding Sita's hand, Rama led her slowly around the sacred fire.

From the upper reaches of the pavilion the gods were heard to exclaim, "Excellent! Bravo!" Celestial flowers rained down upon Rama and Sita. The entire assembly of onlookers erupted with a shout of joy. Both Dasarath and Janaka looked with tearful eyes at the newlywed couple. Rama's complexion, resembling a celestial emerald, contrasted the pure white features of Sita. They were both covered with golden flower petals and their many jewels shone brilliantly. As they walked hand in hand around the fire, Sita looked down in shyness while Rama smiled at the loudly cheering crowds in the pavilion.

Each of Rama's three brothers, one after another in order of their seniority, took the hand of one of the other three princesses. Lakshmana was united with Urmila, Bharata with Mandavi and Shatrughna with Srutakirti. The three effulgent princes, holding the their brides' hands, went around the sacred fire along with Janaka and the many sages.

Cries of happiness filled the pavilion. While the gods played their celestial drums, bevies of Apsaras danced and Gandharvas sang. The sages recited Vedic texts and the blast of conch shells was heard everywhere. All those present in the assembly were lost in ecstasy.

The ceremony ended at midday and the kings and princes gradually retired to their tents, headed by Dasarath, Janaka and the four newly married couples.

The following day, Vishvamitra, after taking permission from both Dasarath and Janaka, left for the northern Himalayan ranges, his mind intent on the performance of asceticism. Janaka bestowed upon his daughters a dowry consisting of hundreds of thousands of cows and an equal number of elephants, horses, chariots and foot soldiers. The king, whose wealth was virtually unlimited, gave away millions of pieces of silken and cotton textiles, tens of thousands of handwoven carpets, heaps of gold, silver and jewels, and hundreds of richly adorned maids for each of the brides.

*   *   *

After a few days Dasarath left for Ayodhya, proceeding at the head of a large army. As the king, surrounded by his sons and the host of sages, was traveling along the broad road that led to Ayodhya, he suddenly saw a strange omen. Birds began to cry out fearfully and swoop low over their heads. Witnessing this foreboding sign, Dasarath's heart quivered and his mind became fearful. The king asked Vasishtha if he knew the cause of those omens.

"These signs portend some grave danger," replied the rishi, "but here are groups of deer crossing our path from left to right. This indicates our deliverance from that danger. You should not fear."

A fierce tempest blew up. The sun was enveloped in darkness and the sky became black. Trees crashed to the ground and the earth shook. A dreadful dust storm swirled around the travelers, confounding their senses. They were rendered virtually unconscious. Suddenly, from out of the darkness, appeared the terrible sage Parasurama. He was dressed in tiger skins and had matted locks coiled at the crown of his head.

Dasarath and his followers immediately recognized him. Although a brahmin, Parasurama was famous for his prowess as a fighter. In former ages he had single-handedly overcome the world's warriors, annihilating them by the millions. The sage had become enraged when his father was killed by warrior kings, and he wreaked an awful vengeance. He had ranged the globe massacring the entire warrior class. He now stood before Dasarath holding a battle-ax in one hand and in the other a fierce arrow which resembled a streak of lightning. He was as tall as two men and he had upon his shoulder a great bow. Appearing as irresistible as the fire of universal destruction, he blocked the path like an impassable mountain.

The sages in Dasarath's party quickly gathered together. They took water to wash Parasurama's feet and hands and offered him gentle words of welcome.

Accepting the honor offered by the sages, Parasurama looked at Rama and said in a grave voice, "O Rama, I have heard of your strength. By breaking Shiva's bow you have performed an incredible feat. How can I, who has formed a great enmity with all warriors, tolerate hearing of such prowess existing in a king? I have here another sacred bow, that of Vishnu. Let us see your power now. Fit this celestial arrow upon this bow and simply draw it to its full length. If you are able to accomplish this task, then I shall challenge you to single combat. When you stand on the battlefield and are swept away by the force of my weapons, you shall earn undying fame."

Dasarath threw up his hands in horror. Knowing well of Parasurama's power, he feared for Rama's life. He approached the sage with joined palms and entreated him to spare Rama. Paying no heed at all to the king, Parasurama continued to speak only to Rama: "Both the bow broken by you and this one here were constructed by the architect of the gods, Vishvakarma. The one you sundered formerly belonged to Shiva. However, this one here was Vishnu's property. It is thus more powerful than the one you broke, for Vishnu is always Shiva's superior."

Parasurama took the bow from his shoulder. With furrowed brows, he gazed at Rama with bloodshot eyes, not immediately recognising the prince's divine identity. "The bow has been passed down from Vishnu to my ancestors and finally to me. I now offer it to you, O Rama. Considering your sacred duty as a warrior to always accept a challenge, exhibit now the strength of your arms!"

Parasurama held out the enormous bow. Rama, smiling slightly, stepped forward. "I have heard of your tremendous feat in fighting and killing all the world's warriors twenty-one times. You have fully avenged your father with this commendable action."

Even as a child Rama had been told the story of Parasurama. The many kings killed by that sage had become debauched, and it was by divine arrangement that they had been annihilated. As a sage Parasurama had performed much asceticism and had finally been personally empowered by Vishnu himself. By dint of Vishnu's own desire and power Parasurama had been able to exterminate the warrior class. Now Vishnu, appearing as Rama, again stood before the sage. He continued to speak: "You are a brahmin sage and are therefore worthy of my worship. However, since you despise me, seeing me to belong to the warrior class, I shall now display to you my personal prowess."

Rama seized the bow along with the blazing arrow from Parasurama's hand. He strung the bow in an instant and drew the arrow back to his ear. Looking angrily at Parasurama, he asked, "Where shall I discharge this deadly shaft, O sage? As you are my superior I dare not aim it at you."

Hosts of gods had assembled in the sky. Seeing the celestial bow drawn in anger by Rama, and fearing that he may destroy the heavens, they cried out, "Vishnu! Save us, save us!"

Rama, standing with the bow, blazed as brilliant as the sun and Parasurama fell back in astonishment. He felt his own power completely eclipsed by Rama. Suddenly realizing Rama's identity, the sage spoke in faltering tones. "You appear invincible and I can understand that you must surely be the imperishable Vishnu himself. I accept defeat but I am not shamed, as you are indeed the Lord of all the worlds."

Parasurama recalled how Vishnu had long ago said he would come again to take back the divine energy he had given to the sage. The warrior-sage folded his palms and said, "O Rama, O all-powerful one, you have already divested me of my power and my pride. Please release this arrow upon my desires for heavenly pleasures and thereby burn them all to ashes. I wish only to serve you. With all my material aspirations destroyed by you, I shall be fit to become your eternal servant. This is my deepest desire."

Parasurama bowed low before Rama, who then fired the fearful shaft. The sage immediately vanished along with the arrow. Then Varuna, the god of the waters, appeared and Rama gave him the celestial bow to keep on behalf of the gods.

The exchange between Rama and the sage was heard and understood only by Vasishtha and a few other spiritually powerful brahmins. The king and the others present had been wholly confounded by the events that had occurred. They were amazed and relieved to see that Rama had somehow appeased the sage. Everything again became calm and the party resumed their journey, soon approaching Ayodhya.

Word had already reached Ayodhya of the approach of Dasarath's party. Thousands of brahmins and citizens had come some miles out of the city to greet them. They stood along the wide roads throwing rice grains and fresh green leaves in front of Dasarath. Seated aboard his chariot, the emperor and his sons waved at the people. They moved slowly through the crowds and entered the city in state. It was decorated with flags and festoons and strewn all over with flowers. Trumpet fanfares sounded and joyous people thronged around the king's party as it went slowly along the main thoroughfare.

Dasarath entered his own white marble palace, which resembled Mount Himavat. He was greeted by his wives, who had organized a ceremonious reception for their sons and new daughters-in-law. After the greeting the princes and princesses went to their respective palaces and began to enjoy life in Ayodhya exactly like the gods in heaven.

After a few weeks, Dasarath asked Bharata and Shatrughna to go to the kingdom of their father-in-law, Kushadhvaja, who himself had no sons. The emperor instructed the princes to assist Kushadhvaja in the affairs of state. Along with their wives and a large army, Bharata and Shatrughna therefore soon left the capital and went to Rajagriha, where Kushadhvaja lived.

CHAPTER FIVE

CROOKED ADVICE FOR QUEEN KAIKEYI

The aging Dasarath, thinking of his retirement, gradually entrusted more and more of the state affairs to Rama and Lakshmana. Those two princes, along with their wives, served the king in every way. They always thought of the welfare of the people. Everyone became pleased with their disposition and conduct. They were gentle and kind, but firm when necessary. They demonstrated complete mastery of the military arts and, having slain the powerful Rakshasas even while boys, were respected as great heroes.

Rama was especially dear to the king and the people. He was always tranquil and softspoken, not retorting even when someone spoke harshly to him. He recognized the smallest of services rendered and did not take to heart any wrongs against him. Rama had conquered anger and was full of compassion. Making all arrangements to protect the people, he surrounded himself with intelligent advisors and never made a decision without due consultation. Despite his power and ability, he always remained humble, mild and self-controlled. He was not influenced by envy or hatred, did not engage in frivolous talks and always sought the good in others. Free from sloth, he was ever vigilant to carry out his duty.

Rama gave delight to even the gods, who would frequently grace Ayodhya with their presence. He was as tolerant as Mother Earth, as wise as Brihaspati, and as valorous as Indra. His personal beauty was as resplendent as the brilliant sun-god.

Dasarath, seeing his son endowed with so many virtues, longed to see him installed as the Prince Regent. The king discussed his desire with his ministers and priests. They all unanimously agreed that Rama, as the eldest son, was the rightful heir to the throne and that he would be the most popular choice of the people. However, when the royal astrologers were calculating a favorable time for the coronation, they discovered dreadful signs in the heavens, portents that indicated that some calamity would soon occur.

Dasarath became concerned. The omens must surely foretell of his own impending death. He decided to perform the ceremony quickly at the earliest opportune moment. Having set a date for Rama's installation, he summoned to Ayodhya rulers and important men from around the globe. But the gods so arranged that Dasarath, in his haste, neglected to invite King Kushadhvaja. Thus neither Bharata nor Shatrughna came for the ceremony. Dasarath realized too late his omission, for it was a journey of some days to Rajagriha. Nevertheless, he considered that his two absent sons would soon receive the delightful news of their elder brother's installation. He felt sure they would be overjoyed and would not take offense.

Soon a large gathering of kings and brahmins appeared in Ayodhya and Dasarath had them assembled in the royal court. Sitting in state in the assembly, the emperor blazed forth like Indra in the midst of the gods. He spoke in a pleasing and melodious voice, which was at the same time sonorous and grave.

"All of you know how the earth has long been protected by me and the kings who previously appeared before me in my line. To the best of my ability I have ruled the people, giving protection even at the expense of personal comforts. My body has become worn out in the shade of the royal umbrella. Carrying on my shoulders the burden of governing the globe, I have become old. I wish now to bestow this kingdom upon one well suited to take my place. Here is my beloved and eldest son Rama, who vies with the king of the gods in all virtues. With the agreement of my closest advisors and in accordance with custom and law, I desire to place Rama at the head of the state. With your permission, therefore, the ceremony will take place tomorrow morning."

Dasarath looked around the vast assembly of kings and sages. All of them gazed at him intently as he spoke. The kings saw Dasarath as the leader of the entire earth. They all had affection for the old emperor, who always administered the law with justice and compassion. They willingly paid him tributes and sought his guidance in the affairs of state management. Dasarath oversaw the world situation, ensuring that the different kings and leaders all ruled according to the codes of religion. All the assembled kings felt that Rama was the perfect choice to succeed Dasarath. As the emperor looked at his obedient and gentle son, he was moved by love. He continued to speak with tears running from his eyes.

"Rama, who possesses every desirable quality, will be your worthy protector and even the universe will be better ruled with him as emperor. If my plan finds favor with you, then be pleased to give your consent. Otherwise, if you consider that some other course should be taken, then speak out. Perhaps you may find me overly attached to Rama, choosing him when a better choice could be found. The views of the dispassionate are always to be sought when deciding a difficult issue."

The whole assembly was filled with delight upon hearing Dasarath speak. They erupted with loud acclamations of joy, even as a crowd of peacocks would acclaim the appearance of a large rain cloud. The sound echoed all around Ayodhya, seeming to shake the earth. "Let it be so! Let it be so!" was heard everywhere, and every man was in agreement.

Stepping forward, a leader of the brahmins said, "You have long protected us with love, O king. Now you have a worthy son and can retire peacefully. Pray install Rama as the Prince Regent, for he alone deserves to be your successor. We long to see Rama riding upon the great royal elephant, his head shielded by the white umbrella."

Upon hearing the assembly voice their unanimous agreement to Rama's installation, Dasaratha stood up, his eyes flooded with tears of joy. "It is fortunate for me and indeed the world that you all wish to see Rama succeed me as king. This confirms my decision. I shall begin the arrangements for Rama's installation immediately."

Dasaratha came down from his throne and approached Vasishtha, touching his feet. "With your permission, O holy brahmin, we shall proceed with the ceremony tomorrow. If you are agreeable, then please make all preparations."

"So be it," Vasishtha replied, and he immediately commanded the king's ministers to set about making ready all of the items required for the installation the following day. The assembly then dispersed with a loud clamor, and shouts of "Victory to Rama!" were heard everywhere.

That night, however, Dasarath remembered the astrological predictions. He became fearful and called for Rama. Speaking with him in private, Dasaratha said, "I have enjoyed a long life and have always protected the people to the best of my ability. In thousands of religious ceremonies, I have bestowed abundant charity. By sacrifice, worship and charity I have repaid my debt to the gods, the brahmins and the forefathers. I have also fully satisfied myself through the enjoyment of numerous pleasures. All that remains for me to do is to install you as my successor."

Dasaratha clasped Rama close to his bosom. The king's body trembled and his eyes shed tears. He desperately longed for his son to succeed him. At last it was imminent. Surely no evil destiny could prevent it now. Would not even the gods desire to see this magnificent prince become the king? Dasarath revealed his concerns to Rama, telling him of the malefic stars. He also told his son of the many bad dreams he had recently experienced.

"My dear Rama, due to seeing all these omens, your installation has been sought swiftly by me before any problems arise. With your good wife,

Sita, make offerings into the sacrificial fire tonight. At sunrise tomorrow we shall commence the installation ceremony."

Rama nodded in agreement and then bowed and took his leave from the king. He went back to his palace and, along with Sita, sat before the sacrificial fire making offerings to Vishnu.

*   *   *

The news of Rama's installation quickly spread around the city, delighting everyone. The temples were thronged with people offering gifts and worshipping the gods. As evening fell the city streets were filled with a flurry of joyous citizens. The large crowds of men moving about Ayodhya resembled the tossing waves of the ocean. Everyone spoke only of the installation. Poets and bards composed songs about the occasion. Flags were hoisted high on the housetops and garlands of forest flowers were draped everywhere. Colorful festoons hung across the streets, which were swept and sprinkled with perfumed water. Shining lamps hung from every tree lining the streets. The city echoed everywhere with the loud chanting of Vedic hymns. Elephants and bulls roared on all sides and the whole atmosphere throbbed with excitement. No one could wait for sunrise, when the ceremony would commence.

In the palace of Kaikeyi, the king's youngest queen, there was a hunchbacked maidservant called Manthara. Upon seeing the celebrations, Manthara approached Rama's former nurse and inquired, "What occasion gives rise to this display of delight on every side? Is the emperor going to perform some great sacrifice?"

The nurse, her face blooming with happiness, told Manthara about the king's decision to install Rama as the heir-apparent. "Tomorrow, under favorable stars, our lord Dasarath will give to the sinless Rama the office of Prince Regent. What greater occasion for joy could there be?"

Manthara's mind recoiled at this news. She was immediately seized with anger. Surely this was a disaster! With Rama installed as king her mistress Kaikeyi would soon fall out of favor, her own son Bharata being left as nothing more than Rama's servant. Manthara raged within herself. She had long enjoyed special privileges as Kaikeyi's senior maidservant. The emperor particularly liked her mistress, who had given Manthara the esteem she desired. As a hunchback she had always been the butt of jokes and abuse among the other servants. But as her mistress became more influential, the other servants, even those of the senior queen Kaushalya, had been obliged to pay her respect.

Sighing with anxiety, Manthara ran to Kaikeyi's room where she found the queen lying upon a couch. With her face flushed she began addressing her bemused mistress in harsh tones. "Get up, foolish woman! How can you lay there when calamity stares you in the face? You languish here at ease even as a flood of misery sweeps towards you. Thoroughly neglected by your husband, you are threatened now with utter ruin."

Kaikeyi looked affectionately at her servant. Manthara had been her childhood nurse and Kaikeyi saw her like her own mother. The queen had not heard the news about Rama and she inquired from Manthara, "Pray tell me what causes you sorrow at this time? You seem sorely afflicted."

Manthara became even more incensed upon hearing Kaikeyi's question. She replied in a low voice trembling with anger. "There is no doubt that disaster now threatens us both. With your destruction will come mine, as much as with your good fortune rests mine. I am therefore saying this only for your benefit."

She grasped Kaikeyi's hand, trying to impress upon her mistress what appeared to her to be the obvious facts. "Although born in a royal line, you seem ignorant of the ways of kings. A king will speak sweet words to a person while at the same time planning their destruction. The emperor has acted as your beloved spouse while performing deeds which will ruin you to the very roots."

Kaikeyi sat up and looked at her servant curiously. Manthara's eyes blazed as she continued. "Having sent your own son Bharata away to a distant kingdom, this wicked king now plans to install Rama as Prince Regent. What greater misfortune could there be for you?"

Kaikeyi smiled. She loved Rama as much as her own dear son, while Rama for his part looked upon Kaikeyi as being equal to his own mother Kaushalya. She felt a surge of joy upon hearing Manthara's report. She could not understand why Manthara was disturbed. Why was she so vehement? If anyone else had spoken about Dasarath and Rama in such a way, she would have had them punished, but Kaikeyi was accustomed to her servant's sullen temperament. She felt there was no malice in Manthara, despite her often angry expressions.

Taking from her bosom a necklace of brilliant diamonds set in gold, Kaikeyi handed it to her servant and said, "My dear Dhatri, this is surely the best news you have ever brought me. My heart swells with pleasure at hearing your words, which seem to me like nectar. I wish to reward you. Take this gift and tell me if there is anything else I can do for you."

Manthara threw down the necklace and began rebuking Kaikeyi. "This is no occasion for joy, foolish lady! What strange frame of mind has seized you? An ocean of grief threatens to overwhelm you and yet you stand here smiling. Your stepson Rama will become king while your own son Bharata is left aside. Bharata's claim to the throne is the same as Rama's and thus Rama will see him as an enemy. Lakshmana serves only Rama, and Shatrughna serves your son. Therefore it is only Rama or Bharata who may be crowned as the sovereign of this world. My mind quakes with fear to think of the danger to your son from the powerful Rama once he is king."

Manthara's eyes grew bloodshot with fury and her face whitened as she spoke. Why was Kaikeyi not understanding? Kaushalya had long been snubbed by the king in favor of Kaikeyi. When Rama became the king that would all change. Kaushalya would be exalted to the highest level, while Kaikeyi would lose her special position as the king's most favored consort. Kaushalya would certainly exact her revenge for her long suffering. Kaikeyi would become Kaushalya's maidservant and Bharata would at best be Rama's servant-more likely he would be exiled. Where would that leave Kaikeyi's servants? Praying to the gods to help her, the hunchbacked maid became more ardent in her plea.

"You must do something! This is a great disaster. Once the crown has passed to the other side of your family, you will in time see your own side sink into oblivion, bereft of all royal fortune."

Hearing this strong submission from her servant, the beautiful Kaikeyi thought of Rama. She could not imagine him bearing any ill will toward Bharata. Manthara's fears were quite groundless. Rama always acted in perfect accord with religious principles. He was devoted to truth, disciplined and always kind. He doubtlessly deserved to be king. After he was crowned he would surely look after his younger brothers like a father. Manthara had no reason to feel such distress. Kaikeyi chided her gently.

"When such an occasion for rejoicing has come, you should by no means give way to grief, my dear maidservant. Nor should you think ill of Rama. My son Bharata will be in no danger from Rama, and in the future he may well succeed him to the throne. There is no need for lamentation."

Manthara would not be placated. In order to improve her own position she wanted her mistress to be the mother of the king. Blinded by her own greed and envy, Manthara considered the emperor to be acting from similar motivations. She continued to beseech Kaikeyi in increasingly rancorous tones.

"Surely it is due only to stupidity that you fail to see your impending doom, O deluded one. Rama will be crowned king and after him will come his son. Where then will Bharata be left? Not all the sons of a king can assume the throne; it falls only to one among them. Having taken hold of the throne, Rama will ensure that it goes to his own son, if necessary by banishing Bharata, or perhaps even by sending him to the next world. You and your line will be lost and forsaken. I am here to awaken you to a great peril now arrived at your door. Do not disregard me."

Manthara's lofty position in the palace had gone to her head. She was furious at the prospect of losing her status and she continued to present many arguments to her mistress. She played upon the natural rivalry existing between the king's co-wives. Kaikeyi's affection for Rama was deep and the discussion went back and forth for some time, but gradually Manthara began to change her mistress's mind. By the gods' arrangement, her arguments swayed Kaikeyi's mind and the queen's intelligence became confused. Although she loved Rama, she began to consider that his installation was an injustice.

Manthara saw in Kaikeyi's face that her mind was wavering. She grasped the queen's hands. "There is a way by which we may not be ruined. If Rama can be sent to the forest and Bharata installed in his place, then the sovereignty may be secured in your line."

This idea had entered Manthara's mind by the sudden inspiration of the gods. Kaikeyi, intrigued, looked at her servant. "How can this be accomplished?"

Manthara recalled a story she had heard from her mistress many years earlier. "Some time ago you told me how you once went with your husband when he was assisting Indra in a battle against the demons. Having fought hard one day, your husband lay unconscious on the battlefield, his body severely wounded. A grave danger beset him then from a demon who would come at night to devour the bodies of the warriors still on the field."

Kaikeyi remembered the incident. Many years back the emperor had gone to the heavens, taking Kaikeyi with him. He was famed as an invincible warrior and the gods had asked his assistance in a fight. At that time he had fought so powerfully that his chariot appeared to be facing ten directions simultaneously and the gods had therefore named him Dasarath, or "ten chariots."

Manthara continued, "At that time, seeing the danger to Dasarath, you rode out in a chariot and rescued your lord. Upon recovering he offered you a couple of boons, but you deferred them to a time when you might need them most. Surely that time has now come. Go to Dasarath and ask that he banish Rama and install Bharata in his place as the Prince Regent. In this way we shall both be saved."

Despite her love for her husband and her attachment for Rama, Kaikeyi became convinced by Manthara's arguments. She was upset. How could the king have treated her in such a way? He was always so kind and loving. Was all that just a show to win her favor? She began to feel angry. The king might have spoken so many sweet words to her, but by his behavior it was obvious that he favored Kaushalya. They had probably even conspired together to have Bharata sent away. Why had she not realized it before? It was obvious! Now the whole situation was revealed. Dasarath had shown his real feelings by completely neglecting her and favoring Kaushalya's son instead.

Kaikeyi heaved a doleful sigh. "Your suggestion finds favor with me, Manthara. I shall this very moment go before the king and ask of him these boons."

Manthara's mind was full of cunning. Her eyes narrowed. "You should ask that Rama be banished for no less than fourteen years. Within that time your son Bharata will become dear to the people and he will be firmly established on the throne."

Manthara intelligently knew that Bharata could never become the king in Rama's presence. The people would not allow it to happen. Even the humble Bharata himself would almost surely not accede to such an arrangement. Rama had to be banished. The maidservant continued, "Do not allow Rama to remain in the kingdom. By his power and influence he will seize the throne, even if Bharata is crowned. Your son has long been away while Rama has been here, winning the hearts of the people. It is imperative that Rama be sent away for a long time."

Kaikeyi listened with full attention as her maidservant revealed her insidious plan. "Listen as I tell you the means of approaching the king. Putting on soiled garments, you should go to the sulking chamber and lie down on the bare floor. With your ornaments cast about and your hair in disarray, lay there weeping."

Manthara knew that her mistress was guileless by nature. The queen would not have acted politically, even though angered, but her servant led her along. She spoke of Dasarath's special affection for his youngest and most beautiful wife. "The king will never be able to tolerate your sullen mood. He cannot ignore your order. For your sake he would enter fire and even lay down his very life. Using the power of your charms you will easily achieve your ends, O beautiful lady."

Clenching her fists, Kaikeyi sat on her bed, spread with a pure white silk sheet. Manthara was right. The king obviously liked her for something, if only her beauty and charms. Every evening he spent time with her. Tonight he would be in for a surprise! Kaikeyi came fully under the sway of anger as Manthara continued.

"When the king sees you distraught, he will take you up and offer you anything. He will present priceless gems and pearls in order to pacify you. Do not be distracted from your goal of banishing Rama. Insist upon the two boons long ago given by your lord. Take those boons now, O queen. Demand the exile of Rama and the coronation of Bharata."

Although Manthara showed her mistress an evil course disguised as good, Kaikeyi accepted her advice. Kind, gentle and wise by nature, Kaikeyi nevertheless lost her good sense under the influence of her envious maid. Considering her husband and Rama as enemies, she spoke with hot, heavy breaths. "You have given me good counsel, O wise woman. I have been cheated by the king. You have acted as my well-wisher by pointing this out. When my son is installed on the throne, I shall confer upon you numerous boons and much wealth."

Manthara smiled and urged Kaikeyi to make haste. "Let us go quickly to the inner rooms, for the king will shortly come for his evening visit with you. You should by no means stand by as Rama is made Prince Regent. Act swiftly for the interests of your son and your own self."

Kaikeyi was pierced again and again by Manthara's sharp words. The servant repeatedly spoke against the king and Rama, stoking Kaikeyi's anger more. Arriving at the sulking chamber, the queen threw herself on the floor and said to Manthara, "Either Rama is exiled and Bharata made king, or I shall remain here in this state, taking neither food nor water. If my desire is not fulfilled, then you shall see me depart from this spot for the region of the dead."

With her ornaments scattered and her garland crushed, Kaikeyi lay on the beautiful mosaic floor, appearing like a goddess fallen from the heavens. Her face dark with rage, she tossed about and sobbed.

CHAPTER SIX

THE KING'S HEARTBREAK

Dasarath, having seen that all the arrangements for the installation were underway, made his way toward Kaikeyi's rooms for his evening rendezvous. The glorious monarch entered Kaikeyi's excellent apartment as the moon might enter the sky at night, spreading its beautiful rays. Peacocks, parrots and other species of colorful birds crowded the palace, their cries augmenting the sounds of various musical instruments. Hundreds of well-dressed maids moved about in the great halls and rooms, in which were hung flowing silk drapes and numerous fine paintings. Along the outer walls grew trees filled with blossoms and fruits. Tall seats of ivory burnished with gold stood everywhere, along with expansive couches covered with soft cushions. Costly handwoven carpets covered the floors. First-class food and drink of every variety were provided in gold and crystal dishes laid out on golden tables.

Dasarath swept through the palace, which rivaled paradise itself. The armed guards at the outer doors bowed low as he passed, while at the inner doors the female servants folded their palms in respect. Coming at last to Kaikeyi's personal quarters, the king did not see her lying on her bed as expected. Dasarath was surprised to find that his beloved spouse had failed to meet him at the usual time. He called out for her. When there was no reply the king was dismayed. What had happened? He searched about and, finding Kaikeyi's doorkeeper, inquired of his wife's whereabouts. With a dejected expression the portress told the king that Kaikeyi had entered the sulking chamber in an angry mood.

Even further dismayed upon hearing this strange report, the king quickly made his way towards his wife. He entered the sulking room and saw her there fallen on the floor in a sorry and unseemly state. Dasarath looked sadly upon his youngest queen, who was dearer to him than his life, but who now held in her heart a wicked and sinful desire. Lying on the ground she looked like a rose creeper violently torn from its tree, or like an Apsara dropped from heaven, or a doe caught in a hunter's snare. Dasarath looked upon her as the lord of elephants might look upon his mate lying pierced by a poisoned arrow. Fondly stroking her tear-streaked face, the agitated emperor spoke to her softly.

"Your anger is surely not meant for me, who only wishes for your unending happiness. Tell me, O gentle lady, by whom you have been insulted or rebuked so that you now lie here rolling in the dust? Who deserves punishment today at my hands? Or do you wish me to release someone who deserves to be punished? By whom have you been offended or whom would you seek to oblige?"

Kaikeyi said nothing and did not even look at the king. Dasarath felt tormented as he sought at length to appease her. "If you are ailing, then I shall call here the royal physicians, who will quickly heal your pain. Speak out whatever is amiss and allow me to make amends. I can by no means tolerate your distress and will quickly perform any work which pleases you. This earth with all its wealth belongs to me. What shall I bestow upon you today? What can you gain by torturing yourself in this way, my beloved queen? Please rise up and tell me the source of your sorrow."

Kaikeyi was comforted and encouraged by her husband's entreaty. He was ready to do anything to please her. She prepared to put forward her terrible proposal. Seeing Dasarath deeply moved by love for her, Kaikeyi spoke in strained tones. "I have not been insulted or offended by anyone, O king. There is, however, something I wish you to accomplish. Make me a solemn vow that you will fulfill my desire and then I shall tell you what it is."

Dasarath placed her head upon his lap and straightened her disheveled hair. He smiled at her and said, "Save for my son Rama, there is none in this world more dear to me than you. I swear then by that invincible high-souled Rama, dearer to me than life, that I shall satisfy your cherished desire. By that very Rama, from whom separation would surely end my life, I swear to carry out your order. Indeed, by Rama, whom I would have in exchange even for my own self, my other sons and the entire earth, I promise to do your bidding. Please, therefore, reveal your mind to me, O good lady."

Kaikeyi saw that her husband had bound himself completely by this thrice-spoken vow. She inwardly rejoiced and felt that her ends were practically achieved. She then said to him what would have been difficult to say even for an enemy, and which was like death arrived at Dasarath's door. "Let all the gods headed by Indra witness your promise. Let the sun, the moon, the sky, fire, day and night, the four quarters with their presiding deities, the universe itself and the indwelling Lord in everyone's heart take heed of your great vow. The highly glorious emperor, who is always true to his word and who knows what is right, has given me his promise."

Looking intently at her bemused husband, Kaikeyi said, "Remember now, O king, how in former times you fought with the gods against the demons and how I saved your life. Surely you recall your offer to me then of two boons. Having kept those with you all this time, I now wish to take them. Grant me those boons, O lord, or see me give up my life this very day."

Held under the powerful sway of passion and bound by his infallible promise, the king, like a deer stepping into a snare, made ready to accord the two boons to his queen. Kaikeyi continued, "For my first boon, let my son Bharata be installed as the Prince Regent in Rama's place. For the second, let Rama be exiled to the forest and remain there for fourteen years. Be true to your promise, O king of kings, and cover both yourself and your race with everlasting glory."

For some time Dasarath gazed at his wife in utter disbelief. He was seized by an agonizing anxiety when he heard her cruel utterance. Surely this could not be happening. Was he really hearing this or was it a dream? Had something experienced in a former life suddenly returned as a vivid hallucination? Maybe he was simply losing his sanity. How could Kaikeyi have made such a request? She had always shown a deep affection for Rama.

As he considered her words again and again, Dasarath became overpowered by grief and fainted away. Upon regaining consciousness he saw before him his wife, sitting with a stern expression, and he remembered again her terrible request. As distressed as a deer at the sight of a lion, the king sat upon the bare floor. He sighed like a poisonous serpent transfixed by the mystic spells of a charmer. Crying out, "Alas, what a calamity!" he swooned once more.

As he again came back to consciousness the king began to feel furious. This was entirely unexpected from Kaikeyi. She was revealing a side of her nature he had never seen before. He thundered at his queen as if about to consume her with his blazing wrath. "O cruel and wicked woman, it seems you are set upon the destruction of my race. What harm have Rama or I ever done you? Why then are you bent on bringing ruin to me and mine at such a time? By harboring you all this while I have held to my bosom a venomous snake. When practically the whole of humanity extols Rama's virtues, how shall I forsake him? I might give up my wives, my kingdom and indeed my life, but I can never part with Rama."

Dasarath broke off, too shocked to continue. Had he not always shown kindness to Kaikeyi? How could she hurt him in this way? Surely she realized that her request would kill him. Deeply impassioned, he spoke with tears in his eyes. "The world may exist without the sun, crops may grow without water, but in no event can life remain in my body without my seeing Rama. Therefore give up your sinful desire, O beautiful lady! Placing my head upon your feet, I beseech you to be gracious to me."

Dasarath held his wife's feet and gazed into her face, but Kaikeyi sat looking at him impassively, without saying a word. In plaintive tones the king continued. "If you feel I have slighted your son Bharata, then let him indeed be installed in place of Rama. But what need is there to send away the lotus-eyed and gentle Rama? I cannot believe that you have alone developed a dislike for Rama. On so many previous occasions you have told me of your love for my beloved son. Surely you are now possessed of an evil spirit."

Dasarath could not imagine how else his wife could behave in this way. She had never been harsh towards him before. He remembered the astrological omens. Surely his wife's strange request was the work of some malevolent influence. He spoke more gently. "I have seen myself how Rama serves you even more than does your own son Bharata. Have you not always told me so yourself? How then have you come to desire Rama's exile to the dreadful forest for a full fourteen years? Let him remain here and let Bharata be king. What objection could you have to that?"

Kaikeyi did not waver. She had lost her trust in Dasarath and she seethed with anger. He was simply trying to win her over with empty words. But she was not going to be fooled any more. She remembered Manthara's warning. The king and his beloved Kaushalya were not going to cheat her this time. She would get her boons no matter what Dasarath said. She sat in silence.

Dasarath could not think clearly. He was torn by his love for Rama and his promise to his wife, who had now seized him violently by the heart. Realizing that he could never order his son to enter the forest, Dasarath feared he would bring infamy to his royal line. No king in his line had ever been known to break his word at any time.

Dasarath implored his wife. "What will you gain by banishing Rama? He will always render you every service and remain entirely devoted to your welfare. I have never received a single complaint against Rama even from his subordinates, let alone elders like you. Truthfulness, charity, asceticism, self-control, kindness, non-duplicity, learning and service to his elders—all these are ever-present in Rama. How could you wish harm to that guileless prince?"

Dasarath could see that Kaikeyi was unmoved. It was obvious her feelings towards Rama had changed. The king decided to try a different approach and he invoked his own love for her. "O Kaikeyi, you should show mercy to me in this, my great misery. An old and worn man, I am fast approaching the end of my days. I have now been subjected to an unbearable grief in the shape of your harsh words. What do you wish to possess? I can offer you anything that may be had in all of this world. Only ask for your desire and consider it done. Joining my palms I fall at your feet. Do not banish Rama. Accept my piteous plea and save my life."

Kaikeyi looked coldly upon her husband. He had fallen weeping to the floor and was tossing about, gripped by an overwhelming agony. He prayed again and again for deliverance, but Kaikeyi felt no pity. With her heart hardened by Manthara and her intelligence confused by the gods, she was fixed in her evil determination. Looking contemptuously at Dasarath, she spoke fiercely. "After granting boons and failing to fulfill them, how will you again proclaim your piety in the world, O noble king? When in an assembly of sages you are asked about your promise, how will you reply? Will you admit that you proved untruthful to your own dear wife, to whom you owe your very life? Having once granted boons, and having again sworn three times to fulfill those boons, will you now falsify your word?"

Kaikeyi was standing, her face flushed with anger. She felt cheated by her husband. He had promised her anything. Now he was trying to back out. This simply confirmed her doubts about his sincerity. He had no intention of giving her what she wanted. Her voice became cold. "What honor will you bring to your line by this action, O king of kings? Do you not recall the many occasions when your forebears were prepared to sacrifice everything, including their own lives, in order to protect the honor of your race? O foolish king! It seems that at the expense of anything you wish to install Rama as your successor and enjoy life with Kaushalya eternally!"

Kaikeyi was furious. The king was prepared to sacrifice anything for the sake of Kaushalya's son, but he cared so little for Kaikeyi that he would deny her rights even if it meant bringing infamy upon himself. She went on, her voice rising to a shout. "Whether your promise was righteous or otherwise and whether you made it sincerely or not, it cannot now be withdrawn. If Rama is installed as Prince Regent I shall swallow poison and give up my life before your eyes! I would prefer death to seeing Kaushalya become the mother of the king. I swear by Bharata and by my own self that I shall not be appeased by anything less than Rama's exile."

The king's body trembled. Consumed by grief, he gazed with unwinking eyes upon the face of his beautiful wife. He was stunned by her words, which struck him with the force of a thunderbolt. He suddenly dropped to the ground like a felled tree, calling out Rama's name. Like one insane, he lost his mental balance and lay motionless on the cold floor for a considerable time. Gradually gathering his senses about him, the king stood up and spoke in a choked and anguished voice. "I cannot believe you are now speaking your own mind. Who has perverted you towards this evil course?

He suddenly dropped to the ground like a felled tree.

As if possessed by some demon you speak shamelessly that which should never be spoken. What has inspired in you this great yet groundless fear? Why are you suddenly seeing Rama as your enemy, uttering such cruel words? What do you expect to gain by Bharata's becoming my successor instead of Rama? I expect that Bharata, whose virtues compare with those of Rama, will not even reside in Ayodhya without Rama, far less accept the throne."

The king had so many times seen Bharata serving Rama with love. There was no question that Bharata would accept the kingdom, leaving Rama aside. What had made Kaikeyi imagine this to be possible? Could it be the hand of the gods? But what purpose of theirs would be achieved by denying Rama the rulership of the world? And even if Bharata should be king, why should Rama be exiled for fourteen years? It was unthinkable. Dasarath spoke aloud his thoughts. "Having said to Rama, 'Go to the forest,' how shall I look upon his crestfallen face, which will exactly resemble the eclipsed moon? Surely the kings assembled from every quarter will say, 'How has this foolish man ruled the world all this while?' When asked by wise and learned men about Rama, how shall I say that I sent him away to the forest, being pressed by Kaikeyi? If I say I was supporting the cause of truth, then what about my declaration that Rama would be installed as my successor?"

Dasarath fell back onto a couch. His arms were outstretched towards Kaikeyi, who had again fallen to the floor on hearing her husband's arguments. The king wailed in agony. "What reply can I make to Kaushalya when she asks why I rendered her such an unkind act? I have always neglected that godly lady in favor of you. Remembering my acts now gives me great pain."

Dasarath's mention of Kaushalya only made Kaikeyi more furious. What a blatant untruth! How did he expect her to believe that she was more favored than Kaushalya? In her desperation the king was ready to say anything. Kaikeyi stared at her husband, her eyes red with anger.

The king continued to speak, his passionate words lost on his implacable queen. "Seeing Rama departed for the forest and Sita weeping, I shall soon lose my life. You may then carry on all the affairs of state along with your son as the undisputed ruler. I have always seen you as my devoted and chaste wife. That was my mistake! Inveigled by your empty inducements, I have long held you close. Now you have finally killed me, even as a hunter kills a deer after enticing it with melodious music."

Dasarath saw that Kaikeyi was not to be swayed from her purpose. His anxiety intensified. In his anger and confusion he began to blame himself. Surely the whole world would condemn him for sacrificing his sinless son for the sake of a sinful woman. This terrible turn of events could only be the result of his own wicked acts in some previous life. He sat with his head in his hands, crying softly as he spoke.

"I lament only for the sake of those who will suffer for my sake when I perform the evil act of exiling Rama. For having deprived a son like Rama of fatherly affection, all honest men will rightly revile me in the following words: 'Alas, this old and foolish king, being bound by lust for his favorite queen, could even reject his dearest son!'"

Unable to contain his grief, Dasarath lamented loudly for a long time. Censuring Kaikeyi and calling upon her to have compassion on her fellow queens, on Sita and on the citizens of Ayodhya, he tried in many ways to change her mind. Kaikeyi remained adamant. The king then began to realize the inevitability of Rama's departure. He spoke to his queen in complete dismay.

"The very moment I ask Rama to depart he will leave, being fully obedient to my order. I shall then be left, cast into the deepest despair with my life's breath quickly expiring. Upon reaching heaven I shall be censured even by the gods for my vicious behavior. You too will earn unending infamy, O lady of wicked resolve. None shall praise you for causing the virtuous and highly popular Rama to be sent into the wilderness."

Dasarath practically writhed in pain as he thought of Rama leaving for the forest. That gentle prince was accustomed to ride upon the finest chariots and elephants. How would he roam the forest on foot? Every day Rama was served by numerous royal cooks, competing to offer him every fine dish. How could he subsist on wild fruits and roots? How could his son put on the coarse garments of the forest dwellers, having always been clad in the costliest of robes? The emperor, devastated, shook with grief. He felt his life slipping away.

Gazing at Kaikeyi, who he now saw as his mortal enemy, Dasarath said, "O wicked woman, it is a wonder that on speaking such cruel and vicious words your teeth do not shatter into a thousand pieces and fall from your mouth. When Rama goes to the forest, Death will surely take me. I will be condemned by all men. Kaushalya and Sumitra will then be cast into abject sorrow and will likely follow me to Death's abode. Having inflicted such miseries upon us, and being left alone with your son to rule over this world, what other indescribable pains will you give to the remaining people, who are all so loved by me?"

Although Dasarath had no intentions of asking Rama to leave, he knew his devoted son would depart immediately upon realizing his father's predicament. The king tried one last desperate plea to Kaikeyi. "Even if, upon my failing to exile my son, you are ready to swallow poison, throw yourself into fire or hang yourself, I shall by no means banish Rama. You have disgraced your family and are intent upon destroying mine. I shall never accede to your ruthless request. O malicious queen, abandon now your evil desire! I fall helpless at your feet. Come to your senses and be gracious to me, who has always been your well-wishing protector."

Exhausted by grief, Dasarath sank to the floor like a man gripped by an illness, his hands stretched out to the feet of his queen.

The unflinching Kaikeyi, who had given up all affection for her husband, saw that her ends were still not achieved. Convinced by Manthara of the king's ill intentions towards her, with her intelligence further confused by the gods, Kaikeyi could not accept Dasarath's entreaties. In a disdainful and harsh voice, she addressed the fallen monarch. "Where now is your honor, O king? Your claim that you adhere to truth is simply an empty boast! Are you to withdraw the boons previously promised to me and further sworn on this very spot? Fulfill my boons as you vowed and protect your far-reaching fame!"

Dasarath, unconscious, could not reply. After some time he revived and looked upon his queen's face. From her cold expression it was obvious that she was not in the least assuaged. The grief-stricken monarch gazed up at the clear night sky. He prayed to Nidra, the night goddess, to stay forever. How could he face the dawn, bringing as it would Rama's departure? Dasarath sat weeping, continuously repeating Rama's name.

Kaikeyi spoke impassively. "I have only asked you to fulfill your promise to me, O king. Why then do you now lie down dejected? The path of morality has been clearly shown by your ancestors. Proceed upon that path now, O truthful one, and send Rama away!"

The educated Kaikeyi, knowing her husband to be devoted to religion and piety, invoked the codes of morality. "Those men who understand right from wrong declare truthfulness as the highest virtue. I simply urge you to act upon truthfulness alone, O king, and do your duty. Truth is the support of all the worlds, the eternal Vedas represent truth, virtue itself is rooted in truth and truth sustains all beings. By following truth one attains the supreme. Therefore set your mind on truth, O king, and grant my prayer: banish Rama to the forest."

Kaikeyi stood up amid her strewn ornaments. Her eyes flashed as she made her final demand to the king. "Three times you promised and therefore three times I ask you. Fulfill my wish to see my son installed on the throne and send Rama away to the woods. This alone will satisfy me and save me from giving up my life, after seeing you abandon your honor."

As the unscrupulous Kaikeyi maintained her pressure on him, Dasarath could see no means to escape from his avowed word. With great difficulty he controlled himself, drawing upon his reserves of fortitude. His heart burned with unbearable anguish as he looked through tear-dimmed eyes at Kaikeyi. How could he any longer consider her his wife? She was fit to be rejected. Her name should never again be associated with his. No one should call her the queen of Dasarath.

The king spoke fiercely. "O perverted woman, here and now do I disown your hand, which I formerly clasped in the presence of the sacred fire and with the utterances of holy mantras. Now the night has passed and soon the people will joyfully urge me to install Rama. However, as at your insistence I shall this day surely breathe my last, Rama should be made to offer the last rites to my departed soul. O woman of evil conduct, you should make no offerings to me, for I fully reject you today."

Kaikeyi fumed. What use were these empty words? Her husband had already rejected her when he favored Kaushalya. She addressed the king in piercing words. "Why do you say such scathing and hurtful things, O monarch? I merely ask that you give me what you have already promised. Summon now your son Rama and give up this needless agonizing. Do your duty and stand fast to virtue!"

Like a first-class horse lashed with a whip, Dasarath controlled his mind and righteously responded to Kaikeyi's words. "Bound with the strong cords of morality, I am helpless. My judgment fails me, and in this evil hour I seek the refuge of Rama. Bring my gentle son before me."

The king fainted away, exhausted with grief and his futile efforts to change his wife's mind.

CHAPTER SEVEN

RAMA AGREES TO DEPART

Towards the end of night, Vasishtha, accompanied by numerous disciples, hastily entered Ayodhya from his hermitage outside the city. He went along the well-swept and watered streets, all thronging with citizens eagerly awaiting Rama's installation. Crossing the outer courtyard of the king's palace, which was decorated all over with rows of flags, he approached Dasarath's inner chambers. The rishi saw the courtyard crowded with large numbers of brahmins reciting sacred hymns from the Vedas. Upon reaching the palace gate he was met by Sumantra, who prostrated himself before the sage and then immediately left to inform Dasarath of his arrival.

As he passed through the palace and approached the inner chambers, Sumantra was entirely ignorant of his master's present plight. He composed in his mind pleasing prayers with which to greet the king, who was dearer to him than his own father. The guards informed Sumantra that the king was in Kaikeyi's chambers and, as he arrived at her door, he began to loudly recite those prayers. "Even as the sun, which sustains all beings, arouses the world, arise now, O Emperor, like the sun rising from the eastern hills. As Matali, the minister of Indra, extolled his master who then rose up and conquered the demons, so do I now extol you to rise up and do your duty, O lord. All of us await you with joined palms. The glorious sage Vasishtha has arrived with other sages and stands ready to perform the sacred installation ceremony of Rama. Order us now to proceed, O mighty monarch."

Hearing Sumantra speaking at the door, Dasarath became overwhelmed with sorrow once more. He went to his charioteer and embraced him. The king looked at Sumantra with eyes reddened with grief. "Today, O Sumantra, your well-chosen words only pierce my heart with pain." Dasarath's happiness had ended. He could not say anything more and simply stood with tears flowing down his face.

Sumantra was unable to fathom the cause of the king's sadness. He stepped back with tightly joined palms. This was strange. Surely this was the happiest day of Dasarath's life. For so long he had desired a successor. At last his desire was about to be fulfilled.

Seeing the mystified Sumantra, Kaikeyi said, "The king has remained awake the entire night, considering Rama's installation. Sleeplessness has made him unwell. He wishes now to see his son. Therefore bring Rama here."

The intelligent minister looked at Dasarath. Something was surely wrong. On such a momentous occasion why was the king not himself going to fetch Rama? Dasarath saw his minister's confusion. Reassuring him, the king told him to fetch Rama. Sumantra considered then that his master might just be exhausted from the preparations for the installation. Saying "It shall be done," he bowed low and left for Rama's palace.

Meanwhile the priests were making ready all the items required for the ceremony. Around a beautifully carved and adorned wooden seat were arranged many gold pitchers filled with water from all the sacred rivers, ready to anoint Rama. Above the seat was a large white umbrella which shone like the full moon on a clear night. Excellent musicians played melodies appropriate to the mood, while brahmins chanted Vedic texts meant to invoke good fortune. The brilliant sun rose in a clear sky and everyone eagerly awaited the arrival of the king and his son.

Sumantra reached Rama's palace, which was as splendid as Mount Kailasha. Secured with oak doors fifty feet tall, and embellished with hundreds of balconies, its main facade was adorned with gold images studded with innumerable gems. The outer gateway was constructed of coral worked with gold and embedded with large precious stones of every description. As Sumantra passed through that gateway he was greeted by delightful music and the aroma of various incenses. Peacocks and cranes crowded the courtyard, which was graced with blossoming trees and bushes.

Sumantra descended from his chariot and entered the palace, which was in no way inferior to the palace of Kuvera, the god of riches. Enlivened by simply seeing that palace, Sumantra passed through three entrances, each guarded by powerful young warriors wielding spears and bows. Rama was as dear to him as his own life and his heart pounded with joy as he approached the inner chambers. The corridors through the palace were cool and delightful, decorated with fine wood carvings and lit by the luster of thousands of celestial gems. Arriving at the gate to Rama's personal quarters, Sumantra asked the doorkeepers there to inform Rama of his arrival. Rama, who was alone with Sita, immediately instructed that Sumantra be shown into his room.

Sumantra went before Rama, whom he found seated upon a gold couch, being fanned gently with a whisk by Sita. Richly adorned with costly garments and smeared with crimson sandal-paste, Rama seemed to shine like the midday sun. He smiled affectionately at Sumantra, who fell prostrate on the ground, offering prayers. Rising up with folded hands, the minister said, "Most blessed is Kaushalya for having had you as her son. Your father, along with Queen Kaikeyi, now desires to see you. Be pleased to go there without delay."

Rama looked at Sita and said, "Surely my father is speaking with his queen about my installation. I think the blessed Kaikeyi, always favorable to my father, must even now be urging the king to make haste with the ceremony, knowing as she does how much the emperor longs for its completion. As he has sent his most trusted messenger to fetch me, the king along with his most beloved queen undoubtedly wish to bless me that my installation will proceed without impediment."

Rama rose to leave and the dark-eyed and lovely Sita invoked divine blessings upon him. Following her husband to the gate she said, "After installing you as Prince Regent, the king should, in course of time, consecrate you as the ruler of this world, even as Brahma installed Indra as the ruler of the gods. I wish to serve you in that state. May the great deities Indra, Yamaraja, Varuna and Kuvera, the guardians of the four quarters, guard you from every side."

Along with Sumantra, Rama went out from his palace quarters as a mighty mountain lion might emerge from his cave. Rama saw Lakshmana standing at the first gate, bent low with joined palms. At the middle gate Rama met his friends and relations and he greeted them all according to their status, offering obeisances or embracing them.

Within the courtyard Rama mounted upon a golden chariot, which shone like fire and was covered over with white tiger skins, and had thousands of small golden bells hanging from its sides. The charioteer spurred on the tall steeds, which were as powerful as young elephants, and the chariot moved away swiftly with a deep rumbling. As the outer gates swung open, Rama's chariot came out from the palace like the moon emerging from behind a cloud.

Rama went along the main road, preceded by a platoon of mailed warriors wearing swords and carrying bows. The prince sat peacefully while Lakshmana fanned him. He smiled at the people who thronged the streets in the thousands. His chariot was followed by great elephants resembling moving mountains. Thousands of horsemen brought up the rear. Poets and singers chanted Rama's praises to the accompaniment of divine music echoing in the heavens. Mixed with these sounds were the shouts of the warriors, which resembled the roaring of lions.

On the balconies and at the windows of the mansions lining the roads stood women who showered Rama on all sides with flowers. The ladies also praised Sita, saying, "Surely that godly lady has performed the highest penances to have been blessed with this great hero Rama as her husband."

The citizens, seeing Rama pass by, uttered blessings. "May victory attend you!" they cried out. Others were heard to say, "Here goes Rama, who will today inherit the royal fortune. Fortunate too are we who will soon be ruled by him."

Being extolled everywhere, Rama rode down the highway, which was lined with white houses appearing like clouds and with shops filled with abundant produce of every variety. The streets were strewn with jewels and with grains of rice and blades of sacred kusha grass. Brahmins made offerings of ghee lamps and incense to Rama as he passed, invoking divine blessings and saying, "We would renounce every worldly happiness simply to see Rama coming out of the palace as Prince Regent today. Indeed, even liberation itself is not so desirable."

None could turn away their eyes or mind from Rama as he went along the road in Ayodhya. Everyone looking upon Rama also felt that he was glancing at them. Gradually Rama and his entourage arrived at Dasarath's palace. Rama passed through the three outer gates on his chariot and then got down and passed through the last two gates on foot. He politely sent back all those persons who had followed him, even though they found it difficult to part from him. At last Rama reached the inner chambers alone and approached Kaikeyi's rooms.

As he entered the rooms, Rama saw the afflicted king seated with Kaikeyi on a golden couch. He bowed at his father's feet, then laid himself low before Kaikeyi, his mind fully composed. Dasarath appeared dejected and distressed, his face streaked with tears. He sat burning with agony and repeatedly sighing, appearing like the eclipsed sun or like a holy brahmin who has told a lie. Seeing his son standing before him with a modest demeanor and folded palms, the monarch said only, "Rama," and could not say another word, being overcome by grief.

Rama was seized with apprehension to see his father in that unusual state. Like the ocean at the rising of the full moon, Rama became agitated. He was devoted to the king and was saddened to see him so sorrowful. How was it that on such a day his father did not greet him? Even when angry he would always rise to bless his son. Why was he now remaining seated, looking downwards and weeping silently? Rama went before Kaikeyi, who sat at a distance from the king, and addressed her alone.

"O godly lady, pray tell me the reason for my father's distress," Rama asked gently. "Even though always affectionate to me, why does he not greet me today? Have I unwittingly committed some offense? Is the king angry with me for my having failed in some way to respect him?"

Kaikeyi remained silent and Rama continued. "I hope no suffering caused by illness or mental anguish has afflicted my father. Truly it is said that everlasting happiness cannot be had in this world. I hope I have not offended anyone dear to the king. If I were unable to please my father or if I failed to do his bidding and thus angered him, I would not survive even for an hour. What wretched man would not devotedly serve his father, a veritable god to him on earth, to whom he owes his own birth in this world?"

Understanding from Kaikeyi's taut expression that there was tension between her and his father, Rama said, "Perhaps my father has been hurt by some utterance of yours, O fair-faced queen, made out of vanity or anger. My dear Kaikeyi, please inform me of the cause of this unprecedented disturbance to the emperor, for I am very curious."

Upon hearing this question from the high-minded Rama, Kaikeyi, who had become impudent and was thinking only of her own interests, replied boldly, "The emperor is neither angry nor anguished, O Rama. However, there is something on his mind which he will not disclose for fear of hurting you, his beloved son. Having made a promise to me, the king now repents and wishes to retract his word, just like any other common man. The ever-truthful monarch wants to build a dam across a stream whose waters have already flowed away. Truth is the root of piety. This is known to the righteous. O Rama, take care lest the king loses now his piety for your sake, angry as he is with me."

Looking into Rama's apprehensive eyes, Kaikeyi said, "If you will undertake to do whatever the king may ask, be it good or bad for you, then I shall explain everything. I shall speak out the king's promise only as long as it shall not fail because of you; but the king himself will not in any event tell you."

Rama was distressed to hear Kaikeyi speaking in this way. Within the hearing of the emperor he replied to her, "Alas, how shameful it is that I should hear words expressing doubt about my devotion to my father! You should never think this, O glorious lady. At my father's command I would this very moment leap into blazing fire, swallow a deadly poison or plunge into the depths of the ocean. Therefore tell me, my dear mother, what is on your mind? By my avowed word I shall without doubt do whatever is desired by the king. Know that Rama's word is always truth!"

Seeing the king mute and the guileless Rama prepared to carry out her desire, Kaikeyi felt her purposes all but accomplished. In an unkind voice she revealed her wicked intentions to Rama.

"It is well known how I once saved the king's life and how, as a result, he granted me a couple of boons. Against those boons I solicited today a promise from the king to fulfill my desire. I wish for Bharata to be installed in your place and for you to go to the forest, remaining there for fourteen years. O descendant of emperors, prove true to your word and to that of your father. Indeed, rescue the king from the ignominy of impiety and leave without delay. Let Bharata be duly consecrated with all the paraphernalia arranged for you. While he remains here to rule this wide and prosperous earth, you shall remain for fourteen years in some distant forest, wearing matted locks and the barks of trees."

The king cried out in pain as Kaikeyi spoke. Rama stood by without showing any emotion as the queen continued. "Overcome by compassion for you, this monarch cannot even look at your face. O Rama, ornament of your line, make good his promise and deliver him from his difficult and awkward situation!"

Even though Kaikeyi uttered such cruel words, Rama did not yield to grief. The king, however, felt increasing agony as he thought about his impending separation from Rama. He listened in silence as Rama replied to Kaikeyi, "So be it! To honor my father's promise I shall put on the dress of an ascetic and depart forthwith for the forest. You need entertain no doubt in this regard, O queen. Why, though, does not my father greet me as before? I could never transgress his order, even as the ocean, by the order of the Supreme Lord, can never trangress its shores."

Rama looked across at his father, who could not return his glance. The king kept his head down and wept softly. Rama turned back to Kaikeyi. "Ordered only by you, O Kaikeyi, I would joyfully part with, in favor of Bharata, not only the kingdom but also all my personal property, my wedded wife Sita and even my own beloved self. How much more gladly would I part with these things when ordered by my father, the emperor himself, in order to please you and honor his pledge? Please reassure my afflicted father, for seeing him sitting there shedding tears pains me greatly. He may feel assured that I shall immediately enact his desire without feeling any sorrow at all. Let swift horses be sent for Bharata. Without questioning my father's command I shall now quickly proceed to the forest!"

The ignoble Kaikeyi then rejoiced at heart. Confident that Rama would soon leave, she urged him to hurry. "Let it be so!" she exclaimed. "Messengers may leave immediately to fetch Bharata from his uncle's kingdom. You should not wait a moment, O Rama, lest some impediment presents itself. Keen as you are to depart, leave right now. Do not be concerned for the king's silence, for he is too shy to ask you himself. Let this apprehension be banished from your mind and make haste. As long as you have not left, the king will take neither food nor water."

Drawing a deep sigh with the words, "Alas, how very painful," the king collapsed unconscious on the couch. Rama gently placed his cool hands on his father's forehead and raised him up. The prince was again urged on by Kaikeyi. Turning towards her, Rama said, "I have no desire to live in this world as a slave to material gains. Like the rishis I am devoted only to righteousness. I will always do whatever is agreeable to my adorable father, even at the cost of my life. The greatest piety lies in serving one's father. Indeed, O gentle lady, greater still is service to the mother, according to sacred texts. Surely you do not see any good points in me, O princess of Kekaya, as you felt it necessary to ask such a minor thing of my father. Your request alone would have sufficed. I shall go to a lonely forest and live there for fourteen years. Please bear with me only as long as it takes for me to take leave of my other mothers and to gain the agreement of Sita. Try to ensure that Bharata protects the kingdom and serves his aged father, for this is the eternal morality."

Unable to speak due to grief, Dasarath wept aloud. Rama bowed low at the feet of his royal father and also before the hard-hearted Kaikeyi. He was moved by acute sorrow but he kept it within himself, showing no external sign. Joining his palms and circumambulating his father and stepmother, Rama departed.

He then made his way towards Kaushalya's rooms. Lakshmana, hearing from Rama of the turn of events, followed close behind, his eyes brimming with tears. Reaching the room where the installation was to be performed, Rama respectfully went around the royal seat without casting his eyes upon it. Despite his renouncing the rulership of the world, no change of mood could be perceived in Rama, any more than in a perfect yogi who has completely transcended all dualities.

Forbidding the use of the royal umbrella which was offered him as he left, as well as the pair of beautiful royal whisks, Rama sent away his ministers, his chariot and the citizens. The news of Rama's impending exile had spread quickly and the people were shocked and dismayed. By mastery over his mind and senses Rama controlled his own agony upon seeing the people's sadness. He exhibited his normal peaceful demeanor and approached Kaushalya's apartments. He was followed by Lakshmana, who, seeing his brother equipoised, was strenuously controlling his own emotions. Rama smiled softly. He was as dear to his relatives as their own lives and he did not wish to display any feelings which would cause them pain.

As he entered Kaushalya's quarters a loud and pathetic cry came from the ladies. "Alas, here is that Rama who has served all of us exactly as he did his own mother. Today he will leave for the forest. How could the foolish king exile the harmless Rama and thus bring ruin to the world?"

Hearing from a distance the piteous wail, Dasarath shrank with shame and hid his head beneath the silken sheets on his couch. Rama went towards Kaushalya's room. He carefully maintained his composure, although he felt agonised at seeing the suffering of his relatives. As he approached the outer entrance of Kaushalya's apartment he saw many door-keepers seated and standing there. They quickly flocked around Rama, uttering blessings on the young prince. At the middle entrance Rama was greeted by elderly brahmins who were constantly reciting Vedic hymns. Bowing low before them, Rama entered and came to the inner door where he was led into Kaushalya's chamber by her personal maidservants.

CHAPTER EIGHT

GRIEF AND FURY

Kaushalya had spent the night in undisturbed prayer and penance on behalf of her son. She was unaware of his meeting with the king and Kaikeyi. Rama found her seated before the sacrificial fire, surrounded by brahmins making offerings to Vishnu. She was clad in white silk and, although fatigued by fasting, she still appeared most beautiful. Upon seeing Rama bowing at her feet, she rose up joyfully to embrace and bless him. "May you attain the age and fame of the virtuous royal sages who have gone before you in our line. Sit with me a little and take breakfast, then go to your father, the ever-truthful monarch, for today he will install you as the Prince Regent."

Kaushalya offered Rama a bejeweled seat next to her, but he merely touched it in respect and said, "O godly lady, surely you do not know that a great calamity has now arrived. What I am going to tell you will cause you unprecedented pain, even as it will my beloved wife Sita. I am about to leave for the forest; therefore, what need have I of this fine seat? The time has arrived for me to occupy a mat made of forest grasses. Indeed, in accord with a promise already made to my father, I shall inhabit a lonely forest region, living on fruits and roots. How then can I partake of this royal fare you offer? The emperor will install Bharata as Prince Regent and has exiled me to the forest, to live like a hermit for fourteen years."

Kaushalya at once fell down, like a tree severed at its root. Her mind confused, she lay on the floor like a goddess fallen from heaven. Rama quickly lifted her, gently stroking her face with his hand. Kaushalya slowly regained her senses. Struck with agony, she looked at Rama, who was controlling his own grief. She knew beyond doubt that her son could not possibly have spoken falsely, nor was he given to flippancy or jest. His words were certainly true and they pierced her heart.

Clasping Rama's hand in hers, she spoke in a choked voice. "For a long time I suffered the terrible pain of being childless, O beloved son. Surely the feeling of being without issue is a grief that consumes a barren woman.

Before your birth every effort your father made to please me was futile,
O Raghava, for I longed only for a child. Your birth ended that pain, but
now I fear that an even greater suffering has arrived."

Kaushalya could not bear the thought of separation from Rama. She
held him tightly as she spoke. "Separation from you will rend my heart in
two. That pain will be compounded by the cruel words of a junior wife.
What could be more painful for a woman? Unending grief and lamentation
has become my lot. Even with you by my side I have been despised; what
then will be my fate when you are gone, O dear child? Surely I shall soon
die."

Kaushalya thought how she had always been neglected by her husband
in favor of Kaikeyi. With Bharata enthroned she would be entirely abandoned. For twenty-seven years she had watched Rama grow to manhood,
awaiting the day when he would assume the throne and end her woes. How
could she any longer suffer Kaikeyi's scorn? Now Rama, her only solace, was
leaving. It seemed her prayers were all in vain. Her fasts and meditations
were useless. What was the value of all her self-discipline and sacred observances? Rather than becoming the king, her son was being cast away.
Kaushalya condemned herself.

"Surely my heart is hard like steel, for it does not shatter upon hearing
this terrible news. Death will not take one before the proper time or else I
should have certainly gone immediately to the court of Yamaraja, the great
lord of death. If by one's own sweet will one could meet with death, then in
your absence I would depart this very day. Without you, O Rama, life will
be useless. Therefore, like a cow following its calf, I shall definitely go with
you to the forest."

Wailing in this way Kaushalya contemplated the calamity about to
befall her. Rama was duty bound to his father and would never oppose his
order. He would certainly leave without delay. Unable to bear her suffering,
Kaushalya collapsed sobbing onto a couch.

Lakshmana stood nearby, writhing in pain. This situation was intolerable. How could Rama accept it? Why did he not do something? Unable to
repress his tumultuous anger, Lakshmana spoke furiously to Kaushalya. "I
also find Rama's imminent departure to be uncceptable, O glorious lady.
Rama should never relinquish the royal fortune for any cause. Perverted by
the words of a woman, the king has lost his good sense. He is desirous of sensual enjoyments and has been overpowered by lust and senility. What will
he not say, urged on by the sinful Kaikeyi? To desire the banishment of the
powerful Rama is nothing short of madness. What vice or offense can be
found in Rama? There is no man in this world, even if he be Rama's deadly
enemy, who could find in him any fault, even in his absence. What man who

respects virtue would forsake such a son, who is equal to the gods, disciplined and kindly disposed even to his enemies? What son would heed such
a command from a father who has abandoned righteousness?"

Lakshmana's furious voice resounded around the chamber. If the king
would not give Rama the kingdom, then it should be taken by force. He
would stand by his brother with bow in hand, exhibiting his valor. Let anyone who dared try to prevent the installation of Rama! He would hold off
the entire city of Ayodhya should they oppose Rama. Whoever supported
Bharata would find himself slain by Lakshmana. This situation called for
strong action. Why should they accept it meekly? Lakshmana tightly
gripped the bow hanging from his shoulder and turned to his brother.

"If, at Kaikeyi's instigation, our father acts like an enemy, then he
should be made captive or even killed without compunction. The scriptures
make clear that even a father or a preceptor can be rejected if they lose their
discrimination, failing to distinguish between right and wrong. On what
authority has the king sought to confer the kingdom upon Kaikeyi's son
when it rightfully belongs to you?"

Breathing hot, heavy sighs, Lakshmana turned back to Kaushalya and
assured her that Rama would be installed as king. He held up his bow.
"O godly lady, I swear by my bow that I am truly devoted to Rama with the
whole of my heart. If Rama enters into blazing fire or retires to the forest,
know that I have already done the same. I shall dispel your sorrow by means
of my arms even as the sun dispels the morning mist. Let your royal high-
ness along with Rama witness today my valor. I shall kill my aged and
wretched father who, as a result of senility, has entered his second childhood
in Kaikeyi's association."

Lakshmana stood blazing like fire, yet Rama remained calm and composed. Kaushalya, weeping, spoke to her son. "Having heard your brother
Lakshmana, who has raised pertinent and proper arguments, consider now
what ought to be done. You should not obey the unjust command of
Kaikeyi, leaving me here to grieve."

Kaushalya knew Rama would act only according to moral laws. He
would never be swayed by sentiment to deviate from scriptural codes. She
called upon Rama as his mother. "Dear son, do I not deserve the same obedience as you offer to the king? Is service to the mother not an even higher
virtue than service to the father? I cannot allow you to leave, nor could I
live in your absence. If you leave I will take a vow to fast until death. You
will then be guilty of killing your own mother."

The queen cried piteously, trying again and again to convince Rama
not to leave. Rama burned with anguish to hear his mother her express her
feelings, but keeping his mind under control, he spoke to her in a gentle

voice. "I do not feel able to flout my father's command, and therefore I wish to enter the forest. The order of one's father is no less than the order of the Supreme Lord. It cannot be transgressed if one wishes to acquire virtue in this world. The king is not ordering me to do anything sinful. By obeying his command I shall be following the path of morality, which has ever been followed by pious men. I only desire to do what is right, never otherwise. For as long as one does the bidding of his father, he is never overcome by evil."

Rama turned towards Lakshmana and admonished him, speaking in soft but firm tones. "I know your unsurpassed love for me, as well as your strength of arms, which cannot be easily withstood, O noble prince. My gentle mother does not deeply understand the imports of morality and is thus experiencing great agony. My father's command is rooted in righteousness and is therefore worthy of being obeyed. Indeed I have already given my word to honor his order. I cannot break my pledge. Since I have been commanded by Kaikeyi according to my father's promise, O valiant prince, how can I, knowing well the path of piety, neglect that command? Therefore give up this unworthy thought of overthrowing the king. Stand firm on righteousness alone and do not give way to anger and a display of strength. Accept my resolution to follow the royal order."

Rama went before his mother and knelt down with folded hands, bowing his head low. He was as devoted to Kaushalya as he was to Dasarath and did not want to leave without her consent. He again asked her permission to depart. Rama swore on his life that after the fourteen years had passed he would return and remain in Ayodhya as her devoted servant. He asked her not to yield to sorrow. In accord with the eternal laws of morality she should serve the king. He also desired to follow the path of piety. For that reason he was anxious to leave for the forest in compliance with his father's order. She should not try to prevent him.

Hearing his request, Kaushalya felt impassioned. How could her son abandon her in this way? She had always carefully observed her duty as a mother. She was always affectionate towards Rama. Surely Rama realized that she would die if he left her now. In a last attempt to change his mind the queen spoke in spirited tones. "As your mother, I do not grant you leave to depart. Am I not as venerable to you as your father? O Rama, I cannot face the thought of your leaving. In your absence I care not for either life or death. What will be the value of life to me without you, whether it be in this world or in heaven? Your presence for even an hour is more preferable to me than the possession of heaven and earth combined."

As his mother wailed piteously, Rama only became all the more desirous to escape, even as a lordly elephant would want to escape when surrounded by men goading it with firebrands towards a trap. Fixed in his determination to do his duty, he replied, "I feel that both you, my dear mother, and the powerful Lakshmana have not properly understood my mind. Thus both of you harass me most painfully. Happiness in this world is temporary and ultimately illusory. Only the foolish think themselves to be the body composed of material elements and thus seek sensual happiness. This body, along with its relations and all its sensual joys, exists for only a few moments. The real self is the eternal soul dwelling in the heart, whose happiness lies only in the pursuit of a godly life."

Both Kaushalya and Lakshmana listened silently as Rama spoke eternal spiritual truths. He described how association of friends and relatives was exactly like the coming together of sticks floating in a river. They are thrown together and very soon parted by the swift current of time. Therefore one's happiness should never depend upon such ephemeral relationships. One should give up all attachment for the body and fix the mind only upon the eternal Supreme Lord, whose order is represented by superiors such as the king. This would bring everlasting happiness. Rama concluded, "How then can I abandon the righteous path of following my father's command simply out of attachment for either the kingdom or my relatives?"

Rama reassured them that he was not at all disturbed to be leaving for the forest. He responded to the suggestion that Dasarath was acting against the codes of morality. "The king has adhered to virtue even at the cost of his own desires and happiness. Suffering intense pain, he is prepared to abandon his beloved son for the sake of truthfulness. My dear mother, it is he who is always your shelter and means of happiness in both this and the other world. You should therefore remain by his side and serve him. Pray grant me leave to go to the forest. I shall never accept the rulership of the earth through unrighteousness."

Rama stopped speaking and approached the anguished Lakshmana, who was still incensed with his father and Kaikeyi. Lakshmana stood with his eyes open wide in rage, like an infuriated elephant. Rama gently restrained his devoted brother. "Control now your anger and grief, O Lakshmana. Take courage and overlook this seeming offense to myself. Experience instead the joy of assisting our father to increase his virtue by implementing his pledge. Gentle brother, please send back all the items gathered for my consecration today. Reassure my mother and help me prepare for my departure."

Rama placed his hand on Lakshmana's shoulder. He was pained to see his brother's distress, but he had no intention of challenging his father. He had to vindicate the king's honor. As long as he remained in Ayodhya the king would suffer the pain of seeing his truthfulness questioned. Only when

Rama had left for the forest, clad in deerskins and wearing matted locks, would Kaikeyi be satisfied and the king's word redeemed.

Lakshmana looked at the ground. He was burning with the thought of the terrible injustice about to be done to his brother, but he could not possibly defy Rama's desire. Rama put his arm around Lakshmana's shoulder and spoke reassuringly. "All this should be seen as the will of Providence, which can never be flouted. No blame should be attached to Kaikeyi, for it was Providence alone who moved her to make her request to our father. How could she have ever decided to send me away? She has always treated me exactly as has my own mother, Kaushalya. Surely she was prompted by Providence to say to the king those terrible words, giving him such grief. I know her to be gentle and kind. She would never, like a vulgar woman, utter words intended to torment both myself and our father."

Rama felt no anger towards Kaikeyi and he did not want her to be blamed for what was, after all, a divine arrangement. He continued, "That which cannot be foreseen or understood must be accepted as the will of Providence alone. What man can ever contend with destiny? Joy and sorrow, gain and loss, birth and death--all of these come one after another by the arrangement of Providence or destiny. None can avoid them nor can anyone alter the strong course of destiny. When even the best laid plans go awry without any apparent cause, it is undoubtedly the work of Providence."

Rama smiled at Lakshmana whom he knew had spoken only out of love. He asked him not to lament for that which was unavoidable, decreed by some unseen destiny. Lakshmana should not censure either their father or Kaikeyi, as they were moved by superior forces. Rama then asked that the sacred waters gathered for his installation be instead used to anoint him at the inauguration of his vow of asceticism. He looked at his younger brother with affection. "Beloved Lakshmana, I will soon depart, for this is surely my destiny."

Lakshmana stood with his head bent low, pondering his brother's words. His mood swung between distress at Rama's impending exile and delight at his brother's steadfast adherence to virtue. But he was still not fully convinced that it was right for Rama to leave. Furrowing his brows, he hissed like an angry cobra in a hole. His frowning face appeared like that of a furious lion and was difficult to gaze upon. Violently shaking his head and arms, he said to Rama, "Your steady devotion to duty is unequalled, O Rama, but carefully consider its result in this case. By accepting the words of that wicked couple you are prepared to do something that is condemned by all people. I am surprised that you do not suspect the motives of our father and Kaikeyi. If there were any truth in this story about the boons granted by the king, then why did Kaikeyi not seek their fulfillment long ago?"

Lakshmana accused the king of conspiring with Kaikeyi. Dasarath must have surely lost his senses under the influence of lust. Along with the covetous Kaikeyi he had made a sinful plan, quite opposed to any morality. He concluded that the king's authority was therefore fit to be rejected. "Please forgive my intolerance, O Raghava, but I cannot accept your present piety, which impels you to take as fate this evil turn of events. Nor can I accept that destiny is supreme."

Lakshmana was a heroic and powerful warrior. His face turned crimson as he went on. Why should one acquiesce to a painful fate as if he is helpless? Only those who are cowardly and weak would trust in destiny alone, Lakshmana argued. The valiant always remain firm of mind. They never become disheartened when their purposes are thwarted by fate. Rather, they exert themselves with all power. Lakshmana stood before Rama with his bow held high. "Today you shall see me rushing at the enemy like an uncontrollable king of elephants! Not even all the gods united together will prevent your consecration today. Those who support your exile will find themselves either deprived of life or sent to the forest. I will dash the hopes of our father and Kaikeyi. Anyone opposing me will find no shelter in destiny as my fierce strength ruthlessly cuts him down!"

Lakshmana drew his sword and cleaved the air. He gave full vent to his rage. The right time for Rama to retire to the forest had certainly not arrived. He should rule the globe for thousands of years. Only when his own sons were ready to take his place should he leave for the forest. That was the proper course of virtue. Lakshmana seemed about to consume the earth as he spoke.

"If you fear censure for the seemingly sinful act of rejecting father's order, you should not worry. I shall personally guard you in every way and forcibly repel all those who object to your accepting this kingdom, even as the coastline holds back the ocean! O Rama, allow yourself to be installed today. I alone am able to prevent any impediments to the ceremony. These arms of mine are not meant simply to add to my attractiveness, nor is this bow a mere ornament, nor are my sword and quivers of arrows hanging on my body as badges of honor. All these are meant for crushing the enemy. Today you will see arrows released like incessant showers of rain. You will witness my sword flashing like lightning as it cuts down all those who stand before me. The earth will be thickly covered with the arms, legs and heads of heroes. Hewn down by my sword, enemies will drop like so many meteors falling from the sky! While I stand on the battlefield with uplifted weapons how can any man alive be proud of his strength? Today I shall demonstrate the king's helplessness and establish your unopposed sovereignty! Tell me which of your enemies should this day be deprived of life, fame and relations? Instruct me how to proceed so that this wide earth will be brought under your control. O glorious lord of our race, I am here to do your bidding alone."

Rama wiped away his brother's angry tears. He knew Lakshmana was only speaking out his devotion to him. Lakshmana knew that ultimately he had to follow Rama. He knew Rama could not possibly act against religion or morality. Nevertheless, in his pain he expressed his powerful feelings. Rama perfectly understood Lakshmana's mind and he comforted him. "O gentle brother, you should know I am firmly obedient to my superiors' command. This is the path trodden by the righteous. Be firm and control your grief and anger. That will be the most pleasing to me."

Kaushalya realized her son was unshakeable in his determination to obey his father's order. Tears streamed down her face. Who could believe this was happening? Rama, the dearest son of the emperor, was being exiled to the dangerous jungle. How could that pious-minded and gentle boy live in such a fearful place? Destiny was surely supreme in a world where one like Rama must retire to the forest. Kaushalya trembled with grief. She held her son's head. "It is well known how a cow will follow her roaming calf. In the same way I shall follow you wherever you may go, for separation from you, my dearest son, will kill me."

Rama addressed his mother with love. "Betrayed by Kaikeyi and seeing me leave for the forest, my father will surely not survive if he is also abandoned by you, O godly queen. It is sheer cruelty for a woman to desert her worthy husband. That should never even be contemplated, for it is always condemned. So long as the king lives you should render him service, for this is the eternal moral code. For a married woman the husband is her deity and her lord."

Rama knew his mother was fully aware of her religious duty, which she would never abandon. He spoke only to give her strength and reassurance. The queen listened in silence as Rama, invoking the ancient religious codes, described the fate of a woman who does not serve her worthy husband. Even if she is devoted to fasts and sacred observances, she will become tainted by sin and suffer the reactions. On the other hand, a woman who devotedly serves her husband, even without any other religious practices, will reach the highest heaven.

Rama folded his palms. "Therefore, O queen, remain devoted to the king and ensure that he does not suffer excessive grief. Leading a holy life, bide the time until I return. When you finally see me duly installed as king and dedicated to your service, you shall achieve all that you desire."

Although dismayed at the prospect of losing her son for fourteen years, the pious Kaushalya nevertheless felt delighted to hear his admonition. It was clear she could not change his carefully considered resolution to depart. Blinded by her tears she said, "Go then with my blessings, O heroic son. May good betide you always. My misery will end only when you again return from the forest and offer me words of consolation. If only that time were already arrived! Leave now with a steady mind, dear Rama. Following in the footsteps of the righteous, repay your debt to your father."

Still in the grip of sorrow, Kaushalya began to worship the gods in order to invoke divine blessings for her son. Praying to each of the principal deities and asking that they guard Rama from all dangers, she offered oblations of ghee into the sacred fire. As she finished her prayers, Rama bowed before her and held her feet for some time, while she wept softly. Embracing him tightly, Kaushalya said, "Please leave in peace, my child, and accomplish your purpose. When at last I see you returned, as one would see the full moon appearing above the horizon, all my sorrow will be gone. Only when I see you ascend your father's throne, wearing the crown and clad in royal robes, will my heart's desire be fulfilled. May all the gods protect you as you sojourn in the dreadful forest. Depart now, O Raghava, I wish you well!"

Rama took leave of the grieving Kaushalya, who followed after him with her eyes. He went out of her apartments feeling agony. Lakshmana, who had resigned himself to accept Rama's determination to depart, followed close behind.

CHAPTER NINE

SITA'S PLEA

Rama moved along the royal highway towards Sita's quarters, praised by the many brahmins who lined the road. Sita still had not heard the news of Rama's impending exile and was eagerly awaiting him, her mind absorbed in thoughts of his installation. As her husband entered the room she sprang from her seat. Rama had left Lakshmana outside and had gone alone to speak with Sita. He was perplexed as he considered how to tell his wife the terrible news. Although striving to control his mind and contain his grief, Rama's face wore a pained expression and his head hung low.

Sita was astonished to see him in that state, his face pale and bathed in perspiration. Apprehensively she inquired, "What troubles you, my lord? Today is the auspicious and joyful day of your installation, but you seem to be covered by the dark shadow of grief."

Sita asked Rama why he was not accompanied by the royal servants carrying the white umbrella. Why was he not wearing regal dress or anointed with sandalwood paste after having gone through the inaugural ceremony? Where was the king and his ministers? What was happening?

Rama steadied his mind and looked upon Sita's face. "My worshipable father has ordered me to enter the forest for fourteen years' exile. O most beautiful princess, according to Kaikeyi's desire, my brother Bharata will be installed in my place. Indeed, in days gone by two boons were granted to Kaikeyi by my ever-truthful father. She has recalled the king's debt now and placed him under his word to send me away, conferring the office of Prince Regent upon the noble Bharata. In obedience to morality I shall therefore depart forthwith to the forest. I have come to see you on my way."

Sita shook like a tree caught in a gale. How could this be true? She listened with astonishment as Rama continued. "O high-minded lady, please remain firm. In my absence you should take to fasts and prayer, remaining disciplined at all times. Worship and serve my father and mother who are both grieving deeply due to my separation from them. Sumitra and Kaikeyi should also be served by you, as should Bharata and Shatrughna, who are both as dear to me as my own self. Be especially careful not to praise me before Bharata, for men endowed with power and wealth cannot tolerate hearing others praised. Indeed, Bharata will be the king and should therefore be served by you with all attention, carefully avoiding any offense."

Sita was dumbfounded. She turned pale and her eyes opened wide. She knew without doubt that Rama meant what he said. The princess listened in horror as he instructed her. Rama told her to remain living peacefully in Ayodhya under the protection of the emperor and Bharata, devoting herself to righteousness and religion. Rama himself would leave immediately for the forest.

After hearing Rama speak, the noble Sita became indignant out of her love for her husband. Her cheeks flushed red and she replied angrily, "How have you uttered such words today, O lord? They are never worthy of one possessed of strength and weapons, who is capable of affording protection to the weak. Your advice is not worth hearing!"

Considering Rama as her only refuge, Sita spoke strongly. She described how the father, mother, brother, or any other relation were never the shelter of a chaste woman with a husband. The wife should share her husband's fortune under all circumstances. She stood in front of Rama, her eyes flashing as she continued, "I am enjoined by ancient religious codes to enter the forest along with you, dearest Rama. I cannot possibly remain in Ayodhya! If you leave today for the forest, I shall walk before you, clearing away the sharp grasses and thorns on the path."

Sita assured Rama that he could take her anywhere with confidence. She would live happily under his protection and would prefer forest life with him to residence in the richest palace or even heaven itself without him. She had been trained in all the arts of service and was well prepared to accompany him. "I need no further advice, O lord. Simply order me to depart. Remaining with you in fragrant woodlands, I shall be as happy as I am now living in your palace."

Sita felt pained that Rama had not considered taking her with him. Raised in a line of warrior kings, the princess was not easily disturbed by difficulty. Again and again she exhorted her husband to take her to the forest. "Certainly you are capable of guarding me from any danger. Indeed, none other can guard me as you can, Rama. Nor is it their sacred duty. I shall therefore go with you today. That is my fixed determination."

Sita was fond of the country. She imagined herself alone with Rama amid beautiful mountains, woods and lakes. Even if it was austere she would nevertheless prefer thousands of years spent with her husband in this way than a single day without him. She spoke her deepest feelings. "I shall enter the forest at your feet. I am exclusively devoted to you, my mind is ever attached to you and I am determined to die if disunited from you. Therefore grant my prayer and take me with you today."

Rama considered the difficulty of living in the forest and he did not feel at all inclined to take Sita with him. He spoke gently to his dear wife, who had buried her face in her hands and was sobbing. "My dearest lady, you are born of a noble line and are always devoted to virtue. Practice that virtue and appease my mind, for I cannot bear to see you suffer. I shall now give you advice meant only for your good, frail Sita. Not only is there no joy in the fearful forest, but it is always fraught with misery. Simply by taking you there I would be neglecting my duty to protect you."

Rama described the forest where he had gone many times for hunting expeditions. There were numerous lions and other fierce beasts. Marshes and rivers abounded in crocodiles and other fierce aquatics. The forest paths were rugged and often impassable. Innumerable thorny trees and stinging bushes made traveling difficult. Sharp grasses grew everywhere. Hornets, gnats, scorpions, spiders and mosquitoes were always present, along with snakes and serpents of every kind. In the deep forest the darkness was dense. Furious winds often blew, lashing a traveler's face with debris.

Rama was determined to dissuade the gentle Sita from following him. "Exhausted after searching all day for food, one must lie down at night upon beds of dry leaves. Baths must be taken in lonely lakes which are the abode of serpents. By day and night the terrible pangs of hunger can be appeased only by one's mind, for food is scarce. O princess, one is subjected to all kinds of illnesses and mental anguish. Anger, greed and fear must be completely controlled. A forest is certainly a place of terrible suffering; therefore, give up this idea of following me there. It is not a secure place for one such as you."

Sita's determination remained unshaken. "All these dangers will be as nothing to me if I am able to remain by your side. I will in any event have no fear whatsoever with you as my protector. Even Indra will not be able to harm me when you are with me. What then of mere beasts? You have always instructed me that a wife can never be independent from her husband, O Rama; indeed she is half of his very self. How then can I not accompany you?"

Sita remembered how, when she was a young girl, an astrologer had predicted that she would one day have to live in the forest. Surely that time had arrived. She continued to plead with Rama. Was this not an opportunity for her to fulfill her religious duty by following him to the forest? Would not any other course be against virtue? The husband was the wife's supreme deity. Sita quoted the scriptures. A chaste woman who remained throughout life by her husband's side surely attained the same destination as him after death. That was her only desire, to be with Rama always. Looking into Rama's eyes, she spoke in a piteous voice. "For what reason then, O great hero, will you leave me behind? I who am devoted and faithful, who shares alike your every pleasure and pain and who desires to follow the religious path? You should certainly bring me with you; otherwise, being sorely afflicted, I shall resort to poison, fire or water in order to bring about my end."

Although Sita's lamentations hurt him, Rama did not relent. He tried to pacify and reassure her, but she only became all the more determined to accompany him. Agitated at the thought of separation from her husband, she taunted him.

"Has my father Janaka obtained as my protector a woman in the form of a man? How, in your absence, could I tolerate the people falsely saying, 'It seems that strength and valor are lacking in Rama, as he could not protect his own dear wife'? What fear has assailed you that you now desire to desert me, although I remain entirely devoted to you? I will not cast my eyes on another man even in thought! How then can you even consider delivering me for protection to another, O my lord?"

Sita continued to beseech Rama. She had no intention of remaining behind without him under any circumstances. Be it heaven or hell, she could only be happy by her husband's side. Sita gazed imploringly at Rama as she begged him to take her with him.

Rama was agonized by the thought of leaving behind his beloved wife. He would miss her. Still, he feared her suffering in the forest. His heart ached as she cried out to him.

"Without you heaven would be exactly as hell to me, while with you hell would be the best of all abodes. How can I remain here under the control of those who are inimical to you and have sent you to the forest? If I must watch you leave without me, then I shall drink poison this very day. I cannot bear the pain of separation from you for even an hour. How, then, shall I stand it for fourteen years? Take me with you or let me give up my life here and now in your presence."

Sita's beautiful face was streaked with tears, which fell continuously from her dark eyes like drops of water from blue lotus flowers. Rama embraced her and gently wiped away her tears. He was still apprehensive about taking her, but he could not see her endure the pain of his separation. She was already almost senseless from grief and he had not even left. What would happen to her during fourteen years of his absence? Making up his mind to take her with him, he spoke to her reassuringly.

"I would find no pleasure even in heaven if I obtained it at the cost of your suffering, O most pious lady! Not knowing your real feelings and being afraid that forest life would cause you pain, I discouraged you from following me. I see now that destiny has decreed you should dwell with me in the forest. Follow me then, O princess, and I shall protect you in strict accord with the moral laws always followed by the virtuous."

Rama made clear his firm intention to go to the deep forest and remain there for the full duration. He wanted Sita to have no doubt of what lay ahead. He was fixed in his determination to obey his parents' command. How could one who disregarded elders and teachers ever hope to please God, who is not so easily seen or obtained? Earth, heaven and the kingdom of God can all be achieved by one who serves his mother, father and teacher. Explaining all this to his devoted wife, Rama said, "Not even truthfulness, charity or sacrifice are comparable to serving one's father and mother. This is the eternal religion. Pious men, devoted to serving their parents, reach the regions of the gods and beyond. I therefore desire to do exactly what my truthful father has enjoined. I shall go to the forest today. As I see that you are set on following me, my resolve to leave you behind has weakened. O lady of bewitching eyes, I shall take you with me and together we shall practice asceticism in the deep forest. I am pleased with you, Sita. Your determination to serve me in every circumstance is worthy of your dynasty and it adds glory to mine. Prepare to leave immediately! Give away all your riches to the brahmins and go with only a simple dress and no belongings. We shall soon depart."

Sita was overjoyed to hear her husband's agreement. Her face bloomed like a full-blown lotus. Excitedly she began following Rama's instructions, giving away all her costly garments and jewels, as well as all the other riches in her palace.

In the meantime Lakshmana, who had been waiting patiently outside Sita's apartments, saw Rama coming out. He bowed down before Rama and held his feet tightly. "If your mind is set upon leaving for the forest, then take me with you," he implored. "I shall walk ahead of you holding my bow and guarding against all dangers. With joy I shall accompany you through beautiful woods resounding with the cries of wild animals. Without you I do not desire even the rulership of all the worlds."

Lakshmana hoped Rama would approve, but Rama tried to dissuade him. "My dearest Lakshmana, you are dearer to me than life itself. Always affectionate, devoted to virtue and firm on the right path, you are my constant and most valued companion. Yet if you follow me to the forest, who will be left to serve your mother Sumitra and the illustrious Kaushalya?"

Rama suggested that Kaikeyi would not be kind to her co-wives once her son obtained the kingdom. Bharata would be devoted to his own mother, Kaikeyi, and thus the other queens would be neglected. Therefore Lakshmana should remain in Ayodhya to care for Kaushalya and Sumitra. By serving Rama's elders, Lakshmana would demonstrate his devotion to Rama. Rama concluded, "Incomparably great religious merit will be earned by you, O noble Lakshmana, and our mothers will be saved from suffering."

Lakshmana was not inclined to accept Rama's advice. How could he live without Rama? In soft but firm words he argued that Bharata and Shatrughna were both devoted to Rama. They would therefore serve all of Rama's elders equally. Lakshmana promised his brother, "If somehow they become proud and arrogant upon attaining the kingdom, abandoning virtue and neglecting their elders, I will return to punish them. For even while we live in the forest, news of the kingdom will reach us through the sages and ascetics living there."

Lakshmana had already anticipated Rama's objections and had carefully considered them. There was no doubt in his mind that he should follow his brother. Continuing to reassure Rama, Lakshmana reminded him how the king had already arranged more than adequate support for Kaushalya and her dependents. The revenue of thousands of villages was under her control. She was capable of maintaining herself as well as Sumitra and even Lakshmana himself. He concluded, "Therefore kindly make me your personal attendant, for there will be no unrighteousness in this act. Going before you with my sword, I shall clear a safe path for you and Sita. In wakefulness or sleep, you shall find me by your side ever ready to do your bidding."

Rama was pleased and comforted to hear Lakshmana speak. Lakshmana was as dear to him as life itself and Rama had been sad at the prospect of leaving him. Holding Lakshmana by the shoulders and looking into his expectant face, Rama said, "Take leave of your near and dear ones, O my brother, for we shall depart shortly." Lakshmana felt a surge of happiness and his limbs trembled. He bowed to his elder brother and asked for his order.

Rama asked Lakshmana to go to Vasishtha's hermitage, where he had left some divine weapons. There were two celestial bows along with a pair of inexhaustible quivers, two impenetrable pieces of body armor and a pair of long, shining swords. Rama had received these as a dowry from Janaka and had left them with Vasishtha so they could receive daily worship in his hermitage. He said to Lakshmana, "Bring all these weapons, dear brother, for I feel we will have need of them soon."

Lakshmana joyfully went and fetched the weapons. Then he and Rama together began to distribute their wealth to the brahmins. Many sages came at that time to offer their blessings to Rama and all of them were given great riches. Gold, silver, jewels, pearls, chariots, horses, silken garments and hundreds of thousands of cows were distributed freely to anyone who came begging charity. Many thousands of brahmins were given sufficient alms to maintain them for the rest of their lives. Rama's relations and dependents, as well as the needy and afflicted were also given much wealth. At that time in Ayodhya there was not a single brahmin or needy person who was not provided with gifts. Being thus honored and gratified by Rama, they all returned to their own homes, praising him in their hearts.

CHAPTER TEN

SAD FAREWELLS

It was time for Rama and his two companions to say their farewells. Holding their weapons and followed by Sita, the brothers made their way towards Dasarath's palace. As they passed along the road many men crowded around to watch them. Plunged in sorrow at seeing their beloved prince leaving, they lamented in various ways.

"Here passes the same Rama who before would move regally in state, followed by a huge retinue," said the people. "Now he walks with only Sita and Lakshmana as his companions. Although used to every luxury, he is going to the terrible forest in obedience to his father's word."

Some citizens censured the king, whom they felt had been gripped by some evil spirit. How could he send his dearest son into exile? Rama's qualities were evident to all; his compassion, learning, gentleness, sense control and mental peace—all were ever visible in that noble prince.

The citizens could not face the prospect of Rama's departure. They felt pain, just as a tree with all its fruits and flowers is hurt when its root is damaged, and they spoke out in public places. "We will give up our homes and villages and go with the pious Rama to the forest. Let us share with him all his joys and sorrows. Let Kaikeyi rule over a deserted kingdom, bereft of its people."

Everyone feared the prospect of Kaikeyi becoming powerful as the mother of the king. They angrily cursed her again and again. All of them would go with Rama. They would abandon the city, leaving its houses to be filled with dust and overrun by mice. The forest would become a city and Ayodhya a forest. They would drive out from the forest all the fierce animals and snakes, sending them to live in Ayodhya with Kaikeyi as their protector.

The two brothers heard the laments of the people, but they kept their minds under strict control. Smiling gently and glancing with affection at the citizens, they walked together like a pair of powerful lions. They entered Dasarath's palace and saw Sumantra, who stood with folded hands and a disconsolate face. Rama asked him to announce their arrival to the king. When Sumantra went before Dasarath he found the king distracted by grief, heaving deep sighs, his eyes red from weeping. The devoted and faithful Sumantra regarded his master to be like the eclipsed sun or a fire covered by ashes. Bowing at the king's feet, Sumantra said, "The illustrious Rama has distributed all his wealth to his dependents and the brahmins, and he now stands at your door awaiting your permission to depart for the forest."

Ordering his minister to show Rama in, the king also asked that all his wives be present. Sumantra brought the queens, who arrived accompanied by numerous maidservants. He then brought Rama and Lakshmana before their father. As Rama entered the room, Dasarath ran impulsively towards him; but being stricken with sorrow, he fell senseless to the floor. Rama and Lakshmana rushed to assist their unconscious father. All the ladies threw up their arms and gave out a wail which mixed with the tinkling of their ornaments. A commotion filled the room, with cries of "Alas! Alas! O Rama!" Kaikeyi alone remained unmoved.

Rama and Lakshmana, both crying, lifted their father and placed him gently on a couch. As the king returned to consciousness, Rama regained his composure and, with folded hands, said, "I have come to take leave of you, father. Please grant me your permission to go to the forest. Also allow Lakshmana and Sita, whom I could not deter even with great effort, to accompany me. O great king, please give up your grief and look favorably upon us, for we wish now to depart."

Rama calmly awaited his father's permission. The king spoke with difficulty. "As a result of a promise made to Kaikeyi I have lost my good sense. Therefore, my dear Rama, take me captive and rule over this kingdom."

Fixed in righteousness, Rama replied, "May you rule the earth for another thousand years. I have no desire for sovereignty. After a mere fourteen years have passed I shall return and once more take hold of your feet, having redeemed your pledge, O ruler of men!"

Dasarath was mortified, but he saw Kaikeyi urging him on with covert gestures. Bound by the fetters of truth he spoke to his son, granting him permission to leave. "Please leave with an undisturbed mind, O Rama, and may your journey be a safe and happy one."

The king was devastated. He could see that Rama's decision to depart was firm and not to be reversed. Rama was devoted to piety and truth. Dasarath requested him to remain for just one night, so that he and Kaushalya might see him a little longer. He wanted to offer Rama all enjoyable things on that last day. Trembling with grief the king said, "I swear to you that I never wanted this to happen. I have been obliged by Kaikeyi, who has abandoned virtue after long concealing her evil intentions. Your willingness to accept even this terrible order, simply to save me from sin, proves beyond doubt your greatness. O gentle Rama, I permit you to leave. Only, go tomorrow with my blessings."

Hearing of his father's request, Rama became concerned. He did not wish to delay his departure any longer and said, "Who will offer me tomorrow the delights I enjoy today? The time for my departure has come and I must now cast aside all thoughts of enjoyment. Let me leave right away. Make over this vast kingdom, with all its riches, to Bharata. My resolution to live in the forest cannot be swayed. Your boons to Kaikeyi should now be implemented in full. I shall live with ascetics for fourteen years and the world should be given to Bharata."

Rama moved closer to his anguished father, who sat shaking his head. He asked the king to be firm and free from sorrow. Rama assured his father that he had no desire at all for the kingdom, nor for any pleasures, nor even for life itself devoid of virtue. He only wished to execute the king's command and prove him true to his word. Comforting the grieving monarch, Rama said, "Since Kaikeyi said to me, 'Go to the forest, O Raghava,' and I replied by saying, 'I am going,' I must now redeem that pledge. Please let me leave. I cannot wait an instant longer."

Rama felt sorrow to see his father suffering such intense agony. Not wanting to increase his father's pain, however, Rama kept his own feelings in check and maintained a calm expression. He spoke gently, assuring his father that he would certainly enjoy his stay in the forest. He would sport happily with Sita in the many delightful woods and groves. Protected by his own weapons and by Lakshmana, there would be no fear for them from the beasts and Rakshasas in the forest. When fourteen years had passed the king would find them returned unharmed and ready to serve him again. Bharata alone could competently and righteously rule the globe in his absence.

Rama added, "I shall never accept the kingdom by bringing infamy to you, O king. Indeed, I could renounce every pleasure, including my own dear wife, in order to satisfy your command. I shall only be happy the moment I enter the forest. You need not feel any pain for me. Be peaceful, my lord, and allow me to leave."

Dasarath, tormented by a burning agony, embraced Rama tightly and then again fell unconscious, showing no signs of life. All the queens, along with their maidservants, cried loudly. Kaikeyi felt her purpose fulfilled and was rejoicing inwardly. Witnessing her silence, the king's intimate friend Sumantra was furious. Beating his head, wringing his hands and grinding his teeth, he spoke scathingly to her, his eyes blazing with wrath.

"Here lies your husband, the support of the whole world, betrayed and forsaken by you, O queen. Surely there is nothing sacred for you. I consider you to be the murderess of your husband and the destroyer of your entire race. Do not despise your lord in this way, for his order is superior to that of even a million sons. Ignoring the time-honored rule of primogeniture, you seek to usurp Rama's rights and bring unbearable pain to the king."

Tears flowed from the old minister's eyes as he spoke. He told Kaikeyi to renounce her evil aim. If her son became the king, then no pious man would remain in the kingdom. What joy would she derive from ruling the empty earth, which was earned through sin? It was a great wonder that the earth did not split apart and swallow her, or that the great sages did not utter fiery curses to consume her on that very spot. Having served the king all his life, Sumantra felt every pain the king felt as if it were his own. As he addressed Kaikeyi he could hardly bring himself to look at her.

"The glorious king will never belie his promise to you. Do not force him to perform an act repugnant to himself and the whole world. Follow the desire of the king and become a protectress of the world. Let Rama be installed on the throne. He will undoubtedly always remain favorable to you in every way. If, however, on your order he is sent to the forest, then your only gain will be unending infamy. Give up your misguided desire, O Kaikeyi, and live happily."

Kaikeyi looked coolly at Sumantra, who stood before her with joined palms, and she made no reply. Her mind remained unmoved as she awaited the execution of her order. Seeing her resolve, Dasarath, who had regained consciousness, sighed and said to Sumantra, "You should immediately order my army to make ready to depart. They should accompany Rama to the forest. So too should wealthy merchants skilled at establishing networks of shops. Search out hunters who know the secrets of forests and send them with Rama. Assemble thousands of capable servants and have them prepare to leave. Indeed, you should arrange for my entire treasury and my granary to be transported along with Rama. He should not have to endure any austerity during the fourteen years of exile."

As Dasarath spoke Kaikeyi became alarmed. The king was going to divest the kingdom of all its wealth before her son was crowned. Dismayed and fearful, she turned towards Dasarath and spoke, her mouth parched and her voice choked. "How can you bestow upon Bharata a kingdom stripped of its wealth? How then will he actually be the ruler of this world, as you have promised?"

The king turned angrily towards Kaikeyi. "After handing me a heavy burden to bear, you are now lashing me as I carry it, O hostile and vulgar woman! When asking for your boons you should have stipulated that Rama could not take anything with him to the forest. Abandoning all sense of righteousness, you have taken to a path leading only to grief. I cannot stay here with you any longer. Along with all the people of Ayodhya I shall follow Rama to the forest!"

Rama approached his father and said politely, "O great king, of what use to me is an army and all your riches? I have renounced the kingdom; how then can I take its wealth? He who has parted with an elephant yet seeks to retain its tether is simply a fool. I am resolved to enter the forest and dwell there with the ascetics, wearing the barks of trees and living on whatever produce I can glean from day to day."

Rama wanted to act only in accord with the scriptural instructions regarding the vow of forest life. He told his father that one living in the forest should not do so in great opulence. Rama asked that the king not bestow upon his brother a kingdom bereft of its riches. He would leave with only his weapons and a spade for digging roots. Turning to the king's servants, Rama said, "Bring me the tree barks and I shall take off these royal garments and make ready to depart."

His request so gladdened Kaikeyi that she personally fetched the spartan forest clothes made from barks and grasses she had already prepared. Shamelessly handing them to Rama, Lakshmana and Sita, she said, "Put these on." Rama and Lakshmana quickly and adroitly changed into those clothes, but the beautiful Sita was perplexed, unsure of how to wear them. Trying again and again to place the bark linen over her other clothes, Sita felt abashed. With her eyes flooded with tears she said to her husband, "How does one wear such dress, my lord?"

Rama personally fastened the bark over Sita's silk dress. Seeing her clad in forest apparel, her many female servants began to wail piteously. "This noble princess has not been ordered to enter the forest!" they cried. "Dear Rama, please let her remain here with us so we may continue to serve her and enjoy the blessing of seeing her divine form. How can this gentle lady live like an ascetic in the forest? She does not deserve to suffer in this way!"

Although hearing their loving remonstrances, Rama continued to tie on Sita's forest clothes as she desired. Suddenly Vasishtha became overwhelmed with distress at seeing the gentle Sita about to enter the forest. Feeling angered and weeping hot tears, he said to Kaikeyi, "O cruel woman, have you no shame? After deceiving the king and bringing disgrace to your family, are you still not satisfied? Will you stand by and watch as this highborn lady leaves for the forest, wearing the coarse garments you prepared? You did not ask that she be exiled along with Rama! These tree barks are not meant for her. Excellent garments and jewels should be brought by you for your daughter-in-law. She should proceed to the forest on first-class conveyances and accompanied by all her servants."

Vasishtha loved Rama and Sita like his own children. He could not stand and watch as they departed while the hard-hearted Kaikeyi looked on gleefully. The sage spoke words which pierced Kaikeyi deeply. He explained that according to scripture the wife was her husband's own self. They were one and the same person. As such Sita should therefore rule over the kingdom, even if Rama himself could not. The forest would become the capital of the world. Indeed, the entire state of Koshala, along with all its people and the city of Ayodhya, would leave along with Rama. The sage blazed with anger as he went on, appearing like a smokeless fire.

"Surely Bharata and his brother Shatrughna will also enter the forest, clad in barks. You may then rule over a desolate kingdom, peopled only by trees, which alone could not rise up and follow Rama!"

Kaikeyi remained silent and looked at Rama and Sita, who were ready to leave. Sita wished only to follow her husband. Even upon hearing Vasishtha's words, she was not swayed in the least from her purpose. She stood next to Rama, covered from head to toe in the grass and bark clothes given by Kaikeyi. All the people present then loudly exclaimed, "Shame upon the powerless king who does nothing to stop this flagrant injustice!"

Hearing their cries the emperor became dispirited and lost interest in life. He turned to Kaikeyi and rebuked her for making Sita wear forest garments, but the queen remained silent. Rama came before his father, who sat with his head bent low, and asked his permission to leave. He requested the king to take special care of Kaushalya, whom he feared would suffer in his absence. Looking at his son clad in the dress of a hermit, the king fell unconscious. After being brought to his senses by his ministers, who gently sprinkled him with cool water, Dasarath lamented loudly.

"I think in my past life I must have given terrible pain to other living beings and thus this pain is now being felt by me. Surely life will not leave one until the appointed time arrives. Otherwise, why does death not claim me now, who am tormented by Kaikeyi and beholding my dearest son wearing the robes of an ascetic?"

Crying out, "O Rama!" the king broke off, choked with tears. With a great effort Dasarath then managed to control his grief and, turning towards Sumantra, he said, "Fetch here the best of my chariots and take the glorious Rama beyond this city. Since I see a virtuous and valiant son being exiled to the forest by his own father and mother, I can only conclude that this is the results of piety, as declared by the scriptures. Religion is undoubtedly difficult to divine."

As Rama and Sita approached the chariot brought by Sumantra, Kaushalya came and tightly embraced Sita, saying, "Wicked are those women who forsake their worthy husbands when fallen upon hard times. Even though such women have in the past been protected and afforded every happiness, they malign and even desert their husbands when misfortune arrives. Such women are heartless, untruthful, lusty and sinful by nature, being quickly estranged in times of trouble. Neither kindness nor education nor gift nor even marriage ties can capture the hearts of these women."

Kaushalya loved Sita as a daughter. She knew that Rama's gentle wife was entirely devoted to piety and she spoke to her only out of motherly affection. She continued, "For virtuous women, who are truthful, pious, obedient to their elders and acting within the bounds of morality the husband is the most sacred object and is never abandoned. Although Rama is being sent to the forest you should never neglect him, dear Sita. Whether wealthy or without any means whatsoever, he is always your worshipable deity."

Sita was filled with joy to hear this advice, which was in accord with her life's aim. Joining her palms, she replied reverentially, "I shall surely do all that your honorable self instructs. I have always heard from you proper advice about how to serve my husband. Even in thought you should not compare me to wicked women, for I am unable to deviate from virtue, even as moonlight cannot be parted from the moon. As a lute is useless without its strings or a chariot without its wheels, so a wife is destitute when separated from her worthy husband. Having learned from my elders all the duties incumbent upon a wife, and knowing the husband to be a veritable deity, how can I ever neglect Rama, O venerable lady?"

Kaushalya's heart was touched by Sita's reply and she shed tears born of both delight and agony, being moved by Sita's piety and at the same time anguished at the thought of her imminent departure.

Rama looked with affection at his mother. It was time for him to leave. He feared Kaushalya would pine away after he left. Rama stood before her with folded palms. "Please do not show my father sad expressions, heightening his grief. Fourteen years will pass quickly, even while you sleep. You will rise one morning to find me returned with Sita and Lakshmana, surrounded by friends and relatives."

Rama looked around at all the royal ladies standing there and said, "Please forgive any unkind words or acts which I may have said or done out of ignorance because we have lived closely together. Now I take leave of you all."

A cry rose up from the ladies that resembled the cry of female cranes. Dasarath's palace, which had always been marked with the joyous sounds of music and festivities, was now filled with the sound of agonized wails.

Catching hold of Dasarath's feet, Rama, Sita and Lakshmana took their final leave of him and walked around him in respect. Numbed by grief, Rama bowed to Kaushalya and climbed up onto the chariot, followed by Sita. As Lakshmana followed them, his own mother Sumitra came up to say good-bye. Embracing her son she said, "Serve well your elder brother Rama, my dear son. The eternal moral law states that the older brother is the refuge of the younger, whether in good times or bad. Never forget the duties of our race, O Lakshmana, which are to practice charity, perform sacrifices for the good of the people and to lay down one's life on the field of battle."

Blinded by tears, Sumitra allowed her son to mount the chariot as she called out, "Farewell, dear son, farewell! Always see Rama as you do your father Dasarath, look upon Sita as myself, your mother, and see the forest as Ayodhya!"

Sumantra took up the reins of the horses and urged them forward. The great golden chariot moved ahead with a thunderous rumbling. As it passed down the royal highway the people assembled were stunned with sorrow. Both old and young alike rushed towards the chariot as thirsty men would rush toward water in the desert. Clinging to the sides and the back of the chariot they looked up at Sumantra, calling out, "Hold fast the reins, O charioteer, and drive slowly. We wish to see Rama a little longer."

Rama, anxious to be gone as quickly as possible, asked them to desist and told Sumantra to drive more swiftly. Ordered by Rama, "Move on!" and at the same time told by the people who filled the road, "Stop!" Sumantra could do neither. With great difficulty the chariot pressed slowly forward.

Seeing Rama leaving and his city plunged into despair, the king fell prostrate. Upon being brought back to consciousness, he got up and, along with Kaushalya, ran after the chariot. Rama looked behind him and saw them trying to make their way through the crowd. He was unable to bear the sight of his father and mother in such distress, but being bound by duty, he urged Sumantra ever forward. The charioteer was perplexed, hearing from behind the king calling out, "Come back!" and then being ordered by Rama to drive quicker. Rama said to him, "This pain should not be prolonged further. Make haste! If my father reprimands you when you return, you should simply say you could not hear him."

Finally breaking free from the crowd, the chariot gathered speed and left the city. Dasarath was still running along the road, his eyes fixed on the dust raised by the chariot's wheels. Breathless and at last losing sight of the chariot in the distance, Dasarath fell down on the road.

As he lay there Kaushalya and Kaikeyi came to raise him up. On seeing Kaikeyi, however, the king became inflamed with anger. "Do not touch me, O sinful woman!" he roared. "I never want to see you again. You are neither my wife nor relation and I have nothing more to say to you. I also reject those who serve and depend upon you. If your son is in any way pleased to receive the sovereignty, then I shall shun him as well!"

Dasarath gazed at the tracks of the chariot. He covered his face in shame, blaming himself for Rama's departure. With Kaushalya's help, he slowly made his way back to the palace. As he passed along the road he saw the city marked by mourning, its shops closed, its streets deserted. Lamenting all the while, Dasarath entered his palace as the sun goes behind a cloud. The great palace was silent and without movement, overladen with a heavy atmosphere of sorrow. Dasarath went into Kaushalya's apartments and, laying down upon a soft couch, cried out, "O Rama, have you really deserted me? Alas! Only those who will endure these coming fourteen years will be happy, seeing again the face of my gentle son. I cannot tolerate life without that tiger among men. O wicked Kaikeyi, you may rule this kingdom as a widow!"

Kaushalya looked sadly upon her husband and said, "Having discharged her poison upon Rama, the crooked Kaikeyi will now wander freely like a female serpent who has shed her skin. With Rama exiled and her own son installed as king, surely she will cause further fear to me, even like a snake living in one's own house. How shall I survive without Rama?"

Thinking of Rama and Sita entering the forest, Kaushalya cried out in pain. How would they survive? Exactly at a time when they should have enjoyed the luxuries of life, they were banished and made to live like ascetics. When again would she see them? Surely in some past life she had committed some grievous sin. For that reason she now suffered such terrible pain. She lamented loudly, "O Rama! O Lakshmana! O Sita! Where are you now? The fire of my grief tortures me today as the blazing sun scorches the earth in summer!"

Sumitra gently reassured Kaushalya, reminding her of the greatness of Rama and Lakshmana. Controlling her own grief and sitting next to Kaushalya, she placed her arms around her co-wife. She spoke about Rama, describing his qualities and immeasurable strength. Simply to prove his noble father to be perfectly truthful, he had renounced the throne and gone to the forest. This was the path of virtue followed always by cultured men. That path led only to regions of never-ending happiness. Kaushalya should therefore not pity her son.

Sumitra spoke softly. "Being ever attended by the loving Lakshmana and followed by his devoted wife, Rama will feel no discomfort. Even the sun will withhold its scorching rays from Rama's body, seeing his boundless virtues. A gentle and soothing breeze will always blow softly on Rama. At night when he lies down to sleep, the cooling rays of the moon will caress him like a loving father."

Sumitra stroked Kaushalya's face. She spoke to assuage her own suffering as much as that of Kaushalya. She told Kaushalya not to worry. Rama would surely be protected by the terrible weapons that Vishvamitra gave him. He would dwell fearlessly in the forest just as he would in his own palace. Sumitra concluded, "Knowing the power of that prince, I have no doubt we will see him returned as soon as his term of exile is concluded. With Rama as your son you should not grieve in the least, for your good fortune is very great indeed. Shed your sorrow now, O sinless lady, for all the people must be comforted by you at this time, pained as they are by Rama's separation."

Comforted by Sumitra, Kaushalya felt relief and embraced her co-wife tightly. The two queens sat together for a long time, lost in thoughts of Rama. Nearby the king lay almost unconscious on a couch, repeatedly murmuring Rama's name.

PART TWO

EXILED

CHAPTER ONE

INTO THE FOREST

After their father had returned, Rama and Lakshmana left the city and went along country paths toward the forest. Even though they urged Sumantra to drive quickly, a large number of citizens continued to follow them. Rama stopped to rest after some time and allowed the people to reach him. He said to them with affection, "You have shown your great love for me beyond any doubt. Now for my pleasure, please bestow this same love upon my brother Bharata. I am sure he will take good care of you in every possible way. Although still a youth, he is old in wisdom and greatly heroic. He will prove a worthy master and dispel all your sorrows and fears. Serve him well, for he has been selected by our lord the emperor. It is also my desire that all of you please him with your service. Be kind to the emperor so that he may not suffer excessive agony in my absence."

Rama tried hard to make the people turn back, but they would not return. The more Rama showed his determination to stick to the path of righteousness and truth, the more the people desired to have him as their ruler. It was as if Rama and Lakshmana, by the cords of their virtuous qualities, had bound the people and were dragging them along.

The chariot began to move forward again and a group of elderly brahmins, their heads shaking with age, ran behind, struggling to keep pace as the chariot picked up speed. They called out, "O swift steeds, stop! Come back and be friendly to your master Rama, who is always intent on pleasing the brahmins. O horses, halt! Although endowed with excellent ears, do you not hear our plaintive cry? You should not bear Rama away. He is pure-minded, heroic and virtuous. Therefore, you should return him to the city to be our king, not carry him away to some distant, lonely place!"

Rama looked back, feeling compassion for the distressed brahmins. He did not want to ride himself while brahmins walked, so he got down from his chariot and continued on foot. Although his heart was breaking to see the people's anguish, Rama looked straight ahead and walked with firm strides, followed by Sita and Lakshmana. Sumantra drove slowly behind them in the chariot. As the brahmins continued to beseech them, they gradually approached the banks of the river Tamasa. Searching out a suitable site, they decided to camp there for the night. The citizens of Ayodhya camped nearby. Rama released the horses and allowed them to drink the clear river water. After bathing, Rama spoke to Lakshmana, indicating the forest across the water.

"There lie the desolate woods, my brother, echoing on all sides with the sounds of birds and beasts. The city of Ayodhya will similarly resound with the cries of forlorn men and women, lamenting for our having left. I fear for my father and mother who must be weeping incessantly and will perhaps even lose their sight."

Rama thought of Bharata. By now he would have been informed of the situation. Thinking of Bharata's nobility, Rama felt reassured as he spoke with Lakshmana. "I am sure the high-minded Bharata will take good care of our parents, consoling them in every way. As I reflect upon Bharata's softheartedness and piety, my mind is pacified. My dear Lakshmana, I am grateful you have chosen to follow me, for this too gives me solace. Fasting for this our first night in the forest in accord with the scriptural codes, I shall now sleep peacefully."

Lakshmana had Sumantra prepare a bed of leaves on the ground and Rama lay upon that with Sita. He soon fell asleep, but Lakshmana stayed awake, guarding his brother. Nearby he could see the many fires lit by the people who were following Rama toward the forest.

In the middle of the night Rama rose and again spoke with his brother. "It seems there is no possibility of us convincing the citizens to return to their homes," he said, looking across to the place where the people had set up camp. "Just see the pains they are taking to follow us, sleeping now on the bare ground. Surely they would sooner give up their lives than go back to the city without us. Let us leave immediately while the people still sleep. They should not have to endure this austerity further on our behalf. As rulers of the people it is our duty to eradicate our subjects' suffering. Certainly we should not cause them pain. Thus we must leave now and throw them off our trail."

Lakshmana agreed and, as Rama woke Sita, he roused Sumantra and had him prepare the chariot. The two princes and Sita climbed aboard, and Sumantra drove it swiftly upstream, away from the sleeping people. The charioteer crossed a shallow part of the river and then, leaving the common road, drove through the woods. Doubling back and going by different paths, sometimes riding through shallow waters for some distance, Sumantra made sure the people would not be able to track them. He drove quickly, and before dawn they had gone a considerable distance from where the citizens were camped.

As dawn approached in the camp, the sound of numerous birds mingled with the lowing of the cows which grazed freely on the riverbank. Roused by these sounds, the citizens arose and soon discovered that Rama and his party had left. They were shocked and began to loudly lament. They condemned sleep for having stolen Rama from them. Falling to the ground, they wept and said, "How could Rama, who is fit to rule the globe, put on the dress of an ascetic and leave for distant lands? How did that jewel among men, who was like a loving father, go to the forest, leaving us forlorn? Let us now meet our end by fasting until death, or by setting out on the final great journey to the north."

Looking all around they found big logs of dry wood. Some of them suggested they pile up the wood to make a funeral pyre and immediately enter it. What use was their life now? What could they say to their near and dear ones in Ayodhya when asked of Rama's whereabouts? How could they say they let him enter the forest even as they slept? When they returned without Rama, the city would surely become desolate and devoid of all happiness. Having gone out with that high-souled hero, firmly determined to follow him anywhere, how could they now go back without him?

Continuously crying out, the citizens sought out the chariot's tracks and began to follow them. When they found themselves thrown off the trail by Sumantra's expert driving, they became utterly despondent. Their anguished voices echoed around the woods. "Alas! What shall we do? We are doomed by Providence!" Gradually the bewildered citizens began to reluctantly head back toward Ayodhya, following the tracks the chariot had made when leaving the previous day.

Depressed and despairing, the citizens finally arrived in the city. They were blinded by grief and hardly able to distinguish between their own relatives and others. They searched for their homes with difficulty, some of them even entering the wrong houses. Afflicted with sorrow, they cast their eyes all around and, although the city and their houses were filled with abundant riches, to them it appeared vacant and nothing gave them pleasure.

Ayodhya seemed at that time to be like the firmament bereft of the moon. Everywhere its citizens shed tears and all of them felt like giving up their lives. No one rejoiced on any occasion, even when coming upon unexpected fortune or seeing the birth of a firstborn son. Merchants did not display their merchandise, nor did the goods even seem attractive. Householders did not cook food and the household deities were neglected.

As the men returned home without Rama, their wives reproached them. "Without seeing Rama what is the use of our house, children or wealth?" the wives said. "It seems the only virtuous man in this world is Lakshmana, who has followed Rama to the forest in order to serve him!"

The men, pained by the loss of Rama, made no reply. Their wives lamented at length. How could they remain under the protection of the old king, who had lost his good sense and sent Rama away? Worse still was the prospect of serving Kaikeyi, whose aim was now completely achieved. Having forsaken her husband and disgraced her family for the sake of power, who else would she not abandon?

The ladies could not contain their feelings. Out of despair they remonstrated with their husbands. "Thanks to Kaikeyi, this kingdom will be ruined. With Rama gone, Dasarath will soon meet his end along with his distinguished line, which has existed for so long. How can there be any good fortune with Kaikeyi in a position of power? We should therefore end our lives. Or we should follow Rama to some distant place where Kaikeyi's name will never be heard. The glorious and ever-truthful Rama shall be our only shelter."

As the ladies of Ayodhya lamented, the sun gradually set on the city, leaving it dark and cheerless, its lights unlit and its temples and public meeting places deserted. Fallen upon evil days, the celebrated city became silent, the sounds of singing, rejoicing and instrumental music having ceased. All the people remained in their own homes, thinking only of Rama.

*   *   *

During that night the chariot carrying the princes covered a long distance. As they traveled, Rama remembered the pain of his relations and people. Reflecting again and again upon his father's command, he kept his determination strong and urged Sumantra to drive swiftly. They passed many villages, seeing on their outskirts well-tilled and cultivated fields, as well as beautiful, blossoming woodlands. People from the villages, to where the news of Rama's exile had already spread, saw the chariot passing, by and they censured the emperor and especially Kaikeyi, saying, "The cruel Kaikeyi has acted without propriety. She has caused the exile of the highly virtuous Rama. What will become of us now? How will the delicate princess Sita survive in the forest? How shameful that the king could abandon all affection for such a son and daughter-in-law!"

Going more slowly as he passed the people, Rama heard their comments and he smiled at them without saying anything. As the chariot moved on more swiftly, the travelers saw innumerable gardens, fruit orchards and lotus ponds. Temples resonant with the sounds of sacred incantations were everywhere. While sitting in the chariot and enjoying the sights of his flourishing kingdom, Rama thought of his coming exile. He would long for the day of his return to this prosperous land of Koshala.

As they at last reached Koshala's southern border, Rama got down from the chariot and stood facing the direction of Ayodhya. With his face covered in tears he spoke in a choked voice. "I take leave of you, O foremost of cities. Protected by the emperor and your presiding deities, may you fare well. When I have squared my debt to my father and fulfilled his pledge, I shall return."

Many country dwellers had gathered around Rama. They were filled with grief to see him bid his sad farewell to Ayodhya. Rama glanced at them with affection. He thanked them for the love they showed for him, and told them to go home.

The people simply stood gazing at Rama, unable to move. Although he urged them to return home, they stood rooted to the spot. They could not turn away from the heroic and handsome prince. As they stood watching, Rama remounted his chariot and it disappeared into the distance, even as the sun sets at the end of the day.

Gradually the party reached the Ganges river in the Ushinara province. Along the banks of the river for as far as the eye could see in both directions were clustered the hermitages of ascetics and rishis. Hundreds of hills ran along the length of the river, and the river flowed with cool water flecked with white foam, making a roaring sound as it rushed past. Somewhere the river ran still and deep and somewhere else it dashed violently against rocks. In places it was covered with white lotuses, while in others thousands of swans, cranes and herons hovered on its waters. It was the resort of even gods and Gandharvas who sported along its banks. Surrounded by trees laden with fruits and flowers and full of varieties of singing birds, the river appeared most beautiful.

Seeing this celestial region, Rama decided to stop for the night. He took shelter under the branches of a large tree and sat down to offer worship to the Ganges. Sumantra unyoked the horses and allowed them to drink and then roll on the grassy riverbank. The charioteer stood with folded hands near Rama, who sat peacefully with Sita by his side.

The king of that territory was named Guha, a dear friend of Rama who ruled over the tribal people known as the Nishadhas. Hearing from his people of Rama's presence, he immediately went to him. Guha found Rama by the bank of the Ganges and he stood at a distance, waiting respectfully for his audience. He was overjoyed to find his friend arrived in his kingdom, but his joy was mixed with sorrow at seeing him dressed as an ascetic. Rama looked up and saw Guha standing there, surrounded by his relations and elderly ministers. Quickly approaching him with Lakshmana, he tightly embraced him and they exchanged greetings. Guha spoke to Rama, whom he had met on many occasions in Ayodhya when going there to pay tribute. "I am honored by your presence in my kingdom. This land here is as much yours as it is mine. Indeed, I am your servant. Only order me and I shall immediately do whatever you wish."

He showed Rama the many varieties of food and drink he had brought, as well as the excellent beds he had prepared for them. Rama thanked him and said, "I have been well honored by you today. You should know that I am under a vow to live in the forest as an ascetic. I accept your offerings but allow you to take them back. Please leave only as much as may be taken by my horses. Since these steeds are dear to my father, you will please me by serving them well."

Reluctantly, Guha commanded his men to do as Rama had requested, having the best of food brought for the horses. He watched with sadness and admiration as Rama accepted only water for himself and then lay down to sleep on a bed of leaves. Lakshmana washed Rama's feet and again kept vigil nearby. Going over to Lakshmana, Guha said, "Here is a bed for you. There is no need to remain awake for I shall stand here, bow in hand, and guard you all from danger. There is nothing in these woods unknown to me. Indeed, along with my men I could withstand the attack of a vast and powerful army coming upon this region."

Guha took Lakshmana by the arm and showed him the bed, but Lakshmana politely refused his offer. "Under your protection we feel not even the least fear, O sinless Guha. But how can I rest while Rama and Sita lie down on the earth?"

Lakshmana looked at his brother lying beneath the tree. His mind was troubled. How could one such as Rama, who was capable of withstanding even the gods in battle, be brought to such a state? Lakshmana's thoughts drifted to Ayodhya. He became restless, thinking of his father and the subjects. Surely Dasarath would soon breathe his last, having sent his dearest son to a life of severe austerity. Probably Kaushalya and the king would die that very night, uttering words of despair and anguish. Losing their beloved monarch after watching Rama depart, the people of Ayodhya would be seized with agony after agony.

Engrossed in such thoughts, Lakshmana breathed heavily like an infuriated serpent. Hot tears glided down his face. Guha placed an arm around his shoulder and gently reassured him. As the two men spoke the night gradually slipped away.

When dawn broke, Guha arranged for a large rowboat to ferry the princes across the fast-flowing Ganges. The time had arrived to leave the chariot and continue on foot. As the princes fastened on their armor and weapons, Sumantra humbly approached them with joined palms and asked for instructions. Rama smiled and said, "You have rendered me excellent service, O Sumantra. Please return now to the king's presence and inform him of our well-being. We shall now proceed on foot."

Sumantra found it difficult to leave Rama. Gazing into his face, he spoke in an anguished voice. "What man in this world has ever had to face such a perverse destiny, O Raghava? What is the value of cultivating piety and truth when we see such a result? We are actually lost and ruined by your departure. Coming under the control of the sinful Kaikeyi, we will simply suffer."

Sumantra broke down and wept for some time and Rama comforted him. As he regained his composure Rama said, "I cannot think of anyone who is as great a friend to our family as you, O noble charioteer. Please act in a way which will not increase my father's grief. Whatever he instructs should be carried out without hesitation, even if he orders you to serve Kaikeyi."

Rama understood all the nuances of statecraft. He was worried that in his absence the king's ministers and servants might try to undermine Kaikeyi. He wanted the kingdom to run smoothly and his father to be spared any unnecessary anxiety in dealing with intrigues. Wanting also to ensure that his family not be left anxious for his sake, Rama added, "Please tell my father that neither Lakshmana nor Sita nor I are grieving in any way. Happily do we commence our sojourn in the woods. The period of fourteen years will soon pass and we shall return."

Rama considered the urgent need to re-establish stability in Ayodhya. He spoke solemnly to Sumantra. "Ask the king to fetch Bharata quickly and duly install him as Prince Regent. Bharata himself should be told to accept the post without any hesitation, for this will be most pleasing to me. He should then serve the king and all the queens with an equally disposed mind."

Rama gave his permission for Sumantra to leave, but the charioteer still stood before him, his mind perplexed. How could he return without Rama? He revealed his mind to Rama. "As we left the city the people were practically rendered senseless with grief even upon seeing you in this chariot. What then will be their state when they see the chariot returning empty? Surely Ayodhya will be torn in two, even as the army of a hero is split apart when it sees his chariot carrying only the charioteer, the hero having been slain."

Sumantra thought of Dasarath and Kaushalya. They would be devastated by grief when they heard that their son had actually entered the forest. Sumantra felt incapable of returning. He pleaded with Rama to let him go to the forest too. He was prepared to remain with Rama for the full fourteen years rather than go back to Ayodhya without him. Falling to the ground and clasping Rama's feet, he spoke with pain in his voice.

"My desire is to convey you back to Ayodhya at the end of your exile. If I must return without you, then seated upon the chariot I shall enter blazing fire. I am your devoted servant and it does not befit you to abandon me now. Let me follow you and render you every service. Fourteen years will be as many moments in your presence, while in your absence it will seem like fourteen ages."

Rama was moved by compassion for Sumantra, who was piteously supplicating him again and again. He lifted the weeping charioteer. "I know your devotion for me, Sumantra. However, I must ask you to return. Kaikeyi will not be satisfied unless she sees the chariot returned without me and hears from you of my entry into the forest. For the good of the king I want her to be convinced that I have fulfilled the terms of her boons, and I also desire that her son Bharata be given the kingdom."

Rama knew that if any doubt remained about whether or not he had really gone to the forest, then, in the hope of his return, they would not install his brother Bharata. He therefore convinced Sumantra of the need for him to return to Ayodhya, carrying the messages he had given. With a heavy heart Sumantra finally assented and got up on the chariot. Rama then turned and spoke to Guha. "It would not be proper for me to stay in a region where I have many men to serve me. I wish to go to some uninhabited part of the forest and live in a simple hermitage, gathering my daily food from wild roots and fruits."

Rama knew Guha and his people were hoping to accommodate him in a nearby wood, but he was devoted to virtue and wanted to properly follow the scriptural instructions, which prescribed a life of strict asceticism for one taking the vow of living in a forest. Using the sap of a banyan tree, Rama and Lakshmana matted their hair into a thick mass. With their matted locks and their bark and grass garments, the two princes looked like a couple of ascetic rishis. Rama helped Sita onto the boat, and then jumped aboard himself, along with Lakshmana. Headed by Guha, the oarsmen plied the boat out across the river. Rama waved to Sumantra, who stood motionless on the sandy river bank, gripped by despondency.

The boat approached the southern shore of the Ganges swiftly and smoothly. Sita folded her palms and prayed to the goddess Ganga for protection in the forest. The river was placid and shone like a sheet of glass under the bright sun. Small ripples spread from the side of the boat as the oars gently and rhythmically splashed the water. Rama and Lakshmana sat silently, thinking of Ayodhya and their family and friends. They watched as Sita sat in the prow of the boat, her eyes closed in prayer. Gradually they approached the shoreline, with its sprawling forest reaching practically to the river's edge.

After the party disembarked, Rama said a fond farewell to Guha. He embraced the forest chieftain and then turned and walked toward the thick forest. Lakshmana went ahead of him, placing Sita between them. As they walked they heard the sounds of beasts and birds--the shrill trills of parrots, the grunts of boars, the cries of monkeys and the occasional growls and roars of tigers.

Rama was apprehensive about Sita's safety. The vast and trackless forest lay immediately ahead. What dangers would they now have to face? But as they began to penetrate into the forest, Rama's fear for Sita gave way to delight. At last the moment had arrived! His father's word would now be redeemed. Despite any danger he would surely stay here for fourteen years, thinking only of the glory of his aged and pious father. Keeping his mind fully alert, Rama gripped the great bow which hung from his shoulder and placed his other hand on the hilt of the blue steel sword strapped to his belt.

The three travelers had become hungry and they searched for roots and bulbs, fit for offering in the sacred fire. After they had cooked and made the offering, they ate, and when the meal was over, they performed their evening worship. Rama and Lakshmana then sat together and Rama spoke a little to his brother. "Surely the king will sleep only fitfully tonight, O Lakshmana! On the other hand, Kaikeyi will rest peacefully with her desired object fulfilled."

Rama was pensive. Until now he had not dwelt upon his own anxiety for fear of increasing the pain of those he loved. Now that he was finally in the solitude of the forest, he felt a deep disquiet. What other terrible suffering would Kaikeyi cause for his father? With Bharata installed as Prince Regent perhaps she would even try to bring about Dasarath's death, so that her own son might more quickly become the king. How could the king protect himself, being weakened by grief? What would become of his mother Kaushalya, as well as Sumitra? Rama appeared anxious as he continued.

"I think that in the morning you should return to Ayodhya, O noble prince! Protect our mothers and our aged father. I do not see anyone else who can guard against Kaikeyi's evil intrigues. Even now she may be plotting to poison our parents."

Although he felt helpless, Rama nevertheless censured himself for failing to secure his parents' happiness. Having undergone great pains to nurture him with love, they were deprived of his company just when they should have found their labors repaid. "Alas," exclaimed Rama, "I am an ungrateful and useless son!"

Rama wept. He could by no means breach the order of Kaikeyi and his father, but he feared he might be acting wrongly if the result was his parents' death. Torn apart by his feelings, he wanted Lakshmana to go back to Ayodhya to protect them. Rama lamented loudly for some time. When he fell silent, Lakshmana replied, "Please do not grieve in this way, dear brother, as you simply cause grief for myself and Sita. It is not possible for me to leave you as I would not survive even for a short while in your absence. Placing your faith in the pious Bharata, you should not send me away. I only wish to remain with you here and do not desire even the highest heaven without you."

Rama remained silent. He knew well that Lakshmana would never leave him. It had grown dark and the brothers sought the shelter of a large tree where Rama and Sita lay down to rest. Lakshmana remained awake a short distance away, vigilantly guarding them from any danger. Gradually the full moon rose and shone through the branches of the high trees, illuminating the beautiful faces of Rama and Sita as they slept, which appeared to Lakshmana like two more moons fallen to the earth.

The following morning after sunrise they went in an easterly direction toward the confluence of the Ganges and the Yamuna. They were keen to find the hermitages of the rishis whom they knew lived in that region. The famous sage Bharadvaja, the leader of all the brahmins inhabiting that forest, dwelt nearby.

As they walked they were enraptured by the colorful beauty of the forest. Huge trees rose up on all sides. In some places the trees opened up into expansive clearings carpeted by innumerable varieties of flowers and shrubs. Lakes of crystal clear water covered with white, blue and reddish lotuses were seen here and there. The trees were laden with blossoms, filling the air with their fragrance. The sounds of cuckoos, parrots and peacocks echoed all around.

Keeping close together, the three travelers walked throughout the day, sometimes moving easily and at other times with difficulty through densely wooded regions. Toward the end of the afternoon they heard in the distance the sound of the two rivers rushing to meet each other. Around them they began seeing signs of life: chopped wood and man-made paths. Catching sight of smoke rising above the trees, they realized they had found the dwellings of the rishis and they quickly went toward them.

At the precincts of the hermitage they were greeted by a young ascetic who was a disciple of Bharadvaja. He led them through the many thatched cottages of the brahmin community, showing them to a great sacrificial arena where Bharadvaja was seated. Surrounded by his disciples, the sage sat before the sacred fire, absorbed in meditation. As soon as the three travelers caught sight of the effulgent rishi they prostrated themselves on the earth in obeisance. They waited respectfully at a distance for the sage to beckon to them.

Bharadvaja had attained virtual omniscience by his long practice of asceticism and meditation. He immediately sensed the presence of his exalted guests and he rose up to greet them. Going before the sage, Rama said with joined palms, "We are Rama and Lakshmana, the sons of Emperor Dasarath, O highly venerable sage. Here is my blessed and irreproachable wife, a princess of Videha and the daughter of King Janaka. Ordered by my ever-pious father, I have come to this forest to live the life of an ascetic for fourteen years, and my brother and wife have chosen to follow me. Please bless us."

Bharadvaja gazed upon the faces of his guests, understanding their divine identities. He offered them various delicious foods prepared from wild roots and fruits. Tears flowed from his eyes as he spoke to Rama. "I already knew of your exile and have been expecting you to pass this way. Your auspicious arrival here at my hermitage signals the success of all my austerities and sacrifices. It is highly difficult to have a sight of you and today I am supremely blessed. My dear Rama, if you so desire you may remain here in this delightful stretch of land, which is quite suitable for the life of asceticism."

Smiling and graciously accepting the sage's offerings of love, Rama replied, "This hermitage is well known and not so far from the state of Ayodhya. The people will soon seek me out if I remain here. Please tell me of some other, more lonely place, for I will not be able to tolerate the pain of the people again beseeching me to return."

Bharadvaja understood Rama's concern. He directed the prince to a mountain named Chitrakuta, lying some fifty miles away. After spending the night at the sage's hermitage, the three travelers set out the next morning toward the mountain. It lay across the Yamuna, which they crossed by means of a raft constructed from timber and bamboo.

As they walked toward Chitrakuta they saw countless varieties of trees and plants spreading everywhere in tableaus of rich colors. The constant singing of thousands of birds resounded on all sides, mingling with the sounds of trickling rivulets and cascading waterfalls. From time to time the trumpeting of an elephant could be heard in the distance. Branches of great trees were bent low under their burden of sweet fruits. From many of them hung large honeycombs, heavy with the thick honey produced by the black bees droning around the fragrant forest flowers.

Sita was captivated by the beauty of the forest, touching and smelling the many blossoms that hung all around. Completely forgetting his grief and anxiety, Rama laughingly held her hand and told her all the names of the trees and plants. The three travelers were elated simply to see such a celestial region. In great happiness they moved toward Chitrakuta.

The part of the forest leading to Chitrakuta had been rendered quite passable due to the regular traffic of ascetics, and the travelers made good progress. Toward the end of the third day of their departure from Bharadvaja's hermitage they approached the foot of the mountain. They saw there a huge banyan tree which spread its branches of dark green leaves away in all directions. Bowing down to the presiding deity of the tree, Sita offered her respects. She prayed that they would successfully complete their exile and return that way again on their way back to Ayodhya. Lakshmana prepared beds of leaves near the foot of the tree. After saying their evening prayers and preparing a meal, the travelers rested for the night.

At sunrise the following day Rama and his party moved on again, with the great Chitrakuta mountain rising ahead of them. Bluish in color, it was covered with copses of green, yellow and red trees. Numerous waterfalls sparkled in the morning sun. The mountain was sheer in places, smoothly sloping elsewhere. Its snow covered peaks disappeared into the clouds. The travelers stopped and stared for some time at its majestic beauty. They began to ascend the mountain and, some way up its side, arrived at the hermitage of the sage Valmiki, situated on a broad plateau.

The sage was joyful to see Rama and his companions. He greeted them with hospitality and respect and they conversed for some time. Valmiki told them of his own history. Although he was now a powerful ascetic, blazing with bodily luster, he had previously been a robber who had maintained his large family by plundering travelers.

The rishi told the whole story. Once, long ago, he encountered the sage Narada in the forest and sought to steal from him. The sage told Valmiki he would happily give him anything he wanted, but he told him to first go to his family and ask them the following question, "Are you prepared to accept a share of the sins which will ensue from my crimes?" Valmiki assented to this request and went to his family. However, they declined to accept his sins, saying that they only wished to receive from him the fruits of his action in the form of money and goods.

Leaving them in disgust, Valmiki returned to the sage, who then told him to renounce his life of crime and become an ascetic. In order to bring about in Valmiki a full sense of the temporality of life, Narada told him to meditate on the word mara, meaning "death." Valmiki thus constantly repeated the word mara, without realizing that he was, in effect, also repeating the holy name of Rama. By his meditation he became a powerful rishi.

Rama decided to stay close to Valmiki's hermitage and he asked Lakshmana to construct a cottage. Lakshmana quickly erected a timber-walled hut with a thatched roof. Rama lit a fire and, with roots gathered from nearby and cooked in the fire, he made offerings to the gods. He prayed to the Lokapalas, the principal deities who guard the universal quarters, asking them to sanctify and protect the dwelling. Then he entered it along with Sita. Within that spacious two-roomed hut, Rama constructed an altar for the worship of Vishnu in accord with the instructions of scripture. Rejoicing at having found such a delightful place for their residence, the three travelers settled down in peace.

CHAPTER TWO

DEVASTATION IN AYODHYA

After Rama and his party had gone into the jungle on the other side of the Ganges, Sumantra and Guha spent some time speaking together about Rama. Both were shocked and saddened to realize his firm intention to spend fourteen years in the deep forest. They had both been hoping that he would relent and perhaps return to Ayodhya to punish the evil Kaikeyi, who did not deserve any kindness. Or he could at least remain with Guha and his people, where he could be reached easily. Now he was gone. Guha heard from his spies about Rama's meeting with Bharadvaja, and his going on from there to the Chitrakuta mountain. Sadly, the Nishadha king returned to his own home in the city of Sringavera, from where he ruled over the forest tribes.

As the reality of Rama's departure sank in, Sumantra drove the chariot back toward Ayodhya. After two days traveling he arrived to find the city subdued and silent, overpowered by grief. Sumantra entered by the southern gate. As the empty chariot moved along the road, hundreds and thousands of people approached it crying, "O Rama! Have you really gone? Where is that faultless hero? Alas, we are forsaken and lost!"

Sumantra, afflicted at hearing their laments, covered his head with his garment. He felt ashamed to have been the one who took Rama away. He made his way along the royal highway to Dasarath's palace, hearing the wails of the women who stood on the balconies of their houses, gazing upon the chariot now bereft of its passengers.

Sumantra reached the palace and went quickly through the first seven gates, arriving at the eighth which led to the king's inner chambers. He entered the large room and found the king seated on a couch, pale and withered from grief. The charioteer described his journey from Ayodhya with Rama. Dasarath listened in complete silence and then, having heard of Rama's definite entrance into the forest, fell senseless to the floor.

Seeing their husband fallen, the ladies burst into tears. Kaushalya, assisted by Sumitra, lifted him up and said, "Why do you not reply to the charioteer, my lord? He has carried out a most difficult task on your behalf. Are you feeling ashamed for perpetrating such an unseemly act? Be fixed in your determination, O king, for you have firmly adhered to truth! Do not submit to this grief, as we who depend upon you will not be able to survive seeing you filled with such despair."

Kaushalya spoke with a faltering voice. Her dear son, whom she had not been able to go without seeing for even a day, was now gone for fourteen years. She dropped in a faint next to her husband. All the ladies flocked around, sprinkling cool scented water on the faces of the monarch and his queen, who lay like a god and his consort fallen from heaven.

When Dasarath awoke from his swoon he summoned Sumantra, who stood silently nearby. The charioteer was covered in dust and his face was streaked with tears. With folded hands, he stood respectfully before the king.

Dasarath sighed dolefully and said to Sumantra, "Where will Rama live now, taking shelter under a tree and sleeping on the bare ground? What will he eat? The prince has known only luxury and deserves the best of everything. Formerly he would always be followed by my great army; how can he now live alone in the desolate forest?"

Although Rama and Lakshmana had grown up to become fierce fighters, to the emperor they were still his tender young sons. Dasarath could hardly tolerate the thought of their living a life of austerity and abnegation, along with the gentle Sita. Anxiously he imagined the scene facing his two boys. How could they survive in the wild among carnivorous animals and venomous snakes?

The king continued, "Did you follow them as they walked alone into some bleak and lonely land? What were their last words? O Sumantra, pray tell me what they uttered as they were leaving, for this shall be my only sustenance for the coming fourteen years."

Dasarath stood up and looked into his charioteer's face, whose head hung down and who was shaking with sorrow. With a choked voice Sumantra replied to the king, "The ever-truthful Rama asked me to touch yours and Kaushalya's feet on his behalf, O great king. He requested me to convey his fond farewell to all the ladies in the royal court, who are to Rama just like his own mother."

After bowing at the feet of the king and queen, Sumantra continued to speak with difficulty, describing his parting from Rama and the others. Faithfully he recounted the exact messages the two princes had given him.

"Rama, who was constantly shedding tears as he spoke, asked that Bharata be quickly installed as the Prince Regent. He left instructions that

Bharata should accord all respect to his aged father and to all of his mothers, especially the grief-stricken Kaushalya."

The charioteer then recalled the final angry words of Lakshmana. "When Rama stopped speaking, Lakshmana, hissing like an enraged cobra, said, 'For what offense has this virtuous prince been exiled? The king has carried out Kaikeyi's order without considering its merit. Regardless of his reasoning, I find no justification whatsoever for the emperor's decision to send away the sinless Rama. Rama's exile will end in remorse. It contradicts all good sense and is against tradition and even scripture. Having performed an act which has caused nothing but pain to all the people, how can father remain as the king any longer? Indeed, I cannot even see in him the qualities of a father. For me, Rama alone is my brother, master and father!'"

Sumantra, having summoned up the vehemence with which Lakshmana had spoken, calmed himself down and described his last sight of Sita. "The blessed princess Sita stood silent as I prepared to leave. As though her mind were possessed by an evil spirit, she remained motionless and distracted, heaving deep sighs. Gazing upon her husband's face, she suddenly burst into tears, covering her own face with her two bejeweled hands, which looked like two white lotuses. Then the three of them stood watching as I drove the chariot away."

Dasarath asked Sumantra to describe his return journey and the charioteer replied, "I remained with Guha for three days, hoping and praying that Rama would return. Finally I concluded that I would not see him again until the full fourteen years had expired. I yoked up the chariot and urged the horses to move, but they remained stationary, shedding tears of grief. After much cajoling they finally moved and I proceeded on the path back to Ayodhya."

Sumantra stopped speaking for some time as he struggled to control his feelings. After sipping a little water he continued describing the scene he had witnessed on his return. On all sides in the kingdom he saw signs of grief and separation from Rama. Even the trees with their flowers and leaves looked withered. The lakes and rivers were dried up and everywhere there were beasts and birds entirely immobile, not even searching for food. The woods were silent and gave off none of their former fragrance. The parks and gardens in the city appeared desolate and deserted. No one greeted him as he entered Ayodhya. Everywhere were sighing men and women, lost in thoughts of Rama. As they saw the empty chariot they let out tremendous cries of grief. Even the animals wore wretched expressions. On the tops of high buildings he saw noble ladies gazing mutely at each other, their eyes overflooded with tears. The city appeared devoid of all happiness, looking exactly like the empress Kaushalya, bereft of her beloved son.

After Sumantra stopped speaking, Dasarath became pensive, feeling extreme regret. How had he stood by as Rama had left? Why did he not reprimand the wicked Kaikeyi? He cursed his foolish attachment to virtue that brought about such an unvirtuous end. Where was the truth in banishing the truthful prince Rama?

In a piteous voice the king exclaimed, "It was out of infatuation for my wife alone that I exiled Rama. I did not seek any counsel with my ministers and wise advisors, being dictated to by the sinful Kaikeyi."

Dasarath wondered how he could have acted so contrary to his own good sense and wisdom. Surely this great calamity had suddenly happened by the will of Providence simply to destroy his race. The king sighed, feeling helpless in the hands of fate.

Turning to Sumantra, Dasarath said, "O charioteer, if I have ever done you any good turn, then please quickly take me to Rama! My mind is drawn irresistibly to the prince. If I am still the king today then let anyone fetch Rama back to Ayodhya! I shall not survive for even an hour longer without Rama! Where is that Rama, whose shining face is adorned with pearl-like teeth? Maybe that mighty-armed prince has gone far into the woods by now. Bring me a chariot and I shall immediately make haste to see him. If I do not soon catch a sight of Rama, I shall reach Death's abode this very day!"

Dasarath had been hoping beyond hope that Sumantra might somehow have returned with his sons. Realizing the finality of Rama's departure, the king gave full vent to his terrible grief.

"O Rama! O Lakshmana! O Sita! What could be more painful for me than not seeing you here? You do not know that I am dying from agony, like a lost and forlorn creature."

The emperor fell senseless onto a couch. Close to him Kaushalya tossed about on the floor as though possessed by a spirit. Seeing Sumantra she exclaimed, "Charioteer! Yoke up the chariot and take me to Rama, for I shall not live another moment without him! Where now is my son reposing, his head placed upon his mighty arm? When again will I see his charming features surrounded by curling black locks? I think my heart is as hard as a diamond; otherwise, why does it not shatter to pieces even though I do not see Rama?"

Sumantra felt all the more agonized himself as he saw the grief of the king and queen. He tried to comfort Kaushalya. "I think your son will settle happily in the forest along with Lakshmana and Sita. Indeed, I did not detect in them any dejection at the prospect of living as ascetics. Shaking off their grief, they appeared pleased upon approaching the forest. Sita seemed especially happy; much delighted at the sights and sounds of the woods."

Kaushalya, not appeased by Sumantra's kind words, turned toward Dasarath, admonishing him out of grief and love. "My lord, you are famous in all the three worlds for your compassion and kindness, yet you thoughtlessly banished your faultless son! How will your two gentle boys, ever accustomed to every luxury, live like hermits? How will the frail Sita, a child of a mere sixteen years, survive the ravages of forest life? She has always been offered the very best of cooked foods and will surely not survive on wild roots. How will she bear the terrible roars of lions and tigers?"

Kaushalya became increasingly angry as she spoke. Her eyes reddened, and black streaks of collyrium ran down her cheeks. She censured Dasarath for his cruelty.

"You have utterly divested Rama of his right to be king," she cried. "Even after returning to Ayodhya, Rama will surely not accept the kingdom. High-class men can never enjoy items left by others. Rama will therefore not accept the kingdom left by his younger brother, even as a tiger would not eat the food brought to him by another animal."

Kaushalya's mind was absorbed in thoughts of her son and she raved inconsolably. How could Dasarath have perpetrated such an evil act? Kaushalya railed at the king, holding her head in her hands.

"Rama has been ruined by his own father, even as a brood of fish are swallowed by their father. I believe, my lord, that you can no longer tell right from wrong. The main support for a woman is her husband; the son is the second. Therefore, like Rama, I am also ruined, my husband having lost his good sense and my son gone away! This whole kingdom has been ruined by you. All your people have been destroyed. Only Kaikeyi and her son are happy!"

Kaushalya stopped speaking and began to sob uncontrollably. Dasarath, already deeply remorseful, felt even more anguish upon hearing his wife's words. Crying out, "O Rama" again and again, he sat disconsolate. With great difficulty he gathered his senses and went before Kaushalya with folded hands, speaking in a trembling voice, his head hanging down.

"Be kind to me, O godly lady. You are merciful even to your enemies. What then to speak of me. The husband is always the lord for the wife in good or evil times. Seeing me to be sorely pained, you should not increase my grief by such harsh words."

Kaushalya immediately felt sorry. She took Dasarath's hands and folded them around her head. Kneeling before him and weeping, she spoke hurriedly through her confusion.

"Now I am surely ruined for having spoken words disagreeable to my husband. I deserve to be punished by you, who I know to be always truthful. She is a wicked and low-born woman who must be beseeched by her worthy and virtuous husband."

Kaushalya was afflicted by many strong feelings and her mind became completely distracted. Her grief, despair and anger at losing Rama were now compounded by remorse and guilt at having upset Dasarath. She had spoken in an almost hysterical manner.

"Pray forgive me, O great king. Overcome by grief I uttered unseemly words. Grief destroys patience, eradicates knowledge and confounds the senses. Indeed, there is no enemy like grief. Even a great blow from an enemy can be endured, but the smallest amount of grief is intolerable. The five nights that Rama has been gone seem to me like five years. Even as I remember Rama again my grief grows like the ocean receiving the rapid flow of many large rivers."

As Kaushalya was speaking the sun set. Dasarath, being comforted by his wife, fell into a fitful slumber for an hour. Upon waking he sat sighing and recalled something he had done when he was a young prince. Realizing that long past deed to be the cause of his present suffering, Dasarath related it to Kaushalya.

"Without doubt a person receives the results of his own actions, good or bad, O gracious queen," the king said. "He who acts without consideration of the results, both immediate and long-term, is surely a fool. If a man cuts down a mango grove because the trees have unattractive blossoms, planting instead the brightly flowering palasha trees, he will later lament when the bitter fruits of the palasha appear. By sending Rama away I have indeed cut down a mango grove just as it was about to bear fruit. Now I am tasting the bitter palasha."

Dasarath felt as if his heart might burst. He maintained his composure with a great effort and continued. "A long time ago, as a youth and before we were married, I went to the forest to hunt. I had acquired great skills at bowmanship and could easily hit even an invisible target by its sound alone. Little did I know that this skill of mine, of which I was so proud, would yield such a disastrous result.

"It was the rainy season and the rivers were swollen. Going out at night on my chariot, I made my way to the Sarayu. I waited there in the darkness by the river bank for a buffalo or an elephant to come by. Soon I heard the sound of gurgling at a point nearby, although I could not see what caused the sound. Thinking the sound to be that of an animal drinking, I took out an arrow and released it. From the quarter where I shot my snake-like arrow there came a loud wail of some forest dweller. In distinct and pain-filled tones I heard the following cry:

"How has this weapon fallen upon a harmless ascetic like myself? To whom have I given any offense? I am a simple seer who has forsworn violence and lives only on fruits and roots. Oh, I am killed! What foolish person has hurled this arrow? This act will result only in evil. I do not grieve so much for myself but for my aged and helpless parents. Without me, their sole support, how will they survive? With a single arrow some ignorant fool of uncontrolled mind has killed me and both my parents!'"

Weeping all the while, Dasarath continued, "When I heard that plaintive shout I was mortified. My bow and arrows fell from my hands. I was all but overwhelmed with grief and dropped to the ground, almost losing my senses. I scrambled toward the source of the voice with my mind utterly perplexed. There, lying on the bank of the river, was an ascetic wearing treebark garments. My arrow was protruding from his chest. Smeared with dust and blood, with his thick mass of matted hair in disarray, he lay groaning. He had come for water and the sound I had heard was the gurgling of his pitcher, which lay nearby with its water run out.

"Seeing me to be royalty, the ascetic looked up at me with bloodshot eyes and spoke angrily. 'What wrong have I done, O king, that I should receive this terrible punishment? I came here to fetch water for my blind parents. Even now, as I lie here dying, my poor father must be wondering where I am. But what can he do? He is old and feeble and cannot even move. He can no more help me than could any tree help another which is about to be hewn down. Seek his forgiveness, O king. You should quickly make your way along this path to where he waits.'"

Dasarath's grief for Rama was compounded by the grief caused by remembering this long past unfortunate incident. With difficulty he continued to speak.

"The young hermit, writhing in agony, asked me to extract the arrow. I hesitated, knowing that the instant the arrow was removed he would die. The boy reassured me, telling me that he was prepared for death. I thus pulled out the arrow. Looking at me in dismay, due to anxiety about his parents, the boy died, uttering the name of Vishnu.

"Seeing the ascetic lying dead, killed by me out of ignorance and folly, I wondered how I could make amends. I quickly filled his pitcher and followed the path he had shown me toward his parents. As I reached the hermitage I saw his aged and blind parents, sitting forlorn like a pair of birds whose wings have been clipped. When he heard me approach, the boy's father said, 'Do not delay, my son. Bring the water immediately. Your poor mother is in anxiety because you have been sporting in the river for a long time. Our lives depend upon you, dear child. You are our only support and indeed our very eyes. Where are you? Why do you not speak?'

"I was gripped by fear to behold the sage and I replied to him in a faltering voice, 'O holy sage, I am not your son but a prince named Dasarath. I have committed a most terrible and evil act out of sheer folly. Hearing your son collecting water, I mistook him for a beast drinking. I released a deadly arrow and killed the boy. As a result of my rash act your son has ascended to heaven, leaving you here. Please tell me what I should do now.'

"When he heard my story, the sage, though rich in ascetic power and thereby capable of burning me with a curse, restrained himself. Sighing in sorrow with his face bathed in tears, that old rishi, who appeared exceptionally glorious, said to me, 'Had you not come here and confessed, then as soon as the news of my boy's death reached me, your head would have been split into a hundred pieces by my anger. Indeed, if one consciously kills a hermit engaged in austerity, then death is the immediate result. You are only surviving now as you performed this deed in ignorance.'

"The sage asked me to take him to the place where his son lay. I immediately lifted both of the elderly ascetics on my two arms and carried them to the river bank. Being placed near the dead boy they cried out in agony and gently stroked his face. The sage said, 'Why do you not greet us today, dearest child? Why are you lying here upon the ground? Have you become displeased with us? Here is your beloved mother. Why do you not embrace her, my tender son? Please speak to us. Whose heart-moving voice will we now hear beautifully reciting the holy Vedic texts? Who now will tend the sacred fire? Who will comfort us with consoling words, deprived as we are now of our only support? My son, how will I be able to support your old mother?'

"The sage sat weeping for some time, lost in grief. Holding his son's head he said, 'Pray wait a while, dear boy, and do not yet proceed to Yamaraja's abode. I shall go with you and speak to the god on your behalf, saying, "Although my son has been killed as a result of some former sin, he has in fact become sinless. Therefore grant to him those regions which are attainable only by brahmins perfect in asceticism and study of scripture, or by heroes who drop their body while fighting fearlessly for the good of the people."'

"Wailing piteously, the ascetic and his wife offered sanctified water to their dead son with mantras and prayers. I then saw the boy appear in an ethereal form along with Indra, the king of heaven. He gently consoled his parents, saying that he had achieved his exalted status as a result of his service to them. He said they would soon join him in heaven. The boy then left, seated next to Indra in a shining celestial car.

"At that time the sage said to me, 'In order to release you from the terrible sin of killing an ascetic, which can drag even the gods down to hell, I shall pronounce upon you a painful curse. Just as I am dying now in the agony of separation from my son, so in the future shall you die in the grief of separation from your son.'

"After saying this, the sage had me light a fire and place upon it his son's body. Along with his wife he then entered the fire. The two ascetics gave up their bodies and went to heaven, leaving me stunned and pondering the sage's words."

Dasarath was suddenly afraid as he realized that, in accord with the sage's infallible curse, his death was now near. Controlling his mind he called out for Kaushalya. His eyes were blinded with tears and his body was trembling. He said to his wife, "That curse uttered so long ago by the sage is now coming to pass. I shall soon die of grief. Come here, Kaushalya, for I cannot see you clearly. Men on the threshold of death have all their senses confounded."

Kaushalya sat close to her husband and comforted him with soft words. Dasarath became deeply absorbed in remembrance of Rama. He longed for one last sight of him. He felt anguished and remorseful, wishing he had somehow been able to stop Rama from leaving. The king lay back upon the couch and spoke in a trembling voice.

"This grief is drying up my vitality even as the blazing summer sun sucks out the earth's moisture. Blessed are they who will see the pious and handsome Rama returned fourteen years from now. I can no longer see or hear anything. All my senses are failing along with my mind, just as the bright rays of a lamp disappear when its oil has run out. This grief born of my own self is rendering me helpless and unconscious, just as the current of a swift river wears away its own bank. O Rama, reliever of my suffering, are you really gone? O Kaushalya, my dear wife! O Sumitra, pious lady! O Kaikeyi, my sworn enemy and disgrace of my family!"

Dasarath lamented and tossed about in agony for some time. Gradually he became silent, his mind fixed only upon Rama. Stricken with the intolerable pain of separation, the great emperor gave up his life during the night and ascended to the highest abode of the Supreme Lord.

CHAPTER THREE

BHARATA'S RETURN

The following morning large numbers of singers and bards assembled at the palace with the intention of waking the king. They stood near his quarters and began their recitations, praising the emperor and telling of his ancestors' glorious deeds. Holy brahmins chanted sacred texts while expert musicians played on various instruments. Those chants and songs mixed with the singing of the birds on the palace trees and created an exquisitely beautiful sound.

The palace attendants, unaware of the king's demise, gathered together the items required for his morning ablutions. Gold pots filled with scented water, along with many soaps and unguents were fetched. In accord with the Vedic tradition, young virgin girls, along with milk cows and other pure items like gold and silver, were brought before the king so that he would see these immediately upon waking, thereby creating an auspicious start to the day.

When everything was made ready just before sunrise, the royal ladies went into the king's chamber to wake him. As they approached his bed they saw him lying motionless and showing no symptoms of life. Nearby Kaushalya and Sumitra were lying asleep, exhausted from grief. Their faces were tear-streaked and withered like lotuses scorched by the sun. The palace ladies fell back in alarm and began to shake like reeds in a stream. They touched the king's body and, finding him cold and lifeless, realized he had died from grief. All those beautiful women began to wail loudly, like a herd of female elephants who have lost their lord in the forest.

Kaushalya and Sumitra were roused by the sound. Looking at the emperor and touching him, they cried out, "My lord!" and dropped to the ground. Kaikeyi ran into the room and she too became afflicted by pain and sorrow, falling down unconscious. The three queens tossed about on the ground lamenting loudly. They appeared like three goddesses fallen from heaven, deprived of their splendor. The whole chamber became crowded with men and women, all alarmed, bustling about excitedly. With the sudden death of the king everyone became perplexed and confused. Loud cries filled the air. The king's three hundred maidservants surrounded him on all sides, weeping piteously.

Kaushalya looked at her husband's face, which seemed like the sun shorn of its luster. Kneeling by his side she held his head and began to loudly reprimand Kaikeyi.

"O cruel Kaikeyi, are you now satisfied? Having killed the king you may now enjoy the throne without fear. Rama has forsaken me and gone to the forest and now my husband has ascended to heaven. I cannot live any longer. Only Kaikeyi, casting all propriety to the winds, could live happily after seeing her husband die in agony. O cruel lady, you have destroyed our noble race!"

Kaushalya embraced her dead husband. She thought of Rama, Sita and Lakshmana. How would they learn of their father's death? What will they do when they hear of it? Even now poor Sita must be clinging fearfully to Rama, terrified by the sights and sounds of the forest. If this painful news should reach her, surely she will die.

Kaushalya could not tolerate any more grief. Tearfully she cried out to Kaikeyi, "You have killed me as surely as you have killed the king. I shall enter the fire clinging to my lord's body."

With difficulty the king's ministers separated Kaushalya from Dasarath. They gently removed her from his chamber and began to perform the necessary rituals for the death of a king. As none of Dasarath's sons were present, they could not perform his funeral. Therefore, in order to preserve the body until Bharata arrived, they immersed it in a vat of fragrant oil.

The city of Ayodhya, already plunged in sorrow, became even more desolate. The people cried out their distress and everything remained still, no one going out for any business. The great city looked like a dark night bereft of the moon and stars. Loudly reproaching Kaikeyi in choked voices, the citizens grieved throughout the day and night, finding no rest.

The following day the king's brahmin counselors assembled together. Looking toward Vasishtha, who was temporarily carrying out the king's duties, the wise sages made different speeches pointing to the need for a prince to be quickly coronated. The sages described how, without a ruler, the kingdom would soon meet with ruin. In a land without a king even the rain would not fall in proper time and the crops would fail. Sons would disobey their fathers and wives their husbands. There could be no personal property without a protector and men could not sleep in peace. Everything would become chaotic and anarchy would soon prevail. Like fishes, men would devour one another. Atheism would become prominent and godless and misbehaved men would become leaders.

One of the chief brahmins concluded, "Even as the eyes protect the body, so the king is ever vigilant to protect the people. The king is truthfulness and virtue incarnate. He is the mother and the father and the best benefactor of all men. All the principal gods reside in the body of the king; indeed he is the powerful representative of the Supreme Lord Vishnu. Therefore, O Vasishtha, have Bharata and Shatrughna brought home. Quickly crown a qualified man as king, before this ancient and prosperous kingdom is thrown into utter confusion and darkness!"

When the brahmin sages had finished speaking they sat awaiting Vasishtha's opinion. Vasishtha looked around the assembly and replied, "We should immediately send swift messengers to the Kekaya capital, Girivraja. Since the emperor has bestowed this kingdom upon Bharata, he must be brought here as quickly as possible and installed as king. No other course of action can be considered."

Vasishtha wanted Bharata to be brought home before the news of his father's death and Rama's exile reached him. Bharata should be informed of the heartbreaking news while surrounded by his intimate family. Vasishtha said to the messengers, "Tell the prince that all is well, but that he is required for some urgent business. Take with you excellent gifts for the Kekaya king and leave at once."

The messengers mounted upon the best of the king's horses, which were capable of covering hundreds of miles a day, and sped westwards toward Girivraja. They took the shortest possible route, at times leaving the road and traversing open countryside and woods. They crossed the Malini River, which flowed between the Aparatala and Pralamba Mountains, and also the Ganges where it flowed through Hastinapura. Moving quickly through the Panchala and Kurujangala provinces, the messengers reached the Saradanda River at the end of the second day. After crossing that river they entered the city of Kulinga, hardly pausing for a moment. Galloping together they passed through the city and soon crossed the Ikshumati River, then the Beas and Salmali Rivers, finally arriving at the Kekaya district at the end of the third day. With their horses all but exhausted, they entered the city of Girivraja and went straight toward the king's palace just as dawn approached.

*   *   *

In his palace Bharata had just risen and was feeling disturbed. He had awoken from a dream filled with inauspicious omens. He sat alone, sunk in thought. Some of his friends approached him and inquired why he looked so sad. Bharata replied, "In a dream I saw my father looking dejected, falling from the peak of a mountain into a filthy pool. He seemed to be laughing and he swam around in that pool. I then saw the ocean dry, the moon fallen upon the earth and the entire world assailed by demons. My father, dressed in black, wearing a crimson garland and smeared with red sandal-paste, got upon a chariot drawn by donkeys and rode southwards."

Bharata knew the science of omens and dreams. He understood that these visions clearly indicated his father's death, or perhaps the death of one of his brothers. Sighing heavily, the prince continued. "My throat feels parched and I am gripped by anxiety. Suddenly I hate myself for no reason. Surely some great calamity is imminent."

As Bharata spoke, a messenger entered his room to announce the arrival of envoys from Ayodhya. They came before Bharata and bowed low, touching his feet and saying, "We have been sent by the sage Vasishtha. He sends word that all is well, but he requires your immediate presence in Ayodhya for some urgent business."

On behalf of Dasarath, the envoys presented their gifts to the Kekaya king and his son. The messengers were feeling fatigued from their journey, so Bharata had them seated and served with the best of food and drink. He tried to find out from them the exact nature of the business for which Vasishtha was summoning him. Thinking of his dream, he asked about his father and other dear relatives. The messengers answered his questions politely, carefully avoiding telling him about his father's death or Rama's exile. Bharata could nevertheless sense that something was terribly wrong. He wanted to depart immediately and he went to King Aswapati, requesting his permission to leave. The king embraced him and said, "In you my daughter Kaikeyi is blessed with a noble son. Leave now with my blessings, but return again when your business is complete."

The king of Kekaya presented Bharata with many gifts to take to Ayodhya. Huge elephants, horses, costly cloth and much gold were given by King Aswapati. He also quickly arranged for a detachment of his best soldiers to accompany Bharata.

Bharata received the gifts with gratitude to the best of his ability, but his mind was distracted. He was anxious and could not wait to depart. Taking leave of his friends and relations, Bharata mounted his chariot along with Shatrughna and they hurriedly left. Followed by hundreds of other chariots, as well as by the thousands of elephants and horses gifted by the king, the prince of Ayodhya went out of the city looking like a god leaving the heavenly city of Indra.

*   *   *

Bharata's chariot went quickly ahead

For seven days Bharata and his party traveled to Ayodhya. The prince longed to race ahead, taking the shorter route through the woods as did the messengers from Ayodhya, but he was hampered by his large retinue. They went along the established roads and passed through many villages and towns, but they did not stop anywhere.

Bharata's mind was filled with apprehension. What could possibly be wrong, especially in the presence of Rama and Lakshmana? Had their father died? Was some powerful enemy besieging the city? Perhaps it was simply that his father wished to install Rama as the king. But why had the messengers not told him?

As the party reached the territory of Koshala, Bharata urged on his charioteer. His chariot went quickly ahead, leaving the army, headed by Shatrughna, to follow slowly behind. He soon arrived at Ayodhya. Looking at the city from a distance, Bharata said to his charioteer, "Something is surely amiss in this great and glorious city. I do not hear the usual clamor of men, nor the sound of sacred recitations made by throngs of brahmins as they perform sacrifices. Even the animals are silent. No one is moving about on the roads and no one has come out to greet me."

As they passed along the main road into the city Bharata became even more concerned. Where were the young couples who would always sport romantically in the gardens lining the road? The trees in those deserted gardens, with their leaves falling all around, seemed to Bharata to be weeping. As he rode quickly into the city he saw various ill omens. Crows and vultures cried on all sides. The sun was enveloped by dark clouds and a chill wind blew, raising up clouds of dust and leaves.

Bharata reached the city's western gate. The guards, gladdened to see him, welcomed him with loud shouts. The prince moved on after politely greeting the sentries. He was tired and his mind was dejected and disturbed. He spoke again to his charioteer. "Why have I been suddenly brought here, O noble one? I wonder what terrible calamity has occurred. Even without any apparent cause my heart is sinking and my mind is consumed by fear."

The prince looked around as the chariot sped toward Dasarath's palace. He saw signs which seemed to him to indicate the king's death. Houses were unswept, dirty-looking and bereft of splendor, their doors standing wide open. There was no smoke from sacrificial fires rising up, nor the usual sweet aroma of aloe and sandalwood drifting from the mansions along the road. Men and women were standing here and there, wearing soiled clothes and looking pale and emaciated, as if they had not eaten for days.

Bharata looked at the closed shop fronts and abandoned market places, the temples with their dusty courtyards and the deities without fresh dresses or garlands—everything seemed desolate. Filled with sorrow to see the unprecedented state of his beloved city, the prince arrived at Dasarath's palace.

Bharata went quickly into his father's rooms and was alarmed to find the king not present. Everyone looked down to avert his gaze. The palace ladies were weeping and a sorrowful silence had replaced the normal sound of drums, lutes and Vedic recitations. Bharata felt his stomach sink and his limbs seemed to dissolve. Too afraid to ask about his father from the people present, he ran to his mother's apartments. As he entered, Kaikeyi sprang up from her golden seat. Bharata bowed and touched his mother's feet and she embraced him. It had been a long time since she had seen him.

Holding her son and seating him on her lap, Kaikeyi inquired, "How was your journey, my son? You must be tired. Are your grandfather and uncle both well? Have you fared well yourself while living in their kingdom? I have missed you here."

After hearing her endearing questions, Bharata told her everything about himself. Still filled with apprehension, he asked, "How is it that I do not see the king seated here with you? Where indeed is my pious father? Why do I find everyone looking disconsolate and not speaking? I long to clasp my father's feet. Tell me, gentle mother, is he just now in Kaushalya's apartments?"

Possessed by greed for the kingdom, Kaikeyi began to tell her son the terrible news as if it were agreeable and pleasant. "Your high-souled and glorious father, who was always the shelter of all living beings, has attained the state of the gods. This kingdom is now yours."

Bharata looked at his mother in disbelief. He fell to his knees. Crying out "Alas, I am ruined!" he struck his arms on the floor. His worst fear was confirmed. With his mind confused and agitated, Bharata lamented. "This golden couch would always appear beautiful being adorned with the king's presence. Now it appears dark and lusterless like the night sky bereft of the moon. Oh, where is my noble father?"

Bharata covered his handsome face with a cloth and cried in anguish. Seeing her son, whose body shone like that of a god, laying on the floor in a wretched state, Kaikeyi raised him and said, "Get up, O king! Why are you lying here like one unfortunate? Virtuous souls like you are never overwhelmed by grief. Steady your mind, which is always fixed in piety and knows the truth. This wide earth now awaits your rule, O sinless one."

Bharata wept for some time, unable to speak. He remembered his father's love and affection, how the king had personally trained him in statecraft, how they had played and sported together, the times he had sat with his father as he related tales of their great ancestors. Now he was gone!

How could it have happened? Bharata could not understand why no one had called him earlier. Calming his mind he said, "Having speculated that the king was to install Rama as the Prince Regent, I came here swiftly. It seems my calculation was wrong, as I do not see either my father or Rama."

The prince was confused. His mother sat calmly as he spoke out his grief. "Of what disease did my father die, O mother? How fortunate are Rama and Lakshmana that they were able to perform the last rites of the great monarch. Or is my father still present? Surely he does not know I have arrived or else he would have come quickly to see me, embracing me and offering his blessings. Where is that gentle hand which would often brush me off when I would fall in the dust as a child?"

Bharata looked up into his mother's face, his eyes streaming. "Please announce my arrival to Rama. For a man who knows what is right, the elder brother is as good as the father. I shall fall at Rama's feet and ask him what final words were spoken by the righteous and ever-truthful king. I wish to hear my father's last kind message to me."

Kaikeyi slowly replied to her son, telling him the course of events exactly as they occurred. "The glorious king, the best among the wise, departed from this world calling out, 'O Rama! O Sita! O Lakshmana!' Bound by the laws of time, even as a powerful elephant is bound by ropes, the king submitted to death saying, 'Only those men who will see Rama returned with Sita and Lakshmana will have their desires fulfilled and be happy.'"

Hearing this news Bharata became even more confused. What did the king mean? Where were his brothers and Sita? He asked his mother.

Kaikeyi began to relate how they had left for the forest, speaking as if it were something Bharata would be pleased to hear. "Prince Rama, with Sita and Lakshmana, left the city clad in tree barks. They have gone to a distant forest and will remain there for fourteen years."

Bharata was shocked. How could it be true? Surely Rama could not have been exiled. What crime could he possibly have committed?

The prince spoke in amazement. "Did Rama wrongly seize property from some elevated brahmin? Did my brother somehow kill a sinless man? Surely he did not look longingly upon another's wife. I cannot imagine Rama ever doing anything even remotely sinful. Why then has he gone into exile accompanied by the delicate Sita and his loyal brother?"

Kaikeyi completely misunderstood Bharata's mood. Out of ignorance she imagined he would be pleased to hear that, thanks to her machinations, he had become the undisputed ruler. She smiled as she spoke to her son.

"Rama has committed no sin. However, entirely neglecting your noble self, the king was intent upon installing him as the Prince Regent. As soon as this news reached me I asked your father to send Rama away and install you instead."

Bharata's face froze as his mother continued.

"Bound by truthfulness, the emperor did my bidding and granted me two boons which were owed from a former occasion. After exiling Rama, who was followed by Sita and Lakshmana, the king was sorely afflicted with an unbearable grief. Overwhelmed with pain and constantly calling Rama's name, the lord of Ayodhya left this world and ascended to heaven."

Kaikeyi saw Bharata's pained expression. "Do not yield to grief, dear son. This city and indeed this earth now depend upon you. Be firm and perform your father's funeral ceremony, O Bharata. Then assume the throne as the undisputed ruler of the globe."

Bharata could not believe what he was hearing. Had his mother gone mad? Did she really think he envied Rama and coveted the throne? Covering his face with his hands and slowly shaking his head, he replied to the shameless Kaikeyi, "What came into your mind, O cruel woman, that you could have perpetrated such an act? What possible gain is there for me in having the sovereignty of the earth while I stand deprived of my dearest relations? By sending my father to the next world and Rama to the forest you have heaped calamity upon calamity!"

The prince was infuriated. His mother's actions were unforgiveable. Kaikeyi shrunk back as he roared, piercing her with volleys of words. "You have appeared in my family like the goddess Kalaratri, the night of universal dissolution! Having clasped you to his bosom my father has brought about his own death and the extermination of his race. O woman who sees evil where there is none, you have ended my family's joy through greed alone. Tell me the reason that impelled you to kill the king and exile the sinless Rama."

Aghast at her son's vehement reaction, Kaikeyi tried to defend herself. She spoke candidly, telling him about her conversation with Manthara. "O prince, I would surely have said nothing to your father, but Manthara pointed out how you were being wronged. My dear son, I simply acted with your interests in mind."

This only angered Bharata all the more. In grief and anger he stood blazing like fire. With copper-red eyes he gazed at his mother who sat on a couch with her head cast downwards. "Alas," he continued, his voice incredulous, "I am shamed by my own mother! Having got you for their co-wife, the godly Kaushalya and Sumitra have been tormented with agony. How did you not grieve, O hard-hearted one, when you saw those gentle ladies weeping as their heroic sons left for the forest? Are you happy to see your husband lying dead, Rama with Sita and Lakshmana banished, and your remaining family seized with unbearable pain?"

Bharata wept aloud while Kaikeyi sat silently. He was astonished at his mother's deeds. What on earth had possessed her? She had never acted like this before. She had always loved Rama as much as her own son. How could she possibly think it would please him to gain the sovereignty in this terrible way?

Bharata went on fiercely. "Blinded by lust you have clearly not understood my devotion to Rama. I will never take this kingdom in his absence! My strength and intelligence depend only upon my powerful brother. Rama should certainly become the king while I become his humble servant. I can no more take the weight of the kingdom than a young calf can take the load borne easily by a bull. Even if I were able to rule without Rama, I will never allow you to achieve your cherished end. I would sooner die!"

Bharata's mind raged. Kaikeyi's insane action had to be somehow reversed. He resolved to go immediately to the forest and find Rama. He first had to establish to Rama that Kaikeyi's abhorrent acts had nothing to do with him. What must Rama be thinking? Surely he would not believe that his own devoted brother was in any way guilty! Did anyone think that? Bharata was horrified. He rounded on Kaikeyi again.

"I cannot stand by and watch the path of morality abandoned as a result of your sinful desires. The eternal moral code prescribes that the king's eldest son should inherit the throne—especially when that son is the most highly qualified and beloved of all the people. I shall doubtlessly bring back Rama from the forest. O evil-minded one, you will never see me installed as the king!"

Bharata continued to reproach his mother with sharp words. Kaikeyi remained silent, her mind bewildered. Bharata's reaction was quite unexpected and she did not know how to reply.

Bharata shook his head. "Since you have committed a hideous sin, you shall surely reside in hell. There you shall wail endlessly with none of your desired objects attained. Do not say anything to me, evil lady. I hereby desert you! You are neither my mother nor the emperor's wife. Without doubt you are a wicked Rakshasi who entered my family in the guise of a relation."

Bharata hissed like an enraged serpent. Immediate remedial action was required. He would bring Rama back and then take his place in the forest to fulfill his vow! How could he possibly remain in Ayodhya among the grieving citizens while Rama sat in some lonely wilderness?

The prince pointed angrily at his mother as he went on. "For your part, cruel woman, you had best either enter fire, swallow poison or go yourself to the forest. There is no other course left for you to free yourself from the stain of your sinful deed. I myself shall be freed of this sin only when Rama has been brought back and installed upon the throne."

Bharata fell to the floor almost senseless with grief. With his garments in dissaray and his jewels tossed about, the prince looked like a banner raised in honor of Indra and suddenly dropped down again.

While Bharata lay absorbed in sorrow, Dasarath's ministers, having heard the commotion in Kaikeyi's rooms, gathered around. After some time Bharata regained his senses and saw the ministers surrounding him. Rising up quickly, the prince again rebuked his mother, who sat, miserable, her eyes full of tears.

Bharata turned toward the king's advisors and said in a loud voice, "At no time did this sinful woman consult with me concerning Rama's exile. I have never coveted the kingdom. Indeed, I knew nothing of the intended installation of Rama. I was far away from Ayodhya. Only today have I learned all the facts from my mother, whom I utterly reject."

Kaushalya, whose rooms were nearby, heard Bharata's voice. She got up, desiring to speak to the prince. Bharata was also thinking of Kaushalya. He ran out of Kaikeyi's apartments accompanied by Shatrughna. As they went toward Kaushalya, they saw her in the passageway. She was dressed in white silks and appeared pale and emaciated. Her body was trembling and she seemed distracted. As she saw the two princes approaching she cried out and collapsed to the floor. Bharata and Shatrughna quickly lifted her up and she embraced the brothers, who were both weeping.

The distraught queen said to Bharata, "You may now enjoy this kingdom stripped of all its enemies. Surely you hankered for the sovereignty and now your mother has fully secured it for you. The cruel Kaikeyi has sent away my son as an ascetic. She should now send me away as well. Otherwise I shall place at my head the sacrificial fire and, followed by Sumitra, proceed happily along the road taken by Rama. In any event I cannot remain here any longer."

Kaushalya sobbed as she spoke. "Your mother has served you well, O Bharata! Your plan has succeeded. Rule now this wide earth abounding in riches, but first, please take me to wherever my high-souled son is staying. I shall spend my days with him in the forest."

The queen bitterly reproached Bharata with many painful words. Hearing this the prince was stunned and he practically lost consciousness, his mind utterly confused. He fell at Kaushalya's feet and cried out. Kneeling before her with joined palms, Bharata said, "Surely you know my love for Rama, O noble lady. How could you even imagine that I am in any way guilty of conspiring with Kaikeyi? I found out only today of this terrible turn of events."

Bharata clasped Kaushalya's feet. Did she really believe he was a party to Rama's exile? The prince spoke from his heart. "Let the man who agrees to Rama's exile reap the sins that follow every kind of wicked act condemned in the scriptures! Let him roam about this world like a madman, clad in rags and begging for his food. Let him never take delight in piety and truth. Let all his wealth be looted by robbers. Let him fall victim to every kind of disease. Let him never attain the higher regions inhabited by the gods. Indeed, let that merciless and evil man fall down to the darkest hell and remain there forever!"

The prince expressed his anger to Kaushalya, pleading his innocence by making numerous difficult oaths. He was mortified to think that anyone could imagine him in any way inimical to Rama.

The queen was reassured by Bharata's words. She had spoken only out of her own anguish. In her heart she knew the prince was innocent. Gently stroking his head she said, "My agony is aggravated by your pain, dear son. Surely you are free of all sins. Your mind has not deviated from righteousness and you are true to your word. You will doubtlessly reach the realms of the virtuous, my child."

As Kaushalya and Bharata spoke together, remembering Rama and the king, they both fell to the floor, overpowered by grief. The palace attendants then helped them to their rooms, where they lay in a fitful sleep.

CHAPTER FOUR

'WE SHALL BRING RAMA BACK'

The next day as twilight approached Vasishtha came to Bharata and said, "Rise up now, O prince, and shake off this grief! The time has come to perform your father's funeral. Come quickly, O Bharata, for the ceremony is long overdue!"

Seeing the sage, Bharata fell prostrate at his feet, saying "So be it." After quickly bathing and changing his clothes, he went with Vasishtha to the place where his father's body was lying in its tank of oil. Vasishtha had Dasarath's body brought out and laid upon a golden bier studded with numerous bright jewels.

As he gazed at his father, Bharata lamented. "O great king, you always knew right from wrong! After sending Rama and Lakshmana into exile, what did you intend to do? How shall I act now, my lord? Alas I am lost! Where have you gone, dear father, leaving this servant of yours distressed and forlorn? Where now is that glorious Rama who performs great deeds with little exertion?"

Bharata stood at his father's feet. Dasarath lay covered with white silks and adorned with royal ornaments. Bharata cried to him piteously. "Now that you have left for the heavens, O king, who will protect the people? Deprived of you this earth no longer appears attractive. Indeed, this city of Ayodhya looks like a dark night bereft of the moon."

Vasishtha came up to Bharata and said, "Gather yourself together, O prince. You should now carry out the last rites for the king with a cool mind."

Bharata asked the priests to proceed with the ceremony. The brahmins brought out from the king's apartments his sacred fire, which he had maintained throughout his life. Placing the fire at their head they carried the king to the cremation ground, their throats choked with sorrow. As the procession made its way along the road, the citizens came out of their houses and walked ahead, scattering flowers and pieces of new cloth on the road.

At the cremation ground on the bank of the Sarayu, the priests prepared a pyre with various types of fragrant woods. They placed Dasarath upon the pyre and began to chant the sacred hymns of the Sama Veda to invoke good fortune. Bharata took a flame from the king's sacrificial fire and lit the pyre. The king's wives, along with the princes and priests, then circumambulated the fire, their hearts burning with grief.

The women wailed piteously. Kaushalya and Sumitra fell to the ground, crying like a pair of female cranes. Although they both longed to ascend the pyre and follow their husband, they longed even more to see Rama and Lakshmana return. As the fire died down, all of the king's relatives went to the riverbank and offered palmfuls of that holy water to his departed soul. They then returned to the city and spent the following ten days grieving, taking little food and lying upon the bare ground, their eyes filled with tears.

On the eleventh day the final obsequial rites were performed and on the twelfth day Bharata gave to the brahmins much charity on his father's behalf. On the following day Bharata and Shatrughna returned to the cremation ground to collect their father's ashes. Upon arriving at the funeral pyre, the two princes saw their father's remains and they cried out in pain. Remembering again the king's various affectionate gestures toward them, they fell to the ground and rolled about.

Shatrughna lamented angrily. "A fierce and formidable sea of grief has been unleashed by Manthara! Kaikeyi's boons are its great waves and her words its fearful alligators. Alas, this violent ocean has swept over us all! Where have you gone, dear father, leaving behind poor Bharata, who is yet a tender boy?"

Shatrughna stood up with his arms outstretched. "How strange that this earth does not split in two, seeing you gone and Rama retired to the forest! We two brothers shall also go to the woods for we cannot return to Ayodhya, rendered desolate without our father and brother."

All the attendants of Bharata and Shatrughna were distressed to see the princes' agony. Comforting the royal brothers, the omniscient Vasishtha said, "Your father has surely ascended to the highest regions of bliss. He was ever pious and never committed a sin, even in his mind. You grieve needlessly, for the soul of your father is eternal and has gone to the Lord's eternal abode."

The two princes stood with folded hands, looking at the royal priest. Putting aside their grief, they listened attentively as the sage continued.

"The body is always dead, being composed of nothing more than lifeless matter. It is born and remains for only a short while, with destruction being its inevitable end. Only a fool grieves for the unavoidable. The wise understand that this entire world will be destroyed along with all its living creatures. It is the soul alone that will survive."

Vasishtha pointed to the king's remains as he spoke. The king had achieved the perfection of life and would not take another birth. Those devoted to God's service leave this temporary world forever. For them there is no more suffering. The princes should shed their grief and perform their duties. Their father now sat in the highest heaven, while the kingdom stood in need of their protection.

After hearing the sage's spiritual instructions the brothers gained strength. They took their father's ashes and placed them in the sacred Sarayu. Along with all their attendants, they made their way back to Ayodhya. As they walked, Shatrughna spoke to Bharata. "How strange it is that the mighty Rama stands exiled by the words of a woman. I cannot understand why Lakshmana did not forcibly restrain the king, seeing him to be straying from the path of righteousness."

Shatrughna was mystified that such an injustice could have taken place. How did Rama allow himself to be sent away, causing his father's death? What sin had that powerful and virtuous prince ever committed? Had he been present, Shatrughna would surely have intervened. Kaikeyi and her evil maid would have been checked and severely rebuked for their unforgiveable behavior!

As Shatrughna thought in this way they arrived at the king's palace and saw Manthara at the gate. She was wearing costly garments and adorned with jeweled ornaments. Seeing the two princes she gasped and shrank back. Immediately the doorkeeper seized her and dragged her to the princes, saying, "Here is the cruel wretch responsible for the exile of our beloved lord! Do with her what you will!"

Shatrughna became inflamed and took hold of Manthara. Pulling her into the palace, he spoke in front of the many other maidservants who were standing there. "This wicked one shall now reap the fruits of her evil deeds! She has brought acute and unbearable pain to all in this house, as well as to all the citizens of Ayodhya. Watch now as I punish her!"

Manthara shrieked loudly, being held tightly by Shatrughna. All her female companions ran away in different directions, fearful that the enraged Shatrughna would also turn on them. The prince dragged Manthara violently across the floor and her ornaments broke and scattered on the blue marble floor like so many stars in the sky.

Kaikeyi heard her servant screaming and came quickly to help her. Seeing her, Shatrughna began rebuking her with harsh words. Kaikeyi was pained by Shatrughna's sharp words and ran to Bharata for protection. Bharata moved away from his mother and spoke to the furious Shatrughna.

"Even when sinful, women should never be slain. You should therefore forgive this maidservant. Indeed, I would have slain my own mother if the eternal moral law did not forbid it—and certainly such an act would never be pleasing to Rama. Our pious brother would never speak with us again if he heard that we killed this woman."

Hearing Bharata's admonition, Shatrughna released Manthara and she fell almost unconscious to the floor. Kaikeyi raised her up and she wailed piteously, her clothes and hair in disarray. Kaikeyi looked fearfully at Shatrughna and gently calmed her servant. Although Manthara had brought about a terrible calamity in Kaikeyi's life, the queen felt no anger toward her. Her son's severe reaction had made Kaikeyi thoughtful. She remembered her husband's words when she asked for the boons. He had been right. She had always loved Rama like her own son. What had possessed her so that she had desired his exile? She considered it the work of all-powerful Providence. Manthara could not be blamed. She was only an instrument in the hands of destiny. Thinking of Rama and feeling she had done him a great injustice, Kaikeyi watched in silence as Bharata and Shatrughna left.

*   *   *

On the fourteenth day after the funeral the king's counselors conferred and then spoke with Bharata. Wanting to install him as king, they said, "As your elder brother has gone to the forest along with Lakshmana, there will be no sin in your superseding him and accepting the throne. Therefore, O jewel among men, be consecrated as our ruler and protect us with justice and compassion."

The counselors showed Bharata the seat and coronation paraphernalia which had been prepared for Rama's installation. Exactly as Rama had done, however, Bharata walked around the seat in respect and said, "I shall never accept the kingdom, passing over the pious Rama. All of you know well the rule in our race. The kingship is always conferred upon the eldest brother. Therefore, Rama will be the ruler of this earth. Let a large and powerful army be made ready, for we shall go to the forest to bring back Rama."

Bharata pointed to the paraphernalia. "Taking all these items, we shall perform Rama's coronation even in the forest. You may then bring him back in honor as the king. I myself shall remain there in his place for fourteen years. I shall never allow my mother to realize her wicked ambition!"

Bharata became enlivened as he contemplated the possibility of bringing Rama home. He felt sure that Rama could be convinced to return when he saw Bharata coming to get him with all the people of Ayodhya. He ordered that expert architects and engineers construct a road to the forest.

The work should begin immediately and they would leave as soon as possible.

All the brahmin counselors applauded Bharata, saying, "Very good! It shall be done!" They blessed Bharata and he felt delighted in mind. His face lit up with joy and tears flowed from his eyes. Thinking of Rama and his imminent return, everyone found their grief dispelled.

Thousands of skilled men were employed in the task of building the road. Absorbed in thoughts of Rama they worked swiftly, leveling the land to lay out a broad road paved with great slabs of red stone. The work was carried out as quickly as possible. Wells were dug and large ponds excavated. Trees were planted along the edge of the road to provide shade, and fragrant gardens were laid out at intervals. The great highway was decorated with festoons and sprinkled with scented water mixed with sandalwood paste. Along the way tent encampments, enclosed by wide moats, were erected for the army. Temples were constructed and images of Vishnu and the gods were installed and worshipped. In some places wealthy men had mansions built and villages grew up around these houses. The road extended from Ayodhya all the way to the Ganges. Strewn with various forest flowers, it appeared like a pathway made by the gods and leading to the heavens.

Within less than a month the road was complete. Bharata summoned Sumantra and ordered him to have the army prepare to leave. In great eagerness the army chiefs prepared everything for the journey to the forest. Mounting upon his own golden car drawn by six pairs of horses, Bharata set out from the city. He was followed by nine thousand elephants, sixty thousand chariots and a hundred thousand infantry. All the royal counselors and priests accompanied him, as well as Dasarath's three wives.

The procession from Ayodhya consisted of thousands of citizens of all classes. It made its way slowly toward the forest. Merchants set out shops and artisans and craftsmen of all kinds plied their trade along the road. Thousands of brahmins, their minds absorbed in meditation, followed the procession on bullock carts, uttering benedictions and prayers.

After some days Bharata arrived near Sringavera, where Rama's friend Guha lived. Halting on the bank of the Ganges, the prince set up camp. Bharata descended from his chariot along with Shatrughna and went down to the riverbank, where he lay down in prostrated obeisance. Along with his brother and Dasarath's wives, he offered Ganges water to the king's departed soul.

Guha had seen Bharata's approach and said to his counselors, "This huge army appears like a sea without any shore. I see in the distance a towering banner bearing the emblem of Bharata. Surely he has come here wishing harm to Rama."

Guha thought Bharata intended to kill Rama in order to establish his unchallenged right to the kingdom. Seeing the tremendous number of people accompanying Bharata, he felt fearful.

"I think this prince will either bind us with chains or kill us, finding us entirely devoted to Rama," Guha continued. "Have our men stand ready with weapons and clothed in mail. The boats should each be filled with one hundred warriors and should wait on the other side of the river. Rama is our lord and master and we should do whatever is in our power to assist him."

Guha decided to go personally to Bharata and discover his purpose. Taking various sweetmeats and fruits as an offering, he went with his chief ministers toward the prince's tent. As he approached nearby, Sumantra saw him and informed Bharata, "Here comes the Nishadha king, Guha, accompanied by a thousand of his men. He is Rama's friend and he knows well everything about the forest. O noble prince, you should allow him to see you, for he will surely know Rama's whereabouts."

Bharata immediately gave orders that Guha be shown into his tent. He came before Bharata and humbly bowed down saying, "This kingdom is yours, O prince. As Rama's friend you are my friend and indeed my lord. Be pleased to accept these foodstuffs and please also stay in my house. Allow my men to entertain your army tonight, and tomorrow you may leave refreshed to accomplish your purpose."

Bharata could understand Guha's mind. He was pleased by his reception and by his devotion to Rama. He spoke gently to the Nishadha ruler. "It is a pleasure to meet you, dear friend of my brother. We are satisfied by your kind hospitality."

Bharata pointed across the Ganges. "I heard Rama went that way, O king, toward Bharadvaja's hermitage. By which route should we proceed in order to find him, O king? Should we cross this river or go along its bank?"

Guha was apprehensive. He looked down as he replied to Bharata. "Seeing your vast army, my mind was filled with fear. I trust that you wish no harm to Rama. If that is the case, then my ferrymen can take you across the river and show you the way."

Bharata reassured Guha. "May the time never come when any wickedness toward Rama enters my heart. Do not have any doubts about me, O Guha. I am here to bring back Rama to Ayodhya. My glorious brother is as good as my father, and I long to see him again. Pray point out his whereabouts to me and I shall go and press his feet to my head."

Tears sprang to Guha's eyes as he replied. "There can be none equal to you on this globe, O jewel among men! Who else could renounce the rulership of the world? Surely your fame will be everlasting. Rest now for the night and tomorrow I shall make all arrangements."

Guha took his leave from Bharata and the prince laid down to sleep. Thinking of Rama, he was seized with sorrow. Perhaps he would not be able to find him. Many months had passed since Rama had left. Who knows where he might be now? Bharata was unable to sleep. He was oppressed with an agony which weighed upon him like a heap of rocks. Heaving sighs Bharata tossed around, immersed in thoughts of Rama. Gradually the dawn approached, and as the sun rose Guha returned.

The forest king spoke again to Bharata. He described how Rama had spent a night there and then, after matting his hair, had left for the deep forest with Lakshmana and Sita. Guha indicated the way they had gone.

Hearing how Rama had matted his hair, Bharata became apprehensive. Surely Rama would not now return. His resolve to remain as an ascetic for fourteen years must be firm. Seized with such thoughts Bharata all of a sudden fell to the ground, saddened at heart. Shatrughna raised his brother, who sat shedding tears. Kaushalya and Sumitra quickly approached him and spoke comforting words. Bharata recovered his composure and said to Guha, "Tell me everything about Rama. What foods did he eat? Where did he sleep? What did he say?"

Guha told Bharata how he had offered Rama many excellent cooked foods, but Rama had refused them, saying "It is never the duty of rulers to accept charity. Indeed, we should always give charity to others."

Guha explained how Rama had drunk only water and then had slept upon a bed of grass laid out by Lakshmana. Bharata asked to be shown the place where Rama slept and Guha took him to the foot of the tree where the bed still lay. Seeing it Bharata loudly exclaimed, "Alas, how could it be that one such as Rama should lay down on a bed of grass? He was ever accustomed to sleep at the top of high palaces, in rooms with golden floors spread with the finest rugs. Having always been awoken by the sweet strains of music and song, how is he now roused by the roar of wild beasts?"

Bharata lamented at length as the reality of Rama's exile and ascetic life struck him. The injustice was insufferable to Bharata and it was made even more excruciating by the thought that he was the cause. His voice was filled with pain. "This is truly incredible! It cannot be real. Surely I am dreaming. See here the strands of gold left by Sita where she lay on these grasses, her delicate limbs pressed to the hard ground. I am ruined indeed, for it is on my account that all this has happened!"

Images of Rama and Sita dressed in forest attire, emaciated due to eating only fruits and roots, filled Bharata's mind. Beating his head he cried out. "From this day I shall wear matted locks and tree bark! I shall lay upon the bare earth to sleep and shall eat only simple forest fare."

Bharata became even more determined to find Rama and bring him back to Ayodhya, staying himself in the forest in Rama's place. After spending another night sleeping on the spot where Rama had lain, Bharata had the army prepare to leave. Guha brought five hundred large boats equipped with oarsmen and sails. He offered his own personal boat to Bharata and his relatives. Some boats were filled with women, some with horses and others with chariots. As the boats plied across the river the elephants swam with the flags on their backs waving in the breeze. Many of the soldiers also swam while their equipment was carried in the boats.

Late in the afternoon the whole party assembled again on the other side of the river. Ordering them to camp at that spot, Bharata went with Vasishtha and other brahmins to look for Bharadvaja's hermitage.

Out of deference to the great sage Bharadvaja, whose only wealth was asceticism, Bharata approached him wearing only simple cloth, leaving his armor and weapons behind. With Vasishtha at their head, the prince and his counselors went on foot and soon arrived at the sage's hermitage.

As soon as he saw them at his door, the sage hurriedly rose and had his disciples fetch water to wash their feet. He embraced Vasishtha and offered blessings to Bharata, who had fallen prostrate at his feet.

Bharadvaja gazed at Bharata, whom he recognized as Rama's brother. The sage knew by his own mystic vision that Dasarath was dead. After inquiring about the situation in Ayodhya the sage asked Bharata, "What brings you all this way, leaving aside the onerous business of managing the state? Because of your mother's words, you are ruling the world as its undisputed monarch. I trust that you have not come here with some dark intention toward the sinless and perfect Rama?"

The sage's words cut into Bharata. Tears flowed from his eyes as he replied in a hurt voice, "If even you impute such motives to me, then I am truly ruined. I never approved my mother's aims! I cannot even imagine doing harm to Rama, nor will I ever accept the kingdom!"

Feeling that no one would believe his innocence, Bharata felt despair. He folded his hands and spoke imploringly. "The powerful Rama is the true ruler of this earth. I have come here to bring him back to Ayodhya. Falling at his feet I shall make him return and then remain here in his place. O all-knowing sage, please be gracious to me and show me where Rama is staying."

Bharata's sincerity was obvious. The all-knowing Bharadvaja smiled. He placed his hand upon Bharata's head, who sat before him weeping, and said, "I surely knew of your intention and spoke only to heighten your resolve and indeed your fame. You are a worthy member of your royal line,

O prince, and are always dedicated to the service of your elders. Your devotion to Rama is beyond doubt."

The sage assured Bharata that he would point out Rama's whereabouts. He asked the prince to stay the night at his hermitage and leave the following morning. Bharata agreed and the sage then offered to feed the entire army. Astonished, Bharata said, "We have already received sufficient hospitality from you, kind sir. As a forest dweller you need only offer simple fruits and this you have done. My army is vast and occupies a huge area of land. If I brought them here, they would all but wreck this holy site."

Bharadvaja laughed and replied, "Have your army brought here forthwith. You should not doubt my ability to receive them, nor will they be any trouble at all."

Commanded by the sage, Bharata assented. Sending back one of his men, he had the army approach the hermitage. As they moved slowly through the forest Bharadvaja sat in meditation. By uttering Vedic mantras he invoked the presence of the principal gods. He then requested them to provide hospitality for the divine prince and his army.

Seated in trance, the sage said within himself, "Let the sacred rivers bear to this region all kinds of celestial beverages. Let the moon-god bring every sort of excellent cooked food. May the heavenly architect Vishvakarma create a suitable site for receiving the army. May Indra send all his Apsaras along with the Gandharva clans to entertain these troops."

As Bharadvaja invoked various divine beings with perfectly pronounced Sanskrit hymns, they all appeared before him. A cool and delightfully fragrant breeze began to blow. Thick showers of flowers fell from the heavens and the sound of celestial music was heard. As the Gandharvas sang and played upon vinas, hosts of Apsaras danced. All of Bharata's entourage, who had assembled at the hermitage, felt their hearts moved by the exquisite sights and sounds seen and heard everywhere.

Before everyone's eyes the entire area around the hermitage changed wonderfully. For a radius of forty miles the ground became even, carpeted with soft blue grass. Numerous types of fruit trees sprang up, full of ripe fruits. Mangos, guavas, peaches, melons and innumerable other soft and hard fruits were seen. Alongside streams of crystal clear water stood large white mansions furnished with seats and couches. A great palace appeared that looked like a white cloud and had a large arched doorway. Delicious food and drink were laid out in these spacious buildings.

With Bharadvaja's permission, Bharata entered the palace, which was adorned with countless flower garlands and sprinkled with scents. Seeing a golden throne, Bharata simply walked around it and sat on the seat next to it, surrounded by his chief ministers.

Streams of sweetened milk and cream flowed past the palace. By Bharadvaja's mystic power, many trees in the hermitage came to life and began playing upon different musical instruments. Some of them assumed the form of dwarfs and began to move about in haste, serving Bharata and his army. All around there appeared thousands of golden vessels containing food of every description. Heaps of steaming white rice were seen, along with tanks filled with milk drinks and yogurt. Pots of honey and large jars filled with intoxicating drinks stood next to platters containing delicious sweetmeats.

Beautiful young maidens attended upon the soldiers, washing them and massaging their feet and bodies with fragrant oils. These celestial damsels, all adorned in pure silk garments, served the men food on golden plates. Being maddened with pleasure, the troops laughed loudly and ran about in all directions. They praised Bharata and Rama again and again as they partook of every kind of enjoyable thing. Although they ate and drank huge amounts they found that they were still not sated. Their senses and minds became more and more enlivened and they felt renewed and refreshed. Even the army's animals were carefully tended and given all kinds of food and drink by the celestial beings invoked by Bharadvaja.

As the night ended, the troops saw before them numerous items of toiletry. Pots of hot water along with soaps and unguents in silver and wooden cases appeared. Combs, brushes, talcs and shining mirrors were in abundance, as well as fresh clothes, shoes and all kinds of ornaments. As the men bathed and put on their clothes and armor, the gods and Apsaras left the hermitage and returned to the heavens. The army was astonished by the night's events, which seemed like a dream. They looked around at the hermitage, which had returned to its normal appearance. Everything had disappeared except for the celestial garlands strewn about, which, although crushed, were as fresh then as they had been at the beginning of the night.

As the sun rose Bharata went to Bharadvaja after the sage's morning prayers. The prince bowed before him and asked his permission to leave. Bharadvaja blessed him and said, "I trust you and your followers spent an enjoyable night. Please tell me if there is anything else I can do for you."

Bharata thanked him for his hospitality and asked to be shown the way toward Rama's hut in the woods. The sage smiled and said, "There is a mountain some twenty miles from here named Chitrakuta, full of lovely caves and groves. On the northern side of that mountain, shaded by blossoming trees, flows the Mandakini River. There, by that river, you will find your two brothers."

As the sage spoke Kaushalya and Sumitra got down from their chariot and clasped his feet. They thanked him profusely as they anticipated seeing

Rama. Kaikeyi also came to the sage and shamefully bowed before him, feeling guilty at heart. Looking at her with compassion the sage asked Bharata, "Please tell me, who are these noble ladies?"

Bharata indicated Kaushalya saying, "This godly lady is the mother of the lion-like Rama. Afflicted with grief, she is emaciated with fasting. Clinging to her arm is the celebrated Sumitra, the mother of Lakshmana and Shatrughna, those two great heroes."

Becoming angry, hissing like a cobra as he spoke, Bharata indicated Kaikeyi. "This one here is my own mother, the wicked and vulgar Kaikeyi. It was by her intrigues that the great emperor Dasarath died from anguish and the mighty Rama now resides in a lonely mountain reach."

Bharadvaja, who knew the plans of the gods and the divine arrangements of the Supreme Lord, said to Bharata, "You should not censure your mother, O great prince. Do not think her guilty, for Rama's banishment will result in good to the entire universe. Indeed, it will bring happiness to the gods, demons and rishis, along with the whole of the creation."

Bharata blushed deeply. He had been piercing his mother with angry looks and he felt rebuked by the sage. Unable to immediately subdue his anger, he averted his gaze and tried to assimilate Bharadvaja's instructions. He stood up and walked respectfully around the sage. Receiving his permission to leave, Bharata ordered the army to depart and mounted upon his chariot. Guha accompanied the two princes. As the huge mass of men moved off through the woods they made a great noise, terrifying the deer and birds dwelling there. Slowly approaching the Chitrakuta mountain they all thought only of Rama, longing to see him again.

CHAPTER FIVE

RAMA REMAINS FIRM

Three months had passed since Rama had settled on the Chitrakuta mountain. Living peacefully in their thatched cottage, Rama, along with Lakshmana and Sita, was happy. From their hut they could see the top of the mountain, some of which was yellow, some red as madder, some glittering silver and some blue-green like a shining emerald. Thousands of other subtle hues shone on the side of the great mountain, and it teemed with deer of every description and hosts of harmless tigers, leopards and bears. Trees laden with flowers and fruits were crowded with varieties of colorful and sweetly singing birds. Clear rivulets flowed from countless springs, and waterfalls sparkled in the sunshine.

Rama felt gladdened at heart to see all this and, sitting at ease on the porch of his hut, he spoke with Sita: "Look at the Kinnaras as they sport on these delightful slopes, having descended from their own planets. See also the Vidhyadharas and Gandharvas courting their womenfolk after hanging their swords and other weapons from the boughs of trees. This place is finer even than heaven. Surely we will easily spend fourteen summers here as if they were a month."

Sita smiled. She felt joyful to be living there with Rama. Despite its simplicity she liked forest life, preferring it even to her life of luxury in the city. She looked down at the Mandakini River where lines of ascetics, clad only in loin cloths, stood in the water with their arms upraised as they worshipped the sun. A cool breeze carried the aroma of tree blossoms, which cascaded on all sides of the mountain. On the sandy bank of the river heavenly Siddhas were appearing and disappearing, moving about in delight. Further down the river she saw a group of elephants standing amid the red and white lotuses as they drank the clear water.

Rama continued, "Let us take our midday bath in the river, O princess. With you by my side I do not miss any of my relatives or even Ayodhya itself. Your beauty puts to shame the so-called beauty of these heavenly damsels, and it gives me newer and newer pleasure."

Rama looked at his brother, who stood at a distance holding his bow. "The godly Lakshmana stands over there equipped with weapons and ready to carry out my every command. Living on the delicious forest fare he gathers, we reside here most happily, dear Sita. What more could I desire even if I lived in Ayodhya?"

Rama and Sita descended to the river and found a secluded spot to take their bath. After bathing and sporting for some time in the cool waters, they came out and sat in the sun on a large flat rock. As Rama conversed with Sita he noticed in the distance a cloud of dust rising to the sky. Looking around he saw frightened animals running in all directions and heard a terrific noise, which became progressively louder.

Rama called out to his brother. "Lakshmana! What do you think is causing this disturbance? A sound like a terrible crash of thunder is coming from the north! Is some king or prince out hunting in the forest, followed by his army? Or is it some vast herd of beasts on the move? Please go and see."

Lakshmana immediately climbed a tall tree and looked all around. Fixing his gaze on the north, he saw in the distance a large army crowded with elephants, horses and chariots, and joined with a mass of marching foot soldiers. He shouted to Rama and informed him.

"Let Sita quickly find a cave," Lakshmana advised Rama. "Extinguish the fire so that the smoke will not be seen. We two shall stand here clothed in mail and holding upraised weapons, for a powerful army approaches!"

Rama, who was not at all fearful, replied to Lakshmana, "Look carefully at the ensigns. Try to determine whose army you think it might be."

Lakshmana stared at the head of the army and saw a tall ensign waving in the breeze, bearing the emblem of a kovidara tree. The prince became infuriated and looked at the army as if he might consume it with his gaze alone.

"Clearly this is Bharata's army!" he exclaimed. "I see there the mark of the kovidara. Evidently he has secured the throne of Ayodhya and now desires to attain undisputed sovereignty by killing us both. Even now I see swift horses going ahead to seek us out."

Lakshmana seethed with anger. "It is fortunate indeed that I shall now see Bharata's face, for whose sake you are enduring this forest life deprived of your sovereign rights. Surely he has come here as an enemy and as such deserves to be killed outright! I see no sin in this action, O Rama, for Bharata has sorely wronged you."

Lakshmana descended from the tree and picked up his weapons. He held his sword aloft. "Today Kaikeyi, who is so desirous of the kingdom, will be seized with sorrow when she sees her son slain by me! I shall then kill her also! Let the earth drink the blood of all these warriors. Beasts of prey will drag about the corpses of elephants and horses, as well as of thousands of men pierced by my arrows. Killing Bharata along with his army, I will repay my debt to my weapons!"

Rama replied gravely to the enraged Lakshmana. "These sentiments do not befit you, dear brother. The mighty Bharata has come here longing to see us and you wish to greet him with weapons. I have given my word of honor to remain in the forest. How then can I forcefully take the kingdom from Bharata, thereby gaining a sovereignty stained with infamy?"

Feeling admonished by his brother, Lakshmana looked down and sheathed his sword. Rama continued, "I will never accept a royal fortune won at the cost of the death of my kinsmen. Indeed, I would only accept the kingdom for the pleasure and protection of my relatives, for I have no personal desire for sovereignty. If any joy should come to me that is not enjoyed by yourself, Bharata or Shatrughna, then let it be reduced to ashes."

Rama knew Bharata's heart. Bharata was no less devoted to him than Lakshmana. He could understand why his brother had come to see him. He also longed to see Bharata. Comforting Lakshmana, Rama said, "When Bharata heard of my exile I am sure he would have felt his heart overwhelmed with affection and his mind distracted by grief. After censuring Kaikeyi with harsh words, he no doubt left Ayodhya intent on bringing me back. Of this I feel certain."

Lakshmana felt ashamed to have spoken angrily about Bharata. He remembered the close and loving relationships the four brothers had enjoyed in childhood. Rama was right. Bharata could not possibly have come in a martial spirit. Lakshmana blushed as Rama continued.

"I cannot imagine Bharata harming us even in his mind," Rama said gently. "Has he somehow previously offended you, dear brother, so that you wax so wrathful toward him now? If you are set upon the slaughter of Bharata, then I shall order him to hand over the kingdom to you this very day. Certainly he will remain here in your place, clad in tree barks, while you rule over this broad earth."

Lakshmana shrank with shame. It had been wrong of him to think so badly of Bharata. There was never a time when any malice or envy had been seen in that prince. Lakshmana tried to make amends for his previous outburst.

"It must be as you say, dear Rama. I think the mighty-armed emperor himself has personally come here accompanied by Bharata. Our father will doubtlessly try to persuade us to return, handing you the sovereignty refused by Bharata. Indeed, I saw father's gigantic elephant, Shatrunjaya, rocking about at the head of the army as it marched."

From their vantage point on the mountainside Rama could see the army coming into view. Spotting the king's elephant he felt a sudden apprehension. Why was there no white umbrella held over its back? Shatrunjaya would not have come out without the king. Unless, that is, there was no king. Rama was fearful. Along with Lakshmana and Sita, he waited near his hut for Bharata's arrival.

* * *

When they reached the mountain, Bharata detailed a number of expert trackers to go in search of Rama's hermitage. He himself went ahead on horseback and began searching on foot when he reached the dense forest on the mountainside. Accompanied by Vasishtha and other brahmins, Bharata pressed ahead into the forest, anxious to see his brothers. He said to Vasishtha, "Blessed is this mountain reach, O sage, where Rama and Sita now roam. How fortunate is Lakshmana who always beholds the moon-like face of Rama. I long to hold Rama's feet on my head. There will be no peace for me until I see him duly consecrated and seated upon Ayodhya's throne."

Bharata climbed a tall tree and gazed all around. Upon seeing a column of smoke he surmised it to be coming from Rama's hermitage. Rejoicing, he descended quickly and went in that direction. Confident that they were now close to Rama, he sent Vasishtha back to bring the queens. Then, along with Shatrughna and Guha, he went as quickly as possible up the mountain slope.

As they arrived at a plateau they suddenly burst into a clearing and saw there, on a leveled piece of ground, Rama's hut. Rama and Lakshmana were sitting in front of the leafy cottage. Bharata saw the sacrificial fire placed on an altar surrounded by blades of kusha grass. Hanging on the sides of the hut were two long bows, plated with gold and shining like rainbows. Large quivers filled with fearful looking arrows stood by the bows, along with two great shields adorned with gold engravings. A couple of swords hung by the bows, sheathed in silver and gold.

When Bharata saw Rama dressed as an ascetic, his hair matted, he let out a cry and fell prostrate. Rising up again he gazed with tear-filled eyes at his beloved brother, who appeared like Brahma seated in his celestial assembly hall. Rama turned and smiled at Bharata, who along with Shatrughna was rushing toward him. Stumbling even as he ran over level ground, Bharata swiftly approached Rama and fell before him. In a choked voice he began to lament.

"Alas, here is my elder brother, who deserves to sit in a royal assembly, seated now in the company of deer," Bharata cried. "What a cruel destiny!

Here is that exalted soul who should wear garments worth many thousands wearing the barks of trees. All this is on my account! Woe to me, condemned by all the world."

Sobs stifled Bharata's voice as he lay near Rama, his hands stretched toward his brother's feet. His face was covered with perspiration and he called out, "Oh, my brother, my noble brother!" Shatrughna also shed tears and bowed before Rama. Rama and Lakshmana quickly got up and closely embraced both of their brothers. The four princes coming together appeared as if the sun and moon had conjoined with Venus and Jupiter in the heavens.

Rama asked Bharata what had brought him away from Ayodhya. Surprised to see him with matted locks and wearing a deerskin, Rama said, "Why have you come here without our father, dearest brother? I hope all is well in Ayodhya. As long as father lives you should surely wait upon him with great attention. Still, I am glad to see you here, although you appear pale and emaciated. Why the ascetic dress, noble Bharata? I think your love for me must be very deep."

Rama gently stroked Bharata's head. Looking up he saw Guha standing at a distance with folded palms and he smiled at him. Rama was fully absorbed in loving exchanges with his friends and relatives. Feeling pain and concern to see Bharata's condition, he continued to speak. "I hope you have not lost the kingdom due to immaturity and inexperience. Surely you know all the facets of diplomacy and kingly science, O powerful prince."

By way of loving instruction, Rama asked after many aspects of the kingdom. He inquired if the people were properly protected, the animals cared for, the army well maintained and the brahmins given sufficient charity. Bharata listened respectfully as his elder brother spoke.

"I see here all my mothers," said Rama. "Indeed it seems that the entire kingdom of Koshala has accompanied you, dear Bharata. This gives rise to grave doubts in my mind. Please tell me why you have all arrived here today, for you have aroused my curiosity."

Bharata knelt before Rama, clasping his feet. "Dear Rama, the act perpetrated by my mother was wicked and never approved by me. Casting you into the forest and afflicting the whole of Ayodhya with unbearable pain, she hoped to see me installed as the king. This will never happen! Please return now with us, O Raghava, and take your rightful position as ruler of this world. Be kind to me and to all these people, O tiger among men."

Rama felt compassion for Bharata. He questioned him again. "What need is there for your adopting this mode of ascetic life, dear Bharata? The order of our father is that you become the king. I too stand enjoined by our father to remain here in the forest. Our pious father's order is supreme.

Therefore, without censuring your mother Kaikeyi, you should enjoy the kingdom. For myself, I am happier staying here in obedience to our father than I would be in attaining to the imperishable abode of Brahma."

Bharata's head sank. He knew his elder brother's mind. It would be impossible to convince Rama to transgress an order given by his elders. Still he felt impelled to try. He could not possibly take the throne in place of Rama. With a heavy heart Bharata informed Rama of what had happened in Ayodhya.

"While I was away in the Kekaya kingdom and you had already gone to the forest, our glorious father ascended to heaven. Thinking only of you and lost in grief at your separation, the king left his mortal body. Now, by the time-honored rule, you, as the elder son, should inherit the kingdom. There cannot be any doubt on this point."

As he heard for the first time the news of his father's death, Rama felt as if his heart had been pierced. Raising his arms and crying out, he sank to the ground like a tree filled with blossoms cut at its root. He lay motionless with the color drained from his face. Bharata quickly sprinkled him with cool water. Rama sat up and held his head, wailing piteously.

"With my father dead and gone what shall I do in Ayodhya? Alas, I am surely a wretched and useless son. My father died because of me. Nor was I even able to cremate him. Even when the fourteen years expires I shall not have the courage to return to the city, seeing it desolate and bereft of its protector. Who will now speak those kind and loving words my father spoke when he saw me well-behaved?"

Rama went over to Sita and Lakshmana who were seated nearby. "Dear Sita, your father-in-law is no more. O Lakshmana, you are now fatherless. Our brother brings the sorrowful news of the king's ascent to heaven. This world now stands without a ruler."

Sita's eyes filled with tears and she was unable to look at her husband. Rama and Lakshmana wept along with Sita as Bharata and Shatrughna comforted them.

Rama controlled his feelings and said, "I must now perform the last sacred rites for the king. Let us go to the river."

The four princes and Sita, stumbling due to their grief, descended with difficulty to the riverbank. They were assisted by Sumantra and other ministers of the king, who stood watching as Rama entered the water along with his brothers and Sita.

Rama faced the southern quarter, over which Yamaraja presides, and held water in his cupped palms. He let the water trickle through his fingers and said in a choked voice, "May this sacred water reach you, O great tiger

among kings! Let this offering serve you, dear father, who have gone forever to the world of our forefathers."

Rama offered prayers for his father and then returned to his hermitage
to prepare an offering of food for the departed king. After the offering was
made, Rama and his brothers clasped each others' hands and began to wail
loudly. The sound was like the roaring of lions and it reverberated all around
the mountain passes.

Hearing that confused noise the soldiers in Bharata's army were
alarmed and they said to one another, "Surely Bharata and Shatrughna have
met Rama and Lakshmana. This sound must be the loud cry of those four
brothers mourning for their deceased father."

The soldiers got up quickly and began running toward the sound.
Crashing through the undergrowth on foot, horseback and in chariots,
everyone in Bharata's entourage rushed toward Rama's hermitage, eager to
see him again. The noise of all those thousands of people moving through
the forest was tumultuous. Deer, buffaloes, boars, lions and elephants ran in
all directions, terrified by the great commotion. Birds of every kind cried
loudly and flew up into the air.

Dasarath's widowed queens got down from their chariot and went on
foot into the woods, accompanied by Vasishtha. Walking with difficulty
along the narrow forest paths, they finally arrived at the spot where Rama
was standing with his brothers. Rama saw them as they entered the clearing
and he ran quickly toward them. He bowed down to Vasishtha and each of
the three queens, touching their feet. After Lakshmana and Sita had also
offered their respects, Rama sat down with Vasishtha on the wooden seats
in front of his hut. The queens wept aloud upon seeing the ascetic dress of
Rama and Sita.

Kaushalya went to Rama and tenderly wiped the dust from his face.
Turning to Sita, she said, "How are you surviving in this lonely forest, dear
Sita? Your face appears pale and withered. Alas, my grief upon seeing you
here blazes up like a fire fed with abundant fuel."

Rama consoled Kaushalya, while Lakshmana spoke with Sumitra, who
was also deeply pained. Bharata then came and sat at Rama's feet. With his
palms folded he said, "Kaikeyi is now satisfied and the kingdom has been
offered to me. If this kingdom is mine, then I hereby give it to you, O Rama.
Please take it without any hesitation."

As Bharata sat before Rama and Lakshmana, the three brothers shone
like three sacrificial fires. Bharata held Rama's feet as he spoke. "The power
to rule this world rests only with you, O Rama. I can no more emulate that
power of yours than a donkey can emulate the gait of a horse or a sparrow
the flight of Garuda. Indeed I am dependent upon you. Let the world behold

you shining with splendor on the Ayodhya's throne. We shall take you there in state this very day!"

All the people gathered there called out, "Well said!" upon hearing Bharata speak. With tears streaming from his eyes Bharata sat looking up at Rama. He hoped desperately that Rama might somehow be persuaded. He could not imagine going back to Ayodhya without him.

Seeing his brother and other relatives weeping, Rama felt compassion. Keeping his own grief in check, he replied, "No man is free to act as he pleases. In this world the embodied soul is dragged here and there by the all-powerful force of Providence. No one can control that force. All gains will end in loss, every meeting ends in separation and all life has its end in death. As there is no fear for a ripe fruit other than a fall, so there is no fear for any man other than death."

Everyone listened attentively as Rama spoke, their feelings of sorrow relieved by his instructions. "The passing of days and nights quickly exhaust the life span of all beings, even as the summer sun sucks up the water in a lake," Rama went on. "You should grieve only for yourself; why do you grieve for another? Death is our constant companion. He walks with us, sits with us and having gone a long distance with us when we travel, he duly returns with us."

Rama still had no desire to return to Ayodhya. He wanted to encourage Bharata and give him strength. Stroking his brother's head, he continued to instruct him.

"Beloved brother, the power to prevent one's own death does not exist in a person grieving for another. Our father departed after a long life of piety and we should by no means grieve. We ourselves have embarked on the very same path trodden by the emperor and will join him in due course. Let us therefore throw off grief and dedicate ourselves to the pursuit of piety by which we too shall attain the blessed regions reached by the king."

Rama looked around his hermitage. Thousands of people were crowding on the mountainside, all looking towards him. There was complete silence as Rama spoke. Even the animals seemed silent. Only the sound of the river and the rustling of leaves in the breeze could be heard. Dappled shadows moved over the ground in the late afternoon sun. With a mild smile Rama continued to address Bharata, within the hearing of everyone there.

"Father has shed his old, worn-out body and, with an ethereal and undecaying form, he now sports in great happiness. Rather than grieve for him we should now carefully do his bidding. For your part you should rule over the earth, dear Bharata, while I for mine should remain in the forest until fourteen years have expired. This will ensure our welfare in both this world and the next. Under no circumstances should we disobey our virtuous father."

Rama spoke for more than an hour and Bharata felt joy to hear his brother's words of instruction. But he was also dispirited to see Rama's determination to stay in the forest.

When Rama stopped speaking, Bharata grasped his feet and replied, "Your position is glorious, O mighty brother. You are never dejected at adversity nor exhilarated at finding joy. You are always able to distinguish truth from untruth. Therefore you know what is real and what is only temporary and thus ultimately unreal. It is certainly the soul and not the body that one should nurture in this world."

Bharata realized that Rama was only acting with philosophical understanding; he knew that Rama could not possibly act outside the codes of religion or morality. Nonetheless, Bharata was himself still doubtful about the justice of Rama's exile. He spoke to Rama in order to clear his doubts. "Were it not for moral codes, I would have surely slain my sinful mother. How did the king allow himself to fall under her sway? Due to infatuation or foolishness our father acted wrongly. As his sons is it not our duty to correct his mistakes? Surely this is the proper religious path for an honest and worthy son."

Bharata turned and indicated the people gathered around. "All these people need your protection. This is the duty of rulers according to scripture. Nowhere is the duty of a ruler stated as being life in the forest. March back to Ayodhya at the head of this vast army. Let your friends feel joy today and your enemies run frightened in all directions. O Rama, if you resolve to stay here, then you shall find me by your side. I can by no means find in myself the strength to rule in your absence."

Bharata sat with his head bowed. Everyone was enthralled by the conversation between the two royal brothers, and they became simultaneously joyful to witness his firm resolve and disconsolate to realize he would not be returning to Ayodhya.

Rama replied to Bharata in a solemn voice. "All his life our father followed the path of piety. This is widely known. Impiety would not have been possible for that truthful man. When our father accepted Kaikeyi's hand he promised her father, as the bride price, that her son would inherit the kingdom. Furthermore, sworn under solemn oath by Kaikeyi, the king promised you the kingdom and ordered me to go to the forest. Whatever the reasons, this was the king's promise. If that promise is broken our father will be liable to sinful reactions. Our duty as his sons is to fulfill his promise and thereby save him. No other course is possible for us."

Rama paused for a moment. He got down from his seat and lifted up Bharata and Shatrughna. "You two should return to Ayodhya and protect the people. O Bharata, get yourself consecrated as king and rule the earth. I shall become the emperor of wild beasts. The white umbrella should be held over your head as you ride on the royal elephant, while for my part I shall go on foot, shielded by a canopy of trees. Leave with joy for the city, my brothers, and I with Lakshmana will joyfully enter the woods. In this way we shall preserve our father's piety."

Bharata said nothing. He felt reassured by Rama's reply, but was profoundly sorrowful at the prospect of leaving him.

At that moment a brahmin named Jabali spoke, trying to convince Rama to return on the basis of atheistic doctrines. "Why are you attached to your father, Rama? He was nothing more than flesh and bones and has now merged again with the earth. People who consider that others are in some way related to them are simply mad. Alone we came to this world and alone we shall leave. As such we should only work toward our own interests. You need not suffer now for the interests of your deceased father. Take the throne and enjoy it, O Rama, for this will be in your own best interests."

Jabali did not himself believe the philosophy he was espousing. He was only trying somehow to change Rama's mind. Perhaps Rama would accept the arguments as a pretext for going back to Ayodhya. Most likely, though, he would defeat Jabali's position and thereby establish the path of religion. Either way Jabali would be satisfied and he continued to speak his atheistic philosophy.

"I lament for those who forsake sense pleasures for the austerities of a religious life," said Jabali, rising to his feet. "Hoping for future happiness they meet only with extermination at death, having led a life of suffering. The scriptures have been written by intelligent brahmins who wished to exalt sacrifice and charity. In this way these brahmins have assured their own livelihood."

Jabali smiled as he spoke his false philosophy. No one in the assembly accepted his words, but they too hoped that Rama would yet be convinced to leave the forest. Everyone listened in silence as Jabali concluded his speech.

"Knowing this truth, O Rama, you should renounce your foolish asceticism. There is nothing beyond this visible universe. Do not depend for your happiness on anything outside of that which you can see and immediately experience. Therefore, O great prince, accept the kingdom and enjoy it as the undisputed ruler."

Rama sat down again as Jabali stopped speaking. Looking at the brahmin he said, "A man is known by his conduct alone. Although posing as a learned and cultured person, one who acts as you direct is to be accepted as sinful and debased. Those who are wise never praise a person who acts only to please his senses. Such a person is mean, selfish and greedy, driven only by lust for pleasure. His immediate happiness soon turns to distress and he sinks into a hellish condition."

Rama appeared angry as he refuted Jabali. His eyes were red and he spoke gravely. "If I were to follow the path espoused by you, O atheistic one, then this entire earth would be cast into ruin. All men follow the king's example. Abandoning the religious path, the people would become licentious and uncontrolled. Chaos would prevail and everyone would suffer."

Jabali sat down before Rama with his palms joined and his head bowed. He said nothing as Rama explained how the attempt to find happiness through sense enjoyment was futile. Both the senses and their enjoyments are soon destroyed. Only the soul and God are eternal, along with the spiritual realms where the Lord resides. Those who are actually learned therefore follow the path of truth which leads to those ever-existing realms of bliss.

Rama paused and gradually his anger subsided. After some minutes he spoke again. "My father was wedded to truth. Following his instruction will lead only to happiness. I shall therefore remain in these woods and Bharata should rule the earth. This will be our only assurance of happiness, both in this world and the next. O Jabali, you should not speak in this way again, for to mislead the people is a very great sin."

Rama, having spoken to instruct all people, fell silent. He knew Jabali's heart and did not feel anger toward him, only toward his words. The people's pain was Rama's pain and he knew that Jabali's presentation of hedonism led only to pain.

Saying "It is exactly as you say," Jabali prostrated himself before Rama and returned to his place among the other brahmins.

Vasishtha stood up and spoke in the midst of the assembly. "This Jabali knows well of the soul and its actual happiness. He spoke only out of his desire to see you installed as the king. This is also my desire, O Raghava. As the emperor's eldest son it behooves you to now accept the throne. You need entertain no doubt in this regard."

Vasishtha recounted the history of Rama's line. One by one he named the previous kings and explained how each had handed the kingdom to their eldest son. Finally he said, "O Rama, this is my instruction to you. I am your preceptor and as such I am even more worthy of your obedience than your father. Indeed, I was also his preceptor. Therefore I command you to accept the throne of Ayodhya."

The sage had spoken only out of love. He was aware that Rama was enacting a divine plan by remaining in the forest, but still he longed for him to return.

Rama looked with affection at Vasishta and replied, "The debt owed to one's parents cannot be easily repaid, O learned sage. They give everything they have for their children. Feeding them, nurturing them, putting them to bed and rubbing them with oil, the father and mother give their love at every moment. My worthy father's word should not prove false due to my negligence, for I wish to render him some service in return for his love."

It was obvious that Rama was not going to be convinced by anyone to leave the forest. Bharata suddenly stood up and exclaimed, "Seated upon blades of kusha grass spread on the ground, I shall remain here in front of Rama's door. Without taking food or water I will not move until Rama agrees to accept the throne."

Quickly grabbing a bunch of grass from near Rama's hut, Bharata spread it out and sat down. Rama said in surprise, "O Bharata, why do you take such a vow? Your duty is to rule the kingdom, not sit upon the ground like a destitute brahmin."

Bharata turned toward the people and implored, "Why do you not plead with my brother to return?"

A leader of the brahmin community stepped forward. "It is clear that Rama will not be swayed from his determination to follow his father's command. What can we do? Our hearts are breaking with the thought of Rama's separation."

Rama glanced lovingly at the brahmin and then said to Bharata, "Get up, O tiger among men. Return to Ayodhya. Become the king and rule with justice. In fourteen years you will see me returned."

Bharata stood up and replied to Rama, "If our father's order must be followed, then allow me to stay here in your place."

Rama gently admonished Bharata, telling him that it was not possible for one's promise to be fulfilled by another person. Rama had given his word and it was he who had to keep that word. He promised that when he returned to Ayodhya he would accept the throne, but he would not under any condition return before the fourteen years had expired.

The many eminent sages who were present had listened intently to the conversation between the two divine brothers. They were thrilled and astonished, thinking of the deep import of their discussion. Hosts of heavenly rishis along with the gods, stood invisible in the sky. The divine beings then spoke so that only Rama and his brothers could hear.

"Hearing this wondrous dialogue between Rama and Bharata, we long to hear it again and again," said one of the gods. "O Bharata, please allow

Rama to fulfill his promise to his father. By virtue of Rama's vow Dasarath has ascended to the highest heaven, freed of his debt to Kaikeyi."

The gods were anxious for Ravana's death which they saw as imminent. They showered celestial flowers on Rama and his brothers and then returned to their heavenly abodes. Encouraged by hearing the demigods, Bharata was prepared to accept the responsibility of ruling Ayodhya. Falling at Rama's feet he voiced his final doubts. "My lord, how does the power to rule our vast kingdom exist in me? I am young and inexperienced. Nor am I possessed of any great ability. Surely the kingdom will meet with ruin under my incapable guidance."

Rama raised his younger brother and placed him on his lap. Stroking his head he said, "Your humility is your real qualification. By virtue of this wisdom you can protect the entire earth. Always seek the counsel of learned brahmins and rule with confidence, O jewel among men."

Bharata then brought before Rama a pair of ornate wooden sandals embellished with gold. He put them on the ground and said, "Please place your feet in these sandals, dear Rama. Let these shoes be the rulers of the kingdom and I shall remain as their servant."

Rama immediately put on the sandals and then took them off again, handing them back to Bharata. Bharata placed the sandals on his head. "For the coming fourteen years I shall live in a hut outside Ayodhya," he said, sighing. "I shall survive on only fruits and roots and my hair shall be matted. If at the end of this time I do not see you return, O Rama, then I shall enter blazing fire."

"So be it," replied Rama and he embraced each of his brothers. He again told Bharata that Kaikeyi should not be condemned and that she should be treated with kindness. Rama paid his respects to all the people there according to their positions, speaking fond farewells to everyone. Kaushalya and the other queens stood in front of Rama unable to say anything, their throats choked and their eyes flooded with tears. Rama bowed to each of them in turn.

As the queens departed Kaikeyi turned and spoke privately to Rama. She censured herself again and again, begging his forgiveness. The queen fell at Rama's feet. "I am entirely ignorant and have acted like a fool," she said tearfully, "but now I understand that you are the eternal Supreme Person. Who would not be bewildered upon seeing your human pastimes? O Lord, please forgive me and destroy my attachments to family and wealth."

Rama smiled at her with affection. "It was I who, for the sake of the gods, prompted you to act as you did," he said. "You are not to blame, nor am I angry with you. Hardly anyone knows my real nature. I am never affected by desire in the same way as ordinary men. I act simply to reciprocate the service and love I am given. Gentle lady, return to Ayodhya and live peacefully. Think of me day and night and you will soon be freed from all your attachments to this temporary world."

Kaikeyi felt deeply relieved and gladdened. With folded hands she circumambulated Rama and again joined the other queens.

Bharata had the golden sandals placed upon the royal elephant and shielded by the white umbrella. With the elephant at their head, the citizens of Ayodhya returned the way they had come.

As they entered Ayodhya some days later, they saw that it had become dark and desolate. The streets were unswept and rubbish was strewn all around. The doors and windows of the empty houses swung open. The city had become overrun by cats and owls, and mice ran everywhere. No offerings were being made in the temples and all the shops and pleasure houses were closed. The streets were deserted and the city, which had always been full of the life and joy of countless people, was now silent and still. The city resembled a vast army which has been defeated in battle, its armor shattered, its ensigns torn down, and its heroes killed.

Bharata made his way to Dasarath's palace, dejected to see the state of his beloved Ayodhya. After entering the palace, which was like a mountain cave abandoned by its lion, Bharata went into the assembly hall with Vasishtha and his other counselors. He placed Rama's sandals on the throne, then sat next to them and said, "I shall not accept the throne of Ayodhya. These sandals should be consecrated as the king and I shall be their servant only. Indeed, I shall live in a hermitage outside the city. When Rama returns I shall again place these sandals on his feet, as he alone is the king."

The brahmins applauded Bharata. "So be it!" they exclaimed. They then duly installed the sandals with the coronation ceremony.

Bharata then moved with Shatraghna into a small wooden hut, eating only forest fare and wearing ascetic dress. Each day he would submit the affairs of state before Rama's sandals. Only then would he carry out any necessary action. Any gifts he received he would also offer to Rama's sandals. In this way he ruled the kingdom.

CHAPTER SIX

THE FOREST SAGES

After Bharata left, Rama continued to live on Chitrakuta Mountain. As the months passed, Rama began to notice that the rishis living nearby were always fearful and anxious. He approached the leading ascetics and, bowing down humbly, asked, "O venerable ones, has something in my behavior given you cause for concern? Have either my brother or I been acting in a way not worthy of our esteemed forefathers? Is Sita behaving in a way unbecoming a young woman?"

Rama had noticed on several occasions that the brahmins spoke together while glancing at him. He knew they were worried about something. Seated before them with folded palms, Rama listened carefully as the leaders replied.

"How could there ever be any fault in the behavior of you or your brother, O Rama?" one rishi said. "What unseemly conduct will ever be seen in the gentle and high-born Sita? We know well your true identity."

The rishis glowed with ascetic power. They constantly chanted various names of God, fingering their wooden beads as they intoned the mantras. With a desire to render service to Rama, they addressed him as if he were an ordinary man.

"There is a powerful Rakshasa called Khara living near here," the rishi continued. "This demon is Ravana's younger brother and he is brutal, haughty and sinful. Angered by your presence, he has been afflicting us with more vehemence than usual."

Rama frowned as he heard about the Rakshasa. He could not tolerate any aggression toward brahmins.

The rishi went on, "Khara and his hordes of Rakshasas, constantly impede our sacrifices. The demons show themselves in hideous, savage and frightening forms. They throw flesh, bones, excrement and urine down from the sky, defiling our sacrificial arenas. They make strange and terrible noises and it is only a matter of time before they become violent toward us. We therefore desire to leave this place."

Seeing sacrifice as their sacred duty, the ascetics wished to go to another forest where they would not be disturbed. As brahmins, they would not themselves fight the Rakshasas, although they were capable of checking them by their mystic power. They also understood that Rama wanted to destroy the demons, especially their leader Ravana.

Rama tried to reassure the rishis, but they were determined to leave. Having stayed on Chitrakuta for some years, the renounced ascetics were also concerned that they may have become attached to their material situation. Normally they moved continously from forest to forest, staying only one or two years in each place. After speaking a little more with Rama, informing him of where Khara lived, the brahmins rose up in a body. With only their water pots and staffs they left the region. Rama followed them for some distance in order to see them off with respect. He then returned to his hermitage, considering in his mind how to deal with the Rakshasas.

When he reached his hut, Rama said to Lakshmana, "I think the time has come for us to leave Chitrakuta. The brahmins have left, and I am afraid that we will again be visited by the people who now know of our whereabouts. We should leave for some other more remote forest."

Rama decided to make his way to the Dandaka forest, which was inhabited by the Rakshasas. He wanted to confront the demons. The two brothers donned their weapons and, with Sita walking between them, immediately left.

After journeying for some days they entered the Dandaka forest and came upon a cluster of hermitages. The rishis there greeted them with respect. Those ascetics were endowed with divine vision, and they were astonished to see Rama and his companions. The Lord of all the worlds was standing before them. Seeing Rama and Sita's simple forest dress, the sages felt wonder and awe. They worshipped Rama with various prayers and offered him a hut for the night.

"Welcome indeed is your arrival in these woods," the rishis said. "The king is the protector of righteousness and the only refuge of the people. He stands with his scepter and metes out justice as God's powerful representative. O Rama, we are your subjects and your servants. We are simple brahmins who have renounced anger and controlled our senses. As such we deserve your protection, even as a fetus is protected by its mother."

Entertaining Rama with forest produce, the ascetics described how the Rakshasas had become increasingly violent. Under Ravana's leadership the demons had become fearless and they attacked the brahmins constantly. Fourteen thousand powerful Rakshasas had taken up their residence in the Dandaka forest, headed by Ravana's two brothers, Khara and Dushana. The situation was becoming unbearable for the sages.

Rama and Lakshmana listened gravely. They resolved to deal with the Rakshasas as soon as possible. While they were conversing with the rishis, Sita met Anasuya, the sage Atri's wife. Anasuya gave Sita a celestial garment, garland and ornaments, along with celestial cosmetics and unguents. Sita accepted the gifts graciously and with her husband's permission adorned herself with them. After decorating herself with the heavenly apparel, she shone brilliantly, exactly like Lakshmi, the eternal consort of Vishnu.

After spending the night with the rishis, the princes left with Sita and they penetrated deep into the Dandaka region. Lakshmana moved ahead and cleared a path with his sword, cutting through the thick creepers and bushes. Sita, her head covered with her cloth to protect herself from the swarms of insects that flew about, walked in the middle. Rama brought up the rear, vigilantly watching on all sides and holding his bow at the ready. The cries of jackals and the shrieks of vultures and birds of prey could be heard all around. Here and there they saw uprooted, broken trees and the carcasses of slain beasts.

As they broke through into a clearing they suddenly saw a dreadful-looking Rakshasa. Powerfully built and as tall as several men, he stood entirely blocking their way. With high pointed ears, fierce teeth protruding from his cavernous mouth, and blood-red eyes staring out from an ugly mis-shapen face, the demon was terrible to behold. He held a long lance on which he had speared four lions, three tigers, a couple of wolves and about ten spotted deer. Around his blackish and hairy body were draped tiger skins, still dripping with blood and fat. He resembled the god of death standing with his staff of justice. When he saw Rama and the others he let out a terrific roar that could be heard for many miles. He rushed furiously toward them and quickly seized Sita.

Taking the princess a little distance away, the Rakshasa spoke to Rama and Lakshmana in a voice resounding like claps of thunder. "Who are you two, looking like ascetics but carrying weapons? You shame the brahmin class with this strange behavior. Why have you brought a woman into this dense forest? Sinful as you are, you shall meet death at my hands. This lady shall become my wife. Today I shall drink your blood on the battlefield."

Sita trembled in the monster's clutches, like a sapling trembling in a storm. Seeing her carried away by the Rakshasha, Rama said to Lakshmana, "It seems that Kaikeyi's cherished desire will today be fulfilled. This hideous demon has taken hold of my sinless wife. There is nothing more painful for me than to see the princess of Videha touched by another. This is more painful even than the death of my father or the loss of the kingdom."

Rama cried tears of sorrow as he spoke. Lakshmana became infuriated with the demon and he hissed like an angry cobra. "Why are you, the Lord of all beings with me as your servant, grieving like an orphan?" he asked. "The earth will soon drink this beast's blood. The anger which I wrongly directed toward Bharata will today be released upon that foul demon. Watch now as my arrow pierces his breast and he whirls around, falling lifeless to the ground."

The Rakshasa, still awaiting a reply to his question, again boomed out, "Who are you and where are you going?"

Rama moved closer to the demon and replied, "We are two warriors of the royal order of Raghu who have come here in exile. Tell us who you are and why you roam this forest, O wicked one."

"So, you are kings from Ayodhya!" the Rakshasa replied. "Know me to be Viradha, a Rakshasa who wanders this forest eating the flesh of sages. You should run away the way you came. I'll not kill you. I have been granted boons by Brahma and cannot be slain by any weapon, O Raghava. Leave quickly and abandon this princess to me. Assuming a human form I shall sport with her as my wife."

Rama grew furious. With bloodshot eyes he spoke in a voice like Indra's. "You pathetic fool! You are certainly seeking death. You will get it today on the battlefield. I shall not leave you with your life."

Without uttering another word Rama shot seven golden-feathered arrows at the demon. The arrows flew with the speed of Garuda and pierced right through Viradha, falling upon the earth drenched with his blood. The Rakshasa roared in pain and released Sita. With his lance upraised he rushed at Rama and Lakshmana. The brothers immediately sent a shower of arrows at the demon.

Even though pierced all over, Viradha remained standing. Laughing aloud he yawned contemptuously. He then hurled his lance at Rama with the force of a tempest. Rama at once fired two arrows which cut the lance into three pieces as it coursed toward him. As it fell to the ground the shattered lance resembled a rocky mountain ledge that had been struck by Indra's thunderbolt. Rama and Lakshmana took out their swords, which resembled two black serpents preparing to attack. They rushed at the Rakshasa and began striking him with great force. Viradha reached down and lifted both brothers, one on each arm. Placing them on his shoulders he ran toward the woods.

As Viradha approached the dense forest Sita cried out, "Alas, where goes my lord? O best of the Rakshasas, please take me also. How can I remain here alone?"

Hearing Sita's plaintive wail, Rama raised his sword high and hacked off the demon's right arm. Lakshmana lopped off his left arm, and Viradha fell upon the ground in a swoon. Although striking him with their swords and with kicks and punches, the brothers saw that the Rakshasa still did not die. Rama said to Lakshmana, "It is clear that due to his boons this demon cannot be killed by force. We should bury him in a pit, for this is the traditional way of disposing of the Rakshasas. Quickly dig a large pit, O tiger among men!"

Rama stood with his foot pressing down upon the Rakshasa's neck. Viradha regained consciousness and said, "O Raghava, I am defeated by you. Your strength is not less than Indra's. I now know you to be the all-powerful Rama and your wife the highly fortunate Sita. I am the Gandharva named Tumburu. Due to not properly serving Kuvera, the lord of wealth, I was cursed by him."

The fallen Rakshasa explained how as Tumburu he had previously been Kuvera's servant. One day Tumburu had been sporting with the Apsaras and had failed to properly attend upon his master. In anger Kuvera had cursed him to enter a demon's fierce form. Tumburu had pleaded for mercy and Kuvera had replied, "When Rama, the son of Dasarath, defeats you in battle, then you will attain your own form and return to heaven."

Viradha spoke with difficulty. "By your grace, O Rama, I am freed from a terrible curse. I shall now go to my own abode. O Lord, ten miles from here lives the sage Sarabhanga, who longs to see you. Go to his hermitage, for he will give you good advice."

Viradha begged Rama to inter him in the pit so that he could die. Rama and Lakshmana rolled the huge body of the Rakshasa into the hole Lakshmana had dug. After covering him with earth and rocks, they comforted Sita and then continued on their way, looking for Sarabhanga's hermitage.

In the sky the gods had witnessed the whole scene. Seeing Rama, whom they knew to be the powerful Vishnu acting like a human, they were astonished. Nothing was beyond Rama's knowledge or power, yet he accepted the feelings and actions of an ordinary man. Pondering upon the import of Rama's deeds, the gods received Tumburu back to them.

Rama searched for Sarabhanga, absorbed in a mood of affection for the sage. As the brothers came near the ascetic's hermitage they saw in the sky a golden chariot. It shone like the midday sun and was drawn by a thousand greenish horses. A brilliant white canopy resembling a large cloud and decorated with magnificent garlands covered the chariot. Seated in the chariot was Indra, who was being fanned with white whisks by two beautiful young girls. In the sky many other gods surrounded Indra. Rama and Lakshmana saw numerous Gandharvas and Siddhas, all dressed in resplendent silk garments and gold ornaments. All these high-souled beings were worshipping Indra with Vedic hymns.

Upon seeing this wondrous sight Rama said to Lakshmana, "O Lakshmana, see here Indra's wonderful chariot, full of grandeur. Those young men
with broad chests and arms like iron clubs, wearing red garments and gold
earrings and surrounding him in the hundreds, appear as unassailable as
tigers."

Lakshmana gazed up at the host of gods assembled in the sky. All of
them appeared youthful and all had garlands as bright as fire on their chests.
As the two princes looked on, the gods rose up into the sky and vanished.
Amazed at this sight Rama and Lakshmana walked on and entered Sarabhanga's hermitage.

Sarabhanga was seated before the sacrificial fire. Having practiced
asceticism for many years, he was able to fix his mind upon the Supreme
Person within his heart. He had realized that Rama was that same person.
In meditation the sage prayed that he might be able to see God in his human
form. Accordingly, Rama approached the old ascetic and bowed low before
him, touching his feet and saying, "I am Rama, and this is my brother Lakshmana and my wife Sita. At Viradha's behest, we have sought your presence. Viradha has now risen to heaven with the gods. Pray tell us what we
should do, O jewel among sages."

Sarabhanga rose immediately, his eyes flooded with tears. He showed
the three travelers a seat. Offering them water and fruits, he said, "O Rama,
there is no one more kind or merciful. After meditating for a very long time
and reaching the end of my attachments to this world, I saw you in my
heart. Now I see you here as the son of Dasarath."

After offering many prayers the sage fell silent. He sat for some time
gazing with love upon Rama's face. Smiling, Rama asked, "Why did I see
here the lord of the gods, O sage?"

The sage said that Indra had come to take him to the higher planets,
which he had earned as a result of his asceticism. Sarabhanga explained
that, desiring to remain on earth to see Rama, he had sent Indra away.

"Now that I have seen your transcendental form I have no desire to go
to the heavenly worlds, O Raghava," Sarabhanga said. "Please take from me
my ascetic merits."

"You will doubtlessly rise beyond even the highest heaven and attain
Vishnu's immortal abode, O learned one," Rama replied. "But before leaving, pray tell me where I should go now."

Sarabhanga directed Rama to the hermitage of another sage named
Sutikshna. He then gazed at Rama and entered a deep meditation. From
within himself Sarabhanga invoked the fire element and immolated his mortal frame, which quickly burned to ashes. The sage appeared in a shining
spiritual body and, after offering his respects to Rama, rose up into the sky.

Rama remained seated in Sarabhanga's hermitage and many other rishis came there and begged him to dispose of the Rakshasas. They told him how the demons were killing thousands of brahmins. Rama assured the rishis that he would annihilate the Rakshasas in due course. He then left and went toward Sutikshna's hermitage, following Sarabhanga's directions.

Upon seeing Rama, Sutikshna offered many prayers and then took him to see the powerful rishi Agastya. On the way to Agastya they saw that the forest resembled the famous Nandana grove in the heavens. The ground was suddenly smooth, carpeted with soft grasses. Trees bent down on both sides under their heavy loads of ripe fruits. The clear lakes were filled with lotuses and crowded with swans, cranes and many other varieties of water birds. Flowers grew and trees blossomed everywhere. The animals were docile and approached the travelers without fear.

Rama looked around at the wonderful scenery. "It seems we are near Agastya's hermitage," he said. "By his austerities the sage has transformed this forest into heaven. We will soon behold that shining rishi."

Requested by Lakshmana, Rama told various stories about Agastya. He kept his brother and Sita entertained as they walked throughout the day. Finally by evening they arrived at the hermitage. As they approached it Rama said, "Let us go see Agastya, for he will surely bless us with all good fortune. I think that with his permission we should remain in this region for the rest of our stay in the forest."

Sutikshna went ahead and informed Agastya of their arrival. The sage quickly had them brought into his hermitage. As they entered the large compound they saw numerous sacrificial fires, each dedicated to a particular god and tended by Agastya's disciples. All the principal deities, including the Supreme Lord, Vishnu, as well as Shiva, Brahma and dozens of other gods were being worshipped. Sacrificial smoke and the sound of mantras filled the air.

Agastya, feeling ecstasy, rose up from his seat and came swiftly toward Rama. Rama saw the sage coming and along with Lakshmana he immediately prostrated himself on the ground. Sita stood close behind with her hands folded and head bowed.

Agastya raised Rama up and said, "I have been thinking of you for a long time, O Raghava. I am blessed by your appearance here. You are always beyond the influence of the insurpassable material energy. Simply by remembering you one can be carried beyond the great ocean of birth, death and suffering. What then can be said of one who sees you?"

Agastya sat the travelers down and after offering oblations into the sacred fire, he presented them with water and food. Seated in meditation the sage then caused a great golden bow to appear. There were also two quivers filled with sharp arrows which blazed like fire, and a long sword sheathed in a golden scabbard. Agastya presented the weapons to Rama, telling him how in a previous age Vishnu had used them to assist the gods in a war against the demons.

Rama accepted the celestial weapons respectfully and then asked the sage to tell him of a place where he could live. After again meditating for a while the sage replied, "By virtue of my austerities and meditation I have come to know you and understand your purpose, O Rama. I therefore suggest you go to a nearby forest called Panchavati. It is beautiful and sanctified. At that place all your desires will be fulfilled."

Agastya gave the brothers directions. After taking leave, Rama, Lakshmana and Sita began the twenty-mile walk to Panchavati, making their way along the narrow forest paths.

After a few miles they came across a huge vulture lying in a clearing. Rama and Lakshmana, assuming it to be a Rakshasa, quickly prepared to fight. Rama carefully approached the vulture, which resembled a hill.

"I am Rama and this is my brother Lakshmana, two descendants of Raghu," he declared. "Who are you and what is your race?"

In gentle speech the bird replied that he was an old friend of Dasarath. His name was Jatayu and he was the king of the vultures. He recounted to Rama his entire lineage, which began with the ancient sage Kardama. In the course of his narration Jatayu described how all the various species of birds and animals had descended. Jatayu was the nephew of Garuda, the invincible eagle carrier of Vishnu.

"This forest is infested with Rakshasas and vicious beasts," Jatayu said. "Allow me to accompany you in the forest. I shall protect Sita when you two brothers go out to gather food."

Rama knew of Jatayu's friendship with his father. He joyfully embraced the great bird and gave his permission for Jatayu to follow him. Rama then continued toward Panchavati, eager to encounter the demons.

After arriving at Panchavati, Rama selected a spot near the sacred river Godavari. Lakshmana sanctified the spot with prayers and water from river. He constructed a large hut with mud walls, supported on strong wooden pillars, its roof thatched with kusha grass and reeds. Rama was delighted to see the beautiful cottage and he embraced Lakshmana. "With you as his son, virtuous and always attentive to my needs and desires, surely the king still lives," Rama said affectionately. "O Lakshmana, you are to me as good as my beloved father."

Rama and Sita settled in the dwelling and lived peacefully, bathing in the Godavari and enjoying the sights and sounds of the forest.

CHAPTER SEVEN

THE RAKSHASI SHURPANAKHA

The time passed quickly for Rama and his companions. They lived in almost complete solitude, seeing only an occasional ascetic. Although Rama wanted to face the Rakshasas, no opportunity presented itself.

One day, just as their tenth winter in exile was ending, a powerful Rakshasi named Shurpanakha, a sister of Ravana, came to the Panchavati region. While she was roaming about looking for food, she saw Rama's footprints and followed them. Soon she arrived at Rama's cottage. As she came near the hermitage she saw Rama seated outside his hut. She was immediately attracted to the handsome Rama, with his powerful frame and majestic bearing. Her mind filled with lust, she assumed the form of a beautiful woman and walked slowly before him.

"Who are you, dressed in ascetic garb yet wielding weapons?" the Rakshasi asked. "Why have you come to this forest which is frequented by Rakshasas? Be pleased to tell me."

Rama looked guilelessly at the Rakshasi. "There was a powerful king named Dasarath," he replied. "I am his son Rama and this is my brother Lakshmana. There is the princess of Videha, my wife Sita. On my father's command I am sojourning here in the forest. Now tell me, who are you, O beautiful maiden? Who is your husband? You seem to me to be a Rakshasi capable of assuming various guises. Tell me truly why you have approached me."

Shurpanakha moved her hips and glanced down coyly. "Know me to be Shurpanakha, sister of the unconquerable Ravana. Living here with my other brothers, Khara and Dushana, I range these woods devouring ascetics and causing fear to all. However, upon seeing you I long to embrace you as my husband."

Shurpanakha hoped that, even if Rama was not attracted to her, out of fear of her he might accede to her request. Hearing that she was a Rakshashi, Rama and Lakshmana looked at her in surprise. In her fine silks and ornaments she appeared exactly like a celestial maiden. She moved closer to Rama and smiled. "O Rama, of what use to you is this skinny and deformed woman?" she asked, throwing a disdainful glance at Sita. "Accept me as your wife. I am possessed of great power. After devouring this wife and brother of yours, I will carry you to high mountain reaches where we can sport together in joy."

Rama laughed heartily. He decided to joke with the infatuated Rakshasi. "O beautiful woman, I am already married. For ladies like you it is always painful to have a co-wife. Here though is my younger brother. He is handsome and highly qualified and is as yet unmarried. Why not take him as your worthy husband?"

Shurpanakha turned quickly toward Lakshmana, who stood smiling with his hand resting on his bow. The Rakshasi moved toward him. "See my alluring form," she said. "I am certainly worthy of becoming your wife, O handsome one. Let us range together happily through these woods."

Lakshmana caught Rama's joking mood. "Why do you seek to become a maidservant, foolish woman?" he asked with a laugh. "I am dependent on my older brother. As my wife you will be Sita's servant. You should seek only Rama as your husband. Who could actually refuse you in favor of a human lady? Surely Rama will soon abandon the weak and worn-out Sita once you are his wife."

Shurpanakha was too simple to catch the joke. She took Lakshmana's words to be true and turned again toward Rama, who sat next to Sita. "Why do you cling to this hideous wife of yours?" she asked, growing impatient. "If it is her who stands between you and me, I shall now devour her, even as you watch. We shall then roam together at ease."

Shurpanakha rushed furiously toward Sita, even as a large meteor would fall toward the earth. She assumed her natural form as a Rakshasi, appearing like a black cloud. Rama immediately roared and checked her by the sound alone. As she fell back Rama said angrily to Lakshmana, "It is clear that jests should not be had with cruel, low-class people. See how we have placed Sita in danger. O mighty brother! Take your sword and quickly disable this ugly, vile and wanton being. Do not slay her, as she is a woman."

Lakshmana drew his sword. He moved swiftly and sliced off the demon's long nose and pointed ears. Shurpanakha screamed in pain. She realized the brothers were formidable and quickly ran off into the woods. Her dissonant and horrible cries could be heard disappearing into the distance as she retreated. She bled profusely and raised her arms as she ran, roaring like a monsoon cloud.

The Rakshasi sought her brother Khara, who was the leader of the Rakshasas in the forest. Going before him drenched in blood and crying

Shurpanaka rushed furiously towards Sita.

loudly, she dropped upon the ground like a bolt from the blue. Khara sat surrounded by numerous powerful Rakshasas. He was holding a massive club. When he saw his sister's state, he frowned.

"What fool has done this to you?" the Rakshasha snarled. "Who has ignorantly goaded a poisonous serpent with his finger? Whoever has assailed you has fastened around his neck the noose of death. Tell me explicitly, O sister, who will today meet with his end at my hands?"

Khara stood up. He was proud and arrogant. He took the offense to his sister as a personal insult. "Who could possibly have been so bold as to provoke me?" he thundered. "Whose foaming blood will soak the earth today? Whose flesh will the vultures delightedly tear from his body when he lies slain by me on the battlefield? Quickly tell me the name and whereabouts of the wretch. I do not see a being in the three worlds of heaven, earth and hell who would dare challenge me, including Indra himself!"

Shurpanakha gathered her senses and answered her furious brother. She told him how she had seen Rama and Lakshmana in the forest, appearing young and tender yet obviously possessed of terrific strength. "These two brothers look like Gandharva kings," she said. "They are dressed like ascetics and seem to be in perfect control of their senses. I could not ascertain if they were humans, gods or some other divine beings. In their midst I saw a young lady of faultless form and beauty who shone like the moon. On account of that lady I was reduced to this state by those two brothers."

Shurpanakha asked Khara to kill them immediately. Holding a cloth to her wounded face she said, "I long to drink the blood of that slender woman as well as of those two brothers. Quickly accomplish my desire, dear brother. Go now to where they are staying and slay them in an encounter."

Khara at once ordered fourteen powerful Rakshasas to go and attack the two princes. He told his sister to accompany them. "Once these Rakshasas have made short work of those three, you may drink their gushing blood. Dragging their corpses on the field of battle, pierce their soft flesh with your long teeth."

Like clouds driven in a storm, the fourteen Rakshasas along with Shurpanakha sped toward Rama's hermitage. As they arrived they saw Rama seated at ease with Sita in front of their hut. Lakshmana was nearby chopping firewood. Rama saw the Rakshasas entering the area of his hermitage and he said to Lakshmana, "Wait here by Sita's side, O son of Sumitra. I shall quickly dispatch these evil marauders of the forest. Indeed, I have long awaited just such an opportunity."

Rama stood up and strung his bow in an instant. He called out to the Rakshasas, "Halt! Why do you seek to injure us? We live here peacefully, harming no one. Armed with my bow I aim to make this forest free from the likes of you. If you have any love of life, then flee now and never return. Otherwise stand on the battlefield and witness my show of strength."

The Rakshasas looked at Rama and laughed. Each of them was twice as tall as Rama. Their bodies were hugely powerful and they were equipped with fierce weapons. They considered Rama's threat comical. It was a rare human who could face even one Rakshasa in battle, and they were fourteen. Their leader replied harshly to Rama.

"Foolish human! What power do you have to face us in battle?" he said, his voice resounding around Rama's hermitage like a great drum. "You have angered our master Khara and thereby brought death upon your head. Hit by our iron clubs and swords, you will soon succumb to our might. Boast while you can, for in a moment you will give up your valor and indeed your life."

All fourteen Rakshasas rushed at Rama. They roared loudly and hurled large iron darts. Rama stood his ground. Releasing fourteen arrows he cut down the darts as they flew at him. The Rakshasas raised their swords and closed on Rama, their mouths open and their eyes bloodshot. Rama, moving more quickly than the eye could see, at once fired fourteen arrows one after another at each of the demons. His long, straight shafts were made wholly of iron with points sharpened on stone. They screamed through the air and hit each demon in the chest. Their hearts ripped apart, the Rakshashas fell to the earth, soaked in blood, like fourteen great trees felled by a storm.

Shurpanakha was astonished to see Rama's prowess. Surely he was not an ordinary man, nor his weapons those of an ordinary warrior. She ran away in fear and disappointment and fell again before Khara.

Khara looked at her in surprise. "Why are you still crying?" he asked. "I have already sent fourteen brave fighters to oblige you. Those Rakshasas are unassailable and devoted to pleasing me. Without doubt they will satisfy your desire. With me and my army as your protector why do you wail?"

Shurpanakha told her brother what had happened. She sat before him trembling, with blood encrusted on her face and clothes. Khara listened in amazement as she spoke.

"Although your fourteen fighters were angry and impetuous, they were quickly slain by Rama. He exhibited fearsome energy and power. His arrows were like rods of death. All fourteen Rakshasas are now prostrate upon the ground, killed easily by Rama. O Khara, my mind is possessed by terror when I think of Rama. Be my protector!"

Shurpanakha rolled about on the ground, beating her chest and shedding tears. She mocked her astonished brother, trying to goad him into battle with Rama. "What is the use of your idle boasts? Go out and face Rama in a fight. You will soon see your energy and pride humbled. Or if you actually do have any power, then let it be proved. Slay the two brothers today and avenge me and your fourteen servants."

Khara rose up like a serpent that had just been kicked. He screamed in anger. In the midst of the other demons he roared, "My fury is immeasurable! It cannot be held in check any more than a mighty ocean wave. By virtue of my strength I hold this human Rama of no account whatsoever. His life is already ended. Dry your tears, sister. Today you will see Rama sent to Yamaraja's abode. After I sever his head with my axe, you will drink his hot blood."

Shurpanakha was delighted. She praised her brother as a giant among the Rakshasas. Despite his boasts, however, Khara considered Rama a formidable opponent. He gave instructions to his brother and general, Dushana. "O valiant one, prepare my chariot. Fill it with every kind of weapon. Order all of the fourteen thousand Rakshasas under my command to prepare themselves for battle. I myself will march at the head of the high-souled Rakshasas to destroy the arrogant Rama."

Dushana fetched Khara's huge golden chariot, which shone like the sun and was drawn by a hundred spotted horses. It resembled a peak of the golden Mount Meru. In its center it had a large ensign pole made of cat's-eye jewels. The chariot was bedecked with small gold bells and its sides were studded with red and blue gems and embellished with carvings of alligators, flowers, trees, mountains, lions, tigers and flocks of birds. Many flags flew from tall poles and it had eight golden wheels. Khara indignantly ascended the chariot and, raising his sword, ordered the army to advance. With a great clamor the vast army sallied forth from the Janasthana forest. Holding clubs, darts, razor-sharp axes, javelins, maces, swords, scimitars, bows and sharpened discuses, they moved off, all shouting their battle cries.

Khara urged his charioteer to spur on the horses. The sound of the swift moving chariot filled the four quarters. The army followed behind Khara, some running on foot, some coursing through the air, others riding horses and still others on the backs of elephants. They were all seized with a desire to kill the enemy.

As they drove forward, however, they saw various evil omens. The sky above them was covered with a huge grey cloud which poured down blood-red water. Khara's horses stumbled and fell even on level ground. The sun appeared to be surrounded by a dark, red-edged halo. A gigantic, frightful vulture settled on Khara's ensign pole. Carnivorous beasts and birds cried in discordant notes and jackals yelled. The wind blew violently and thick darkness covered the four quarters. Stars flashed in the sky and meteors descended with roaring sounds.

Khara felt his left arm throbbing violently. His voice grew faint and his eyes were filled with tears. A sharp pain filled his head and he heard a loud ringing in his ears. Even though he saw these omens, however, out of folly Khara did not return. He laughed loudly and said to his followers, "Disregard these evil portents, O Rakshasas. They do not bother me in the least, although they are terrible and inauspicious. I am able to stand before Death himself. With my sharp arrows I can shoot the stars from the sky."

Khara railed foolishly, considering the omens to be sent by the gods, for whom he cared little. He raised his battle-ax and bellowed, making the earth shake. "How can I return without slaying Rama and Lakshmana, who are so proud of their strength? Today my sister will be gratified with the blood of those humans. I have never been defeated in battle and am unafraid even of Indra when he stands with the whole heavenly host."

The demons felt joy upon hearing Khara's valiant speech. As if bound and dragged by the noose of death they raced toward Rama's hermitage.

In the sky many rishis assembled to witness the encounter. Gods, Gandharvas, Siddhas and Charanas came in their aerial cars. The celestial beings, who were friendly to all, spoke together. "May all be well with the brahmins," they said. "Even as Vishnu conquered the foremost demons with his discus weapon, may Rama annihilate the Rakshasas."

While the gods looked on, Khara, surrounded by his powerful generals, rushed forward, eagerly seeking combat. The Rakshasas suddenly approached the two princes, even as a group of planets might rush toward the sun and the moon.

From his hermitage Rama had also seen the evil omens. "Behold these portents, O brother, foreboding the imminent destruction of the Rakshasas. These grey clouds are raining blood, while my arrows are shaking in their quivers. This undoubtedly means death will soon overtake the entire Rakshasa horde."

Rama felt his right arm throb and his mind becoming enlivened. Such favorable omens indicated his victory, although all around him he saw evil portents. He concluded that there would shortly be an encounter between himself and the Rakshasas, from which he would emerge victorious.

As Rama contemplated in this way he heard the distant crash of Khara's advancing army. The sound of beating drums and roaring Rakshasas filled the air. Quickly taking Sita by the hand, Rama said to Lakshmana, "Take this delicate princess to some safe cave on the mountain. Please don't hesitate."

Rama knew his brother was longing to confront the Rakshasas, but Sita had to be protected. Lakshmana obeyed Rama's order immediately and took

Sita to a concealed cave which was difficult to reach. After placing her inside he stood at the entrance holding his bow.

Rama put on the golden coat of mail Agastya had given him. He strapped on the two inexhaustible quivers of arrows and tied his sword to his belt. Standing rooted to the spot Rama looked like a brilliant flame suddenly appearing in darkness. He twanged his bow, which filled the quarters with its terrifying sound.

The gods looked on, eager for the Rakshasas to be destroyed. They gazed at Rama, who stood fearlessly before the charging Rakshasas. He resembled the invincible Shiva seized with fury, but he was single-handedly facing fourteen thousand terrible demons. Curious to see the outcome, the gods watched in anticipation.

As the Rakshasa army rushed toward Rama they seemed like a mass of dark blue clouds. The forest animals fled, terrified by the sound of the approaching army. Rama suddenly saw the Rakshasas coming at him from all sides. They screamed in fury and hurled their spears, darts and clubs. From his chariot Khara released a thousand flaming arrows and roared loudly.

Rama stood firm. He was pierced with numerous arrows and his limbs were smeared with blood. With his own arrows he cut down the rain of weapons. Axes, swords, lances and spiked maces were thrown at him with the force of a tempest. Rama whirled around and parried the weapons with his straight-flying arrows. As the foremost Rakshasas closed in on him, mounted on elephants, Rama seemed like Mount Sumeru assailed by thunderclouds. He did not feel afflicted even though struck again and again. Fully hemmed in on all sides, Rama looked like the sun screened by evening clouds.

The gods felt dejected and fearful, beholding Rama standing alone amid thousands of Rakshasas. They cried out, "Victory to Rama!" Understanding their fear, Rama resolved to kill the Rakshasas. He began shooting his gold-tipped arrows, three or four at a time, in all directions. With his bow drawn constantly into a circle, Rama moved with the speed of a hawk. An unbroken line of deadly shafts left his bow. Those arrows passed right through the bodies of a dozen Rakshasas before falling to the earth. Rama's arrows smashed the Rakshasas' weapons and chariots and tore apart their golden armors.

With their arms, legs and heads severed, countless Rakshasas fell lifeless to the ground. Rama was enraged. He shot innumerable shafts that could not be intercepted or endured and which killed the demons by the thousands. Horses, elephants and Rakshasas lay mangled on the ground. Crushed by Rama, the Rakshasas sent up a piteous wail.

Some fierce and brave Rakshasas, who were leaders of the army and possessed of terrible might, rushed at Rama, hurling their barbed missiles and iron pikes. But Rama smashed their weapons to pieces even as they flew at him. With razor-headed arrows he cut off the Rakshasas' heads. They toppled over like trees knocked down by a blast from Garuda's wings. The surviving Rakshasas, wounded and dispirited, ran to Khara for protection. Khara consoled them and ordered Dushana to attack Rama.

The mighty Dushana was capable of contending with ten thousand warriors at once. With a great roar he urged his chariot forward. The Rakshasas were encouraged to see their leader advance. Uprooting trees and lifting massive stone slabs, they charged once more at Rama.

The dreadful encounter between Rama and the Rakshasas was fearful to witness. Rama alone appeared like hundreds of warriors. The demons could not tell when he took out his arrows or placed them on his bow. They only saw him pulling his bowstring and an endless stream of arrows being fired. The demons rallied themselves and rushed at Rama all at once from every side. They hurled trees and rocks with great force. A diverse shower of weapons fell upon Rama, along with volleys of barbed arrows.

Smothered by weapons, Rama invoked the celestial missile presided over by the Gandharvas. As he released the weapon, all directions became covered by blazing shafts. Under a canopy of arrows, darkness enveloped the battlefield and the demons fell back in fear. Hundreds dropped dead at once. The ground was strewn with heads wrapped in turbans adorned with bright jewels. Severed arms still clutching weapons lay everywhere. Headless trunks spouting forth blood ran about wildly before falling to the ground. Everywhere were bodies of Rakshasas, horses and elephants, along with broken chariots, shattered weapons, rocks smashed into powder and trees torn to pieces.

The surviving Rakshasas were unable to face Rama. They stood frozen with fear. Dushana, seeing his army routed, sent up a great battle cry. He ordered his five thousand personal guards to attack. These Rakshasas had never known defeat. They were energetic and never turned their backs on the battlefield. With terrible impetuosity they incessantly assailed Rama on all sides. Fearful showers of scimitars, spiked maces, huge rocks and long swords fell upon Rama. Rama, becoming increasingly enraged, intercepted the volley of weapons with his arrows. Some weapons he struck down with his whirling sword as he slayed the Rakshasas, who fell like so many great oak trees cut at their roots.

Dushana then rushed toward Rama in his chariot, discharging innumerable arrows like thunderbolts. Rama released a razor-like arrow which split apart Dushana's bow. With four more shafts he killed the four horses drawing Dushana's chariot. He then released a crescent-headed arrow which severed the head of Dushana's charioteer. With three more arrows Rama pierced Dushana's chest.

The demon jumped down from his chariot holding a mace which resembled a mountain peak. The glowing club was studded with sharp iron pikes and belted with gold. It was capable of crushing the celestial army and smashing down the gates of their citadels. Dushana tightly grasped that weapon, which resembled a large serpent and was stained with his enemies' blood. Raising it above his head, he rushed at Rama with a huge roar.

As Dushana bore down on him, Rama lopped off his arms with a pair of arrows. Along with his bejeweled arms, Dushana's club fell to the ground. With a third crescent-headed shaft Rama cut off Dushana's head. Seeing Dushana slain, the gods exclaimed, "Excellent! Well done!"

Rama then swiftly dispatched all of Dushana's five thousand warriors to Death's abode.

Khara was practically stupefied with anger. Seeing his army all but annihilated he charged Rama. He sent ahead of him his own guards, a dozen of the mightiest Rakshasas. As one might greet guests, Rama greeted each of those demons with his sharp arrows. Those mystical shafts, given by Agastya, were encrusted with gold and diamonds and they blazed like fire. They emitted smoke and sparks as they sped through the air. Tearing into the demons' bodies, they split their hearts in two.

Khara looked on in astonishment. Who was this human? Besides his personal guard, the three-headed Trishira was the only other demon alive. Khara advanced toward Rama but Trishira checked him. "Simply command me, O lord, and I shall vanquish this man," Trishira said, raising his mace. "See him thrown down today by my might. This wicked one deserves death at the hands of all Rakshasas. I shall kill him now, or I will lay down my life on the battlefield. Then you may march against Rama yourself. Therefore, order me to fight."

Trishira, who was wishing only for death, received Khara's permission. He mounted his glittering chariot and rushed against Rama. The demon appeared like a moving three-peaked mountain. His volleys of arrows resembled a black cloud. As he charged at Rama, he roared like the crash of a gigantic drum. Rama met him with a profuse number of swift arrows. Although the arrows dug into Trishira's body he simply laughed. He hurled a golden lance, tipped with steel and fastened all over with many small bells. The lance glowed like fire as it sped toward Rama. Firing three arrows at once, Rama cut the lance into four pieces. It fell at his feet like four shining stars dropped from the heavens.

Trishira immediately shot three barbed arrows which struck Rama on the forehead. With blood gushing from his head, Rama appeared beautiful, like a mountain tipped with red oxide. Provoked by Trishira's attack, he laughingly shouted, "Just see this demon's strength and valor. But what will it avail him? His arrows, although fired with all his power, strike me like so many flowers. O demon, now see my prowess!"

Rama became excited. He shot fourteen serpent-like arrows into Trishira's chest. With four more shafts he killed the Rakshasa's four horses. Rama severed the head of his charioteer with a broad-headed arrow. He then struck down the demon's ensign and shattered his chariot. As Trishira leapt from his broken chariot, Rama struck him on the chest with an arrow imbued with the force of a thunderbolt. The Rakshasa stood stunned by that arrow. Rama quickly fired three razor-headed arrows which lopped off the demon's three heads, and the heads rolled on the ground with their golden earrings glittering. Trishira's body fell like an uprooted tree and the ground shook.

Khara felt fear enter his heart. His entire army was slain. Fierce Rakshasas who could face even the gods now lay dead on the battlefield. He looked at Rama, who stood as immovable as the Himalayan mountains. Still Khara urged his charioteer forward. He drew his great bow to a full circle and fired innumerable arrows at Rama. His blood-sucking shafts sped through the air like angry serpents. Khara then displayed his mystic power and filled the four quarters with arrows.

Rama at once countered Khara's shafts with his own. The sky was soon covered with arrows and not even the sun was visible. The two warriors fought furiously, the battle resembling a fight between a lion and an elephant. Like a driver striking a lordly elephant with a goad, Khara struck Rama with a number of fierce arrows. The demon stood firmly rooted in his chariot like Death himself with noose in hand.

Thinking Rama tired, the Rakshasa felt the moment opportune for his victory. He stood tall in his chariot and raised his frightful-looking bow. Rama, however, was no more concerned than a lion would be on seeing a small deer. Khara approached Rama as a moth approaches a fire. Displaying his dexterity, he split Rama's bow in two with a razor-faced arrow. With seven more shafts each resembling Indra's thunderbolt he pierced Rama at his vital points. He then covered Rama with another thousand arrows fired with blinding speed.

Hit hard by Khara's shafts, Rama's bright armor fell in pieces to the ground. With arrows piercing him all over his body, Rama became enraged. He shone on the battlefield like a smokeless fire. Rama raised Vishnu's terrible bow and darted toward Khara. He cut down the demon's ensign with a dozen gold-winged arrows. That gold ensign descended to earth like the setting sun. Khara continued to rain arrows on Rama, aiming for the vulnerable parts of his body.

Rama became more and more furious. Grasping his bow tightly, he fired six carefully aimed arrows. One struck the demon in the head, two in his arms and three in his chest. Rama then shot thirteen more shafts as if they were one. With one he cut the chariot yoke; with four he killed the horses; with the sixth he cut off the head of Khara's charioteer; the next four arrows shattered the chariot; the twelfth cut Khara's bow; and the thirteenth pierced him deeply in the chest. All this happened in a matter of seconds. Screaming in fury Khara leapt clear of his smashed chariot, and he stood on the ground, mace in hand.

Collected together in the sky, the gods and rishis applauded Rama, encouraging him to quickly slay Khara.

Rama then said to the Rakshasa, "You have pursued a ruthless and wicked course, O Rakshasa. With your vast army you have inflicted pain on all created beings. Only those who are sinful and hard-hearted perpetrate such acts. Therefore, you deserve to die at the hands of all beings, even as a venomous serpent should be killed."

Even though challenging the Rakshasa, Rama felt no malice toward the demon. As a ruler, he saw it as his duty to punish the wicked to correct them. Like a father correcting an errant son, he apprised Khara of his sins even as he meted out his punishment. He continued to castigate the Rakshasa in a booming voice that echoed throughout the forest. "One who continuously commits sinful acts soon sees the terrible results, O night-ranger. Just as a man who eats poisoned food soon dies, so one who performs sinful acts is quickly dragged down by his sins. I am here to punish sinners like you, O Khara. Pierced through by my arrows, you will today follow the path of those ascetics whom you have killed. Fight to the best of your ability; I will strike down your head like a ripe fruit!"

Khara laughed. He was impervious to any good instructions. Beside himself with anger, the demon roared back, "Having killed only ordinary Rakshasas, O human, why are you vainly ranting? Those who are truly brave speak nothing of their valor. Only the vulgar brag as you are doing, O disgrace to the royal class! Just as brass taken for gold reveals its baseness when placed in fire, so you have shown your baseness now that the hour of your death has arrived."

Khara raised his heavy mace. "Obviously you do not see me standing here wielding my mace and holding the earth, with her heavy load of mountains, in balance," he bellowed. "I am capable of killing you along with all the creatures in the three worlds. But enough talk! You have killed fourteen thousand Rakshasas. Now I shall wipe away their relatives' tears by slaying you."

Khara whirled the mace and released it for Rama's destruction. As it coursed swiftly through the air it shot out searing flames which burned the surrounding trees to ashes.

With twenty steel-tipped arrows Rama shattered Khara's mace to pieces. It fell to the ground like an angry serpent checked by mantras. Rama laughed at Khara. "Is that your best effort, O vile demon? It seems you are bold only in speech. Even as Garuda snatched nectar from the gods, so I shall snatch away your life. The earth will drink deeply your foaming blood. With your head severed you will lie closely embracing the earth, like a man embracing his lover."

Rama continued to taunt Khara, reminding him of the many sages he had killed. Closely watching the demon all the time, Rama said, "When you are laid low by me in protracted slumber, this forest will again become a happy abode for ascetics. Your wives and kinsmen will grieve today, as do the kinsmen of those you have slain. Try again, if you will, for your death is near."

Khara's anger was again incited by Rama's words. He foamed at the mouth. Looking around for another weapon he screamed, "Your mad talk is born of vanity alone. It is said that at the moment of death one cannot discern right from wrong. I see this to be true. Evidently your mind is thrown into confusion as your death approaches."

Khara saw a large tree nearby. He tore it from the earth and hurled it at Rama, exclaiming, "You are killed!"

Rama was unmoved. He met the fast-flying tree with a volley of arrows. It fell in splinters and a shower of leaves. Determining to kill the Rakshasa at once, Rama became violently angry. He was covered in perspiration, and his face shone brightly. He pierced Khara with a thousand arrows. Torrents of foaming blood ran from the demon's wounds like rivulets running down a mountainside. Khara was maddened and ran furiously at Rama. Taking a few steps backwards, Rama took out a shaft resembling Yamaraja's mace. He placed it on his bow and imbued it with the celestial force of Indra's thunderbolt. When the Rakshasa was almost upon him, Rama released the arrow. It struck Khara full on the breast with a sound like thunder. The demon fell to the ground, a huge burning hole in his chest.

As Khara fell dead, the Charanas sounded their celestial drums as a shower of flowers fell upon Rama, while the gods applauded, saying, "These violent Rakshasas, unslayable by any other, have been slain by Rama in less than two hours. His resolve and power exactly resembles that of Vishnu!"

The sage Agastya, standing in the sky at the head of a large group of rishis, also spoke to Rama, "At Indra's prompting and for this very purpose of killing the Rakshasas, Sarabhanga had you sent here. The rishis will now again inhabit this region to practice their austerities."

Lakshmana then came out of the cave where he had hidden Sita. Along with the gods and great sages, he praised Rama's achievements. Sita ran to her husband and embraced him tightly. She ran her cool hands over his many wounds, crying tears of joy to see him victorious over the Rakshasas. As night fell, thousands of carnivorous animals and birds descended on the battlefield. Rama and Sita retired into their hut and Lakshmana sat nearby, keeping a lonely vigil.

CHAPTER EIGHT

RAVANA'S LUST IS INCITED

There was one Rakshasa named Akampana who escaped from Rama. After seeing all his companions killed, Akampana fled to Lanka to inform Ravana of the news. Going before the lord of the Rakshasas, who was the scourge of all created beings and who took pleasure in giving pain to others, Akampana fell at his feet and said, "O great king, your entire army which was stationed in the Janasthana forest is now no more. Even the mighty Khara and Dushana are dead. Only I have somehow survived."

Ravana shook with anger when he heard this news. He gazed with his ten heads at the disheveled and fearful Rakshasa lying at his feet. The demon king rose up quickly from his golden throne. He was pitiless and rough, and he felt no compassion for the trembling Akampana. As he spoke he appeared about to consume Akampana in his rage. "Who, with his life all but ended, is responsible for this rash act?" he demanded. "O weak Rakshasa, what fool would dare antagonize Ravana? Even Indra, Kuvera or the great Yamaraja would not be safe if they offended me. I can burn fire and kill even Death himself!"

Under the protection of Brahma's boon Ravana had become utterly conceited and arrogant. He considered himself unconquerable. Even the the principal gods had been forced to retreat in battle against him. None of them could contradict Brahma's order. They would therefore not kill Ravana, even if capable. He had thus ranged the universe creating havoc and fearing nothing. He grabbed hold of Akampana. "Tell me the name of the wicked wretch who has slain my followers. You need not fear, for whoever it is will certainly die at my hands today."

Akampana was reassured by Ravana's words. At least the demon king was not going to vent his anger on him. He replied, "It was a man who carried out this astonishing feat of killing the Rakshasa army. He is a son of Dasarath named Rama. Tall and powerfully built, the prince possesses matchless strength. He alone annihilated the entire host of Rakshasas."

Ravana listened in disbelief. How was it possible? One Rakshasa against a large number of men was easy to believe, but a single man killing fourteen thousand Rakshasas was incredible. Ravana hissed like an angry snake. "Was this Rama accompanied by Indra and all the gods?"

Seeing Ravana's incredulity, Akampana went on describing Rama's power. "It is difficult to even look upon Rama as he stands on the battlefield. His golden-winged arrows fall in thousands with the force of a tempest. He has mastered the celestial weapons and looks like Death incarnate while fighting. Whichever way the Rakshasas ran, stricken with fear, they saw Rama standing in their front. No gods assisted him, O great one; he alone devastated your army."

Ravana snorted derisively. He would not be humiliated by any mere man. He thought of his own power. Thousands of years ago he had gone to the Himalayas, intent on performing austerities in order to gain unmatched material opulence. It was then that he approached Brahma. Surviving on air alone, he took only one breath a day. When he failed after a long time to propitiate Brahma, he began a sacrifice. He cut off his twenty arms one by one and offered them into the fire to please Brahma. When Brahma still did not appear, the demon began to cut off each of his ten heads and place them in the fire. At last Brahma appeared before him. Ravana then secured his boon, which he now recalled. He had not asked for immunity to humans, but how could any human even look at him, never mind fight with him? Even the gods fled in fear when he mounted his chariot for battle. This Rama sounded most unusual but, nevertheless, Ravana was proud of his hard-won strength and felt sure he could kill Rama without difficulty. Standing with his back to Akampana, he said, "I shall go immediately and finish this Rama."

Akampana was intelligent. He had already realized Rama's irresistible strength when he saw him fighting. The Rakshasa had thus stood back from the fight and made his escape. He considered that Ravana's chances of defeating Rama were slight. Therefore he advised his king. "When Rama is enraged, he cannot be tamed by any warrior. In my opinion he could, by the force of his arrows, tear down the very heavens with the sun, moon and constellations. He could stem the current of a flooded river or break down the shores of the ocean and deluge the entire world. With his arrows Rama could lift the earth itself. Indeed, that illustrious man could dissolve all the worlds and then create them again."

Ravana turned and looked pensively at Akampana. Clearly Rama was no ordinary man. Akampana was himself a powerful commander of the Rakshasa forces. He knew how to estimate the strength of the enemy. The Rakshasa king listened carefully as Akampana continued. "I do not think you

will be able to defeat Rama in battle, any more than a sinful man can attain
the regions of heaven. However, there is a way by which you can probably
overcome him. Listen as I tell you." Ravana sat on his throne and leaned
forward attentively as Akampana went on.

"Rama has come to the forest with his wife, Sita. I have heard she is
more beautiful than any goddess, female Gandharva or Apsara. From all
accounts she is a stunning jewel among women who cannot be compared to
any other. Surely she is dearer to Rama than his own life, as he has brought
her with him even to the lonely forest. O king, by means of some trick kidnap Sita. Rama will be overcome by grief and either die or be weakened
enough for you to defeat him."

Ravana pondered Akampana's suggestion. He liked the idea. Thanking
Akampana, he decided to go the next day to find Sita. He first needed to
seek the help of Maricha, the son of Tataka, who was well known for his
magical powers. Ravana mounted his chariot, which shone like the sun and
was drawn by great mules with the heads of fiends. As he sat in his golden
chariot, which had a white canopy spread over it, he was fanned by attractive maidens. His strongly built body was the color of glossy black gems.
With his ten heads and twenty arms he resembled a ten-peaked mountain.
As his chariot rose up to the sky, he cast his splendor like a thundercloud
with flashes of lightning.

The mighty Rakshasa moved swiftly ahead, surveying the scene below.
Heading north toward the Himalayas, he saw beneath him the beautiful
coastline. It was crowded with hermitages and graced with numerous woods
and lakes filled with lotuses. Many Siddhas, Charanas, Gandharvas and
other divine beings sported in great joy in and around those lakes. Thousands of Apsaras danced and played with the gods. Ravana saw in the sky
wonderful aerial cars, like white mansions, adorned with celestial garlands
and carrying the residents of heaven. From the cars came the sounds of
delightful music, which enlivened the heart and mind.

Passing over great forests, Ravana came at last to the northern mountains. There he found Maricha's hermitage. Defeated and punished by
Rama, Maricha had retired to the forest and dedicated himself to the practice of penance. He looked up in surprise as Ravana's chariot descended
from the sky. Maricha rose up quickly and greeted the overlord of all the
Rakshasas. "Welcome, great king," he said reverentially. "I hope everything
is well in Lanka. What has brought you to this lonely forest, inhabited only
by ascetics?"

Maricha offered Ravana celestial foods unknown to humans. He sat
him on a mat of kusha grass and served him personally. Ravana only looked
at the food and said to Maricha, "My entire army of Rakshasas led by the

powerful Khara has been destroyed by Rama, a son of king Dasarath, con-tending single-handedly and on foot. I am here to seek your assistance in abducting Rama's wife Sita. By this means only will I be able to overpower Rama."

Maricha stood up with a start. "By what enemy in the guise of a friend have you been tendered this advice?" he asked in horror. "Who have you offended so that they should suggest that you kidnap Rama's wife? That per-son clearly seeks to rid the world of the Rakshasas' lord. Using you as his tool, he desires to extract a fang from the jaws of a serpent. Who is it, O king, who has dealt you a powerful blow on the head, even as you slept peacefully?"

Maricha paced up and down, shaking his head. He had already been convinced of Rama's incomparable power. Hearing that he alone had killed Khara and his army only confirmed it all the more. He trembled as he con-tinued to speak. "O Ravana, you should not even think of staring at Rama. That lion among men, whose sharp teeth are his numberless arrows, easily kills small animals in the form of Rakshasas skilled in battle. Do not hurl yourself into the vast and dreadful ocean of the angry Rama, whose arms are its alligators and whose weapons are its tossing waves. Remain peacefully in Lanka, enjoying with your wives, and allow Rama to sport in the woods with his wife Sita."

Maricha spoke passionately. He continued to argue against the wisdom of Ravana's antagonizing Rama. Ravana listened thoughtfully. He again recalled his omission to ask Brahma for invincibility against humans. The Rakshasa king asked Maricha why he considered Rama so powerful. Telling him about the incident of Vishvamitra's sacrifice, Maricha replied, "I was ranging the earth, my body appearing like a mountain, with a huge iron club in my hand. My might exceeded that of a thousand elephants. I would roam about in the forest eating the flesh of rishis. Considering me more powerful than even the gods, the sage Vishvamitra sought only Rama as his protec-tor. Rama was a mere boy at that time. When I saw him in Vishvamitra's hermitage, I disregarded him, thinking him to be simply a child. However, with a single arrow Rama hit and threw me eight hundred miles into the ocean, and he slaughtered all of my powerful companions."

Maricha told Ravana how he returned to the forest again. He assumed the form of a sharabha, a fierce eight-legged carnivorous beast capable of killing even lions. In that form, accompanied by two other Rakshasas in sim-ilar forms, he continued to terrorize the rishis. One day he again came across Rama seated in his hermitage. Rakshasas in the form of sharabhas rushed at Rama, remembering their previous enmity. In an instant Rama had lifted and strung his bow, releasing three gold-tipped arrows which sped like thunderbolts. Maricha's two companions were killed outright. Maricha himself had dodged the arrows and retreated in fear. He then decided to abandon his life of antagonizing rishis and retire to the mountains.

Concluding his speech, Maricha said, "My fear of Rama has made me adopt this life of asceticism. Indeed, I live in continuous dread of that prince. In every tree I see Rama, clad in barks and wielding his bow, looking like Death personified standing with noose in hand. I actually see thousands of Ramas all around me. Indeed this whole forest appears to have turned into Rama. I see him everywhere, even in dreams and meditations. If someone speaks out a word beginning with 'R', I shake with terror. O king, under no circumstances shall I be convinced to again stand before Rama."

Ravana sat silently after Maricha stopped speaking. Out of pride, the Rakshasa king still felt capable of dealing with Rama. He was not going to be afraid of a mere human. However, seeing Maricha's reluctance to assist him, he decided to return to Lanka and await another opportunity. He felt sure that his path would soon cross with Rama's.

Soon after he arrived back at Lanka, Shurpanakha visited him. As he sat atop his seven-storied palace, surrounded by his ministers, his sister came and fell at his feet. Wailing piteously, she rolled about on the ground. She looked up at Ravana, who sat on his golden throne glowing like a fire fed with abundant fuel. His huge blackish body was covered by celestial robes, adorned with jeweled ornaments taken from the gods. His twenty arms, which could arrest the movement of the planets, looked like great tree trunks. They were marked by scars made by Indra's thunderbolt and the other weapons of the gods. He stared down at Shurpanakha with his twenty reddish eyes.

Ravana told his sister to get up and asked her why she was lamenting. Shurpanakha, displaying her mutilated face, answered him harshly. "Do you not see my disfigured face? What kind of protector are you, O king? I am a helpless woman and your sister, but I have been humiliated at the hands of a man. Do you not care for this, O powerful Rakshasa?"

The Rakshasi shook with fear and anger as she continued to address the demon king. "Everyone reviles a monarch who is licentious and overly attached to sensual enjoyment. Such a king, who fails to properly attend to his state affairs, is soon ruined. O Ravana, are you not aware that you are losing control of your territories? Having formed enmity with the gods and the brahmins, how can you expect to rest here in peace, enjoying the pleasures of life? You are childish and without any intelligence. You do not know what should be done and will therefore lose your kingdom before long."

Hearing such a searing rebuke in the midst of his ministers enraged Ravana. Short-tempered and intolerant, he replied angrily, "Tell me who has attacked you, wretched woman? Why are you afraid?"

Shurpanakha told Ravana what had happened. She also described to him Rama's annihilation of the Rakshasas exactly as Ravana had already heard it from Akampana. Ravana's curiousity about Rama was aroused. He said, "Tell me more about Rama. Why is he living in the forest? What is his strength and his weakness? How has he overpowered the unassailable Khara, Dushana and Trishira?"

After telling Ravana that Rama had been sent to the forest by his father, Shurpanakha described how she had personally witnessed Rama's power. "I could not see when Rama took up his arrows or bent his bow, which shone brightly like a rainbow. I only saw the Rakshasa army falling like hewn trees. The demons resembled a wheat field destroyed by a downpour of hailstones. I also saw by Rama's side his brother Lakshmana. He too seems exceptionally glorious and is clearly devoted to Rama. Indeed, he appears like Rama's second self. I hold these two brothers to be practically unconquerable in battle."

Shurpanakha, as a Rakshasi, possessed celestial intelligence. Like Akampana, she was able to recognize Rama's power, although she did not understand his identity. She spoke cunningly, wanting to incite her brother to confront Rama. "I saw by Rama's side his beloved wife Sita, whose beauty is hard to describe. Her dark eyes and hair contrast vividly with the hue and luster of her body, which resembles molten gold. Her breasts, hips and thighs are exquisitely shaped and she shines like another Goddess Lakshmi."

Shurpanakha knew that her brother was lusty. He had absolutely no regard for moral laws and took pleasure in enjoying other's wives. The Rakshasi went on describing Sita. "Her countenance is like the full moon. With her thin waist and delicate limbs, Sita is beyond compare. I have seen no woman like her on the face of the earth, be she a goddess, Gandharva or Yaksha. Any man embraced with delight by Sita will enjoy a happiness greater than that of Indra. Without doubt that peerless female, who is of a gentle disposition, would be a worthy consort for you, O king of demons."

Ravana's mind was captivated by her description. He considered how he might win her. Arrogantly he assumed that she would be attracted to him, the great and powerful king of the Rakshasas. But how could she be taken from Rama? Ravana was beginning to think that he needed to exercise caution in his approach to Rama. He listened as his sister continued.

"I wanted to snatch away Sita and bring her to you, O brother. But I was viciously attacked by the wicked and cruel-minded Lakshmana. No one but you, O mighty king, will be capable of taking Sita from Rama. Surely she should be your wife. Why not go the forest and see her wondrous beauty for yourself?"

Shurpanakha longed for revenge. Sita was the cause of her being mutilated. The Rakshasa woman wanted the princess to be taken from Rama so that both Rama and Sita would feel intolerable pain. Perhaps then Ravana would be able to overpower the grief-stricken Rama. Shurpanakha gazed imploringly at her brother. "Snatch away the incomparable Sita from Rama. Then, standing in the forefront of battle, defeat and kill that human along with his evil brother."

Ravana was convinced. He was already angered by Rama's killing of the Rakshasa army in Janasthana. Now here was his own sister, disfigured and humiliated by the human brothers. Ravana took that personally. He especially could not tolerate the sharp and taunting words Shurpanakha delivered in front of his ministers. He had to prove his power. And above all he wanted to have Sita. Thinking again of Maricha, he called for his chariot. This time he would not be deterred from his purpose. Maricha's refusal to help him was unacceptable. Ravana mounted his great chariot and rose up swiftly into the sky.

CHAPTER NINE

THE KIDNAPPING OF SITA

Again arriving at Maricha's hermitage, Ravana quickly sought him out. Maricha, clad in black deerskins and seated in meditation, spoke in surprise when he saw Ravana. "Why have you returned so soon, O king? I trust all is well in Lanka."

Maricha sat the Rakshasa king on a grass mat. He offered him food and drink, but Ravana waved it aside and said, "No doubt you recall my earlier request, O Maricha. I am here now to insist that you comply. Not only has Rama annihilated my army in the forest, but he has attacked and mutilated my sister Shurpanakha. He must by all means be punished. Prepare to leave. You will assist me in Sita's abduction."

Ravana had made up his mind. He told Maricha to come with him to Rama's hermitage. Once there he should use magic to assume the form of an enchanting deer. Ravana calculated that Sita, due to her womanly nature, would become captivated by the deer. She would then send Rama to capture it. As soon as Maricha had taken Rama to a distance, he should further use his magical powers to allure Lakshmana. Imitating Rama's voice, the Rakshasa should cry out in distress. When Lakshmana heard the cry he would come after Rama, leaving Ravana to abduct the unprotected Sita. Ravana spoke derisively of Rama, knowing that Maricha considered the prince formidable.

"This worthless human has been exiled by his father. Abandoning virtue, he caused my sister to be violently assaulted. He is a disgrace to the royal class and a threat to all beings. His time is now all but run out. Once he has lost his wife, his strength will be gone. I shall then make short work of him."

Maricha's face whitened. This was his worst fear. Ravana was bent on a purpose which would surely end in both their deaths. He stared at Ravana with unblinking eyes. His mouth felt dry and his limbs weak. He folded his palms and addressed the Rakshasa king in a trembling voice. "People speaking agreeable words are easy to find, O lord. On the other hand, rare are those who will speak words for one's good which are nevertheless unpalatable. O Ravana, you have clearly not heeded my earlier advice. You have not sought to establish for yourself Rama's actual power. This dereliction of your duty will lead to the extinction of the race of Rakshasas, there is no doubt."

Ravana's expression hardened. He was not interested in Maricha's advice. He listened impatiently as Maricha went on. "Rama has not been abandoned by his father nor is he devoid of virtue. Indeed, he is devoted to piety and truth. Listen as I tell you his history."

He told Ravana how the prince had gone to the forest to prove his father truthful. Both Maricha and Ravana understood that warriors derived power from virtuous behavior. Maricha made it clear that Rama was virtue incarnate. He again described Rama's power and the consequences of facing him in battle.

"Do not cast yourself headlong into the fierce fire of Rama blazing on the battlefield," Maricha beseeched the Rakshasa king. "Upon encountering, Rama you will relinquish for good your throne, your happiness and your very life. Rama's glory is immeasurable. You will no more prove able to remove Sita from Rama than you could take from the sun its brilliance. O Ravana, remain peacefully in Lanka. Do not bring about your own destruction, along with that of your relatives, friends and entire kingdom."

Ravana blazed up with anger. He cared nothing for Maricha's well-intended advice. Rising, he spoke harshly to the fearful demon. "Your words, like seeds sown in barren soil, are entirely fruitless. I cannot be deterred from my aim of kidnapping Sita. O ignoble Rakshasa, I did not ask you about the merits or demerits of my intentions. Indeed, a king should never be advised except when he requests such advice. I have told you what I require. All that remains for you to do is to carry out my order."

Ravana reiterated his idea. He knew that Maricha could, by his unique magical abilities, transform himself into the most wonderful-looking creature. He felt sure his plan would work. Speaking slowly and deliberately he told Maricha the consequences of non-cooperation. "Perhaps upon approaching Rama you will face some danger, but if you reject my request then death at my hands will be certain and immediate. Carefully weigh things in the balance of reason, O Maricha, and do what you feel is best."

Maricha tried one last time to sway Ravana from his plan. "Whoever advised you to confront Rama should be executed, O king, not me. That sinful person obviously desires only your imminent ruin. The minister who counsels violent measures against a powerful enemy is himself the enemy. Such advice will lead to the destruction of the counseled along with the counselor, and indeed the state itself."

Maricha saw that Ravana was silent, fixed in his purpose. Obviously his counsel was useless. Maricha then realized that his death was near. Understanding the inevitability of his fate, he spoke fearlessly to Ravana. "Being a slave to your senses, cruel and evil-minded, you have adopted this course of action. People with leaders who are not self-controlled cannot prosper any more than sheep protected by a jackal. A terrible and unforeseen calamity has arrived at Lanka's door, O king, which will bring an end to the city as well as to you. Therefore I simply pity you. I shall fulfill your order. It is better to be killed by the enemy than executed by the king. Take me as already slain at the very sight of Rama, and consider yourself dead with all your followers the moment you bear away Sita. Those on the verge of death cannot understand right from wrong. No advice can help them."

Maricha rose slowly and prepared to go with Ravana, saying, "Let us now depart." Ravana became joyous. He had heard little of what Maricha had said. The Rakshasa king was thinking only of Rama and, more particularly, of Sita. When he saw Maricha ready to follow his command, Ravana embraced him and said, "Here is my real Maricha. Before now, some other demon must have possessed you, robbing you of your valor. We shall proceed fearlessly on my chariot. Once you have bewitched Sita with your magic, you may go wherever you please. I shall do the rest."

The two Rakshasas got aboard the great chariot; the goblin-headed asses bore it away into the skies. Moving swiftly they soon arrived at the Dandaka forest. As they circled overhead, they saw below Rama's hermitage. They landed nearby and Ravana instructed Maricha, "Now work your wonderful magic, my friend. I shall wait here."

Ravana had no intention of immediately encountering the two brothers. He wanted first to steal and enjoy Sita, anticipating that this would weaken Rama. Ravana knew that Rama would soon come after him, but that would give him the opportunity to gauge the strength and weakness of Rama and his forces. The Rakshasa felt confident that he could confront Rama from the security of Lanka, surrounded by his powerful troops. After transforming himself into a human ascetic wearing matted locks and simple dress, he waited in the woods near Rama's hermitage.

Meanwhile, Maricha turned himself into a magical deer. His head was partly white and partly dark with horns like bright sapphires. The upper part of his snout had the hue of a red lotus, while the lower part had that of a blue lotus. His perfectly formed body had slender white legs, with hoofs like glossy black gems. The deer's belly was dark blue and its flanks golden. All over its shining skin were a number of jewel-like spots. Its tail resembled a rainbow and it glanced about with eyes that shone like diamonds.

In that deer form Maricha wandered slowly about. Other deer approached him but quickly ran in all directions, sensing that this was not actually a deer. Maricha strenuously controlled his Rakshasa nature, which was impelling him to kill and eat the deer which came near to him. Nibbling at leaves here and there, he went into the region of Rama's hermitage. Sita was outside the hut plucking flowers. She immediately saw the wonderful-looking deer.

Seeing that he had caught her attention, Maricha playfully came near to Sita and then moved away again. As the deer gamboled about, Sita's mind became enchanted. Her eyes opened wide in wonder as she surveyed the stunning form of that magical animal. It seemed to illumine the forest on all sides as it moved around with grace and elegance, making delightful sounds. Sita called out to Rama, "Come quickly, my lord, and bring Lakshmana! Here is a sight to behold."

Hearing Sita calling out again and again, the two princes came to her and saw the deer for themselves. Lakshmana was immediately suspicious. "This animal cannot actually be a deer. Never has such a deer, looking like a bright jewel, been seen anywhere upon the earth. This must surely be a Rakshasa come in disguise. I suspect it is probably Maricha."

Lakshmana recalled how Rama had spared Maricha's life previously. He knew the demon was capable of great mysticism and strongly suspected that some evil plan was afoot. But Sita was captivated. She interrupted Lakshmana. "O Rama, this wonderful animal has stolen my mind. Please fetch it to me. I would love to show it to my mothers-in-law and your brothers. When we return to Ayodhya we can keep it in the palace as a pet. I do not think that such a beautiful creature can be a Rakshasa. My lord, I must possess this gentle animal."

Sita repeatedly beseeched Rama to capture the deer, which remained close by. Rama felt obliged to satisfy his wife. He turned to Lakshmana. "Dear brother, see how this deer has created such a burning desire in Sita. I must try to catch it for her. I have never seen a deer like this anywhere before. It defies description. If, as you say, it is a Rakshasa in disguise, then it must be put to death. Therefore I shall chase it through these woods. Either I will bring it alive or, having determined it to be a Rakshasa, slay it with my sharp arrows. Perhaps then I may take its superb skin for Sita."

Rama asked his brother to stand close to Sita and guard her while he was gone. Like Lakshmana, he also feared an attack from the Rakshasas. He told Lakshmana that Jatayu was nearby and could assist him if necessary. Rama then fastened his sword to his belt and, after tying on his two quivers, he grasped his bow. He then went toward the deer, which bounded away into the woods.

In fear Maricha ran swiftly into the deep forest. Rama pursued him, moving through the trees with agility and speed. But Maricha kept ahead, sometimes appearing for a moment and then disappearing again. Acting exactly like a deer, he bounded high in the air and glanced about fearfully. In this way Maricha took Rama a long distance from his hermitage. Rama felt helpless, seeing the deer maintaining a constant lead over him. He stopped and leaned on a tree, exhausted and perspiring. He decided that Lakshmana's assessment was correct. This could not be an ordinary deer. He would have captured it by now if it were. Rama concluded that the deer was certainly a Rakshasa.

Spotting it emerging from a distant cluster of trees like the moon appearing from behind clouds, Rama took out an arrow. He imbued that shaft with celestial power and shot it at the deer. It streaked through the air glowing like fire, seeking out its target. In a moment it struck Maricha and pierced him in the heart. The Rakshasa bounded as high as a palm tree and screamed in pain. As he crashed to the ground he again assumed his actual form.

Rama ran toward the dying Rakshasa. Maricha saw him approaching and remembered Ravana's instruction. With his dying breath he let out a cry that could be heard for miles. Perfectly imitating Rama's voice, which he vividly remembered from their previous encounters, Maricha cried, "Lakshmana! Help me! Alas, Sita!"

With that final cry the Rakshasa died, his gigantic form covered in blood lying prostrate on the ground. Rama stood before the dead Rakshasa, filled with apprehension. This was obviously a plot by the demons. When Lakshmana and Sita heard that cry, they would become confused. Rama looked at Maricha's massive body. The voice of a Rakshasa was hundreds of times more powerful than that of a man. Rama had been chasing the deer for an hour at least and was miles from the hermitage. The only thing to do was to run back. Rama immediately began to retrace his steps. Thinking of Sita, he feared the worst.

At the hermitage Lakshmana and Sita had heard the Rakshasa's cry. Sita was struck with anxiety. Turning to Lakshmana, who stood calmly, she said, "Did you not hear your brother's cry? Surely he has fallen into the hands of the demons, even as a bull might be seized by a group of lions. O Lakshmana, go quickly to help Rama! My heart is all but stopping and my breath hardly comes. Please act swiftly!"

Lakshmana did not move. He remembered Rama's instruction to guard Sita. He did not at all fear for Rama and considered the cry to have been uttered by a demon. Sita became even more anxious when she saw Lakshmana unperturbed. Bewildered by fear, she spoke angrily. "O son of Sumitra, you are an enemy in the guise of a friend. It seems you are glad to see the plight of your brother. Surely you desire to possess me for yourself. Therefore you do not rush to Rama's aid. What is the value of protecting me when our leader is in such danger?"

Sita shook with fear and sobbed loudly. Lakshmana felt pained by her words and he tried to reassure her. "Your husband cannot be overcome by the gods or demons assembled in any number, O gentle princess. Rama cannot be killed in a fight by any created being, of that there is no doubt whatsoever. Be at ease. Rama will soon return, having slain the Rakshasa who assumed the form of the deer and who no doubt uttered that cry."

Lakshmana was certain that Rama was not in any danger. He could guess that the demon had been killed by Rama and had imitated Rama's voice as he died. After Rama had annilihated the Rakshasa army at Janasthana the Rakshasas must have formulated a plot for revenge. Lakshmana tried to explain this to Sita, but she became even more angry. She stood blazing like fire, her eyes red with fury. Because of her fear for Rama, she was confused. Despite her respect for the virtuous and gentle Lakshmana, who had never once looked her in the face, her anxiety for Rama made her rebuke him harshly.

"O ignoble and merciless Lakshmana! It is obvious that you care nothing for your brother. Indeed you are happy to see him in peril. I can understand that you have been concealing your true nature. Posing as Rama's friend you have all the while been coveting me. Your sinful desire shall never be fulfilled. I shall give up my life even in your presence. Having become Rama's wife, how could I accept an ordinary and wicked man like you?"

Lakshmana was deeply hurt. Sita was as worshipable to him as Rama. He could not even imagine what she was suggesting. His mind raced, confounded by agony. He could not remain with Sita while she was in this mood. Her words were unbearable. How could she make such accusations? He had to look for Rama. But what would happen to Sita? Fearful and angered by Sita's castigation, Lakshmana controlled his mind and replied, "Your words pierce me like a heated steel arrow. I cannot argue with you since you are a deity to me, O princess. Alas, it seems that the nature of women is to be fickle and given to sentimentality. Although I feel sure I am right, I must nevertheless follow a dangerous course, driven by your sharp words. I shall depart and search for Rama, but I fear I may not find you here when I return."

Sita continued to cry out, saying to Lakshmana, "I shall never remain with another man in Rama's absence! I would sooner drown myself in the river, fall from a high precipice or enter blazing fire."

Lakshmana was enraged by Sita's insinuations. He tried consoling her, but she would not say anything. He prayed to the forest deities to protect her. Then, bowing to her with folded hands, he left to look for Rama, Sita's words still ringing in his ears.

As soon as Lakshmana had gone Ravana came out of hiding. In a human form he approached Sita, who was without Rama and Lakshmana, even as thick darkness overtakes dusk when devoid of the sun and moon. He saw the youthful princess sitting and weeping in front of her hut. As he came near, all the animals fled in all directions. Even the breeze did not blow and the river slowed her swift current till she almost stopped flowing. Appearing like a holy man, Ravana was like a deep well covered by grass. He looked intently at Sita, marveling at her beauty. As he gazed at her the demon was pierced by Cupid's arrow. Continuously chanting Vedic mantras he moved close to Rama's beautiful consort. In his guise as a brahmin ascetic he stood before Sita and praised her in various ways.

"O most beautiful lady, you possess the splendor of gold and silver adorned with celestial gems." Ravana spoke poetically, his deep voice resonating around the forest grove. "Your form is radiant and your face, eyes and delicate limbs are like so many blooming lotuses. Are you a goddess or an Apsara descended from heaven? Your body is perfectly formed and your face resembles the full moon. With your dark eyes and full lips playing over teeth resembling rows of pearls you have captured my heart. My mind is stolen away by your beauty, which is surely unmatched anywhere in the three worlds."

Ravana thought that by praising Sita he would attract her to him. His mind was full of lust. With wide opened eyes he continued, "Why are you residing in a dark forest, frequented by wild beasts and haunted by Rakshasas? You deserve to live at the top of a magnificent palace of gold. Sweet-smelling gardens should be your playground, not fearful forests. Tell me, O charming lady, who are you and who is your protector? Are you the consort of some powerful deity? Why are you alone in this dangerous region?"

Sita looked up and saw Ravana dressed as an ascetic. She had encountered numerous brahmins during her stay in the forest and she was not surprised to see this one. The pious and open-hearted princess offered Ravana a seat and water to wash his feet. Acting perfectly in accord with religious codes, she fetched food from the hut and placed it before him, saying, "You are welcome."

Ravana watched her closely. He was stunned by her grace and elegance. He made up his mind to carry her away by force if necessary. As she tended to her unexpected guest, Sita looked around for signs of Rama returning, but she saw only the vast green forest. She began to reply to

Ravana's questions. "I am the daughter of Janaka, the king of Mithila, and my name is Sita. I am the consort of the high-souled Rama, a prince of Ayodhya. With him and his powerful brother Lakshmana I reside here peacefully."

With a guileless mind Sita told him how she and Rama came to be living in the forest. She explained everything in brief and then said, "Soon my husband and his brother will return, bringing with them varieties of forest produce. Rest here awhile and they will no doubt sumptuously entertain you. But tell me, O sage, who are you and how do you come to be wandering this lonely forest?"

Ravana decided to reveal his true identity. He stood up and replied proudly to Sita, "I am Ravana, the celebrated ruler of all the Rakshasas. The gods, demons and human beings are struck with terror upon hearing my name, O Sita. Now that I have seen you, O most beautiful woman, I can no longer find delight in my own consorts. Become my foremost queen! Roam with me at ease in my golden city, Lanka. You will live in a splendid palace adorned with jewels, and five thousand handmaidens will wait upon you."

Sita was shocked. She became enraged and said to the Rakshasa, "I have taken a vow to follow Rama, who is as unshakeable as a great mountain, as powerful as Indra and as wise as Brihaspati. I cannot be swerved from Rama's service. He is virtuous and always true to his word. I am dedicated to Rama, who will never abandon his devoted servant. I belong to that Rama who is like a mighty lion and destroys his enemies with ease and speed. How have you, O Ravana, a jackal, been so brazen as to covet me?"

Sita looked disdainfully at Ravana, who stared at her lustfully. She felt sickened. What a disgusting creature! How could he even imagine that she would go with him? How disgraceful that he should pretend to be a brahmin ascetic, the holiest of men. She spoke with fury. "You could no more touch me than you could the sun's fiery orb. Your desire is sure to bring about your death, O vile Rakshasa. You seek to extract a tooth from the jaws of a powerful and hungry lion. You wish to carry in one hand the massive Mount Mandara. You desire to swim across the ocean, having tied around your neck a stone slab. You who would steal the beloved consort of Rama are trying to snatch away the sun and moon with your bare hands."

Sita reproached Ravana again and again. She scorned and derided him with sharp words, warning him against his evil intentions. "After stealing me away, where will you go? How will you retain me while Rama stands on the battlefield, bow in hand? Your pathetic might is nothing against that of Rama's. Next to Rama you are like a crow compared to Garuda."

Sita shook like a sapling caught in a storm. She turned away from Ravana and prayed for Rama to return quickly. The Rakshasa was provoked by her harsh words and he began to boast about his own strength. "I have won from Kuvera the celestial city of Lanka, chasing him away by my own power. Why, I have even taken from him the Pushpaka, his celebrated and beautiful airplane which can range anywhere according to one's will. Wherever I stand, the sun withholds its fierce rays, the wind blows gently and the rivers become still and calm."

Ravana tried to intimidate Sita. He was annoyed that she was not interested in him. How could she remain attached to Rama, an insignificant human, when Ravana, the immensely powerful king of the Rakshasas, sought her favor? Surely she did not know of his strength and exploits. Even the gods feared his angry gaze. And as well as power, what about his unlimited opulence? Ravana described the city of Lanka, with its innumerable gold palaces.

"Come with me to Lanka, O princess. There you will enjoy human and celestial delights you have never even imagined. You will soon forget the mortal Rama, whose life is well-nigh ended. Rama has lost everything and, having no power, lives in fear in the forest. I can dispose of him with a single finger. By your good fortune Ravana is here in person to beseech your love. Accept me, O Sita, and abandon the worthless Rama."

Sita could not even look at Ravana. She clenched her fists and flushed a deep crimson, sharply rebuking the demon. She told him that once he had laid hands on her, he would soon die at Rama's hands. Crying and calling for Rama, she moved away from the Rakshasa. Ravana became furious. He struck one hand against another and roared. The Rakshasa then assumed his original form with its ten heads and twenty arms. He moved closer to Sita. "Look at me, O proud lady! I can lift up the earth, drink the ocean and kill even Death himself."

Ravana's red eyes burned like fire. Wearing a red robe and bedecked with fine gold ornaments, he looked like a dark cloud lit up by lightning. He had lost all patience and he spoke angrily to the trembling Sita. "Here is a husband fit for you, O charming one. I shall take good care of you and never do anything you dislike. Leave aside the useless Rama and serve me. You do not deserve a life in the forest. Give up your affection for the soon-to-die human and become the queen of Lanka."

Ravana had no intention of leaving her behind, but Sita was clearly not going to go with him willingly. He would have to force her. The demon grasped hold of the delicate Sita, taking her hair in one hand and her legs in another. Seeing him looking like Death, with mighty arms and sharp teeth, the forest deities all ran away. At that moment Ravana's chariot appeared close by, drawn by its ugly mules. Ravana took Sita in his arms, scolding her sharply, and he placed her in the chariot. Sita writhed in

Ravana's grasp. As the chariot rose up she called for Rama at the top of her voice. Distracted with grief and anguish, Sita wailed like a mad woman.

"O Lakshmana, where are you? I am being seized by a vile Rakshasa. O Rama, your life has been sacrificed for virtue. How then do you not see me being unrighteously carried away? You always chastise the wicked. Why then do you not punish the evil Ravana?"

Sita began calling to the trees. She cried to the river and forest deities, to the animals and the birds, asking them all to tell Rama what had happened. Turning to Ravana she said, "The fruits of sinful deeds are not immediately received, O Rakshasa, but in time they destroy the perpetrator to his very roots. O Ravana, your time is all but over. Rama will certainly recover me and end your life."

As the chariot rose higher, Sita looked down and saw Jatayu perched on a large tree. She called out to him. "O bird, help me! I am being seized by an evil Rakshasa! Don't try to stop him. He is too powerful. Quickly find Rama."

Jatayu heard Sita and looked up. He saw the chariot with Ravana and Sita on board. From the tree he called out to the Rakshasa, whom he immediately recognized. "O Ravana, I am the king of the vultures, Jatayu. I possess might and am devoted to virtue. I shall not allow you to carry away Sita in my presence. You who are also a king should not bear away another's wife against the eternal codes of morality."

Jatayu flew up from his perch, continuously reproaching Ravana and reminding him of what had happened to Khara and Dushana. Soaring upwards, he kept pace with Ravana's chariot. He spoke in a loud voice, disturbing the demon's mind. "Release Sita now, O evil-minded one! You have placed the noose of Death around your neck. You have tied a poisonous snake in your cloth. O fool, your act will bring you nothing but suffering. If Rama were here, you would no more be able to carry away Sita by force than one could alter a Vedic text by the force of logic."

Jatayu was infuriated. He challenged Ravana. "I am here to stop you, O night-ranger! Stand and fight. Although I am old and weak I cannot watch you take away this princess. Struck by my bill you will fall from your chariot like a ripe fruit from a tree."

When Ravana heard Jatayu's challenge he veered his chariot toward him and rushed angrily at the king of birds, raining him with blows from his twenty arms. But Jatayu swooped and avoided Ravana's attack. Then he assailed Ravana with his sharp talons. As the great bird screamed, Ravana roared. The clash between the two combatants was tumultuous and frightening to witness. It resembled an encounter between two winged mountains. Ravana fired terrible-looking arrows that sped through the air like streaks of fire. Jatayu was suddenly struck all over with hundreds of sharp arrows. Ignoring his wounds, he rushed at Ravana, inflicting many wounds on him with his beak and claws. Jatayu then broke Ravana's large jewel-encrusted bow, which fell glittering from the sky. Ravana swiftly strung another bow and shot thousands of arrows at Jatayu, entirely covering his body. The king of birds looked as if he had found shelter in a nest. He shook off the network of arrows with his wings and again flew at Ravana's chariot. The great bird tore off the heads of Ravana's mules. With a blow from his bill he killed the charioteer. Swooping again and again, Jatayu then smashed Ravana's chariot. As his chariot fell in pieces, the Rakshasa grabbed hold of Sita and dropped to the ground.

The gods, witnessing the battle from above, applauded Jatayu. Then Ravana again rose into the air. In two of his arms he held Sita, while in another hand he clutched his fierce-looking sword. He faced Jatayu, who again rebuked the demon.

"Your act is condemned by all virtuous men," thundered Jatayu. "It is not even heroic. You are simply a thief, and like a thief you will be caught and punished by Rama. O cowardly one, how do you hope to survive? Surely it is only for the annihilation of the Rakshasas that you have stolen Sita. Wait a short while and Rama will return. Or fight me now, Ravana, for I shall never allow you to leave with Sita."

Jatayu flew at Ravana. He tore the demon's back with his talons and struck his heads with his beak. The fearless bird pulled the Rakshasa's hair and dragged him about. Ravana shook with anger. His eyes blazed and his lips twitched with indignation. Tormented by Jatayu he decided to kill him. He rushed at the bird and struck him violently with his fists. Jatayu then tore off Ravana's ten left arms. Even as the arms fell to the ground, ten more grew immediately in their place, like serpents coming out of an ant hill. The Rakshasa then placed Sita on the ground. He darted toward Jatayu and began striking him with his fists and feet. Taking his razor-sharp sword, he lopped off Jatayu's wings. The great vulture fell on the ground, dying. With his white breast reddened with blood, he resembled a large cloud tinged by the setting sun. Sita cried out and ran toward him. Gently stroking his head, she called out to Rama.

"My lord! Where are you? Do you not see this terrible calamity? The sky is filled with evil omens. Come quickly. Here lies the brave Jatayu, mortally wounded on my account. O Rama! O Lakshmana! Save me!"

Sita cried bitterly. From the sky, Ravana saw that his adversary was overcome. He descended swiftly and went toward Sita. She ran away and embraced a tree, crying out, "Hold me, trees, hold me!"

Ravana grabbed her forcefully by the hair. In the grip of his own destiny he dragged Sita away as she cried out, "Rama! Rama!" again and again. Pulling her onto his lap, Ravana rose up into the sky.

At that time the wind stopped blowing and the sun appeared lusterless and dull. The whole creation seemed out of order and a dense darkness enveloped the four quarters. Brahma saw by his divine vision that Sita had been seized violently by Ravana and he said to the gods, "Our purpose is accomplished!" The great sages in the forest also saw Sita being taken. Knowing Ravana's destruction to be imminent, they felt simultaneously agonized and joyful.

Ravana held Sita tightly and flew toward Lanka. With her body shining like molten gold and adorned with jeweled ornaments, Sita looked like lightning against a black cloud. Ravana appeared like a dark mountain illumined by fire as he traveled with haste toward his city. Sita's face pressed against Ravana, resembled the full moon splitting a cloud. She burst into tears again and again and called out for Rama. Lotus petals fell in showers from her crushed garland. A bejeweled golden anklet dropped from her foot like a circular flash of lightning. Her necklace of pearls fell from her breast, appearing like the Ganges descending from the heavens.

As Ravana soared over the treetops the leaves shook violently, seeming to say to Sita, "Don't be afraid." Forest ponds, with their faded lotuses and frightened fishes, appeared sorry for the princess. Lions and tigers, along with birds and other beasts, angrily rushed behind, following Ravana's shadow. The mountains, their faces bathed in tears in the form of rivulets and with arms upraised in the form of peaks, seemed to scream as the wind from Ravana's passage rushed over them. Seeing Sita held in the grasp of the ten-headed monster, the forest deities wept and their limbs trembled with fear.

Sita, her face pale and her eyes reddened, chastised Ravana. "Have you no shame at all? Resorting only to stealth and trickery, you have stolen away the chaste wife of another. O coward! You have killed the old and helpless Jatayu and now you flee in fear from Rama. You are proud of your valor, but people throughout the world will scorn and deride you, O vile demon!"

Sita struggled in Ravana's grip. She preferred to fall to earth and die than be carried away by him. She censured Ravana continuously, goading him to turn and fight with Rama and Lakshmana. The tearful princess told him that even if he carried her to Lanka she would soon die, being unable to see Rama. Ravana, ignoring her sharp words, continued to bear her away through the skies.

As they flew, Sita looked down and caught sight of a group of large monkeys sitting on a mountain peak. She pulled off her silken head covering and quickly bound up her golden bracelets and other shining jewels, dropping the bundle as Ravana flew over the monkeys. Sita hoped they would meet Rama and show him the jewels. He would then know which direction Ravana had taken her. The Rakshasa king did not notice Sita's cloth falling to earth.

The monkeys caught sight of it as it fell. They looked up and saw Ravana speeding past with the beautiful princess held in his arms. The Rakshasa coursed through the air like an arrow shot from a bow. Delighted in mind, he raced toward his own destruction. Crossing over the fearsome ocean, which teemed with sharks and other fierce aquatics, he went in the direction of his celestial city. Even as he flew overhead the wind died and the ocean waves were stilled out of fear of him.

The many Siddhas and Charanas in the sky who witnessed Ravana's flight with Sita said, "This marks Ravana's end."

Soon Ravana arrived in Lanka and entered his palace, going straight to the inner section where he kept his many wives. There he spoke with the Rakshasas who were entrusted with guarding his women. "Take good care that no man looks upon Sita. Give her every item of enjoyment the moment she asks. Gold, gems, pearls, silks--whatever she may desire should be provided. Those who slight or upset her, knowingly or unknowingly, must not hold life dear."

Ravana then left and went to his own rooms. He called for eight of his most powerful generals. After praising them for their strength and valor, he said, "Armed with various weapons, go at once to the Dandaka. Seek out Rama and observe him closely. Be wary, for Rama has single-handedly destroyed the entire army I had stationed in that forest. Because of that I feel a rage that burns my insides. That rage will only be calmed when Rama lies dead, slain by me. Therefore you should learn of Rama's strengths and weaknesses. Report these to me and I shall then do what is required."

Ravana gave them detailed instructions, repeatedly extolling them with pleasant words. The powerful Rakshasas then made their bodies invisible and set out toward the Dandaka forest. Ravana, having set up a bitter enmity with Rama, felt secure and rejoiced within himself. He decided to visit his inner quarters where Sita was lodged. Stricken with love for the dark-eyed princess, he hurried to see her.

Ravana found Sita bathed in tears and fallen to the floor amid the Rakshasis. She resembled a female deer beset by a number of hounds. Even though she was unwilling, Ravana had her forcibly brought as he showed her his palace. It comprised a large number of shining buildings supported by pillars of ivory, gold and crystal. The palace was astonishing to behold and highly pleasing to the mind. Ravana took Sita up the magnificent central stairway of gold, showing her the vast extent of his home. The walls were set thickly with celestial gems, which threw off a brilliant luster, lighting the whole palace. On each level of Ravana's palace were differently furnished rooms, meant to evoke different moods. The palace resounded with the delightful music of kettledrums and other instruments. Various scents filled the air. There were fountains and ponds surrounded by flowers of every description.

Hoping to seduce her, Ravana spoke to Sita. "I have under my control millions of Rakshasas. Ten thousand of them are my personal servants. My city extends for eight hundred miles and is constructed everywhere with gold and gems. Everything I have I now give over to you, O lovely princess. You are more dear to me than life. Become my wife and the queen of all the women who are mine. What is the use of remaining attached to Rama, who is deprived of his kingdom, given to austerities and travels the earth on foot?"

Ravana tried at length to impress Sita. He bragged of his power, telling her how he could conquer even the gods in heaven. Ravana also derided Rama in various ways, saying that he would not be able to reach Lanka even in thought. Indeed, Ravana boasted, there was not a being anywhere in the three worlds who would now be able to rescue Sita from Lanka. "Therefore, O delightful lady, share with me all these celestial pleasures. Range freely with me in the Pushpaka. Cast aside any thought of Rama, whose life is soon to end, for I alone am a husband worthy of you."

Sita sat sobbing for some time, not looking at Ravana. She had no desire to speak to him, but seeing the Rakshasa's insistence she composed herself and addressed him reproachfully. "O sinful demon, had you dared lay hands upon me in Rama's presence, you would now be lying prostrate on the battlefield. Give up your vain boasting! Your life has all but ended. Your royal fortune is gone. Gone too is your strength and intelligence. Soon a shower of arrows will rain down upon Lanka, annihilating the Rakshasa forces. Thanks to you, O vile Rakshasa, this city will soon be filled with weeping widows."

Sita spoke furiously to Ravana. How could he even dare to suggest that she abandon Rama for him? He was like a crow trying to steal a sacrificial offering from amid an assembly of brahmins. Her mind would not for a single moment contemplate a sinful act. It was only with deep regret that she looked at Ravana at all. Obviously, virtue was entirely unknown to him. He could imprison her or kill her as he liked, for she had no use of life without Rama.

Hearing Sita's stinging words, Ravana's bodily hair stood on end. He spoke threateningly. "O most beautiful lady, hear my warning. If you do not yield to me within one year, you shall be killed by my cooks and served to me as my meal."

Ravana then stormed away. He instructed the Rakshasis to break her pride. "By fearful threats alternated with soft words, tame this lady as one would tame a wild animal!"

He told them to keep her in his beautiful gardens, which were filled with trees laden with fruits and flowers. They should guard her carefully and continue to inform her of Ravana's power and glory. Gradually her mind would change. Otherwise she would be put to death. Ravana left in anger, his footsteps causing the earth to vibrate.

Placed in the midst of a grove of trees, Sita fell weeping to the ground. She felt her limbs overpowered with grief and could find no peace of mind. Threatened by the Rakshasa women, who had misshapen faces and deformed figures, she was like a young deer fallen into the clutches of tigresses. With her mind rapt in thought of Rama, she fell unconscious, oppressed by fear and sorrow.

CHAPTER TEN

RAMA'S TERRIBLE DISCOVERY

Rama raced toward his hermitage. He was filled with foreboding. As he crashed through the bushes he heard a jackal's fierce yell behind him. Recognizing the evil omen he became even more anxious. Had Sita been devoured by Rakshasas? Lakshmana must have left her when he heard Maricha's cry; Sita would have insisted upon it. The Rakshasas had plotted successfully. Surely they had now taken Sita.

Rama saw other frightening omens and his mind became even more distressed. As he rushed through the forest he suddenly saw Lakshmana coming toward him. Rama ran to him and took hold of his hand. He spoke sternly. "My dear brother, what have you done? Why have you abandoned the helpless Sita? Without doubt she is now dead or stolen by the Rakshasas."

Rama pointed out to Lakshmana the various omens. He told him about Maricha's trickery. It was now obvious. The Rakshasas had arranged everything so they could abduct Sita. Tears flowed from Rama's eyes as he thought of his wife. If she were killed, he would give up his own life. Desperately he asked Lakshmana, "Did you fail to protect her? Where is that gentle lady who willingly gave up every happiness to follow me here? Where is Sita now? You should know that I cannot live without her for even a moment."

Feeling dispirited, Lakshmana replied, "I did not leave Sita willingly. Urged by her strong and painful words I came looking for you. She would by no means allow me to stay with her. Forgive me, my lord."

Lakshmana explained everything to Rama--how he had tried hard to convince Sita of Rama's invincibility, how she had accused him of having ulterior motives--but Rama only became angry and reprimanded him. Why had he taken Sita's words seriously when she was overwhelmed by sentiment? Why had he allowed himself to fall prey to anger? He had failed to carry out Rama's order. Now they would surely meet calamity. Rama turned and continued to run toward his hermitage, his mind fixed on Sita.

As Rama ran he felt a tremor run through his limbs. His left eye throbbed violently. Greatly perturbed by these baleful omens, Rama crashed through the forest. He seemed almost to fly, oblivious of the creepers and bushes which lashed him. Breaking into the clearing where he had his hermitage, he ran about wildly, looking for Sita. He called her name again and again, but on finding no sign of her, his heart sank.

Rama examined his hut and the surrounding grounds closely. It resembled a lotus flower blighted by winter and deprived of its charm. The trees seemed to cry as they creaked in the wind. The flowers appeared faded and dull. Deer and birds were restless and ill at ease. Rama saw blades of kusha grass scattered around, along with flower petals fallen from Sita's garland. He wailed loudly. "Surely Sita has been snatched away. Or perhaps she lies dead somewhere. Or has she gone out playfully, hiding now in sport?"

Rama searched frantically, but Sita was nowhere to be found. He feared the worst. This was surely the work of the Rakshasas. Even now Sita must be in their clutches. Rama imagined Sita as she was carried away. She must have cried out for him in plaintive tones. As she was borne upwards, her beautiful face streaked with tears, fear would have gripped that timid princess. Perhaps at that very moment she was being devoured by demons who were cutting open her soft neck and drinking her blood.

As Rama ran from tree to tree, his eyes red from sorrow, he appeared almost crazy. He questioned the trees, "O Kadamba, O Bilva, O Arjuna tree, where is Janaka's frail daughter? Is she alive or not?"

In the madness of grief he spoke to animals, the river, the sky and the earth itself, but they all remained silent, heightening Rama's anguish. The forest and river deities, remembering Ravana's frightful form, were petrified with fear and could make no reply. As Rama gazed around, it seemed to him that he saw Sita in the sights of the forest. The yellow flowers looked like her silk garment. The creepers flowing in the wind became her limbs. Rama thought he saw his beloved wife everywhere. He ran toward her crying, but found only the desolate and echoing forest.

Rama rebuked himself for leaving Sita. What would he say to Kaushalya? How could he even look at Janaka, that ever-truthful monarch? Rama felt as if he would die. But then what would his father say upon seeing him arrived in heaven, killed by grief? Surely the emperor would reproach him for becoming a liar by not completing the term of his exile.

Rama lamented piteously. "I shall never return to Ayodhya. Kaikeyi may rejoice, her purpose fulfilled. O Lakshmana, you should embrace Bharata and tell him to long rule over this wide earth, for Rama is no more. Without Sita I shall not accept even heaven, what then of this world? With

Sita's death has come mine. For failing to protect that gentle princess I shall reach unending regions of hell."

Rama fell weeping to the ground. He censured himself in many ways. Surely this awful misfortune was the result of sinful acts performed in a past life. It was undoubtedly his destiny. Such suffering—the loss of the kingdom, separation from his loved ones, the king's death, and now Sita's loss—could only have been caused by his own past evil deeds. Rama tossed about in pain.

Seeing Rama's agony, Lakshmana, himself gripped by despondency, approached his brother and said, "Do not give way to despair, O mighty prince. Men of your caliber are never bewildered by even the greatest disaster. We shall yet find Sita. She cannot be far away. It is less than an hour since I left her. Let us continue our search."

Rama composed himself and got up. He sighed and gazed about, wondering which way to go. As he looked at the seat outside his hut, he remembered how he had sat there with Sita by his side—how they had talked and laughed together; how she had teased him, pretending to be hurt by his words, or cajoling him to fetch a particular flower from deep in the woods. As he thought of his lotus-eyed wife, Rama's grief rose in repeated waves.

A couple of large deer came close to the brothers. Rama asked if they had seen Sita. The deer then stood with their heads pointed toward the south. Rama and Lakshmana took that as a clue and sped off in that direction. They soon came upon a trail of flowers fallen on the ground. Rama dropped to his knees and picked up the petals. They were from the braid on Sita's hair. He cried out in a resounding voice, "Sita! Sita!"

The two brothers kept running. Suddenly they saw enormous footprints, probably of a Rakshasa. Near to it were Sita's footprints going here and there as she evidently ran in fear. As they looked about they found a huge bow lying in pieces, along with many fearsome arrows tipped with blue steel barbs. A chariot lay smashed there, still yoked to great mules with goblin heads, some of which had been torn off in what was obviously a terrible fight. The headless body of the charioteer still sat holding the reins and whip. There were strands of gold fallen from Sita's ornaments, along with her crushed garland.

Rama pointed to the ground. "See here the many drops of blood! Look at these shattered weapons. And this mighty bow, encrusted with pearls and gems. Whose chariot is this, with its hundred-ribbed canopy torn apart? Look over there! Glowing golden armor studded with emeralds and rubies. All these items could only belong to gods or demons."

Rama fell to the ground wailing piteously. "O Lakshmana, it is clear that Sita is dead. Here at this place two Rakshasas fought for her sake. The victor would surely have consumed my darling wife. Alas, I am lost."

Lakshmana carefully examined the scene. There had obviously been an encounter between two very powerful beings. Perhaps Rama was right. But from the footprints there did not appear to be more than one Rakshasa. Lakshmana felt that somehow Sita was still living. He reassured Rama, telling him to take heart, for Sita would surely soon be recovered.

As he checked his grief Rama felt consumed by anger. The corners of his eyes turned coppery as he stood holding his bow. "The Rakshasa race will soon be extinct. They have borne away Sita even as she practiced virtue. How did the gods stand by and allow this to happen? Do they not fear my wrath? Do they think I am powerless? For too long I have been mild and compassionate. Today the world will see a different Rama!"

Rama roared, giving vent to his anger. He would fill the heavens with his missiles. With his weapons he would annihilate the entire creation. All living beings would find themselves oppressed as he discharged endless flaming arrows. The planets would be brought to a standstill, the sun obscured and the moon brought down from the sky. The mountains would lie crushed to a powder and the oceans would be dried up. If the gods did not bring back Sita, they would find no shelter anywhere in the universe. All the worlds would be torn to pieces by Rama's arrows and nothing would remain. A blazing fire would rage through all the quarters, leaving total devastation in its wake.

Rama tightened his clothes. His lips trembled and he pressed them against his teeth. He looked like Shiva intent upon the destruction of the universe at the end of an age. Taking from his quiver a dreadful-looking arrow, he placed it upon his bow. "Today I shall not be checked by conciliation or force. See now, dear Lakshmana, as I bring down the gods from heaven."

Lakshmana grabbed hold of Rama's arm and stopped him from releasing his arrow. With palms joined he spoke gently to the infuriated Rama. "You have always been dedicated to the good of all beings. Do not abandon your nature today, O Rama. Do not be swayed by anger. You should not destroy the worlds for one person's offense. Lords of this world are always just in their punishment. Therefore display your forbearance, for it is as deep as that of the earth itself. Be calm and consider the situation with care."

Lakshmana pointed out that they could see only the footprints of a single Rakshasa. It appeared that someone had fought against the demon, probably to protect Sita. Whoever had abducted Sita was obviously possessed of great power. Perhaps no one was able to prevent the kidnapping.

After all, who would approve of the destruction or kidnapping of Rama's spouse? The gods and Gandharvas, the rivers, seas, mountains and indeed all living beings were not capable of giving offense to Rama, any more than the priests at a sacrifice could offend the person for whom they were performing the ritual.

Rama felt slightly pacified as Lakshmana continued, "Let us seek out the assistance of the great sages. With me by your side we shall search the whole earth with all its mountains and forests. If we still do not find Sita we shall go to the depths of the ocean and up to the realms of the gods. O Rama, we shall not rest until we find your beloved wife."

Lakshmana suggested that if still they did not find Sita, then Rama could let loose his venomous missiles upon the worlds. But first he should control his anger and seek his wife through peaceful means. Otherwise, what example would he set for the world? If the earth's ruler immediately resorted to violence when under duress, then what would ordinary men do? Could they be expected to exercise any control when in distress? In this world calamities visited everyone in due course of time, but they also disappeared again. Happiness and distress follow one another in swift succession. One should not give way to either. Even the gods were subject to suffering. One should neither rejoice nor grieve for material things, but with a peaceful mind carry out one's duties. This was the path to everlasting happiness. Lakshmana looked into Rama's eyes.

"O Rama, you have often instructed me in this way. Indeed, who can teach you, even if he be Brihaspati himself? I am only trying now to awaken your intelligence, which has been dulled by grief. Dear brother, people like you do not give way to grief even when faced with the gravest perils. Therefore spare the worlds. Seek out only the sinful adversary who has stolen Sita."

Rama put down his bow and replaced his arrow in its quiver. He was moved by his brother's beautifully worded advice. Controlling his anger, he thanked Lakshmana and asked him what they should do next. Where should they begin to look? The two princes continued to walk south, discussing what to do. Soon they came upon Jatayu lying upon the ground. Seeing from a distance the mountainous bird drenched in blood, Rama exclaimed, "Lakshmana! Here is a Rakshasa in the guise of a bird. Surely this beast has devoured Sita. I shall make short work of it with my fiery arrows."

Rama fitted a razor-headed arrow to his bow and bounded toward Jatayu, but as soon as he recognized the great bird he lowered his weapon. Jatayu, close to death, saw Rama coming and raised his head. Vomiting blood he spoke in a strained voice. "O Rama, the godly Sita and indeed my life have both been snatched away by Ravana. I flew to her assistance and fought with the demon. Although I smashed his chariot and killed his horses, I was finally cut down by him."

Jatayu then described what had taken place. Upon hearing his story Rama fell weeping to the ground. He embraced Jatayu and stroked his head. In great pain Rama cried out, "Alas, who is more unfortunate than I? My sovereignty is lost, I am exiled, my wife is stolen and now my father's friend lies mortally wounded, having tried his best to help me."

Rama questioned Jatayu. Where did Ravana take Sita? What did she say as she was being dragged away? How powerful was the Rakshasa and where was his abode? Rama spoke wildly in a tearful voice.

Jatayu looked at him fondly. Speaking in barely a whisper he replied, "The demon conjured up a storm as he flew in the sky. As I contended with him I soon became exhausted, being old and worn out. He then lopped off my wings. He sped away with his face pointing south."

The bird lay gasping. He reassured Rama that Sita would soon be found. The Rakshasa had kidnapped her at an hour which was favorable for her return. "Although he knew it not," Jatayu said, "it was the 'vinda' hour. According to scripture, a treasure lost during that time is again recovered."

Jatayu told Rama that Ravana was the son of the sage Vishrava and the half-brother of Kuvera. Although he was immensely powerful Rama would soon slay him; Jatayu was sure of it. As the old bird spoke he felt his life departing. Blood flowing continuously from his mouth, he looked at Rama with tears in his eyes. Repeating Rama's name over and over, Jatayu gradually became silent. His head fell to the ground and his body slumped back.

Rama stood with folded hands looking at his father's dear friend. He cried out in anguish. "Speak more, O noble bird. Speak more!"

But Jatayu was dead. Rama gazed at him sorrowfully. Turning to Lakshmana he said, "Alas, this bird has laid down his life for my sake, dear brother. It is clear that valiant souls who practice piety and virtue are found even in the lower species of life and not just among humans. The pain of seeing this vulture's death afflicts me as much as that caused by Sita's loss."

Rama considered Jatayu to be as worthy of his worship as Dasarath. He asked Lakshmana to fetch logs so that they could build a funeral pyre. Rama looked at the bird and said, "You will attain unsurpassed realms of happiness, O king of birds. Never again will you take birth in this mortal world of pain and suffering."

The brothers placed Jatayu on the wood pile and set it alight. Rama personally recited the sacred mantras and performed the ritual, cremating Jatayu as he would his own relative. Both brothers then went to the Godavari and, after bathing in the river, offered its sacred water to Jatayu's

departed soul. When the ritual was complete Rama and Lakshmana felt
pleased, knowing that Jatayu had gone to divine regions of unending happiness. They fixed their minds on recovering Sita. Going in a southerly direction they entered the deep forest, appearing like Vishnu and Indra going out
to encounter the Asuras.

Lakshmana went ahead wielding his long sword and hewing down the
shrubs and creepers that blocked their progress. The forest was trackless and
difficult to traverse, but the brothers moved swiftly. Distressed and eager to
find Sita, they looked on all sides, but saw only the dense forest. Lions
roared and birds of prey screamed above them. Thick darkness enveloped
them as they penetrated deeply into the jungle. As they moved ahead vigorously and without fear, they began to perceive evil omens. Rama's left arm
throbbed and his mind became disturbed. Jackals howled and crows emitted
shrill cries. Rama said, "Be wary, O Lakshmana. These signs definitely indicate some imminent danger."

Even as he spoke a loud noise suddenly resounded from ahead of them.
It was deafening and it filled the four quarters. Rama and Lakshmana, with
swords in hand, ran toward the sound. Here must be the demon responsible
for taking Sita. They would soon dispatch him. Perhaps Sita was still there.
The brothers raced ahead.

They suddenly broke into a clearing and saw a colossal Rakshasa
seated there. Taller than the surrounding trees, the demon looked like a
mountain peak. He had no neck or head and his huge mouth was in his
belly. The demon was dark blue in color and covered all over with sharp
bristling hair. At the top of his body was a single fearful eye which blazed like
fire. His long pointed tongue darted in and out, licking his lips. He had arms
eight miles long and they drew toward him all kinds of animals. As Rama
and Lakshmana looked on, the Rakshasa devoured bears, tigers and deer,
which he crammed into his gaping mouth.

The brothers saw the Rakshasa from a distance of a mile. They looked
in amazement. As they stood there, the demon saw them and reached out
with his two arms, which snaked about like two enormous creepers. Tightly
grasping both brothers he lifted them high above the ground. Lakshmana
cried out to Rama, "Free yourself, O Rama! Leave me as an offering to this
devil. Make good your escape. I cannot release myself from this demon's
clutches. After recovering Sita and the throne of Ayodhya, always remember me there."

Already torn by anguish due to having allowed Sita to be captured,
Lakshmana was overcome by the demon. Rama replied to his distraught
brother, "Do not yield to fear, O Lakshmana. A man like you should never
feel dejected."

The massive Rakshasa pulled the brothers toward him. "Who are you two with shoulders like those of bulls, dressed like ascetics yet wielding swords and large bows?" he boomed. "By the will of Providence you have fallen within the range of my sight at a time when I stand oppressed by hunger. Your life is now of short duration."

Rama felt despair. What would happen next? Was there no end to his suffering? He called out to Lakshmana. "Powerful indeed is destiny. Calamity upon calamity is heaped upon us. We are now threatened with death even before we could find the beautiful Sita. What should be done now?"

The demon spoke again. "Today you two shall serve as my food. Exert yourself if you have any strength."

Lakshmana, who had gathered himself together, became infuriated. He shouted to Rama, "The strength of this repulsive demon lies in his arms alone. Let us quickly cut off his vast arms with our swords."

As Lakshmana spoke the Rakshasa roared and opened his mouth wide. He began drawing the brothers toward him. Without delay they both brought their swords down upon his arms with great force. The razor-sharp weapons sliced through the demon's flesh and his arms fell upon the ground, releasing Rama and Lakshmana. Emitting a terrible bellowing scream, which echoed for miles, the demon slumped back, bathed in a stream of blood which gushed from the stumps of his arms. He called out to the princes, "Who are you?"

Lakshmana replied, "We are two sons of Dasarath, in the line of Iksvaku. This is Rama and I am Lakshmana. We are here at the behest of our noble father. While my mighty brother wandered in the forest, his consort was stolen away by a Rakshasa, whom we now seek. But who are you? Why do you reside in this forest in such a form with a flaming mouth in your belly?"

The demon became joyful upon hearing Lakshmana speak. "Welcome, O tigers among men. It is my good luck that I see you here today. By good fortune only have my arms been severed by you."

The Rakshasa, whose name was Kabandha, told the brothers his story. He had previously been a Gandharva. Once, out of pride in his divine beauty, he had laughed at a rishi named Ashtavakra, whose body is bent in eight places. In order to free Kabandha from his pride the rishi had pronounced a curse, turning the Gandharva into a Rakshasa. Kabandha had begged for mercy and the rishi had said, "When Rama and Lakshmana cremate you in a lonely forest, only then shall you be released from my curse."

Kabandha continued, "In the form of a Rakshasa I ranged the forest. After once performing severe asceticism, I received from Brahma the boon of a long life. Becoming fearless I then challenged Indra to battle. That invincible god hurled his thunderbolt at me. It hit me and forced my head, arms and legs into my trunk. Although I begged him, Indra would not kill me, saying, 'Let the words of Brahma prove true.'

"I asked Indra how I could survive in such a form, a mere trunk with no head or limbs. Out of compassion he gave me these two arms and this huge mouth. He then said, 'When Rama and Lakshmana sever your arms, you will ascend to heaven.'

"Thus have I sat here, stretching out my arms and pulling into my mouth lions, leopards, bears, tigers and deer. I always thought to myself, 'One day Rama and Lakshmana will fall within my grip.'"

Kabandha implored the princes to throw him in a pit and cremate him. Rama asked that he first tell them if he knew anything about Sita's whereabouts. He said to the Rakshasa, "We only know the name of Sita's abductor. We do not know where he lives, nor even his appearance."

Kabandha said he would be able to give them good advice as soon as he could assume his original celestial form because only then would he be possessed of his former divine intelligence. The brothers dug a great pit next to the demon and placed in it many logs. They pushed Kabandha into the pit and set fire to the logs. As the Rakshasa's body burned he looked like a large lump of ghee, with fat running down on all sides. Suddenly from the pit there arose a shining personality dressed in blazing yellow garments and wearing a bright garland. A splendid aerial chariot drawn by swans also appeared and Kabandha took his seat on it. He then spoke to Rama. "O Raghava, I shall now tell you how you shall recover Sita. One who has fallen upon misfortune is served by another in the same circumstances. You must befriend someone who has suffered a similar fate as you."

Kabandha told Rama that he should seek out the monkey Sugriva. This monkey lived on a nearby mountain with four friends. He was powerful, intelligent, cultured and true to his promise. His enraged brother Vali had exiled him for the sake of sovereignty and he was in need of help. By forming a pact with Sugriva, Rama would render him good and in return the monkey would assist Rama in finding Sita.

Kabandha went on, "Having restored the kingdom to Sugriva, the monkey will send out thousands of his followers to search every part of the world. O Rama, even if your wife has been taken to the highest or lowest planet, she will be found and returned to you with Sugriva's help."

Kabandha then told Rama how he could find Sugriva. With his divine vision the Gandharva could see exactly what Rama would encounter and he told him in detail. Rama would meet with the monkeys near the hermitage of the rishi Matanga on the side of Lake Pampa, where there now lived only an old ascetic lady named Sabari. After explaining everything, Kabandha remained in the sky, shining like the sun. Rama thanked him and said, "Please depart now for your own abode. You have rendered me excellent service."

Kabandha bowed his head and offered prayers to the brothers, recognizing who they were. His golden chariot then rose upwards. As he disappeared into the skies the Gandharva called out, "Enter an alliance with Sugriva."

Rama and Lakshmana immediately headed west as suggested by Kabandha. After some time they reached Lake Pampa and stayed one night by its side. In the morning the princes looked about and located the site of Matanga's hermitage. It was hemmed in by trees laden with fruits and flowers. Varieties of colorful birds played in the trees and their singing was beautiful. Deer, rabbits and other timid creatures moved about peacefully.

The princes walked over the soft grass and soon found the hut where Sabari lived. She was seated outside the hut and rose respectfully as they approached. Joining her palms, the ascetic lady fell down before the brothers and clasped their feet. Sabari offered them grass mats and brought water to wash their feet, saying, "You are welcome."

Rama and Lakshmana sat at ease and Rama spoke. "O noble lady, is your asceticism proceeding without impediment? Have you mastered your senses? Are you fully freed from anger and is your diet controlled? O gentle one, has your service to your guru borne fruit?"

Sabari looked at Rama with tear-filled eyes. She had been practicing austerities and yoga for many years. Being fully self-realized, she could understand the identities of the two princes. She spoke in a pleasing voice. "Today the full fruition of my asceticism and meditation has been attained. Today my life is perfected. My teachers have now been served and satisfied and I have achieved heaven. Indeed, O Rama, after seeing your divine form I shall reach those realms that know no decay."

Sabari told Rama that her preceptor Matanga had not long before ascended to heaven. Before leaving he had informed Sabari that Rama, accompanied by Lakshmana, would soon come there. She should serve the two princes and then, when they left, she would rise up to the eternal regions. With shaking hands Sabari began offering the brothers fruits and vegetables of every description.

After graciously accepting Sabari's offerings, Rama asked to be shown the hermitage. "I wish to see for myself the glory of your guru," he said. "Please show me where he lived and worshipped."

Sabari took the brothers to where Matanga had his altar. It shone with a brilliant luster which illuminated the surrounding area. In a pond nearby were the waters of the seven oceans, brought there by Matanga's ascetic powers. Flower garlands made by the sage lay on the ground, still fresh and unfaded.

After she had shown the brothers around, Sabari said, "I long now to join those great rishis in heaven. I am ever their servant. Please permit me to leave, O Rama."

Rama and Lakshmana looked around, saying, "Wonderful." Rama turned to the old ascetic woman. "You have properly honored us, O blessed lady. Please depart at will."

Sabari bowed low to Rama and, approaching the sacrificial fire, cast herself into it. As her body was consumed she arose in a brilliant ethereal form. Adorned with celestial jewels and garlands, she appeared resplendent. Like a streak of lightning she rose into the sky, illuminating the whole region. She went upwards toward the holy realm now inhabited by the sages whom she had always served.

Having watched Sabari depart, Rama spoke to Lakshmana. "This hermitage shines with splendor. By simply coming here we have been freed of the stain of sinful karma. Dear brother, surely now our fortunes will change. I feel that we shall soon meet with Sugriva."

Rama felt joy as he anticipated meeting the monkey. He remembered Kabandha's words. Soon Sita would be found, he felt sure. The two brothers left the hermitage and walked around the edge of the lake, carefully surveying the area. The sounds of peacocks and parrots perched on the trees nearby echoed all around. It was noon and the princes took their midday bath in the lake. The water was crystal clear and covered with innumerable lotuses, making it appear like a many-colored carpet. The lake had gently sloping banks of golden sand covered with tall trees. Long creepers reached down to the water and shining fishes nibbled at their ends.

As the brothers continued around the bank of the Pampa, which stretched for miles, they came to the foot of the Rishyamukha mountain. Rama gazed up at it. "Surely this is the mountain where Sugriva dwells. O Lakshmana, my heart is torn with grief for Sita. I feel I cannot live much longer unless the princess is found. Please quickly search for the monkey."

Thinking of Sita, Rama burst into a loud wail. Where was Janaka's daughter now? Perhaps she had pined away in his absence, dying of grief. As Rama looked around at the beautiful scenery his pain only heightened. Everything reminded him of Sita. The peahen's mating dance brought to mind the way Sita would approach him in love. The fragrant breeze was like the scented breath of his beloved wife. Yellow champaka flowers resembled her shining silk garment. Bright red tree blossoms looked like the princess's full lips. Deer moved about with their mates, piercing Rama's heart as he remembered how he would wander with Sita. The white swans reminded Rama of his wife's complexion. Indeed, he saw her everywhere he looked.

Rama cried out in anguish, his heart burning with the pain of separation. Lakshmana comforted his brother, again reassuring him that Sita would be found. As he spoke to Rama his voice rose in anger. "The sinful Ravana will find no shelter, even if he enters the darkest region of the universe. I shall seek him out. Either the Rakshasa will yield Sita or meet with his end at my hands. Throw off your grief, dear brother, and together we shall strenuously exert ourselves to find Sugriva. High-class men never give way to despondency, even when faced with the most terrible calamities. Rather, they become more and more determined to overcome their difficulties."

Rama was heartened by Lakshmana's assurances. The two brothers continued their search for Sugriva.

CHAPTER ELEVEN

RAMA MEETS THE MONKEYS

High on a peak of the Rishyamukha hill, Sugriva had heard Rama's cries. He looked around and saw the two princes on the edge of the lake. He was immediately seized with fear. The two humans appeared like a couple of powerful gods. Sugriva wondered if they had been sent by his brother Vali, who bore him constant enmity. The princes' large bows and swords struck fear into Sugriva's heart. He ran back to his cave and said to his four companions. "Two mighty warriors, disguised as ascetics, have come here. Surely this is Vali's doing. Dispatched by him with the purpose of seeking me out and killing me, those two heroes will soon arrive here. What should I do?"

The five great apes, who were all incarnations of the gods and who belonged to the celestial race of Vanaras, sat together and discussed. They decided to ascend a high peak and observe the warriors. Coming out from their cave they leapt from crag to crag. As they bounded impetuously upward, they broke down large trees with their powerful arms. Tigers and leopards dashed away in fear, seeing the apes jumping about the side of the mountain. After reaching a high place, they came together and gazed down upon Lake Pampa. Sugriva's main advisor, Hanuman, who was a son of the wind-god Vayu, then said, "What cause is there for concern, O Sugriva? Here are only two men. I do not see Vali, the actual source of your fear, nor can Vali ever come here because of Matanga's curse."

Hanuman advised Sugriva to closely observe the warriors. From their movements and gestures he would be able to ascertain their actual purpose. He should not give way to unnecessary fear. Perhaps the two men had come as friends.

Sugriva was still not sure. He had experienced Vali's malicious anger on numerous occasions. He replied to Hanuman, "No trust can placed in kings, O wise one. They will never rest until all their enemies are destroyed. I feel that these two warriors are Vali's emissaries. Even if they exhibit friendship, we should be wary. Otherwise, having gained our trust, they will then fulfill my brother's wicked purpose."

Sugriva told Hanuman to assume the form of a brahmin and meet with the warriors. He should study them carefully and then report back. Hanuman, who accepted Sugriva as his king, bowed respectfully and left, leaping down to the base of the mountain. As a son of Vayu, he possessed great mystic power. He thus assumed a human form and, appearing as a wandering mendicant, approached Rama and Lakshmana.

Hanuman prostrated himself before the princes and inquired in respectful tones, "What brings you two shining ascetics to this region? You appear like a pair of royal sages fit to rule the entire world. Your massive bows glow like rainbows, your swords appear dreadful, and your arms are like the trunks of mighty elephants. Yet you are dressed as brahmins. And why do you wail so despondently? Why do you search about this lake? Your presence here is a mystery, although you are indeed welcome. You seem like the sun-god and moon-god descended to earth, illuminating this large mountain by your own luster. Perhaps you are even powerful expansions of the Supreme Lord."

The astute Hanuman closely examined the two brothers. He could understand they were not ordinary men. The monkey had a deep devotion for Vishnu and as he looked at Rama, he felt his love being awakened. It seemed he had known this human all his life, although he had never met him before. Hanuman thought carefully. Surely this was the Lord incarnate. What profound purpose had brought him here?

Hanuman decided to reveal his identity. Folding his palms he told them he was Sugriva's minister. Sugriva was the king of the Vanaras, but he had been banished by his brother. He now sought the princes' friendship and was waiting high upon the mountainside.

The brothers were relaxed and smiling. They had listened attentively to Hanuman. Rama had become cheerful upon hearing his words and he said to Lakshmana, "This meeting is fortunate indeed, dear brother. Here stands Sugriva's minister, who is the monkey we seek. My heart and mind are moved by this noble Vanara's speech. Surely he has studied every facet of Sanskrit grammar, for his words were faultless and delivered in a gentle and highly poetic style. Even an enemy with upraised sword would be made friendly by such a speech."

Rama asked his brother to reply to Hanuman. Lakshmana then informed the monkey that they had heard about Sugriva and wished to meet with him in friendship. Hanuman smiled. Realizing that the two god-like brothers were seeking his master's assistance, he felt that Sugriva's kingdom was already recovered. The monkey joyfully spoke again. "Pray tell me your purpose in having come to this lonely forest region in the first place."

By gestures Rama urged Lakshmana to explain everything to Hanuman. Lakshmana told him in brief all that had happened to Rama from the point of his being exiled. The narration of Rama's many misfortunes distressed Lakshmana and he spoke with tears streaming from his eyes. Describing how Kabandha had directed them to find Sugriva, the prince concluded, "This Rama, whose father Dasarath was daily honored by all the kings of earth and who himself possesses limitless virtues, now seeks the refuge of Sugriva, the lord of monkeys."

When the prince stopped speaking, Hanuman stood with folded palms. He looked at Rama and said, "Fortunate indeed is Sugriva that you have sought him as an ally. He too is fully afflicted by grief, having lost his home and family at the hands of his powerful brother. He now lives in fear on this high mountain. Come, I shall take you to him."

Rama and Lakshmana looked at each other joyfully. Hanuman then assumed his form as a monkey and, kneeling, told the princes to mount his shoulders. Then the powerful ape leapt up the mountainside, carrying both Rama and Lakshmana with ease.

Within a few minutes Hanuman reached Sugriva. Setting the brothers down, he introduced them to the monkey chief. He told Sugriva all that Lakshmana had said about their exile and search for Sita. Hanuman praised the princes highly and recommended to Sugriva that he accept their proffered friendship.

Sugriva looked at the two brothers, his mind awed by their brilliance and obvious power. Like Hanuman, he felt a strong love and devotion awakening in his heart. He stood up and spoke to Rama. "I am highly honored that you have sought my alliance, O Rama. Your righteousness, your virtues and your kindness to all beings is well known. It is my gain only that you have arrived here today. O noble one, if my friendship is acceptable to you, then please take my hand. Let us enter into an abiding pact."

Sugriva extended his hand to Rama, who clasped it firmly in his own. Rama vigorously embraced the monkey and they both felt great happiness. Hanuman then lit a fire and sanctified it with Vedic mantras. Rama and Sugriva sat by the fire and swore their alliance together. They went clockwise around the fire, hand in hand. As they gazed happily at each other, Sugriva said, "May our friendship last forever. Our woes and joys are now one."

Hanuman broke off a large bough from a flowering sal tree and set it on the ground as a seat for Rama and Sugriva. He broke off another from a blossoming sandalwood tree and offered it to Lakshmana. When they were all seated Sugriva began telling Rama about himself. "I have been banished and antagonized by my elder brother Vali, O Rama, and I move about these woods in great fear. He has stolen my wife and wrested the kingdom from me. Even now he seeks to destroy me. Please grant me security from my hostile brother."

Rama laughed heartily and replied, "Certainly service is the fruit of friendship, O mighty monkey. You need have no fear from Vali. That immoral monkey will soon lie dead, killed by my infallible arrows. You will see Vali struck down and lying on the earth like a shattered mountain."

Sugriva was reassured. He was certain he would soon recover his wife and kingdom. He again clasped Rama's hand and thanked him. Sugriva assured Rama that he would search out and find Sita, whether she was in the bowels of the earth or the vaults of heaven. "You should know for sure," he said, "that neither god nor demon can hold Sita any more than a man can digest poisoned food."

Even as that friendship between Rama and Vali was forged, the left eyes of Sita, Vali and Ravana all throbbed violently and simultaneously, foreboding good to the princess and evil to the other two.

After the brothers and the monkeys had eaten a meal of cooked roots and forest vegetables prepared by Hanuman, they again spoke together. Sugriva told Rama that he had seen, not long ago, a great Rakshasa flying overhead clutching a crying lady. He had heard her plaintive calls of, "Rama! Lakshmana!" This must surely have been Sita being stolen by Ravana. Sugriva continued, "I saw the princess wriggling like a snake in the demon's grasp. She spotted me sitting with my four companions on the mountaintop. She then threw down her jewels wrapped in a cloth."

Rama grasped the monkey's arm. "You saw my beloved Sita? Where are those jewels? Bring them quickly!"

Sugriva got up and entered deeply into his cave. After a few minutes he returned, holding the cloth bundle Sita had thrown. He laid it out before Rama and the brilliant jewels shone in the bright sunshine. Rama dropped to his knees and began sobbing. "Sita! My darling!" He pressed the jewels to his bosom. Thinking of his kidnapped wife he began to hiss like a serpent provoked in its hole. He turned to Lakshmana, who had knelt by his side. "See here, O Lakshmana, Sita's bright jewels. The Rakshasa must have carried her this way."

Lakshmana gazed at the jewels and replied to Rama. "I do not recognize the armlets or earrings, for I have never looked at the face or body of the princess. But I recognize the anklets, which I saw each day as I bowed at her feet."

Rama stood quickly and spoke to Sugriva. "Tell me where the demon has taken Sita? Where does he dwell, O Sugriva? On account of that demon I shall exterminate the entire Rakshasa horde. By carrying off Sita he has opened wide the portals of death. Let me know his whereabouts and I shall dispatch him to Death's presence this very day, accompanied by all his followers."

Sugriva's head fell. He told Rama he had no knowledge of Ravana's whereabouts. The city of the Rakshasas was unknown to the monkeys, as it was to humans. Perhaps it even lay on some other planet, for the Rakshasas could move freely anywhere. But Sugriva solemnly swore that he would find Sita. Rama should not lament. Whatever it took to locate the princess, Sugriva and his monkeys would undertake.

Sugriva reassured Rama. "Do not allow grief to overpower you, O great hero. Wise men face every calamity with fortitude and do not yield to sorrow. Only the foolish are overcome by lamentation, losing their intelligence and strength and sinking like an overloaded boat. O Rama, I am here to help you. Cast away your grief."

Rama wiped his face with his cloth and smiled at Sugriva. He felt comforted by the monkey's words and thanked him for his counsel. He urged Sugriva to begin the search for Sita immediately and he again promised to kill Vali. Sugriva and his ministers felt immense pleasure to hear Rama's promise and they considered their purpose accomplished. Sugriva vowed his unending and unswerving friendship and service to Rama, who then asked, "Tell me how you came to be exiled, dear friend. Why do you tarry here on this lonely mountain, suffering grief and fear?"

Sugriva then told Rama his story. "Although I had ascended the throne of the monkeys under the instruction of Vali's ministers, I was deposed and chased away violently by Vali. Even my dear wife was stolen by my powerful brother. Still he antagonizes me. Many times I have killed monkeys sent by him for my destruction. Thus it was that I feared even you when I first saw you arrive here."

Rama wanted to hear all the details about Vali. He asked Sugriva to relate the whole history. What were Vali's strengths and weaknesses? Why had he insulted Sugriva? Rama was already feeling anger toward Vali. He wanted to know everything about the arrogant monkey. Then he would take the necessary steps. He again reassured Sugriva. "Speak with confidence. Soon you will see my arrow streak toward Vali's chest and him falling like a cleft mountain."

Sugriva, feeling delight, said, "Vali and I are the two sons of Riksaraja, the king of the monkeys. My father and I always held Vali in the highest esteem. When the king died it was Vali, as the elder prince, who was duly installed as the ruler. I always remained subservient to my brother, standing by his side."

Sugriva described how, one day, a demon named Mayavi had come to Kishkindha, the monkeys' city. He had a dispute with Vali over a woman and he stood outside the city gates, bellowing fearfully and challenging Vali to a duel. Vali was sleeping and Mayavi's roars woke him. He got up furiously and immediately rushed out of the city with Sugriva by his side. When Mayavi saw the two huge monkeys emerging from the city he became fearful and ran away. Vali and Sugriva gave chase and were gaining on the demon when he suddenly entered a large hole in the earth.

Upon reaching the hole, Vali decided to go after Mayavi and he told Sugriva to wait for him. Although Sugriva implored his brother to take him, Vali went alone into the hole. He bound Sugriva on oath to remain at the entrance of the hole until he returned.

A year passed and Sugriva waited. There was no sign of Vali. Sugriva began to fear his brother had been killed. He stayed at the hole, feeling misgivings. Then, as he sat watching the hole, a large amount of foaming blood began to seep out. Sugriva also heard the roaring sound of the demon, but he could not hear his brother's voice. Thinking carefully, Sugriva concluded with great sorrow that Vali must have been killed. Not wanting the demon to escape, Sugriva placed an enormous boulder over the hole. He then returned grieving to Kishkindha.

Vali's ministers then installed Sugriva on the throne, although he was reluctant to accept it. However, after only a short time elapsed, Vali returned, having killed the demon. When he saw Sugriva on the throne he became enraged. He bound the ministers in chains and spoke harshly to Sugriva, explaining that he had found Mayavi after a full year of searching and had slain him and all his kinsmen. He then turned back, only to find the entrance to the hole blocked and Sugriva gone.

Sugriva was full of reverence toward his brother and bowed before him, touching his feet with the crown. He told Vali how pleased and relieved he was to see him returned. Sugriva would again happily become his brother's servant, but Vali would not be placated. He accused Sugriva of deliberately shutting him up in the hole out of a desire to gain the kingdom. He threw Sugriva out of the city with only a single cloth wrapped around him. Vali also stole his brother's wife.

Sugriva concluded his story. "Thus it was that I came to be wandering about, accompanied by only a few close friends and advisors. Ranging the earth in fear of Vali, I finally sought shelter upon this mountain, knowing that he cannot come here due to a curse."

Rama smiled at Sugriva. Once more he gave him every assurance that the cruel and immoral Vali would soon be punished. "I will soon dispel your grief at losing your wife, O king of monkeys, even as the sun dispels a morning mist."

Sugriva looked at Rama. With his powerful frame and huge bow he was truly an impressive sight. Surely he could easily overpower even the mightiest of warriors. But Vali was no ordinary opponent. Although raised by Riksharaj, Vali had been born the son of Indra. He possessed strength beyond compare. No one could face him in battle. Therefore Sugriva felt uncertain. He began to describe Vali's prowess. "Each day upon rising, Vali, for exercise, strides from the western to the eastern ocean. Then he moves to the southern shore and again bounds from there to the northernmost coast. He knows no fatigue and climbs to the tops of mountains, hurling down their huge peaks with his bare hands. I have seen Vali snap numerous massive trees as if they were small sticks."

Sugriva then told Rama about Vali's encounter with another celestial demon named Dundubhi. This demon was accustomed to roam about in the form of a terrible-looking buffalo. He possessed the strength of ten thousand elephants and was wandering around looking for a suitable opponent. Coming to the god of the seas, the demon challenged him to battle, but the god declined, saying, "I am not competent to fight with you." The deity sent Dundubhi to the Himavan mountain, telling him that he would get battle there, but the mountain also declined to fight with Dundubhi. The demon roared angrily and demanded to know who could possibly face him. Himavan then said that Vali would prove a worthy combatant for him, and he directed Dundubhi to Kishkindha.

The furious demon, still in the form of a tremendous buffalo, rushed toward Vali's city. He appeared like a black cloud racing through the skies in the rainy season. Dundubhi arrived at the gates of Kishkindha and thundered like a large drum being violently beaten. That sound reverberated for miles and it broke down the surrounding trees. Vali was enjoying with his wives in his palace. Drunk with wine and passion, he stood up and gazed about with reddened eyes. He was intolerant by nature and the sound of the demon maddened him. He ran out of his palace, followed by his wives. Going before Dundubhi he said, "Why do you bellow like this, O demon? If you are challenging me, then you had best flee immediately before I take your life."

The demon laughed loudly. He said to Vali, "You should not challenge me in the presence of ladies. O gallant monkey, fight with all your power and I shall kill you today. Or, if you prefer, you may remain for this night with your wives and we shall fight tomorrow. It is improper to fight one who is drunk or blinded by passion. Return to your city and gaze upon it for one last time. Say fond farewells to your near and dear ones. Install your son upon the throne and then come out for battle. Soon you will lie dead upon the earth."

Vali laughed to hear this arrogant boasting. He sent his wives back into the city and said to Dundubhi, "Do not make excuses to hide your fear. Take my inebriety to be the drunkeness of a warrior just prior to a battle. We shall fight now!"

Vali tightened his cloth and stood like a mountain in front of Dundubhi. The demon roared and, lowering his pointed horns, charged furiously at Vali. The monkey at once seized Dundubhi by his horns and swung him around, throwing him down on the ground. Blood flowed from the demon's ears and he got up and charged again. Rising up on his hind legs, he began pounding Vali with his hooves, making a sound like thunderclaps. He thrust his horns into Vali's body, but the monkey stood firm.

The battle raged for some time as the two opponents beat each other furiously. Vali struck the demon with fists, knees, feet, rocks and trees. Gradually he overpowered Dundubhi, who became exhausted. Vali then took hold of his horns and dashed him to the ground with great force. He whirled the lifeless demon around and tossed him to a distance of eight miles. As he flew through the air large amounts of blood flowed from his smashed body. Some drops fell upon the hermitage of the sage Matanga. The rishi stood up in a rage and looked around. He saw Dundubhi's carcass and by his mystic vision could understand that Vali had thrown the dead demon there. He immediately uttered a curse: "If the monkey who threw this corpse ever steps within a four-mile radius of this hermitage, he will immediately turn to stone."

Thus Sugriva explained why Vali did not dare come near Rishyamukha. He pointed to what appeared to be a massive heap of shining white rocks. "Here are Dundubhi's bones, tossed away by Vali. Even these bare bones can hardly be moved by any other person."

Lakshmana laughed contemptuously. "What feat have you seen that Rama cannot easily equal? O Sugriva, I have not heard anything yet to indicate that this brother of yours is formidable."

Sugriva assured Lakshmana that he was convinced of Rama's prowess, but he had not yet seen any demonstration of Rama's power, while on many occasions he had witnessed the power of Vali. He asked Rama to show him his strength by kicking away Dundubhi's skeleton.

Rama laughed again and with his foot he playfully lifted the huge bones, flicking them high into the sky. That skeleton flew out of sight, landing some eighty miles away. Seeing the bones vanishing into the distance

Sugriva was impressed, but he still remained doubtful. He said to Rama, "You have thrown the dried-up bones of Dundubhi, but he was hurled by Vali when still a carcass full of flesh and blood. O Rama, forgive me, but there is one other test I should like to witness."

Sugriva showed Rama and Lakshmana seven sal trees, each more than thirty arms' length in diameter. In the past Vali had easily broken down many such trees. Sugriva asked Rama to show his strength by piercing one of those trees right through with an arrow.

Rama smilingly took up his bow and strung it, placing on the string a dreadful-looking arrow. He took aim and released the arrow which passed cleanly through all seven trees. The arrow, gilded with gold, entered the earth and descended to the subterranean regions. Forcing its way back up and out of the earth, it again entered Rama's quiver.

Sugriva was astonished and fell flat on the ground at Rama's feet. He considered Vali as good as slain. Kneeling before Rama he said, "You could kill with your arrows the gods and demons combined. Who can stand before you in battle? With you as my ally, my grief has totally dried up. O Rama, let us go quickly and make short work of Vali."

Rama agreed and they all left immediately for Kishkindha. Rama told Sugriva to go ahead and challenge Vali to a fight and he would wait nearby. When Vali came out of the city, Rama would kill him.

Sugriva stood outside Kishkindha and began to roar. Vali heard his brother and rushed out to fight. The two monkeys began a tumultuous and terrible combat that resembled a clash between Mars and Mercury in the heavens. Blinded by anger they threw blows like thunderbolts at each other. Striking with their fists, palms and feet, they pummeled each other, screaming with fury.

Rama watched closely, bow in hand. He could not distinguish who was who. The two monkey brothers resembled each other closely, like the twin Ashvini gods. Rama did not therefore release his arrow for fear of hitting Sugriva.

Vali soon got the upper hand and the battered Sugriva ran for his life. He dashed back to the Rishyamukha, closely followed by Vali, who stopped at the edge of the forest near to Matanga's hermitage, saying, "Today you are spared."

Sugriva lay gasping on the ground as Rama ran up to him. The monkey looked at the prince in surprise. "Why did you not say truthfully that you had no intention of slaying Vali? Look at me now. I have been half-killed by that fearful ape. O Rama, had I known you were reluctant I would not have moved from this place."

Rama consoled Sugriva, explaining that he was unable to distinguish the monkey from his brother. Their features, dress and ornaments were too similar. He suggested that Sugriva again challenge Vali, but this time wearing some distinctive mark so that Rama could tell one from the other. Lakshmana tied round Sugriva's neck a flowering creeper. Reassured, Sugriva got up and left again for Kishkindha.

Lakshmana and Sugriva strode in front, followed by Rama, Hanuman and the other three monkeys. They soon reached the city and again Sugriva went to the gates. He looked at Rama, still feeling fearful. The beating from Vali had shaken him.

Rama saw Sugriva's anxious expression. He took the monkey by his shoulders and said, "Do not hesitate. Vali will presently roll in the dust, struck down by my arrow. I have never uttered a falsehood, even though I have been in adversity for a long time. Let go your mighty shout, O Sugriva, and Vali will quickly proceed to this spot. How can he brook a challenge in the presence of women? This shall be his last battle and indeed his last day on earth."

Sugriva accepted Rama's firm assurance. While the two princes remained concealed in a clump of bushes, he again began to shout out his challenge. His roar rent the air pitilessly. Animals fled confused in all directions like women assailed by wicked men due to the failure of leaders to protect them. Birds dropped from the sky like gods whose pious merits have been exhausted. As Sugriva emitted his fierce cry he sounded like the ocean lashed by a gale.

Vali was in his inner chambers with his wives. Hearing Sugriva's challenge, he sat up in surprise. How had his brother returned so soon? Was he not satisfied with one thrashing? This time there would be no escape for that arrogant monkey. Vali was seized with fury. His limbs trembled and his eyes turned crimson. Grinding his teeth he leapt from his bed and ran toward the door.

His wife Tara, seeing him about to go out, ran to him and held his arm. Her womanly intuition told her something was wrong. She spoke fearfully. "My lord, shake off this anger. Do not enter another combat with Sugriva. Although you are more powerful than your brother, I nevertheless feel misgivings. How has Sugriva become so fearless even though he was only just beaten by you? Why does he now stand there roaring like a monsoon cloud? Surely he has found a powerful ally."

Vali stopped and looked at his beautiful wife. She told him that she had heard how Sugriva had formed a friendship with two princes from Ayodhya. Tara described the power and glory of Rama, which she had heard described by Angada, Vali's son. Rama was unassailable in battle and capable of crushing vast armies. He was the supreme resort for the afflicted and had given an assurance of safety to Sugriva. The Vanara queen begged her husband not to go out and fight. Instead he should welcome Sugriva and install him as the Prince Regent.

Tara implored her husband. "I consider Sugriva to be your foremost friend. You need not maintain this animosity. Bring him close with gifts and kind words. Along with Rama he will prove your greatest ally. O valiant monarch, please do not enter another combat with Sugriva, for I fear it will be your last."

Gripped by death, Vali could not accept his wife's wise advice. He reproached her as she stood before him weeping. "How can I tolerate this insolence? For a warrior who has never known defeat, brooking an insult is worse than death. I am not able to stand the arrogance of the weak Sugriva, much less his roar. O timid one, I shall not tarry here longer. Sugriva shall meet his end today."

Vali told Tara she need not fear on Rama's account. He knew about the human prince. Rama was devoted to virtue and piety; he would never commit the sin of killing innocent person. Nor could he intervene in the fair fights of others. Vali ordered Tara to stay in the palace. He was going out to face Sugriva and would soon return, having either killed his brother or sent him flying in fear. The queen bowed her head and, praying for her husband, returned sorrowfully to her rooms.

Filled with rage and breathing heavily, Vali rushed out of the city gates. He saw Sugriva standing firm like a mountain, his reddish brown body glowing like fire. Vali tightened his loin cloth. Raising his fist he charged furiously at his brother, shouting, "This iron-like fist, hurled at you like a mace, will return after taking your life!"

Remembering his brother's treatment of him, Sugriva was also worked up with anger. He threw a great punch at the onrushing Vali. The two monkeys clashed together roaring like maddened bulls. Struck a swinging blow on the chest by Vali's two clenched hands, Sugriva vomited blood and looked like a mountain covered with a cascade of red oxides. He tore up a sal tree and dashed his brother over the head. Vali shook like a ship tossed in the ocean. He fell upon Sugriva and began pounding him with his knees and fists. The two monkeys fought fiercely and gradually Vali once more gained the upper hand.

Sugriva, with his vanity shattered, began fearfully looking about for Rama. He was becoming weaker and weaker. From behind the bush Rama saw his chance. Vali stood over his collapsed brother, his arms upraised. Rama swiftly placed an arrow on his bow, releasing it with a sound resembling a crash of thunder. The arrow sped like a streak of lightning and hit Vali on the breast, sounding like another thunderclap.

Vali fell to the ground like a hewn tree, uttering a great cry. He lay unconscious with his body bathed in blood. Although struck by Rama's powerful arrow, the monkey did not die, as he was wearing a gold chain Indra had given him. By Indra's blessings that chain was capable of preserving the life of whoever wore it. Lying there with his scattered garments and shining ornaments, and the glowing arrow of Rama protruding from his chest, Vali looked like a colorful banner suddenly dropped to the ground.

Rama and Lakshmana slowly approached the mortally wounded monkey. Vali opened his eyes and looked up at Rama, who was smiling at him. The fallen monkey spoke with difficulty. "You are famous for your truth and virtue, O Rama. How then have you commited such an abominable act? What was my crime that I should be punished in this way? I did not attack you. Indeed I was engaged in fair combat with another. Why then have you killed me, remaining concealed at a distance?"

Vali accused Rama of irreligion, saying that he only posed as a virtuous person. This heinous deed surely proved him to be otherwise. He had lost control of his mind and senses, overcome by desire and swayed by sentiment. Out of friendship for Sugriva, he had abandoned righteousness.

Gasping for breath, Vali went on, "I cannot understand why you have acted in this way, O Rama. What did you have to gain by killing me, a mere monkey living in the forest on wild fruits? The scriptures condemn the eating of monkey flesh or the using of their skins. There was no reason to slay me. I have done you no harm at all. Surely this act will be condemned by all holy men and you will go to hell."

Vali censured Rama at length, speaking passionately. After some time he closed his eyes and fell back exhausted. He felt regret. Why had he not listened to Tara? She had tendered him wise advice. By ignoring her he had reaped the results of his impetuosity. The arrow in his chest burned like fire. Vali was shocked. How could the virtuous Rama have perpetrated such a vile deed?

Rama waited for Vali to regain a little strength. When the monkey again opened his eyes, Rama said, "O Vali, you clearly do not understand righteousness and religion. This entire earth belongs to the descendants of Manu, having been bequeathed to them by that great deity and speaker of religious codes. Bharata now rules this world and we, his brothers, are his servants. It is thus our duty to roam the earth, promoting virtue and punishing the wicked. You, O proud monkey, are indeed wicked."

Rama then explained to Vali rules of morality. The younger brother should be regarded as one's own son, and his wife as one's daughter-in-law.

Vali had therefore been guilty of a great sin in punishing the sinless Sugriva and co-habiting with Ruma, Sugriva's wife. The scriptures prescribed death as the punishment for one who has illicit sexual relations with his own daughter or a wife of his younger brother. There was no doubt that Rama's punishing him was just.

Rama continued to address the pain-stricken Vali. "You are now freed from the sinful reaction which would have sent you to hell. A person punished by the king is released from all sins and ascends to heaven, but if the king fails to punish a sinner, then he himself incurs the sin. O Vali, you should not grieve, for you have been fortunate to receive the proper punishment, making you eligible for the higher planets after death. Nor did I act wrongly by remaining concealed. Since you are a monkey, this was the appropriate way to kill you. Just as when hunting the king shoots arrows at animals while hidden from view, so I shot you."

Vali could not argue. He had always felt remorseful for the way he had treated Sugriva, but had denied those feelings, remaining fiercely antagonistic toward his brother. Now he had finally received the result. All creatures had to accept the fruits of their own acts alone. No suffering or happiness came other than as a result of one's former acts. Understanding this, Vali accepted Rama's words as true and gave up his anger and grief. With difficulty he replied, "How can a dwarf argue with a giant? O Rama, you are the best knower of all religious principles. I am justly punished. Please forgive my harsh words spoken earlier out of sorrow and confusion. I have certainly strayed from the path of virtue."

Vali feared that after his death his brother Sugriva would be antagonistic to his son Angada. He begged Rama to establish a friendship between the two monkeys. Rama assured Vali that Sugriva would rule the Vanaras with righteousness, treating Angada like a younger brother.

Vali lost consciousness, his life all but ended. At that moment Tara ran out of the city crying for her husband. She saw the monkeys who were Vali's followers running about in all directions, seized with fear of Rama. Tara stopped some of them and asked them why they were fleeing.

"See there your mighty husband struck down by Rama's arrow," they replied. "Death in the form of Rama is bearing him away. Leave quickly with us, for soon Sugriva will take over the city and drive us out, assisted by Rama's deadly arrows."

Tara looked around and saw Vali lying on the ground. Nearby Rama leant on his great bow. With a wail she ran toward her fallen husband, beating her breast and head. She fell at Vali's feet. The lordly ape resembled a mountain struck down by Indra's thunderbolt. Crying out, "My lord!" she rolled about in agony. Angada also came there and dropped to the ground at his father's feet, overwhelmed with grief.

Tara lamented loudly. "Get up, O tiger among monkeys! Why do you not greet me? Come with me now and lay upon your excellent couch. The bare ground is no place for a king to lay. Alas, it is obvious that the earth is more dear to you than myself, for you lie there embracing her with your out-stretched arms. What shall I do? Where shall I go? I am lost!"

Crying like a female osprey, the intelligent Tara thought how her husband had banished Sugriva and stolen his wife. Surely this was the fruit of those sinful deeds. How could she live now as a widow under the care of Sugriva, Vali's enemy? What would happen now to her dear son Angada? Tara held Vali's feet, who still lay unconscious and was barely breathing.

Hanuman gently comforted Tara. "This is the sure end of everybody, O gentle lady. All of us shall reap the results of our own deeds only, good or bad. As such, we gain nothing and do nothing for others by lamenting. Vali has reached the end of his allotted life span and will now rise to the higher regions. Do not grieve."

Tara cried out in pain. She had no desire to live without Vali. Laying next to her husband she determined to fast until death, following the path taken by Vali.

As Tara sobbed, Vali opened his eyes and looked slowly about. Seeing Sugriva he spoke to him affectionately. "O brother, please forgive my evil acts against you. Destiny did not decree that we should share happiness together. Accept now the rulership of the monkeys. I shall soon depart for Yamaraja's abode."

Vali asked his brother to be kind to Angada. He also asked that Sugriva carefully protect Tara, always seeking her advice on important matters. Rama's order should be closely followed and Sugriva should always seek to please him.

Sugriva, feeling despondent, nodded in assent to Vali's instructions. Vali then took off his celestial gold chain and gave it to Sugriva. Turning to Angada he said in a whisper, "Dear son, I shall now depart from this world. Remain ever devoted to Sugriva's service, seeing him as you do myself."

With his eyes rolling in pain and his teeth exposed, Vali gave up his life. His head fell to the side as his last breath gasped out. A great howl of sorrow went up from the many monkeys who stood surrounding Vali. "Alas, our lord is gone! Who will protect us now? Who can equal Vali in strength and splendor?"

Tara and Angada embraced Vali's body, wailing loudly. Sugriva was filled with remorse. He went before Rama and said, "I am a wretch who has caused the death of my own brother. Although he was always capable, my brother never killed me. But at the first opportunity I have had him slain. How can I take the kingdom now, stained as it is with Vali's blood? How can I tolerate seeing Tara and Angada weeping bitterly on my account?"

Sugriva became overwhelmed by his feelings. He felt sure he would reap the terrible results of the sin of fratricide and indeed the killing of a king. Vali was noble and had ruled the monkeys with justice and compassion. Having killed him, Sugriva was not fit to himself become a monarch. Everyone would simply condemn him. His only recourse was to enter fire along with the body of his brother. Sugriva begged Rama's permission to give up his life. The other monkeys could assist Rama in finding Sita.

Rama was moved to tears upon hearing Sugriva's piteous lamentations. As he considered the monkey's sorrowful words, Tara approached him and said, "O all-powerful one, I too shall enter the fire along with Vali. I have no desire for life without my husband. Surely he will miss me, even among the Apsaras in heaven, for I have always been his most devoted servant."

Tara begged Rama to kill her with the arrow which had slain Vali. "O Rama, the wife is always considered one with her husband. Therefore you need not fear the sin of killing a woman. You will only be completing the task of killing Vali by taking my life. I cannot tolerate the pain of separation from my spouse. Surely you know only too well what that terrible pain is like."

Rama looked compassionately at Tara, who had fallen to the ground. He consoled her most gently. "O wife of a hero, do not think in this way. This entire creation yields happiness and distress one after another for all created beings in accord with their destiny. Where will you go to avoid your fate? Be peaceful here; having duly mourned for your husband, you will soon enjoy as much delight under Sugriva's protection as you did with Vali. Your son will become Prince Regent and you will be honored. All this is ordained by Providence. O Tara, the wives of heroes never lament as you are doing now."

Rama instructed Tara according to the moral codes which applied to her race. On the death of her husband, she should accept his brother as her spouse and serve him as she had Vali. Tara became silent, gazing at Rama, who now turned to Sugriva to comfort him.

Rama told Sugriva to take heart and attend to Vali's funeral. The soul of the monkey king would not be helped by simply grieving for him. "The time for grieving must soon end and duties must be performed," Rama said gravely. "Time controls everything. Vali has succumbed to all-powerful Time, going to the regions he has earned by his own acts. Now Time is urging you to perform your religious duties toward your brother."

Sugriva stood looking at Rama. His mind was bewildered with grief and remorse. Lakshmana took hold of the monkey's arm and told him to proceed with Vali's cremation. Lakshmana gave detailed instructions to the confused Sugriva. Hearing the prince speak, Sugriva's attendants ran to carry out his orders.

Rama again spoke to the grieving Tara. "O Vanara queen, carefully consider whether or not this dead body of Vali was ever related to you. It is nothing but a collection of inert chemicals. The real person is the soul, not the body. In ignorance only do we form relationships based upon bodily considerations, calling others 'husband,' 'son,' or 'friend.'"

Rama explained that the soul is without designations. It is eternal and dwells for only a short time in the body. During our brief sojourn in our bodies we form so many illusory relationships, but all of these will undoubtedly be broken by the force of time. The soul's real happiness lies in its relationship with God. Vali had now moved closer to that eternal relationship and no one need lament for him.

As Rama spoke, Vali's grieving relatives felt relief. Gathering themselves together they prepared for Vali's funeral. A beautiful wooden palanquin was fetched. Vali's body was carefully laid on it and it was lifted up by eight powerful monkeys. Vali looked like a fallen god. The palanquin was adorned by numerous carvings of birds, trees and fighting soldiers. Over its top was lattice work covered with a net and many garlands and jeweled ornaments. The sides of the palanquin were daubed with red sandal-paste, and lotus flowers were laid out all along its edges.

Sugriva and Angada bore the palanquin along with the other monkeys. Sugriva had regained his composure and he issued orders to the monkeys. "Walk ahead of us, scattering the ground with jewels of every description. Let learned monkeys recite the scriptures and we shall proceed slowly to the cremation ground."

The procession moved off, heading toward the river bank. A great wail was sent up by the many females who walked in front. Gradually they came to the river and a funeral pyre was built on its bank. The palanquin was set down next to the pyre and Tara again fell to the ground, crying mounfully. "O hero! Why do you not cast your glance upon me today? See here your wives, all weeping, who have trodden the long path behind you. Here are your ministers, sunk in a sea of dejection. O Vali, dismiss your counselors now as you did in the past. Then we shall sport together, intoxicated with love."

The other women gently raised Tara, who was overwhelmed with sorrow. With the help of Sugriva and the weeping Angada, they lifted Vali's body onto the pyre. Angada then lit the pyre and walked around his father,

who had set out on his journey to the next world. All the others joined him
in slowly circumambulating the blazing pyre.

Everyone then entered the river and offered sacred water to Vali's soul.
After the obsequies were performed, Sugriva and his counselors surrounded
Rama and Lakshmana.

Hanuman, who resembled a golden peak of Mount Meru, folded his
hands and said to Rama, "By your grace, O Raghava, has Sugriva acquired
the ancestral kingdom of the Vanaras. Please enter this city of Kishkindha
in state and, with your permission, we will perform the coronation
ceremony."

Rama looked stern as he replied. "Commanded by my father I shall not
enter even a village for fourteen years, much less a city. You may proceed
into the city and duly install Sugriva as your king. I shall remain outside,
finding some suitable cave for my residence."

Rama instructed Sugriva to remain in Kishkindha for the coming few
months. It was the beginning of the monsoon season, so it would be impossible to search for Sita. When the rains ended Sugriva should dispatch the
monkeys in all directions to look for Ravana and the princess.

Sugriva took leave of Rama and went into his city, which was situated
within a vast mountain cave. In accordance with scriptural injunctions, a
grand coronation ceremony was performed. Everyone repeatedly extolled
Rama and Lakshmana, feeling honored by the friendship of the two princes
from Ayodhya. Sugriva was reunited with his wife, Ruma, and he entered
Vali's magnificent palace. Awaiting the end of the rainy season he lived happily, surrounded by his wives and ministers.

CHAPTER TWELVE

THE SEARCH BEGINS

Rama and Lakshmana moved to the nearby Mount Prashravana and sought out a large cave close to its summit. They settled in, spending their time talking together and performing sacrifice. But Rama's mind rarely left Sita. His only consolation was to describe her qualities to Lakshmana. He longed for the rainy season to end so that he could search for his beloved wife. Gradually the rains subsided. The sky cleared and the resonant cries of cranes filled the air. Although the monsoons were over, however, Sugriva still did not prepare his army to search for Sita. Realizing this, Rama discussed the situation with Lakshmana.

"It seems the Vanara king has forgotten his debt to us, noble brother. Why have his messengers not arrived here with news of their search? O Lakshmana, I fear that the gentle Sita is lost forever. What is she doing now? Surely her mind dwells on me, even as mine never leaves her. Surely she weeps in agony, even as I weep here."

Rama's grief was as strong as it had been when Sita was abducted four months ago. Rama felt powerless. He was still no closer to finding Sita than the day she was kidnapped, and now Sugriva, upon whom his hopes were resting, was letting him down. Rama sat distracted by sorrow. Lakshmana reassured him. "This is not the time to grieve, dear brother. We must strenuously exert ourselves to find Sita. With you as her protector, no one can hold the princess for long. Compose yourself, Rama! Let us do what must be done."

Rama sighed and looked around. On a plateau beneath his cave, a large pond had been formed by the rains. Swans and cranes sported joyfully in the water among clusters of white and red lotuses. Rama could hear the croaks of frogs and the cries of peacocks. In the distance he heard the trumpeting sound of elephants in rut. Large black bees droned around the bright forest flowers, intoxicated with nectar. The sky was a deep blue and the wind, which had blown fiercely during the monsoons, had become a gentle breeze. The sights and sounds of autumn were visible everywhere. Rama was reflective. Where was Sugriva? Had he forgotten his promise now that his own problem had been solved? How could he so ungrateful? Rama's brow furrowed with anger and he turned to Lakshmana.

"These past four months have seemed like a hundred years for me. I have longed for the end of the rains, O Lakshmana, so that we might find Sita as we agreed with Sugriva. Although I have rendered him a great favor, the evil-minded monkey king obviously holds me in contempt. Seeing me forlorn and deprived of my kingdom, living helplessly like an ascetic in the forest, the wicked fellow entirely disregards me."

Rama told Lakshmana to go to Kishkindha. He should tell Sugriva that there is no viler being than one who is ungrateful. Had he forgotten the favor Rama had done for him, and the promise he had made in return? Did he wish to again see Rama's golden bow drawn to its full length? Did he desire to see Rama angry on the battlefield? Did he long to hear again the crash of Rama's bowstring sounding like so many claps of thunder? It was strange that Sugriva seemed to have forgotten how Vali was slain by a single arrow from Rama, although Sugriva himself could never overcome his brother. Rama's eyes were crimson with anger as he spoke.

"It is clear that Sugriva is lost in sensual pleasures, having regained his kingdom after a long time. Drunk and surrounded by women, he has all but forgotten his pledged word to me. Tell him, O brother, that the path taken by Vali still lies open. Along with all his kinsmen, Sugriva may proceed along that path if he does not care for his promise. He should take heed of this warning. Otherwise he will meet again soon with Vali."

Lakshmana himself became furious as he listened to Rama. He told Rama that he would go immediately to Kishkindha. With upraised weapons he would dispatch Sugriva to Death's abode. Clearly the licentious and unvirtuous Sugriva was not fit to rule a kingdom. Angada should be installed as king and he could organize the search for Sita. Sugriva should be punished without delay.

Lakshmana stood up and reached for his weapons. Rama, whose anger had already begun to subside, then checked his brother. "I think it not fitting that you kill Sugriva. Try at first to pursue a gentler path. Remind him of our friendship and his promise. O Lakshmana, do not use harsh words immediately. After all, Sugriva is but a monkey. Perhaps you can awaken him to a sense of his duty by conciliatory speech."

Lakshmana bowed in assent to Rama's words, although he could not subdue his anger. He left the cave and began running toward Kishkindha, thinking of what he would say to Sugriva. He could not disobey Rama's order, but he would not tolerate any resistance from Sugriva. If that lazy monkey did not immediately set about his duty, he would be sorry. How dare he be so negligent of his promise to Rama! Who did he think he was? Lakshmana bit his lips in fury as he bounded down the mountainside.

*   *   *

In the city of Kishkindha, Hanuman had also noticed the season change and Sugriva not stirring. The intelligent minister thought carefully about the situation. Rama would certainly take stern action if Sugriva failed to fulfill his pledge. Hanuman approached the Vanara king, who was absorbed in sensuality, and spoke to him in a friendly and pleasing manner.

"You have regained sovereignty, fame and prosperity, O Sugriva. It now remains for you to win the goodwill of your allies. The dominion, fame and glory of a king who acts well toward his allies will always grow. That king who regards equally his exchequer, his army, his allies and his own self, will gain a great kingdom. However, he who fails to take care of any one of these meets with disaster."

Hanuman then reminded Sugriva of his promise to Rama. The time had arrived to begin the search for Sita. The king should immediately send out monkeys in all directions. Rama should not need to ask. It would be shameful if Sugriva did not act quickly to repay a debt to his friend and ally.

Sugriva thanked Hanuman for his wise and timely advice. The monkey king realized his laxity and he immediately summoned his ministers and counselors. He issued orders. "Let all the Vanara generals be quickly assembled. Swift-footed and energetic monkeys are needed. Ten thousand of my army should immediately depart for every country where the Vanaras dwell. Have them fetch the very best of the monkey warriors here to Kishkindha. Anyone sent out and failing to return within fifteen days should be executed." Ordering Hanuman and Angada to organize the army, Sugriva again retired to his rooms.

Within a few days the monkey hordes began to assemble outside the city. Monkeys resembling elephants, mountains and clouds gathered together. Those powerful Vanaras were like mighty tigers and were all heroic. They were dark and terrible and they made one's hair stand erect just to see them. Some were as strong as a hundred elephants, some ten times stronger than that, and others ten times stronger again. They stood awaiting Sugriva's orders.

As the monkeys milled about in their tens of thousands outside Kishkindha, they noticed Lakshmana approaching in the distance. When they saw the prince running toward the city, his face glowing with anger and his bow grasped tightly, they became fearful. Some of them, not recognizing him, lifted up trees and boulders, ready to defend Kishkindha. Others ran in all directions as Lakshmana arrived near the city gates, holding aloft his bow and calling for Sugriva. Seeing the monkeys prepared to attack him, Lakshmana became even more angry. He heaved deep and burning sighs and licked the corners of his mouth.

Angada quickly came out of the city and, checking the monkeys from fleeing, went before Lakshmana. Rama's brother appeared to the monkey prince like the blazing fire of universal destruction. In great fear he bowed low at Lakshmana's feet and greeted him respectfully. Although furious, Lakshmana contained his anger and spoke kindly to Angada. "Pray tell Sugriva of my arrival, dear child. I stand here tormented by grief due to Rama's plight. Please ask the king to hear from me Rama's advice."

Angada bowed again and left swiftly, running to Sugriva. He burst into his chambers and told him to come quickly. But Sugriva was asleep, groggy from the night's pleasures. He lay upon his bed with only garlands as his dress. As he slowly stirred, many more monkeys came near his room, raising a great clamor. They were terrified of the wrathful Lakshmana. Sugriva heard the tumult and came to his senses. He stood up, troubled in mind, and Angada explained the situation.

Sugriva told Angada to bring Lakshmana immediately. "Why have you left him standing at the gates?" he demanded. "He should be offered every respect, even as much as myself." Angada, joined by Hanuman, quickly left to fetch Lakshmana.

Within a few minutes Lakshmana was led into Kishkindha by Angada and Hanuman. Still fuming, the prince surveyed the city. Great mansions and temples lined the wide avenues, each building set with celestial jewels of every description. The city was illuminated by the jewels' glow. Rivulets flowed by the avenues and groves of trees grew here and there, yielding all kinds of delightful fruits. As he went along the main highway, Lakshmana saw the large white palaces of the chief monkeys. They shone like clouds lit by the sun. Long wreaths of flowers hung from those palaces and the scent of aloe and sandalwood issued from the latticed windows.

Lakshmana was led into Sugriva's palace, the most magnificent of all. After passing through seven heavily guarded gates, he entered Sugriva's inner chambers. Here and there were numerous gold and silver couches, spread with costly silk covers. Many beautiful Vanara ladies, wearing garlands and gold ornaments, moved about, their anklets tinkling. As they reached Sugriva's private chambers Lakshmana heard the strains of celestial music from within. He became even more annoyed with Sugriva. The insolent monkey was reveling while Rama suffered agony! Lakshmana twanged his bowstring, and the sound reverberated through the entire palace.

Sugriva was startled. Realizing at once that Lakshmana had arrived, he spoke urgently to Tara, who sat by his side. "Go quickly and greet Lakshmana. He will never display anger in the presence of a woman. Pacify him with gentle words. Only then will I be able to face him."

Tara rose up and went out of the room. The gold string of her girdle hung loose and she tottered slightly from intoxication. Bending her slender body low, she covered her head with her cloth and respectfully greeted Lakshmana. As soon as he saw Tara, Lakshmana looked down modestly. His anger abated as Tara spoke gently. "My lord, what gives rise to your angry mood? Who has disobeyed your order? Who has recklessly gone before a forest fire while it rushed toward a thicket of dried trees?"

Still annoyed, Lakshmana replied, "This husband of yours appears to have forgotten his duty. He seems intent only on pursuing pleasures. Four months have already passed since Rama left and we still see no signs of Sugriva keeping his word. He remains drunk here, enjoying with you and unaware of the passage of time. O Tara, drinking is always condemned by the wise as the root of irreligion. Please remind Sugriva of his religious obligation."

Tara begged Lakshmana to forgive Sugriva. After all, he was but a monkey. It was no surprise he had fallen a victim to lust. Even great sages in the forest were sometimes overcome by desire. What then of a monkey living among beautiful women? One under the sway of carnal desire loses all sense of time and place. Forgetting his duty, he casts decorum to the winds and absorbs himself in pleasure. Tara told Lakshmana that Sugriva was regretful. He was always Rama's devoted servant and he longed to fulfill Rama's order. Even now he was waiting eagerly to speak with Lakshmana.

Tara led Lakshmana into Sugriva's chamber. As the prince entered the apartment he saw Sugriva seated on a golden couch next to his wife Ruma. He was surrounded by youthful Vanara ladies adorned with shining jewels and heavenly garlands. His eyes were bloodshot and his limbs were smeared with sandal-paste. Sugriva's costly silk garment hung loose on his powerful body, and Vali's brilliant gold chain shone from his chest.

Seeing Sugriva absorbed in sensual delights, Lakshmana's anger was rekindled. His eyes opened wide and his lips set in a firm line. The furious prince breathed heavily and wrung his hands, looking with blood-red eyes at Sugriva. The monkey king jumped from his couch, like a tall flag suddenly raised in honor of Indra. He went before Lakshmana with folded palms and bowed at his feet.

Lakshmana addressed him in angry tones. "Who is more hard-hearted than he who makes a false promise to a friend, especially when that friend has done him a great favor? O lord of the monkeys, one who ungratefully fails to repay the service of friends deserves to be killed!"

Lakshmana quite forgot Rama's request to first speak kindly to Sugriva. He glared at him. This selfish monkey deserved no pity. He lay here at ease while Rama was pining away. Lakshmana vented his fury, his voice thundering about Sugriva's spacious chamber.

"Ingratitude is the worst of all sins, O thoughtless one! You are lustful and a liar. You have achieved your own ends, made some empty promise, and then simply abandoned yourself to pleasure. Surely you will regret your omission when Rama's blazing arrow speeds toward you. Before long you will meet with Vali again!"

Tara again beseeched Lakshmana to be patient. Sugriva was an ordinary being subject to the sway of his senses. No one could easily avert the strong urges of the body. Even the great Vishvamitra had once lost himself in sexual pleasure for a hundred years, thinking it to be a day. Sugriva had now been awakened to his duty. He had taken action and sent out many monkeys to raise an army to find Sita.

Tara spoke passionately to the angry Lakshmana. "Vali told me there are a hundred million powerful Rakshasas in Lanka. These must be overcome if Ravana is to be defeated. Therefore Sugriva is now amassing a force sufficient to encounter all the Rakshasas. The army will be ready within some days. Do not be angry. The search for Sita will soon begin."

Lakshmana was pacified when he heard that Sugriva had already made arrangements. He nodded his head and relaxed.

Seeing Lakshmana relaxing, Sugriva said, "Everything I have depends upon Rama. How can I ever repay him? Rama alone is powerful enough to recover Sita and is merely using me as his instrument. This again is his kindness on me. I only wish to serve him in whatever way I can. Please forgive any transgression on my part, for there is no servant who is without fault."

Lakshmana began to feel ashamed of his angry outburst. He spoke kindly to Sugriva. "With you as his supporter my brother is blessed in every way, O gallant monkey. I feel sure he will soon destroy his enemy with your assistance. Please forgive my harsh words, for I am sorely afflicted by my brother's plight."

Lakshmana asked Sugriva to come with him to see Rama. Sugriva immediately had a large palanquin fetched and he mounted it along with Lakshmana. Accompanied by Sugriva's ministers, they departed toward Prashravana.

The golden palanquin, covered by a white canopy, was carried swiftly toward the mountain where Rama waited. Conches and kettledrums were sounded as the procession of monkeys moved in state. Sugriva was surrounded by many warlike monkeys bearing weapons in their hands. He was fanned on both sides by his servants and eulogized by bards as they traveled.

They soon arrived at Rama's cave. Sugriva jumped from the palanquin and prostrated himself at Rama's feet, who lifted the monkey and embraced him with love. Rama seated Sugriva on the ground and, sitting next to him, spoke in a gentle voice. "A wise king is he who pursues in their proper order religion, wealth and pleasure, allotting proper time to each. He who pursues only pleasure, neglecting the other two, wakes up after falling, like one asleep on a treetop. The king who wins pious allies and destroys sinful foes gains great religious merit, O Sugriva. The time has come for you to make an effort for merit. What then has been done, O King?"

Sugriva replied that he was ever indebted to Rama for his kindness and favor. The Vanara king explained how he had dispatched thousands of monkeys to gather an army. Soon there would be millions of fierce monkeys, bears and baboons gathering at Kishkindha. All of them were sprung from the loins of gods and Gandharvas and all were terrible warriors capable of changing their forms at will. Sugriva would have at his command a vast army, countless in number. They would quickly find Ravana, completely uproot him, and recover Sita.

Rama was delighted and he looked like a blue lotus in full bloom. He embraced Sugriva tightly. "It is no surprise that one of your caliber renders such good to his friends. With you by my side I shall easily conquer my enemies. O Sugriva, you are my greatest well-wisher and are fit to help me in every way."

Rama and Sugriva discussed for some time, planning how to make their search. Sugriva then left to meet with his emissaries who were returning with the troops they had gathered.

As millions of fierce monkey warriors came to Kishkindha the earth vibrated. A massive dust cloud rose up and veiled the sun. The trees shook, sending down showers of leaves and blossoms. The entire region for miles around became thickly populated by monkeys who looked like mountains. Some were golden-hued like the rising sun, some were as red as copper and some blue as the sky. Others were as white as the moon and still others as blackish as thunderclouds. All of them, like great mountain lions, had frightening teeth and claws.

The troop leaders approached Sugriva and asked for his command. Sugriva took all of them and went again into Rama's presence. One by one he introduced the Vanara chiefs, and they all bowed low at Rama's feet. Sugriva concluded, "These warriors are righteous, brave and powerful. They can move on land, water and through the air. They have conquered fatigue and are famous for their exploits. All of them have arrived bringing thousands and millions of followers. O Rama, these Vanaras are ready to do your bidding. Please give your command."

Rama stood up and embraced Sugriva. "It must be ascertained whether or not Sita still lives. O noble one, find out where Ravana's land is located. Once we have this information we shall then do what is necessary."

Sugriva then assigned four parties to search the four directions. He gave detailed descriptions of the countries where they should look and then added, "This search should be conducted only over the next month. Then you should return. Anyone returning after a month will be subject to death. Rama and his great purpose should be constantly remembered by all of you. May success be yours!"

Sugriva had asked Hanuman to assist Angada in leading the search party to the south. This was the direction where Ravana would most likely be found, as he had been seen flying that way with Sita. Sugriva spoke with Hanuman just before he left. "There is nothing on earth or in the heavens that can obstruct your movement, O valiant son of the wind-god. You are no less than your great father in prowess. There is no created being on earth equal to you in strength and vigor. On you rests my main hope of finding Sita."

Rama heard Sugriva speaking with Hanuman and he saw his eager expression. It was clear he was confident of success, as much as Sugriva was sure that his minister would find Sita. Rama was overjoyed. He went to Hanuman and gave the monkey a ring inscribed with his name. "Take this token, O jewel among monkeys, and show it to Sita. This will reassure her that I sent you. I feel sure you will soon see the princess."

Hanuman took the ring and touched it to his head. He prostrated himself at Rama's feet and prayed for his blessings. Then, looking like the full moon surrounded by a galaxy of stars, he left with his party.

The Vanaras and bears all left with great haste. Shouting and howling, thundering and roaring, growling and shrieking, they ran in the four directions. The monkey chiefs cried out in different ways. "I shall destroy Ravana and bring back Sita!"

"Single-handed I shall kill that demon and rescue Janaka's daughter, even from the fires of hell."

"I shall smash down trees, cleave great mountains and churn up the oceans. I will certainly find the princess!"

"I can leap across the sea a distance of eight hundred miles."

"I will bound up Mount Meru and enter the bowels of the earth until Sita is found!"

While boasting of their power in this and other ways, the monkeys gradually disappeared.

After the monkeys had left, Rama spoke to Sugriva. "I was surprised to hear your extensive descriptions of this earth. How do you know it so well?"

Sugriva replied that he had seen every part of the world while running away from Vali. "My angry brother chased me in all directions," he said. "As I dashed away in fear I saw every part of the wide earth as if it were the impression of a calf's hoof. With Vali always behind me I ran with tremendous speed. Finally I remembered Matanga's curse and came to the Rishyamukha, whereupon Vali left me alone."

Rama laughed to hear Sugriva. The two friends sat speaking together for some time, then Sugriva left for Kishkindha to await the return of the search parties.

* * *

The monkeys dispatched by Sugriva began their search. They scanned cities, towns and villages. Scouring woods and forests, they climbed mountains and dived into lakes and rivers. They explored deep caverns and entered holes in the earth. Going as far as possible in the directions they were assigned, they scrupulously searched everywhere for Ravana and Sita. Even after searching for a month, however, they were not successful. One by one the parties returned, fearful, to Sugriva.

From the north came Satabali, disappointedly reporting his failure. Vinata returned from the east, also without success. From the west came Sushena, again without having discovered Sita's whereabouts.

In the south Hanuman and Angada and their party had traveled a great distance. The month had almost passed and still there were no signs of Sita. They reached the plains surrounding the Vindhya mountains. It was a desolate region, full of caves and thick forests, waterless and uninhabited. The whole area had been rendered a wilderness by the curse of a sage many years previous who had been angered by his young son's death.

Thousands of monkeys combed the entire terrain. Penetrating more and more into the frightful area, they suddenly came upon a huge Rakshasa. Seeing the demon, who looked like a hill, the monkeys stood with their loins tightly girded, ready to fight. The demon saw the monkeys and bellowed out, "You are gone!"

Angada thought the demon to be Ravana. He became enraged and rushed straight toward the roaring Rakshasa, who raised his massive hand to strike the monkey. Angada leapt high and dodged the blow. Swinging his powerful arm as he flew, the Vanara hit the Rakshasa on the head with his outstretched palm. The blow was tremendous and the demon vomited

blood and fell to the ground. After examining the dead Rakshasa and realizing that it he was not Ravana, the monkeys continued their search.

The vast Vindhyan range was filled with innumerable caves. The monkeys systematically entered each and every one. They climbed every mountain and scoured all woods and groves. Gradually they moved further and
further south. Not finding Ravana or Sita anywhere, they became more and
more fatigued and disappointed. The month allotted by Sugriva passed and
still they had no clue as to where Sita had been taken.

One day when they were exhausted and wracked by thirst, they came
upon the entrance to a huge cavern. They saw birds emerging from it with
their wings dripping with water. The monkeys decided to enter the dark
cave. They formed a long, eight mile chain to avoid getting lost. Bats
shrieked and birds flew past them. Occasionally the growl of a lion or tiger
was heard.

As they went deeper into the cave they saw ahead of them a bright
light. They moved quickly toward the light and came upon a huge open
area, brilliantly lit by thousands of shining golden trees. The trees were
adorned with brightly colored flowers and leaves, and they bore fruits which
shone like rubies and emeralds. The trees hemmed in large lotus ponds of
clear water, filled with golden fish. The monkeys saw palaces of gold and silver, set with cat's-eye gems and covered with lattices of pearls.

On all sides were spacious couches and seats studded with various
kinds of gems. Mounds of gold and silver vessels lay here and there, as well
as piles of colored jewels. There were collections of sandalwood and aloe-
wood carvings, as well as many first class palanquins lying about. Piles of
costly ethereal textiles of indescribable beauty lay on the floor. Celestial food
and drink of every kind was spread on gold tables, and there were dazzling
heaps of gold everywhere.

The monkeys were stunned by the sight and they stood looking all
around, their mouths hanging open. Then they saw an ascetic lady clad in
black deerskins sitting some distance from them. She shone with yogic
power as she sat in meditation. Hanuman approached her and respectfully
inquired who she was and in whose cave they now found themselves.

The woman's name was Swayamprabha, and she explained that the
cave and all its wonders had been created by Maya, the architect of the
celestial demons. He had dwelt there for some time, being finally slain by
Indra for the sake of an Apsara whom Indra himself had coveted. The
Apsara had lived in the cave with Swayamprabha as her servant. She had
now returned to heaven, leaving Swayamprabha to her meditations.

The ascetic lady gazed at the monkeys. She could understand that they
were Rama's servants. She had seen Rama in her meditations and under-

stood his divine identity. She was pleased to have the opportunity to serve Rama by entertaining his servants. The yogini gave the monkeys delicious food and drinks, which invigorated them. As they ate they told her of their mission.

When they had finished eating the hermitess asked them to close their eyes and she would take them out of the cave. The monkeys complied and in a moment they mysteriously found themselves again standing at the entrance to the cavern. Swayamprabha told them to continue their search and then took her leave, disappearing back inside.

The monkeys stood outside the cave, amazed but refreshed from their celestial repast. They carried on vigorously searching and soon reached the southern ocean. Realizing that they had looked everywhere in the whole southern region without success, they fell prey to anxiety. It was now more than six weeks since they had left. The monkeys were fearful of Sugriva's anger when they returned and they sat together discussing what to do.

Angada spoke, "The king will certainly have us all put to death upon our late return, unsuccessful in our mission. Therefore I suggest that rather than return in shame we sit here and fast until life leaves our bodies. How can we go back and face execution in front of our near and dear ones?"

Some of the monkeys agreed and others recommended they continue searching for some time before giving up. One of them suggested they re-enter Swayamprabha's cave and live out the rest of their days happily. This met with approval from other monkeys, but Hanuman disagreed. "I don't approve of this course of action, O Vanaras," he chided. "Forgetting our master's cause, and actually forming an enmity by abandoning him, is not at all a wise move. Nor will Rama and Lakshmana tolerate it. Those princes will tear Maya's cave asunder in no time. Their arrows fall with the force of Indra's thunderbolt. All of us will be annihilated."

Hanuman continued to speak, praising Sugriva's qualities. "We need not fear the monkey king. He regards all his subjects with love and would certainly not kill Angada, the son of his dear wife Tara. Nor will Sugriva be harsh toward you others. We have all tried our best to find Sita and should now return to Kishkindha, reporting to the king for further orders."

Angada did not appreciate Hanuman's speech. He especially disliked hearing Sugriva praised. The monkey prince became angry. "No good qualities are to be found in Sugriva. Indeed, that worthless monkey has taken to wife his mother in the shape of Tara. He locked up my father in a cave and usurped his kingdom. Although Rama rendered him a great favor, that ungrateful wretch soon forgot his debt to the prince of Ayodhya. What piety does he possess? He only instigated this search for Sita out of a fear of Lakshmana."

Angada still burned within from the killing of his father brought about by Sugriva. How could Sugriva ever be kind toward the son of his mortal enemy? Now there would be more than sufficient excuse for him to punish Angada, who had failed in his mission and had committed treason by sowing dissension among the other monkeys. He was sure that Sugriva would either kill him outright or cast him into chains for the rest of his life.

Angada determined to sit there on the beach and fast until death. He sank to the ground weeping, his mind confounded by grief and despair. With the exception of Hanuman, the other monkeys sat next to him, denouncing Sugriva and praising Vali. They all sat on kusha grass with their faces turned to the east. Thinking of Sugriva's fury and Rama's prowess, they prepared for death.

As they sat there roaring in dismay, they suddenly saw an enormous bird come out of a mountain cave. The bird looked upon the line of monkeys appearing like a row of mountain peaks on the plateau beneath him. Realizing they were observing the praya vow of fasting until death, he said to himself, "Surely this food has been ordained for me by Providence. After a long time I shall eat sumptuously, feasting upon this line of monkeys one by one as they fall dead from starvation."

The bird dropped down and perched near the monkeys. Seeing him there Angada turned to Hanuman and said, "Surely this is Yamaraja come in person to punish us for failing to serve Rama's purpose. This bird reminds me of Jatayu, about whom we have heard from Sugriva. That glorious bird laid down his life for Rama in a fierce battle with Ravana. We shall also now give up our lives in Rama's service. Alas, like that heroic vulture we too have failed to save Sita."

The great bird heard him speak. He called out to Angada. "Who is this who mentions Jatayu? Where is that younger brother of mine? I have not seen him for so long. My heart trembles as I hear you speak of his death. How did he encounter the king of the Rakshasas? If it pleases you, O monkey, pray tell me everything you know."

The bird told them that his name was Sampati. He lived high in the mountains, unable to fly because his wings had been burnt by the sun. He had lost touch with his brother Jatayu for many years.

Angada told the bird everything about himself and his companions. He narrated the story of how Jatayu had died protecting Sita. Now they were searching for the princess and had given up hope. Thus they sat there, fearful of Sugriva and Rama, and awaiting only death.

Sampati cried out in anguish. His eyes filled with tears and he said to Angada, "Jatayu was dearer to me than life. Now he is killed by the Rakshasa and I can do nothing to avenge him. O monkeys, I am old and worn out. What then can I do upon hearing this terrible news?"

Sampati explained how a long time ago he had flown with Jatayu to heaven. "As we soared upwards we perceived the earth with her numerous mountains as if she were covered with pebbles. Her rivers looked like so many threads. Great cities seemed like chariot wheels and forests like grassy plots."

Tears fell from the bird's eyes as he recounted how he had lost his brother. "We had wanted to follow the sun as it coursed through the heavens. When we reached the track of that fiery globe, however, we became overpowered by its rays. Jatayu had grown weak from heat and exhaustion. I therefore covered him with my wings to protect him. We then fell back to earth, where we became separated. I fell onto the Vindhya mountain, with my wings completely destroyed by the scorching rays of the sun."

Angada looked at the wingless bird. He must know all the regions of the universe. Surely he knew where Ravana lived. Perhaps there was still hope. The Vanara asked Sampati, "Can you tell us where lies the abode of that vilest of all beings, Ravana?"

Sampati had slumped down in sorrow. But upon hearing Angada's question he lifted his head and opened wide his eyes. "Although I am an old and useless bird I can still render some service to Rama, if only with my speech. I do indeed know where Ravana lives. In fact as I lay upon this mountain some while back I saw him flying by, holding Sita. The princess was constantly crying out, "Rama! O Rama! Lakshmana! Help!"

The bird told Angada that Ravana dwelt in Lanka, which was situated in the midst of the southern ocean eight hundred miles away. The princess was being held captive in Ravana's garden, guarded by fierce Rakshasis. Sampati possessed the ability to see Lanka even as he spoke to the monkeys. He said, "Although my wings are broken, my vision is not impaired. We vultures are capable of sighting objects at a great distance. Furthermore, by my intuition I can understand that one of you will soon see Sita, and then you will return again to Rama's presence."

Requested by Sampati, the monkeys took the bird to the seashore where he offered water to the departed soul of his brother. He then told them more about himself. When he had first fallen to the Vindhya mountain he had spoken with a rishi named Chandrama, who was living there. The bird had fallen at the sage's feet and related his sad tale. Weeping, Sampati had said that he wished to throw himself from the mountain peak and end his life. The rishi restrained him, telling him that in the future some monkeys would arrive at that spot, searching for Rama's divine consort. "Although I am able to give you your wings back, I will not do so, as you are

destined to render a service to Rama through those monkeys. You must
remain here and tell them where to find Sita. At that time your wings will
again be restored."

Sampati said the rishi had then enlightened the bird with spiritual
knowledge. He had told him that bodily sufferings must be borne by everyone as a reaction to their own past deeds. One should nevertheless realize
that the real self is different from the body. Without being overly attached
to the body one should try to fix the mind on the Supreme Lord, with whom
all beings have an eternal relationship. Thus Sampati should not lament for
his broken body. He should live there patiently, thinking of Rama and waiting for his chance to render him some service.

Sampati concluded, "That was eight thousand years ago and I have
survived here all this time, being brought food by my son. Now at last I have
performed my service to Rama."

Even as Sampati spoke a beautiful pair of wings sprouted from his body.
He rose at once into the air and called down to the monkeys. "O Vanaras,
Chandrama rishi told me you would succeed in your mission. Indeed he said
that the servants of Rama could easily cross the terrible ocean of birth and
death; what then of this small sea? Take heart and go to the south. Cross the
ocean and you will find Lanka, where Sita is held. Farewell."

The bird disappeared into the sky, leaving the monkeys to continue
their search. They were overjoyed. Abandoning all thoughts of fasting until
death, they leapt into the air, raced down to the beach and roared with glee.
Then they saw the billowing waves. How could they possibly cross the
ocean? They did not possess the power of flight. The vast sea stretched into
the distance looking as insurmountable as the sky.

Angada asked, "Which one among us can leap across this sea? Who
shall become the deliverer of the monkeys today? If any among you can
jump over the ocean and reach Lanka, speak out and remove our fears."

The monkeys all remained silent, gazing with unblinking eyes at the
roaring sea. Angada spoke again, trying to inspire them with confidence. "I
have no doubt any one of you is capable of this feat. As far as I am concerned, I can certainly leap eight hundred miles, but I do not know if I shall
be able to return safely."

Angada looked around at the party. Among them was Jambavan, a
great leader of the bears, who replied, "It is not right that you, our Prince
Regent, should go on this expedition, although you could leap a thousand
or even ten thousand miles if you wished. One of us should go instead."

Jambavan said that he himself could only cover seven hundred miles,
having grown old. Each of the monkeys then stated how far he could leap.

Some said one hundred, some two hundred and some five hundred miles. But none said they could leap the full distance and return again.

Jambavan then spoke to Hanuman who was sitting silently. "O valiant monkey, you have not told us of your strength. I know you to be possessed of tremendous ability."

Jambavan described Hanuman's birth and power. The monkey was begotten by Vayu and soon after his birth he had leapt into the sky for thousands of miles, wanting to catch the sun. At that time he had been struck down by Indra. Hanuman's father, the wind-god, became aggrieved at seeing his son killed and had ceased to blow. All created beings then began to suffocate due to the stoppage of air in the universe. The gods sought to appease Vayu by bringing Hanuman back to life. They had also blessed the monkey with many wonderful powers.

On the strength of the gods' blessings Hanuman had become fearless even as a young child. He had played in the hermitages of the rishis, mischievously throwing about their paraphernalia and stopping their sacrifices. To check him the rishis had uttered an imprecation. "You will forget your great power. Only when you hear your powers described by another will you again remember them."

Jambavan concluded his narration about Hanuman. There was no doubt that he could leap to Lanka. Why then was he sitting there indifferently? Could he not see the monkeys plunged in despair?

Hanuman stood up. Jambavan's speech had ended the rishis' curse. He remembered his great prowess and felt encouraged by Jambavan. With a great roar he said, "I shall jump across this mighty ocean!"

He then expanded his body to fifty times his normal height. Stretching his arms and yawning, he spoke in a voice that resounded like thunder. "I claim my descent from the mighty Vayu, who circulates through all of space and easily smashes down mountain peaks. I could leap to the outer limits of the universe. I am quite able to overtake the blazing sun as it moves from the east across to the western mountain. Today I shall leap from Mount Mahendra, scattering the clouds, shaking the mountains and drying up the sea. I will swiftly and easily reach Lanka in one great bound. Have no fear."

Hanuman roared again and again, filling the monkeys with joy. Jambavan replied, "Our grief is now dispelled. We are depending on you, O gallant monkey. We shall stand on one foot in yogic meditation here upon the seashore, praying for your success, until you return."

Hanuman reassured the monkeys further. He asked them what he should do. Should he annihilate the entire Rakshasa horde and rescue Sita? Or should he single-handedly kill Ravana, uproot Lanka and carry it, along with Sita, back to Rama?

Angada asked him to first locate Sita and then report back, for that was Sugriva's order. In consultation with Rama and Sugriva they could then decide on their next course of action.

Hanuman bowed to that instruction and bounded to Mount Mahendra a few miles away, its peak piercing the clouds. He ranged up the side of the mountain and stood on its summit. As he stood there roaring, gods and Siddhas assembled in the sky above him uttering benedictory hymns. They dropped celestial flowers and beat their drums.

The huge monkey folded his hands to the east and offered respects to Vayu, his father. He concentrated his mind and gazed south toward Lanka. Hanuman felt honored to have such an opportunity to render Rama a service. From his first meeting with the prince he knew Rama to be his eternal master. He felt Rama's ring bound in his cloth. Sita would be overjoyed to receive that token and know that Rama would soon arrive to rescue her. With a sense of elation Hanuman contemplated approaching Rama with news of Sita. He squatted down and prepared to jump.

With a great cry of "Victory to Rama!" Hanuman sprang upwards with tremendous force, pressing the mountain deep into the earth. Animals rushed down the mountainside in all directions. The rishis engaged in meditation in the mountain forests were startled and rose into the air. Great serpents moving about on the side of the mountain became furious and bit the rocks, which then glowed red from the serpents' virulent poison. All the trees shook and shed their blossoms, and the whole mountain appeared covered with flowers. Large fissures appeared in the mountain and different colored streams issued out. As Hanuman leapt upwards, Mount Mahendra presented a beautiful sight and the monkeys gazed up in wonder and awe. Then they went down onto the beach to begin their wait for Hanuman's return.

CHAPTER THIRTEEN

HANUMAN LEAPS TO LANKA

Hanuman flew forcefully into the morning sky. Trees, shrubs and flowers flew behind him in the wind raised by his movement, like relatives following a dear one setting out on a long journey. Hanuman thought of Rama. Sampati was right. Simply by remembering Rama's name at the end of life, anyone could cross the entire ocean of material suffering. These eight hundred miles were nothing. Hanuman felt confident of success as he soared toward Lanka. Soon he would reach Sita and reassure her. If any Rakshasas tried to stop him, that would be their last act on earth. He would dispense swift justice to the Rakshasas. Then, returning to Rama's presence, he would await further commands.

As the flowers following Hanuman fell into the dark blue ocean, they made the sea appear like the star-spangled firmament. The trees dropped with great splashes like meteors fallen from heaven. Hanuman's outstretched arms looked like a pair of five-hooded serpents risen from the mountaintop. The great monkey seemed as if he were drinking up the vast ocean and swallowing the sky. His eyes blazed like two sacrificial fires and his coiled tail flew behind him like a flag. His reddish brown face shone like the sun, and the wind rushing past his armpits thundered like a cloud. He seemed like a comet moving through the heavens with its fiery tail.

Hanuman's reflection in the blue sea appeared like a ship rocking with speed over the large waves that were raised by the wind of his flight. As the sea rose up it revealed whales, sharks and serpents, thrown about in confusion. Hanuman rushed through the sky like a winged mountain, drawing behind him white and red-hued clouds. As he entered and came out again from the clouds, he appeared like the shrouded and visible moon. Gandharvas with their wives rained flowers on him. Even the sun, honoring his service to Rama, did not scorch him. The wind-god raced with him, fanning him with a gentle breeze. Gods and rishis extolled him, along with Nagas, Yakshas and other celestial beings.

Hanuman flew forcefully into the morning sky.

The god of the ocean observed Hanuman flying above him. He considered how to render him a service, thereby pleasing Rama himself. In his depths there was a large mountain named Mainaka. The ocean-god approached Mainaka and asked him to rise above the waters, offering his peaks to Hanuman as a resting place. The mountain assented and began to grow upwards. It emerged from the sea with a great roar, foaming billows falling with a crash on all sides. The golden-peaked mountain rose swiftly and shone beautifully, with Nagas and Kinnaras sporting on its slopes.

Hanuman saw the mountain ahead of him filling the whole sky, and he thought it to be an obstruction. He prepared to strike it with his chest. The mountain deity assumed a human form and stood on its peak: "O Hanuman, requested by the god of the seas who wishes to serve Rama, I am here to offer you shelter. The sea-god was formerly rendered a service by Rama's ancestor, Sagara, who filled the ocean when it had been dried up by the angry Agastya Rishi. I too am indebted to your father Vayu, who once saved me from Indra."

Mainaka told Hanuman that, in a long past age, many mountains flew in the sky. Afraid of the mountains, the rishis asked Indra to cut their wings with his thunderbolt. Vayu had saved Mainaka from Indra. The mountain therefore wished to repay his debt to Vayu by serving Hanuman. He asked the monkey to alight on his peaks and rest for a while.

But Hanuman was not inclined to stop. He replied to Mainaka, "I am grateful and I thank you for your offer, but the time for resting has not yet arrived. My duty is not yet done. Please forgive me. You have already rendered me service by your kind words. Now please allow me to continue."

Hanuman respectfully touched the peak of the mountain and then rose still higher into the sky. The mountain and the sea-god both looked up at him and offered prayers and benedictions for his success.

Indra and the other gods also watched Hanuman. They were astonished to see his power. Desiring to test him and see more of his prowess they approached Surasa, the mother of the Nagas. They asked the snake goddess to assume the form of a Rakshasi and stand before Hanuman. Indra said, "We want to see his power, as well as further expand the fame of this great servant of Rama. Let us see how he overcomes you, O Naga lady, for he will be greatly tested when he reaches Lanka."

Surasa went into the sea and suddenly rose up in front of Hanuman in the form of a vast and terrible Rakshasi. She boomed out to Hanuman, "The gods have ordained you to be my food. O jewel among monkeys, quickly enter my mouth. Brahma has granted me a boon that none who come before me can escape being eaten!"

Surasa opened her cavernous mouth, which was set with rows of fierce teeth. Hanuman smiled and said to the Naga goddess, "I am on a mission to serve Rama, the lord of creation. You should not impede me. If I must be eaten by you, then pray wait here. Once I have completed my duty I shall doubtlessly return and you may devour me then as you please."

The Naga replied that he would not be able to pass her by, for such was the boon given by Brahma. She expanded her mouth even more as Hanuman came closer. Her jaws stretched for eight miles, but Hanuman quickly grew to sixteen miles. She then expanded her mouth to twenty miles and Hanuman again exceeded that size with his body. As the Naga grew even further Hanuman suddenly contracted himself down to the size of a thumb. Entering her mouth he went inside her throat and quickly came out again. He returned to his normal size and said, "I have honored Brahma's boon. Now let me pass and fulfill my mission. I wish you well."

The Naga goddess resumed her original form and praised Hanuman, blessing him to be successful in his quest. Hanuman moved on with the speed of Garuda. He saw many celestial chariots drawn by lions, tigers, elephants, birds and serpents as he coursed along the heavenly airways. Gandharvas, Yakshas, Vidhyadharas and other celestial beings were thronging the skys. Great heroes, who had lain down their lives in battle, rose upwards through the lofty region, their ethereal bodies shining like fire.

As Hanuman shot through the sky he was seen from below by a Rakshasa woman called Simhika. She gazed hungrily upon the monkey's enormous body. Desiring to devour him, she used her mystic power to suddenly seize his shadow as it sped over the water. Hanuman felt his progress arrested. He looked all around and saw beneath him Simhika's hideous form rising up from the sea, her terrific mouth open wide to swallow him. She thundered like a mass of clouds. Hanuman fearlessly entered her mouth. As he entered her body the Siddhas and gods cried out, "Alas!"

But Hanuman, whose body was as hard as a diamond, began to tear the demon's vital parts. He cleft her heart in two and burst out from the side of her body. The Rakshasi screamed and fell dead into the sea. Seeing Hanuman unscathed and flying onwards, the gods praised him saying, "Your success is certain. He who possesses firmness, vision, understanding and skill never fails in his undertakings."

Hanuman continued on, adored by the divine beings. Soon he saw in the distance a large island which appeared like a mass of clouds on the horizon. As he came closer he saw the shore of Lanka, skirted by forests and high mountains. Hanuman returned to his normal size in order to avoid being seen. Flying over the island he came upon the city of Lanka, which was perched on the summit of Trikuta mountain. As he climbed down the mountainside he considered how to best enter the city.

Hanuman surveyed the region. It was covered with beautiful woods filled with flowering and fruit-bearing trees of all kinds. There were meadows and lotus ponds and pleasure groves of every description. The aroma of flowers wafted on cool breezes and the sounds of various birds filled the air. Hanuman made his way to the edge of the city, which was encircled by a wide, deep moat. A golden wall ran around the city. Large pennants with small golden bells tied to them blew in the wind atop that wall. Ferocious Rakshasas ranged on the ramparts that ran along the wall. In their hands they held formidable-looking bows and other fierce weapons.

Behind the wall Hanuman could see lofty mansions and palaces, some golden and others as white as the moon. He climbed a high tree and gazed upon the city. Hundreds of tall and impressive buildings ran along elevated white-tiled roads. In front of them were many wonderful golden archways adorned with flowering creepers. The city gave off a roaring sound and appeared like the capital of the gods. To Hanuman it seemed to be sailing in the air. Lanka, which had been constructed by the celestial architect Vishvakarma, was inconceivably splendid and it awed Hanuman's mind.

Reaching the northern gate Hanuman sat in thought. He looked upon Lanka, which was guarded by innumerable gallant and terrible Rakshasas, as one might view a cave full of venomous serpents. As he gazed up at the high wall Hanuman reflected. How would the monkeys ever overpower this city? For a start, only he, Sugriva, Angada and Nila, the monkey general, could even cross the ocean and reach there. Then they would only be four against an uncountable horde of Rakshasas, headed by the invincible Ravana himself. What would they do?

Hanuman decided to first find Sita and ensure that she was safe. After all, those were his instructions. Then he could consider further action. He pondered deeply how to go about searching for the princess and yet not be discovered. Having taken such a great leap over the ocean, he did not want to fail now. It would be best to enter Lanka under the cover of darkness in an inconspicuous form. Hanuman decided to wait until sunset and enter the city as a small monkey. Going from house to house, he would locate Sita and then decide how to approach her.

That night the full moon rose in a clear sky, appearing like a swan swimming in a lake. Hanuman stood up, ready to enter the city. As he approached the wall, however, the presiding deity of Lanka came before him. She was fierce and ugly and she gave out a horrible yell. In a discordant voice she asked Hanuman, "Who are you, trying to covertly enter this city? You shall never be allowed to pass by me, O monkey!"

Hanuman cared little for the Rakshasa goddess. He did not reveal his name but rather asked her to first identify herself. She replied in harsh tones that she was Ravana's servant. She guarded Lanka and would now kill Hanuman for his insolence in trying to assail the city.

Hanuman stood as firm as a mountain. He replied that he would enter the city no matter who tried to prevent him. The Rakshasi immediately struck him with her hand. Unmoved by that blow and becoming furious, Hanuman clenched his fist and hit her but without his full force, as she was a woman. Nevertheless, struck by Hanuman, the demon goddess fell prostrate to the ground. After some moments she recovered and begged Hanuman to spare her. She revealed to Hanuman that Brahma had told her the end of the Rakshasas would come soon after she was overpowered by a monkey. That time had clearly arrived. The words of Brahma could never prove false. The time for the destruction of Ravana and the Rakshasas was nigh.

The Rakshasi told Hanuman to proceed into the city and then she disappeared. Hanuman assumed a form no bigger than a cat. Springing up, he climbed over the outer wall and began to penetrate the city. He moved along the main road, which was lit by celestial gems studding the golden archways along its sides. The road was covered with brightly colored flowers. From the houses he heard sounds of laughter and music, as well as the tinkling of ornaments and jewels. Those houses had crystal entrances and verandas of coral and lapis lazuli. They were adorned with golden images of thunderbolts and planets, and lattice windows of gold embedded with diamonds, rubies and emeralds.

Hanuman went quickly from house to house, searching for signs of Sita. He saw many demons engaged in amorous activities in their houses with damsels resembling Apsaras. In some places there were groups of Rakshasas praising Ravana. In other places some Rakshasas known as Yatudhanas were studying the scriptures and chanting sacred hymns. In public squares Hanuman beheld wrestling matches between Rakshasas of huge proportions, roaring at each other in anger. Hanuman also saw thousands of Rakshasa warriors, holding bows, swords and other terrible-looking weapons. As he moved unnoticed along the city streets, Hanuman, himself a military expert, could recognize Ravana's many variously disguised spies.

Gradually he approached Ravana's palace. In front of it was a garrison of soldiers, one hundred thousand in number. The palace itself stood on the summit of the Trikuta mountain, looking like a great white cloud. It was circled by a number of moats adorned with lotuses and lilies. Hanuman swam across the moats and, in his diminutive form, easily entered through the latticed gates in the gold brick walls. Thousands of exceptionally powerful Rakshasas stood on guard, but they paid him no heed.

As Hanuman moved through the first courtyard he saw numerous wonderful conveyances such as golden chariots, palanquins and large aerial cars. There were thousands of horses, some as black as night, some red-hued and others as white as snow. Massive elephants bedecked with jewels stood looking like clouds with flashes of lightning.

Within the courtyard were mansions occupied by arrogant and intoxicated demons. Hanuman could hear them laughing and shouting at one another in diverse tones. He silently entered each of the mansions, looking everywhere for Sita. Within every house he saw many women, some embracing their partners, some adorning themselves with excellent dresses, some sleeping and others, angered out of love, hissing like serpents. All of the women were highly attractive, with countenances like the full moon, and their dark eyes covered by curling lashes. Although Hanuman saw innumerable women, he did not see Sita anywhere.

Hanuman wandered through dozens of seven-storeyed mansions and finally entered the inner palace building where Ravana kept his women. It was embellished everywhere with pearls and gems of great value. The scent of aloe and sandalwood incense wafted and the sound of celestial music could be heard. Hanuman padded over the highly polished marble floor, which was spread with celestial textiles. The walls were made of gold decorated with silver carvings studded with gems. Thousands of exquisitely beautiful maidens moved about, their tinkling gold ornaments sounding together like the gentle waves of the sea. Adding to that delightful sound was the deep vibration of meghas and kettledrums.

Hanuman considered Ravana's palace to be the ornament of Lanka. In some rooms he found galleries of heavenly paintings and carvings of every kind. Sometimes the palace opened out to large grassy enclosures with ponds full of swans, surrounded by blossoming trees full of peacocks and other colorful birds. Hanuman saw sacrificial fires attended by ascetic Rakshasas who chanted Vedic mantras. Here and there were heaps of precious stones and other collected treasures. Couches, seats and beds were all of the most wonderful design and made of gold, coral and celestial woods. With his mind awed, Hanuman moved on without stopping, intent on discovering Sita.

He found the Pushpaka chariot lying in the center of Ravana's palace. It resembled a large mansion and shone like the midday sun. The chariot was embellished with every kind of celestial jewel and adorned with carvings of gold and silver. Birds made of cat's-eye, as well as others fashioned of coral and silver, decorated the chariot, along with lovely serpents made of jewels. Horses and elephants made entirely of refined gold stood on the sides of the Pushpaka. There were also large gold and crystal pleasure

houses containing many excellent seats. Golden stairways led up to plat-
forms radiant with sapphires and emeralds. Garlands and wreaths of heavenly flowers hung everywhere. Seen on the spacious central floor of the
chariot was a lotus pond, in which a number of carved elephants stood,
holding golden lotuses in their trunks and offering worship to a breathtak-
ingly beautiful form of Goddess Lakshmi.

Hanuman was astonished to see the mountain-like chariot, which
hung suspended in the air. The monkey moved on quickly, searching
Ravana's apartments, which covered four miles in width and eight in length.
Everywhere were powerful looking Rakshasas who held terrible weapons
and looked alertly in all directions. By his powers of illusion Hanuman kept
himself invisible to all the guards. He then entered Ravana's personal bed-
chambers. Its floor was covered with slabs of crystal, inlaid with figures made
of ivory, pearls, diamonds, coral, silver and gold. Large pillars of gems rose
up to the roof, which was studded with innumerable jewels and looked like
the star-spangled sky at night. On the walls were carvings of eagles with
huge outspread wings. Murals depicting the heavenly planets hung there on
the walls and the floors were covered by large silk carpets embroidered with
designs of mountains, forests and rivers.

The odor of celestial foods reached Hanuman's nostrils, calling him
like a loved one beckoning a dear relative. He felt all five senses being simultaneously attracted by the delights in Ravana's palace. The monkey considered that he had entered the highest abode of Paradise. He compared it only
to Indra's palace or the abode of Brahma himself. Fixing his mind upon his
purpose, like a consummate yogi meditating on the Supreme, Hanuman
continued to search for Sita.

As he went into each separate chamber Hanuman saw many maidens
looking like heavenly nymphs. They were half-dressed and lying asleep,
overpowered by intoxication and lovemaking. Adorned with jeweled girdles
and anklets, they emitted a fragrance like lotus flowers. Their large lips, red
like copper, parted slightly showing rows of teeth that resembled pearls.
Crushed garlands lay here and there, along with discarded silk raiments.
The delicate-limbed ladies lay with their clothes and necklaces thrown
about, and other ornaments fallen to the floor by their beds. With their
large, dark-lashed eyes closed, they looked like lotuses with their petals
closed at night. To Hanuman they appeared like a number of brilliant meteors fallen from heaven and united there in Ravana's chambers.

Although Ravana's wives, who were daughters of Gandharvas, rishis
and powerful demons, were beautiful beyond compare, Hanuman considered them nothing in comparison to Sita. His mind did not waver even
slightly from his mission upon seeing them. As he went by the sleeping

maidens, he came to a prominent dais made of crystal and bedecked with precious stones. It appeared like a celestial structure with a large gold and ivory couch placed on it. Over the top of the brilliant couch a hung a white canopy wreathed with garlands of lotuses and red ashoka flowers.

Lying there fast asleep was Ravana himself. Hanuman saw he was extremely handsome, with a complexion like a dark cloud. He was adorned with bright flashing earrings and clad in robes of gold and crimson. His limbs were smeared with red sandal-paste and he resembled a cloud reddened by the sunset and lit by flashes of lightning. Decorated with garlands and jewels he seemed like Mount Mandara covered with clusters of trees and flowers.

Hanuman looked with disgust upon the great demon, who lay snoring like an elephant. He shrank back and gazed upon the demon from a distance. Ravana was only displaying one of his ten heads and two of his arms. To Hanuman those arms appeared to be a couple of large five-hooded serpents lying asleep in a cave on Mount Mandara. They were well-muscled and as thick as tree trunks, scarred from the many battles Ravana had fought with the gods. On his head Ravana wore a brilliant diadem, and around his neck hung a string of pearls and gold chains. As the demon breathed out, the odor of liquor mixed with mango and nutmeg filled the room.

At his feet were many youthful women. They had all fallen asleep in various positions, one of them hugging her vina, another seated with a small drum under her arm, and another clutching a pair of tambourines. Next to Ravana on the couch was a lady of astounding beauty, golden-complexioned with exquisitely formed limbs decorated with the best of jewels. Seeing her lying there, endowed with celestial splendor and the exuberance of youth, Hanuman thought for a moment that she might be Sita. Filled with delight, he leapt about, waving his arms and kissing his tail. Displaying his monkey nature, he frolicked around, climbing the pillars and dropping to the floor, pacing back and forth and flipping over again and again.

Suddenly he paused and thought, "This surely could not be Sita. Separated from Rama, the princess would never be able to sleep or eat or even adorn herself. Nor would she consort with another man even in her mind, even if he be the lord of the celestials himself. None could equal Rama, that divine lady's beloved husband."

Hanuman examined the sleeping maiden by Ravana's side closely. Her face showed no signs of grieving or sorrow. There was no doubt; this could not be Sita. He moved on quickly, keener than ever to locate the princess.

He continued searching Ravana's vast bedchamber. There were thousands of women lying everywhere. All of them were beautiful and adorned with blazing golden ornaments. Hanuman saw tables spread with every kind of food and drink placed in gold and crystal vessels. The floor was strewn with celestial flowers and looked most charming, shedding a bright luster into that great hall. But although he scrupulously examined every part of the room, he did not see Sita anywhere.

As Hanuman looked upon the many semi-clad women, he felt a grave misgiving. Was this not sinful? To look upon the wives of others, especially in such a condition, was always condemned by scripture. Even looking upon the sinful Ravana, who had stolen other's wives, was itself sinful. Hanuman felt disturbed, but he considered his mission. Where else could he find Sita? He had to look for her among Ravana's women. And he had not looked at them with even a slight tinge of lust. His mind was steady, firmly fixed on Rama's service. It was not possible that sin could overcome him in such circumstances.

Feeling reassured but simultaneously despondent at not finding Sita, Hanuman came out of the bed chamber. Where should he look now? How could he return without finding Sita? What would he say to Sugriva and Rama when they asked him, "What did you accomplish upon reaching Lanka?" Maybe that sorrowful lady had died of grief. Or perhaps the Rakshasas had devoured her. Hanuman could not bear such thoughts. He had to keep looking. If he could not find Sita, then he would fast until death.

Thinking in this way he went along the paths outside the palace. As he walked he saw ahead of him the palace gardens. They had not yet been searched. Hanuman prayed to the gods that he might at last succeed in finding Sita. He paused as he reached the gardens and thought of Rama. Thrilled at the prospect of finding the princess, he leapt up onto the top of the surrounding wall.

From his vantage point Hanuman surveyed the lovely grove, which was lit by the moon. A sweet fragrance reached his nostrils as he looked over the large enclosure. He saw blossoming trees of every kind, as well as silvery creepers and golden shrubs. Flowers grew everywhere along the sides of immaculate lawns. Peacocks and parrots perched on the trees, along with many other varieties of colorful birds. Hanuman ran quickly along the wall, carefully examining the garden. He jumped from tree to tree and they shed their flowers, making the earth appear like a richly adorned woman. As he leapt he awoke flocks of birds who flew upwards, shaking the branches of the trees and showering Hanuman with blossoms.

Hanuman moved impetuously, anxious to find Sita. He saw ponds of different shapes full of lotuses and sleeping swans. There were bathing pools with golden steps leading down to them and banks of fine sand made entirely of crushed pearls. Rivulets ran between silver trees covered over by flowers of gold. Fruits such as Hanuman had never seen hung from the boughs of the trees. Everywhere the monkey looked he was wonderstruck at the opulence. In the center of the garden he came upon a large simshapa tree. He climbed to its top and gazed around in all directions, eager to catch sight of Sita. At a distance away he saw a temple situated in a large grove of ashoka trees. Those trees, with their thousands of bright red blossoms appearing in every season, seemed as though made entirely of flowers. Simply by looking upon those splendid trees, a man would feel his grief dispelled. The lofty temple amid the trees was standing on a thousand marble pillars. It looked like Mount Kailash, Shiva's glorious abode. Steps of coral rose up to a large terrace of refined gold.

Hanuman spotted a woman lying near the temple. She was surrounded by Rakshasis and tossing about on the ground. Hanuman leapt through the trees to take a closer look. The woman was clad in soiled garments, but she was beautiful, like a diamond covered in dust. Her slender body was smeared with dirt. She lay repeatedly sighing and seemed distraught, her face streaked with tears.

This was surely Sita. Hanuman felt his heart leap with joy, but it was agony to see her in such a wretched condition, appearing in every way like the eclipsed moon. Although fallen to the ground and weeping, she spread about her a golden luster. Enmeshed in a mighty web of grief, she seemed like a flame intertwined by smoke. Her dark eyes, with their long black lashes, darted about helplessly, like those of a fawn snared by a hunter.

Hanuman gazed upon her. He recognized the celestial yellow garment he had seen waving in the breeze when Ravana had passed over the Rishyamukha. This was undoubtedly the lady seized by that demon. The monkey gazed with sorrow at the princess. How powerful and inscrutable was destiny! Sita was the daughter of a king and the wife of an invincible hero, yet she was now suffering torment. She was gentle, kind and always virtuous, undeserving of any pain. How then had she been placed in such terrible circumstances? It was inconceivable.

Hanuman thought of Rama. How could he now best fulfill his Lord's purpose? Sita was difficult to approach because she was surrounded by hundreds of fierce Rakshasis. Hanuman examined them carefully. All of the Rakshasis were ugly and grossly misshapen. Some had one eye in their foreheads, others had huge ears that covered their bodies, some had heads like boars, tigers, buffalos, goats, deer or foxes. Some had their head sunk into their chests. They were all sizes, some very tall, others dwarf humpbacks. Some had the legs and feet of elephants, camels or horses. Some had abnormally long and twisted noses, some had large pointed ears or fierce lion-like teeth. Others had hair down to their feet and hands with claws.

The sight of the Rakshasis made one's hair stand on end. They clutched various types of weapons and stood or sat about Sita, watching in all directions. In their midst the noble princess seemed like the moon beseiged by malevolent planets. Hanuman thought carefully. He remained hiding among the boughs of the tree. Dawn was approaching and the sky to the east was beginning to lighten.

Just at that time Ravana was being awakened. Musical instruments were played and poets sang his glories. The demon rose up with his hair and garments in disarray, still intoxicated by the strong liquors he had drunk the night before. Immediately he thought of Sita. Quickly arranging his dress and adorning himself with every kind of ornament, Ravana went out of his rooms toward the gardens and made his way hastily to the ashoka grove. Behind him came one hundred beautiful maidens, their large hips and breasts swaying as they struggled to keep up with him. They carried whisks with golden handles, oil torches, pitchers of wine and pure white umbrellas. Their gold ornaments jangled together and flowers fell from their hair and garlands as they ran. Moving behind the demon they appeared like flashes of lightning following a cloud.

Although he possessed great power, the evil-minded Ravana was a slave to his lusty desires. With his mind fixed upon Sita, he passed through the golden, gem-encrusted arches at the entrance to the ashoka grove. In a god-like human form he headed straight for the place where Sita lay, longing to get another sight of the divine princess. As he walked he composed poetic phrases in his mind to win Sita over.

Hanuman, concealed in his tree, heard the tinkling of ankle bells approaching. He looked around and saw Ravana making his way along the path, illumined on all sides by bright torches. The demon moved quickly with his slanted coppery eyes staring straight ahead. He was adjusting his upper garment of pure white silk embellished with flowers and pearls. Preoccupied with his thoughts of Sita, he got his golden armlet entangled with his necklace of shining jewels, and he struggled to release it as he strode along the path.

Hanuman remained completely still as Ravana passed by the tree where he was hidden. Once the group of women had passed him, however, Hanuman leapt down and silently followed them toward Sita. The monkey hid behind the trunk of a large tree close to Sita and cautiously peered around it to see Rama's glorious consort seated on the ground, trembling at the sight of Ravana approaching her. Her knees were drawn up to her chest and she held them tight with her arms.

Ravana, who appeared youthful and majestic, and who shone with a brilliant aura, stood before the princess. She looked miserable and stricken, like a rose creeper torn from a tree and thrown to the ground. She appeared like a shattered faith, or a frustrated hope, or an abandoned treasure. She was covered with dirt yet charming as a pure white lotus stained with mud. Weeping incessantly, she tossed about on the bare earth, her mind absorbed in thoughts of Rama.

The Rakshasa king sought to seduce her, as a fool would walk heedlessly toward a steep precipice. He gazed down at the forlorn Sita, who did not even glance up at him. With her palms folded she prayed to Vishnu that he might soon bring Rama to her presence.

Ravana said, "O most splendid jewel among women, do not be afraid of me. I am here only to render you service. Why do you lie here in a wretched condition? Rise up and enjoy with me. I shall provide you with pleasures only the gods know."

Sita turned her face away in contempt, her body wracked by sobs. Ravana had tried to win her over each day since taking her captive, but his attempts sickened her. She longed for the day when Rama would come and destroy the demon. Surely that time would soon come. She did not feel that she could take much more of Ravana's torment.

Sita's resistance only made Ravana's desire for her the more insistent. He stared at her imcomparably beautiful form. Even though she had been fasting and had not washed since he had kidnapped her, she was still far more lovely than any of his consorts. Indeed, if it were not for Nalakuvera's curse. . .

The demon folded his hands in supplication. "What will you gain by lying here grieving? Your youth is passing swiftly and will soon be gone. Enjoy with me now while you can. There are none in the universe who can compare with me in virility and power. You are the finest of all women. I believe that after creating you the celebrated Brahma must have retired, seeing his work to have reached perfection."

Ravana offered her the position of his principal queen. He would subjugate the entire world and offer it to her father Janaka. He had already conquered the gods in heaven and now stood unchallenged as the most powerful person in the universe. What could Rama do against him? Sita should stop thinking of her puny prince, who was clad in rags and lived in a lonely forest. Perhaps, Ravana suggested, Rama had already died. There was no chance that she would ever see him again. And even if he should somehow find his way to Lanka, he would be immediately destroyed by Ravana, standing at the head of an unlimited number of invincible Rakshasas.

The demon went on, his voice rising and falling melodiously as he implored Sita. "Become my wife, O most beloved one, and enjoy life. Put on the best of garments and gold ornaments. Shake off your grief and range freely with me in delightful groves along the seashore."

Sita shuddered at Ravana's sinful suggestion. Without looking at him, and placing a symbolic blade of grass between herself and the demon, she replied, "Give up your futile hope. You no more deserve me than a sinful man deserves perfection. How do you expect me to perform an act condemned by all pious women? How do you imagine that I will rest upon the arm of any other man after I have once rested upon Rama's arm? Do you not realize that molesting the wives of others leads only to destruction? Evidently there is no one in Lanka who knows morality. Or perhaps you have become so degraded that you are simply unable to heed good advice."

Ravana snorted in anger. He clenched and unclenched his fists. There seemed to be no way of winning this woman. His eyes remained fixed upon her as she continued without looking at him. "You should know me to be as inseparable from Rama as sunlight is inseparable from the sun. Unite me with Rama at once if you wish to do good for yourself and your Rakshasa race. Make friends with Rama. Otherwise, see your city, yourself and all the demons destroyed for good. If I am kept here, you will soon see well-aimed arrows joined end to end filling the sky. They will rain down upon Lanka like so many fire-mouthed serpents. You were able to steal me only when Rama and his brother were not present. Indeed, O weak one, it is not possible for you to stand in the sight of Rama and Lakshmana any more than a dog can remain under the gaze of a pair of lions."

Sita rebuked Ravana further. Even if he sought shelter on the peak of Mount Meru or descended to Varuna's abode, he would not escape from Rama. By his wicked act of stealing Sita he was already killed by his own destiny. Rama would be the instrument to fulfill that fate. With the evil Ravana remaining their leader, the Rakshasa race would be destroyed to their roots.

Sita spoke harshly. "I would burn you to ashes myself by the power of my asceticism and chastity, but I do not have my lord's order. Nor do I wish to waste my ascetic merits on such a wretch as yourself."

Ravana was furious. Breathing heavily he spoke slowly, his deep voice barely constraining his rage. "Because of your insolent words you deserve to be put to death. Only my love for you prevents me from having you immediately killed. You have a few more months left of your one-year reprieve. If by then you have not submitted to me, then my cooks will mince you up for my morning meal."

The demon then turned away from Sita. His eyes flamed and his tongue darted out of his mouth. His shining diadem and his broad, powerful shoulders shook with his anger. His red robes swirled about him as he walked away and his large reddish-gold earrings swung back and forth. With his dark blue waist cloth he appeared like a mountain topped with crimson oxides and lit by lightning bolts. As he left the grove he turned to the Rakshasis. "Use whatever means you can to change this princess's mind. By soft words, coercion and threats, force her to submit. Dissuade her from thoughts of Rama and convince her to accept me. This will be in your own interests, O Rakshasis."

With a roar of frustration Ravana left the garden, his heavy footfalls receding into the distance. As Hanuman continued to watch, the fierce Rakshasis began to harass Sita, asking in rasping and grating voices why she was reluctant to accept Ravana as her lord. The Rakshasa king was the son of a great rishi. He had vanquished the thirty-three principal gods in battle. Even Indra could not stand before him. Now that very Ravana was bowing at her feet, begging for her favor. He was prepared to renounce his principal consort, the chaste and beautiful Mandodari for Sita's sake.

Numerous Rakshasis cajoled Sita in various ways. They told her to stop pining foolishly for Rama, a mere human. Of what consequence was Rama when compared to Ravana? She obviously had no idea what was best for her.

Sita turned away from the Rakshasis. Their advice was useless. She could no more abandon Rama than heat could abandon fire. She spoke with tear-filled eyes. "Devour me if you will, I shall never become Ravana's wife. As Sachi waits upon Indra, as Arundhati upon Vasishtha and Rohini upon the moon-god, so do I always wait upon my lord."

The Rakshasis were filled with rage when Sita rejected their counsel. They resorted to harsh and threatening language. Licking their protruding lips with their dart-like tongues, they raised their axes and other weapons at Sita. Sita stood up and walked toward the tree were Hanuman was hiding, with a group of Rakshasis surrounding and intimidating her. Seeing her approach, the monkey quickly climbed up into the branches of the tree. As he looked down from the tree he saw Sita severely afflicted by her Rakshasi guards. They spoke fiercely. "Submit to Ravana, O princess, or this very day I shall tear out your heart and eat it!"

Brandishing a huge dart one Rakshasi said, "For a long time I have wanted to feast on your liver and spleen, as well as your swollen breasts and indeed all your limbs."

Hanuman burned with anger. He felt the impulse to leap down amid the Rakshasis and immediately thrash them, but he restrained himself, intelligently waiting for an opportunity to first speak with Sita. If he revealed himself now, there would be chaos and the chance to reassure Sita would be lost.

Continuously tormented, Sita fell to the ground weeping. She cried out
to the Rakshasis, "A human woman is not fit to be the wife of the Rakshasa
king. Therefore finish me now, Rakshasis. End my misery!"

Sita embraced the tree, calling out Rama's name. Her face was pale and
she shook with sobs. As she tossed her head about her long braid of hair
writhed like a black snake. She wondered what kind of sin she must have
committed in her past life that she must now endure this suffering. If it were
not for her longing to again see Rama, she would have ended her own life.
How could she endure another visit from Ravana?

Sita turned to the Rakshasis, who were still threatening her as she lay
clutching the tree. "O wicked ones, I would not touch Ravana even with my
left foot. That evil one should understand it now. I would not go to him
even under threat of being transfixed, hacked to pieces, roasted in fire or
hurled down from mountain peaks."

The princess thought continuously of Rama. Why had he not come to
rescue her? Surely he had not abandoned her. Perhaps he did not know
where she was. But Jatayu must have told him. Or maybe the bird died
before getting the chance. If Rama knew her to be in Lanka, then without
doubt he would have reduced the city to ashes by now. The ocean would
present no problem. Rama's fiery arrows would dry it up in an instant. But
what if Rama had perished from grief, being unable to find her? Lakshmana
would also die, seeing his brother gone. Maybe, after losing her, Rama had
practiced yoga and become detached from worldy things such as love for his
wife. But that could not be possible in one like Rama; he would never
become detached from his duty. Protecting one's wife was always the duty
of pious men.

Sita lamented, thinking only of her husband. She envied the perfect
mystics who had transcended the dualities of happiness and distress. For
them the loss of relatives did not cause any sorrow, nor did they long for any
pleasing thing. If only she could experience their peace. As she lay absorbed
in such thoughts, a Rakshasi named Trijata stepped forward and restrained
her companions. She had just risen from sleep and told them of a dream she
had experienced.

"I saw a shining personality, who was surely Rama, mounted upon a
celestial chariot drawn by a thousand horses and coursing through the air.
He was united with Sita. The couple wore white robes and white garlands
and were ablaze with splendor. I also saw Ravana, robed in black with a red
garland and sitting on a chariot drawn by asses."

Trijata described her dream in detail: Ravana had entered a fearful
darkness, his body smeared with excrement. She saw all of Ravana's sons
and ministers with their heads shaved and bodies bathed with oil. She saw

Lanka being set alight by an agile monkey and all of the Rakshasas disappearing into a pool of cow dung.

The Rakshasis knew the science of interpreting dreams. It seemed from Trijata's dream that a great calamity was about to befall Ravana. Sita was heartened by Trijata. She sat up and as she did so she felt her left eye throbbing and her left arm palpitating. This was an auspicious omen. That omen, along with Trijata's dream, gave Sita hope. She felt that Rama must surely be near. The Rakshasis fell away from her, some of them running to report to Ravana.

CHAPTER FOURTEEN

SITA IS FOUND

In the tree Hanuman considered what to do next. He wanted to comfort Sita and give her Rama's ring, but he was not sure how to approach her. She would likely think him to be Ravana in disguise using sorcery to trick her. She might cry out and alert the Rakshasas. What then? He could be killed or captured. How would Rama's purpose be served if that happened? What other monkey could leap across the ocean and return?

Hanuman thought carefully. He decided to remain in the tree and sing praises of Rama so that Sita could hear. The Rakshasis had moved away to a distance and would not notice. Hanuman started to speak out loud. "In the city of Ayodhya there lived a great ruler named Dasarath. That lordly king begot a valiant son named Rama, who possesses every good quality. Going to the forest in obedience to his aged and pious father, Prince Rama slayed in battle many violent demons."

Hanuman related in brief Rama's history up until the time of Sita's abduction. He described what had happened to Rama in her absence since then, leading up to his own leap across the ocean and arrival in the ashoka grove.

Sita was struck with wonder to hear the voice from the tree. She looked up and all around her, feeling joy upon hearing Rama's activities described. As she gazed into the boughs of the tree she saw among the leaves Hanuman's tawny figure. The small monkey sat humbly with his palms folded. Immediately she became afraid. Who was this creature? What was he doing in the tree? Was this Ravana's trick? But remembering the auspicious omens, Sita became thoughtful. She prayed to the gods that Hanuman's words might prove true.

Hanuman slipped down from the tree and bowed low before Sita with his joined palms raised above his head. "I assume you are Sita, consort of the highly blessed Rama. I am an envoy dispatched by Rama to seek you, O noble lady. Along with his brother Lakshmana, Rama waits in grief for some news of your whereabouts."

Sita felt overjoyed to hear of Rama, but she was still suspicious. What if this was Ravana? Nevertheless, upon seeing the monkey she was feeling a strange calm and peace of mind. She looked carefully at Hanuman and asked, "How can I know that you are not Ravana?"

Hanuman reassured her. He described the features of both Rama and Lakshmana in great detail, telling her everything he knew about the two princes. Hanuman then told her about himself and how he had come to meet with Rama. He spoke confidently. "Now that I have found you I will soon return to Rama. You will see your lord arrive here before long, marching at the head of an unlimited number of powerful monkeys and bears."

Hanuman showed her the ring Rama had given him. He handed it to Sita and she immediately recognized it. She was now convinced by Hanuman. Standing up in excitement she felt unlimited joy. Her eyes shed tears of happiness and her face shone brightly. She praised Hanuman. "You have achieved a great feat in crossing the wide ocean and entering this fortified city. O noble monkey, surely you are the foremost of Rama's servants."

Sita wondered why Rama himself had not come there. Why had he not smashed the city of Lanka and taken her back? Was he still strong in mind and body? Was Lakshmana well? Sita questioned Hanuman eagerly and the monkey replied, "Rama does not know your exact whereabouts, O godly lady, but he is well and awaiting news of you. As soon as he hears my report he will come here with his army and rid the world of Rakshasas. There can be no doubt whatsoever."

Hanuman assured Sita that Rama was always thinking of her. Indeed, his mind was distracted by grief due to her separation. He could not eat properly and hardly slept. Rama sat for long periods gazing into the distance, sighing heavily. He would not even brush from his body gnats and mosquitoes, oblivious to everything as he thought of Sita. From time to time he would call out her name and shed tears.

Sita felt simultaneous joy and grief as she heard of her husband and his own grief for her. She sat lost in thought of Rama for some time, looking like the bright moon seen through a veil of clouds. The monkey's words were like nectar mixed with poison. She could not tolerate hearing of Rama's sorrow. Her beautiful eyelids with their long black lashes fluttered as she blinked away her tears. She spoke to Hanuman, who sat with his palms folded and head bowed. "O valiant monkey, you must quickly bring Rama. Only a short time remains till the merciless Ravana will have me killed. The demon will not heed any good advice and is bent on bringing about his own destruction, held as he is in the grip of Death."

Sita told Hanuman that she had heard how Ravana's brother and minister, Vibhishana, had repeatedly exhorted the demon king to return Sita. He and other wise Rakshasas warned Ravana that keeping Sita would result in the annilihation of the Rakshasas. But Ravana would not listen. Sita had heard this from Vibhishana's wife, who had befriended the princess.

When he heard that Sita's life was threatened, Hanuman became alarmed. He spoke urgently. "Let me take you from this place immediately, O princess of Mithila. You may climb upon my back and I shall leap across the sea with ease. Do not be fearful. I could easily carry the whole of Lanka, Ravana and all. Therefore mount upon my back and I shall transport you to Rama's presence this very day."

Sita looked at Hanuman, who still appeared as a normal monkey less than half her size. She spoke in surprise. "Your proposal is surely quite monkey-like, O gallant one. How shall I even get on your back?"

Hanuman was piqued. This was the first time his strength and power had been questioned. Obviously Sita was not aware of his abilities. He needed to give her a demonstration. Hanuman began to expand his body, growing up to a huge size. He looked down at Sita and said, "I have the capacity to lift up this entire island, with its hills, woodlands, lakes, city, defensive walls and the very lord of Lanka, Ravana himself. Be done with your hesitation, O princess, and allow me to carry you to Rama."

Sita gazed up in amazement at Hanuman, who stood before her like a tawny mountain. She was reassured of his ability, but was still doubtful about traveling on his back. She said, "You are like the wind-god himself, dear monkey. When you fly with great speed it will be difficult for me to hold fast to you. The force of your flight will likely render me unconscious. I will then fall into the ocean, only to be devoured by fierce aquatics."

Sita also feared that Hanuman would not be able to leave Lanka with her. The Rakshasas would spot them and give chase. They were capable of fighting in the air with powerful weapons and Hanuman would be hard-pressed to retaliate as he flew with Sita on his back.

Sita explained that there were still other reasons why she could not take up Hanuman's offer. "I have vowed never to touch the body of any man other than Rama. I am already mortified due to being grasped by the sinful Ravana. I could not voluntarily touch another man. Nor could I allow anyone other than Rama to rescue me, thereby diminishing Rama's fame. I therefore prefer to wait for my lord, confident that he will soon arrive."

Hanuman nodded in assent to Sita's words. She was right. It would not be possible for her to cling to him while he flew swiftly back. And he respected her chastity, which was without comparison in the world. Resuming his normal size he said, "I shall now go back to Rama. Please give me some token so that he will know that I have actually met with you."

Sita replied to him in a voice choked with tears. "You may give him this token in the form of a message. Remind him of the time when we lived together on the Chitrakuta mountain and how I was once attacked by a crow and Rama gave me protection."

Sita told Hanuman in detail about the incident. The crow in question was Indra's son and he had wanted to witness Rama's prowess. He had attacked Sita, whereupon Rama had thrown a blade of grass at him, imbuing it with the power of the Brahmastra. The empowered grass had chased the crow across the universe and finally destroyed one of his eyes. Rama would remember that incident and know that only Sita could have recalled it.

Hanuman asked if Sita had any message for Rama. The princess replied, "You should report to Rama my wretched condition. Although I have the invincible Rama as my protector, I now appear like one forlorn. He should lose no time in rescuing me. He is capable of advancing against the entire host of gods and demons united together, what to speak of Ravana."

Sita took from her cloth a brilliant celestial gem which she had used to decorate her hair. Handing the yellow jewel to Hanuman she said, "Give this gem to Rama and say to him, 'Even as Vishnu rescued the Goddess Earth from the depths of the ocean, you should descend into the midst of the Rakshasas and save me.' O monkey, deliver this message to my lord."

Hanuman took the jewel and bowed low to Sita. It was time to leave. But he wanted first to test the Rakshasas' strength. Now that he had actually penetrated into Lanka he saw his opportunity. If he could incite the Rakshasas to fight with him, it would give him some idea of their force and power. And besides that, Hanuman wanted to do some damage to the demon forces before he left.

Thinking in this way, Hanuman, still in a vast form, began ripping up the trees and bushes in the gardens. He tore down the walls and archways and hurled them into the ponds. Moving like a tempest and roaring all the while, the Vanara created havoc in the grove. He took up a huge iron bar and stood at the entrance to the garden, eagerly awaiting the arrival of Rakshasa troops.

The inhabitants of Ravana's palace were terrified to hear Hanuman's roar, along with the crash of trees and the cries of frightened animals. The Rakshasis, who had been buried in sleep, woke with a start. They saw Hanuman standing at the gate of the garden like a towering hill. Some of them had already noticed that Sita was speaking to a monkey and they questioned her about his identity.

"How should I know anything about this wonderful being?" she replied. "You are the ones skilled in sorcery and magic. Why then can you not ascertain for yourselves the nature of this creature?"

Some of the Rakshasis ran in fear to Ravana. They reported to him that the monkey had entirely destroyed the beautiful gardens, leaving only the large simshapa tree under which Sita lay.

Ravana flared up. His eyes blazed and hot tears fell from them like drops of burning oil from a lamp. He thought for a moment. This attacker was probably a powerful emissary of the gods or even Vishnu. No one else would dare assail Lanka. Ravana ordered a select band of Rakshasa warriors, the Kinkaras, to capture Hanuman. Eighty thousand of them immediately gathered and left for the garden. The massive Rakshasas were endowed with extraordinary might, had large teeth and held fierce weapons. They rushed in a body toward the ashoka grove, keen to lay hold of Hanuman.

Seeing the colossal monkey they darted at him like moths toward a flame. They attacked Hanuman with their sharp-edged spears, maces, clubs, iron pikes and scimitars, surrounding him and shouting loudly. Waves of arrows sped toward Hanuman, rushing through the air and sounding like a roaring gale.

Hanuman assumed an even larger form. He lashed the ground with his tail and uttered a great cry. "Victory to Rama and Lakshmana! I am Hanuman, the son of the wind-god, and I am here as Rama's servant. Not even a thousand Ravanas can withstand me. I shall destroy Lanka and then return to my master."

The Kinkaras were struck with fear upon seeing Hanuman's size and hearing his booming voice, which shook the earth. They closed in on him in thousands. Hanuman whirled the iron bar and began striking the demons down. Bounding into the air and tearing through the Rakshasa ranks, Hanuman swiftly annihilated them. He moved like the wind and could hardly be seen by the Rakshasas. In a short time they were virtually wiped out. A few of them survived and ran back to Ravana.

The demon king became even more furious. He ordered one of his great generals, Jambumali, to attack Hanuman. The Rakshasa bowed to Ravana and went out for battle clutching his golden bow. Jambumali mounted a chariot drawn by a hundred tall steeds with the heads of fiends. He twanged his bowstring, making a sound like thunder and, roaring with anger, raced toward the palace gardens.

Meanwhile Hanuman had been looking around to see what further destruction he could cause. He saw an enormous temple atop a great hill where the Rakshasas worshipped their guardian deity. He quickly climbed the hill and scaled the side of the temple, which appeared like the sheer face of a mountain. As he went up the wall of the temple, the effulgent Hanuman resembled the rising sun. Repeatedly crying out, "Victory to Rama!" he began tearing down the buttresses and large stone arches all around the temple. In minutes he reduced the entire edifice to a pile of rubble.

Hanuman leapt down from the hill and spotted Jambumali coming toward him. The demon was dressed in crimson robes with a garland of bright red flowers round his neck and a chaplet of red jewels on his head. Large gold earrings shone brilliantly from his blackish-blue pointed ears. He roared loudly and fired a hundred long shafts from his bow.

Hanuman also roared when he saw the demon. He stood joyfully in front of the bellowing Rakshasa. Jambumali pierced the monkey all over with his terrible arrows. With one large crescent-headed shaft he struck Hanuman in the mouth, while with a number of barbed arrows he hit him in his arms and legs. His head stained with blood, Hanuman looked like a large red lotus in the sky. He was infuriated and he took up an immense boulder, hurling it with tremendous force at Jambumali.

The demon laughed and instantly released ten powerful arrows which smashed the flying rock into fragments. Enraged, Hanuman then uprooted a sal tree and whirled it about. Jambumali again shot his razor-sharp arrows and cut the tree to pieces. He continued to pierce Hanuman with more and more arrows.

The monkey lost his patience and again took up the great iron rod with which he had slain the Kinkaras. With innumerable arrows sticking from his body he rushed toward the demon. He bounded into the air and came down onto Jambumali's chariot, bringing the rod down onto his skull. Smashed by Hanuman, the demon's head was pressed into his body, which itself was crushed into a shapeless mass. The chariot was shattered and the demonic donkeys ran here and there, bellowing in fear.

Ravana was astounded to hear that Jambumali had been slain. He again ordered seven more of his generals to go out for battle. The Rakshasa warriors went out to meet Hanuman shouting in joy, each of them eager to excel the others in battle. They mounted large chariots overlaid with golden armor and decked with banners and flags. Rumbling like thunderclouds, the chariots rushed toward Hanuman. The demons were expert in the use of celestial weapons and they began to release all kinds of missiles at the great monkey.

Hanuman leapt into the sky and wheeled about with his arms and legs outstretched. He dodged the arrows and missiles of the Rakshasas, who themselves rose into the sky to fight him. As he sported with the Rakshasas, who each held a golden bow, Hanuman looked like the powerful wind-god

playing among thunderclouds with streaks of lightning. He swept down
upon the demons one by one, striking them with his hands and feet. Hanuman killed all of them, and they fell to the ground like mountains struck
down by Indra's thunderbolt.

Hanuman then descended to earth and stood again at the gateway to
the gardens, eager to fight with more demons. The ground was strewn with
the bodies of Rakshasas and smashed chariots. Elephants and horses cried
in dissonant tones and blood flowed everywhere. In order to strike terror
into the Rakshasas and create dissension among their ranks, Hanuman
shouted, "Send out your best fighters, Ravana! They will meet the same fate
as these here. I am Hanuman, servant of Rama. Soon millions of monkeys
like myself will arrive here, accompanied by Rama himself. What use is your
fighting? Release Sita now and restore her to Rama!"

Ravana decided that Hanuman could not possibly be a monkey. Surely he was a divine being created by the gods. The demon had seen some
mighty Vanaras, but this one seemed extraordinarily powerful. Still, surely
he could be vanquished. Ravana and his warriors had overcome the gods
themselves; it should not be too difficult to overpower this monkey,
whoever he may be. Ravana summoned five more exceptionally powerful
leaders of his army. Encouraging them by praising their strength and skill in
battle, he sent them out to capture Hanuman. He had to find out who this
monkey was and why he had come to Lanka.

But one after another Hanuman slew the Rakshasa generals. He struck
down the first three with his thunderbolt-like fists. The other two then
assailed Hanuman from his two sides, hurling their fierce weapons with
great force. Hanuman, who himself looked like a mountain, tore off the top
of the nearby hill, complete with its beasts, snakes and trees. Soaring
upwards with that great crag, he brought it down upon the two demons and
completely crushed them.

Hanuman then began slaying thousands of other Rakshasas who were
gathered there. He killed warriors by striking them with other warriors, elephants with other elephants, and horses with horses. The ground was covered with corpses. Hanuman appeared like the Time Spirit bent upon the
destruction of all created beings.

Ravana considered the situation. This being was formidable. He had
wiped out a number of near invincible Rakshasa chiefs. Nevertheless, how
could anyone ever defeat Ravana? That was impossible. Admittedly the
goddess Lanka had previously come screaming to him, speaking of his imminent destruction, but Ravana was still confident. If necessary he himself
would deal with the monkey, but first let him contend with Ravana's powerful sons. That should take care of him. Ravana turned to Prince Aksha,

who sat by his side. Spurred on by his father's glance, Aksha rose from his seat and went out for battle.

He mounted his golden chariot which shone like the sun. It was yoked to eight celestial steeds, all as swift as thought. A large red standard, studded with bright gems, flew from a bejeweled pole. Rows of fierce lances and javelins were arranged alongside numerous quivers of razor-headed arrows. Eight long and terrible-looking swords were fastened to the sides of the chariot in silver scabbards emblazoned with golden moons and stars. Urging on his steeds Aksha rose above the ground and swept toward the gardens, accompanied by thousands of other demons on elephants, horses and chariots.

The Rakshasa prince arrived before Hanuman in a few moments. He paused for a minute to assess his opponent's strength. Aksha was awestruck to see the mountainous monkey standing ready for combat. Hanuman looked to him like the blazing fire of universal dissolution. But the prince was accomplished in battle and he felt no fear. He gazed at Hanuman with his large red eyes, which resembled those of a lion. Aksha drew his great bow to its full length and sent three powerful arrows toward the monkey. The arrows struck Hanuman's head and he bled profusely, giving him the appearance of the newly risen sun.

Hanuman, his eyes bulging in indignation, looked down at the Rakshasa. Aksha wore a breastplate which seemed to be made entirely from gems, it shone so brilliantly. His golden armlets flashed while he worked his beautiful ornate bow. As he assailed Hanuman, Aksha seemed like a dark cloud covered by a rainbow, pouring a shower of flaming arrows onto a large mountain.

Seeing an opportunity to again display his prowess for Rama's cause, Hanuman roared in joy and sprang into the air. He darted about evading Aksha's arrows with the speed of the wind. Aksha's chariot followed him through the air like an elephant approaching a large covered well. The prince continuously fired his deadly weapons at Hanuman, who wheeled about like a firebrand.

Witnessing the fearful encounter between the Vanara and the Rakshasa, the gods were amazed. The sun grew dim, the wind ceased blowing and the sky echoed with loud shrieks. Even the sea convulsed and the Trikuta mountain shook.

Hanuman considered that the prince was a worthy opponent, although only a boy. The Rakshasa was growing in strength as he fought. He stuck to Hanuman wherever the monkey flew and pierced him with thousands of razor-sharp arrows. Hanuman became more and more infuriated and he made up his mind to kill Aksha. Suddenly turning as he was pursued by the prince, Hanuman struck the eight steeds with his palms and killed them outright. As his chariot descended to the earth, Aksha rose up into the air, holding his bow and sword. He resembled an effulgent rishi who had quit his body through yoga and was ascending to the realm of the gods.

As the prince flew through the sky Hanuman met him and took hold of his two legs. Spinning him around violently, the monkey swiftly descended from the air and dashed him to the ground. With his bones smashed and body bathed in blood Aksha fell dead.

Hosts of rishis, Yakshas and Nagas who ranged the stellar sphere had gathered in a body in the canopy of the sky to watch the conflict. Observing Hanuman's stupendous feat in killing Aksha, they applauded and rained down celestial flowers.

Ravana was filled with grief and rage. He turned to his eldest son, Indrajit. This prince had earned his name, 'the conqueror of Indra,' by once taking captive the mighty king of the gods. He had command of all the mystic missiles, including even the infallible Brahmastra, presided over by Brahma himself. Ravana extolled his son at length. He ordered him to go out and take Hanuman captive. The Rakshasa king felt confident that Indrajit would succeed and he watched with affection as the obedient prince marched out for combat.

Indrajit rushed out like the sea on a full moon day. He mounted a chariot drawn by four sabre-tooth tigers of immense size. With an arrow fitted to his bow he swiftly arrived before Hanuman. Upon seeing the banner Indrajit had seized from Indra, Hanuman roared loudly in joy, realizing that he faced the famous conqueror of Indra. The crash of the wooden tom-toms and war drums which accompanied Indrajit increased Hanuman's martial ardor. He grew even further in size and again leapt into the sky.

Indrajit fired his long-shafted arrows, which were covered in gold and had beautifully feathered ends. They screamed through the air with their steel points glowing bright red. Hanuman moved rapidly in all directions and skillfully avoided them. The Rakshasa released more and more deadly shafts and they traveled in long lines, like streaks of lightning, but the Rakshasa could not hit the swiftly moving monkey. Nor could Hanuman find any opportunity to take hold of Indrajit. The gods and rishis were struck with wonder as they watched the two accomplished warriors wheeling about in the sky.

The Rakshasa realized that Hanuman was formidable. But if he was a created being then he would surely succumb to the might of the creator's weapon, the Brahmastra. Indrajit fitted to his bow the special arrow he reserved for the Brahmastra. He chanted the mantras sacred to Brahma and released the missile. Hanuman, instantly bound by the divine force of the irresistible weapon, fell to the earth with his limbs stunned. He understood that the Brahmastra had overpowered him and considered the situation.

Hanuman had been given a boon by Brahma that the Brahmastra would only be effective upon him for a short while. He knew he would soon be released. But this was an opportunity for him to be taken before Ravana himself. That would be useful. He could deliver a stern ultimatum to the Rakshasa on Rama's behalf and then make his escape.

Having reduced his body to its normal size, Hanuman was surrounded by a large number of fierce Rakshasas who quickly bound him with large ropes. Hitting and kicking Hanuman, they began dragging him toward Ravana's palace on Indrajit's order. Hanuman feigned fear and, even as the effect of the Brahmastra wore off, allowed himself to be taken to Ravana. Within his mind the monkey thought only of Rama and how he could best serve him now.

The demons dragged Hanuman into Ravana's great assembly hall and threw him before the Rakshasa king. Ravana's fierce-looking ministers reviled Hanuman. Some said, "Let him be thrashed, roasted alive and devoured." But Ravana was inquisitive. Who was this being? Why had he caused so much havoc in Lanka? The demon turned to his chief minister and ordered him to interrogate Hanuman. The monkey immediately said, "I am a messenger arrived from Sugriva, king of the Vanaras. Both he and I are the servants of Rama, the lord of this world."

Hanuman looked up at Ravana. He was awestruck by the demon's opulence. Ravana sat upon a vast crystal throne studded with gems and raised on a platform of gold. On his head he wore a brilliant diadem set with priceless jewels and encircled by strings of pearls. His limbs were decorated with numerous gold ornaments inlaid with diamonds. He wore valuable silk robes and was adorned with crimson sandal-paste, painted with peculiar designs. His ruddy eyes were at once terrible and yet as attractive as large lotus petals. With his twenty powerful arms he looked like a mountain infested by five-hooded serpents. On both sides he was being fanned by elegantly adorned young women. Next to him sat his four principal advisors, who leaned across to him offering advice and reassurance.

Hanuman gazed intently upon Ravana, admiring his power and opulence. Surely the demon could have been the leader of the gods and the protector of the universe were he not given to violent and sinful acts. If this demon were enraged, he could doubtlessly turn the entire world into one large ocean.

Prahasta, Ravana's chief minister, was doubtful about Hanuman's identity and he questioned him. "Take heart, O monkey. We will soon release you. But first tell us who you really are. Are you an envoy of Vishnu, thirsty as he is for conquest over the demons? Perhaps you are sent by Indra or one of the other gods. Speak the truth! We do not hold you to be a monkey, for your power is very great indeed."

Hanuman responded that he was indeed a monkey. He again declared himself to be Sugriva's messenger. "We are Rama's servants. He cannot be conquered by any being in all the worlds. Take heed of the advice I shall now offer you for your own good, O Ravana."

Hanuman told Ravana the history of Rama and his exile to the forest, leading right up to the assembling of the Vanara hordes at Kishkinda. All these monkeys, Hanuman warned, were as swift and powerful as Hanuman himself. No one could resist them in battle. Seeking to create fear and dissension among the Rakshasas, Hanuman spoke boldly. "You should immediately release Sita before it is too late. Otherwise you will soon see an ocean of monkeys and bears descend upon Lanka. Rama and Lakshmana will stand at their heads, loosing arrows which are as powerful as Indra's thunderbolt. Not even all the gods united together could keep the princess of Mithila from Rama. If you value your life, restore her to Rama today."

Hanuman then described Rama's prowess. Rama could dissolve the universe with his arrows and immediately create it anew. Not even Brahma or Shiva could not stand before Rama in battle. Lanka and its Rakshasas would not present even the smallest obstacle to him. Ravana had placed the noose of death around his neck when he stole Sita. His only hope now was to go before Rama and beg for forgiveness and mercy.

Ravana was overcome with wrath. Opening his eyes wide he exclaimed, "Kill this insolent monkey!"

Hearing this command, Ravana's brother and counselor Vibhishana immediately objected. "It is never acceptable to kill a messenger. No virtuous ruler would even consider such an action. If necessary the monkey can be punished in some other way."

Ravana angrily replied that Hanuman had acted sinfully. He had destroyed the ashoka grove and killed many Rakshasas. But Hanuman replied that he had acted only in self-defense. He was only a monkey. His monkey nature had made him playfully tear down the gardens, and he had then been attacked by many fierce warriors. What could he do but fight back?

When Hanuman stopped speaking, Vibhishana continued to argue against his execution. Ravana's eyes blazed with fury. He always found his brother's advice hard to accept. But Vibhishana was wise; that much Ravana could accept. The demon king decided to inflict another punishment upon Hanuman. "Monkeys are fond of their tails," Ravana said with a smile. "Set his tail alight. Then parade him around the streets of Lanka.

After that, if he survives, he can return home in a wretched and mutilated state."

The Rakshasas quickly carried out Ravana's command. They tied oil-soaked cloths around Hanuman's tail and set them alight. Hanuman furiously expanded his body and began lashing the demons around him. Cursing, they dragged him from the hall and out into the streets of Lanka. His tail ablaze, the giant monkey marched behind his captors, carefully surveying the city. After all, this was an opportunity for further reconnaissance so he could advise Rama how the city could best be attacked.

Some of the Rakshasis reported to Sita that Hanuman was being paraded through the city with his tail alight. Upon hearing this news Sita felt aggrieved. She prayed mentally to the fire-god, Agni, "If I possess any merit from service to my husband and if I am truly devoted to Rama, then please prove cool to Hanuman."

At once Hanuman felt the fire on his tail to be cold. He wondered how that could be possible. Surely it was due to Rama's power, or perhaps it was due to Sita's mercy. Rama's god-like spouse is dear to all beings, Hanuman thought. The fire-god would certainly try to please those devoted to her service.

As Hanuman went along Lanka's streets he was derided and abused by the demons. The monkey decided to make his escape. He was tied around his torso with thick ropes that bound his arms to his body. Hanuman suddenly reduced his size and slipped free of those ropes. With a shout of "Victory to Rama!" he sprang into the air. He bounded across the rooftops and made his way toward the city's northern gate. As he leapt he set fire to the mansions of the Rakshasas with his flaming tail. Assisted by his father Vayu and by Agni himself, Hanuman soon had a large part of Lanka blazing.

Hanuman again assumed his colossal size and roared like the thundercloud that appears at the time of universal dissolution. Many buildings in Lanka cracked and fell, blazing, to the ground. Rakshasas ran and flew in all directions, shouting in terror. Seeing Hanuman standing like a mountain they considered that Agni himself had come to destroy Lanka. Rakshasas fell from the high windows of their mansions, their blazing bodies resembling meteors. Molten gold and silver flowed in rivulets carrying sparkling gems of every description. It seemed as if the whole of the Trikuta mountain was ablaze. Huge scarlet and orange flames leapt up and dense palls of black smoke hung like clouds around the mountain.

Some of the powerful Rakshasas attacked Hanuman. He took up a massive club and smashed them, killing thousands. "Here is the mighty and vengeful Indra!" some cried. "Surely this is Yamaraja meting out his awful punishments!" said others. Still others considered that Shiva had come there blazing with fury. Indeed, it might be any powerful deity, for the sinful Ravana had angered them all at different times. Perhaps it was even the infallible and unassailable Vishnu, Lord of the entire creation.

Hanuman stood on the northern rampart and looked around at the blazing city. Scenes of chaos and turmoil met his eyes on all sides. He felt satisfied with his work and decided that it was time to return to the mainland. In the sky above him the gods and rishis had assembled and were extolling him with choice poems.

But a sudden apprehension seized Hanuman. What about Sita? Surely the princess had been burned alive in this immense conflagration. How had he been so impetuous? Hanuman cursed himself for falling a victim to anger. Under the impulse of anger a person could kill his elders or rebuke those worthy of worship. He had let himself come fully under the sway of his fury with no thought of the terrible consequences. What would happen now if Sita were killed? The monkey felt gripped by despondency.

Even as Hanuman thought this, however, he heard from the sky the Charanas saying, "Hanuman has achieved a great and marvelous feat. This city of Lanka, thickly crowded with demons, has been burnt on all sides. It now stands as if shrieking and yet the gentle Sita has not been harmed in the least."

Reassured by their words, Hanuman decided then to depart. He leapt across to the Arista mountain on the northern shore of Lanka. As he ascended the mountain, which reached up to the clouds, large rocks broke under his feet and scattered down the mountainside. Deer and lions started and fled in fear. Large trees were crushed beneath Hanuman's tread, making a loud cracking sound. On the summit of Arista, Hanuman crouched down, ready to leap across the ocean once more.

Shouting Rama's name, Hanuman leapt into the air. Again the pressure of his leap pressed the mountain down into the earth. All its trees shook and shed their blossoms. Vidhyadharas, Kinnaras and Gandharvas, who were sporting on the mountain slopes, rose into the air as the mountain vibrated violently. Thousands of lions living in the mountain caves roared together with a terrific noise.

Hanuman rose high into the sky and soared away from Lanka, his mission accomplished.

PART THREE

WAR

CHAPTER ONE

THE ARMY SETS OFF

Hanuman sailed across the firmament feeling overjoyed at his success. He would soon see Sugriva and Rama and give them the good news that Sita had been found. Leaving Lanka in a state of confusion, he moved with the speed of the wind. No Rakshasas gave chase, as they were all engaged in trying to save their afflicted city.

Out of fear of Ravana, the fire-god had not burned his palace. The Rakshasa king fumed as he gazed out at his blazing city. He should have killed the monkey when he had the chance. Without doubt Rama and his troops would soon arrive in Lanka, and there would be a great battle. Ravana thought of his boon from Brahma. The demon had no immunity from humans. Would this human king Rama be the cause of his death? Was he Vishnu incarnate? He would need to be, mused Ravana. Let the fight go ahead. We will soon see Rama's power. Ravana would not cower before anyone. Death would be preferable. Indeed, death at Vishnu's hands was no shame. Some even said that such a death awarded one the highest regions of bliss. But under no conditions would he surrender Sita. Rama would have to take her by force or not at all. The demon stood lost in reverie.

Hanuman sped through the sky like an arrow loosed from a mighty bow. Within an hour, he again saw Mount Mahendra looming large in the distance. The monkey roared again and again, filling the sky with the thunder of his voice. Angada and the others heard his roar and stood on the seashore gazing up at the sky, relieved to realize that Hanuman's roar indicated success. Overpowered by happiness, they leapt and sprang about on the beach, shouting with joy.

Within a few minutes they saw Hanuman bursting through the clouds, appearing like Garuda in full flight. The Vanaras stood with joined palms in respect and appreciation of their compatriot as he descended upon the Mahendra mountain, which shook with the force of his landing. Hanuman quickly descended from the mountain and, again assuming his normal size, ran toward his friends. The monkeys surrounded him, raising cries of joy.

They offered Hanuman roots and fruits and laughingly embraced him with tearful eyes.

Taking Angada by the hand, Hanuman sat down in a wooded grove near the beach to tell him everything that had happened. "I have seen the godly Sita. She sits pining for her lord, surrounded by fierce Rakshasis and constantly harassed by Ravana. We should lose no time in rescuing the princess."

Hearing of Hanuman's success the monkeys sent up great shouts. Some roared like lions and others bellowed like bulls. Some raised ululations while dancing around and waving their long curly tails. In the midst of the foremost monkeys, Angada said to Hanuman, "Your feat is without compare. You have saved our lives and rendered a great service to Rama, who will soon be freed of his grief. What marvelous determination and valor you have displayed, dear Hanuman!"

Angada and Hanuman sat encircled by powerful Vanaras, even as Indra and Surya are surrounded by the other gods. As Angada questioned him, Hanuman described in detail all the events that had occurred since he left. The monkeys were delighted to hear how he had killed so many powerful Rakshasas and wrought havoc in Lanka, but they were horrified to learn of Ravana's terrible threat to Sita. Angada decided that immediate action was required. "How can we report to Rama that Sita lies in such a sorry state? We must recover her from Lanka. Here are monkeys as powerful as the gods. We shall all of us proceed swiftly to Lanka. Let us destroy that city, kill the evil Ravana and rescue Sita. Then we can return to Sugriva and Rama."

Jambavan did not agree with Angada. "Your suggestion is not wise, O mighty monkey. We were not enjoined to kill Ravana or bring back Sita; we have been asked only to locate her and report to Rama of her whereabouts. That prince has vowed to rescue her himself. Even if we should somehow succeed without Rama, we would falsify his vow."

The monkeys accepted Jambavan's advice. The old king of the bears was always wise and he considered everything carefully. He was right. It was better to report back to Kishkindha. Then they could go to Lanka united with all the other monkeys, headed by Rama and Lakshmana. There would be plenty of opportunities for fighting at that time.

The monkeys got up and immediately set out toward Kishkindha. With Hanuman at their head they bounded back as fast as they could. Within a few days they reached the Madhuvan forest, which lay not far from Kishkindha. The forest was extensive and filled with trees loaded with fruits and honeycombs. The monkeys took Angada's permission to drink the honey, which was actually meant for Sugriva, and they consumed it in large quantities. They became intoxicated and danced merrily here and there. Some of them sang loudly while others laughed hysterically. Some leaned unsteadily upon one another and still others lay flat on the ground. They rolled about and slapped their sides. Rolling the beeswax into balls they pelted one another in sport. They ripped down boughs from the trees and whirled them around in mock fights. Leaping from tree to tree they raised a great tumult in the forest.

The Madhuvan forest was guarded by a Vanara general named Dadhimukha. When he saw that thousands of monkeys were tearing down the trees and taking the honey he became infuriated. He dispatched a number of his guards to stop them. Accosted by the guards, the monkeys in Angada's party laughed and fought with them. They took hold of the guards by their legs and dragged them about. Others they tossed into the air and slapped around with their palms.

When even Dadhimukha himself was beaten by Angada, he decided to go and inform Sugriva of the situation. Dadhimukha told the monkey king how Angada and Hanuman, along with thousands of other monkeys, were wrecking the king's personal orchard and stealing his honey. However, upon hearing this report, the intelligent Sugriva became joyful. He turned and spoke to Lakshmana, who was by his side. "There can be no doubt that Angada's party has returned successful. O noble Lakshmana, my guess is that Hanuman has found Sita. These monkeys would not make so bold with my grove and its honey had they failed in their mission."

Lakshmana rejoiced and ran to tell Rama the news. Sugriva told Dadhimukha that he should tolerate the misbehavior of the search party and send the monkeys into Kishkindha.

Dadhimukha bowed to Sugriva and left at once. Realizing that Hanuman had accomplished a great service to the king he felt gladdened. As he raced back to the Madhuvan with Sugriva's message he forgot all about the beating he had received. Back in the orchard he saw all the monkeys, who by now had become sober, standing about urinating on the trees. He sought out Angada and bowed before him. "Please forgive me, O prince. I should not have tried to restrain you. Sugriva very much desires to see you and Hanuman. Please go there with all speed."

Angada spoke kindly to Dadhimukha. Then he raised his arm and shouted to the other monkeys, "All right. Let us now go to Kishkindha! Sugriva and Rama are expecting us!"

Sugriva awaited their arrival eagerly. He was sure that they had succeeded. It had been almost three months since their departure. There was no possibility that Angada would have returned if he had failed. The monkey king reassured Rama, who was experiencing deep anxiety over Sita.

Rama looked up with tear-stained eyes at Sugriva. This was their last chance. All the other parties had returned without success. What if Angada's group had also failed? Rama sat by Sugriva, anxiously waiting Angada's news.

Suddenly they heard cries in the distance and saw a cloud of dust rising upwards as Angada and his party rushed toward Kishkindha. Sugriva stretched and curled his tail in joy. He saw Angada and Hanuman at the head of the party, bounding swiftly toward him. They appeared like thundering clouds driven along by the wind. Within a few minutes they had arrived and were prostrating themselves before Sugriva and Rama. Hanuman sat before Rama with folded palms. "My lord, Sita has been found," he said.

Tears sprang to Rama's eyes. He jumped up and said eagerly, "Tell me everything about that godly lady, O gallant one. Is she well? Where is she? Where indeed is that wicked wretch Ravana?"

With Angada's permission, Hanuman related everything to Rama and Sugriva, describing in detail how he had jumped across the ocean and wrought havoc in Lanka. He told them how Sita was pining for Rama and would not even look at Ravana. He then gave Sita's message to Rama, along with her ornament.

Rama took Sita's yellow jewel from Hanuman. He pressed it to his bosom and wept softly. Comforted by Lakshmana he said, "Even as a cow sheds milk upon seeing its calf, so my heart melts upon seeing this jewel. It originally belonged to Indra and was given to Sita by King Janaka. By seeing this brilliant gem I have directly gained sight of my noble father-in-law as well as my beloved wife Sita."

Rama asked Hanuman to repeat Sita's speech again and again. He was pained to learn of her sorry plight and felt her words to be his only consolation. The monkey narrated to Rama his entire conversation with Sita. When he stopped speaking Rama sat silently for some time absorbed in thoughts of Sita. At last he said to Hanuman, "You have accomplished a great deed, dear Hanuman. None but Garuda or the wind-god himself could have achieved this feat. Who could leap across the expansive ocean? Who, having once entered Lanka as an enemy, could ever hope to emerge alive? You are a first-class servant, O monkey. You have achieved all that was asked of you and more."

Praising Hanuman in various ways, Rama lamented that he could not repay the monkey for the service he had rendered. All he could offer him was his embrace. "O Hanuman, that is all I can call my own at this time," Rama said as he took hold of Hanuman and tightly hugged him.

Rama then began to consider how to recover Sita. How could he and millions of monkeys cross the ocean? He again felt despondent and asked Sugriva if he had any ideas. The monkey replied, "In my opinion, a bridge should be constructed across the ocean. There is no need to lament. We now know Sita's whereabouts, and we have amassed an army that is more than capable of annihilating the demons. I am confident, for I perceive many good omens and my mind feels delighted."

After hearing Sugriva speak, Rama became determined. He said to the monkeys, "I am surely able to cross this sea, either by the mystic power I have acquired through asceticism, by throwing a bridge over it, or by drying it up with my fiery arrows. O Hanuman, tell us of Lanka's fortifications and defenses, for we shall soon arrive there for battle."

Hanuman described everything he had seen in Lanka. The city was atop a great mountain thickly covered with forests. At the edge of the city was a wide moat infested with alligators. All around Lanka were vast ramparts with steel-barred drawbridges and gates. Hordes of Rakshasas prowled about the ramparts, holding spiked clubs which could kill a hundred warriors with a single blow. Great catapults were lined along the defensive walls, as well as machines which could fire blazing iron darts to a distance of ten miles. Ravana's forces were all but unlimited in number. They were highly trained and could use every kind of weapon, and they remained constantly alert to any danger. They had already had enough time to repair the damage caused by Hanuman and would now be especially vigilant, expecting Rama's attack.

When Hanuman finished speaking, Rama said fearlessly, "Without delay I shall destroy this great city of Lanka. Let us immediately prepare to depart. It is the auspicious midday hour. Favorable constellations augur our success. Having abducted Sita, the despicable Ravana shall not escape with his life."

Sugriva warmly applauded Rama, who then began issuing orders. He asked Sugriva's commander of troops, Nila, to lead an advance party out of Kishkindha. They should prepare the way for the whole army, ensuring that no hostile troops lay in ambush. Only the most powerful monkeys should go, as a difficult task lay ahead. Rama personally named the best monkey warriors: Gaja, Gavaya, Gandhamadana, Rishabha, Dwivida, Mainda and others. Then he said, "Mounting Hanuman's back, I myself shall go, even as Indra rides upon his elephant Airavata. I shall march in the center of the army cheering the troops as they rush like a flood. Lakshmana should mount Angada's back, as Kuvera would ride upon the elephant Sarvabhauma, who guards the eastern quarter of the universe."

Sugriva bowed to Rama and then gave detailed instructions to his monkeys. Gradually, the many millions of powerful monkeys moved off in a southerly direction. Springing and bounding in joy they proceeded swiftly like masses of clouds driven by a gale. They roared and shouted their determination, "We will slaughter Ravana and the Rakshasas. Not one shall survive!"

The monkeys sportingly lifted and tossed each other around. They leapt up trees and hills and jumped upon one another's backs. As they pressed forward they roared like the tumultuous ocean. At the rear of the monkeys came Jambavan and his contingent of bears. In the midst of them all were Rama and Lakshmana, seated upon the backs of Hanuman and Angada. They looked like the sun and moon conjoined with Jupiter and Venus and surrounded by innumerable stars.

Lakshmana spoke to his elder brother. "The omens are all good, Rama. A gentle breeze follows us and the sun shines brightly. The beasts and birds run and fly along with us. This army of monkeys and bears are roaring in joy and they are ablaze with splendor. In the night skies I have observed numerous auspicious portents. Undoubtedly your success is imminent, dear brother."

Rama smiled as he rocked about on the back of Hanuman, who was racing ahead with swift steps. The vast party raised an enormous dust cloud which screened the sky. They were like a continuous line of clouds covering the heavens. When they crossed rivers, the currents flowed backwards for many miles. Bounding through lakes, they caused them to overflow and flood the surrounding land. They broke down trees and smashed rocks, haughtily vaunting their prowess to one another. Traveling by day and by night they quickly approached the southern shore of the sea.

When they reached the ocean Rama spoke to Sugriva. "Here lies the vast sea, O valiant monkey. This lord of the rivers cannot be crossed easily. Some device is required. Let us camp here and deliberate upon our next course of action."

When the army came down onto the beach it stretched for miles like a second ocean. It created a noise that drowned out the roar of the sea as the monkeys discussed how to reach Lanka. None was capable of emulating Hanuman's incredible leap. The Vanaras and bears stared out at the tossing waves, wondering what Rama and Sugriva would decide to do next.

CHAPTER TWO

PANIC IN LANKA

In Lanka, Ravana had assembled his ministers for a full council meeting. Seeing the terrible carnage and destruction wrought by Hanuman, the demon spoke to his advisors. "This city, which we previously thought unassailable, has been penetrated and wrecked by a mere monkey. My gardens are destroyed, our temple has been outraged and some of the topmost Rakshasas have been slain, including my own son Prince Aksha. Indeed, that wretched monkey has single-handedly turned the city upside down."

Ravana looked around at his advisors. He asked them to carefully deliberate and then decide on their next course of action. The demon king was apprehensive. He was sure that Rama and his army would somehow cross the ocean before long. And Hanuman's demonstration of strength and power had been astonishing. If the rest of the monkeys were like him...

Ravana continued, "I am depending upon your advice, O Rakshasas. It is said that he is a wise person who, before an undertaking, seeks the counsel of learned persons versed in the scripture. However, he who simply acts without due consideration and advice will quickly come to ruin."

The demon king's generals were all powerful, but they lacked intelligence and political wisdom. Without understanding the full extent and power of the Vanara forces they spoke of them derisively. The Rakshasas boasted of their own prowess, dismissing Rama and his army as being of no consequence. They reminded Ravana how he had defeated the gods, Gandharvas, Yakshas, Nagas, Daityas, Danavas and other foes in battle. Ravana had even repulsed Death himself. What fear could he have of an army of humans and animals?

One of the mightiest Rakshasas, Prahasta, stood up and, with his palms folded toward Ravana, spoke in a voice that boomed like thunder. "We were caught unawares by Hanuman, who sneaked into Lanka. Had I been prepared for him, then that monkey would not have left this city alive. Indeed,

I can sweep the entire globe clean of monkeys in no time at all. Simply command me, O lord."

Another powerful Rakshasa named Virupaksha stood up and spoke furiously, holding aloft his frightful iron bludgeon which was stained with flesh and blood. "How can we tolerate this monkey's affront? Order me and I shall leave this very hour! I will smash Rama and Lakshmana with my iron club and crush the entire monkey army. Even if they flee into the dread deep or take refuge in the heavens, they shall not escape my wrath."

One Rakshasa suggested that they employ trickery, disguising themselves as humans and infiltrating Rama's army. They could pretend to be a contingent dispatched by Rama's brother Bharata. Once they entered his army, the rest of the Rakshasas could attack from the air. The Vanara army would then be torn to be pieces by a two-pronged assault both from within and without.

One after another, each of the leading Rakshasas declared that he alone could defeat Rama and his troops. Ravana should remain peacefully in Lanka. The demon forces would swiftly cross the ocean and annihilate the monkeys before they could even approach the city. Standing together, the Rakshasa generals raised a great tumult in Ravana's assembly hall. They grasped their bows, arrows, spears, pikes, javelins and iron maces and asked Ravana for his order to depart for battle.

Vibhishana, Ravana's younger brother, then stood up. As the clamor of the other demons died down he spoke to Ravana. "The wise declare that force should only be used after other methods of achieving one's aim have failed. Furthermore, force is said to be likely to succeed only when the enemy is weaker, devoid of virtue or condemned by their own adverse fate. Rama is ever alert and possesses boundless might. He is virtue incarnate and is assisted by every divine power. No one who knows what is best would counsel an attack upon Rama."

Vibhishana was not like the other Rakshasas. He did not share their inclination for wanton living and violent behavior. Although he was Ravana's blood brother, Vibhishana was given to meditation and the practice of virtue. He also realized Rama's divine nature. He spoke gravely, intent on his brother's welfare. "Have you forgotten how Rama disposed of Khara and his troops? Think carefully about Hanuman's feat in leaping across the ocean and wrecking Lanka. Do not underestimate the power of Rama and his servants."

Vibhishana advised Ravana to give Sita back to Rama. If he did not do so, then before long he would witness the total destruction of Lanka. All the heroic Rakshasas would perish like moths entering a fire. Ravana should

pursue the path of righteousness if he wanted to see his city and his followers survive.

Ravana listened to his brother without comment. He did not like
Vibhishana's advice, but it made him somewhat circumspect. The demon
king then dismissed his assembly saying he would decide the next day what
should be done.

The following day at dawn, Vibhishana again approached Ravana. As
he passed through the long, wide passageways of Ravana's palace he heard
the sound of Vedic hymns being chanted by the Yatudhanas, blessing the
Rakshasa king that he might attain victory. Vibhishana knew that Ravana
was not going to achieve victory against Rama. He had to avert the total
devastation of his people, which he now saw as imminent.

Vibhishana entered Ravana's chambers and greeted his brother with
gentle and soothing words. Ravana glanced over at an ornate golden seat
and Vibhishana sat down looking intently upon his brother. Vibhishana had
studied all the codes of religion. He knew what was right in every circumstance and he now tendered beneficial advice to Ravana. "Ever since Sita
was abducted, there have been numerous bad omens in Lanka. The sacrificial fire emits sparks and is enveloped by smoke. The cows' milk has dried
up. Horses neigh dolefully even though well-fed and tended. Crows swarm
about, uttering harsh cries. Jackals howl ominously day and night."

Vibhishana described many other types of evil portents and again asked
Ravana to return Sita to Rama. "This action alone will save you, all the
other Rakshasas, and this city from destruction," Vibhishana said. "Even if
you find me in some way self-motivated you should not ignore my advice,
for doing so will have terrible consequences."

Ravana sat shaking his head. He grunted contemptuously and replied
to his brother. "How can Rama stand before me in battle? Under no
circumstances shall I return Sita. Today in council I shall issue orders for
battle."

Vibhishana shook his head sorrowfully. It was hopeless. Ravana seemed
bent upon his own destruction.

Ravana dismissed Vibhishana and sat brooding for a while. He had to
have Sita. For the last ten months he had tried everything to win her over
and was not going to give up now. If he could only kill Rama, then surely
she would be won. But this Rama was no ordinary man; that much was obvious. And if the monkeys were all like Hanuman, then he had a real battle
on his hands. No matter. There was no question of an ignominious surrender. A fight to the last was the only thing acceptable. If Rama were a mere
mortal man, then he would certainly succumb to the might of the

Rakshasas. And if he were Vishnu himself? Well, defeat at the hands of a powerful foe was never shameful.

Ravana would not be cowed by any enemy. He would fight. The demon rose up and swept toward his assembly hall followed by bards who uttered poems in his praise. Coming from his inner chambers he mounted a golden chariot and sped down the wide road that led to the hall. He was surrounded on all sides by Rakshasas attired in diversely styled robes and adorned with every kind of jewel. These powerful Rakshasas, capable of contending single-handedly with tens of thousands of warriors, roared loudly. They held upraised weapons of every sort in their hands.

As Ravana and his generals approached the hall, trumpets blared and conch shells blasted. Innumerable kettledrums were beaten as the demon king went through the great doorway into his hall. Ravana strode across the golden floor of the hall toward his crystal throne, which was spread with the skins of the priyaka deer. After taking his seat he ordered that a full council of war be assembled.

Immediately swift messengers flew off to every part of the city, calling for all the Rakshasa leaders. Hearing Ravana's order, the mighty Rakshasas rushed toward the assembly hall from all directions. Some mounted great chariots, some rode elephants, and others ran on foot. They quickly entered the assembly hall as lions might enter a rocky mountain cave. After prostrating themselves before Ravana, they took their seats, each according to his rank. As they sat gazing on their ruler's face, they appeared like the Vasus surrounding Indra.

Vibhishana took his seat next to Ravana on a throne of gold. When Ravana saw that everyone was present and sitting silently he turned to Prahasta and spoke. "You should issue orders to ensure that Lanka's defenses are fortified. All four kinds of troops should be made ready, for a great fight is at hand."

Prahasta immediately rose and gave orders to his key Rakshasas. Within a short time he returned to Ravana and said, "It is done."

Ravana then addressed the entire assembly. "All of you know well your duty in all circumstances. My undertakings executed through all of you have never proved futile. I wish to enjoy the royal fortune forever, ruling over Lanka with justice and compassion. However, we now stand threatened by Rama and his army for the sake of Sita, whom I abducted. I cannot part with that lovely lady, smitten as I am by the shafts of love. Although she has not yet submitted to my advances, she has promised me that after one year has passed she will be mine. Therefore I must by all means repulse Rama's attack. O Rakshasas, tell me if this meets with your approval or not."

Ravana lied about Sita. She had never indicated that she would accept him at any time. He gazed around the assembly with his ten heads, looking for his subjects' agreement. Except perhaps for Vibhishana, he did not expect that any would argue with him. But suddenly his powerful brother Kumbhakarna stood up in a rage.

"O Rakshasa, you now seek our counsel, but what advice did you ask when you stole Sita from Rama?" he thundered. "Actions taken without due consideration of their righteousness and without recourse to proper counsel lead only to grief. On an impulse alone you abducted Sita from Rama, and now you face a severe consequence. Fortunately, however, you have me as your well-wisher. I shall make good your foolish action by standing against Rama and Lakshmana on the battlefield. Give up your fear and rest at ease. The two human brothers will not return with life once they face me."

Kumbhakarna was as powerful as Ravana, but he had once been tricked by the gods into asking a boon from Brahma that he might enjoy six months of sleep at a time. Brahma had thus said he would remain awake for only one day every six months. The day of the council happened to be his one day of wakefulness. The following day he would again fall into a deep slumber. He was nevertheless devoted to his brother and was prepared to do whatever he could to help him. Kumbhakarna was wise and he knew Rama was a formidable foe. He wanted to fight him and either attain a glorious victory or, as was more likely, die gloriously at Rama's hands. But first he would need to be awakened.

Although smarting from his brother's admonishment, Ravana thanked Kumbhakarna for his support. Then Mahaparsva, a leader of some of Ravana's troops, stood and asked him a question. "My lord, having secured the beautiful Sita, why do you not simply enjoy her by force? Who can prevent you or do anything about it?"

Ravana then told them of the long-past incident with Rambha. "This is a secret I have never revealed," he said. "Nalakuvera's curse was reinforced by the words of Brahma himself. Indeed, the powerful creator, upon whom my own strength rests, said that if I ever again violate a woman, my life will end immediately."

Ravana looked around the assembly. The Rakshasas were dedicated to him and ready to fight with any enemy on his behalf. They sat awaiting his command. The demon king boasted to them of his power. "Surely Rama has not seen me in battle, as furious as the raging ocean and as swift as the wind. Otherwise, he would not be so foolish as to march on Lanka. He has not seen arrows like flaming serpents with forked tongues loosed in millions from my bow. Rama wants to face Death himself standing enraged on the battlefield. I shall consume Rama in no time. I will disperse his army as a the sun disperses a morning mist."

Ravana railed on for some time. When he at last became silent, Vibhishana stood up to speak. He knew it was more or less hopeless— Ravana was already set on battle—but he had to make one last attempt to make his brother see sense. His voice echoed around the silent hall as every-one listened to his words. "By whom has the immense and highly venomous serpent, known as Sita, been tied around your neck? That serpent has for its sharp fangs Sita's sweet smiles. Her bosom is its coils, her five fingers are its five hoods and her thoughts of Rama are its deadly poison. O Ravana, do not destroy your race. Before we see monkeys like great mountains bound-ing toward Lanka and arrows like thunderbolts falling on the heads of our warriors, return Sita to Rama."

Vibhishana tried at length to convince Ravana of his folly. Although he was rebuked by various Rakshasas he insisted that the only way to save Lanka was to return Sita. He made it clear that it was his duty as a coun-selor to tender advice conducive to the interests of his master. He would not neglect that duty out of weakness or fear, nor out of a desire to say some-thing pleasing. Even if advice were distasteful, it should still be given by a counselor who properly understood his duty. And a wise leader was he who was able to hear both palatable and unpalatable advice, giving equal con-sideration to both.

Indrajit became impatient and agitated upon hearing Vibhishana speak. He retorted. "How do you call yourself a Rakshasa, O weak uncle? Surely you are devoid of courage, virility, prowess, heroism and spirit. These two men can be slain by any Rakshasa, even the most insignif-icant among us. Why then do you tremble in fear?"

Indrajit bragged about his own strength. He had overcome hosts of gods headed by Indra riding upon the celestial elephant Airavata. He vowed that he would kill Rama and Lakshmana personally. Vibhishana rebuked him with strong words. "Being a mere boy, your intelligence is not mature. You cannot see what is right or wrong, dear child. Although called a son, you are actually your father's enemy. You are evil-minded and deserve death, for your counsel will lead only to the death of all those who listen to you. You are indiscriminate, dull-witted, wicked and ignorant. You do not understand Rama's power. There are none among the gods, Daityas, Danavas or Rakshasas who can withstand the flaming arrows Rama will loose in combat."

Ravana had heard enough. He would not accept Vibhishana's advice. All he wanted now was to get on with the fight that lay ahead. He spoke furiously. "It is better to live with an enraged serpent than a person who, although pretending to be a friend, is actually in league with the enemy. It is a fact that kinsfolk usually despise their chief even though he may be carrying out all his duties. The greatest danger lies in one's own relatives, O disgrace of our race, for they may turn on one at any time. Although a brother, you are unworthy of my affection. Indeed, one bestowing love upon the unworthy obtains only grief."

Ravana vented his anger, insulting Vibhishana in various ways. He told him that had he not been his brother he would surely have killed him for his words.

Vibhishana realized that there was nothing he could do to help the proud demon king. Along with his four ministers, who were his close followers and friends, he rose up into the air. Stationed in space, with mace in hand, he spoke to Ravana. "You who have addressed me with harsh words, O king, are deluded. Say what you will, for your intelligence is lost. Those speaking pleasant words can easily be found, O Ravana, but one who speaks unpalatable truth is rare. One fallen under Death's Sway does not heed the words of wisdom offered by a well-wisher. I have tried my best, wishing to save you from certain destruction. Now be happy in my absence. I can no longer tolerate your abusive speech, even though you are my elder. Farewell. I shall now depart."

Vibhishana soared away from the assembly hall, accompanied by his four friends. Ravana made no attempt to stop him and was glad to see him go. Now there were none who would oppose his desires. He issued orders to prepare for battle.

CHAPTER THREE

RAMA CONFRONTS THE OCEAN

Vibhishana had decided to join Rama. He crossed the ocean and arrived at Rama's camp in less than an hour. The intelligent Rakshasa stayed in the air and asked to see the leader of the monkeys. Sugriva quickly appeared. Seeing the five huge Rakshasas in the sky wearing armor and adorned with celestial jewels, he was apprehensive. He thought carefully. Had the Rakshasas come to attack the monkeys? Perhaps this was some kind of cunning trick, of which Rakshasas were so fond. Sugriva looked closely at Vibhishana. The Rakshasa looked like a mountain or a cloud and vied with Indra in splendor. All five Rakshasas were holding various weapons.

Sugriva spoke to Hanuman. "Surely these Rakshasas have some malicious intentions at heart. Let us take up rocks and trees. Leaping into the air we shall quickly finish them before they can execute their plan."

As Sugriva spoke, Vibhishana addressed him from the sky. "There is an evil Rakshasa by the name of Ravana. I am his brother Vibhishana. He has carried away Rama's consort by using trickery and deceit. Although I repeatedly advised him to return the princess, the demon would not listen. I have thus come here to seek Rama's shelter."

Vibhishana asked the monkeys to inform Rama of his presence. Sugriva was still highly suspicious. He ran up to Rama and said, "One of the enemy has suddenly made his appearance here. No doubt he seeks an opportunity to kill us when we are unaware. Perhaps he is a spy. There may be other invisible Rakshasas around. No trust should ever be reposed in these demons. Please tell us how we should deal with this one."

Sugriva told Rama Vibhishana's name and who he was, as well as what he said. The monkey king was sure that Vibhishana had evil intentions and had been sent there by Ravana himself. He suggested that the Rakshasa and his followers be killed immediately.

The Rakshasa stayed in the air

Rama listened carefully. He looked around at the other monkey chiefs who sat with him. "You have heard Sugriva's suggestion. What do the rest of you think?"

Each of them gave their opinion. They all felt that Vibhishana was to be treated with the utmost caution and suspicion, that he should be interrogated and tested before they placed any trust in him.

Rama then turned to Hanuman and asked his opinion. The monkey had studied all the scriptures, and bowing to Rama he replied, "Although you are well able to ascertain for yourself this Rakshasa's intentions, you nevertheless seek our opinion out of humility and kindness. I shall therefore speak my feelings in this regard. In my view we should accept Vibhishana as our own. I do not think he has any devious purpose."

Hanuman said that he had not detected any deceit in the speech or expression of Vibhishana. If a person has ill motives, then it is always revealed in their expression. Hanuman felt that Vibhishana had wisely decided that Rama's cause was superior to Ravana's. It appeared that the Rakshasa was moral and desired to assist Rama.

Having given his opinion, which differed from that of his companions, Hanuman asked Rama for his view. Rama thanked all of them for their suggestions and then said, "I cannot refuse to receive a person who has sought my shelter. Whatever his intentions I must accept a supplicant. This is never condemned in the eyes of good people."

Sugriva was alarmed by Rama's statement. He was still convinced that Vibhishana was inimical. The monkey king tried again to convince Rama. "What does it matter whether his intentions are good or bad?" Sugriva argued. "After all, he is a Rakshasa and will always revert to his own nature. Furthermore, if he can abandon even his own brother, then how can we ever trust him as our friend?"

Sugriva wanted Vibhishana to be taken captive and perhaps even killed. The Rakshasa was Ravana's brother. His allegiance to Rama would never exceed his deeper attachment to his own people. Sugriva looked anxiously at Rama, who smiled and replied gently, "Your concerns are well-founded, O noble Vanara, but I have given it careful thought. Even if this demon is malevolent, what harm can he do? I can annihilate the entire horde of Rakshasas with my fingertip. We should not have any fear. And we should always abide by the instructions of the Vedas."

Rama explained that even an enemy must be received with hospitality according to scriptural rules. If a person comes seeking shelter, then one must offer him protection even at the cost of one's own life. No consideration should be made of his intentions, good or bad. If a supplicant is turned away and perishes as a result, then he takes all the pious merits of the man who turned him away. Great sin is incurred by such neglect. Rama concluded, "If a person comes to me saying, 'I am yours' only once, then I shall give him courage and protection from all danger forever after. This is my solemn vow made here before you all. Even if Ravana himself came to me, I would not refuse him shelter. Bring Vibhishana here, for I have already granted him safety."

Everyone present was moved deeply by Rama's speech. With tears flowing from his eyes Sugriva said, "It is no wonder that you should speak in this way, O Rama. You are the best knower of what is right and are always devoted to virtue. My doubts are gone. Let Vibhishana enjoy our friendship on an equal level with all of us."

Sugriva gave Vibhishana Rama's message. Feeling reassured, the Rakshasa descended to the earth along with his devoted followers. He went before Rama and lay flat on the ground with his bejeweled hands touching Rama's feet. Getting up onto his knees, he addressed Rama respectfully. "I am Vibhishana, the younger half-brother of Ravana. Insulted by him, I have come here, abandoning my family, friends and home. O Rama, you are the only shelter of all beings. My very life now depends upon you."

Rama glanced affectionately at Vibhishana. He spoke soothingly to the Rakshasa, welcoming him. Rama then asked him about Ravana's strengths and weaknesses. "Please tell me in truth all that you know about Ravana and Lanka."

Vibhishana told Rama about Ravana's boon. He described the power of Ravana's chief warriors--Kumbhakarna, Indrajit, Prahasta, Mahodara and others. All of them were capable of facing the mightiest fighters even among the gods. Accompanied by them, Ravana had given battle to the four guardians of the universe, all of whom he routed.

Rama replied to Vibhishana, "I have indeed heard of all these exploits of Ravana which you have truthfully related. Hear me now! After killing in battle the ten-headed Ravana along with all his followers, I shall crown you king of Lanka. There need be no doubt whatsoever. I swear by my three brothers that I shall not return to Ayodhya without slaying Ravana with his sons, kinsfolk and people."

Vibhishana again bowed to Rama and promised to render him every assistance in the upcoming battle. Rama ordered Lakshmana to go at once and fetch some seawater. With that water Rama immediately consecrated Vibhishana as the ruler of Lanka. Witnessing this display of grace all the monkeys leapt about joyfully, roaring and shouting, while Vibhishana sat with his head bowed.

Hanuman then approached Vibhishana and asked how the army could possibly cross the ocean. After thinking for some while, Vibhishana suggested that Rama personally ask the ocean-god to reveal some means of crossing. The ocean had been excavated by a great king in Rama's line and thus the deity would no doubt wish to render him some service in return. Rama was pleased with Vibhishana's advice and he spread a seat of kusha grass on the seashore. He sat there and began to pray to the god to reveal himself.

As Rama sat on the beach Ravana's spy flew over the Vanara army. He determined its size and power and returned with all speed to Ravana. Falling before the demon king the spy submitted, "Like another sea, a deep and immeasurable flood of monkeys and bears is moving toward Lanka. They are spread out for one hundred miles in all directions. At their head are the two powerful princes, Rama and Lakshmana. Even now they are camped on the seashore, determining some means of crossing over it."

Ravana became perturbed. He ordered a demon named Suka to carry a message to Sugriva. "Tell the monkey that he has nothing to gain by assaulting Lanka," he ordered. "I have never done him any harm. What does it matter to him if I have carried off Sita?"

Ravana told Suka to warn Sugriva off. It would not be possible for monkeys and bears to defeat Rakshasas. Not even the gods could overpower Lanka; what then could a few mere mortal creatures do? They had best return peacefully to their own country.

The powerful Suka turned himself into a large bird and flew swiftly across the sea. He swooped over the monkey army and found Sugriva. From the air the Rakshasa delivered Ravana's message, but even as he was speaking the monkeys suddenly sprang up and dragged him down. They began to beat him violently. Suka cried out to Rama for mercy. "Only an envoy who has spoken his own view rather than his master's message deserves death. O Rama, I have faithfully related Ravana's message and should therefore not be slain."

Rama ordered the monkeys to let Suka go. The demon again rose into the air and asked for Sugriva's reply to Ravana. The monkey king said to the demon, "Ravana should be informed that I am neither his friend nor his well-wisher. Indeed, he has formed an enmity with Rama and is thus my sworn enemy as well. For stealing Sita from Rama the demon deserves death at my hands, and that he shall receive in due course."

Sugriva sent a message that Ravana would not escape even if he sought shelter in the furthermost part of the universe. He would certainly be killed along with his entire demon force. The Rakshasa was no match for Rama and his army. Ravana obviously lacked prowess because he stole Sita when Rama was absent. He now faced a terrible calamity in the shape of Sugriva and his army.

After Suka had left, Rama sat with a concentrated mind at the edge of the sea. He meditated on the sea-god Samudra and waited patiently for him to appear. Three days and nights passed as Rama sat motionless on the beach, but still the ocean deity did not come. Rama became enraged and he spoke to Lakshmana. "Just see the vanity of this god. Although I have sat here humbly beseeching his audience, he has not appeared. Alas, forbearance, gentleness and politeness of speech are construed as weaknesses by the wicked. The world regards with respect only those who are arrogant, harsh and given to meting out strong punishments. O Lakshmana, neither fame, nor victory, nor even popularity can be won by conciliation. I shall therefore stand with my bow and flaming arrows. I shall dry up the ocean this very day. The monkeys may go on foot to Lanka. Watch now as I exhibit my prowess."

Rama was furious with Samudra. Feeling insulted, he stood firmly on the beach, forcibly stringing his great bow. His eyes were red and he blazed like the fire of universal destruction. He instantaneously released hundreds of fleet arrows toward the sea. The ocean began to roar and rise up in massive billows. Clouds of steam covered its surface as the flaming arrows entered the water. Long, writhing sea serpents and great dark whales were thrown about. Waves resembling the Mandara mountain were seen to rise up one after another. Even far beneath the ocean the Danavas and Nagas felt disturbed and cried out in distress.

Lakshmana rushed toward Rama and held onto his bow. "There is no need for this display, dear brother!" he exclaimed. "Men of your caliber never give way to anger. Your purpose will surely be achieved without such violence."

In the sky invisible rishis called out, "O Rama. Hold! Be at peace!"

But Rama's anger did not abate. He placed upon his bow a large golden arrow and began thinking of the mantras to invoke the Brahmastra. Stretching his bow with vehemence he gazed furiously at the raging sea. Suddenly the heavens were enveloped by darkness and fierce winds blew. Large bolts of lightning were seen and the earth itself shook. The ocean surged back a distance of ten miles and rose up to a tremendous height. Rama stood immovable with his arrow trained on the waters.

Then suddenly before everyone's sight, Samudra appeared. Rising up from the ocean, he seemed like the bright sun at dawn. He shone like a glossy black gem and was adorned with brilliant gold ornaments. Clad in red robes with a garland of red flowers, he had eyes like large lotuses. A wreath of celestial flowers crowned his head. On his chest was a prominent jewel which shed a white luster all around. Surrounded by many river goddesses he came before Rama and placed before him a large heap of shining jewels taken from the ocean depths. He spoke in a sonorous voice.

"Every element has its natural state, O Rama. My nature is to be fathomless and unfordable. I did not wish to deviate from my constitutional position, neither from infatuation nor from fear. Nevertheless, I shall tell you the means by which I may be crossed by your army. The monkey named Nala is a son of Vishvakarma, the heavenly architect. He can construct a bridge over me which I will sustain."

Samudra assured Rama that he would be able to cross him without fear. The deity would ensure that the fierce creatures inhabiting his depths would not be aggressive. Rama still stood with his arrow at the ready on his bow. However, he was now pleased with the sea-god and he said, "This unfailing shaft must be released. Tell me, O abode of Varuna, where I should send this arrow?"

Samudra asked Rama to fire the arrow upon a part of his waters to the north. There were numerous sinful demons inhabiting that region and Samudra did not like his waters being polluted by this touch. Rama assented and shot his fiery arrow to the north, drying up that whole section of the ocean. Samudra then disappeared from view.

Nala was enlivened by the task that faced him. He informed Rama that he had been granted a boon by Vishvakarma, the gods' engineer, who decreed that Nala's abilities would equal his own. Nala was confident that he could build the bridge. He ordered the monkeys to fetch the necessary materials. The monkeys leapt about joyfully, applying themselves to the work with great energy.

Soon there were thousands of trees and massive heaps of rocks piled on the beach. Nala had them thrown in the sea and they sent up huge splashes of water. Using lengths of creepers to measure and make straight lines Nala gradually constructed his bridge over the sea. The ocean allowed even great rocks to float on his waters. Binding together tree trunks, rocks and reeds, the monkeys built the bridge toward Lanka. On the first day they covered over one hundred miles. Becoming even more enthusiastic, they built one hundred and fifty miles on the second day and nearly two hundred on the third. In this way the bridge was completed in only five days and reached right across the ocean to the shores of Lanka. On the southern shore of Lanka stood Vibhishana and his ministers, maces in hand, ready to repulse any Rakshasas who tried to attack the bridge.

The gods and Gandharvas, along with the celestial rishis, all stood in amazement as they gazed upon the bridge. It was eighty miles wide and eight hundred miles long. The monkeys and bears swarmed onto it shouting and roaring in joy. Like a great flood they swept toward Lanka. In their forefront

were Rama and Lakshmana mounted upon the backs of Hanuman and
Angada. They soon reached Lanka and ordered the army to encamp on the
shore.

Rama sat with Lakshmana and Sugriva. He told the monkey king to
have his troops ready for battle at any time. He spoke of evil portents he had
witnessed. "Winds full of dust are blowing. The earth is quaking and trees
are falling. Dark clouds are thundering and giving forth drops of blood. On
all sides there are ferocious beasts uttering fierce screams as they face the
sun."

Rama described many omens and said that they foretold the destruction of both armies. "Eminent heroes among the Vanaras, bears and
Rakshasas will soon be killed," Rama said gravely.

Sugriva had the army arrayed in battle formation. They spread out and
surrounded the city of the Rakshasas from the eastern to the western side.
As they approached Lanka they heard a deafening clamor of war drums
from within. The monkeys rejoiced at hearing that hair-raising sound and
they roared loudly, drowning out the drums. Hearing the terrifying roars, the
demons clasped their weapons more tightly.

Rama looked upon Lanka and felt a pang of separation from Sita. Here
she was at last. The vile Ravana also lay within this city tormenting the
anguished princess. Rama was anxious to face the demon. He spoke to
Lakshmana. "Here is the splendid city of Lanka, built long ago by
Vishvakarma. It looks like the sky filled with white clouds."

Rama had the army deployed in a human-shaped formation with its
arms reaching around the city. The most powerful monkeys were stationed
at the various key points. Rama himself, along with his brother, stood at the
head of the formation. The monkeys took up gigantic trees and rocks, saying to one another, "Let us dash this city to pieces!"

CHAPTER FOUR

RAVANA'S EVIL TRICKERY

In Lanka, Ravana received reports from his spies that the monkeys were amassed outside the city. The terrified Suka told him that Rama's army was inestimable in size and power. He recommended that Ravana immediately return Sita to Rama. Suka's suggestion infuriated Ravana. "I would not give back Sita even if the entire host of gods now stood outside Lanka!" he bellowed. "Oh, when shall my arrows dart toward Rama like bees toward flowers in spring? I shall eclipse his army even as the rising sun obscures the stars."

Ravana bragged of his power at length. He had no intention of making peace with Rama. The demon arrogantly asserted that his power was without compare. It would be a one-sided fight.

The demon king was nevertheless impressed by the fact that the army had crossed the ocean by building a great bridge. He needed to more carefully assess their power and he ordered Suka and another Rakshasa, Sarana, to enter the enemy ranks. "Disguise yourselves well and ascertain the exact size of this army. Find out who are the generals and who are Rama's counselors. Tell me who is their commander-in-chief."

Suka and Sarana disguised themselves as monkeys and penetrated deep into Rama's army, but they could not find the end of his troops. The monkey forces occupied woods, mountains, rivers and flatland for as far as could be seen. It stretched back across the bridge all the way to the opposite shore, still moving toward Lanka. The sound of Rama's army was tumultuous, and it struck fear into the hearts of the Rakshasas.

As the two spies wandered amid Rama's soldiers, Vibhishana detected them. He had them captured and brought before Rama. The monkeys kicked and pummelled them as they were dragged toward Rama, and the Rakshasas were terrified and afraid for their lives. They joined their palms and implored Rama, "Dear sir, we are two spies sent by Ravana to find out everything about your army. Please spare us."

Rama laughed heartily and replied, "You need have no fear for your lives, O night-rangers. If you have seen the entire army, then return to Ravana at once. If not, then I shall have Vibhishana show you whatever you wish to see. Then you may deliver the following message to your king."

Rama wanted Ravana to be fully informed of the immensity of the forces that now surrounded his city. Perhaps the foolish demon would see sense. Rama asked the spies to tell Ravana to display all his strength. The next day he would see his city with its defensive walls and arches broken down by Rama's arrows. At daybreak, Rama said, he would let loose his terrible anger on the Rakshasas.

The two spies were released and they sped back into the city. They went trembling before Ravana and spoke. "It seems to us that Rama and Lakshmana alone could uproot Lanka with its walls, palaces and the entire host of Rakshasas. The glory and power of these brothers is limitless. They are united with an army of Vanaras who appear frightful and who are bellowing joyfully at the prospect of war. O lord, abandon your policy of antagonism while there is still time. Return Sita to Rama."

Ravana roared angrily. Again his weak-hearted followers were suggesting something to which he could never agree. Again he said that Lanka was impenetrable even by the denizens of heaven, never mind a few monkeys. The spies were obviously afraid because they had been beaten by the monkeys, but Ravana would never give way to fear under any circumstances. Followed by Suka and Sarana he went up to the top of his palace, wanting to see for himself the monkey army.

Standing atop his snow-white palace, which was as high as dozens of tall palm trees, Ravana gazed around. Near the walls of the city he saw an ocean of dark-colored monkeys and bears. He focused his gaze upon the head of the army and asked Sarana the names of the chief monkeys. Sarana replied, "That colossal monkey who stands facing Lanka and roaring like a furious bull is Sugriva, their king. The one by his side who looks and thunders like a dark storm cloud is Nila, his commander. Near him the massive monkey who is pacing about and repeatedly yawning in fury is Angada, the crown prince. And there is Hanuman, who single-handedly laid waste to Lanka. You have already met him."

Sarana went on to describe all of the powerful monkey generals, pointing them out one by one. The awestruck Rakshasa praised the power of Rama's army, which he felt was unassailable.

Ravana looked carefully at the foremost monkeys. They were all standing firm with their faces toward the city. Brandishing thick trees and rocks resembling mountain peaks, they shouted and roared, eager for the battle to commence. Behind them stretched the vast army covering every visible part of the island of Lanka. Ravana saw Rama with Lakshmana, shining together like the sun and the moon. Near them Vibhishana stood, holding his mace and surrounded by his four ministers.

The demon king, agitated at heart and indignant, spoke harshly and angrily to his two spies, who stood with their heads bent low. "How have you dared to glorify in my presence the enemy forces? No wisdom or good sense exists in either of you. Indeed, the load of ignorance is borne by you both alone. By sheer good luck I have been able to retain the sovereignty of Lanka with stupid ministers like yourselves. I should have you both put to death at once. My anger is hardly abated even when I think of all your past services. Get out of here! I do not want to see your faces again."

Ravana ordered that some other spies be quickly brought. He told them to go among Rama's army and try to ascertain their exact battle plan. They should discover everything about Rama: when he slept, when he ate, what were his habits. Equipped with this knowledge, Ravana felt confident he could repulse his enemy.

The spies, headed by a demon named Sardula, quickly left in obedience to Ravana's command. Reaching the top of the Suvala mountain they gazed around at the army of monkeys. The Rakshasas were beside themselves with fear as they scanned Rama's vast forces. As they moved toward the army they were again discovered by Vibhishana, who was constantly on the lookout for Ravana's emissaries. The monkeys beat the demons severely and dragged them before Rama, but the compassionate prince again ordered their release.

The spies returned hastily to Lanka. Panting and stupefied with terror they fell before Ravana. The demon king said to Sardula, "You appear somewhat off-color, O mighty Rakshasa. I trust you did not fall into the hands of enraged enemies."

Sardula replied in a faint voice. "O lord, it is simply not possible to spy upon this army. They are guarded on all sides by monkeys like mountains and are headed by the invincible Rama. There is no possibility of even asking them a single question. I had hardly penetrated the army before I was arrested and brought before Rama. The monkeys paraded me about, having me march back and forth in various unusual gaits. They attacked me with knees, fists, palms and teeth, throwing me before Rama in a wretched state."

Sardula described to Ravana the enormous bridge over the sea and how it was filled with monkeys and bears still pouring into Lanka. Like the other spies before him the Rakshasa recommended that Ravana hand back Sita; but the demon king remained resolute. He would not give up Sita even if threatened by all the worlds joined together.

Ravana dismissed the spies and went into his rooms thinking of Sita. Perhaps there was now an opportunity to win her over. If he could somehow convince her that Rama was dead, she might succumb. It was worth a try. And in any event, perhaps, just perhaps, he may end up losing her to Rama. Now might be his last chance to gain her favor. The demon decided to play a trick upon Sita. He summoned a Rakshasa named Vidyujiva, an expert magician, and ordered him to create a head that looked exactly like Rama's head, and a bow resembling Rama's own.

Saying, "So be it," Vidyujiva soon produced the head and bow, and showed them to Ravana. The demon king was pleased and he handed the magician a priceless necklace of gems. Ravana then told Vidyujiva to accompany him to the ashoka grove to see Sita.

He found Sita lying beneath a tree, sighing repeatedly, still guarded by numerous Rakshasis. With Vidyujiva close behind him Ravana went before her and began to speak. "Your husband, on whose account you have rebuked me, now lies killed. O blessed lady, your roots are torn out and your vanity is crushed. Of what use to you now is your dead spouse? Become mine today. I shall be a better protector to you than any other. Let me tell you how Rama and his army were slain."

Ravana fabricated a whole story about how the army of monkeys was annihilated by the Rakshasas. He told Sita they had been wiped out during the night as they slept, exhausted from their journey across the sea. All of the principal monkeys, including even Hanuman, were now dead. Rama's head had been severed by the commander of the Rakshasas. Ravana had Vidyujiva show her the trick head. The magician placed the head on the ground in front of Sita. He handed the bow he had created to Ravana and then promptly vanished from the spot.

Throwing down the bow next to the head, Ravana said, "Look now upon your husband. There is his famed bow, fetched here by Prahasta after he had disposed of that mortal being during the night."

Sita looked at the head. It resembled Rama closely with the same large eyes and the same splendid jewel in his hair. The princess burst into a wail and fell to the ground. She cried out, censuring Kaikeyi. "O cruel woman, be now satisfied with your work! See what you have done to the noble house of Raghu. How can I continue to live? Everything is finished. The death of a husband before his wife is declared to be a catastrophe."

Sita lamented at length. How had this happened? The royal astrologers had predicted that Rama would live a long life and rule over the earth. "The Time Spirit is irresistible to all beings," cried Sita. "O Rama! Surely you are now reunited with your father. But what of me? Do you not recall the solemn vow you made at our wedding? You declared you would always protect me and take me to the next world with you. How have you deserted me now?"

The princess was torn apart. She thought of Kaushalya and Sumitra. They would both die immediately upon hearing the terrible news. Considering that she was the cause of Rama's death, Sita condemned herself. She said to Ravana, "Kill me at once, O demon. Lay my dead body on top of Rama and unite a husband with his wife."

While Sita was wailing in this way a messenger came to Ravana. He called the demon aside and told him that he was needed urgently in the council chamber. Prahasta had arrived and was awaiting orders to commence the battle.

Ravana turned away from Sita. There was no time to lose. Rama's formidable forces had to be checked at once. The demon immediately left the ashoka grove and walked swiftly toward his chambers. As soon as he left, a Rakshasi named Sarama, the wife of Vibhishana, came toward Sita. Taking her away from the other Rakshasi guards, she reassured the distraught princess. "I heard what Ravana said to you, but you should not believe him. He is a great trickster and a liar. O gentle princess, be fully restored to confidence. Rama is not dead. Even now the demon king is making plans to defend the city from the monkey forces, headed by your inconquerable husband and his brother."

Sarama spoke with affection to Sita. The Rakshasi was as pious as her husband and she had often comforted the grieving princess. She assured Sita that Rama's so-called head was an illusion conjured up by Ravana and his henchman.

As Sarama and Sita spoke they heard the crash of war drums as well as the clamor of troops and the blare of countless trumpets. It was obvious that a battle was about to commence.

Sarama had heard from her husband all about Rama. She said to Sita, "This mighty fight will result in the complete destruction of the demons. Ravana will undoubtedly be slain by Rama. No other outcome is possible. Dear Sita, I am certain you will soon be reunited with your husband."

After gladdening Sita, Sarama asked if there was any service she could do for the princess. She offered to carry a message to Rama. "If you wish, I can go invisibly through the skies and reassure Rama of your safety," she suggested. But Sita instead asked to be informed of Ravana's plans. She wanted to know if Ravana had any intention of releasing her or of even killing her before Rama came. If so, then perhaps a message should be taken to Rama.

Sarama went unobserved into Ravana's chambers and listened to the discussions. After some hours she returned again to Sita and informed her what was happening. "Ravana has been exhorted by his own dear mother to return you to Rama," Sarama said. "Along with one of his elderly and affectionate counselors, she tried at length to make him see sense. Other wise ministers have also put forward a case for your return. They warned Ravana that battle with Rama and the monkeys will have a disastrous result for the Rakshasas. But Ravana will no more let you go than a miser would leave his hold on treasure. He is not prepared to release you until he has laid down his life in combat, O godly one."

Sita thanked Sarama for her kindness and friendship. Feeling reassured that her husband would soon arrive to rescue her, she sat beneath the simshapa tree, absorbing herself in thoughts of Rama.

*   *   *

In his council chamber Ravana gazed around at his ministers. They all sat mutely looking at one another. Rama's feat in crossing the ocean with an unlimited number of bears and monkeys was astonishing. And that was on top of the incredible display by a single monkey in Lanka. Surely battle with Rama would be foolhardy. Seeing the timidity of his advisors, Ravana spoke in a voice which rang around the silent chamber. "I have heard everything about Rama and his prowess. I feel that we will be able to overcome him in battle. I know the Rakshasas to be unfailing and resolute. You should entertain no fears."

An elderly counselor named Malayavan, Ravana's maternal grandfather, replied, "O king, there are different ways to deal with a hostile enemy. Battle is only one and it is only recommended in situations where the enemy is clearly weaker or where every other means of diplomacy has failed. You have not explored any other avenues with Rama. Let us first try to make an alliance. Give Sita back to Rama. The outcome of battle is always unsure; there must be a loser. On the other hand, O intelligent Rakshasa, negotiations can produce a favorable result for both parties."

Malayavan spoke strongly. Ravana had abandoned virtue. He would now be swallowed up by evil. Rama however was devoted to virtue and his cause was just. The gods and rishis whom Ravana had assaulted were all supporting Rama. Furthermore, Ravana had no immunity from humans and animals. Nor was Rama an ordinary human. He was surely Vishnu himself. Therefore peace should be secured by any means.

Having delivered his sagacious advice, Malayavan fell silent, eyeing the ruler of Lanka and awaiting his response. Ravana knitted his brows. He breathed heavily in anger. Clenching, his fists he replied furiously, "How have you uttered such harsh and ill-considered words? Surely you have come under the sway of the enemy. On what basis do you hold as powerful the wretched Rama, a mere human who has been abandoned by his father and has as his support only a band of monkeys? See him struck down by me in a short while! Having somehow crossed the sea and reached Lanka, he will nevertheless not return with his life. There is no doubt whatsoever."

Malayavan made no reply. It seemed that Ravana was bent on his own ruin. After uttering benedictions wishing him victory, the old minister left for his own residence.

Ravana set about making all arrangements for Lanka's defense. He posted powerful generals at each of the city's four gates, all of them equipped with a force of hundreds of thousands of fierce Rakshasas. Ravana himself would visit each gate in turn. Satisfied that everything was secure, the demon then retired to his own chambers.

CHAPTER FIVE

THE WAR BEGINS

Outside Lanka, Rama held counsel with his chiefs. They discussed how to assail the city. Vibhishana reported that his four ministers had entered the city in the form of birds. They had carefully surveyed everything. Vibhishana described the defensive arrangements. "At the eastern gate stands Prahasta, the commander-in-chief. At the southern gate is Mahaparshwa and Mahodara, two almost invincible Rakshasas. Stationed at the western gate is Ravana's cunning and fearful son Indrajit, who is highly dangerous in battle. At the northern gate is Ravana himself."

Vibhishana told Rama how many Rakshasas they faced. They numbered tens of millions, all of them equipped with fierce weapons of every description. It was not going to be an easy fight.

Rama smiled. He issued orders detailing different monkeys to attack each gate. Sugriva, Jambavan and Vibhishana should remain at the center of the army. Nila would assault the eastern side, Angada the south, Hanuman the west, and Rama himself would attack the northern gate. He wanted to waste no time in confronting Ravana directly. Rama ordered that the monkeys should fight in their natural forms only. This would be their distinguishing mark. Rama expected that the demons would try trickery and assume different forms. The monkeys would have the best chance of recognizing each other if they remained in their own forms.

Evening was approaching. The battle would commence the next day. Rama decided to ascend the Suvela mountain and spend the night there. As he climbed the mountain he spoke with Lakshmana. "We shall be able to survey Lanka from this vantage point. I long now for the battle to begin. My anger toward Ravana is growing at every moment. The whole Rakshasa race will perish on account of their mean-minded and stubborn king."

Rama reached the top of Mount Suvela along with hundreds of the foremost monkey warriors. They gazed at Lanka, which glowed red in the light of the setting sun. Along its defensive wall, which appeared like a sheer cliff face, there seemed to be another dark wall in the shape of a compact row of Rakshasas. No gap could be seen anywhere in the lines of heavily armed demons. The monkeys roared in anticipation. As they stared at their enemy, the sun set and a full moon rose. Rama and the monkeys alertly watched for any signs of a treacherous night assault by the Rakshasas.

After sunrise the following day the monkeys closely surveyed Lanka again. Atop the Trikuta mountain the city appeared charming with its tow-ering white gates and gold and silver fortifications. Mansions and palaces and tall, golden-domed temples crowded the city. The monkeys saw various devices lined up along the outer wall ready for the battle. As the Rakshasas readied themselves for battle the thunder of drums and the blowing of conches and trumpets was tumultuous.

As Rama and the monkeys looked across at Lanka they saw in the dis-tance Ravana himself. The demon appeared at the top of the city gate, clad in red robes and adorned with shining scarlet gems. He was being fanned on all sides and a large white parasol was held over his head.

Seeing him there, Sugriva became impetuous. He immediately sprang from the mountaintop and with one mighty bound landed near the demon king. He rushed up to him and said, "I am a friend and servant of Rama, ruler of this world. Display your power, O Rakshasa, for I shall not spare you today."

With that, Sugriva leapt upon Ravana and dashed his shining diadem to the ground. The Rakshasa shook him off and stood for the fight. He spoke harshly. "Today I will break your beautiful neck, O monkey."

Ravana caught hold of Sugriva and threw him forcefully to the ground, but the monkey bounced up like a ball. He closed on Ravana and grasped him tightly. As they pummeled, kneed and scratched one another they appeared like two tall trees intertwined together and shaken by a gale. Their limbs were bathed in blood and perspiration as they locked together, grunt-ing furiously. Both were endowed with extraordinary might and they fought with tremendous power. They fell to the ground and rolled over, dropping from the flat roof of the gate to the ground below, still violently belaboring each other. As both were experts at wrestling, they employed various maneuvers with great skill. They appeared like a lion and a tiger engaged in a furious fight to the death. Breaking apart, they moved around in a circle, each rebuking the other with harsh words.

They stood in diverse postures and moved about in many ways-now rushing, now wheeling, now leaping high and now crouching. As they struck and dodged one another with blinding speed they appeared graceful, but neither could overpower the other. Becoming tired of the bout, Ravana decided to exhibit his supernatural power. Sugriva realized this and immediately sprang high, landing again on the roof of the gate. Taking another great bound he soared across to the Suvela mountain. Ravana was left standing angrily on the ground. Seeing that he had returned to the side of Rama and Lakshmana, the demon decided not to pursue the monkey. The battle with the prince would come soon enough.

Rama embraced Sugriva and examined the wounds Ravana had inflicted upon him. Feeling a little annoyed with the monkey, Rama admonished him out of love. "Kings should not act in such rash ways, O mighty one. If anything had happened to you, then what would have become of me? If you had been slain, then I surely would not have survived. Please do not be so impetuous again."

Sugriva bowed to Rama and replied, "Seeing that disgusting demon who has borne away your wife, I lost control of myself. I had to give him a beating. I am sorry."

Rama praised Sugriva's courage and strength and then turned to Lakshmana. "O valiant brother, the time for battle has arrived. We should array our forces in preparation. Many terrible omens are visible, boding massive destruction and death. The earth will soon be covered with rocks, darts, arrows and swords, hurled by monkeys and Rakshasas. Soon a thick morass of flesh and blood will spread on all sides. Surrounded by monkeys and bears, we should immediately march on Lanka."

Rama rapidly descended the mountain, followed by his brother. Upon reaching the foot of the mountain he reviewed the army. Then, with Sugriva's assistance, he marshalled the troops ready for the battle. At an auspicious moment he ordered them to advance. The army moved off sending up a roar which made the earth shake and the walls of Lanka vibrate. The different Vanara commanders soon reached their respective positions at the gates of Lanka. Rama himself stood at the northern gate. Sugriva remained at a distance from the city. Along with Lakshmana and Vibhishana he detailed divisions of troops to support each of the commanders.

Seizing hold of fully grown trees and massive boulders, the monkeys rushed forward. Their long tails raised in anger and their terrible teeth bared. Their eyes were bloodshot and their faces contorted with fury. As they bounded high in the air, they seemed like a swarm of locusts. The growls and roars of the fierce bears led by Jambavan sounded like the rush of a mighty ocean.

The army quickly surrounded the city of Lanka, making it difficult even for the wind to approach. Looking out from the walls, the Rakshasas were filled with wonder upon seeing the flood of monkeys and bears. They ran about in all directions, making ready to defend their city.

Rama summoned Angada and asked him to carry a message to Ravana. This was the demon's last chance. If he returned Sita now, then a battle could be averted. Rama said to Angada, "You should approach the ten-headed monster on my behalf. Tell him that his cup of sins has now overflowed. Fierce retribution will shortly ensue for all his acts of violence against the rishis, gods, Gandharvas, Apsaras, Yakshas and others-what to speak of his depraved act of stealing Sita from me. His arrogance born of Brahma's boon will shortly be smashed by me. Soon he will see his city rent asunder and the Rakshasas lying lifeless upon the ground. Standing firm in battle, I will soon force him to throw down his body."

Rama offered Ravana the opportunity to surrender. He could return Sita now and the army would leave peacefully. Otherwise, the world would soon be rid of Rakshasas, barring those who sought Rama's shelter.

Angada leapt high and crossed over the walls of Lanka. Confounding the demons by his speed and movement, he swiftly arrived before Ravana. He stood a short distance from the Rakshasa and announced himself to be Rama's messenger. He then delivered the message exactly as he had heard it from Rama.

Ravana was seized by fury. He commanded his ministers to capture and kill Angada. Four huge demons immediately took hold of Angada by his arms. The monkey, who blazed like a fire, allowed the Rakshasas to hold him. Taking all four of them still clinging to his arms, he leapt up onto a high ledge. He then dashed the demons together and they fell senseless to the ground. The monkey let out a great shout proclaiming his name and roaring, "Victory to Rama!" With a great leap he returned to Rama, smashing down the wall from which he jumped. Ravana's reply to Rama was clear enough.

Witnessing this display of power, Ravana became morose. He foresaw his own destruction. The demon sat sighing amid his ministers, but still he gave no thought to the possibility of surrender.

Rama affectionately received Angada back. Hearing then of Ravana's cruel response, he resolved to fight and immediately gave the order to charge. Mounted upon the back of a monkey, Rama led the attack himself. The entire earth around Lanka was rendered brown by the mass of monkeys and bears. They filled the moats and completely covered the defensive walls as they rapidly scaled them. The air was filled with cries of "Victory to Rama and Sugriva!" Many mighty monkeys rose quickly to the tops of the walls, screaming ferociously. They poured onto the ramparts and tore into the Rakshasas with their teeth and nails.

Ravana ordered his troops to rush against the enemy. A great clamor was raised. Thousands of drums were beaten with golden sticks, creating a terrible din. Rakshasas of hideous features blew conches and trumpets and rallied Ravana's vast forces to the fight. With their dark limbs adorned with brilliant jewels the Rakshasas seemed like so many clouds lit by lightning. They joyfully rushed forth like the waves of an ocean swollen with the rains of universal destruction. The trumpeting of elephants, the neighing of horses, the clatter of chariots and the shouts of demons made the earth and sky resound.

The Rakshasas struck the monkeys with their flaming maces, javelins, pikes and axes. The monkeys grasped hold of the demons with their powerful arms and hauled them down from the walls. They aimed terrible blows at the Rakshasas with their fists and feet. The demons replied with darts and arrows. As they fought, they shouted out their respective names. All around Lanka there were monkeys, bears and Rakshasas locked in fierce combat. The earth quickly became covered with a mire of flesh and blood.

Great heroes among the Rakshasas mounted brilliant chariots and came out of the city. With their dazzling coats of mail they shone like fire. Others sallied forth on the backs of gigantic elephants, while others charged out on great steeds. They were supported by tens of thousands of Rakshasas on foot, their frightening faces twisted in fury. Shouting, "Victory to the king," the Rakshasas issued out for battle like a black river gushing out of the city gates. Some of them took to the air and swooped down upon Rama's army wheeling huge scimitars. Others fought on foot, raising their frightful weapons and screaming in anger. The Vanaras met them, surging toward them with shouts of joy. The two armies appeared like heaven and earth colliding in the sky.

Great duels took place between the heroes on both sides. Angada fought with Indrajit even as Shiva had contended with the demon Andhaka. Hanuman fought a furious battle with the huge Rakshasa Sharabha, while Vibhishana battled with a violent Rakshasa called Suparshwa. Sugriva closed with Praghasha and Lakshmana with Durmukha. Four of the most powerful Rakshasas charged Rama, who stood on the battlefield, shining like a smokeless fire.

A fierce and confused fight raged. All of the combatants sought a quick victory and they fought with tremendous force. A stream of blood flowed across the ground floating dead bodies that looked like logs with hair resembling weeds. Heads, arms, legs and trunks rolled about. The clamor of the fight was deafening. It struck terror in the hearts of all those who were not heroes in battle.

Sharabha hurled at Hanuman a blazing lance which pierced the monkey in the breast. Not tolerating the attack, Hanuman sprang onto the demon's chariot and with his bare hands smashed it along with the

Rakshasa himself. Sugriva took up a massive sal tree and brought it down upon Praghasha's chariot, killing the Rakshasa outright. A fierce and notorious demon named Pratapana rushed yelling toward Nala and lacerated him with hundreds of sharp arrows. With one of those arrows Nala bounded onto the demon's chariot and gouged out his eyes. With a hail of arrows Lakshmana overwhelmed Durmukha, and with one swift shaft he pierced the demon in the heart. Rama quickly lopped off the heads of the four Rakshasas who surrounded him.

The powerful Mainda, a commander among the monkeys, leapt into the sky and fought the Rakshasas who flew overhead. Catching hold of the powerful demon named Vajramusti he smashed him to the ground along with his chariot and four great steeds. Nikhumbha, the son of Kumbhakarna, shot a hundred swift arrows at Nila. The monkey took up a chariot wheel and rushed toward the Rakshasa who stood laughing in his chariot. Nikhumbha loosed another hundred fierce shafts at the advancing Nila. Not minding the arrows, Nila whirled the iron wheel and jumped onto the Rakshasa's chariot. Even as Vishnu severs the heads of demons with his Chakra, Nila cut off the head of Nikhumbha, as well as that of his charioteer.

Vidyunmali, a leader among the Rakshasas, attacked Sushena with his gold-encrusted arrows. Roaring again and again he pierced the monkey with hundreds of sharp arrows. In a rage Sushena took up a mountainous boulder and hurled it at the demon. Vidyunmali hastily leapt from his chariot as the boulder descended and smashed it to pieces. The demon stood on the ground, mace in hand. Sushena seized a huge rock and darted toward the Rakshasa, who swung his fierce mace at the monkey and caught him on the breast. Unmoved by the blow Sushena brought the rock down upon the demon's head with the force of a thunderbolt. Vidyunmali fell lifeless to the ground like a tree smashed in a storm.

Many valiant Rakshasas were crushed in this way by mighty heroes among the monkeys and bears. The battlefield was strewn with spears and maces, as well as javelins, lances and arrows. Smashed chariots lay amid the carcasses of horses and elephants. The headless trunks of Rakshasas and monkeys bounded here and there, spurting blood and finally falling to the ground. Vultures and jackals moved about the field, feasting on flesh and blood.

As night fell, the Rakshasas felt their strength and enthusiasm increase. The fight continued into the night with the combatants hardly able to recognize one another. Voices were heard to call out, "Are you a monkey or a Rakshasa?" Shouts of "Stand and fight!" and "Why do you flee?" mixed with the cries of wounded and dying soldiers. The monkeys could see the golden armor of the Rakshasas glinting in the moonlight, and they sprang upon them, tearing them with their sharp teeth and pounding them with their fists. Powerful monkeys dragged down the elephants and horses mounted by demons. Monkey heroes picked up Rakshasas, crushed them in their embrace and then dropped them lifeless to the ground to be devoured by jackals.

Rama and Lakshmana stood together like two brilliant gods. They killed numerous Rakshasas with swift arrows, including those who ranged invisible through the sky. Not even the heroes among the Rakshasas could approach the two princes as they fought in the midst of the battle.

A terrible sound arose as the Rakshasas beat countless kettledrums and large wooden tom-toms and blew thousands of conches and trumpets. This sound, mixed with roars of pain and the clash of weapons, created a horrifying uproar. It was difficult to move across the ground due to the countless corpses lying there. Monkeys and Rakshasas lay on the battlefield with lances and arrows protruding from their lifeless bodies. That first night of battle was like the night of universal dissolution. Millions of warriors were slain. Ghosts and nocturnal fiends ranged about the battlefield, reveling in the scenes of carnage and death.

The Rakshasas rallied, and headed by six of their mighty chiefs riding in a line, they rushed in a body toward Rama and Lakshmana. Rama released thousands of flaming arrows which lit up the ground like flares. Almost instantaneously he struck down the six foremost Rakshasas with six straight-flying arrows. With other golden-feathered arrows he tore to pieces hundreds of other Rakshasas who came near him. Lakshmana stood behind him and fended off the treacherous demons who attacked Rama from his rear. The demons that approached the princes perished like moths entering a fire.

Angada fought a furious battle with Indrajit. With a rock that looked like a mountain peak he smashed the demon's chariot. Indrajit rose into the air and became invisible. Fatigued from the fight he retreated.

Seeing Angada besting Indrajit, the gods and rishis praised him. Rama and Lakshmana also praised the valor of the monkey prince. They called out, "Well done! Bravo!"

Hearing his enemy praised, Indrajit fell into a terrible rage. Remaining invisible, the demon loosed sharp arrows which shone like lightning. They seemed to appear out of nowhere and sped toward Rama and Lakshmana, piercing them all over. The Rakshasa used his supernatural power to send arrows like venomous snakes which caught and bound Rama and Lakshmana. The two princes fell to the ground enmeshed in a tight network of writhing serpents with glowing ethereal bodies.

Rama immediately ordered ten monkeys to search out Indrajit. Hanuman, Angada and eight other Vanara general bounded into the air and darted about, whirling trees and maces, but they could not locate the demon who continuously fired at them his swift iron arrows bedecked with buzzard feathers. Laughing all the while and keeping out of sight, Indrajit shot hundreds of arrows into the bodies of Rama and Lakshmana. No part of their bodies remained visible. Blood flowed profusely from their wounds and they appeared like trees giving forth red blossoms in spring. Indrajit shouted to them, "Even the ruler of the gods, Indra, could not discern me as I fight invisibly. What then of you two humans? I shall now dispatch you to the abode of Yamaraja with my sharp arrows."

The demon continued firing his arrows at the two bound brothers who felt distressed and afflicted. They lay upon the ground with their bows fallen from their hands. Arrows with the heads of axes, others with razor heads and others with heads shaped like calves' teeth whistled toward them from the sky. Seeing them lying there bathed in blood, the monkeys screeched in agony and fear. They surrounded the fallen princes and shed tears, giving way to despondency.

Indrajit considered his enemy defeated. He joyfully left the battlefield and went toward Lanka to give the happy news to his father.

The monkeys felt hopeless. They stood beating their breasts and crying in anguish. As they gazed around at the sky, fearing further attacks from the invisible Indrajit, they saw Vibhishana coming toward them. Some of the monkeys mistook the Rakshasa for Indrajit and they fled here and there, but Vibhishana reassured them. Looking around with his occult vision he could discern that Indrajit had left. He told the monkeys not to worry and knelt down by Rama's side.

Vibhishana spoke to Sugriva with pain in his voice. "These two brothers who always depend on virtue have been struck down by Indrajit's treachery. The wicked demon cannot face them in a fair fight. Therefore he resorts to sorcery and cowardice."

Vibhishana told the monkeys that Rama and Lakshmana had been bound by a mystical weapon which Indrajit had received as a boon from Brahma. Even the gods would not be able to release them. This made the monkeys even more anguished. Sugriva lamented loudly. "All Rama's hopes have been dashed today. Our efforts are in vain and everything is lost. What shall we do now?"

Vibhishana took hold of Sugriva's arm and reassured him. "Take heart, O monkey king. Conflicts are always of this nature. Victory is never certain. Heroes do not lament when faced with setbacks. Rather, they exert themselves with even more energy. My feeling is that these two princes will recover. Somehow they will shake off these bonds, I am sure. Be strong, for the fear of death should never haunt those devoted to truth and piety."

Vibhishana dipped his hand in cool water and wiped Sugriva's eyes. He told him to look closely at Rama and Lakshmana. They were still breathing and their bodies were lustrous. It was clear they were only in a temporary faint. Vibhishana felt sure they would soon return to consciousness and find a way out of their predicament. He left with Jambavan to reassure and rally the rest of the army, as the news of Rama's fall had spread quickly. Sugriva, along with Hanuman and the other leading monkeys, stood by Rama's side waiting for him to awaken.

CHAPTER SIX

GARUDA TO THE RESCUE

Indrajit entered Lanka surrounded by the chief Rakshasas, all of them bellowing in joy. The Rakshasa prince went quickly to his father's palace and told him the news. "Your two mortal enemies lie killed on the battlefield, struck down by my sharp arrows. Dispel your fear, O king. Victory is now ours."

Ravana sprang to his feet and embraced his son. He was elated and immediately called for the Rakshasis guarding Sita. He instructed them to take the princess in the Pushpaka chariot and show her Rama and Lakshmana. He felt sure that Sita would now accept him as her husband.

The Rakshasis left at once and brought Sita. They placed her on the chariot along with Trijata, who was friendly with the princess. Ordered by Ravana, the chariot rose high above Lanka and went over the battlefield. Sita then saw Rama and Lakshmana lying in a pool of blood and covered all over with arrows. She was stricken with agony. Suspecting their death, she held on to Trijata and cried vehemently, "How has this happened? Learned astrologers foretold that I would never be widowed. They predicted that I would be the wife of a pious ruler of the world and would have powerful sons by him. Today they have all been proven false."

Sita was completely bewildered. Her body shook as she grieved, comforted by Trijata. She thought of Kaushalya and Sumitra. How would those godly ladies live after hearing that their sons had been killed? Indeed, the whole of Ayodhya would be plunged into despair. Surely destiny was unfathomable and all-powerful. If Rama and Lakshmana could be struck down in battle, then even Death itself could be killed.

Trijata carefully surveyed the scene below. She spoke gently to Sita. "From the appearance of the monkeys I deduce that your husband still lives. An army whose leader is slain is cast about like a rudderless boat on a high sea. These monkeys are standing firm in their battle array. Clearly they expect Rama to recover. I also see that Rama and Lakshmana are still possessed of bodily luster. They are surely still living. Do not lament, O princess."

Sita embraced Trijata saying, "May your words prove true." She felt a little reassured and prayed that the princes would soon be restored to strength. The chariot returned to Lanka carrying the mournful princess back to the ashoka grove.

*   *   *

The monkeys surrounding Rama softly called out his name, trying to awaken him. Slowly Rama opened his eyes and looked around. He saw Lakshmana lying unconscious by his side, his face streaked with blood. Rama spoke in a voice choked with sobs. "What purpose of mine will be served by recovering Sita when my gallant brother lies slain in battle. I might find another wife like Sita, but I could never find a companion like Lakshmana anywhere in this world. This prince followed me to the forest, sharing with me every happiness and distress. I shall now follow him to Yamaraja's abode."

Rama condemned himself. It was his fault that Lakshmana had been killed. What was the use of his vain boasting that Ravana would be slain and Vibhishana installed as the ruler of Lanka? Now everything was finished. Rama told Sugriva to return to Kishkindha. He thanked him and all the other monkeys and bears for their service. Now they could go home.

The monkeys stood with tears falling from their eyes. Sugriva burned with fury. He looked toward Lanka. The Rakshasas would pay for this outrage. He would personally annihilate every last one of them, including Ravana and Indrajit. Then he would recover Sita and bring her back to Rama. Clenching his fists he said to Angada, "Take Rama and Lakshmana back to Kishkindha. Expert physicians may heal them with celestial herbs. For my part I shall remain here until the business is finished. No Rakshasa will survive today."

As Sugriva spoke, there suddenly arose a fierce wind. Dark clouds appeared with flashes of lightning. The ground shook and trees toppled over. A sound like the steady beat of some gigantic drum was heard. The monkeys gazed around and saw in the sky Garuda, Vishnu's great eagle carrier. The powerful bird glided down, landing near Rama. As he descended the serpent bonds of the brothers immediately fell away. The ethereal snakes that had wrapped themselves around the princes quickly disappeared into the sky.

Garuda, who appeared in a half-human form with two arms, bowed before Rama with folded palms. He knelt by the brothers and gently wiped

their faces. At once their wounds were healed and their bodies became brilliant. Lakshmana opened his eyes and sat up. All of the monkeys cheered
loudly and leapt about with screeches of joy. Garuda raised the two brothers. Rama embraced him with affection, saying, "It is fortunate indeed that
you have appeared here, O gallant bird. We have been saved from a great
calamity at the hands of Indrajit. Pray tell us, who are you, glowing with
celestial brilliance and adorned with heavenly jewels and garlands?"

Garuda told Rama his name. "Surely you know me, O Rama, as I am
always your servant. Consider me your own breath moving outside of your
body. I heard that Indrajit had employed the Naga sons of Kadru. He converted those powerful serpents into arrows by means of sorcery. I came here
quickly with a desire to dispatch my venomous prey, but they fled away simply upon seeing me. Grant me leave to pursue them."

Rama again embraced Garuda and gave him permission to leave. The
bird assured Rama that the Rakshasas would soon be overcome. Indrajit
would not again be able to employ the serpent weapon. Then, after going
respectfully around the two princes, he rose into the skies, shining like the
sun and filling the whole region with the wind raised by his wings.

Rama and Lakshmana stood ready for battle. The monkeys and bears
roared in joy, uprooting huge trees and brandishing them. They swarmed
toward the gates of Lanka, shouting for the Rakshasas to come out and
fight. Beating clay drums and blowing their conches, the army raised a massive tumult, which terrified the Rakshasas, who gazed from the city walls in
amazement.

*   *   *

Ravana sat in his palace. He had spent the night celebrating, having
sent messengers all around Lanka to declare that Rama and Lakshmana
were dead. As dawn approached, he was thinking of Sita. Now she would
surely be his. He straightened his disheveled clothes and prepared to go to
the princess. Suddenly from outside the city he heard the crashing of drums
and the shouts of Rama's army. "What is this?" he exclaimed in surprise. He
got up with a start and shouted for his ministers. How could the monkeys
rally with their leader slain? Something was wrong.

The demon ordered his ministers to find out what was happening.
Spies left at once and went to the top of the city walls. From there they saw
Rama, Lakshmana and Sugriva at the head of the army, beseiging the city.
The spies reported to Ravana. "The two human brothers are standing like a
pair of lordly elephants that have broken their fetters. All around them
stand the monkeys and bears roaring for battle."

Ravana turned pale. This was a disaster. Surely the Rakshasas were in danger now. Rama had escaped from a weapon which had even overpowered Indra. It seemed that some invincible power protected this human.

The Rakshasa king turned to his commander-in-chief Dhumraksha and ordered him to march at once to fight with Rama. "Take with you the mightiest of the Rakshasas," Ravana commanded. "Use any means whatsoever. Rama must be defeated!"

Dhumraksha left Ravana's palace roaring exultantly and longing for battle. He was surrounded by demons with fierce features who clutched spiked maces, razor-sharp spears and heavy iron cudgels. Clad in golden mail and mounted upon chariots drawn by fiends, they rushed out of the city gates. They were followed by waves of other Rakshasas, some riding massive black steeds and others on elephants as large as hills. Laughing loudly, they went out the western gate where Hanuman was stationed.

As the Rakshasas advanced, they saw numerous terrible omens. Ferocious birds of prey circled screaming over the demons. They descended upon Dhumraksha's standard and fought together, sending a shower of feathers onto the demon. A headless trunk, wet with blood, rose from the ground and ran across the path of the charging Rakshasas. The earth shook and blood fell from the heavens. Darkness enveloped the four quarters and the wind blew strongly into the demons' faces.

Not deterred, Dhumraksha raced on at the head of his troops. He shouted out challenges in a voice resembling the braying of a donkey. The monkeys roared back and charged. The two armies appeared like two oceans surging toward one another and then meeting with a tumultuous crash. Demons and monkeys fell by the hundreds of thousands, pierced and smashed by weapons and trees.

Some monkeys were transfixed by lances and spears. Others were cut to pieces by waves of arrows. Some were hacked down with swords, and still others were trampled by elephants. In response the monkeys crushed the Rakshasas with great boulders. They reduced some of the demons to pulp by bringing tree trunks down onto them. They leapt upon the chariots and tore at the Rakshasas with their nails and teeth. Monkeys lifted demons and dashed them to the ground. Enraged, the Rakshasas fought back throwing punches and kicks that felt like the striking of thunderbolts.

Dhumraksha was possessed by a madness for battle. He wrought havoc among the Vanara troops. He could hardly be seen as he rushed about whirling his various weapons. Arrows loosed from his bow seemed to fly in all directions at once. Monkeys fell on all sides, vomiting blood. Heads, arms and legs flew about. The monkey army was dispersed and put to flight by the enraged Dhumraksha, who thundered like autumnal clouds.

Seeing his troops routed by the Rakshasa, Hanuman became furious. His eyes turned red and he took hold of an enormous boulder. With a roar he hurled the rock at Dhumraksha's chariot, but Dhumraksha nimbly leapt clear. The chariot, along with its horses and driver, was reduced to a mangled heap. Hanuman then took up a sal tree and whirled it around, attacking Dhumraksha's guards. Within moments he pounded hundreds of demons to death. The monkey then grasped a mountain peak and raced toward Dhumraksha, who stood with his mace uplifted. As Hanuman approached him the Rakshasa brought down his mace, which was bedecked with numerous shining points, upon Hanuman's head. It sounded like an explosion, but the monkey was not shaken. Hanuman smashed his mountain peak on Dhumraksha's skull. With his head crushed and all his limbs shattered, Dhumraksha fell dead to the ground.

The other demons ran back toward the city howling in fear. Ravana heard of Dhumraksha's death and he hissed like an enraged serpent. He spoke at once to Vajradamstra, another of the great Rakshasa champions. "Sally forth, O hero! Make short work of our enemies."

Replying "So be it," Vajradamstra circumambulated Ravana and left his palace.

Vajradamstra was artistically adorned with gem-encrusted armlets and a shining diadem. He put on a golden coat of mail that blazed like fire. Taking up his bow he mounted his brilliant chariot, which was dressed with hundreds of pennants and decorated with carvings of refined gold. He came out of the southern gate followed by countless troops holding scimitars, strangely-shaped iron clubs, polished maces, bows, javelins, spears, razor-edged discuses, swords and double-headed axes. They raised a great uproar as they rushed toward the monkey army.

Again many evil omens were seen. Dazzling meteors fell and hideous jackals belched tongues of fire. The demon troops stumbled and fell on level ground. Vajradamstra paid no heed to the grim portents foretelling his defeat. He thundered out his war cry, rallying the Rakshasas to the fight.

The monkeys met them with furious impetuosity. Demons and monkeys collided like mountains clashing together. Warriors fell with their heads and limbs severed. Others dropped down, being sliced in half from head to toe. Some were crushed and some beaten to a pulp. The fighters found their feet sinking in a mire of flesh and blood-soaked earth. From a distance the battle produced a sound that resembled a musical performance, with the clash of weapons for its drums, the twang of bowstrings its vinas and the roar of warriors its loud singing.

Vajradamstra created havoc on the battlefield. From his chariot he released tens of thousands of steel arrows with razor-sharp heads. He moved with the speed of the wind, seeming like Death himself come for the destruction of all beings. The formidable Rakshasa employed mystical weapons of every kind and mowed down the monkey troops like wheat in a field.

Seeing the destruction, Angada became maddened. With his two serpent-like arms he clasped a great tree and whirled it around with blinding speed. The monkey prince danced with the tree on the battlefield and crushed innumerable Rakshasas. He moved through the demon troops like a lion through a flock of deer. The Rakshasas fell back in terror as Angada wheeled. Chariots, elephants, horses and Rakshasas fell on all sides, smashed by the infuriated Vanara.

The earth became decorated with golden poles fallen from chariots, as well as with bejeweled armlets, necklaces and diadems of every sort. A stream of blood flowed on the battlefield carrying the heads and limbs of Rakshasas slain by Angada, who could not be checked.

Vajradamstra saw his troops being routed and, roaring in fury, he rushed toward Angada and shouted out a challenge. He released arrows that flew with unerring accuracy and pierced eight or nine monkeys at a time. In his wake the demon left heaps of slain monkey warriors, who lay with their teeth clenched and eyes still staring in anger.

Angada stood firm to receive the fast-approaching Rakshasa. Vajradamstra shot a thousand arrows at Angada and sent up a great shout. The monkey was pierced all over, but he was not shaken. He hurled his tree at the demon and it whirled through the air with a sound like a rushing gale. Without effort, Vajradamstra tore the tree to pieces with his arrows even as it flew toward him. Angada leapt up a nearby hill and tore off a crag. Spinning around several times he threw it with tremendous force at the Rakshasa. Vajradamstra immediately jumped down from his chariot with his iron mace in his hand.

The rock descended upon the Rakshasa's chariot and shattered it into small pieces, crushing the driver and horses. Even as the crag fell Angada had taken up another and hurled it at the Rakshasa himself. It hit him full on the head and he fell to the earth, vomiting blood. He lay there unconscious for some minutes with his mace clasped to his bosom. Coming again to his senses, he got up and flew at Angada, hitting him in the chest with his mace. The monkey remained steady and the demon began striking him with his fists. Angada returned his blows and the two fought a fierce hand-to-hand battle for some time, both spitting blood and breathing heavily.

Angada uprooted another tree and he stood adorned by its flowers and fruit. The demon seized hold of a shield made of bull hide and a great shining sword decorated with golden bells. The two combatants circled one another, each looking for an opportunity to strike the other. They closed and separated again and again, raining down fierce blows. Both became exhausted and sank to their knees.

Suddenly Angada, who was thinking of Rama, sprang to his feet. He took up a fierce-looking sword and swung it at Vajradamstra's neck, lopping off his head. The Rakshasa dropped to the earth, spurting forth a jet of dark-red blood.

With their leader slain the other Rakshasas fled in fear, pursued by the monkeys. Hanging their heads in shame they swiftly re-entered Lanka. The monkeys surrounded the overjoyed Angada and praised his wonderful feat in killing Vajradamstra.

CHAPTER SEVEN

RAVANA ENTERS THE FRAY

Ravana saw his bedraggled troops returning defeated. His eyes were crimson with rage and he breathed heavily. He ordered the next of his powerful commanders, Durdharsha, to march out for battle. The demon had faced the gods and Danavas in battle and he feared nothing. Mounting his jewel-encrusted chariot, which had eight iron wheels that stood as tall as two men, he raced out of the city. His voice resounded like thunderclaps as he rallied the Rakshasa forces who followed him in the hundreds of thousands. Like the other Rakshasa chiefs before him he observed numerous ill omens, but he too ignored the portents and rushed toward the monkeys.

Another terrible carnage ensued. Rains of sharp arrows and weapons from the Rakshasas were met with volleys of rocks and trees from the monkeys. The combatants fell upon one another in a frenzy, each seeking to violently kill his adversary. No mercy was shown in the furious fight. A great dust cloud rose above the battlefield which screened the sky and enveloped the fighters. They could hardly perceive one another, and monkeys struck monkeys, while demons cut down other demons. Soon hundreds of thousands of Vanaras and Rakshasas lay stretched out on the ground, prey for vultures and jackals.

Durdharsha exhibited a wild rage. Standing on his chariot he loosed venomous shafts that tore the monkeys apart, breaking and routing the ranks of Rama's army. Seeing this, Hanuman advanced toward him. Durdharsha immediately showered him with innumerable sharp arrows, but Hanuman received the shafts like a mountain receiving rainfall. Laughing heartily, Hanuman ran at the Rakshasa, causing the earth to shake. With one hand he took up a great boulder and raised it above his head.

As Hanuman stood with the uplifted rock, Durdharsha shot crescent-headed arrows that smashed it to pieces. Hanuman laughed again and uprooted an ashwakarna tree as big as a mountain. He whirled it around and ran at the demon who was stationed some distance from him. As Hanuman bounded with the tree spinning, he struck down dozens of Rakshasas mounted upon elephants and chariots. Durdharsha saw him approach like a furious tempest, and full of trepidation, began to work his massive bow more furiously. The demon shot hundreds of fierce-looking arrows into Hanuman's body. As the valiant monkey bled, he appeared like a mountain overgrown with trees full of red blossoms.

Determining to kill Durdharsha, Hanuman shouted, "Victory to Rama!" and rushed at the Rakshasa with the tree raised aloft. The demon hardly had time to place another arrow upon his bow before Hanuman reached him. The furious monkey brought the tree down onto the Rakshasa's head with his full force. Durdharsha fell from his chariot dead. The other Rakshasas wailed in despair. They dropped their weapons and fled in all directions, falling over each other in their panic.

The monkeys cheered Hanuman and taunted the defeated demons. Rama and Lakshmana then personally honored the victorious monkey. In the sky the gods assembled and chanted auspicious hymns in Hanuman's praise. Hanuman enjoyed the glory even as Vishnu had upon killing the demons in days gone by.

In Lanka, Ravana was becoming more and more exasperated. He looked at Prahasta, the mightiest of his Rakshasa commanders. "I do not see many who are capable of saving Lanka at this critical juncture, O courageous one. Apart from you, Indrajit, Kumbhakarna and myself, there are none who can undertake such a burden. Rama and his troops are indeed formidable, but the fickle-minded monkeys will be put to flight when they hear your roar on the battlefield. O Prahasta, not even the mightiest gods could stand before you."

Although resolute to fight to the end the demon king was beginning to feel misgivings. There was something exceptional about these monkeys and bears. Some divine force was empowering them. Ravana thought of Rama. No doubt the final battle would be between himself and that human prince. The demon reflected upon his boon. Only a human could kill him. Would it be Rama? He recoiled from the thought. This was not the time for fear. The battle must continue.

Ravana urged Prahasta to march out with another enormous contingent. He told the Rakshasa chief to be firm. Even though victory was never certain, it was always preferable for a warrior to die in battle than in any other way. Ravana asked Prahasta if there was anything he needed. The demon replied, "I need only your blessings, my lord. Having ever been honored by you with gifts and kind words, how can I not render service to you when the time has come? Neither wife, sons, wealth nor even life itself is dearer to me than your service. Today the vultures will feast heartily on the flesh of monkeys."

Prahasta walked around Ravana with folded palms and then left for the battle. He assembled a horde of Rakshasas, all eager to fight. In less than an hour a force of over five hundred thousand Rakshasas was ready. They adorned themselves with garlands sanctified by sacred mantras, put on armor and grasped their weapons. They thronged around Prahasta, waiting to depart.

The demon commander had the iron portcullis at the northern gate lifted and the army swarmed out with a great cry. Prahasta rode at their head in his terrific war chariot furnished with every kind of weapon and driven by a hundred steeds. A large standard of brilliant cat's-eye stones bearing the emblem of a serpent stood in the middle of his bejeweled chariot. Prahasta shone like the sun as he charged laughing toward the enemy.

Dozens of vultures rose up and began circling anticlockwise around Prahasta. A large meteor dropped from the heavens. Clouds rumbled with a sound resembling the braying of a donkey, and showers of blood fell.

Prahasta ignored the omens and pressed ahead with full speed. He met the advancing monkeys and penetrated deeply into their ranks. They immediately surrounded the Rakshasa and assailed him with rocks and trees. The demon simply shrugged off the missiles without being disturbed. He sent volleys of arrows at the monkeys and roared like a thundercloud. His vast Rakshasa force fell upon the monkey troops with shouts of joy.

Monkeys and demons were again destroyed in large numbers. Some monkeys were run through with pikes and lances, some cut down with razor-sharp discuses and some hacked to pieces with axes. Still others were clubbed to death with iron mallets, while others were crushed with huge maces. The monkeys smashed thousands of Rakshasas with mountainous crags and trees. They struck down the Rakshasas with their bare hands and pounded them to death. A tumultuous clamor arose as heroic fighters roared in exultation or screamed in pain.

Prahasta himself caused terrible havoc among the monkeys. He knew the secrets of all kinds of mystic weapons and sent arrows in such numbers that they resembled dark clouds. All around his chariot waves of monkeys fell to the ground, pierced in their vital parts. The battlefield resembled a swirling river with heaps of slain warriors as its banks, lances and spears its trees and torrents of blood for its vast sheet of water. That river rushed toward the sea of death, sweeping away all in its path.

Seeing Prahasta annihilating his troops, the Vanara commander-in-chief Nila rushed toward the demon. Prahasta saw Nila approach and he drew his bow to full length, releasing deadly shafts that pierced the monkey.

Not minding his wounds, Nila took up a tree and struck the Rakshasa as he
stood upon his chariot. Prahasta roared in fury and sent hundreds of arrows
at Nila. The monkey could not check the shafts and he received them with
closed eyes. Nila fell to his knees and braced himself against the arrows'
impact, with his mind absorbed in thought of Rama. Rallying himself, the
Vanara chief took up a sal tree. He brought it down with tremendous force
onto Prahasta's chariot, smashing it to pieces and killing the horses.

Prahasta clutched hold of a fearsome iron mallet and leapt down from
his shattered chariot. He ran at Nila and a fierce fight ensued at close quarters. Prahasta struck Nila on the forehead with his terrible weapon. Blood
flowed in waves from the monkey's head. He hurled a boulder onto
Prahasta's chest but, unmoved by that rock, the Rakshasa again lifted his
massive iron mallet and rushed at Nila. Even as the Rakshasa closed on him,
Nila took up a mountain peak and smashed it onto his head. The demon's
head split apart and he fell to the ground, deprived of his splendor and his
life.

The Rakshasas were thrown into complete confusion. With their commander-in-chief slain, they did not know which way to turn. The jubilant
monkeys overran them and put them to flight. Downcast and defeated, the
Rakshasas re-entered their city.

Rama and Lakshmana warmly applauded Nila and then the monkeys
rested, awaiting the next wave of Rakshasas.

*   *   *

Ravana was shocked to hear news of Prahasta's death; his mind tormented with grief and anger. In an anguished voice he said to his ministers,
"Our enemy should be held in the highest regard. They have killed
Prahasta, who was capable of exterminating Indra's army. It seems it is time
for me to make my appearance at the battle. With a steady stream of blazing arrows I shall consume the army of monkeys. Today I will throw down
Rama and Lakshmana."

Ravana looked around at his ministers. They cheered his decision and
felt encouraged. Now the monkeys would surely be crushed.

Without losing time, Ravana sent for his chariot. Honored with auspicious hymns and conch blasts, and to the accompaniment of beating
kettledrums, Ravana mounted his splendid vehicle. He went out of Lanka
surrounded by innumerable dark Rakshasas, who resembled big mountains.
The demon appeared like Shiva in the midst of his ghostly followers. He saw
ahead of him the immense monkey army springing up with trees and rocks
in readiness to receive them.

As the vast Rakshasa army poured from the city, Rama turned to Vibhishana and asked him the names of the principal fighters. Vibhishana named them all and then pointed to Ravana. "That one who looks like the Himalaya mountain, who is surrounded by terrific demons with the heads of tigers, elephants, camels and deer, who shines like the sun and is adorned with a blazing diadem, he is the sovereign lord of all the Rakshasas, Ravana."

Rama gazed at Ravana and exclaimed, "There at last is the evil one I seek. I can hardly perceive his actual form, bathed as it is in a brilliant efful-gence. Even the gods are not possessed of such brilliance. This demon is accompanied by warriors who seem entirely unapproachable. Indeed, he looks like Death himself surrounded by fiery and hideous fiends. By good fortune this wicked demon has come within my sight. Today I shall freely vent my anger that was born from Sita's abduction."

Rama took from his quiver a long arrow with a barbed steel head and placed it on his bow. With Lakshmana by his side he faced the rapidly advancing Rakshasa hordes.

Ravana raced at the head of his army. He carved his way through the monkeys like a killer whale dividing the ocean waters. Sugriva took hold of a great mountain crag and ran toward Ravana, holding it aloft. As the mon-key king approached the demon, he hurled the mountain-top, which was covered in numerous trees, straight at his chariot. Ravana laughed as the mountain sailed through the air. He tore it apart with a hail of golden arrows that resembled streaks of fire.

The Rakshasa then took out an arrow resembling a huge serpent and released it for Sugriva's destruction. The arrow sped like Indra's thunderbolt and emitted a stream of sparks. It struck Sugriva on the chest and the mon-key groaned in pain and fell senseless to the ground.

As Sugriva fell the Rakshasas shouted exultantly. Other powerful Vanara generals immediately took up crags and rushed at Ravana. They rained down their rocks and trees, but the demon smashed all of them to pieces with his swift arrows. He pierced all of the monkeys with numbers of golden shafts bedecked with jewels. The monkeys fell down, shrieking and crying out to Rama for protection.

Rama heard their cries and he advanced toward the demon, but Lakshmana stood before him and asked that Rama permit him to fight with Ravana first. Rama looked at his younger brother, who was eager for battle. He assented to his request, but warned him to be on guard. Ravana was no ordinary foe.

Lakshmana folded his palms and bowed to Rama who tightly embraced him. The young prince then moved off and surveyed Ravana fighting the monkeys. As he watched he saw Hanuman approach the ten-headed Rakshasa. The fearless monkey shouted at Ravana, "You are proud of your boon, O demon. No fear exists in you of gods, demons, Yakshas or Gandharvas. But beware. There is danger to you from monkeys. My fist will now expel from your body your very life-breath. Try your best to fight with me for your death is now close."

Hanuman raised his fist and moved toward Ravana who shouted back at him, "Strike me at once without fear, O monkey. Earn for yourself lasting fame. Having seen the limits of your power, I shall immediately destroy you!"

Hanuman laughed and reminded Ravana of the fight in the ashoka grove, and of Aksha and the other powerful Rakshasas he had slain. As he spoke he rushed straight at the demon. Ravana threw a great blow which hit Hanuman on the chest and sent him reeling. But Hanuman regained his balance and whirling round he struck the demon with his outstretched palm.

Ravana shook like a mountain in an earthquake. In the heavens the rishis and Siddhas, who were observing the battle, shouted with joy. Ravana recovered his senses and called out to Hanuman. "Well done, monkey! Your strength and valor are worthy of my praise."

Hanuman replied that his strength was lamentable as Ravana still lived. Ravana rushed at Hanuman and dealt him another tremendous blow, which sent the monkey spinning away. The demon then speedily drove his chariot toward Nila, who was standing nearby. Ravana shot thousands of arrows at the monkey chief. Hanuman shouted after him to come back and fight, but the demon paid no heed. He continued to engage with Nila, who took up a mountaintop and hurled it at the Rakshasa. With seven crescent-headed arrows Ravana cut the rock to pieces. Nila threw great trees at the Rakshasa, one after another. Sal, aswakarna and mango trees in full blossom flew with speed toward Ravana. The demon loosed sharp arrows that ripped all the trees to shreds. He then covered Nila with a hail of sharp-pointed shafts.

Nila sprang clear of Ravana's arrows and, reducing himself to a very small size, he leapt onto the top of Ravana's standard. The monkey sprang from the standard to the end of Ravana's bow, then onto his diadem and back again to the standard. Ravana blazed with fury upon seeing Nila's insolence. He set an arrow on his bow and charged it with the power of the Agneyastra, the dangerous fire weapon. Being struck with that missile Nila fell unconscious to the ground. The monkey was burned all over, but by the grace of his father the fire-god, he was not slain.

Ravana then looked around and saw Lakshmana. He directed his charioteer to go quickly toward the prince. Lakshmana saw him approach and called out to him, "Here I am to do battle with you, O king of the Rakshasas. Leave aside the monkeys and fight with me."

Ravana shouted back, "It is fortunate indeed that you have fallen within my sight. Today you shall meet your end at my hands. Fight with all your strength, O Raghava!" Ravana addressed him derisively as a descendent of the powerful King Raghu.

"What is the use of your bragging?" Lakshmana answered. "Those who are actually strong do not engage in such talk. O sinful one, I know your valor and power. Stand firmly now and fight, for the hour of your demise draws near."

Ravana immediately shot seven beautifully plumed arrows at Lakshmana. The prince instantly responded with seven of his own arrows, which struck down Ravana's shafts from the air. Again and again Ravana released deadly arrows, but Lakshmana cut them all down. The demon was astonished at Lakshmana's speed and skill. He became incensed and fired more and more arrows in swift succession. Lakshmana responded with equal numbers. From his fully drawn bow, he shot at Ravana arrows that shone like fire and flew with the velocity of lightning.

Suddenly seeing an opportunity, Ravana released a celestial arrow that penetrated Lakshmana's defenses and struck him on the forehead. Lakshmana reeled and his grip on his bow loosened. Crouching down for only a moment he recovered his senses and stood up, instantly releasing an arrow which cut Ravana's bow in two. The prince then shot three sharp-pointed arrows which hit the demon on the chest and made him swoon.

When he regained his senses, Ravana took up from his chariot a huge javelin he had taken from the gods. He hurled it with great force at Lakshmana, and it sped through the air emitting fire and sparks.

Lakshmana struck the javelin with his arrows, but it coursed on and hit him full in the chest. Stunned by the javelin Lakshmana fell down in a faint. As he lay there burning in agony, Ravana quickly ran up to him and attempted to take him captive. The demon violently caught hold of Lakshmana with his twenty arms and tried to lift him, but despite exerting himself with all his power, Ravana was unable to even raise the prince's arms. He fell back in amazement and quickly leapt back onto his chariot.

Hanuman, who had been observing the battle between Ravana and Lakshmana, took the opportunity to jump onto Ravana's chariot. Whirling his two fists he struck the demon on the chest, making a sound like a great thunderclap which filled the four quarters. Ravana fell to his knees, blood flowing from his mouths, eyes and ears. He lost consciousness and sank motionless to the floor of his chariot. The gods and rishis, witnessing Hanuman's incredible feat, shouted in joy.

Feeling anxiety for Lakshmana, Hanuman left aside his dazed foe. He quickly leapt down and gathered up Lakshmana in his arms. The monkey easily lifted the prince although Ravana, the lifter of Mount Kailash, had not been able to budge him. Hanuman carried the unconscious Lakshmana into Rama's presence.

Rama ran his hand over his brother's face. Slowly Lakshmana came back to consciousness and Rama said to him, "The demon tried to take you captive, but that sinful being could not lift you, protected as you are by virtue. I cannot brook this attack upon you, dear brother. I shall immediately go and destroy this demon."

Hearing this Hanuman folded his palms and asked Rama, "Please mount upon my back and allow me to carry you to Ravana. Fight the demon from my back even as Vishnu fights upon Garuda."

Rama at once climbed onto Hanuman's shoulders and the monkey swiftly went to Ravana. Twanging his bowstring and making a sharp sound that reverberated like thunder, Rama called out to the demon, "Stand, O best of the Rakshasas. You will not escape today. Soon you will follow the path trodden by your fourteen thousand followers in Janasthana."

Ravana was seized with anger. He let go hundreds of flaming arrows, which struck Hanuman all over his body. Keeping a tight hold on Rama, the monkey bore the arrows without flinching. His energy and vigor only grew as Ravana assailed him.

Rama was infuriated by Ravana's attack on Hanuman. He drew his bow to a circle and fired shafts which tore Ravana's chariot to pieces. Its standard, wheels, horses, canopy, shields and driver all fell to the ground. Rama then struck Ravana himself on the chest with arrows that flew with blinding speed. The demon, who had withstood Indra's thunderbolt, was rocked by Rama's arrows and he dropped his bow. He swooned and lay gasping. Rama took up a crescent-headed shaft and tore off Ravana's diadem, of which he was so proud. Rama did not consider the Rakshasa to be a king in any way. With another arrow he broke apart the demon's bow. He then spoke to the half-conscious Ravana.

"You are clearly exhausted from the battle. As you are unable to properly defend yourself, it is not right that I kill you this time. Therefore, O valiant one, return to Lanka. Once you have rested, come out again and you shall witness my strength in battle."

Ravana scrambled to his feet. With his chariot shattered, his diadem ripped off and his bow destroyed, the Rakshasa was a sorry sight. He turned and flew toward Lanka with his vanity crushed. The other Rakshasas followed him and the battle ceased for the time being. Rama and Lakshmana comforted the wounded monkeys and they all rested, awaiting the return of Ravana and his troops.

CHAPTER EIGHT

THE COLOSSAL DEMON

Ravana returned to Lanka feeling highly disturbed. Overcome by Rama like an elephant defeated by a lion, he felt humiliated. Remembering the force of Rama's irresistible arrows, he wondered what action to take. He summoned his counselors, who then entered the council chamber and surrounded Ravana as he sat upon his throne. The demon looked around and spoke to them, still shaking from his fight with Rama.

"It seems that all my asceticism has proved useless, for I have been utterly vanquished by a mere mortal. I am now recalling Brahma's boon, which excluded protection from humans. I think this Rama is the one referred to by King Anaranya, long ago slain by me. Again the curse of Vedavati comes to mind. Surely that lady has been born as Sita. The predictions of those endowed with divine sight always come to pass. Considering all this, O mighty Rakshasas, strive in every way to protect me. A great danger has now arrived at my door."

Ravana then thought of Kumbhakarna. It was time to rouse him. When his fearsome brother marched out, the monkeys would flee in all directions. In battle his body grew to immense proportions. With each step he took he could crush an entire division of warriors. He would make short work of Rama's army. But how to wake him? Brahma's boon to him was more like a curse. He remained buried in the deepest sleep for six months, impervious to everything. It had only been ten days since he had last gone to sleep.

Ravana issued orders for the Rakshasas to go in their thousands to Kumbhakarna's chamber. They should raise a terrific din and try to wake him. The Rakshasas left at once and went quickly to Kumbhakarna's abode which was in a subterranean cavern. Pushing back the enormous gates, the Rakshasas entered his cavern. They were deafened by the sound of his snoring and almost blown over by the blast of his breath. The Rakshasas then saw Kumbhakarna's stupendous body lying in slumber within the vast cave, which was lit by innumerable celestial gems. They piled up great mounds of meat and other foods by his side. Heaps of antelopes, buffaloes and boars were placed next to him, along with massive pails of blood. They anointed him with heavenly perfumes and daubed him with the finest sandal-paste. Costly incense was lit and crowds of Yatudhanas began to extol Kumbhakarna with poetic phrases. Other Rakshasas thundered like clouds and blew their great conchshells with full force. Clapping their arms, beating drums and roaring like lions, the demons raised a tremendous uproar. As the noise issued from the cave, beasts fled in all directions and birds fell down stunned.

But Kumbhakarna did not stir. The Rakshasas then took hold of maces, mallets, boulders and flat swords. They beat the limbs of the colossal Rakshasa. Hundreds of demons mounted Kumbhakarna's chest and pounded him with their fists, but were thrown off by the wind of his breath. Ten thousand Rakshasas surrounded him and all at once began to roar and strike his body with their hard fists. Still he would not awaken.

Unable to rouse Kumbhakarna, the Rakshasas became more and more furious. They made an even louder noise, hitting huge drums with all their strength and blowing their conches taken from the bottom of the ocean. Some of them tore out his hair while others bit his ears. Hundreds of pails of water were thrown on Kumbhakarna's face.

The Rakshasas then had a thousand elephants run up and down Kumbhakarna's monstrous body while at the same time striking him with fully grown sal trees. At last he began to stir. Feeling a light touch on his body Kumbhakarna opened his eyes and stretched his limbs. The Rakshasas and elephants were thrown to the ground and scattered as he sat up and yawned. His mouth appeared like another great cavern and his luminous eyes resembled two blazing planets.

Kumbhakarna reached out and scooped up the food that lay around him. He consumed all of it and quaffed down many pails of blood and wine. When he was sated, the other demons came and respectfully bowed before him. Looking at them with eyes still heavy from sleep, Kumbhakarna questioned them.

"Why have I been roused from my slumber? I hope everything is well with Ravana and with Lanka. Or perhaps some great peril has arrived. If so, then I shall proceed from here at once to remove the cause of your fear without delay. Tell me, O Rakshasas, what should I do?"

A minister of Ravana named Yupaksha replied. "A formidable danger has beset us all of a sudden. Monkeys like great mountains have laid seige to the city. Each of them resembles the single monkey who killed Prince Aksha and set fire to Lanka. At their head is Rama, sorely grieved and angered by Sita's abduction. Even our lord Ravana was overpowered by him in an encounter and then released."

Kumbhakarna was not surprised. He had already warned his brother about Rama. It seemed that the time for the inevitable battle had arrived. Rama's power would now be tested to the full. Kumbhakarna spoke in a voice that boomed around the cavern. "This very day I shall wipe out the entire army of monkeys. The Rakshasas may gorge themselves with their flesh. I myself shall drink the blood of Rama and Lakshmana."

Kumbhakarna sprang to his feet and washed his face. He called for more drink and quickly swallowed two thousand pails of strong wine. Slightly inebriated and anticipating the excitement of battle, the Rakshasa left his cave and marched toward Ravana's palace, shaking the earth with his every step. He was surrounded by Rakshasas who ran with joined palms and continuously sang his praises.

From outside the city, the monkeys saw Kumbhakarna rising above the city walls like a mountain peak. They cried in fear and fell stunned to the earth. Some fled in all directions, seized by panic. Seeing Kumbhakarna, who was adorned with a blazing diadem, moving within the city, the monkeys were struck with terror. They rushed to Rama's tent, calling for him to come out quickly.

Rama came out holding his bow. He saw the huge Rakshasa, glowing with a brilliant effulgence. Rama's eyes opened wide with astonishment. He asked Vibhishana, "Who is this fellow resembling in every way a shining mountain? Simply upon seeing him, the monkeys have been put to flight. I have never seen such a creature before."

Vibhishana told Rama everything about Kumbhakarna. Describing the power of Ravana's immense brother, he said, "This demon has defeated Indra and all the gods in battle. He has crushed and devoured tens of thousands of mighty Daityas and Danavas. Indeed, this one has consumed innumerable living beings. It was for this reason that Brahma contrived to have him sent into continuous slumber. The gods feared that he would render all the worlds bereft of creatures, all of them eaten by him. Obviously Ravana, fearful of you, has roused him for the battle."

Vibhishana suggested that Rama inform the monkeys that Kumbhakarna was only a mechanical device. Otherwise they would never be able to muster up the courage to face him in battle.

Rama smiled. There was no need for that; he would himself deal with this massive mountain of a Rakshasa. He ordered Nila to quickly array the troops for battle. They should be reassured that Rama would himself face the colossus. Taking hold of mountain peaks, trees and various weapons, the monkeys deployed themselves around Lanka, awaiting Kumbhakarna's appearance. Rama himself stood with Lakshmana, both of them holding their bows and facing the city.

In Lanka, Kumbhakarna, who could change his form and size at will, had reached Ravana's palace. He found his elder brother seated in the Pushpaka chariot appearing perturbed and anxious. Bowing low at his feet, Kumbhakarna inquired what service he could render.

Ravana was joyous upon seeing his brother and he directed him to sit down on a splendid heavenly seat. He then told him what had transpired. "O mighty one, just see how the woods and groves of Lanka have been converted into a sea of monkeys. Already they have slain many of the foremost fighters among the Rakshasas. I have been unable to overcome them by any means. Therefore I have sought you as my only shelter. I can think of no other way to defeat this simian army. Beloved brother, you have routed the gods and Danavas many times. Be my saviour today and crush Rama and his followers without delay."

Kumbhakarna became angry. "Were you not warned?" he retorted. "You are now reaping the fruits of your rash and sinful act of stealing Sita. Had you heeded the advice of your well-wishers and acted in accord with political wisdom, you would never have found yourself in such a mess."

Hearing Ravana reprimanded by Kumbhakarna, the minister Mahodara came to his defense. "Ravana acted properly in stealing Sita," he argued. "The duty of all beings is to secure their happiness by any means. Even virtue is only a means to ensure one's happiness. Therefore Ravana's theft of Sita, meant as it was for his pleasure, was rightly done."

Ravana also did not like his brother's speech and he answered angrily. "What use is this lecturing now? We face the greatest danger we have ever known. This is the time for action, not words. Whether I have acted wisely or not is of little consequence now. Let us do what must be done."

Kumbhakarna smiled. "Be at ease, dear brother," he said soothingly. "I spoke only out of my love for you. It is always the duty of a well-wisher to tender proper advice. I shall now fight. You should cast away your fears. Soon you will see the monkey army stretched out on the battlefield. Rama's head will be brought before you. Sugriva and the other monkey chiefs will be thrown about like so many pieces of dust."

Kumbhakarna vaunted his prowess at length, growing more and more enraged. He did not care if Brahma, Indra and Yamaraja appeared on the battlefield. There would be no shelter for Rama and his army.

Mahodara spoke again. "O Kumbhakarna, you are powerful and brave, but you should give up any thought of defeating Rama. That human has already killed fourteen thousand powerful Rakshasas single-handedly. He is now decimating our army. I do not think further battle with him is at all wise."

Mahodara was afraid. He suggested that Ravana use trickery to win over Sita. The demon king should convince her that Rama was dead, and then she would submit to him. This would deprive Rama of all energy.

Both Ravana and Kumbhakarna told Mahodara to be quiet. That plan had already failed. There was no avoiding the battle now, short of returning Sita--and that was out of the question.

Kumbhakarna boomed, "I shall now march out to make good the disastrous policy you have initiated, O king. You are surrounded by useless ministers like Mahodara. They simply aquiesce out of fear and lead you into more and more danger, which they are then powerless to prevent. It is fortunate for you that I am here as your protector."

Ravana laughed heartily to see his brother's resolve. Surely he would now be saved. No one could face Kumbhakarna and live. This would be a glorious day for the Rakshasas. Ravana sprang up and placed a beautiful gold necklace around his brother's neck. He also adorned him with numerous other gem-studded ornaments and had many fragrant garlands put on him.

Kumbhakarna donned an impenetrable golden coat of mail and a huge dark blue girdle. As he marched out for battle, he shone like the western mountains receiving the setting sun. He went first to Ravana's weapon room and took up a great pike, which was embellished with gold and which emitted flames even as it lay there. It shone like Indra's thunderbolt and was no less powerful. The pike was wreathed with garlands of crimson flowers and smeared with the finest sandal-paste. Clutching his fierce weapon, the demon stormed toward the city gates.

Thousands of drums were beaten and conches blew. Kumbhakarna assumed a form six hundred bow-lengths high and more than a hundred in breadth. He strode toward the battlefield surrounded by gigantic Rakshasas driving chariots and mounted upon elephants. Others followed him on camels, donkeys, lions, serpents, antelopes and birds. The Rakshasas, who all had terrifying forms and faces, raised their maces, swords, lances, bludgeons and bows, sending up a terrific roar.

As the Rakshasas moved off, there were many grim omens. Massive gray clouds full of thunder and lightning covered the sun. The earth shook. Birds wheeled from right to left and a large vulture perched on Kumbhakarna's pike. The Rakshasa's left eye and arm throbbed. A flaming meteor fell from the sky and descended to the ground with a terrible crash. Jackals howled and a strong wind blew into their faces.

Kumbhakarna strode towards the battlefield.

Kumbhakarna paid no heed to the omens. He stepped over Lanka's defensive wall and laughed out loud. The Rakshasa gazed around at the army of monkeys, which appeared like a mass of clouds. Seeing the stupendous Rakshasa's sudden appearance, the monkeys dispersed in all directions, even as clouds are scattered by a gale. Kumbhakarna roared repeatedly, filling the four quarters with an unbearable thundering which agitated the ocean and made the mountains quake. Numerous monkeys fell unconscious simply from hearing the sound. Others fled screeching in terror.

As the monkeys stampeded, Angada called out to them, "Have you forgotten your prowess, your valor and your lineage? Why are you fleeing like ordinary monkeys? This gigantic nightmare of a Rakshasa will not be able to stand for long against us, protected as we are by Rama and Lakshmana. Stand and fight, O Vanaras!"

The monkeys regained confidence upon hearing Angada's words. Turning back and taking hold of trees and rocks, they stood firm as Kumbhakarna rushed toward them. They smashed the Rakshasa with mountain peaks and fully-grown trees, but these had no effect whatsoever, falling shattered to the ground. Kumbhakarna reached down and scooped up hundreds of monkeys. He dashed them furiously to the earth. The Rakshasa began destroying the ranks of the Vanara troops like a fire consuming dry wood. Innumerable huge monkeys soon lay senseless on the ground, covered with blood.

The monkeys again hastily retreated. They bounded away without looking back or sideways. Some rushed back over the ocean bridge. Others were seen sailing through the air, having been struck or tossed by the Rakshasa. With their faces turned pale, the monkeys scrambled up mountains or dived into the sea. Bears climbed trees and hid in caves. The whole army ran about in fear, not knowing which way to turn.

Angada tried again and again to rally the monkeys. He called out to them, "Come back! Where will you hide from this monster? He must be faced. What will you say to your wives after you have fled in fear from the battlefield? Have you forgotten your boasting words, 'We shall annihilate the Rakshasas'? How have you become such cowards? No regions of bliss are ever attained by cowards. Indeed, they are always condemned by good men."

Although Angada tried in many ways to convince his troops to fight, they would not listen. They continued fleeing, some of them replying to the prince as they ran, "This Rakshasa cannot be faced in battle. This is no time to exhibit bravery, for life is dear. We are going."

Although their troops fled in all directions, Angada and Sugriva remained firm, along with Hanuman and some of the other powerful commanders of the monkey troops. The Vanara leaders then somehow managed to check the monkeys and reminded them of Rama's invincibility. With heartening arguments they convinced the monkeys to once more advance against Kumbhakarna. With Angada at their head the Vanara forces turned again to face the mighty Rakshasa.

Thousands of monkeys rushed in a body at Kumbhakarna, but he swept them aside with his pike. He ran about crushing and devouring the monkeys even as Garuda would devour serpents. With great difficulty the monkeys remained standing in the forefront of battle. Waves of other Rakshasas rushed forward in support of Kumbhakarna, roaring in joy. The battle raged furiously with Kumbhakarna wreaking havoc among the monkey army.

The powerful Dwivida hurled an immense boulder at Kumbhakarna. The Rakshasa evaded the rock and it fell among the other Rakshasas, crushing chariots, horses and elephants, along with hundreds of demons. The Rakshasa warriors fought back, severing the heads of the yelling monkeys with their deadly arrows.

Hanuman leapt into the air and rained down rocks and trees upon Kumbhakarna's head. The Rakshasa fended off the missiles with his pike. Hanuman, who had grown to huge proportions, came down on the ground and stood firmly in front of Kumbhakarna. He smashed him on the breast with a mountain peak and the Rakshasa reeled back in pain. Quickly recovering, the Rakshasa struck Hanuman a terrible blow with his pike. The monkey was rendered almost senseless and he fell back, vomiting blood.

Seeing Hanuman thrown down, the Rakshasa forces cheered loudly and the monkeys fled in fear. Nila quickly came forward and rallied the troops. He took up a great boulder and flung it violently at Kumbhakarna. The Rakshasa saw it coming and smashed it to pieces with his fist, sending up a shower of flames and sparks.

Five huge monkey chiefs then attacked Kumbhakarna from all sides. They struck him with crags, trees, the palms of their hands and their feet. They climbed up his legs and tore at him with their nails and teeth. Then hundreds of other monkeys rushed at the Rakshasa and leapt upon him. Kumbhakarna plucked the monkeys from his body and thrust them into his huge open mouth. Monkeys were seen to issue out of his nostrils and his ears as the demon repeatedly thrust them into his mouth.

Kumbhakarna looked like Death incarnate appearing for the destruction of all living beings. One by one the powerful monkey leaders assailed him and were repulsed. Sugriva took up a great mountain-top and boldly challenged the Rakshasa. "See now my prowess, O Rakshasa. Leave aside the other monkeys and face me. With this mountain peak I shall dash you to the ground."

The Rakshasa laughed. "I know you, monkey. You are a grandson of Brahma and the son of the mighty Riksaraja. Thus you stand there roaring. Show me then the limits of your strength."

Sugriva immediately hurled the vast crag upon the demon's chest. It smashed to pieces and fell to the earth, but the Rakshasa was hardly moved. In a rage he threw his flaming pike at Sugriva but Hanuman intercepted it as it flew. The monkey placed the pike across his knees and broke it in two, making the Vanara troops roar with joy.

Kumbhakarna became maddened. He stormed across to the Malaya mountain and tore from it a massive peak. Spinning around, the Rakshasa hurled it at Sugriva. The monkey king was caught by the whirling crag and he fell unconscious. The Rakshasas shouted in triumph, thinking Sugriva to be slain. Kumbhakarna quickly ran over and took up the fallen monkey. Pressing him under his arm, the demon made his way back to the city. If Sugriva were killed or captured, then the entire monkey army would be finished.

As the Rakshasa stepped over the city wall, he was greeted by cheering citizens. They showered flowers and scented water on him. Sugriva felt the cool water on his face and he regained consciousness. He saw himself being carried toward Ravana's palace. Bending his body violently, Sugriva spun round and ripped off the demon's ear with his nails. He then bit off the end of his nose and clawed his side. Kumbhakarna roared in pain and threw the monkey down.

Sugriva bounced up like a ball. He sprang onto a rooftop and quickly bounded over the city wall and back to the monkeys. Kumbhakarna stood with blood running down his face. He screamed in anger and turned back toward the battle holding a terrible-looking mace. Rushing into the monkey forces, he continued annihilating them by the thousands.

Lakshmana then appeared before the Rakshasa. He immediately shot two dozen flaming arrows into Kumbhakarna's arms. The prince continuously released arrows which covered Kumbhakarna on all sides like a golden cloud. Brushing aside the shafts the Rakshasa laughed and spoke to Lakshmana. "You have shown me your prowess, O prince. I am impressed with your valor. Even Indra or Yamaraja would not dare to face me in an encounter. But I wish to fight only with Rama. Where is your brother? By slaying him I shall put an end to this conflict. My army will then finish the rest of the monkeys."

Rama heard the Rakshasa's haughty challenge. He called out, "Stand ready for battle!" and shot from a distance a number of arrows that pierced the huge demon all over. Kumbhakarna at once rushed toward him, clutching his mighty mace. Rama sent volleys of arrows, which shattered the

Rakshasa's mace even as he raised it for Rama's destruction. Shafts bedecked with golden feathers thudded into the demon's body by the thousands. Blood poured from his wounds like streams from a mountain.

Kumbhakarna ran about in fury, crushing monkeys and demons alike. He seized hold of a tremendous rock and flung it at Rama. The prince released sharp-pointed arrows which smashed the crag as it flew toward him. The pieces of the rock killed two hundred Rakshasas as the shards fell to earth.

Thousands of monkeys rushed at Kumbhakarna and leapt upon him, trying to drag him down, but the Rakshasa shook them off like so many insects. He dashed about intoxicated with battle and slaying both friend and foe. Rama determined that the time to kill him had arrived. Firmly grasping his bow he called out, "Take heart and fight, O lord of the Rakshasas. Know me to be the destroyer of the Rakshasa race. You will now be slain by me."

Kumbhakarna whirled around and faced Rama, but suddenly Vibhishana came between them with mace in hand. Seeing him there, Kumbhakarna said, "Yes, my brother. Come forward and strike at once. Abandon all filial affection and remain devoted to the duty of a warrior. O Vibhishana, you alone are the redeemer of our race. Among the Rakshasas you are the best knower of virtue. Indeed, I will not slay you today, for you deserve protection at my hands. Stand aside! I cannot check my nature and am given to wantonly killing all creatures."

Vibhishana replied, "With the interests of my race in mind I always tendered advice to Ravana, but neglected by him I sought Rama's shelter. Hence I stand before you in battle today."

Tears sprang to Vibhishana's eyes as he spoke. Rama consoled him and told him to stand aside; the time for Kumbhakarna's destruction had come. Seeing Rama standing firmly before him, Kumbhakarna laughed hideously and said, "I am neither Viradha nor Kabhandha. Nor am I Khara, Dushana, Vali or Maricha. I am Kumbhakarna, arrived here as your death. Do not hold me in contempt. Show me the full limit of your power and I shall then devour you, O Rama."

Rama at once released arrows which flew with the speed of lightning and struck the Rakshasa's body. Those arrows, which had formerly pierced seven sal trees and the very earth itself, did not even shake the demon. The Rakshasa took up a massive club and whirled it about, knocking down Rama's arrows as they flew. Laughing again and again, Kumbhakarna stood with his great club uplifted.

Rama released an arrow imbued with the force of Vayu. It roared through the air and severed the Rakshasa's arm. That arm, still clutching the club, fell to earth and killed a thousand monkeys and Rakshasas.

Kumbhakarna shrieked with pain, making the sky vibrate and the mountains break open. He looked like a mountain whose summit had been cut off with a gigantic sword. With his remaining arm he tore up a large palmyra tree and rushed toward Rama. With each step the earth vibrated and trees toppled over in distant forests.

Rama released another mystic missile, which cut off the Rakshasa's other arm. It fell with an enormous crash, sending Rakshasas and monkeys scattering in all directions. With blood spurting from the stumps of his arms the Rakshasa continued to rush at Rama. He bellowed furiously and the monkeys covered their ears, unable to tolerate the noise. Rama shot a pair of crescent-headed arrows imbued with the force of Indra's thunderbolt and they severed the Rakshasa's feet.

Not deterred, Kumbhakarna still somehow moved swiftly toward the prince. His mouth was wide open and he emitted savage, deafening cries which shook the earth. In an instant Rama filled his mouth with arrows and the demon was silenced. Rama then took up an arrow which was encrusted with gems and which shone brilliantly. Empowering it with the force of the Brahmastra, he released it for Kumbhakarna's destruction.

As it flew with terrible speed, the arrow illuminated all directions like a blazing comet descending to earth. It tore off the Rakshasa's head, which looked like a peak of the Himalaya mountains. Adorned with a pair of blazing gold earrings, his head shone as it was carried through the air by the force of Brahma's weapon. It seemed like the rising moon moving through the heavens. It fell upon the defensive wall of Lanka and demolished the great northern gate. The head then rolled along the royal highway. By the power of Brahma's mystic missile the Rakshasa's body was lifted and thrown into the ocean, creating a tidal wave which swept the coast of Lanka.

Hosts of gods and rishis assembled in the sky and joyously praised Rama. The monkeys surrounded him roaring in exultation. All the remaining Rakshasas fled, astonished and dismayed. Rama felt elated and shone brightly amid the monkeys, even as the sun shines after an eclipse.

CHAPTER NINE

CARNAGE AMONG THE RAKSHASAS

The Rakshasas ran quickly to Ravana and told him the news. "After wreaking havoc among the monkeys for some time, your glorious brother has been slain by Rama. His limbless and headless trunk lies half-submerged in the sea, and his head now blocks the city's main gate."

Ravana was shocked and seized by grief. He fainted. All around him his sons and other relatives sent up a wail of sorrow. They could not believe their ears. How could the invincible Kumbhakarna be killed by a mere human?

Gradually Ravana came around and began to lament. "Alas, my brother, where have you gone? Without removing the thorn from my side how have you left me alone? What use now is my kingdom, or Sita, or even life itself? I am deprived of my right arm, depending on which I had no fear from the assembled gods headed by Indra. Now those gods stand in the sky raising shouts of joy. I cannot brook this turn of events. I shall follow the path trodden by my brother. Either I shall slay Rama or Death may claim me too."

Ravana wept and tossed about in agony. He remembered Vibhishana's advice. His virtuous brother had spoken wisely. He had been wrongly expelled from Lanka. Now Ravana was tasting the bitter fruit of that action. One who ignores the good advice of wise well-wishers always comes to grief.

The Rakshasa king sank down in distress. Seeing him fallen into abject sorrow, his son Devantaka, who was not very thoughtful, said, "Why are you lamenting in this way, O king? Those endowed with power and valor do not give way to grief. The time has come for firm action, not lamentation. Only command me and I shall go out and exterminate your enemies."

Ravana's other sons were heartened by Devantaka's words. They also began boasting of their power. All of them clamored for the order to fight. They were all mighty in battle and had never experienced defeat. All of them knew the mystic missiles and all had received various boons from their practices of asceticism. Bragging loudly, they declared that they would all go out together and finish Rama and the monkeys in no time.

Ravana was encouraged. Driven by his destiny, the demon stood up and embraced his sons, ordering them to march out for battle. Four of the Rakshasa's sons, Trishira, Devantaka, Narantaka and Atikaya, along with two of his half-brothers, Mahaparshwa and Mahodara, were dispatched for the fight. Those gigantic warriors anointed themselves with medicinal herbs capable of warding off injuries, as well as with perfumes and sandalwood paste. They put on golden armor and took up their fierce weapons.

Mahodara mounted an elephant that resembled a dark cloud. Trishira mounted a fine chariot drawn by the best of horses and equipped with thousands of weapons. Atikaya, who stood with a flaming crown on his head, mounted another superb chariot. On either side of him stood Devantaka and Narantaka, clutching frightful maces, both of them appearing like Vishnu holding the Mandara mountain. Mahaparshwa came behind them, mounted upon another elephant which resembled Airavata, the carrier of Indra.

They came out of the western gate of Lanka, like six brilliant planets suddenly appearing in the heavens. Followed by the massed ranks of Rakshasa warriors, they raised their weapons and rushed joyfully toward the monkey army.

The monkeys saw them advancing like a row of dark clouds. The earth shook and the sky resounded with their roars. Drums crashed and conches blew, filling the four quarters with a deafening clamor.

The Vanara army thundered in response and took up crags and tree trunks. The two armies met with a clash and a terrible, confused fight ensued. Demons and monkeys gave out leonine roars as they assailed one another with fury. The monkeys sprang high, dragging down the airborne Rakshasas and dashing them to the earth. They smashed the demons with rocks and pounded them with their fists and feet.

The Rakshasas sent volley after volley of arrows at the monkeys. They whirled their spiked maces and swords, viciously hacking down the enemy troops. The monkeys picked up one Rakshasa to strike another, and the Rakshasas did the same with the monkeys. Arrows with crescent or horseshoe heads sped through the air and lopped off arms, legs and heads.

Narantaka sent up a tremendous roar and began carving a path deep into the monkey army. He left a trail of flesh and blood strewn with mountain-like monkeys lying stretched on the ground. The demon sundered the ranks of his enemy, piercing them with his spear and killing dozens at a time. The monkeys howled in fear as Narantaka fought with a maniacal fury. None could face him.

Seeing the awful destruction being wrought by Narantaka, Angada came forward. He shouted to the demon. "Wait! Why are you showing your strength against ordinary monkeys? Throw your spear, which strikes like lightning, at my breast."

Narantaka spun round and glared at Angada. He hurled his great flaming spear at the monkey who stood firmly before him. The spear broke against Angada's chest and fell to the ground. Angada leapt forward and dealt a blow to the head of the Rakshasa's horse. The horse's feet sank deeply into the ground and its eyes popped out. Narantaka jumped off the back of his slain horse and roared in anger. He struck Angada a terrible blow on the side of his head. The monkey vomited hot blood and fell back dazed.

Crouching down and regaining his senses, Angada, who was thinking only of Rama, suddenly sprang forward. He swung his fist with all his might and hit the Rakshasa on the chest. Narantaka's breast was split asunder by that blow. He sank to the ground with his limbs soaked in blood and gave up his life.

The monkeys sent up a cry of joy and the gods beat their heavenly drums. Observing Angada's incredible feat, even Rama was struck with wonder. Angada stood infused with vigor ready to continue the battle.

Seeing his brother killed, Devantaka cried loudly with grief and fury. He gazed with bloodshot eyes at Angada. Followed by Trishira and Mahodara, he rushed toward the son of Vali, releasing thousands of arrows. Angada immediately seized a huge tree and swept aside all the arrows. He then hurled the tree at Devantaka, but it was torn to pieces by the arrows of Trishira standing close behind him. Angada threw trees and rocks one after another. Mahodara whirled his club and shattered them as they flew toward him. Suddenly the three powerful Rakshasas rushed simultaneously at Angada. Each of them struck him furiously with their clubs. Angada stood his ground tolerating the blows. He leapt toward Mahodara and struck the Rakshasa's elephant with his palm. The elephant fell to its knees and toppled over. Angada then tore out a tusk from the dead elephant and struck Devantaka a terrific blow on the head. The demon reeled about, vomiting blood.

Hanuman saw Angada engaged with the three towering Rakshasas and he ran over to assist the prince. Nila also rushed to Angada's aid, hurling a mountain peak at Trishira, but the Rakshasa smashed the massive crag with his arrows. Devantaka swung his club in a full circle and caught the running Hanuman on his breast. Not minding that blow, although it was forceful enough to have rent the earth, Hanuman swung his fist at the Rakshasa. He caught him on his head with a crack resembling a peal of thunder. The demon's teeth and eyes were forced out and his skull was shattered. He fell like a tree cut at its root.

Hanuman roared loudly and sprang at Trishira. He clawed at the Rakshasa's massive steed even as a lion would claw an elephant. Trishira took up a terrible javelin and hurled it straight at Hanuman. The monkey immediately caught it and snapped it in two. Trishira lifted his sword and thrust it at Hanuman, piercing him in the breast. Not shaken by the wound, Hanuman struck the Rakshasa a blow on the breast with his palm. Trishira fell unconscious and his sword slipped from his grasp. Hanuman snatched the sword and roared. The demon regained consciousness, awakened by Hanuman's roar. He could not tolerate the sound and leapt up furiously, striking the monkey with his fist. Hanuman seized the Rakshasa by his hair, which was covered by a diadem. Pulling the demon's head toward him, Hanuman severed it with the demon's own sword.

Even as Hanuman was slaying Trishira, Nila killed Mahodara with a tremendous blow from a fully grown sal tree. The mountain-like monkey Rishabha then engaged in a fierce fight with Mahaparshwa. The two combatants rendered each other unconscious again and again. Finally Rishabha pounded the Rakshasa to death with the demon's own mace.

Seeing five of their heroes killed in duels with the monkeys, the Rakshasas fled in all directions, resembling an ocean that has burst its shores. The demon Atikaya then came to the forefront of the battle and rallied the terrified Rakshasas. As the huge-bodied demon advanced the monkeys ran away howling. They thought that Kumbhakarna had somehow returned to life. Surrounding Rama, they cried for protection.

Rama saw in the distance Atikaya, who resembled a great mountain. Amazed at this sight, Rama turned to Vibhishana and asked, "Who is that monstrous Rakshasa seated in a chariot drawn by a thousand horses? Surrounded by flaming pikes, he seems like a dark cloud encircled by lightning flashes. Indeed, with his golden bows on all sides of the shining chariot, he is illuminating the battlefield like the newly-risen sun. His blazing arrows going in all directions are like so many sunbeams. Tell me the name of this lion-like warrior."

Vibhishana replied that this was Ravana's son, a powerful fighter who had performed much asceticism and had thus acquired from Brahma different boons. The creator of the universe had made him invincible to gods and demons and had bestowed upon him many mystical weapons as well as the wonderful chariot he was now driving. With his arrows, the demon had even checked Indra's thunderbolt and cut down Varuna's noose. Vibhishana advised Rama to tackle him at once before he annihilated the entire army of monkeys.

Rama watched as Atikaya penetrated into the monkey ranks. At once he was surrounded by Nila, Dwivida, Mainda, Kumuda and Sarabha, five great heroes among the monkeys. They assailed the Rakshasa from all sides, hurling huge rocks and trees at him. The demon easily repulsed all of their missiles with his arrows, which were bedecked with bright red jewels. He pierced all five of the monkeys and sent them running. The demon struck fear into the monkey army as a furious lion would terrify a flock of deer. He looked around and saw Rama. Leaving aside the monkeys, the Rakshasa drove across to Rama and issued a proud challenge. "I do not care to fight with common warriors. If you have the courage and the strength, then stand against me today. I shall soon end your power and your fame."

Hearing this, Lakshmana was infuriated. He seized his bow and twanged the string making a sound which reverberated all around the battlefield. Lakshmana gazed at Atikaya with bloodshot eyes, placing a long shaft on his bow.

The demon laughed derisively. "How do you dare to challenge me, O son of Sumitra? You are only a boy, unskilled in warfare. I cannot be faced by the Himalaya mountain nor even the earth itself. You seek to rouse the fire of universal destruction as it slumbers peacefully. Do not lose your life in this way. Depart swiftly! Or if you choose to stand here, then be prepared for my arrows, which will quaff your lifeblood, even as a lion would quaff the blood of a deer."

Lakshmana could not tolerate Atikaya's arrogant words. He thundered back at the Rakshasa, "Mere speech does not prove your prowess, O demon. Give up this empty boasting and demonstrate your strength at once. After you send at me the best of your arrows and missiles, I will strike your head off even as the wind blows a ripe fruit from a tree. Whether I am old or young is of no matter; you should know me as your death arrived here today. The three worlds were taken by Vishnu even while he was yet a child."

Atikaya flared up in anger. He instantly fired an arrow which flew with the speed of the wind, resembling a meteor and shooting tongues of fire. Lakshmana loosed his own arrow, which intercepted Atikaya's in mid-flight and split it in two. Atikaya grew even more enraged and fitted five more arrows to his bow, sending them at Lakshmana in a moment. Again Lakshmana cut down his shafts as they sped toward him.

Lakshmana seized a sharpened arrow which shone with splendor. Pulling his bow into a full circle he released the shaft and it pierced the demon in the brow. Atikaya shook like a mountain in an earthquake. Profuse blood ran down his head like oxides exuding from a mountain. The Rakshasa praised Lakshmana's feat. He quickly sent two dozen arrows at the prince which seemed to light up the sky, but Lakshmana struck all of them down.

Seizing his opportunity as Lakshmana parried the arrows, Atikaya sent another fierce shaft which struck the prince on his breast. Lakshmana bled profusely but pulled out the arrow and tossed it aside. He then charged an arrow with the force of the Agneyastra, the powerful fire weapon. Seeing the arrow loosed for his destruction and blazing in the sky, Atikaya responded with an arrow imbued with the power of the sun-god. The two mystic missiles met in space like two blazing planets colliding in the heavens. Reduced to ashes, they both fell to earth.

Atikaya fired at Lakshmana a weapon presided over by Yamaraja, but the prince countered it with a missile empowered with the force of the wind-god. Lakshmana quickly responded by covering the son of Ravana with countless arrows, so that neither the demon nor his chariot were visible. Sweeping away those arrows with a sword, the demon did not feel at all harassed. He shot a deadly arrow at Lakshmana, which hit him in the chest and caused the prince to faint for some moments. Regaining consciousness, he shot razor-headed arrows which cut down the demon's standard. He killed the charioteer and several rows of the Rakshasa's horses. But although he struck the demon's body with innumerable arrows, he could not hurt him in the least.

As Lakshmana stood confounded, the wind-god Vayu approached him and said, "This demon is clad in an impenetrable armor bestowed upon him by Brahma himself. Indeed, the Rakshasa cannot be slain except with Brahma's weapon."

Hearing the celestial voice, Lakshmana took out a large golden arrow and fitted it to his bow. He recited the incantations to invoke Brahma's missile. As he chanted the mantras, the sky seemed to shake and the earth groaned. With that arrow on his fully stretched bow, Lakshmana appeared like Death incarnate. He released the arrow and it sped with a terrible cracking sound toward the demon.

Atikaya saw the diamond-bedecked arrow approach him blazing like the midday sun. The demon was struck with fear. Moving with blinding speed he hurled javelins, spears, pikes, maces and axes at the arrow. He also struck it with numerous arrows of his own. But the shaft could not be checked. It baffled the demon's weapons and continued to course swiftly through the air. The blazing arrow caught Atikaya in the neck, severing his head and throwing it some distance onto the battlefield.

When Ravana's son was slain, the remaining Rakshasas sent up a wail. Crying in discordant, tones they ran about in fear, unable to find a protector. They turned their faces toward the city and hastily retreated. The monkeys surrounded Lakshmana and praised him, shouting with joy. The prince smiled and returned to Rama's side. Rama embraced his brother and glorified his wondrous feat. Flowers fell from the sky and heavenly drums sounded.

CHAPTER TEN

RAMA AND LAKSHMANA LAID LOW

Ravana was becoming increasingly anxious. His fear overpowered the grief of losing his sons and brothers. He sat lost in thought on his golden throne. One after another his most powerful fighters were being slain. Even when the two human princes had been overcome and thrown down by Indrajit's irresistible weapons, still they somehow recovered. When Rama had killed even the formidable Kumbhakarna, who was there left who could face the prince and live? Surely he was Vishnu himself, the Rakshasas' supreme enemy.

Ravana's eyes narrowed. He now faced a great peril. He ordered his ministers to check every defensive post around the city. Extra guards should be posted. Day and night there should be extreme vigilance. Anyone found neglectful of his duty would be immediately executed.

The demon hissed with anger. The thought of surrender did not cross his mind for a moment. Victory or death were the only choices. Brooding on Atikaya's fall, he went into his chambers and sat disconsolately on a golden couch.

Indrajit then approached him and said, "O lord of the Rakshasas, why are you held in the grip of sorrow? Do you not see me by your side? How will those two humans survive when I go out again for battle? They were lucky to escape last time, but their luck has now run out. Behold them today lying prostrate on the ground, torn to pieces by my weapons."

Indrajit consoled his father by vowing that he would kill Rama and Lakshmana. Ravana felt heartened. He gave his assent to his son and without delay Indrajit prepared for battle.

The prince donned his impenetrable armor and mounted his great chariot drawn by tigers. Blowing his massive conch he proceeded along Lanka's main highway. At once many other fierce Rakshasas began to follow. Some rode horses, some boars and some giant donkeys. Others mounted lions, jackals and even huge scorpions. Other Rakshasas, who had hideous, twisted faces, mounted crows, vultures and peacocks. Soon an enormous number of Rakshasas were assembled for battle, headed by Indrajit.

Those demon warriors, equipped with every kind of weapon, marched to the sound of kettledrums and conches, making the earth vibrate. Indrajit sat aboard his chariot, which was covered over with a white parasol. He was being fanned by beautiful golden-handled whisks and worshipped by Yatudhanas chanting sacred hymns. As he proceeded for battle he shone like Indra amid the gods.

Ravana stood upon a high rampart watching his son. He felt confident. No one in all the worlds could stand against Indrajit, be they gods, Danavas or Daityas. What then of humans and monkeys? After all, Indrajit had already overpowered the two humans. Surely this time there would be no lucky escapes.

Ravana shouted a blessing to Indrajit as he reached the northern gate. The demon prince turned to his father with palms joined, then raised his hand, and the army rushed out with a mighty roar.

As the Rakshasas reached the battlefield, Indrajit halted them and had them surround him. He dismounted from his chariot and lit a fire. While reciting Vedic mantras the demon worshipped the sacred fire. He poured oblations of ghee into the fire and made offerings of lances, spears and swords in place of the traditional reeds and grasses. Clasping the neck of a dark-hued goat, the demon slit its throat and placed it on the fire.

As the fire burst into flames, the fire-god appeared in person. Shining like refined gold he personally accepted the offerings. Indrajit then climbed back aboard his chariot. He sat in meditation and invoked the Brahmastra. While the Rakshasa was charging all his weapons and his chariot with the force of that celestial missile, the heavens seemed to quake in fear.

Having finished his incantations Indrajit blazed like a smokeless fire. By his own mystic power he became invisible, along with his weapons, chariot and all. He gave the order to charge and the army of Rakshasas went forward roaring in various dissonant tones. They struck the monkeys from a distance with their ornamented arrows and lances thrown with tremendous velocity. The Rakshasas then fell upon the monkeys in a fury.

Remaining invisible, Indrajit assailed the monkey army with razor-headed arrows, lances and maces. The monkeys realized the demon was fighting invisibly and surrounded the place from where his weapons flew. They hurled numerous trees and boulders at him, but the demon cut them to pieces. He tore apart the bodies of the monkeys with his irresistible arrows. With a single arrow the Rakshasa pierced as many as five, seven, or even a dozen monkeys.

Even though they were being exterminated by Indrajit, the monkeys, who had dedicated their lives to Rama's cause, stood their ground. They repeatedly surrounded the deadly demon, sending an endless shower of rocks and trees in his direction.

Indrajit moved off invisibly and searched for the chief monkey warriors. One after another he pierced Nila, Jambavan, Sugriva, Angada, Rishabha, Dwivida and many other monkey heroes. He rendered all of them them virtually unconscious with his terrible shafts. With great joy the Rakshasa beheld the Vanara army being overwhelmed on all sides by his cruel weapons. He rose into the sky above the monkeys and continued to rain down countless arrows, like a dark cloud in the monsoon season.

With their bodies ripped apart, the monkeys fell shrieking like mountains thrown down by Indra's thunderbolt. They could not see the demon or his chariot, but saw only an endless stream of sharp-pointed shafts falling from the heavens. Indrajit sent forth a shower of violent weapons which gave off sparks and incandescent flames. He covered the monkeys with axes, swords, lances and pikes, all of those weapons charged with mystic power.

Indrajit then sought out Rama and Lakshmana, covering them with torrents of arrows. Not minding the arrows any more than a mountain would mind a shower of rain, Rama said to his brother, "This demon Indrajit has engaged the invincible weapon of Brahma. Behold, our entire army has been virtually overpowered. We too will have to succumb to Brahma's weapon, I fear."

Rama knew that no being in the universe could resist the Brahmastra, except by invoking the same weapon to counter it. But the meeting of two Brahmastras was highly dangerous. It could bring about the destruction of the whole cosmos and would likely cause the death of millions of innocent creatures. Rama did not want that to happen. He and Lakshmana sent hundreds and thousands of powerful shafts toward the Rakshasa, but Indrajit shrugged off their arrows and continued aiming his weapons at the two brothers.

The demon again and again recited the incantations sacred to Brahma and sent fierce arrows at Rama and Lakshmana. The princes were completely covered by Indrajit's arrows. They bled all over and appeared like a couple of kinshuka trees covered in red blossoms. Grievously wounded by Indrajit's assault, they both fell to the ground and dropped their bows.

Indrajit sent up a cry of victory. He considered Rama and Lakshmana dead. The demon looked around the battlefield and saw that only a few thousand monkeys remained standing. The battle was surely won. Seeing the sun approaching the western horizon, Indrajit decided to return to

Lanka and tell his father the good news. If any of the monkey army remained on the battlefield, he could finish them tomorrow. Appearing in the sky like a blazing planet, Indrajit commanded the Rakshasa troops to withdraw and they quickly entered Lanka, roaring in joy.

On the battlefield Hanuman still remained standing. He looked around at the scene of devastation wrought by Indrajit. Even Rama and Lakshmana, along with Sugriva, Angada, Nila and all the other powerful Vanara commanders, lay prostrate. The monkey ran up to the two princes and knelt by their side. He was joined by Vibhishana who had also survived Indrajit's attack. Tears fell from Hanuman's eyes as he gazed at the unconscious brothers. They appeared to be severely wounded. Placing his hand on Hanuman's shoulder, Vibhishana reassured him gently.

"Do not give way to despondency, my valiant friend. These two brothers are not killed. Surely they have allowed themselves to be brought under the power of Brahma's weapon in honor of the self-born creator of the universe. Rama and Lakshmana are always protected by virtue. Indeed, they are virtue personified. We will yet see them rise to defeat Ravana and his evil forces."

Hanuman embraced the Rakshasa and thanked him for his kind words. But what could he do now? How could the battle continue with only a handful of monkeys and bears still standing? Even Rama and Lakshmana seemed in no condition to fight.

As Hanuman and Vibhishana looked around they saw Jambavan lying nearby. The wise old leader of the bears was covered with arrows but his head was moving slightly. Vibhishana ran over to him and knelt down calling his name. Jambavan opened his eyes and looked at the Rakshasa. He spoke barely in a whisper.

"O Vibhishana, I can hardly see you, wounded as I am by Indrajit's arrows. Our army is now in grave danger, but if Hanuman still survives then there is hope. Tell me, does the son of the wind-god live?"

Vibhishana was surprised that Jambavan had first inquired after Hanuman rather than Rama or Lakshmana. He called Hanuman over and the monkey came quickly and knelt before Jambavan. Mustering his strength, the old bear began to speak. "My dear Hanuman, it is you alone who can save this army. Only you possess the power to fly from here to the Himalayas. You must go there at once to fetch the celestial healing herbs."

Jambavan explained that there was a mountain standing near Mount Kailash on which grew four precious herbs, placed there by the gods themselves. Jambavan described the four plants. "First there is sanjivakarani, capable of bringing a dead person back to life. Then you must find vishalyakarani, which can completely heal all weapon wounds. The other two herbs are sandhani and suvarnakarani, which together can restore a broken body back to its pristine state. They all grow together atop this mountain. O Hanuman, leave at once and bring them here."

Hanuman immediately stood up. He bounded across to the Trikuta mountain and quickly climbed to its summit. From there he leapt over to the Malaya mountain on Lanka's coast. Standing there the monkey expanded his body till he appeared like a second mountain on top of the Malaya. He thought of Rama and Lakshmana, and of Sugriva and all the other monkeys and bears lying mortally wounded. There was no time to lose. He crouched down and with a great shout of "Victory to Rama!" leapt toward the north.

As he jumped he pushed down the mountain and made the whole island of Lanka shake. The city seemed to be dancing at night as its lights shook with the force of Hanuman's leap. The Rakshasas were seized with fear, thinking that Lanka was about to be consumed by an earthquake.

Hanuman soared through the heavens. Being followed by the wind, he felt no resistance and sped faster and faster toward the Himalayas. In a short time he saw the great range appearing ahead of him. From a distance the mountains appeared like masses of white clouds. As Hanuman came closer he saw the golden Rishabha mountain with the gods' numerous residences atop it. Passing beyond Rishabha he saw Mount Kailash in the distance.

Between Rishabha and Kailash, Hanuman saw the mountain where the celestial herbs grew. It shone brightly and the herbs growing upon its sides appeared like flashing lights. Hanuman came down upon the mountain and began to search for the four herbs Jambavan had described. As he moved among the lush foliage, however, the herbs, perceiving that someone had come to take them, hid themselves from view. Only the gods were able to use those divine medicines; no one else could find them.

Hanuman ran about looking for the herbs. Where were they? What if he could not find them? What would happen to Rama and Lakshmana? Could it be possible that the two brothers would die? No. He could not let that happen. He had to fetch the herbs even if it meant bringing the entire mountain.

The monkey realized that the herbs had concealed themselves from his view. He became furious and roared loudly, thundering at the mountain, "O lord of mountains, as you have not shown any compassion even to Rama and Lakshmana, you shall pay the price today. Watch now as I tear away your shining peak. I shall not return without the herbs."

Hanuman plunged his hands into the side of the mountain and broke off the entire section containing all the herbs. Lifting the huge mountain summit above his head, the monkey sprang into the air. Hanuman soared high into the sky, bearing aloft the mountain with its trees, elephants, tigers, deer and herbs. He blazed with his own splendor and, with the effulgent mountain held in his hands, he looked like the sun coursing through the sky.

Once again, his father Vayu raced behind him and he soon arrived near Lanka. Having accomplished such an inconceivable feat in Rama's service, Hanuman descended near the Trikuta and set down the celestial hill of herbs. Vibhishana rushed over and embraced the monkey. The Rakshasa then set about finding the medicinal herbs, perceiving them by virtue of his occult vision.

Taking a handful of the herbs from Vibhishana, Hanuman went quickly to Rama and Lakshmana. Both he and Vibhishana looked anxiously at the two princes, who appeared like the sun and the moon fallen to earth. They were hardly breathing. Hanuman dropped to his knees by their side. Was he in time to save them? Would the herbs work? His hand shook as he placed a bunch of herbs under Rama's nostrils.

For some time Rama showed no signs of movement. Hanuman was beside himself with anxiety. Then slowly, the prince began to stir. He breathed deeply, inhaling the celestial fragrance. Gradually his eyes opened. He looked up at Hanuman and smiled. The monkey breathed a deep sigh of relief. Quickly he began administering the herbs to Lakshmana. Slowly, he too returned to consciousness.

Sugriva then had Sushena, a monkey expert in healing, come and tend to the princes. Using the other herbs brought by Hanuman, Sushena healed their arrow wounds. In a short time the arrows fell from their bodies and their wounds closed up and healed. Both brothers sprang to their feet, their bodies renewed and invigorated. With tears in his eyes, Rama embraced Hanuman and thanked him for his service.

The surviving monkeys moved swiftly among the wounded troops, administering the herbs to them. They crushed the herbs and allowed the wind to carry the pungent fragrance. No demons lay on the battlefield, as Ravana had ordered that they be tossed into the sea when they were slain. The demon did not want the monkeys to gain strength from seeing how many Rakshasas were killed.

By the potency of the healing herbs hundreds of thousands of the Vanara warriors were restored to consciousness and they jumped up shouting with joy. Even some monkeys who had been killed, but whose bodies were not destroyed, were brought back to life by the herbs' potency. They felt as if they had awakened from a restful night of sleep. Soon the monkey army stood again in their millions, ready and eager for the fight.

The night was drawing to a close and Sugriva, after consulting with Rama and Lakshmana, decided to attack Lanka before the Rakshasas were aware of the situation. The monkeys took up flaming torches and moved like a surging ocean toward the city walls. Shocked and amazed to find so many monkeys clambering over the ramparts, the Rakshasa guards fled in fear. The monkeys set fire to the gates, houses and mansions in Lanka. Rama and Lakshmana sent innumerable flaming arrows into the city and a great fire raged.

Panic-stricken demons ran in all directions with their clothes and hair ablaze. Great mansions and palaces were completely consumed by flames. Golden archways and walls melted and crumbled to the ground. In less than an hour the city gave the appearance of the earth being consumed by the dread fire of annihilation. Searing red flames rose up to the sky and were reflected upon the ocean, making it appear like a charming sea of red waters. As the monkeys ran about setting fire to anything and everything, the Rakshasas' screams were heard everywhere. They dashed out of their houses and were immediately assailed by the monkeys.

Ravana was aroused from his intoxicated slumber by the clamor. He sat up in shock. What was happening? Surely this could not be the monkeys. There were only a few of them left. How could they attack Lanka while their leaders were both prostrate on the battlefield?

Pulling his silk garment around his waist, the demon ran out of his chamber and called for his ministers. Seized with fear they ran to Ravana and told him that Rama and Lakshmana had somehow risen up and attacked the city. The demon king was amazed. He immediately issued orders for the Rakshasa chiefs to march out. Tens of thousands of demons clad in golden armor came onto the city streets. They were led by Kumbha and Nikumbha, Kumbhakarna's two powerful sons. The Rakshasas rushed roaring toward the monkeys, attacking them with swords, pikes, maces, javelins and countless arrows that screamed through the air.

Numerous garlands, broken wine casks and burning incenses made the city fragrant as the bellicose opponents tore at each other in a frenzy. Monkeys picked up Rakshasas and whirled them about, striking down other Rakshasas, while the Rakshasas lanced five or seven monkeys at once with their terrible spears. Infuriated monkeys bit off the ears and crushed the skulls of the demons, pummeling them to a pulp with their fists and feet. Powerful Rakshasas tore off the heads of the Vanaras and lopped off their limbs with great scimitars. Everywhere there were shouts of "Stay!" "Give battle!" and "You are killed!"

Gradually the battle spilled out of the city. Great duels were fought between the principal fighters on both sides. The Rakshasa Kampana challenged Angada and was slain by him with a blow from a mountain peak. Along with the two powerful Vanaras, Mainda and Dwivida, Angada also

Great duels were fought between the principal fighters on both sides.

made short work of Sonitaksha, Yupaksha and Prajangha, three of the mightiest Rakshasas.

Seeing his comrades killed, Kumbha roared with fury. Kumbhakarna's son appeared awful and unassailable. He took up his tremendous bow, in no way inferior to Indra's, and loosed venomous shafts by the thousand. Monkeys fell on all sides, screaming in pain. Mainda and Dwivida rushed toward the Rakshasa and challenged him to fight. Those monkey brothers looked like a couple of moving mountains approaching a third.

As they neared Kumbha, the demon fitted a fierce arrow onto his bow and shot it at Dwivida's chest. Hit by the arrow, Dwivida fell to the ground and lay there wriggling and gasping for breath. Mainda at once took up an enormous crag and hurled it with force at the Rakshasa. Kumbha shot five arrows that shattered the rock and it fell in pieces at his feet. Taking another long shaft, he struck Mainda on the breast and the monkey fell unconscious.

Angada saw his two uncles laid low by Kumbha and he dashed across to challenge the Rakshasa. Kumbha laughed, making an ass-like sound which reverberated all over the battlefield. His eyes blazed like two red fires and he stood in his chariot looking like Death personified. As Angada ran toward him, Kumbha shot dozens of deadly arrows which penetrated the monkey's body. Not shaken, Angada sent a shower of rocks and trees at the demon. Kumbha easily smashed the missiles with his arrows, laughing all the while.

Kumbha then fired arrows, which hit Angada on the forehead and made a stream of blood flow down the monkey's face. Pressing his wounds with one hand, Angada seized hold of a massive tree with the other. He whirled around and tossed that tree at the Rakshasa. It flew with the speed of the wind. Kumbha dropped to one knee and instantly shot seven steel arrows which sliced the flying tree to pieces. Without pausing for a moment Kumbha released seven more shafts, which struck Angada on the chest and sent him reeling.

Rama saw that Angada was sinking to the ground under the force of Kumbha's arrows. He immediately ordered Jambavan and a number of powerful monkeys to go to Angada's assistance. They bounded toward Kumbha, throwing trees and boulders at the bellowing demon. Kumbha spun round and shot his fierce arrows, hitting all of the monkey warriors as they approached him. No one could get near the Rakshasa as he stood with his uplifted bow, any more than one could approach the orb of the sun.

Sugriva then came forward to challenge the Rakshasa. He hurled huge rocks one after another at the demon's chariot, advancing continually toward him. Kumbha smashed all the rocks thrown at him with arrows shot in a solid line. He moved with astonishing speed, striking down the rocks and simultaneously sending arrows at Sugriva. The monkey king was pierced all over, but he did not flinch. He suddenly sprang onto Kumbha's chariot and snatched his bow, even as the Rakshasa fired arrows at him. Sugriva broke the bow in two and hurled it away. The monkey then leapt to the ground and addressed the Rakshasa.

"O Kumbha, you are the equal of Indra, Kuvera and even the mighty Bali. Indeed, you are no less powerful than your uncle Ravana or your cousin Indrajit. You have struck down many powerful monkeys today, O demon, and this is most wonderful. But now your exploits will end. Fight with me, if you dare. I shall make short work of you."

Kumbha was flattered by Sugriva, and his martial enthusiasm increased like a fire fed with oil. Without a word, he leapt down from his chariot and rushed toward the monkey, who stood with his arms outsretched. The two heroes clasped each other and grappled together. The earth shook with their heavy steps. Sugriva leaned backwards and lifted the demon above his head. Spinning around, he tossed Kumbha into the sea. The Rakshasa sank down to the seabed, but soon swam upwards again.

Suddenly emerging from the ocean, the demon flew up and struck Sugriva on the chest with his fist, with a blow that sounded like a peal of thunder and which emitted a brilliant flash. Sugriva did not budge and at once clenched his own fist, which was as hard as adamant. He swung around and brought his fist down upon Kumbha's breast like one planet striking another. The demon's heart was split by the blow, and he fell dead to the ground as Mars would drop from the heavens.

Nikumbha saw his brother slain and his anger flared. He took up his terrific mace and gazed at Sugriva as if about to consume him with his wrath. His club was fitted with iron plates and steel spikes, inlaid with gold and bedecked with diamonds and other gems. The demon wore black iron armor studded with jewels, as well as brilliant golden armlets and earrings. With a garland of celestial flowers on his breast, he looked like a cloud flashing with numerous lightning bolts. He brandished his weapon, whirling it around above his head. His mace shot forth tongues of fire and it seemed to cause the very atmosphere to spin around. The monkey warriors fell back in terror, unable to even look at Nikumbha.

Hanuman came forward and stood directly before the Rakshasa. He pulled back his arms and bared his massive chest. "Strike me at once, O demon," he challenged.

With all his strength Nikumbha brought down the mace upon Hanuman's chest. The club splintered into a hundred fragments and fell to the ground like so many blazing meteors. Hanuman stood unmoved and he smashed Nikumbha on the breast with his fist. The Rakshasa's armor was shattered and blood shot from his breast. He reeled but quickly recovered and seized hold of Hanuman, lifting him from the ground. Seeing this the other Rakshasas roared in joy.

Taking hold of Hanuman, Nikumbha ran toward Lanka. The monkey struck Nikumbha on the head and disengaged himself from the Rakshasa's grip. He landed on the ground in front of the demon. Hanuman struck Nikumbha down and then hurled himself onto the Rakshasa's body. Pressing down all of Nikumbha's limbs, Hanuman took hold of his neck and twisted it ferociously. He tore off the Rakshasa's screaming head and hurled it into the ocean. Observing this incredible feat, the Rakshasa army fled pell-mell in all directions, some rushing into the city, some jumping into the sea, and others flying into the sky. Hanuman raised a great roar of victory and the monkeys surrounding him shouted for joy.

CHAPTER ELEVEN

LAKSHMANA BATTLES INDRAJIT

In Lanka, Ravana was stunned. Twice he had celebrated his seeming victory and twice he had been forced to think again. He sat brooding in his palace. This monkey army was charmed. They had been virtually wiped out by Indrajit, but suddenly they were back on their feet and fighting again. Now Kumbhakarna's two invincible sons had been killed. Things were becoming desperate. Ravana looked across at Indrajit. This time he must not fail. Ravana spoke to his son, who was as powerful as his father in every way.

"O heroic prince, these two mortals must die. Although twice defeated by you, they have somehow miraculously escaped death. Now their luck must have run out. You are the conqueror of Indra. What then of two humans? Go forth again my son. Use any means whatsoever and kill them!"

Once again Indrajit went out from Lanka, accompanied by the remaining force of Rakshasas. After again worshipping the fire on the battlefield he stood up and began to brag of his power. "The two human brothers may be taken as killed. Today I shall secure an eminent victory for my anxious father. This evening he will rest peacefully, experiencing the highest happiness."

The Rakshasa prince used his powers of sorcery to create a thick blanket of darkness. Rising into the sky, he rushed toward the Vanara army, who were thrown into confusion. He rained down steel arrows in the hundreds of thousands. Again he targeted Rama and Lakshmana. The two princes were enraged by his treacherous attack. Rama blazed up like a huge fire fed with volumes of ghee. He bent his great bow into a full circle and released deadly golden shafts that went toward Indrajit in the sky. Using the Shabda-astra, which sought out an invisible opponent, Rama grievously pierced the demon. He saw his arrows fall to the ground, soaked in the demon's blood.

Indrajit drove away from the princes, sending arrows at the monkeys and killing thousands. Seeing this, Lakshmana lost all patience. He fitted an arrow to his bow and spoke to Rama. "I shall now release the Brahmastra, charging it with the power to kill all the Rakshasas at once. We need toler-ate their insolence no longer."

Rama reached out and checked his brother. "We should not slay inno-cent creatures unnecessarily," he told him. "The Rakshasas in Lanka have been sufficiently punished by our assault on their city. Let us now simply annihilate the remaining warriors. I shall myself immediately kill this Indrajit if he remains on the battlefield for even a moment."

Rama declared that the time for Indrajit's destruction had come. Even if the Rakshasa fled for shelter to the farthest reaches of the universe, he would not escape. Rama raised his bow and looked up to the sky.

Divining Rama's intentions, Indrajit quickly withdrew from the battle-field. He entered Lanka and considered what tactic he should use to kill Rama and his brother. Using his prodigious mystic powers, he conjured an illusory image of Sita. Placing this false form on his chariot, he again went out onto the battlefield, this time remaining visible in the sky.

Hanuman spotted the chariot of Indrajit drawn by its demonic tigers and he rushed toward it with a mountainous crag in his hands. As he looked up, however, he saw a woman held in the demon's grasp. Although beauti-ful, she appeared wretched and sorrowful. She was clad in a single garment, unadorned, with her limbs covered in dust and mud. Gazing at her for a while, Hanuman recognized her as Sita.

As the monkeys looked on, Indrajit took out his sword and grabbed Sita by her hair. He began to strike her and she cried out, "Rama! O Rama!"

Hanuman was seized with agony upon seeing this and hot tears fell from his eyes. He angrily rebuked Indrajit. "O wicked one, your act is meant only for your own destruction. Although descended from a brahmin rishi, you are ignoble, mean and sinful. How can you kill a helpless woman, torn from her home and her husband, weak, wretched and crying for protection? Your own death is close. You shall then descend to a dark and condemned region, inhabited by the lowest of creatures."

Indrajit laughed. Dropping the form of Sita, he grabbed his bow and loosed off a thousand fierce arrows at Hanuman and the other monkeys. He then took hold of Sita's hair again and replied harshly to Hanuman. "She for whom you have all come so far and fought so hard I will now slay. I shall then make short work of Rama and Lakshmana as well as you, O monkey. I care not for the immorality of my acts, for whatever causes pain to one's enemy must be achieved by any means."

Indrajit raised his sword and cut the form of Sita into two parts. Laughing loudly, he called out to the monkeys, "Here is Sita now killed by me. Your efforts to recover her have all been in vain. Fight on, if you must, but all of you will meet the same end as she."

The demon rose high into the sky, wheeling about in his golden chariot. Hanuman was seized with grief and anger. Completely infuriated, he fell upon the Rakshasas in a frenzy. Repeatedly roaring he consumed the Rakshasa army like the fire of universal dissolution. He took up a massive rock and hurled it straight at Indrajit's chariot, but the demon rose still higher and the rock fell short. It dropped to the earth, crushing hundreds of demons and opening a chasm in the ground.

Hanuman was filled with despair. Looking around the at monkey army, he shouted to them, "Cease fighting! The object of our battle is now impossible to achieve, for Sita lies killed. Let us withdraw and ask Rama what should be done next."

The monkeys pulled away from the fight and moved back toward Rama and Lakshmana. Seeing this, Indrajit also withdrew, taking the demons with him. He made his way to a sanctuary in a cavern known as Nikumbhila. There he began to perform a ritual for assuring his victory in the battle. Worshipping the powerful goddess Kali, a fearful form of the personified material energy, he made offerings of blood into a sacrificial fire. The demon knew the final battle would soon be fought. He had been granted a boon by Brahma that once having peformed the ritual at Nikumbhila, he would remain completely invincible in battle until his enemy was defeated. The time for realizing that boon had arrived. Surrounded by other Rakshasas, Indrajit sat before the fire reciting the sacred mantras.

* * *

On the battlefield, Hanuman came before Rama and told him the terrible news. Rama at once collapsed to the ground and lay there insensible, like a great tree cut at the root. The monkeys quickly brought cool, scented water and sprinkled his face. Lakshmana, tormented by agony, knelt down and lifted Rama up. He spoke to his brother in a choked voice. "What is the value of a virtuous life? O Rama, how can one like you suffer such reverses? If righteousness brought any good results, then this calamity could never have occurred. Indeed, if good and bad fruits accrued to the righteous and unrighteous respectively, then Ravana would have long ago sunk into hell, while you would now be reunited with your spouse. What can influence all-powerful destiny? It moves only according to its own will. Our acts are all feeble and their results always uncertain."

Lakshmana cried out in pain. Thinking of the sinful Indrajit, his eyes blazed with fury. He urged Rama to rise up and avenge Sita. Together they should at once completely destroy Lanka with all its buildings and citizens.

As Lakshmana spoke to Rama, Vibhishana arrived. He saw Rama lying in a swoon with his head on Lakshmana's lap. All around the monkeys were given over to grief and were lying on the ground and shedding tears. Vibhishana was gripped by despondency upon seeing Rama's state. He knelt by Lakshmana and asked him what had happened. The prince told him about Sita.

Vibhishana, after reflecting for some moments, began to nod slowly. "The report of Sita's death is as absurd as the drying up of the ocean," he said. "There is no possibility that Ravana would allow the princess to be killed. He is consumed by desire to possess her. Even though he was well apprised by me of the consequences of keeping her, the sinful demon would by no means return her to you, O Rama. You have been tricked by the devious Indrajit. Know that woman killed by him to be mere illusion. There is no doubt in my mind."

Rama opened his eyes and looked up at Vibhishana. The Rakshasa explained that Indrajit must have created the illusion in order to weaken Rama and to buy time. He would now be performing a ritual in the Nikumbhila sanctuary. If allowed to finish his ritual, he would be impossible to overcome. There was no time to lose. The monkeys should go at once to the sanctuary and stop the ritual. Vibhishana recommended that Lakshmana go, while Rama remained stationed on the battlefield.

Still overcome by grief, Rama did not fully comprehend Vibhishana's words. He asked the Rakshasa to repeat what he had said. Vibhishana told him everything again and then said, "Rise up and take courage. Sita will yet be recovered. Marshal the troops and send them with Lakshmana. Surely Lakshmana will be able to bring about Indrajit's end with his deadly arrows."

Vibhishana explained to Rama about the boon granted by Brahma. There was a condition that if Indrajit was disturbed during the course of the ritual, he could be killed. That was why he had created the illusion of Sita's death. He obviously considered that this would throw Rama and his army into total confusion for long enough. Vibhishana urged Lakshmana on. "Go now, O valiant one. When Indrajit is killed, Ravana and his army will be finished for sure."

Rama stood up and spoke to Vibhishana. "What you say is true, O night-ranger. Indrajit's prowess in sorcery and in battle is formidable. He cannot be discerned even by the gods when he rides on his chariot in the sky. This one must be slain at once."

Rama turned to Lakshmana and ordered him to leave for Nikumbhila. Vibhishana would show him the way and the foremost monkeys, headed by Sugriva and Hanuman, would accompany him.

Lakshmana felt delighted in mind. He bent down and touched Rama's feet. Taking up his bow and sword, he stood ready for battle and said in a thunderous voice, "Today my swift-coursing arrows will pierce through Indrajit's body and tear him to pieces. That Rakshasa is now as good as dead."

Rama uttered benedictory Vedic mantras and the monkeys cheered. Followed by the vast monkey army, Lakshmana set off for the Nikumbhila sanctuary. After they had covered many miles Vibhishana pointed to the Rakshasa army laying ahead. Indrajit had placed them all around the sanctuary, in the distance they appeared like a great black cloud descended to earth.

The monkeys and bears took up trees and rocks and charged straight at the Rakshasa army. The Rakshasas replied with all kinds of weapons and the sky between the two armies became filled with missiles of various shapes. The monkey army pressed forward and began to overrun the Rakshasas, who had been caught by surprise. The Rakshasas ran about crying in fear. They called for Indrajit to help them. Indrajit became indignant upon realizing that he was being disturbed. Who had been so insolent as to attack him during his sacrifice? With the ritual still unfinished he stood up and went out of the sanctuary. Seeing the battle raging, he quickly mounted his chariot and went out amid the Rakshasas.

Hanuman had taken the lead in the battle and was wreaking havoc among the demons. With an enormous tree he battered innumerable Rakshasas to death. The Rakshasas surrounded him and rained down a shower of arrows, spears, swords and javelins. Hanuman laughed off those weapons and continued thrashing the demons with trees and boulders. Indrajit, seeing Hanuman destroying the Rakshasa army, ordered his charioteer to go quickly before the monkey.

As Indrajit appeared before Hanuman, the monkey challenged him to a duel. "Stand here before me and display your strength of arms, O evil one. You shall not return with your life today." Indrajit took up his bow and prepared to shoot arrows at Hanuman. Seeing this, Vibhishana urged Lakshmana to engage with Indrajit immediately. Lakshmana twanged his bow, making a terrific sound. Indrajit turned and saw the prince who called out to him, "I challenge you to battle. Stay before my vision and fight fairly, if you dare. Death now awaits you, O vile Rakshasa."

Indrajit spotted Vibhishana next to Lakshmana and began to rebuke him with harsh words. "You are the disgrace of our race, O uncle. How can you display enmity toward me, who am as good as your own son? What do you know of virtue? You have abandoned your own people and sided with the enemy. Pointing out my vulnerability, O degraded one, you have rendered great harm to your own brother. Surely you do not know right from wrong."

Vibhishana replied that he did not share Rakshasa disposition. Although born in their race he did not take pleasure in the sinful acts they enjoyed. Citing texts from the Vedas, Vibhishana said to his nephew, "One should always abandon an unrighteous relative, even as one should quickly abandon a burning house. There is no greater sin than stealing another's wife. By killing eminent rishis and waging war on the gods, Ravana has lost all sense of propriety. Now, having stolen Rama's wife, he has filled his cup of sins to overflowing. Along with all his kinsmen he will soon die. But first, you shall die today at Lakshmana's hands."

Indrajit replied harshly to his uncle. Lifting his ornate bow he derided Lakshmana, who was mounted upon Hanuman's back. "How will you withstand my arrows loosed with the force of a thunderbolt? It is clear that you have already embarked upon the road to Yamaraja's abode. I shall send you there at once, along with all these monkeys."

Lakshmana was enraged to hear Indrajit's bragging. He thundered back at him. "You are strong only with your words, O Rakshasa! Those possessed of actual prowess show it with deeds, not boasts. Heroes never need to fight invisibly. You are simply a thief and a coward. If you have any prowess, then show it today! Here I am within the range of your arrows."

Indrajit at once released dozens of arrows that hissed through the air like serpents. They struck Lakshmana and pierced through his armor. The prince began to bleed and, swelling with fury, he appeared like a smokeless fire. Without the least hesitation, he took out five steel arrows worked with gold and fitted with eagle feathers. Pulling his bowstring back to his ear, he shot them at Indrajit. They flew like the rays of the sun, penetrating the Rakshasa's breast. The demon replied with three more arrows of his own, which sped through the air in flames.

The two combatants fought furiously, each seeking a quick victory. They appeared like two lions as they stood firmly on the battlefield hurling their weapons at each other. Fighting from Hanuman's back, Lakshmana displayed great dexterity. His arrows fell upon Indrajit from all sides, striking him like thunderbolts.

The Rakshasa was stunned by Lakshmana's attack, and he reeled in his chariot. Regaining his senses, the demon shouted at Lakshmana, trying to create fear in the prince. Indrajit reminded him how he had been overcome by the Rakshasa's weapons on two former occasions. Surely Lakshmana had forgotten that or else how could he be so foolish as to stand before him again?

The Rakshasa at once pierced Lakshmana, Hanuman and Vibhishana, each with a dozen fierce arrows. Lakshmana laughed and derided the demon's strength. "These arrows are nothing. They strike me like so many flowers and simply increase my desire to fight." Lakshmana covered the Rakshasa with swift-coursing arrows that tore off his heavy golden armor, which dropped from the demon like stars falling from heaven. He was covered in blood and he shone like the morning sun.

In reply, Indrajit sent a thousand arrows at Lakshmana and shattered his armor. The two warriors, lacerated with arrows, battled strenuously for some hours. Neither of them retreated nor felt any fatigue. Hails of arrows sped through the sky like showers falling from autumnal clouds. Both were expert in mystic missiles and they fired and countered those weapons again and again. Networks of arrows clashed together in the heavens, emitting fire and sparks. Huge fireballs were countered by sheets of water, while weapons producing roaring gales were checked by others which created immovable mountains.

A vehement and terrible struggle ensued for a long time. The earth was covered with a mass of arrows that looked like a carpet of sacred kusha grass. The two princes, arrows sticking from every part of their bodies, bled profusely, appearing like mountains covered with trees and giving forth shining red oxides.

As they fought, Vibhishana exhorted the monkeys to engage with the other Rakshasas. He told them that Indrajit was accompanied by all that was left of the Rakshasa army. Vibhishana named all the Rakshasa heroes who had been slain, thereby giving joy to the monkeys and increasing their enthusiasm. They lashed the ground with their tails and bared their terrible teeth. The monkeys stood gazing intently at the Rakshasas. Vibhishana himself then took up his bow and began sending his deadly shafts toward the Rakshasas. Roaring like lions, the monkeys leapt toward the Rakshasas and a fearful battle took place.

Lakshmana dismounted from Hanuman's back, and the monkey dashed into the fray, whirling a great tree trunk and mowing down the Rakshasas in hundreds. Jambavan led his army of fierce bears straight into the battle and a melee spread in all directions, as monkeys, bears and Rakshasas tore and struck each other wildly.

Lakshmana stood on the ground facing Indrajit. The Rakshasa remained in his chariot and continued to release volumes of arrows at the prince. Becoming enraged, Lakshmana sped four arrows at the four frightful-looking tigers drawing the demon's chariot. The chariot halted as the beasts were struck by Lakshmana's shafts. He then took a crescent-tipped arrow and forcefully released it at Indrajit's charioteer, severing his head from his body. As the charioteer fell to the ground, four heroic monkeys bounded over to Indrajit's chariot and fell upon the four tigers. Crushing and pounding them, the monkeys reduced them to a lifeless mass and then ran back to Lakshmana's side.

Indrajit leapt to the ground and retreated back among the other Rakshasas. He ordered them to hold off the monkeys and keep Lakshmana engaged. Then the Rakshasa prince rose swiftly into the air and entered Lanka to get another chariot. Within a short while he appeared again on the battlefield, driving a golden chariot equipped with every kind of weapon. Full of vigour for the fight, Indrajit at once assailed Lakshmana and Vibhishana, while simultaneously firing innumerable shafts at the monkey warriors. So swift was his movement that it was impossible to see when he lifted his bow, pulled back the string or took out and fitted his arrows. All that could be perceived was an endless stream of whetted shafts being sent in all directions.

Indrajit tore thousands of monkeys to pieces. They fell down, screaming and crying out to Lakshmana for protection. His eyes blazing in anger, Lakshmana shot five straight-going arrows which smashed Indrajit's bow. Seeing this wondrous feat, the gods and rishis, assembled in the sky, applauded Lakshmana. The prince then pierced Indrajit with a dozen more arrows, which went right through the Rakshasa's body and fell to the ground like red serpents entering the earth.

Vomiting blood, Indrajit grasped another bow and immediately released a hundred arrows at Lakshmana. Those arrows screamed through the air shooting forth bright red flames. Lakshmana remained calm and intercepted the blazing shafts with his own infallible arrows. Indrajit sped innumerable other arrows toward Lakshmana but the prince parried them all. He answered the demon's attack by again severing his charioteer's head with another crescent-headed shaft. Although deprived of their controller, however, Indrajit's steeds continued to pull the chariot, rising into the air and describing various circular movements.

Lakshmana displayed astonishing prowess. He completely covered Indrajit's chariot with arrows and then pierced all of the other demons surrounding the Rakshasa prince. Indrajit again descended and shot three arrows which embedded themselves in Lakshmana's forehead, making him appear like a three-peaked mountain. Lakshmana at once replied with five searing shafts that thudded into Indrajit's head. The two opponents, bleeding profusely from their wounds, looked like a couple of kinshuka trees in full blossom.

As Indrajit reeled from his attack, Lakshmana quickly shot four deadly arrows which killed the demon's four horses. The Rakshasa leapt down from the chariot. As he jumped, he hurled a golden lance at Vibhishana that resembled a bolt of heaven. Lakshmana instantly shot five arrows at that speeding lance and cut it to pieces. Vibhishana took up his bow and pierced Indrajit in the breast with a number of arrows that struck him with a sound like thunderclaps.

Indrajit bellowed in anger. He took from his quiver a glowing arrow which he had received from Yamaraja. Seeing the Rakshasa fitting this mystic missile to his bow, Lakshmana quickly invoked a weapon he had obtained in a dream from Kuvera. The two infuriated combatants pulled back their bowstrings with the divine weapons fitted. Both bows emitted a piercing noise like a pair of cranes. When released, the two weapons collided violently in mid-air and lit up the heavens. A great fire appeared in the sky along with billows of smoke. The missiles fell to the ground in hundreds of blazing pieces.

Lakshmana invoked the Varunastra, the weapon presided over by the god of the waters. Perceiving this, Indrajit countered the weapon with another imbued with the divine energy of Shiva. The Rakshasa then released the Agneyastra, but this was countered by Lakshmana with the Suryastra, the missile charged with the immense potency of the sun-god. Remaining firm on the battlefield, Indrajit placed a long golden arrow on his bow and began reciting sacred incantations. Darts, maces, swords, axes, hammers and other weapons flew from his bow by the hundreds. Not disturbed, Lakshmana invoked a missile presided over by the wind-god and immediately neutralized Indrajit's weapon.

The battle between man and demon raged furiously. Both of them relentlessly hurled their deadly missiles and filled the sky with volleys of arrows. Neither showed any sign of fatigue and both were worked up with a terrible anger. All around them the monkeys and Rakshasas clashed violently in a fearful and bloody battle. The gods, headed by Indra and accompanied by the great rishis, stood in the canopy of the sky. They prayed to Vishnu and showered blessings upon Lakshmana and the Vanaras, wishing them victory.

Lakshmana saw numerous omens indicative of victory and he considered the time for Indrajit's destruction to have arrived. After reflecting for a moment the prince invoked a divine arrow he had received from Rama which had formerly belonged to Indra. That beautiful shining arrow was imbued with inconceivable power. It was worked with gold and gems and fitted with peacock feathers. The arrow had rounded golden joints, its large steel tip was flat and broad, and its razor-sharp edges were inlaid with diamonds. As Lakshmana placed it upon his bow and drew back the string he invoked the divine Aindrastra, presided over by the king of the gods. Within himself he prayed, "If Rama is always true to his word and fixed in virtue, and if he possesses unrivaled power, then let this arrow end Indrajit's life."

The heroic Lakshmana concentrated his mind and released the arrow. It screamed toward Indrajit with blinding speed. Before the Rakshasa could make any move to counter the weapon it severed his head from his shoulders. That handsome head with its jeweled helmet and blazing earrings rolled on the ground, bathed in blood and shining like gold. Ravana's son dropped to the ground with his bow falling from his hand. All the monkeys and bears, along with Vibhishana, loudly rejoiced; and in the heavens the gods, Gandharvas and rishis raised a shout of victory.

Their leader slain, the Rakshasas lost all enthusiasm for the fight. Terror-stricken they flung down their weapons and fled in every direction. Some rushed into Lanka, some hid in mountain caves and others dropped into the sea. Seeing Indrajit lying dead, they all vanished from the battlefield, even as the rays of the sun disappear when the sun has set. The Rakshasa prince lay on the ground like an extinguished fire.

A roll of celestial drums sounded in the skies and the singing of Gandharvas and Apsaras could be heard. The sky became clear and the sea calm. As the dust settled on the battlefield golden flowers rained from the heavens. Siddhas, Charanas and Gandharvas appeared there and gazed upon the dead Rakshasa. The monkeys leapt for joy, thundering and roaring, and applauding Lakshmana.

Surrounded by Hanuman, Jambavan and Vibhishana, Lakshmana returned to Rama. After respectfully circumambulating him, he stood by Rama's side with bow in hand, even as Indra might stand by the side of Vishnu. Rama smiled, realizing that Lakshmana had succeeded in his difficult mission. He looked with affection upon his brother. Vibhishana described how Indrajit had been slain. Rama cheered Lakshmana upon hearing this report and he addressed him with great delight. "Well done, Lakshmana! You have achieved a great feat today. Without doubt this has assured our victory. You have cut off Ravana's right arm and his best hope of success in the battle. Now that the merciless and evil-minded Indrajit is killed, we will see the sinful Ravana issuing forth for battle. I shall then dispatch him to Death's abode, along with all his army."

Rama thanked all of the warriors who had accompanied Lakshmana. They had fought solidly for three days. All of them were badly wounded. Lakshmana himself was severely lacerated with arrow wounds, his body covered in blood. He was tormented with pain and breathing heavily. Rama summoned Sushena, the monkey skilled in healing. He ordered him to treat Lakshmana and the others with the celestial remedies. They then rested on the field of battle, awaiting Ravana's next move.

CHAPTER TWELVE

RAVANA EXHIBITS HIS PROWESS

The terrified Rakshasas ran to Ravana and informed him of Indrajit's fall. "Having closed with a greater hero, your powerful son has met his end," they reported. "The highly glorious Indrajit, after gratifying Lakshmana with innumerable arrows, has gone to the next world."

Ravana looked at his ministers for some moments in a state of utter dismay. He then fell to the ground in a swoon and remained unconscious for some time. When he recovered he fell back onto his throne and sat with a downcast face, lamenting loudly. "O my son, where have you gone? You conquered Indra and chased away all the gods; how then have you been overpowered by Lakshmana? When angered you were capable of terrorizing even Death himself. Your arrows could smash down the peaks of Mount Mandara. Time is truly all-powerful, for today you have been thrown down by that inconquerable force, even as you stood on the battlefield, weapons in hand."

Ravana was inconsolable. He praised his dead son in many ways. Surely Indrajit had now reached the regions reserved for heroes. Now that he was dead, the gods, rishis and guardians of the worlds would rejoice, their thorn being removed.

Thinking of Mandodari, Ravana cried out in agony. "Your mother, the blessed queen, will surely lose her life today. Soon I will hear the cries of the Rakshasa women as they toss about on the ground. What perverse destiny has brought about your end before mine? O my dear Indrajit, how could you leave me here while Rama and Lakshmana still live?"

Seized by unbearable grief, the demon king fell from his throne and rolled about on the golden floor of his palace. A violent anger then took possession of him and he breathed heavily. Jumping to his feet, he knitted his brows and roared furiously. Flames blazed forth from his wide open mouths. He looked like Time personified about to consume all the worlds.

The demon thought only of revenge. His eyes, red by nature, glowed brilliant red with anger. Tears fell from them like drops of molten metal. He ground his teeth, making a sound like two mountains being rubbed together. Taking up his long razor-edged sword, which shone like the bright blue sky, he held it aloft and thundered in fury. "Pleasing the self-born creator of all the worlds by rigorous austerities, I received from him an infallible boon. Not even the gods and demons combined can kill me in battle, what then of a couple of humans? Bring my bow! Fetch my impenetrable armor! Today I shall march out and make short work of Rama and his entire army."

Looking as if he might destroy the universe itself, Ravana glared all around him. His ministers shrank back in fear, uttering plaintive sounds. The demon king said to them, "My dear son played a hoax upon Rama by killing an illusory Sita. That hoax shall now become reality. I shall finish Sita, who is so dear to Rama."

Bent on his evil purpose, Ravana immediately rushed out of his palace toward the ashoka grove. Seeing the infuriated demon coming out of his palace with upraised sword, the other Rakshasas felt heartened. Surely now the war would soon be ended. Ravana had overcome the four guardians of the world. He would certainly have no problem with an army of monkeys and bears.

The demon stormed toward his gardens, but as he moved swiftly along the pathways his ministers ran up to him. They stood before him trying to dissuade him from his intention of killing Sita. Already a terrible carnage among the Rakshasas had been wrought simply due to her being kidnapped. What might happen if Ravana actually killed her?

Ravana would not be swayed. He strode into the gardens. Sita saw him from a distance and began to tremble. Seeing his furious disposition and uplifted sword, she could understand that he intended to kill her. The princess wondered about her husband. Had he been slain? Why was Ravana so bold? If only she had gone with Hanuman. Why had she decided to stay in Lanka, tormented by this cruel Rakshasa? This was all the fault of the cruel Manthara. Soon that wicked maid would rejoice with her purpose fulfilled. If not already dead, then Rama would certainly not survive long when he heard of his beloved wife's death.

As Ravana came close to Sita, a minister named Suparshwa got before of him, saying, "How are you contemplating such a mean and pointless act, O ten-headed monarch? No good can ever come from killing a woman, for it is condemned by everyone. This lady should be protected. You should vent your wrath on Rama and Lakshmana, your actual enemies. If you kill them, this princess will then be yours to enjoy."

Ravana considered this advice. Perhaps Suparshwa was right. It would be foolish to needlessly lose the princess now after so much effort to retain her. And Rama might yet be overcome. There was no need to kill Sita now. Better to kill Rama; then she would surely submit to him.

Overcome by anger and lust as well as a burning grief, the demon turned away from Sita and made his way to his council chamber. Surrounded by his ministers, he entered the great hall, afflicted by agony. He sank onto his gem-encrusted throne and sat there snorting like a furious lion. With folded hands he addressed the assembly. "I now depend fully on all of you. The time to destroy our arrogant enemy has come. Tomorrow I shall march out to kill Rama. First, all of you should go out, weapons held high, and weaken the human prince and his army. I shall soon follow you."

The Rakshasas roared in joy. They rose up in a body and rushed out of the hall. Mounting horses, chariots, elephants and other carriers, they stormed out of the city. They immediately hurled a massive shower of axes, maces, spears, darts and iron clubs upon the monkeys, who replied with trees and rocks. The two armies again fell upon one another with a tremendous clamor.

Rama decided it was time he demonstrated his own insurmountable prowess. He immediately penetrated deep into the ranks of the Rakshasas. He moved like a whirlwind, leaving a trail of slaughtered demons in his wake. The Rakshasas could hardly look at him. No one could see his movements as he took out arrows from his inexhaustible quiver and sent them in all directions. By releasing the weapon of the Gandharvas, Rama made himself appear in a multitude of forms. To the confused Rakshasas he seemed to be everywhere at once. They saw the curved golden ends of his bow whirling like a firebrand and seeming to completely surround them. His arrows flew from all directions simultaneously. They sliced the Rakshasas to pieces. In less than two hours, Rama had exterminated two hundred thousand Rakshasas, along with eighteen thousand elephants and fourteen thousand horses.

The Rakshasas were completely routed and they fled in panic. Their chariots lay smashed and their armor and weapons littered the ground. With the mangled corpses of Rakshasas and animals lying everywhere, the battlefield appeared ghastly. The surviving Rakshasas rushed back to Lanka, looking back in fear of Rama.

The monkeys cheered and surrounded Rama. Having withdrawn his divine weapons, he stood at ease, blazing with splendor. Sugriva, Hanuman and Vibhishana looked in awe at Rama who said to them, "Only the glorious Shiva and I can exhibit such ability with the celestial missiles."

As the monkeys walked around Rama with folded palms, the gods and rishis praised him from the skies and a shower of flowers dropped down.

*   *   *

Ravana sat sighing in his palace. All around him he could hear the woeful laments of Rakshasa women who had lost their husbands and sons. He was at his wit's end. How had all this happened? What kind of humans were Rama and Lakshmana? This was unimaginable. There were only a few powerful heroes left in the Rakshasa army. Even the gods could not have reduced him to such a plight. What then of an army of monkeys and bears led by a human?

Ravana bit his lips and clenched his fists. His eyes were crimson, and he snorted loudly. Like a losing gambler impelled to stake his all, the demon summoned the last of his commanders and ordered them to again march out for battle. This time he would accompany them. Reluctantly, the Rakshasas accepted Ravana's command. They were stricken with terror as they thought of Rama.

Seeing his commanders trembling in fear, Ravana laughed and began to speak. "With an endless shower of arrows resembling the rays of the sun, I shall dispatch Rama and Lakshmana to Yamaraja's abode. Today I shall avenge my kinsmen and followers. I will wipe out the monkey battalions with waves of weapons surging like a violent ocean. Heads transfixed on arrows will appear on the battlefield like so many lotuses upon golden stalks. Each of my arrows will pierce one hundred monkeys. The vultures and jackals will be fully sated with the flesh of my enemies today. Fetch my chariot and weapons! I shall immediately march at the head of my army."

Ravana stood bellowing out his war cry. The demons felt heartened that their king was coming out to fight. That lordly Rakshasa had never been defeated in battle. Surely this spelled the end of Rama, Lakshmana and all the monkeys.

Quickly Ravana's charioteer brought his golden war chariot. It was equipped with all the divine weapons and adorned with celestial gems. Around its sides were thousands of bright golden pinnacles. Rows of bejeweled pillars held its great canopy and a standard of cat's-eye rose from its center like a massive palm tree. As it moved off, it thundered like a number of clouds, and it produced a beautiful ringing sound from thousands of small golden bells hanging around its sides.

The Rakshasas were struck with wonder to see Ravana mounted on the chariot, which shone like the sun. The charioteer urged on the eight celestial steeds and the chariot sped along Lanka's central highway. Right behind him came the last of his generals, Mahaparshwa, Virupaksha and Surantaka. Following them were the remainder of the Rakshasa forces: three hundred thousand elephants, a hundred thousand chariots, six hundred thousand horsemen and the same number of infantry. Ravana led his force through Lanka's northern gate and they rushed toward Rama's army, sending up loud shouts.

Even as Ravana charged, the sun became dim and the four quarters were enveloped in gloom. Birds shrieked hideously and the earth shook. Clouds rained blood and a meteor fell from the sky with a crash. Ravana felt his left eye twitching and his face became pale. A large vulture perched upon his standard and crows circled above him.

Not minding these fearful omens, Ravana careered madly toward the massed ranks of the monkey army. He plunged into them, immediately creating havoc. With arrows decked with gold he severed the heads of thousands of monkeys. Others were pierced in the heart and still others had their limbs lopped off. Some were crushed by his chariot and some smashed by his mace. Wherever his chariot moved, the monkeys could not stand and face him. An irresistible hail of arrows flew in all directions from Ravana's chariot. He was as hard to approach as the scorching sun.

Soon the battlefield was strewn with the corpses of slain monkeys. As Ravana ploughed into the Vanara forces they fled, tortured by his weapons. The demon king dispersed the simian ranks like the wind dissipating clouds. Having cut through the monkeys, Ravana searched for Rama.

Sugriva became maddened upon seeing the destruction of his army. He threw himself into the battle and began annihilating the Rakshasas on all sides. Roaring at a high pitch, the Vanara king rushed at the Rakshasas, whirling a massive tree. He killed them even as the wind of destruction would knock down trees at the end of an age. Sugriva hurled upon the Rakshasas a formidable number of huge rocks in rapid succession, like a shower of hailstones falling upon a flock of birds. The Rakshasas fell by the hundreds, their heads smashed. They appeared like so many crumbling mountains hit by thunderbolts.

Virupaksha leapt down from his chariot and challenged Sugriva. He shot a hundred fierce arrows at the monkey. The Rakshasa then mounted upon a great elephant and roared. Sugriva turned toward the demon and seized hold of a huge tree. He bounded into the air and brought the tree down upon the elephant's head. The colossal beast staggered backwards and sank to its knees. Virupaksha leapt down and took out his sword. He rushed at Sugriva, who hurled a heavy crag at the demon. Dodging the rock, Virupaksha bounded forward and struck Sugriva a terrible blow with his sword. The monkey flew back and fell to the ground, breathing heavily.

Coming back to his senses after some moments, Sugriva sprang up and aimed a blow at the Rakshasa with his fist. Virupaksha avoided the blow and again struck the monkey on the chest. Sugriva, blazing with anger, swung his hand with the speed of the wind. He struck the Rakshasa on his temple with the force of Indra's thunderbolt. Virupaksha dropped to the ground with blood streaming from his mouth, nose, eyes and ears. He tossed about, bellowing in pain. Losing consciousness, the Rakshasa gave up his life.

Headed by Rama and Lakshmana, the chief monkeys fought in a frenzy. Sugriva, Angada, Hanuman and other principal Vanaras cut down the Rakshasa forces like a field of ripe wheat. The demon king Ravana agonized at seeing his army overwhelmed. He turned to Mahaparshwa and said, "O heroic one, my hopes now rest with you. Repay your debt to your master and destroy this hostile army of monkeys. Do not delay."

The Rakshasa folded his palms and bowed slightly to Ravana. Raising his mighty bow he rushed into the Vanara forces like a moth entering a flame. Endowed with extraordinary strength, he carved a path through the monkeys with his blazing arrows. With deadly accuracy he severed the arms, legs and heads of the monkeys, sending up his fearful war cry. Struck hard and reeling from Mahaparshwa's attack, the monkeys ran to Sugriva for protection.

The monkey king rushed at the Rakshasa and hurled a tremendous crag straight at his chariot. Mahaparshwa saw the rock flying at him and, unperturbed, released swift arrows that broke it to pieces. Shattered into a thousand fragments by a stream of arrows, the rock descended to the ground like a flock of vultures. Sugriva immediately tore up a tree and threw it at the demon with all his strength. Again Mahaparshwa fired arrows, which sliced the tree into pieces.

Sugriva then picked up an iron bludgeon that lay on the ground nearby. He leapt forward and killed the team of horses yoked to the demon's chariot. The Rakshasa jumped down clutching his dreadful mace. He hurled the spiked mace at Sugriva and the monkey struck it with his bludgeon. With a great explosion the two weapons shattered and fell to the ground.

The two heroes fell upon each other and wrestled for some time. They struck each other with their fists, knees and heads, roaring and rolling about on the ground. Sugriva lifted the Rakshasa and threw him to a distance. Getting up at once, Mahaparshwa took hold of a sword and shield and rushed at Sugriva. The monkey quickly looked around and found another sword. With upraised weapons, the two powerful combatants met together, shouting in joy.

A fierce sword fight ensued, creating a shower of sparks as the weapons clashed together. Suddenly Mahaparshwa brought down his sword with full force onto Sugriva's shoulder. It embedded itself in the monkey's armor. As the Rakshasa tried to extract it, Sugriva quickly swung his own weapon in a short arc and severed the demon's head from his shoulders.

As the gods and Siddhas looked on, the Rakshasa fell lifeless to the ground. His head rolled away with its teeth clenched and its golden earrings glittering. Sugriva stood with his blood-soaked sword, looking like a dark cloud graced by a bright sunbeam. The monkeys, overjoyed, cheered their leader and thronged around him. The Rakshasas fled toward Ravana, howling in fear.

In the meantime the other powerful Rakshasa commander Surantaka had been slain in a duel with Angada. Now Ravana alone remained among the great Rakshasa heroes. He was consumed by rage. Looking around at his devastated army, he saw Rama and Lakshmana fighting in the distance. The demon ordered his charioteer to go toward the princes. As his chariot moved across the earth, it gave off a sound like the rumbling of a thousand thundering clouds. The ground shook and the monkeys fled simply from hearing the terrifying sound.

The demon king took out a brilliant arrow and placed it on his bow. He then invoked a missile presided over by Rahu, a malevolent and powerful enemy of the gods. Ravana released the fearful weapon, which then annihilated the monkeys by the hundreds of thousands. Blazing steel shafts sped in all directions, dispersing Rama's army as the sun disperses a morning mist. None dared face the Rakshasa king as he rushed toward Rama.

Seeing the demon approach like an onrushing comet, Lakshmana sped innumerable arrows toward him. Those arrows could hardly be seen as they screamed through the air, but the demon displayed astonishing dexterity and cut them all down. Ravana went straight past Lakshmana and approached Rama. He loosed a shower of arrows on Rama which were like venomous serpents with flaming heads. Rama stood on the battlefield like an immovable mountain. He immediately countered Ravana's arrows with crescent-headed shafts that cut them to pieces.

Ravana continued to send volleys of arrows at Rama, and the prince replied with equal numbers of his own. The sky was filled with arrows resembling flocks of golden birds. Rama and the demon circled each other from left to right, each fixing his gaze on the other. They appeared like Death personified and Yamaraja himself, meeting for a violent encounter. They completely covered the sky with their arrows and caused a shadow to envelop the battlefield. Both kept their bows bent to a full circle and both moved with great speed, keeping their weapons trained on the other.

Rama's blazing golden armor deflected Ravana's shafts, while the demon's impenetrable mail rendered Rama's arrows ineffective. Seeing his arrows falling uselessly to the ground, Ravana sent a dozen fierce shafts which pierced Rama's brow. With those golden arrows protruding from his head and producing profuse blood, Rama appeared to be wearing a shining crown decorated with a red garland. Impervious to the pain, Rama invoked the Rudrastra, presided over by Shiva, and sent a fearful hail of flaming arrows at the demon. They struck Ravana on every part of his body, seeking out his vulnerable points, but the demon's celestial armor again repelled the shafts and they entered the earth, hissing like furious snakes.

Ravana then invoked the fearful Rakshasa weapon, imbuing it with his own enormous personal power. As he released it all kinds of strange missiles sped toward Rama. Some had the heads of terrible lions with wide open mouths, and others had the heads of wolves, jackals, donkeys, boars, dogs, alligators and venomous serpents. Ravana's mystic weapon produced a frightening and discordant sound. It assailed Rama from every side.

Unshaken, Rama moved with great agility and dodged the shafts as they fell. He dropped to one knee and took out a blazing golden arrow. Fitting it to his bow, he invoked the Agneyastra. With that weapon he produced arrows of every description. Some resembled the radiant sun, others the moon, and others appeared like blazing meteors. Some flew like flashes of lightning and some were flaming crescents. Others rose into the sky like shining planets, descending to the earth like brilliant constellations fallen from heaven. Those divine arrows struck down all of Ravana's missiles which were killing the monkeys all over the battlefield.

Ravana blazed up in anger as he saw his wonderful weapon neutralized. He took out another dreadful missile, which had been fashioned by Maya, the architect of the celestial demons known as Asuras. Ravana charged the weapon with the potency of Rudra and fired it into the sky. At once there dropped from all sides innumerable flaming pikes and maces, along with massive iron clubs. Mystical nooses and thunderbolts fell upon the monkey army, accompanied by a piercing gale, like the wind which blows at the end of an age. That demoniac weapon began to annihilate the monkeys. A vast number of blazing missiles directed themselves at Rama, who responded by invoking the Gandharva weapon.

Immediately, countless arrows swept like a sheet across the entire battlefield. Without striking any of the monkeys, the arrows struck and disabled Ravana's missiles. All of them were cut to pieces and they fell to the earth. Without a second's delay Ravana employed the Suryastra. It brought into being a stream of large brilliant discuses which flew from Ravana's bow. As they rose into view they lit up all directions as if a hundred suns had risen on the battlefield.

Rama stood firm and pierced every one of the discuses with his own shafts, charging them with a force equal to that of Ravana's weapon. They split apart the flaming missiles and rendered them harmless as soon as they left Ravana's bow. As Rama countered his missile, Ravana sent ten barbed arrows which pierced the prince all over his body. Enraged, Rama instantly responded with a hundred of his own arrows which thudded deeply into Ravana's limbs.

Lakshmana then came forward and challenged the demon. Raising his bow he sped a number of shafts at Ravana that cut to pieces the demon's standard, which bore the emblem of a man's head. With a single crescent-headed arrow, Lakshmana severed the head of Ravana's charioteer. Then with five more well-aimed arrows, he broke apart the Rakshasa's gleaming bow. At the same time Vibhishana leapt forward and struck down with his mace the demon's steeds, which were as tall as hills.

Ravana quickly leapt from his chariot and gazed at his younger brother with flaming eyes. He hurled a blazing lance at Vibhishana which looked like a thunderbolt, but as it flew toward Vibhishana, Lakshmana cut it to pieces with three razor-headed arrows. That golden lance, which was bedecked with jewels, fell to the earth like a shower of meteors.

Ravana took up another lance even more terrible than the first. It shone with a lurid glow and emitted bright blue tongues of fire. Ravana raised his lance and fixed his gaze on Vibhishana. Lakshmana saw his friend in danger and covered the demon king with countless shafts. Ravana was stunned by the ferocity of Lakshmana's arrows and he turned to face the prince. He shouted out in anger. "You have saved Vibhishana but now you are yourself in grave danger. O proud one, stand ready! This lance, made by Maya Danava for the destruction of the gods, will pierce your heart, leaving your body only after taking your life."

Ravana leveled his infallible lance at Lakshmana. It was adorned with eight golden bells and gave off a loud chiming as the demon pulled it back. With his bludgeon-like arm, Ravana hurled the lance with full force. It sped through the air cracking like thunder and spread a shower of brilliant sparks in its wake. Seeing it approach, Lakshmana uttered an imprecation. "May you prove ineffectual. May your attempt to take my life fail. May all be well with Lakshmana."

As the prince spoke the lance struck him full on the chest. Grievously hurt by the weapon, Lakshmana collapsed unconscious to the ground. Rama was seized with sorrow to see his brother reduced to that state. His eyes filled with tears and his mouth became parched and dry. As furious as the all-devouring fire of universal destruction, he glared at the demon.

Rama ran over to his brother. The lance had pierced his armor and stuck into his body. Rama carefully extracted the lance and snapped it in two. He gently lifted Lakshmana and embraced him. As he held the grievously wounded prince, Ravana shot serpent-like arrows at him. Without caring for the arrows Rama called to Hanuman and Sugriva. "Guard this prince carefully. The time has come for me to manifest my strength. I shall make short work of this ten-headed monster. Here is my unfailing promise: the world will soon be devoid of either Ravana or myself. Let the three worlds witness my power today in battle. I shall achieve a feat which will be spoken of by all beings for as long as the world exists."

Rama stood up and immediately released an endless stream of ferocious shafts at Ravana. Greatly harassed, the demon replied with a shower of flaming steel arrows and iron clubs. Rama countered Ravana's missiles as they sped through the air, striking each and every one of them down. He fought wildly, sending screaming arrows that struck Ravana on every part of his body.

The demon fell back as Rama closed on him. He was entirely covered by Rama's golden-plumed shafts. Ravana could hardly do anything in response as Rama unleashed his fury. Completely overwhelmed, the Rakshasa turned and took to his heels.

CHAPTER THIRTEEN

THE FINAL BATTLE

As Ravana retreated in fear, Rama went back to Lakshmana. He dropped down by his side and cradled the prince's head in his hands. Lakshmana seemed dead. The wound in his chest looked terrible and Lakshmana did not appear to be breathing. Choked by tears Rama spoke aloud, giving vent to his grief. "Oh, how painful it is to see my beloved brother in such a state. My strength is deserting me as I look upon him lying here. Even if I win this fight I will feel no joy at all without Lakshmana. Indeed, this prince has followed me through thick and thin. If he has now departed for the regions of Death, then I too shall follow him."

Rama lamented loudly for some time. What would he say to Sumitra if he returned without Lakshmana? How could he face Bharata and Shatrughna? Surely they would censure him for failing to protect his younger brother. It would be better to give up his own life than hear the reproaches of those most dear to him. Rama fell weeping to the ground.

Hanuman raised him up and comforted him. He called for Sushena, the Vanara physician. Perhaps Lakshmana would respond to his treatment of celestial herbs. Sushena approached the fallen prince and examined him carefully. He looked up at Rama and said, "Your brother still lives. See how his bodily luster has not departed. And I can detect the movement of his life air and the beat of his heart. But he needs urgent treatment."

Sushena asked for more of the celestial herbs which Hanuman had fetched from the Himalayas. The herbs were brought quickly and Sushena administered them to Lakshmana. By the divine power of the herb *sanjivakarani* the prince slowly returned to consciousness. Then Sushena carefully administered the herbs *vishalyakarani* and *sandhani*, which together healed Lakshmana's grievous wound and repaired his bones. Slowly he sat up and looked around. Rama was overjoyed. He pressed Lakshmana to his bosom with tears in his eyes and said, "By good fortune you have been saved from the jaws of death. If you had died, I would not have been able to carry on this fight."

Lakshmana, pained to hear his brother speak in that way, replied, "You have taken a solemn vow to kill Ravana and install Vibhishana on the throne of Lanka. You should not make that false for any reason. O great hero, fulfill your vow at once! Let us see the evil Ravana lying dead on the battlefield, cut down by your arrows."

Rama seized his bow. A terrible anger took hold of him. Lakshmana had spoken well. The time for the arrogant demon's destruction had arrived. As Rama looked around he saw Ravana seated aboard his golden chariot. Having rested, the demon was again rushing at Rama as the malefic planet Rahu rushes toward the sun. From where he stood, Rama immediately shot a steady stream of arrows that shone like fire. They rained down upon the demon, who in turn loosed off torrents of shafts that hissed like serpents as they flew at Rama.

From the sky the gods observed the combat. Seeing Rama standing upon the ground, Indra desired to assist him. He summoned Matali, his charioteer, and asked him to fetch his chariot. In a moment Indra's radiant chariot appeared, drawn by its thousand steeds. Indra ordered Matali to take it to Rama and the charioteer at once descended onto the battlefield next to the prince. With folded palms he respectfully addressed Rama. "Here is my Lord Indra's chariot, O Raghava. Here also is his mighty bow and other infallible weapons, as well as his invincible golden armor. Please use all these to attain victory over Ravana, the enemy of the gods. I shall act as your charioteer."

Rama gazed with amazement at the wonderful vehicle. It was bedecked with glowing gems and wreaths of celestial flowers. A tall pole of cat's-eye stood in its center bearing a brilliant golden standard. The chariot was suspended a bow length above the ground and a crystal staircase came down to Rama's feet. He circumambulated the chariot and then climbed aboard. The prince quickly donned Indra's armor and took up his bow and celestial arrows. As he stood upon that divine chariot, he looked like the sun illumining all the quarters. At Matali's command the heavenly steeds surged forward and the chariot moved off with a rumbling sound that filled the earth and sky.

Ravana, realizing that Rama was being assisted by his mortal enemy Indra, became even more enraged. He fired a celestial missile which unleashed hundreds of thousands of dreadful-looking serpents, their wide open mouths vomiting fire. Writhing and hissing they came from all sides and sped toward Rama.

As the venomous snakes descended upon him, Rama at once invoked a weapon presided over by Garuda. A shower of arrows shot from his bow, turning as they flew into golden eagles with fierce talons and sharply curved beaks. The mystical eagles intercepted and destroyed all of Ravana's serpents.

The demon roared furiously. He struck Matali and all of his steeds with a forcible torrent of shafts with glowing steel heads. The Rakshasa then sent a crescent-headed arrow which tore down the chariot's golden standard. He followed this with countless other straight-flying arrows that struck Rama on every part of his body. In seconds Indra's great chariot was completely covered by Ravana's arrows, so that no part of it was visible.

With his ten heads and massive bow Ravana stood in his chariot looking like the Mainaka mountain risen from the ocean. Observing the demon overwhelming Rama with his arrows, the gods and rishis felt despondent. The monkeys became fearful and they observed grim-looking omens. The sun became dim and the sea tossed with waves that seemed to rise up to the sky. Jackals howled and ghosts and wraiths darted about on the battlefield.

So intense was Ravana's assault that Rama was unable to lift his bow and fit his arrows. Rama's eyes turned crimson with rage. He began to think of the destruction of the entire Rakshasa race. With great expertise Matali drove the chariot upwards and away from the hail of Ravana's arrows. It burst forth like the sun emerging from a cloud. The gods showered blessings on Rama while the Daityas and Danavas uttered benedictions upon Ravana.

When the king of the Rakshasas saw his adversary again stationed before him, he took up a fearful looking dart. That terrific weapon had spikes resembling mountain peaks. It had a flaming point which glowed with a brilliance that could not be looked upon. That dart was dear to Ravana and had been carefully kept and worshipped by him, reserved for a time when he faced a deadly enemy. It was irresistible to gods and demons alike. Ravana raised it with his serpent-like arm and roared with full force. The earth shook and the mountains trembled, sending their lions and elephants fleeing in fear. Looking at Rama, the Rakshasa thundered, "This dart, powerful like a thunderbolt, will now take your life. Hurled by me it will strike both you and your brother, leveling you with all the Rakshasas you have slain. Guard yourself if you can!"

The demon at once threw the dart. It flashed through the air, covered by a circle of lightning and emitting a deafening scream. Rama instantly sent a hundred arrows at the dart but they were deflected and fell useless to the ground. Without losing a moment, Rama took up Indra's celestial javelin. He forcefully hurled it and it flew like a blazing meteor straight at the dart. Struck by the divine lance, Ravana's weapon was split apart and dropped to the earth. The javelin, giving off a delightful sound from the many bells tied around it, returned again to Indra's chariot.

Rama immediately followed that astonishing feat by sending a fierce volley of arrows at the demon. They struck Ravana in all his limbs and pierced his ten heads. The demon blazed with anger and replied with an equal number of his own arrows. Rama intercepted Ravana's arrows while simultaneously continuing to strike him. The Rakshasa then released an even greater number of shafts which penetrated Rama's defense and pierced through his armor. With blood shining on his breast Rama looked like a great kinshuka tree in full blossom.

Neither opponent could easily see the other, so great was the number of arrows filling the air. Rama pulled clear of Ravana's attack and laughed heartily. He rebuked the demon. "You are proud of your strength, O Rakshasa, but it will not save you now. Indeed, since you stole away my consort while I was not present, you cannot be considered heroic. You are a shameless coward given over to vanity alone, vaunting yourself as a hero. Had you tried taking Sita from my presence you would not be alive today. By good fortune I see you now on the battlefield. Prepare to receive the results of your despicable and evil acts, O vile one! Carnivorous birds and beasts will soon feast upon your flesh and blood."

With redoubled strength Rama then sent wave upon wave of arrows straight at Ravana. The prince felt increased enthusiasm for the fight. He invoked all the celestial missiles and they immediately appeared before him on the battlefield. In great joy, Rama fired the weapons at the demon one after another. He recited the incantations with full concentration as he released his arrows. Charged with the mystic power of the divine astras the arrows tore into Ravana and sent him reeling. As he staggered about on his chariot, the Rakshasa was showered with rocks and trees by the monkeys. The demon was reduced to a sorry plight, being unable to lift his bow or do anything in his defense. He sank down on the floor of his chariot. Seeing this, his charioteer veered away from the fight and retreated.

Ravana remained stunned for some time. Gradually returning to his senses, he saw that his charioteer had taken him away from the battlefield. He immediately chastised the charioteer with harsh words. "How have you disdained me in this way, O evil-minded one? Obviously considering me to be bereft of power, heroism and prowess, you have covered me with shame. Today you have nullified my valor, dignity and fame. While my enemy stood expectantly before me, deserving to be gratified by my arrows, you have made me into a coward."

Ravana was beside himself with fury. He accused the charioteer of siding with the enemy and ordered him to return immediately to Rama's presence. The charioteer replied that he had only done what he felt was his proper duty. Ravana had been completely overpowered by Rama's weapons.

Out of affection he had desired to save his master's life. Citing verses from scripture supporting his actions, the charioteer begged Ravana's forgiveness. The demon king was appeased. He nodded at his charioteer and commanded him to return with all speed to the fight. Urged on by Ravana, the charioteer lashed his horses and within a few moments the chariot stood again before Rama.

On the battlefield, Rama was himself expressing his exhaustion from the fight. In the heavens the great rishi Agastya saw this and desired to assist him. Agastya had been observing the battle from the sky along with the gods. He now descended to Rama's chariot and spoke to him. "O mighty-armed Rama, please listen as I tell you the secret of a highly confidential prayer, the Aditya-Hridaya. This prayer will invoke the powerful spiritual energy from the heart of the sun. This is the very effulgence of the supreme Vishnu himself. With this power one can overcome any obstacle and destroy to the roots all one's enemies."

Agastya instructed Rama how to recite the prayer, which would summon the combined power of all the gods, emanating from the bodily rays of Vishnu. With that power Rama would be able to quickly overcome Ravana before nightfall, when the demon's own power would be doubled.

The rishi returned to the heavens and Rama turned toward the sun. After sipping water for purification he recited the Aditya-Hridaya. At once he felt extreme happiness, and his mind became highly enlivened. All his fatigue vanished and he took up his bow. He stood firmly on Indra's chariot. Fixing his gaze upon Ravana, who had again appeared before him, he urged Matali forward toward the demon.

In the heavens the sun-god stood in person amid the other gods and uttered benedictions upon Rama, saying, "May victory attend you!"

Rama saw Ravana's chariot flying toward him, filling all quarters with its thunderous rumbling. That chariot was drawn by huge black steeds with the heads of hideous fiends. It shone with a dreadful luster and was adorned all over with brilliant rubies and celestial sapphires, with rows of pennants flying from its sides. Moving rapidly through space it looked like a cloud containing streams of shining water and issuing forth torrents in the form of arrows.

Rama said to Matali, "From the way in which he is darting back into the fray it appears that this Rakshasa is bent upon his own destruction. Close upon him with care. I shall destroy his chariot even as the wind would blow away a cloud."

Grasping Indra's bow, Rama tempered his anger with patience as he awaited his opportunity to attack the demon, who was maneuvering on the battlefield. Matali skillfully drove the chariot in circles and gradually closed on Ravana, the two opponents releasing streams of arrows and appearing like two proud lions intent on killing each other.

Suddenly many frightful omens appeared. Blood rained down on Ravana's chariot while violent whirlwinds tossed it about. A flock of vultures circled over the demon. In the distance Lanka was shrouded in a red glow. Great meteors fell from the sky and the earth shook. The sky became darkened even while the sun shone. Terrible thunderbolts and flashes of lightning fell upon the Rakshasa army. Ravana's steeds shed hot tears and emitted sparks from their mouths.

Around Rama were seen many favorable signs that portended his imminent victory. The sun illuminated him brilliantly and a gentle breeze blew behind him. He felt his right eye and arm throb and his mind felt joyful.

As Rama and Ravana met in fearful combat, the two armies stood motionless with their weapons held fast in their hands. Observing the man and demon engaged in a desperate duel, all the warriors, along with the gods, Gandharvas and rishis, watched in wonderment. The two belligerent opponents each exhibited their full prowess on the battlefield as they hurled blazing weapons at each other.

Rama fitted a highly-sharpened shaft to his bow, as irresistible as a thunderbolt and shining with splendor. Drawing back his bow to a full circle, he released the arrow at Ravana's standard. It severed the tall pole and the demon's ensign fluttered to the ground.

Ravana burned with indignation. He sent a hail of flaming steel arrows at Rama's steeds. Struck by the arrows the celestial horses neither flinched nor shook but continued to draw the great chariot, describing various circles and movements and baffling Ravana's arrows. The demon fired a tremendous shower of maces, iron clubs, discuses and mallets, as well as mountain peaks, trees, pikes and double-headed axes. At the same time he released tremendous volleys of arrows which fell toward Rama's chariot like streaks of golden lightning.

By Matali's expert handling, Indra's chariot constantly foiled Ravana's weapons. The Rakshasa became more and more infuriated and he directed his mystic missiles upon the army of monkeys. Seeing this, Rama fitted celestial weapons to his bow which sent innumerable arrows into the sky. Those arrows fell upon Ravana's weapons and smashed them to pieces. No arrow shot by Rama failed to find its mark. The sky was completely filled with his golden-plumed shafts. The missiles of the two fighters met together in hundreds and thousands. They created explosions of fire and billows of smoke across the whole battlefield.

Rama and Ravana fought vehemently for hours without interruption. Exchanging blow for blow, neither felt wearied nor inclined to give an inch to the other. Those observing the fight felt their hairs standing on end. No one could take their eyes off the furious fighters as they battled on, relentlessly seeking victory. Ravana sent twenty, then sixty, then a hundred and then a thousand arrows at Rama, aiming at his vital parts, or seeking to kill the charioteer and his horses. Rama responded with twice that number, digging shafts into Ravana's steeds and charioteer, while at the same time constantly covering the demon.

Even after fighting for half a day, neither seemed to have the upper hand. Ravana then composed himself and once again invoked the Rakshasa-astra, imbuing it with all his mystic potency. Immediately the air was filled with a thick shower of every kind of weapon. The entire globe seemed to shake and the ocean became agitated. Serpents and devils appeared screaming in the sky and emitting fire from their mouths. The sun lost its brilliance and the wind ceased to blow.

In the heavens the gods themselves became fearful and cried out, "May all be well with the worlds."

With full concentration, Rama again invoked the Gandharva-astra, which caused hundreds of thousands of arrows to appear and counter Ravana's weapons. Those awful and demoniac missiles fell to the ground and burned up, being pierced by Rama's fiery shafts.

The battle between Rama and Ravana could only be compared to itself. Such a fight had never been seen at any time even by the gods. They watched anxiously as Rama came under repeated ferocious attacks from the lord of the Rakshasas. Rama remained calm. He took from his bow a great razor-headed arrow that resembled a venomous serpent. In an instant he fitted and fired the arrow at Ravana. That arrow, imbued with mystic power, divided into ten and tore off the demon's heads. But they immediately grew again. Rama sent another weapon which again severed the Rakshasa's heads and again they grew back.

Rama struck down one hundred heads, but the demon remained standing. Without slowing his attack for even a moment Rama contemplated this wonderful phenomenon. How was this demon to be killed? No weapon seemed able to take his life. It looked like the fight might go on forever.

Vibhishana quickly approached Rama. He told him that the demon had a boon from Brahma that his heads and arms could never be destroyed. In Ravana's heart was a store of celestial nectar which renewed the life in his body. The only way to kill him was to strike at his heart with a divine weapon that could dry up the nectar.

As Rama considered his next move, all the while raining arrows upon Ravana, Matali turned to Rama and spoke. "O Rama, the time for this one's death has come. Recall now the prayer Agastya told you. Agastya also gave you an arrow when you were in the forest. Imbue that arrow with the force of the Brahmastra and kill the demon by piercing his heart."

Accepting Matali's advice, Rama remembered the celestial arrow which Agastya had given him long ago in the forest. At once it appeared in his hand and he fitted it to his bow. Its shaft was made of ether and its weight consisted of the Mandara and Meru mountains. The wind-god presided over its shaft, the fire-god over its plumes, and the sun-god was installed at its point. It looked like the rod of universal destruction wielded by the Time-spirit himself. Rama again chanted the Aditya-Hridaya prayer and then invoked the infallible Brahmastra.

As Rama drew back the arrow, he shone so brilliantly that no one could look at him. He released the weapon and it flew at Ravana, lighting up the earth and sky and roaring like a tumultuous ocean. It struck the demon on his chest even as he stood firing his own weapons at Rama. Piercing right through his heart, the arrow emerged from Ravana's body soaked in blood and entered the earth. Ravana whirled around and let out a cry which seemed to shake the entire creation. His bow dropped from his hands and he fell from his chariot like a mountain struck down by Indra's thunderbolt.

The Rakshasas fled panic-stricken in every direction. They shed tears of grief on seeing their lord slain. The monkeys leapt about, chasing the fleeing Rakshasas and shouting with joy. The sound of drums and other celestial instruments sounded from the sky. Delightful breezes blew on the battlefield carrying heavenly odors. A dazzling shower of brilliant flowers fell from the sky and covered Rama's chariot. The gods and rishis praised Rama, who stood blazing with splendor. The battle was over. Rama climbed down from the chariot and was surrounded by Lakshmana, Sugriva, Hanuman, Angada, Jambavan and Vibhishana, who all praised and cheered him for his incredible feat.

As he gazed upon his brother's dead body, Vibhishana then began to lament. "Alas, O Ravana, how have you been killed? After displaying your power for a long time you now lie motionless with your brilliant diadem thrown off. The very fate which I predicted has come to pass. Why did you not heed my counsel that was meant always for your good? Overcome by lust, greed and anger, you have met the sure result of harboring these three mortal enemies of the soul. O my brother, now that you have been slain everything seems void; the sun has fallen to earth, the moon has merged in darkness, fire does not emit flames and all energy has become bereft of effort. All of Lanka is lost."

Although shunned by Ravana, Vibhishana had loved his brother and had always desired his welfare. He fell by his side and continued to cry out. Rama approached him and placed an arm around him, consoling him with soft words. "Your brother has died a hero's death. No hero has ever been known to be always victorious. Sooner or later a warrior will die at the edge of weapons. This is the end sought by all great fighters. O Vibhishana, there is no need to mourn for Ravana, for his death was glorious."

Lakshmana also consoled the grief-stricken Vibhishana by telling him spiritual truths. Although Ravana's body had fallen, his soul remained alive. Indeed, having been purified by Rama's weapons and by his death in battle, he would surely have attained an exalted destination. There was no gain in lamenting over a corpse once the soul has departed. Vibhishana should now perform the last rites for his brother and then assume the rulership of Lanka.

As Lakshmana finished speaking with Vibhishana, Ravana's wives suddenly appeared on the battlefield. Crying like female elephants, they fell upon their husband's body and bathed him with tears. Dozens of Rakshasis, their hair and garments in disarray, surrounded the fallen Rakshasa. They rolled on the ground and wailed in agony. Ravana's principal wife, Mandodari was at their head. She swooned upon seeing her husband dead on the battlefield. After regaining her senses, she gazed upon his face and lamented loudly, her voice choked with tears.

"Alas, my lord! How have you fallen at the hands of a man? You—who struck terror into the hearts of the gods, Gandharvas, Siddhas and even great rishis—now lie killed by a mere mortal who came walking from Ayodhya, a city of humans. I do not consider Rama to be an ordinary man. He must surely be Vishnu, the sustainer of all the worlds, the unborn, inconceivable and all-powerful Supreme Person. None other could have laid you low.

"O Ravana, although you conquered your senses, winning great boons from your austerities, in the end you have been conquered by those senses. Fallen prey to lust, you desired to enjoy the sinless Sita. By stealing away that godly lady, the very emblem of chastity and nobility, you brought destruction upon yourself and all your kinsfolk."

Mandodari could not contain her grief. She slumped over Ravana's body and continued to wail in piteous tones.

"O hero, where have you gone now, leaving me forlorn? When I was always your devoted servant, why did you long for Sita? Alas, my life is useless as I could not satisfy my lord. Although we roamed and sported together in every delightful region of heaven, I am now fallen into a fearful ocean of grief. Woe be to the fleeting fortune of kings."

Mandodari looked up with tear-filled eyes and saw Ravana's brother nearby. "Here stands the pious Vibhishana," she cried. "Having ignored his wise advice, you now lie slain. Surely a sinner always reaps the results of sin in the end, just as the virtuous also receive their results. Your brother will now enjoy royal fortune while you are sent to the next world."

Mandodari cried over her husband's body for a long time. Everyone stood by silently, allowing her to vent her grief. Finally the Rakshasa king's other wives gently lifted her up. They supported her on both sides and led her away while she continued to wail.

Rama spoke again to Vibhishana. "Death has ended all animosity. Ravana is now the same to me as you. Please peform the proper rites for his everlasting spiritual good." In accordance with time-honored custom, Rama wanted to immediately perform the last rites for his fallen foe.

Vibhishana stood reflecting for some moments. He told Rama that he felt unable to perform the funeral rites for his brother. Ravana was cruel, merciless and given to heinous sins. Although his brother, he was not worthy of Vibhishana's respect. Ravana's obsequies were an act of worship he could not honestly perform.

Rama smiled. "O Vibhishana, no disdain should ever be felt for the soul. Once dead, a person's soul leaves his body and proceeds to its next life. Ravana's sinful body is now dead, but his pure soul continues to live. The soul is always worthy of respect. You should therefore carry out the rites for the eternal good of your brother's immortal soul."

Vibhishana looked down at Ravana's body. It was a fact. The soul of all beings was a pure part of the Supreme Lord. Ignorance only exists in the external material body, not the soul. Ravana's sins, which proceeded from his ignorance, had ended with the end of his body. Especially as he had been slain by the Lord himself. All taints of sin were surely cleansed by such a death.

Vibhishana at once began the necessary rituals. He had his brother's body brought into Lanka and he lit a sacrificial fire, making offerings of grains and ghee and worshipping Vishnu on Ravana's behalf. Along with the elderly Rakshasas and Yatudhanas, headed by Ravana's grandfather Malayavan, Vibhishana carried out all the rituals strictly in accord with the instructions of scripture.

Ravana's body was placed on a huge bier. He was draped with golden silks and covered with flower garlands. To the sound of various musical instruments, the dead Rakshasa was borne by a hundred demons to a consecrated spot. Brahmins among the Rakshasas carried the sacrificial fire in front of Ravana. They built a pyre out of logs of fragrant sandal and padmaka wood along with ushira roots and bhadrakali grass.

The demons then placed Ravana upon the pyre and threw handfuls of parched rice, sesame seeds and kusha grass. After uttering sacred mantras and sprinkling the pyre with ghee, Vibhishana set it alight. It quickly blazed up, and within moments the Rakshasas king's body was reduced to ashes.

CHAPTER FOURTEEN

SITA'S ORDEAL

After witnessing Ravana's destruction, the gods and rishis departed joyfully for their various heavenly abodes. Matali bowed before Rama and received permission to return with his chariot to Indra. Rama watched as the celestial vehicle rose high into the sky and disappeared. His fury with the Rakshasas had completely subsided. He now thought of Vibhishana's installation as the new king of Lanka. As the city was upon the earth, it was within the jurisdiction of the earth's emperors, although inhabited by the Rakshasas. Thus Rama desired to install the pious Vibhishana as its righteous ruler so as to quickly reestablish order in the devastated city.

Rama asked Lakshmana to perform the ceremony of consecrating Vibhishana on Lanka's throne. Lakshmana immediately had the monkeys fetch seawater in large golden jars. With that water he duly consecrated Vibhishana, carefully following the directions given in the Vedas. Vibhishana sat upon the throne and blazed with regal splendor. The Rakshasas were joyful to see Ravana's brother assume the rulership of Lanka, and they brought him many gifts and offerings. Vibhishana offered all of these to Rama, who accepted them out of his love for the Rakshasa.

When the ceremony was complete, Rama asked Hanuman to go quickly to Sita. He was aching to see her again and he said to Hanuman, "Please inform the princess of the good news. I long to see her. Tell her to make herself ready so that very soon I may meet with her."

Hanuman at once left for the gardens. As he made his way through Lanka he was honored by the Rakshasas, who folded their palms as he passed by. Quickly reaching the ashoka grove, he saw Sita still lying at the foot of the simshapa tree. She was unaware of Rama's victory and appeared mournful. Upon seeing Hanuman, however, she quickly stood up in hope. Surely the monkey must be bearing good news. The princess listened expectantly as Hanuman told her all that had happened.

"O godly lady, your husband has come out victorious. The demon Ravana is no more and the virtuous Vibhishana is now the ruler of Lanka. Dear mother, your woes are ended. Please prepare yourself to see your Lord Rama."

Sita was stunned with joy. She could not make any reply and simply stood for some time gazing at Hanuman with tears flowing from her eyes. At last she said in a choked voice, "O good monkey, I cannot think of anything I can offer you in return for this news. Not gold nor silver nor gems nor even the sovereignty of all the worlds is equal to the value of this message."

Hanuman replied that hearing her joyful reply was itself more valuable than any gift. And, having seen Rama emerge victorious and happy, Hanuman desired nothing more.

Sita praised Hanuman again and again as the monkey stood with his head bowed and palms joined together. When the princess stopped speaking he said to her, "If you permit me, I shall punish these wicked Rakshasis who have made your life so miserable. I would like to give them a good thrashing. They surely deserve death for their evil conduct against you, O divine lady."

Sita pondered for some moments within herself. She looked at the Rakshasis who sat at a distance, no longer concerned with her now that Ravana was dead. Turning to Hanuman, Sita replied, "These Rakshasis were simply carrying out Ravana's order. No blame should be attached to them. Furthermore, any suffering I felt was surely the result of my own past misdeeds, for such is the universal law. Indeed, there is an ancient maxim which is always the code of the virtuous: 'A righteous man does not consider the offenses of others against him. At all costs he always observes the vow of not returning evil for evil, for the virtuous consider good conduct their ornament.'" Sita said that compassion should always be shown toward sinners, for no one was ever found to be free of sin.

Admonished in this way, Hanuman bowed to her and made no argument. Sita had spoken well, quite in accord with her noble character. After reflecting on her words for some moments the monkey then asked, "I wish to return now to Rama. Please give me a message for him."

Sita replied that she only wished to see him. Hanuman assured her that she would very soon see Rama. Bowing once again he left and made his way back to Vibhishana's palace, where Rama was waiting.

Hearing of Sita's condition, Rama asked Vibhishana to arrange that she be given celestial clothes and ornaments. "O king of the Rakshasas, please have that princess bathed with heavenly unguents and dressed in the finest silks. Then have her brought here. My heart is burning with desire to see her again."

Vibhishana personally went to Sita with Rama's instruction, but Sita, anxious to see Rama said, "I wish to see my husband immediately, without having bathed and dressed."

Sita had suffered through almost a year of torture. She had never stopped thinking of the day she would be reunited with Rama. Here it was at last. How could she possibly wait another moment?

Vibhishana replied gently that it was Rama's desire that she prepare herself. Sita, accepting Rama's word as her order, aquiesced, and Vibhishana immediately arranged for her bath and clothing. In a short while the princess was adorned in costly robes and jewels worthy of the consorts of the gods. She mounted a golden palanquin bedecked with celestial gems and was borne into Rama's presence.

Crowds of Rakshasas and monkeys filled the streets, all anxious for a glimpse of the princess. Seated on the palanquin behind a silk veil, Sita shone like the sun shrouded by a cloud. Rakshasas wearing dark jackets and turbans and carrying staffs fitted with bells cleared a path for her. The crowds of onlookers, who were roaring like the ocean, parted as the palanquin made its way slowly along the main highway.

Vibhishana went ahead and informed Rama that his wife was on her way. Hearing that she was on a palanquin, Rama said to Vibhishana, "The princess should be asked to dismount and proceed on foot. The people desire to see her and that is not condemned by scripture. A house, a veil or a costume are never the protection of a chaste woman. Her character alone is her shield."

Lakshmana, Sugriva and Hanuman looked at Rama with surprise. He appeared to be displeased with Sita. His expression was stern and thoughtful. As Vibhishana conducted Sita into his presence Rama looked at her without smiling.

Sita was overjoyed to see Rama again and her face shone like the moon, but she felt abashed when she saw his grave expression. Her limbs trembled and she stood before him with her head bowed and hands folded.

Rama's heart was torn. He deeply wanted to show his love for Sita and to take her back at once, but he feared public censure. As a king he wanted to set the highest example for the people. Sita had been in the house of another man for almost a year. Whatever the circumstances, that would surely be criticized by some of the people. Questions about her chastity might be raised. That would never be acceptable for the wife of an emperor.

Looking at Sita, whose face was bathed in tears, Rama said, "O blessed one, I have won you back today. After conquering my enemies in battle, I have avenged the insult given me through your abduction. You, too, are fully avenged, O princess. The evil Ravana is no more."

Rama stopped speaking, his heart balking at what he had to say next. Steadying his mind he continued to address the tremulous Sita. "Now that I have wiped off the stain of insult on my noble house and established my truthfulness and resolve, no further purpose remains for me in this matter. O gentle lady, I have not undergone this endeavor out of a desire to again have you as my wife. You have long dwelt in the house of another. How then can I take you back into my house? Your good character has become suspect. Ravana clasped you in his arms and looked upon you with a lustful eye. Therefore, my attachment for you has ended. Please go wherever you may desire. Perhaps you may now find shelter with Lakshmana or Bharata or Shatrughna, or even Vibhishana. As beautiful as you are, O Sita, how could Ravana have left you alone?"

Sita was shocked. She wept loudly and shook like a sapling caught in a storm. Greatly shamed by her husband's words, she shrank into herself. Rama's speech had pierced her like poisoned arrows and she cried in pain for a long time. Gradually gathering her senses she replied to Rama in faltering tones.

"Why do you address me with such unkind words, O hero, like a common man addressing some vulgar woman? You are judging all women by the standards of a degraded few. Give up your doubts in me for I am without blame. When Ravana snatched me I was helpless and dragged against my will. Although I could not control my limbs, my heart remained under my control and did not deviate from you even slightly. If, in spite of our living together in love for so long, you still do not trust me, then I am surely undone for good."

Angry, Sita admonished and taunted Rama. Why had he gone to such great endeavors? He could have sent a message with Hanuman telling her that he was rejecting her. Then she would have immediately given up her life and saved him all the effort of war. It seemed he had given way to anger alone, just like an ordinary man. Like a mean man, he had not considered her devotion and chastity toward him. He had forgotten her divine origins and taken her to be an ordinary woman.

Sita, still weeping, turned to Lakshmana. "O prince, please raise for me a pyre. This is my only recourse now. I no longer desire to live, being smitten with false reproaches. As my husband has renounced me in a public gathering, I shall enter fire and give up my life."

Lakshmana was indignant. How could Rama act in this way? He looked at his brother, but Rama remained impassive. He returned

Lakshmana's glance with a slight nod. Lakshmana understood his desire and, feeling deeply pained and perplexed, constructed a pyre.

Rama stood like Yamaraja, the god of justice. No one dared approach him or say anything. Only Sita came near him. She walked around him in respect and approached the blazing fire. The princess then prayed with folded hands. "If I have never been unfaithful to Rama either in mind, words or body, may the fire-god protect me on all sides. As my heart ever abides in Rama, so may the fire-god save me now. As all the gods are witness to my chastity, let the fire-god protect me."

After uttering this prayer Sita walked around the fire and then fearlessly entered it before the vast assembly. Sita seemed like a golden altar with its sacred fire. Gods, rishis, Gandharvas, Siddhas and other divine beings observed Sita walking deep into the fire and all the women in the assembly sent up a great cry as they watched her ascend the pyre, like a goddess fallen from heaven and entering hell. A gasp of amazement and shock came from the crowd as she disappeared into the flames.

Rama was blinded by tears. He was afflicted to hear the cries of the people. With his mind set on virtue and his heart wracked with grief, he watched Sita walk into the fire. From the sky the gods, headed by Brahma, addressed Rama. "How are you allowing this divine lady to enter fire? Do you not recall your actual identity? What is this play of yours, O Lord?"

Rama looked at the gods and folded his palms. He replied, "I take myself to be a human. My name is Rama, the son of Dasarath. Let Brahma tell me who I was in my former lives."

From the sky the four-headed Brahma, seated upon his swan carrier, replied, "O Rama, I know you as the original creator of the cosmos. You are Vishnu and Narayana, the one supreme person who is known by many names. All the gods come from you and the worlds rest upon your energy. You exist within and without all things and reside in the heart of every being. Your existence and actions are inconceivable. You have appeared as Rama for the destruction of Ravana and the deliverance of your devoted servants. Now that you have accomplished your purposes you should return to your own abode."

Rama bowed his head and said nothing. At that moment the fire-god emerged from the fire holding Sita in his arms. The princess was dressed in a red robe and she shone brightly like the rising sun. She wore a garland of celestial flowers and she was adorned with brilliant gems. Her dark, curly hair framed her face, which glowed with transcendent beauty.

Agni placed Sita before Rama and spoke in a voice that boomed out like thunder. "Here is your wife Sita. No sin exists in her. Neither by word, deed nor thought, not even by glance has she ever been unfaithful to you.

Sita walked around the fire.

Ravana forcefully snatched her away while she was helpless and forlorn. Although kept captive by him, her mind and heart remained focused
on you at every moment. She did not give a single thought to Ravana
despite being tempted and threatened by him in many ways. Therefore, O
Rama, accept her back with an open heart."

Rama experienced great joy upon hearing Agni's speech. His eyes
flooded with tears as he replied to the fire-god: "Sita needed this purifica-
tory ordeal. Otherwise the world would have condemned me as foolish and
controlled by lust. She dwelt in Ravana's house for a long time and her
chastity had to be proven to the world, although I know of her undivided
love for me. Indeed, guarded as she is by her own moral power, Ravana
could not have violated Sita any more than the sea could transgress its
bounds."

Rama declared Sita to be as inseparable from him as sunlight from the
sun. He could no more renounce her than a virtuous man could renounce
righteousness.

Sita bloomed with happiness. She sat next to Rama on a golden throne.
The gods and rishis appeared in the assembly offering praises to Rama.
Shiva personally came before Rama and said, "You have killed the scourge
and dread of the universe, O Rama. You should now depart for Ayodhya and
comfort your relatives there. Then be pleased to rule over this world for a
long time."

Shiva told Rama that his father Dasarath was present, seated in a celestial chariot in the sky. Rama looked up and saw the chariot descending
slowly. His father, appearing in a body that shone with celestial splendor,
gazed down at him. Leaving the chariot, he came down to earth and
embraced Rama tightly. He sat next to his son and began to speak.

"Although I reside with Indra, I do not feel as much pleasure there as I
do now upon seeing you again. The words uttered by Kaikeyi when sending
you into exile are still impressed upon my heart, but today I am fully rid of
my sorrow. I have been redeemed by you, dear Rama. Fourteen years have
passed and your exile is ended. I long to see you return to Ayodhya and
assume the throne, after pacifying Kaushalya and the mighty Bharata.
O Rama, I now understand your identity. You are the Supreme Lord, born
on earth for the good of the world."

Rama asked his father to retract the words he had uttered when he had
disowned Kaikeyi and her son. They were both blameless in every respect.
Dasarath assented to Rama's request. He embraced Lakshmana and praised
him for his selfless service to Rama, asking him to continue that service
when Rama became the emperor.

Dasarath then spoke to Sita. "O daughter, do not think ill of Rama for his repudiation of you. He only desired to prove your absolute purity. Your entering the fire was an act which will forever overshadow the renown of all virtuous ladies."

Sita folded her palms and bowed to her father-in-law, who rose again to his aerial chariot and left for the heavens. The other gods paid their respects to Rama and then left for their own abodes. Indra approached Rama and said, "A sight of the gods can never go in vain. O Rama, pray tell us what you desire and it shall be done at once."

Smiling, Rama asked Indra to return to life all the slain monkeys, even those whose bodies had been torn and devoured. He also asked that wherever the monkeys may live there should be abundant fruits and roots for their food.

Indra replied, "Although difficult to grant, your desire shall be fulfilled. Let all the monkeys rise again, even those whose heads and limbs have been severed. Let them be reunited with their families and let trees full of fruits, even out of season, forever grow where they dwell."

The powerful god sprinkled celestial nectar from the sky. The monkeys who were killed then rose from the ground, amazed to see themselves healed and restored to life. They looked at one another and asked, "What miracle is this?" They leapt and shouted for joy, coming together like a great roaring ocean.

Indra bid farewell to Rama and departed along with all the other gods. As the gods' blazing chariots disappeared into the sky Rama ordered that the monkeys camp for the night, while he and Sita rested in Vibhishana's palace.

CHAPTER FIFTEEN

BACK TO AYODHYA

The following morning Vibhishana approached Rama and told him his bath was ready. The Rakshasa said, "Hot and cold baths, as well as every sort of cosmetic, unguents and perfume are ready, and we have prepared heavenly garments and garlands. Excellent maidservants, well-versed in the arts of decoration, are at your service, O Rama."

Rama replied that he had no desire for any kind of pleasure until after he had seen Bharata. He told Vibhishana, "That prince is now living in austerity. He bathes in cold rivers and eats only roots and fruits gleaned from the forest. How can I accept any luxuries?"

Rama asked Vibhishana to find some means by which he could return quickly to Ayodhya. Vibhishana replied that the heavenly Pushpaka chariot was available. "Ravana took this chariot, which moves according to one's will, from Kuvera. It still remains in Lanka, desiring to render you service, O Rama."

Vibhishana bowed low before Rama and repeatedly requested him to stay for a while in Lanka and accept his hospitality, but Rama was anxious to depart. He thought of his mother and of Bharata—how they must long to see him again! His exile was now over. He had promised to return immediately. If he did not return, they would surely be consumed by grief and anxiety. Bharata might even give up his life.

Rama said, "You have already fully honored me with your first-class counsel and advice. You have served me well on the battlefield and I am deeply indebted to you. But now you must grant me leave, O valiant Rakshasa. My task is accomplished and I must return quickly to Ayodhya."

Vibhishana acceded. He at once invoked the Pushpaka, and it appeared in the sky. Rama gazed with wonder at the glowing golden chariot, with its lofty, jewel-encrusted mansions and countless golden trellises wreathed with garlands of heavenly flowers.

After inviting Rama to board the chariot, Vibhishana said, "Is there any final service I can render you before you leave?"

Rama asked the Rakshasa to bestow riches upon all the monkeys. "Give them abundant gold and jewels to take back with them. The king should always reward his army. They should be well cared for and given everything they desire, for they must lay down their lives for his sake."

Vibhishana at once made arrangements for profuse wealth to be distributed to the monkeys. Then he helped Rama and Sita to ascend the chariot. Rama again thanked Vibhishana for his service and the Rakshasa sorrowfully watched him prepare to leave.

Just as Rama was about to depart, Sugriva approached him. "O Rama, pray take the monkeys with you," he begged. "We all desire to see you installed as the emperor. After that we will return to our own lands."

Rama smiled and agreed. He invited all the monkeys to mount the celestial chariot, which was like a golden city. Looking at Vibhishana he added, "You too should accompany me, O noble one. With all your kinsfolk and friends, please mount this chariot and come to Ayodhya."

Once everyone was on board, the Pushpaka rose high into the air. It flew gracefully, with an image of a great swan at its front seeming to draw it along. As it flew Rama pointed out to Sita the sights below. He showed her the battlefield, telling her how all the principal Rakshasas had been slain. While they crossed the sea he explained how Hanuman had leapt to Lanka.

As the chariot reached Kishkindha, Rama had it stop and he told Sugriva, "Quickly descend and fetch your wives and kinsfolk, O monkey. They too should be brought to Ayodhya."

With all the monkeys back aboard, the chariot continued. Soon they passed over the forest where Rama had spent his exile. When they reached Bharadvaja's hermitage, Rama desired to meet with the rishi. He stopped the chariot and went down to see the sage, bowing low before him. Bharadvaja offered his blessings and informed Rama that Bharata was anxious to see him. The sage knew of everything in Ayodhya from his disciples, who visited the city frequently. He told Rama that everyone was expecting his return at any moment.

Rama replied, "Please exert your power and make all the trees surrounding Ayodhya fill with heavenly fruits. All those who will travel to the city to witness my coronation should be amply fed."

At once Bharadvaja meditated and, by his mystic power, all the trees for twenty miles around Ayodhya became heavy with fruits. The sage said to Rama, "You should enter Ayodhya tomorrow after sending ahead a messenger."

Rama agreed and turned to Hanuman. He asked the monkey to proceed ahead to the city and inform Bharata that he would soon arrive. On the way the monkey should stop at Sringavera and inform Guha of the news.

Rama then said to Hanuman, "Closely observe Bharata's features when you tell him that I am returning. I wish to know his reaction. A kingdom rich in lands and wealth could surely attract anyone's mind. If he has developed an attachment for the kingdom, then I shall let him continue to rule as emperor."

Hanuman left at once. He bounded swiftly through the forestlands and soon reached Guha's abode, telling him the happy news. The Nishadha king was overjoyed and he immediately set about preparing to leave for Ayodhya.

Without delay Hanuman continued on to Ayodhya and he arrived early the following morning. At a distance of two miles from the city he found Bharata's dwelling. There he saw the prince, clad in black deerskins, emaciated from fasting, his hair matted. He sat by his wooden hut and shone with ascetic glory, and he was surrounded by his ministers and priests, dressed in similar ascetic clothing.

Hanuman approached Bharata and found him continuously repeating Rama's name. The monkey at once lay flat on the ground, offering his obeisances. Then, with folded palms, he stood before the prince and said, "Having completed his exile and slain Ravana, Rama will soon arrive, accompanied by Sita and Lakshmana. He has asked after your welfare and he longs to be reunited with you."

Bharata was overwhelmed with joy and sank to the ground in a faint. After regaining consciousness he stood up and embraced Hanuman. The prince shed tears of happiness and he spoke in an exuberant voice. "O monkey, I do not know if you are a god, a rishi or what, but you have told me the most wonderful news! I shall give you a hundred thousand cows and many beautiful maidens, adorned with gold and jewels."

Bharata asked Hanuman to tell him in full what had happened to Rama since his departure and the monkey recounted the tale. Bharata was delighted. He told Shatrughna to go into the city and spread the news of Rama's impending return. Bharata ordered that the city be fully decorated with pennants and garlands, and everyone should come out to greet Rama.

Hanuman could easily understand Bharata's heart. Rama should have no doubt about his brother. His devotion for Rama was obviously no less than the devotion Hanuman himself felt. The monkey shed tears of joy as he witnessed Bharata's display of love for Rama.

Shatrughna, along with Bharata's ministers, went into the city and began to prepare. They had Kaushalya and Sumitra placed upon palanquins and brought to Nandigram, where Bharata was living. Behind them came thousands of citizens, some walking, some on elephants or horseback, and others in chariots. The blast of conches and the roll of drums was tumultuous. A great roar came from the huge crowds, and it appeared as if the entire population of Ayodhya had come out of the city. The fourteen years of Rama's exile had already ended and all the citizens longed only for his return. Many other monarchs were also present in Ayodhya, having been invited by Bharata to be present when Rama returned.

By the end of day the whole region of Nandigram was completely crowded with people, all hoping for a glimpse of Rama. Bharata stood gazing to the south. He felt anxious. Had this monkey been telling the truth? Was Rama really about to return? When would he arrive? He questioned Hanuman again and again, and the monkey repeatedly reassured him.

Suddenly Bharata saw in the distance the shining Pushpaka. Hanuman then shouted, pointing it out to Bharata. "Here comes the highly glorious Rama!" he cried.

The shout was echoed by the crowd of citizens and a great clamor arose. They looked with amazement at the celestial vehicle carrying Rama and Sita, which appeared above the horizon like the sun and moon joined together. Bharata fell to the ground like a rod, offering his prostrated obeisances with his arms outstretched toward the chariot.

The Pushpaka descended to earth and Rama dismounted along with Lakshmana and Sita. Bharata ran over to them with Shatrughna, and the four brothers embraced each other for a long time. All the principal monkeys, headed by Sugriva, Angada and Hanuman, assumed human forms and disembarked from the chariot. Along with Vibhishana they were greeted warmly by Bharata, who embraced them all. Bharata said to Sugriva, "You are like a fifth brother to all of us, O monkey king!"

Rama saw Kaushalya nearby and he broke free from the crowd of people who were pressing in around him. Quickly approaching his mother, he fell before her and clasped her feet. She was pale and emaciated through grief and separation from her son. Next to her was Sumitra, who appeared in a similar condition. Rama also bowed before her and touched her feet with reverence. As they met Rama the faces of both of those ladies looked like celestial lotuses in full bloom.

Rama greeted Kaikeyi and the other royal ladies who had come there. He offered his obeisance to Vasishtha and the brahmins, who uttered auspicious hymns from the Vedas. Rama then bowed at the feet of his father-in-law Janaka, who shed tears of joy to see him returned safe with Sita. As he stood up and looked around, Rama smiled at the citizens, bringing joy to their hearts.

Bharata brought Rama's sandals, which had been kept upon Ayodhya's throne. He placed them before Rama and said, "Here is the entire kingdom, held in trust by me on your behalf. Now I render it back to you, O Rama. My birth has borne fruit today and my deepest desire is fulfilled, for I see you returned as the king of Ayodhya."

Bharata told Rama that everything in the kingdom, its exchequer, storehouses, army and crops, had increased tenfold while he was gone. "All this is due to your influence alone, O Rama, for I ruled the kingdom thinking only of your example."

Rama embraced Bharata again and again, and the two brothers shed tears of joy. Seeing the display of affection between them, the monkeys and Vibhishana wept.

Rama then looked up at the Pushpaka and said, "O Pushpaka, you may now return to your master, Kuvera. I thank you for your service." The heavenly chariot then rose into the sky and disappeared.

When everyone was seated, Bharata addressed Rama. "Please assume the rulership of this world. Although I have officiated in your absence, I can no more rule in your presence than a candle can give light in the presence of the sun. Let the world see you shining with dazzling splendor after being consecrated upon the throne of Ayodhya. We all long only for this, O Raghava."

Rama replied, "Let it be so," and a great cheer went up from the assembly. Rama then had the royal barbers cut his hair which was still in a mass of matted locks. He took his bath and dressed in costly silks and brilliant gold ornaments. Many garlands of celestial flowers were hung around his neck and he was daubed with sandal-paste of various colors.

Emperor Dasarath's widows dressed and decorated Sita. Her splendid beauty captivated the soul of whoever looked upon her. When Rama and his three brothers were all prepared, Bharata summoned Sumantra and the royal chariot. He personally took the reins and Rama climbed aboard with Sita. As the chariot proceeded toward the city, Lakshmana and Vibhishana fanned Rama on either side with white whisks, while Shatrughna held the royal parasol over his head.

Hundreds of sages walked in front of the chariot chanting mantras and hymns. Behind the chariot came Sugriva, still in human semblance, riding upon a great elephant and followed by nine thousand other elephants bearing other monkeys. The procession moved in state through Ayodhya accompanied by the blast of countless conches and the roll of thousands of drums. They were followed by crowds of citizens all anxious to see Rama's coronation.

The city streets were beautifully decorated with flags and garlands. From the balconies of the mansions women threw handfuls of flower petals and parched rice. Rama looked around at everyone and smiled, raising his hand in blessing.

Rama entered his father's palace and ordered Bharata to take Sugriva to his own palace. Bharata left Rama to rest for the night and, after arranging for all the monkey's accommodations, he told Sugriva, "The coronation will take place tomorrow. Please arrange to fetch water from the ocean and rivers."

Sugriva agreed and summoned Hanuman, Jambavan, Rishabha and Gavaya. He gave each of them a golden pail encrusted with gems and told them to bring water from each of the four oceans in the north, south, east and west. The monkeys bounded away and swiftly carried out the order. Another five hundred monkeys fetched water from different sacred rivers all over the country. By morning all this water had been given to Vasishtha for the ceremony.

The coronation began early in the morning and Rama was ritualistically bathed by the brahmins. Sixteen beautiful virgin girls consecrated him, in accordance with the scriptural procedure. Following this, Rama was bathed by his ministers and chief warriors, and then by the leaders of the trading community.

From the air the four guardians of the worlds sprinkled Rama with celestial nectar. When the bathing was over Vasishtha had the crown placed on Rama's head. This crown had been created by Brahma and was first worn by Manu himself. It shone with the brilliance of the sun. Wearing that golden crown and seated upon a throne made of precious stones, Rama was radiant and difficult to behold. Seated next to him was the exquisitely adorned Sita, enhancing Rama's grandeur and magnificence.

Vayu came in person and presented to Rama an unfading garland of a hundred celestial lotuses, which imbued its wearer with unfailing vigor and energy. At the urging of Indra he also gave Rama a priceless necklace of pearls interspersed with heavenly jewels of every variety. Taking that necklace, Rama turned and placed it on Sita's breast. She immediately lifted it in her two delicate hands and glanced over at Hanuman. Understanding her desire, Hanuman knelt before the princess and she placed the necklace over his head. Rising up again with that celestial ornament on his chest, Hanuman appeared like a a dark thundercloud decorated with lightning bolts.

Gandharvas sang while the Apsaras danced their mind-stealing dances, filled with movements and gestures deep with meaning. The huge crowds cried out "Victory to Rama!" and "All glories to Sita and Rama!"

The earth itself seemed to rejoice and gave forth abundant crops and fruits, as well as flowers which released a delightful fragrance carried on gentle breezes. The gods filled the canopy of the sky, and all the divine beings experienced the highest ecstasy upon seeing Rama united with Sita. Rama turned to Sita and smiled. His purpose was fulfilled.

EPILOGUE

A month had passed since the coronation. Gradually the celebrations ended and life in Ayodhya returned to normal. Knowing that his guests were thinking of returning to their own kingdoms, Rama began to say his farewells. He spoke first to his father-in-law, Janaka, who had been staying with him in his palace. Folding his palms in reverence, Rama said, "My lord, surely you are our immovable support. We stand protected by you, O king. By virtue of your ascetic power and your blessings I was able to slay Ravana. The bonds of affection between our two families are unbreakable. Please accept these gifts and then feel free to proceed back to Mithila at your pleasure. Bharata and Shatrughna will follow at your heels to escort you there."

Tears filled Janaka's eyes as he witnessed Rama's humility. He looked over at the great pile of riches Rama was offering him. "I feel gratified simply by your sight, O Rama. Let all this wealth be bestowed upon my daughter Sita. I have no wish to leave, but duty dictates that I return to Mithila. I shall now depart, but my mind will never leave you."

Janaka rose to leave and tightly embraced Rama. He then went out of the chamber followed by his ministers and by Bharat and Shatrughna.

One by one, Rama said fond farewells to all the other kings who had come for the coronation, offering each of them gold and other wealth as parting gifts. Those kings all expressed their sorrow to be leaving and gazed at Rama's face without feeling satiated. After circumambulating him in respect, they gathered together their followers and armies and slowly marched out of Ayodhya. The earth shook as the many hundreds of kings and princes left the city on their golden chariots, accompanied by their multitudes of troops. As they left they expressed their disappointment that they and their armies had not been able to join Rama in his fight against Ravana. "Surely this great display of might is useless as we were not able to engage it in Rama's service," they lamented. "Bharata summoned us too late."

When all the kings had gone, Rama spoke with the monkey chiefs. He thanked them again for all their service and embraced them with love. Taking valuable ornaments from his own body, Rama placed them on the bodies of Angada and Hanuman. He spoke affectionately to all the monkeys, offering them profuse quantities of riches. "O Vanaras, you should depart now for Kishkindha. Rule over your subjects with justice and love. You have all rendered me a very great service which I shall never forget."

Hanuman knelt before Rama and folded his palms. "O Rama, I do not know how I can leave you. I have one request before I go. Please let my supreme affection for you stand forever. May my devotion remain constant and may life remain in my body for as long as your story is being told on this earth. Let me stay in some heavenly region, continuously hearing your story being told to me by Apsaras and other celestial beings. In this way my pain of separation from you will be allayed."

Rama smiled. "It shall be so, O prince of monkeys. Your life and indeed your fame will endure for as long as my story lasts in the world. That will be for as long as the worlds themselves last. I am forever indebted to you, O monkey. May my obligation to you stay always in my heart. May the time never come when I need to repay your service, for such times are times of difficulty."

The monkeys, who felt as if the past month in Rama's company had been only a day, reluctantly departed from Ayodhya, their eyes filled with tears and their minds absorbed in thoughts of Rama.

Rama then said his farewell to Vibhishana, asking him to rule Lanka with righteousness. He also instructed the Pushpaka chariot to make its way back to Kuvera in the heavenly planets. Within a few days everyone had left and Rama began his rule of Ayodhya, assisted by Lakshmana and guided by the rishis. Within some days of his guests' departure, Rama was visited by a number of great sages, headed by Agastya. After they had been received with all respect by Rama, they took their seats in his assembly hall. Questioned by Rama, Agastya related everything about Ravana's birth and history, as well as that of all the principal Rakshasas. The sage also told the royal court about the history of the great Vanaras.

After Agastya had finished speaking, Rama said, "O all-powerful sage, I am amazed at hearing your wonderful narrations. By your very sight we have all been blessed, but I have one request. Soon I shall perform sacrifices for the good of the world. Please bless me that these will be successful. Indeed, if it pleases you, then come again to Ayodhya at that time to grace us with your holy presence."

Rama requested all the sages to attend his sacrifice and they replied, "It shall be so." Then they rose in a body and left the assembly.

*   *   *

As Rama ruled over Ayodhya everything became auspicious. It was seen that nobody died prematurely, nor was their any fear of diseases. The world had no robbers and no one suffered any harm from others. Every crea-ture felt pleased and all men were devoted to righteousness. They performed all their duties as service to Rama, and they always thought of him within their hearts. Rains fell when desired and the earth gave forth abundant pro-duce. All people had everything they needed and were fully satisfied, being free from avarice.

Two years passed. One day Rama was walking with Sita in the palace gardens. Having just heard that she had become pregnant, he smiled broadly and exclaimed, "Excellent! O beautiful lady, tell me what desire of yours should be fulfilled."

As they strolled Sita admired the many blossoming trees and bushes in the garden. She was reminded of her time with Rama in the forest. Remembering the celestial beauty of the forest, she said, "O Lord, I have a longing to once more visit the penance groves inhabited by the sages. Let me stay there for a night at the feet of those rishis."

Rama squeezed Sita's hand. "O princess, be it so. You will surely go tomorrow."

The couple sat down in a shaded bower where they were entertained by Apsaras and Naga damsels, who danced to the exquisite music played by Gandharvas. Soon the sun set and they retired for the evening into the palace inner chambers.

The following morning after he had performed his religious rituals Rama entered his council hall. Taking his seat on a great golden throne, he enquired from his chief minister, "O Bhadra, tell me what are the talks of the people? What do they say about me and about my rule? Kings who are not devoted to duty are criticized everywhere."

With joined palms Bhadra replied, "O King, delightful are the talks I have heard from the people. Mostly they discuss your conquest over Ravana and recovery of Mother Sita."

Bhadra glanced downward as he spoke and Rama, catching the ges-ture, asked, "What else do they say, O minister? Leave nothing out. Tell me both the good and the ill words which are spoken. I shall then know what must be done by myself. O Bhadra, speak without any fear or anguish."

Bhadra took a deep breath. "O Lord, listen as I relate the words I have heard while moving among the people. Everywhere—in market places, pub-lic squares, crossroads and in the forests—the people are heard to recite the glories of your wonderful victory. However, O great emperor, I have also heard criticism."

Bhadra described how some of the citizens were questioning Rama's acceptance of Sita back into his home. "They say that the princess, having been taken onto Ravana's lap and kept by him for almost one year, cannot now be considered pure. Because, O Rama, you have allowed her back into your house, these people say they will have to tolerate similar unchaste behavior from their own wives. Whatever a king does becomes acceptable behavior for all the people."

Bhadra looked down at the mosaic floor. Tears fell from the corners of his eyes. He had not wanted to tell his master about the criticisms, but he knew that nothing could be kept concealed from Rama.

Rama appeared shocked. He looked around at his other ministers. "Is this true? Are such talks indulged in by the citizens?"

All the ministers appeared aggrieved. They affirmed what Bhadra had said, each of them bowing low before Rama as he spoke.

Rama became pensive. He dismissed the court and asked that Lakshmana be summoned. As the prince entered the court he saw Rama sitting with downcast expression, seeming like an eclipsed sun. He hurried to his side and asked what was wrong. Rama explained everything, then said, "Dear brother, the calumny of the people eats into my very vitals. It can never be tolerated by a virtuous monarch. Surely I knew that this criticism would ensue, and thus did I test Sita at the time of her return. However, it seems that even though the gods have attested to her purity the citizens are still not satisfied. Alas, surely one's infamy is easily proclaimed in this world."

Rama shook his head as he went on, "Infamy is to be avoided by all means. It is censured even by the gods. As long as one's infamy remains current on earth one stays in hell. Great souls always endeavour for fame and good repute in this world. To avoid disrepute I would give up my brothers or even my own life—what then of Sita?"

Rama instructed the astonished Lakshmana to immediately take Sita out of Ayodhya and into the forest, where she should be left. She was already expecting to go there for a visit, so he would not need to tell her the truth. Rama spoke gravely, "I will not hear any arguments against this, dear brother. Sita should be taken this very day to Valmiki's ashrama which lies on the banks of the Ganges. After leaving her there, come back alone to Ayodhya."

Having spoken, Rama left the court and went with a heavy heart to his personal quarters. Lakshmana slowly made his way toward Sita's rooms. Surely this was the most difficult task he had ever faced. If it were left to him, thought Lakshmana, he would go out and find the men who were criticizing Rama and put them straight. Where was the question that Sita could ever be unchaste? What fault had Rama committed? But Rama's order could not be avoided. Lakshmana had Sumantra prepare his chariot and he

went before Sita, telling ther that Rama had asked him to fulfill her desire
to visit the forest.

Highly pleased, Sita asked her servants to gather together many costly
garments and precious jewels. "I shall distribute these to the wives of the
rishis," she said, smiling.

Lakshmana said nothing in reply. He turned and walked toward the
chariot, with Sita following behind. As she walked she began to notice
unusual omens. She spoke in surprise. "O son of Sumitra, why is it that my
right eye throbs and my limbs shiver? My heart feels heavy and my mind is
filled with anxiety. The earth itself seems distressed and all quarters appear
desolate. May all be well with my lord and indeed with all living beings."

Sita prayed with folded hands as she made her way out of the palace.
Reaching the chariot, Lakshmana said, "All is well, O Queen. There is no
cause for fear. I think your mind is disturbed at the thought of separation
from Rama for even a day. Ascend the chariot and we shall leave at once for
the banks of the auspicious Ganges."

Feeling reassured, Sita climbed aboard the large chariot and
Lakshmana jumped up next to Sumantra in the front. The charioteer urged
on the horses and they set off for the forest. After journeying for most of the
day they arrived at the riverbank, close to Valmiki's ashrama. The three
travellers got down and offered their respects to the holy river, bowing their
heads to the ground.

Thinking of Rama's order that he return at once, Lakshmana looked at
Sita, who was kneeling by the side of the river offering prayers. The time had
come to leave her. She would have no difficulty finding Valmiki's ashrama,
which lay only a short distance away along a smooth forest path. Ashamed
of himself for abandoning the queen, the prince did not want to enter the
ashrama. He sighed deeply. Now he would have to tell Sita the truth. Losing
control of himself, he suddenly let out a great cry and fell to the earth.

Sita looked up in surprise. "What ails you, O Lakshmana? We are here
by the banks of the sacred Ganges and about to see the great rishis. Why do
you wail at such a happy moment? You are making me sad. I know you are
always by Rama's side. Is it that separation from him for even two days is so
intolerable? O hero, take heart. Rama is just as dear to me, but I do not give
way to such sorrow."

Sita asked Lakshmana to take her to the ascetics's hermitage. "Let us
spend a single night with those sages, dear Lakshmana, and then return to
Rama's presence."

Lakshmana slowly got up. His face was covered with tears and his body
trembled. He folded his palms and replied with difficulty, "O auspicious one,
my heart feels as though pierced with a dart. I have been entrusted with a

task that will make me worthy of the whole world's censure. Surely I would
rather die."

Sita was mystified. She had no idea what he meant. Feeling perturbed,
she asked, "What is wrong, my dear brother? Is something amiss with Rama.
Speak out the truth at once."

Lakshmana sighed. Gazing downwards, he said, "O Janaki, before we
left Ayodhya your husband was told about a most painful rumour circulating among the people. The words he heard cannot be repeated by me. Yet
even though you have been proven to be free from blame by the gods themselves, Rama could not ignore the complaints. Struck with grief, he ordered
me to bring you here and then return alone. O gentle lady, you have been
forsaken by him out of fear of disrepute."

Lakshmana broke off, too pained to continue. Sita stood as though petrified. She could hardly believe what she was hearing. Had she been born
only to experience grief? Covering her face with her two bejewelled hands,
she dropped to the earth with a piteous wail.

Getting a grip on himself, Lakshmana said, "Do not give way to sorrow,
O queen. Here is Valmiki's delightful ashrama. Approach him for shelter
and live here peacefully. Remain loyal to your husband, observe fasts and
practice prayer and meditation. Keeping Rama forever in your heart, you
will doubtlessly secure your everlasting welfare."

Sita fainted and lay on the ground looking like a wild creeper bedecked
with blossoms and torn from a tree. Coming round after some moments, she
began to lament, "Alas, this mortal frame was certainly fashioned by the creator simply for sorrow. Indeed, today it seems like the very embodiment of
grief. What sin did I commit that I should suffer in this way? How can I live
all alone in the hermitages of the sages? What will I say to those ascetics
when they ask me why I was abandoned by the great Raghava? I would at
once drown myself in the flowing Ganges, but I would thus break Rama's
line by killing his unborn child. O Lakshmana, do what you must. Forsake
me, the miserable one, but listen first to what I have to say now."

Sita got to her feet. Shaking with sorrow, she held onto a tree for support as she spoke to Lakshmana. "O tiger among men, go then to Ayodhya
and leave me here. After offering my respects to all my seniors, please say
this to my lord: 'O Raghava, you should always act in such a way as to
ensure your unrivalled fame in this world. Surely my abandonment is necessary to save you from ill-repute. Thus, although torn by grief, I feel no
anger. For a chaste woman the husband is the master, deity and preceptor.'"

Having spoken her message for Rama, Sita dropped again to the
ground. Lakshmana looked at her with tear-filled eyes. Unable to make any
reply, he cried loudly and bowed his head to the earth. He then walked

around Sita with his palms folded. After regaining his balance of mind, he said, "O faultless one, to say farewell I now look upon your face for the first time. Oh, how can I bear to see you separated from Rama and dwelling in the deep forest?"

Crying, Lakshmana bowed again to Sita and then ascended his chariot, where Sumantra sat in silent sorrow. He urged on the horses and the chariot moved off. As he went along the path away from the river, the grief-stricken Lakshmana could hear Sita's plaintive cries echoing through the woods, resembling those of a peacock calling for its mate.

Shortly after Lakshmana had left, a couple of young ascetics were walking in the woods to gather firewood when they heard Sita's sobs. Spying her through the trees, they ran back to their hermitage and spoke to Valmiki. "Sir, some noble lady looking exactly like the Goddess of Fortune lies near the riverbank, crying loudly in despair. Perhaps she has descended from the heavens. She certainly does not deserve any pain or sorrow. In our view she is a divine woman who has sought your shelter. O lord, we feel she is worthy of your protection."

Valmiki could understand everything by virtue of his inner vision. Taking up an offering of arghya, he went quickly toward the river followed by his disciples. The effulgent sage found Sita lying with her arms outstretched, weeping. He spoke to her comfortingly. "O gentle one, I know you are Dasarath's daughter-in-law and the beloved queen of Rama. I am Valmiki. Welcome to my hermitage. By my meditations I have understood why you are here. Indeed, all that exists within the three worlds is known to me. I thus know of your purity and blamelessness. O child, be composed and accept this offering. Come with me to the ashrama of the female ascetics. They will surely take care of you as if you were their own daughter. It will be exactly like your own home."

Sita bowed respectfully to the sage and accepted the arghya he was proffering. She replied, "Let it be as you say, O great rishi."

Valmiki led the way to the ladies' ashrama. As they reached that secluded and delightful part of the woods, some of the elder ladies came out to greet them. One of them asked, "What would you have us do, O greatest of sages?"

Valmiki introduced Sita to the ladies and asked that they take good care of her. He told them that she was expecting Rama's child and should be afforded all affection and respect, exactly as they would show the sage himself. Receiving their assurances, he then returned back to his own ashrama, Sita began to reside with the ascetics, her mind always rapt in thought of Rama.

* * *

For some time Lakshmana and Sumantra travelled in silence, thinking of Sita. Finally, as the chariot came out of the forest and onto the main road leading to Ayodhya, Lakshmana said, "O charioteer, how great must be Rama's grief that he is again separated from Sita. Truly this is the effect of destiny. Fate is inexorable. Is it not astonishing that Rama, who could extirpate the entire celestial hosts, should have to submit to fate? It seems to me that Rama was more pained by banishing Sita than he was by his own exile and even her abduction. Why did he submit to the cruel words of the citizens? What virtue did he acquire?"

Sumantra comforted Lakshmana. He then told him of a story he had long ago heard from the rishi Durvasa. "This sage once stayed at Vasishta's hermitage. O prince, at that time your father went there and I drove his chariot. He enquired from Durvasa about the prospects for his sons—how long they would live and rule over the world. Durvasa then narrated the following history."

Lakshmana listened attentively as Sumantra repeated what he had heard from the rishi. Durvasa had described how in ancient times the Daityas had been conquered in battle by the gods. They had fled and sought shelter in the ashrama of the powerful sage Bhrgu. Only the sage's wife had been present and, out of compassion, she let them hide in the ashrama. When Vishnu, who was assisting the gods in their campaign against the Daityas, learned of this, he became angry with Bhrgu's wife and severed her head with his discus. Bhrgu had then returned and seen his wife slain by Vishnu. He immediately cursed Vishnu, saying, "As you have killed my innocent spouse, so you will take birth in the mortal world and meet with separation from your wife for many years."

Sumantra concluded his story. "As soon as he uttered the curse Bhrgu became sorry and he bowed at Vishnu's feet and worshipped him. However, Vishnu said, 'O sage, for the good of the world I shall accept this curse.' Durvasa then went on to explain that, although Rama would become the lord of Ayodhya and rule over the earth for eleven thousand years, he would be separated from Sita. Thus it has come to pass, O Lakshmana, for the words of the rishis can never fail."

As Sumantra ended his story the chariot approached Ayodhya. Entering the city, Lakshmana went at once to the royal court. He found Rama seated on his throne with his face downcast. Lakshmana fell at his feet and told him that Sita had been left at Valmiki's ashrama. In a pained voice he said, "Do not grieve, O tiger among men. All gains end in loss, all elevations end in a fall, all union must end in separation, and life itself always ends in death. The wise therefore do not become attached to wives, sons, friends or riches. You know this well, O Rama, therefore take heart and shake off your sorrow."

Lakshmana assured Rama that the disrepute among the people would now be destroyed by Rama's act of sending Sita away. Rama appeared encouraged by Lakshmana. He smiled and replied, "What you say is true, O hero. I shall take joy in the execution of my duties, for this is the path to everlasting happiness. Let us rest now for the night."

Rama stood up and embraced his brother, and they then retired to their quarters.

*   *   *

Twelve years of Rama's rule went by. During that period his dominion over the earth became firmly established as all other monarchs paid him tribute. His brother Shatrughna slew a powerful demon named Lavana and all other demonic elements were subdued. Rama then thought of performing an Ashvamedha sacrifice for the benefit of the world. Arrangements were made and invitations sent out to all the kings of the earth, as well as to many great rishis. Valmiki was also invited and he prepared himself to go to Ayodhya.

While in Valmiki's ashrama Sita had given birth to twin sons named Lava and Kusha. The boys had been lovingly raised by Valmiki as if they were his own sons. Despite never having seen their father, they had flourished in Valmiki's ashrama and grown into powerful youths. Valmiki had taught them all Vedic knowledge and had also taught them Rama's story, which they became expert in reciting.

As the time for Rama's sacrifice approached, Valmiki took both Lava and Kusha, as well as hundreds of his other disciples, and went to Ayodhya. He entered the sacrificial arena like the sun surrounded by glowing planets. As soon as Rama saw him he immediately ordered that he be worshipped and offered a place of honour in the sacrifice. After he had been shown to his quarters, Valmiki said to Lava and Kusha, "Tomorrow you two should go among the brahmins here and sing the Ramayana. Go also to Rama's palace and sing this most holy narration where the king will hear it. If Rama calls you before him, then you should recite to him the poem in its entirety. Sing it to the best of your ability and with a pure heart. Do not let your minds be captivated by the opulence and wealth that you see. If Rama should ask whose sons you are, you should tell him that you are two disciples of Valmiki."

The two humble and obedient boys replied, "We shall do exactly as you ask, O lord." The boys were eager to meet Rama. As well as knowing the Ramayana by heart, they had heard their mother speak many times about Rama and, although they had come to see Valmiki as their father, they knew they were Rama's actual sons. Looking forward to meeting Rama the next day, they lay down happily for sleep by the side of the sage.

Two hours before sunrise the boys rose and performed their ablutions. After saying their morning prayers they made their way to the assembly of brahmins and began to sing the Ramayana. As they sang they expertly played upon lutes, and the music they produced stole the heart and captivated the mind. The brahmin sages were enthralled and they repeatedly applauded the boys. "Excellent! Well done! We are all amazed by this magnificent poem. Its exquisite music and metre are without compare. It is replete with the nine sentiments of love, pathos, mirth, heroism, terror, wrath, disgust, wonder and serenity. The boys' expert singing creates a vivid picture of the story they are telling, and we feel as if we are seeing it actually happen."

The sages gazed in wonder at the twins. They both looked like Rama himself and were endowed with many auspicious marks. After making various gifts to the boys, the brahmins said, "This song, composed by Valmiki, will be sung by poets throughout all the ages. It is conducive to long life, begets prosperity, invokes all good fortune and ravishes the ears and mind of the hearer. Go now, dear boys, and recite it for the pleasure of Rama himself."

The twins offered their obeisances to the sages and went at once to the palace compound, where they again began to sing. Hearing them from within the palace, Rama immediately ordered that they be brought in. They were offered golden seats within the royal court and Rama said to them, "O ascetics, we have heard your excellent singing. Please recite your poem here for the pleasure of the brahmins in this court, as well as my brothers and myself. I think there is no song its equal, nor indeed singers such as yourselves."

Rama looked carefully at the two boys. He turned to Lakshmana and said, "Although dressed as ascetics, these two appear like rulers of the earth. Surely they are from royal stock, or even have some divine origin. Let us listen now as they repeat their wonderful poem."

The entire royal assembly sat enchanted while the boys sang. As evening approached and they completed their recitation, Rama said, "Wonderful, wonderful! O boys, we desire to know who you are and from where you have come. I wish to bestow upon you gold and other gifts in abundance."

The boys replied that they were Valmiki's disciples. Remembering the rishi's instructions, they politely declined Rama's offer of wealth and asked his permission that they be allowed to return to Valmiki. Rama agreed and the boys departed, leaving the assembly astonished and entranced by what they had heard.

After they had gone Rama dismissed the assembly and sat alone. Hearing his sons recite his life story had made him think of Sita. He longed to see her again and it was ordained by scripture that a king should perform sacrifice with his wife. It had been twelve years since Sita's departure and he had not seen her since. His heart had often ached with her separation but he had wanted to make absolutely certain that the people had no cause at all to criticize him. Feeling that this had now been achieved, Rama desired to bring Sita to the sacrifice. He summoned Bhadra and said, "Please have the venerable sage Valmiki informed that I would like him to fetch Sita. Let both he and the queen herself take oath before the assembly that she has always remained pure. I do not want any further obloquy about myself or Sita circulating in the kingdom."

Bhadra, surprised and gladdened by Rama's request, replied, "It shall be done as you wish, my Lord." Envoys left at once and told Valmiki of Rama's desire. The sage immediately made arrangements for Sita to be brought from his hermitage. He told the messengers that she would be present the following day and they left to inform Rama.

The next morning Rama addressed the royal court. "Today the noble Sita will come to the sacrifice. There she will take oath as to her purity, supported by the great rishi Valmiki, who has given her shelter these last twelve years. I desire that all the kings and sages hear this testimony. Indeed, let as many people as may desire be present."

The assembly cheered Rama and everyone began to make their way to the sacrifical arena outside the city. All of them longed to see Rama and Sita united again. Although they did not question Rama's judgement, it had broken their hearts when he had sent the queen away. For twelve years they had prayed for this day when she might return.

Gradually the vast arena filled up with royalty and rishis. All the greatest sages in the world came there. Narada, Parvata, Vasishta, Vamadeva, Kashyapa, Vishvamitra, Durvasa, Chyavana, and hundreds more were seen there. Representatives of the Rakshasas, as well as many Vanaras, Gandharvas and other celestials arrived. In the sky the gods assembled and Rama took his place in the arena.

Valmiki then made his way into the center of the arena, followed by Sita. She was dressed in an ochre-colored sari and her golden earrings glinted in the sunshine as she walked with her head down. Although she thought only of Rama within her heart, out of fear she did not look up at him. She folded her palms in respect and stood silently before her husband.

Seeing the queen with downcast expression, the assembly was agitated and gave out various cries. Some were sorrowful, some praised Rama, and still others praised Sita. When everyone finally settled down, Valmiki began to speak.

"O son of Dasarath, out of fear of criticism this pious Sita of righteous conduct was left by you near my hermitage. She will now testify to you as to her unfailing purity. I too can swear that this chaste lady is sinless. I do not remember ever having spoken an untruth. O Rama, know for sure that Sita is entirely free from wicked conduct of any kind. Know also that the two boys who recited the Ramayana to you are certainly both your sons. I have practiced penance for many thousands of years and if my words are false, then may I not obtain the fruit of that asceticism. Knowing that Sita was innocent, I accepted her into my ashrama. She is devoted to you only, O Raghava, and will never sway from you under any circumstances."

Rama smiled. "It is exactly as you say, O brahmin. I also know Sita to be without blame. This was previously established by even the gods and thus did I allow her to enter my house. Only due to public censure did I send her away again, even though I never doubted her innocence. Please forgive me. I hereby proclaim my love for the chaste Sita. I also accept these two boys, Lava and Kusha, as my sons. Let her now take oath before this assembly and establish her purity once and for all."

Sita slowly looked up at her husband who gazed at her with affection. She glanced around the assembly. As well as many kings and rishis, she saw all classes of celestials standing there—Adityas, Vasus, Rudras, Sadhyas, Vishvadevas, Nagas and numerous others. Above the assembly on his swan carrier sat Brahma, the universal creator, surrounded by all the principal gods. Everyone waited silently for Sita to speak.

With her hands folded in front of her face, Sita looked down again and said in a tremulous voice, "If I have never even thought about anyone other than Rama, then may the earth goddess grant me shelter. As I worship only Rama in mind, speech and action, so may the earth give me space. If I have truthfully said that I know only Rama as my lord, let the earth receive me now."

Sita felt that she had become a problem for Rama. Despite having been declared pure by even the ever-truthful gods, still the doubts remained. It seemed that as long as she was present there would be those who would find fault with Rama. She would have given up her life the very day she had been sent away to the forest if she had not been pregnant with Rama's sons. Now the boys were old enough to join their father in the city. It was time for her to depart. Rama's reputation could not be sullied by even the slightest doubt and only her departure could ensure that.

As Sita finished speaking the ground next to her opened up and a celestial throne rose up. That brilliant, bejewelled seat was borne on the heads of four great Naga snakes. Sitting on it was Bhumi, the earth goddess, glowing with her divine effulgence. She rose up and held out her hand to Sita with gentle words of welcome. Sita got onto the throne and sat next to Bhumi. Suddenly a great shower of fragrant flowers fell from the sky and covered Sita. The gods loudly praised Sita and, as all the kings and rishis looked on in amazement, the throne slowly re-entered the earth. Everyone glorified Sita for her incomparable devotion and chastity to Rama.

Rama himself cried out as Sita disappeared into the earth, which again closed as the throne entered within. He leaned on the side of his seat and wept in grief. Wringing his hands in despair, he said, "Upon seeing Sita enter the earth I am afflicted with a sorrow greater than I have ever known before. How can I tolerate it? How shall I allow Sita to be taken by the earth? When she was stolen by Ravana I crossed the vast ocean on foot to recover her. I shall again bring her back or go with her for good."

Rama looked down at the earth. Becoming angry, he said, "O goddess, you should return Sita to me or you will feel my wrath. Sita was formerly brought out from your womb, thus you are my mother-in-law. Therefore be kind to me and return Sita, or else grant space to me also. I will stay with Sita wherever she has gone, whether it be heaven or the nether regions. O earth-goddess, hear my words or else I shall destroy you with all your mountains and forests."

Rama's eyes blazed in anger and he stood up, reaching for the bow by his side. Brahma then spoke from his position above the sacrifice.

"O Rama, Lord of all the worlds, do not be grieved. Remember your identity as Vishnu. By your own arrangement has this separation from Sita been ordained. The pure and noble daughter of Janaka has gone to celestial realms where you will see her again without doubt. O Lord, listen now as your sons finish the narration of Ramayana. They will recite to you all of your future acts, culminating in your return to your spiritual abode. Everything is happening according to your will, O Rama. Do not therefore destroy the world."

Rama was pacified by Brahma's speech and he sat down again. Seeing him peaceful, the gods departed for the heavens. As evening fell the assembly dispersed and Rama went sorrowfully back to his palace, taking his two sons with him.

The following morning Rama had Lava and Kusha sing the remaining portion of Ramayana, dealing with future events. Sitting amid his ministers and the court brahmins, Rama listened as the two boys recited the beautiful poetry they had heard from Valmiki. They briefly described the period of Rama's rule over the earth, a time of unparalleled peace and opulence. Their narration was concluded with a description of how Rama and his brothers would finally leave the world.

* * *

After Sita's departure from the world, Rama often thought of her. He could not even think of taking another wife and he had an exquisite gold image of Sita made by expert artisans. That statue sat next to him in the royal court and at sacrifices, serving as the queen. A period of eleven thousand years passed with Rama ruling the world, assisted by his three brothers. He performed ten thousand great sacrifices and the earth enjoyed unprecedented opulence. All creatures were happy and everything functioned in accordance with the arrangement of the Supreme Lord. Religion was firmly established and everyone led pious lives.

One day, toward the end of his rule, Rama was visited by an unusual ascetic, who glowed with a divine radiance. That brahmin, having been worshiped by Rama, introduced himself as a messenger of Brahma. He asked for a private audience with Rama, saying, "O emperor, no one should hear the words that pass between us. If anyone should interrupt us, then they must be killed by you." Agreeing to this request from the brahmin, Rama brought him into his personal quarters. He told Lakshmana to stand outside and prevent anyone from entering, explaining to him what the ascetic had said.

When they were alone, the ascetic said to Rama, "O Lord, you should know that I am Death. Brahma has asked me to come here and inform you that the time allotted for your earthly pastimes is drawing to a close. You have achieved all that you desired to achieve. Now, if it so pleases you, you may return to your own eternal abode."

Death described to Rama some of his former incarnations in the material world, concluding by saying, "O Rama, you are the eternal Supreme Being. You appear in the world to establish religion and destroy the demons. The time set by yourself for this incarnation is now almost over. Be pleased then to resume your place as the Lord and protector of the gods."

Rama laughingly replied, "O destroyer of all, welcome is your visit here. Surely your words fill me with pleasure. It is indeed time for my departure. Please return to Brahma and tell him that I and all my brothers shall leave within a short time."

As Rama spoke with Death, the great mystic Durvasa came to the city. Desiring to see Rama, he was shown into the palace, where he was met by Lakshmana. He asked for an audience with Rama, but Lakshmana told him Rama was busy at that time. Immediately blazing up with anger, Durvasa said, "I will not be kept waiting. Go at once, O son of Sumitra, and inform Rama of my presence. Otherwise know that I shall curse you, your brothers, this territory and all your descendents. Indeed, my anger is already difficult to contain."

Seeing the irascible sage preparing to utter a curse, Lakshmana bowed to him and quickly went towards Rama's quarters. Thinking, "Let there be only my death rather than that of all my kinsmen," he entered the room, where he saw Rama speaking with Death.

When Rama heard that Durvasa was waiting, he immediately came out to greet him. Touching the rishi's feet, he asked, "What shall I do to please you, O great one?"

Durvasa replied that he had been fasting for one thousand years and desired to take food that day and break his fast. "Kindly bring me cooked foods, O Rama, so that I may end my long penance."

Rama had Durvasa seated comfortably in the palace and he personally served him with varieties of excellent food. After the sage had left, and Death had also departed, Lakshmana said to Rama, "I must now die, dear brother, for that was the promise you made to Death. Punish me in accord with your word to that deity."

Remembering his discussion with Death, Rama felt shocked. Speechless with grief at the thought of separation from Lakshmana, he shed tears and stood gazing at his beloved brother. How could he be killed?

Lakshmana folded his palms and said, "Do not feel sorrow for me, O gracious one. Time is all-powerful. Bound by our former acts, we must all come under death's sway. O King, keep your promise without fear. Those men who break their promises will go to hell."

Rama sat down on his throne, struck with sorrow. He called for his ministers and informed them of what had taken place. Vasishta then said, "O Rama, all this was foreseen by me. The time for the conclusion of your pastimes has arrived. You should abandon Lakshmana now. Do not give up your promise, for if you do, then righteousness in this world will perish. Along with righteousness all beings will also be destroyed. Therefore, O lion among men, be separated from Lakshmana today."

Rama looked at Lakshmana. "I leave you, O son of Sumitra. Let not virtue suffer. Desertion and slaying are considered equal according to the wise. Therefore do I abandon you today."

Lakshmana prostrated himself before Rama with tears in his eyes. He then stood up and left the palace, going directly to the forest. Reaching the banks of the Sarayu, he sat down in meditation, preparing to observe the praya vow of fasting till death. With his eyes half-closed, he suspended his breathing and entered a deep trance. As he sat absorbed in thought of the Supreme, Indra came there invisible to all and took him away to the heavens. Thus it appeared to all men that Lakshmana had died.

Hearing of this, Rama was overcome by grief. He felt that he could not remain on earth any longer. Crying out in pain, he said, "I shall confer the kingdom on Bharat. This very day I will follow the path taken by Lakshmana."

Bharat replied, "How can I think of ruling the world in your absence, O Rama? Along with Shatrughna, we shall all leave together. Bestow the kingdom upon your two sons."

Vasishta agreed with Bharat. "This is proper, O Rama. The time fixed by yourself for your rule has all but ended. Surely you must now depart, taking your brothers who are all a part of yourself. Knowing this, the people have become afflicted with sorrow. They are lying prostrate on the ground, mortified at the thought of losing you."

Rama was upset to hear of the citizens' unhappiness. He called for their chief representatives and said, "What should I do to assuage your grief? I must now leave this world."

The citizens begged Rama to take them all with him. "Wherever you are going, O Lord, be it the forest, mountains, ocean, heaven or even hell, we desire to follow you. If it pleases you, let us accompany you."

Rama assented. "It shall be so." He then arranged for his sons to be coronated. Lava and Kusha could hardly face the prospect of separation from their father. They loudly lamented and fell to the earth when they heard that Rama was departing. Rama gently raised them and said, "Dear sons, you must remain on earth to carry on a righteous rule. Establish your capitals in the northern and southern territories. Always thinking of me, lead the people with justice and compassion. Surely we will be united again in the future."

Lava and Kusha tightly embraced their father and then left Ayodhya for their respective kingdoms, which became known as Kushavati and Sravasti, taking vast amounts of wealth with them.

After this Rama dressed himself in pure white silks and prepared to leave Ayodhya. The next morning he had brahmins take his sacred fire from the palace and lead the way toward the forest. With Vasishta reciting hymns from the Sama Veda, Rama went slowly out of the city seated on a great golden chariot. Those with divine sight could see by his two sides the goddesses Lakshmi and Bhumi. Ahead of him went the personified power of resolution, while all around him were his weapons in human forms. Rama was followed by the Vedas in the form of brahmins, as well by the goddess Gayatri and the personified form of Omkara, the divine syllable always meditated upon by great yogis.

All the female inhabitants of the palace then followed, accompanied by Bharat and Shatrughna. Crowds of ascetics, chanting Vedic mantras, came at the head of the citizens, who were grouped according to their respective classes. Hundreds of thousands of Vanaras, Rakshasas and bears also followed behind. Everyone left Ayodhya to go with Rama. Even the animals and birds left the city and went with the procession. No living creature of any kind remained in Ayodhya and they all made their way westward to the banks of the Sarayu.

As they travelled Rama met one last time with Hanuman to say his farewells. Embracing the monkey, he said, "You have made your decision to remain here on earth, so do not let your words become false."

Hanuman replied, "Surely I shall always be in your presence simply by hearing of your glories, O Lord. So long as your divine narration circulates in this world, so I shall remain."

Rama also asked two other Vanaras, Mainda and Dwivida, to stay behind, as well as the king of the bears Jambavan. They all bowed before Rama saying, "So be it." Meeting with Vibhishana, Rama said to him, "O best of the Rakshasas, you should stay in the world to rule over your people. As long as the sun and moon stay in the heavens, so will your rule last. Always worship Vishnu in his form as Jagannatha, the presiding deity of the Iksvakus." Accepting that order, Vibhishana prostrated himself before Rama and then left for Lanka.

Followed by his vast entourage, Rama traveled upriver to the point where it joined the Ganges, then went along the course of that holy river until he reached the foot of the mountain from where it emanated. At that place, where the path to heaven could be found, millions of divine chariots appeared. All the gods, headed by Brahma, were visible. Celestial music played by the Gandharvas could be heard and showers of flowers fell from the skies.

It was seen that Vishnu appeared in the sky on the back of Garuda. Within the sight of all, and being praised by the gods, Rama and his two brothers entered Vishnu's form. Every creature present, who were all absorbed in thoughts of Rama, then gave up their mortal bodies and assumed their eternal spiritual forms. The gods saw them rising up on celestial chariots toward Rama's undecaying abode in the spiritual world. It seemed to those celestials that the very city of Ayodhya went with Rama.

Astonished by this unprecedented sight, Brahma and the gods left for their own abodes, praising Rama within their hearts. His pastimes were complete.

JAYA SRI RAMA!

THE END

APPENDIX ONE

THE STORY OF THE RIVER GANGES

*Told by Vishvamitra to Rama and Lakshmana
upon reaching the Ganges*

In the far north there stands Himalaya, the king of mountains, whose presiding deity is known as Himavan. This Himavan, through his consort Mena, the daughter of the celestial Mount Meru, begot two charming daughters, both matchless in beauty. The elder of the two was named Ganga and, upon the supplication of the gods, she later became this holy river. The other girl was called Uma, and her father conferred her upon the unlimitedly powerful Shiva to be his wife. After marrying that girl, who is also known in this world as Parvati, Shiva sported with her in regions of celestial bliss.

Becoming concerned, the gods with Brahma at their head went before Shiva. They fell prostrate before him and said to him, "O lord, the worlds will not be able to bear your seed should it be released into Uma. The combined power of you and your consort will surely be unbearable to all beings. Please therefore retain your vital energy within your supremely splendid self. You will thereby preserve the worlds from being burned by the brilliance of your progeny."

Shiva, who always remains fixed in thought of Vishnu and is ever compassionate to all beings, replied, "It shall be as you say, for the words of the gods can never be denied. But my vital seed already stands dislodged from my heart. Where then shall it fall?"

Brahma replied, "Your seed should fall upon earth, for she alone is capable of withstanding its power, bearing as she does the weight of all creatures."

Shiva let fall his seed, which covered the whole globe. Brahma instructed Agni, the god of fire, "Accompanied by Vayu, move quickly across the surface of the earth and suck up Shiva's mighty seed. Previously the gods had asked me that I provide them with a powerful commander for their army. Cause Shiva's seed to be borne by Ganga, so that she may bring forth a blazing son who will become the general of the gods."

Agni at once caught up all of Shiva's vital fluid and went before Ganga, saying, "Be pleased to receive Shiva's seed, O Goddess!"

Ganga assumed an ethereal human form of exceptionally exquisite beauty. Upon seeing this form, Shiva's seed melted and the god of fire impregnated Ganga all over with that glowing fluid.

Burning with Shiva's fiery seed coursing through her veins, Goddess Ganga said to Agni, "O shining one, I cannot bear this flaming seed, which has been made even more powerful by your touch."

Agni told her to discharge the seed upon the Himalayas and Ganga immediately expelled it from her body. It emerged from her in a brilliant stream and fell upon the earth, forming vast veins of gold and silver. Even at a great distance mines of copper, lead and tin were created by that divine fluid.

At the exact spot where Shiva's vital seed landed there grew up a thicket of brilliant white reeds. The union of Ganga with the seed of Shiva conceived a child who was born from out of those reeds. He has become known in all the worlds as Skanda. Indeed, he is the powerful general of the gods, also famous as Karttikeya, for he was raised by the six goddesses known as the Krittikas. Even now that god can be seen in the sky shining amid the constellation of Krittika.

After Karttikeya's birth the gods approached Shiva's consort and, pleased in mind, worshipped her. However, she felt angry at having been denied union with her consort and, with bloodshot eyes, she pronounced a curse upon both the gods and the earth. "As I was denied my desire of getting a son, so too shall all you gods remain always issueless. This earth shall have a jagged surface of many shapes and forms and shall have many masters. She shall never enjoy the delight of having a son since she has deprived me of my own child."

Some time after this, a king named Sagara ruled over Ayodhya. From out of his two wives the king had sixty thousand and one sons. By the gods' arrangement, one wife gave birth to a fetus shaped like a gourd, which then split into sixty thousand pieces. These pieces were placed in sixty thousand pots of ghee and gradually they grew into babies. The other wife gave birth to a boy in the normal way.

The sixty thousand sons were of wicked conduct and caused pain to all living beings. The one son, however, was pious and became the beloved of all the people.

One day King Sagara performed a horse sacrifice for the good of the world. Upon seeing the sacrifice, Indra became concerned that Sagara may exceed him in pious merits and thereby take his post in heaven, which Indra himself had won by the performance of pious acts of sacrifice. Indra thus assumed the form of a fierce Rakshasa and seized the sacrificial horse, taking it away to a distant place.

King Sagara ordered his sixty thousand sons to search out that horse. The princes traveled all over the earth, but could not see the horse. They excavated the earth's surface and searched the subterranean regions, but still to no avail. Excavating and looking in all directions, the princes created havoc and killed innumerable creatures. The gods went before Brahma and asked that he stop them. Brahma informed them that Mother Earth is always protected by the Supreme Lord Vishnu, who was at at that time dwelling in the earth's subterranean region. Sagara's sons would soon be destroyed by that very Lord, who had assumed the form of a sage named Kapila.

In time the princes arrived before Kapila and found him seated in meditation. The sacrificial horse was grazing nearby, left there by Indra. Becoming furious they said to Kapila, "O evil-minded one, you have stolen this horse! We shall now kill you and take it back!"

Hearing this threat and seeing before him the sixty thousand sons of Sagara, Kapila, a sage of immeasurable power, became angry. Due to their offense in having assailed the divine rishi Kapila, all the princes were immediately burned to ashes by a fire which emanated from their own bodies.

After some time King Sagara became concerned about his sons. He ordered his one remaining son, Amsuman, to go after them. Amsuman also found Kapila sitting in meditation and saw before him his brothers' ashes, destroyed by their offense against the sage. Grieved by his brothers' deaths, Amsuman looked all around and saw Garuda, Vishnu's great eagle carrier who had come to serve his master. Garuda told Amsuman that he should devise some plan to bring the Ganges to earth so that her waters could flow across his brothers' ashes and thus liberate them from hell. Amsuman offered prayers to Kapila and received from him the horse, whereupon he went back to his father.

Despite every attempt to perform sacrifice and pray to the gods, neither Sagara nor his son were able to cause the Ganges to flow across the earth. It was several generations later that the famous King Bhagiratha finally succeeded. By dint of his great asceticism he pleased Brahma, who ordered the Ganges to fall to earth.

The river Ganges, known in heaven as the Mandakini, emanated originally from Vishnu's foot. When he kicked a small hole in the shell of the universe, the waters of the causal ocean, in which all the innumerable universes float, entered. Falling down to the heavens, the water was entered by the goddess Ganga who then, on Brahma's order, brought it down to earth. This water filled the huge excavation made by Sagara's sons and thereby became the great ocean. It flowed down to the subterranean region where it liberated the sixty thousand princes by covering their ashes. It is that same sacred river, made holy by the touch of Vishnu's foot, which you now see before you, O valiant princes. To this very day anyone whose ashes are placed in this river is immediately liberated.

APPENDIX TWO

THE HISTORY OF VISHVAMITRA

Told to Rama by Satananda, the priest of King Janaka

The sage Vishvamitra was once a king who ruled over the earth for many thousands of years. Collecting a great army comprising hundreds of thousands of soldiers on elephants, chariots, horses and foot, he set out on an expedition to examine his kingdom. Marching through many cities and states, over mountains and rivers, Vishvamitra came at last to the dwellings of the rishis. There he reached the hermitage of Vasishtha, the leader best and indeed the best of all the rishis. This most beautiful site was rich with all kinds of flowers, creepers and trees and was graced by the gods, Gandharvas, Siddhas and Charanas. It thronged with multitudes of celestial seers and sages, who shone like fire, and it hummed with the constant recitation of sacred Vedic hymns. Some of the sages there lived on water and air alone, others on leaves fallen from the trees, while others subsisted on a spare diet of fruits and roots. All of them had mastered their senses and minds and were engaged in asceticism and meditation. The mighty Vishvamitra looked upon this region as if it were the residence of Brahma himself.

Approaching Vasishtha and bowing low before him, Vishvamitra greeted him with praises and prayers. Vasishtha then said to Vishvamitra, "Welcome is your appearance here, O king. Please be seated comfortably and ask of me anything you desire."

The two of them spoke for some time in great delight, partaking of simple forest fare. Vasishtha saw that Vishvamitra was accompanied by a vast army and he said to the king, "I wish to offer full hospitality to you and all your troops. Please accept my desire without any question, O king. I am not satisfied by simply offering you fruits and water."

Vishvamitra was unwilling to take anything from Vasishtha, whom he viewed as his superior. He declined politely, saying, "I am fully honored by your words and audience alone. Indeed your very sight is sufficient. How could I ask anything more? I am satisfied with the fruits you have offered. With your permission, I shall now depart. Please look upon me with love and let me leave taking only your blessings."

But the sage was intent on offering Vishvamitra further hospitality. Vishvamitra tried again and again to dissuade him, but the pious-minded Vasishtha would not be refused. He continuously requested the king to remain there longer. At last, seeing that this would be most pleasing to the sage, Vishvamitra relented and agreed.

Vasishtha felt joy and he stood up and called for his celestial cow, Sabala. "Come, come, my beloved Sabala," he said. "I wish to entertain this king, Vishvamitra, and all his army with a sumptuous feast. Please make every preparation."

Vasishtha's wonderful cow began to produce from her body all kinds of food and drink in enormous quantities—steaming rice heaped high as hills, cooked vegetables of every variety, soups, breads, cakes, pies, pastries, sweetmeats, butter, cream and yogurt—all in silver dishes and plates filled to the brim. Streams of delicious juices flowed and pots filled with ambrosial milk drinks appeared there. Vishvamitra and his entire army were fully satisfied by that splendid array of foodstuffs, every morsel of which tasted like nectar.

The king was astounded to see that it had all been produced from a cow, and he went before Vasishtha, saying, "Your cow is highly amazing, O magnanimous one. I wish to ask from you that she be given to me in exchange for a hundred thousand other cows. As the king I should always be offered the best of everything and I see this cow to be the very best of her species. Therefore kindly give her to me, O sage."

But Vasishtha replied, "I shall never part with Sabala, even in exchange for a thousand million cows. Not even for heaps of gold and silver. Sabala is inseparable from me even as glory is inseparable from a man practicing asceticism."

Vasishtha had no interest in worldly wealth. His life was dedicated to the practice of sacrifice and austerity. All his happiness was derived from within himself. Even if Vishvamitra had offered him the entire world, the sage would not have been interested. But Sabala was dear to him. She had long served the rishi. Assisted by her Vasishtha was able to perform many sacrifices for the good of the world. This was his sacred duty and he had no intention of renouncing it. He continued, "My very life depends upon this cow. For a long time she has sustained me with her milk. Each day she provides me with all the requisites for my sacrificial performances. She has become as dear to me as my own self and I shall not part with her under any circumstances."

Vishvamitra was not used to being refused anything. He was incensed by the sage's insistence on keeping the cow. He did not want to be denied and spoke angrily to Vasishtha. "How is it you are refusing to give this cow to your king? I am a warrior by nature and therefore see strength as the means of achieving my ends. If you will not give me this wonderful creature, then I shall remove her by force."

The king was overwhelmed by pride and anger. Taking hold of Sabala with his exceptionally powerful arms, he began to drag her away, surrounded by his soldiers.

Vasishtha looked sorrowfully upon the scene and said to Vishvamitra, "As the king it is appropriate for you to use such force to achieve your purpose. As a brahmin it also behooves me to exercise forgiveness, for that is my sacred duty in all circumstances. Nor can I ever use force, for gentleness is always prescribed for the brahmins. Therefore, O king, I forgive you."

Although deeply pained to see his cow being dragged away, Vasishtha controlled his feelings. By his own power he was able to prevent her being taken, but he stood by silently, without doing anything. Sabala cried out in distress as the king seized her and she spoke to Vasishtha, "Are you now abandoning me, O lord? What wrong have I done that I am now being removed in this wretched condition by wretched men, even as my master, the all-powerful Vasishtha, looks on?"

Sabala broke loose from the king. She ran to Vasishtha with tears in her eyes and all her exquisitely formed limbs trembling. Looking up at Vasishtha she implored, "Am I now to be forsaken by you, O almighty son of Brahma?"

Vasishtha, his heart tormented with grief, replied to Sabala, "I am not abandoning you, nor have you ever wronged me, O Sabala. Intoxicated with power and depending upon his huge army, this great king, the ruler of the earth, is taking you away. What then can I do, being only a poor brahmin?"

Sabala divined his deeper meaning and answered, "The wise have declared that a brahmin's strength is always superior to that of a warrior. The strength of the sages is spiritual while that of the warriors exists in their arms only. Therefore simply order me to stay and this arrogant king will not succeed in taking me away."

Vasishtha at once said to Sabala, "Stay!"

Immediately the wish-fulfilling cow brought forth from her body a vast army of fierce fighters, equipped with weapons of every kind, who fell upon the army of the king with terrible cries.

Seeing his own army routed by the fighters created by Sabala, Vishvamitra stood his ground and released various kinds of weapons to beat them back. Wave after wave of ferocious looking warriors issued forth from Sabala, some rising up from her roar, some coming out of her udders, while others appeared from her anus. They rushed at the army of the king and in a short time Vishvamitra saw his forces completely defeated and dispersed by the warriors of mystic creation.

Vishvamitra had been accompanied by his one hundred sons. They became furious with Vasishtha and surrounded him. They shot powerful weapons at the sage which sped toward him like blazing comets. Vasishtha, not roused to anger, uttered a powerful Vedic mantra to check the weapons. Simply by the power of Vasishtha's utterance the princes were instantly reduced to ashes. Only one was left standing.

Vishvamitra looked on in complete astonishment. He stood alone, filled with fear and shame. Resembling the furious ocean after it has become becalmed, he became lusterless like the eclipsed sun. He had lost his sons and his army and he felt miserable, his strength and spirit shattered. Ordering his remaining son to take on the earth's administration, he resolved to retire to the forest to practice asceticism in order to increase his power.

After a long period of ascetic practice aimed at pleasing Shiva, the extremely powerful and beneficent god finally appeared and said, "Why are you engaging in such austerities, O king? What do you wish to achieve? I am capable of bestowing boons. Therefore ask from me whatever you may desire."

At that time Vishvamitra had only the knowledge of lesser celestial weapons and did not know how to use the missiles presided over by the principal gods. He fell prostrate before Shiva and offered many prayers, saying, "If you are pleased with me, O lord, then please bestow upon me the knowledge of every divine weapon presided over by all the gods, including the weapons of yourself and Brahma. Tell me the complete science of archery and warfare with all its innermost secrets."

Saying "So be it," Shiva immediately disappeared, and by his mystic power he conferred upon Vishvamitra the knowledge of warfare along with all the mystic weapons. After receiving the weapons, Vishvamitra, who was already full of pride, became even more arrogant. Swelling with power like the ocean on the full moon, he took Vasishtha, the most eminent of all seers, to be dead there and then.

He went at once to the hermitage and began to discharge all his weapons in Vasishtha's direction. The beautiful grove was consumed by the fire of the missiles and the sages rushed about in all directions, tormented and alarmed by the attack.

Vasishtha saw the sages, as well as the beasts and birds, fleeing by the thousands, afflicted by Vishvamitra's weapons. He called out, "Do not fear!

I shall now put an end to Vishvamitra's display of might, even as the sun dispels a morning mist."

Vasishtha was enraged. He went before Vishvamitra, shouting, "Here I am, O wicked fellow. Show me, then, the limits of your strength!"

Vishvamitra aimed at Vasishtha the missile presided over by the fire-god, and it went toward him glowing like the sun.

Smiling even as the weapon raced toward him, Vasishtha called out to Vishvamitra. "What use is your martial power, O unworthy disgrace of your race? See today the power of the brahmins!"

Vasishtha was standing with only his staff. He held it up and the fire weapon was immediately absorbed into it. Vishvamitra then let go each of the divine weapons one after another, including those presided over by Vayu, Varuna, Indra, Yamaraja, Brahma, the immortal Shiva, Dharma the god of virtue, and even Vishnu, the supreme controller. All of them were drawn into Vasishtha's staff and entirely neutralized.

As he stood there blazing in his own glory, Vasishtha looked like the smokeless fire of universal destruction. Imbued with the force of the divine weapons, he shot forth tongues of flame from all his pores. Hosts of gods and celestial rishis assembled in the canopy of the sky and, being fearful, spoke to Vasishtha, "Today you have humbled the mighty Vishvamitra. Your power is infallible, O most noble soul. Extinguish the fire blazing from your body and save the world."

When he heard the heavenly voices, Vasishtha regained his calm and stood silently with his mind controlled. Freed from anger, he told Vishvamitra, "You may leave in peace. Do not act again in such a foolish way."

Vishvamitra, dejected, heaved a deep sigh. He considered his strength useless and said, "Weak indeed are my weapons when used against a brahmin. Where is my pride now? The might of a warrior's arms are nothing in comparison to brahminical powers. I shall therefore return to the forest and perform severe penance until I attain the status of a brahmin."

Vishvamitra went again to the forest, having made enemies with a highly exalted soul. Meanwhile, Vasishtha recreated his hermitage by his mystic powers and began again the performance of his religious duties, meant only for the benefit of mankind.

Vishvamitra practiced extremely difficult austerities. He lived only on fruits and roots and sat in meditation, perfectly controlling his mind by fixing it upon the Supreme and not indulging in any thoughts of sensual enjoyment. During the cold winters he would remain submerged in water up to his neck. In the blazing heat of the summer he sat surrounded by sacrificial fires on four sides. Once, for a very long period of time, he stood upon one leg with his arms upraised. A thousand years passed by as Vishvamitra practiced his asceticism.

While Vishvamitra remained in the forest, Vasishtha had become the royal priest in Ayodhya. A king named Trishanku, a distant ancestor of Dasarath, appeared in the line of emperors who ruled from Ayodhya. King Trishanku desired to attain the heavens in his own bodily form and he asked Vasishtha to perform a sacrifice for that purpose. Vasishtha replied, "O king, no man can attain heaven other than at the end of his life after the performance of piety and religion. This is the universal rule established by God. Therefore I shall not perform any sacrifice with the aim of placing you in heaven in your present body. You should give up this sinful desire."

Trishanku, however, was set upon his aim and did not care for Vasishtha's good advice. He decided to seek out Vishvamitra, knowing him to possess great powers as a result of his long practice of asceticism. He considered that Vishvamitra, being a king who had preceded him in his own line, might be more amenable to his desire. Trishanku also intelligently considered the animosity of Vishvamitra toward Vasishtha, feeling that this would provide a further impetus to Vishvamitra to perform the sacrifice refused by Vasishtha.

After reaching the forest and finding Vishvamitra, the king requested him to perform the sacrifice. Vishvamitra, hearing that Vasishtha had refused and remembering his enmity with the great mystic, agreed.

Vishvamitra then began a sacrifice, carefully following the procedures laid down in the Vedas. He sat before a blazing fire and uttered prayers to all the gods headed by Vishnu, pouring offerings of ghee into the flames. At the proper moment he said, "Witness now my ascetic powers! By my command this king shall rise to heaven, even in this body of flesh and bones. O Trishanku, by virtue of the merits of my austerities, ascend now to heaven where you shall attain the state of the gods!"

As soon as Vishvamitra said this, Trishanku rose up to the skies, but as he approached heaven, Indra checked him. Indra said in a voice booming like thunder, "O king, how are you trying now to enter heaven? You have earned no place here through religion or piety. Indeed, your own preceptor Vasishtha has refused your illegal desire for heaven. O foolish man, fall headlong back to earth!"

Trishanku began to drop swiftly toward the earth and he cried out to Vishvamitra, "Save me!"

Vishvamitra, seeing Trishanku falling back down, called out, "Stop!"

Immediately the king's downward progress was halted and he remained situated in the sky. Seated amid many rishis the great sage Vishvamitra became overwhelmed with anger at seeing Indra's refusal to allow Trishanku into heaven. He said, "Since this jealous god will not let the king attain the heavenly regions, I shall now create a second heaven by dint of my mystic power. Trishanku shall then live there in peace."

Like another Brahma, Vishvamitra evolved from his mind a galaxy consisting of twenty-seven lunar mansions which appeared in the sky. The sage then set about creating another hierarchy of gods to inhabit those heavenly planets. Observing this disturbance to the universal situation, Indra and the gods became alarmed and approached Vishvamitra, saying, "This king does not deserve a place in heaven, O blessed sage. Rejected by his own guru, he now stands divested of all his pious merits."

Vishvamitra replied, "As I have pledged my word to this king, how shall I make it false? A promise of heaven has been given by me. Therefore please let this king enjoy heavenly bliss and let the lunar mansions I created remain in existence."

Indra, out of respect for the great Vishvamitra's request, replied, "It shall be so. Your planets will endure in the heavens in the southern quarter beyond the celestial sphere. Trishanku shall remain in their midst, as happy as a god and shining brightly. All those stars shall circumambulate him, even as all the planets circle the pole star. May you be blessed."

Vishvamitra became pleased, but after ending the sacrifice he considered, "Driven by my anger toward Vasishtha, I have now placed the impious Trishanku in the heavens here in the southern quarter. He will certainly exert a malefic influence upon this region. I shall now therefore move to some other place."

Vishvamitra realized he had considerably diminished his ascetic merits, expending them on the task of raising Trishanku to heaven. Still strongly desiring to attain the full status of a brahmin sage, he continued to perform severe penances, gradually building his stock of pious credits and increasing his power. Indra became concerned, believing that Vishvamitra may soon attain enough power to overthrow him from his post in heaven. The king of the gods desired to impede the sage's penance and he sent the Apsara Menaka to where Vishvamitra sat in meditation.

Menaka entered a lake near to the sage and began to bathe. Hearing her anklets tinkling, and fully opening his half-closed eyes, Vishvamitra saw the heavenly damsel, with her translucent clothes wet and clinging to her divinely formed body. Struck with passion the sage said, "You are most welcome, O celestial lady. Indeed, please dwell here in my hermitage. Heavenly Apsaras are not bound by earthly morality, so I will incur no sin by enjoying with you."

Menaka took up her residence in the sage's abode and they sported together in the beautiful grassy glades in that region. One hundred years passed as if it were only a day. Eventually realizing that he had again been diverted from his purpose, Vishvamitra felt shame and he remonstrated himself, "Alas, I have been overcome by the ignorance born of lust. My mind has been completely bewildered by the beauty of this maiden. Surely this is the work of the gods."

Menaka stood before him trembling. She feared his terrible curse, but Vishvamitra dismissed her with kind and gentle words. Resolving then upon lifelong celibacy, the sage went to the bank of the Kaushiki River, his own sister, and continued his asceticism.

The sage practiced the most rigid austerities, eating only air. A thousand years passed by and he began to emit a blazing fire from his body, born from the power of his asceticism.

Again Indra became alarmed. He approached another Apsara named Rambha and asked her to divert the sage from his austerity. She duly went to where he was sitting and began to dance alluringly before his gaze. However, Vishvamitra did not allow his mind to give way to lust. Becoming angry with her he uttered a curse: "O nymph, since you have maliciously attempted to prevent my penance, you shall remain at this spot as a stone for one thousand years. You may then return to heaven."

The sage realized that he had again diminished his piety, this time by becoming angry. He determined that he would never again give way to anger, nor even speak at all, and he resumed his austerities in that beautiful Himalayan region, suspending even his breathing as well as taking neither food nor water.

Finally, after another thousand years had elapsed, the gods went to Brahma and, seized with anxiety, implored him, "Be pleased to grant this Vishvamitra his desire. By his powerful penance we see the entire energy of the universe becoming disturbed. The earth is quaking with her mountains riven and her seas roaring in great turbulence. Violent winds are blowing and the four quarters are enveloped in darkness. If Vishvamitra does not cease his practice of penance, then universal destruction will surely ensue!"

At this Brahma went before Vishvamitra and said to him in a gentle voice, "O highly blessed sage, you have attained your desire. You now stand equal to Vasishtha as a brahmin rishi. All the Vedic knowledge will become manifest in your pure heart. Stop your austerities."

Requested by Brahma, the sage Vasishtha also came there and befriended Vishvamitra, saying, "You have surpassed all with your tremendous asceticism and have become a worthy brahmin. No anger toward you exists in my heart. Be blessed, O great rishi!"

Falling prostrate before Vasishtha, Vishvamitra sought his forgiveness and, forming a firm friendship with that son of Brahma, left that place with his purpose fulfilled.

APPENDIX THREE

THE BIRTH AND HISTORY OF HANUMAN

As told to Rama by Agastya Rishi

There lived on Mount Sumeru a powerful Vanara leader named Keshari. His wife, Anjana, was beautiful beyond compare. One day Vayu, the wind god, saw her standing alone and he desired union with her. After uniting with her in his mystical yoga form, she con-ceived a child who was named Hanuman. He cried out in hunger and Anjana placed him down amid some reeds while she went to collect forest fruits. Hanuman looked up from where he lay and saw the sun. Thinking it to be a large fruit he sprang upwards with outstretched hands. Gifted with the power of his divine father, he soared through the heavens toward the sun. Vayu went with him, covering him with a cool breeze so that he would not be burned by the sun. The sun-god also withheld his blazing rays as he understood that Hanuman was a great servant of Vishnu who would later assist him on earth.

As Hanuman went swiftly upwards through the skies, a demon named Rahu was also approaching the sun with a view to envelop him. It was the day ordained for that demon to swallow the fiery sun-god, thus creating an eclipse, but Hanuman saw him and pushed him aside. Afraid of the mighty Vanara, Rahu sped away toward Indra's abode in the heavens. Going before the deity he said, "O king of the gods, having allotted to me the sun and moon as my regular food, how is it that you have now given over my share to another? See how another Rahu has appeared in the sky, intent on con-suming the sun."

Indra immediately left his seat and, mounting his celestial elephant, Airavata, he rose up into the heavens. He approached Hanuman, who was streaking through the sky like a blazing meteor. When the Vanara saw the effulgent god nearby, he considered him to be another fruit and he turned toward him. Indra then released his thunderbolt, which struck Hanuman and caused him to drop back down to earth.

The Vanara fell onto a mountain top and lay there apparently dead. Seeing this Vayu became angry and he caused all creatures to begin to suffocate. Interrupting the flow of the vital life airs in all beings, Vayu created a great disturbance in the universe.

Indra and all the other gods quickly approached Vayu, who stood by the fallen Hanuman, and prayed to him to desist from causing so much suffering. Brahma also appeared there and asked Vayu what was the cause of his actions. Vayu replied, "It is on account of my son being slain. See now how that innocent child lays here motionless, struck down by Indra's terrible thunderbolt."

Brahma then reached out and ran his hand over Hanuman. The Vanara immediately sat up and looked around. The relieved Vayu again began to move in the bodies of living creatures, and Brahma said, "Listen, O gods, as I tell you about this Vanara. He will accomplish your purpose on earth and become a famous servant of Vishnu. You should therefore all grant him boons."

Pleased to hear Brahma's words, Indra took off his garland and placed it around Hanuman's neck, saying, "From this day on he shall be invulnerable to my thunderbolt."

The sun-god then said, "I shall bestow upon him a hundredth part of my brilliance. Also, when he begins to study the scriptures I shall enable him to quickly learn all aspects of knowledge. None shall exceed him in scriptural understanding."

Yamaraja granted him invulnerability to his rod and freedom from ailment. Kuvera also blessed him that he would remain unwearied in battle. Shiva said, "He shall be immune to my weapons and from death at my hands." Vishvakarma added, "This Vanara shall be invulnerable to all celestial weapons forged by me and he shall be long-lived."

Finally, Brahma said, "O wind-god, your son shall be invincible in battle. He will prove the terror of his foes and the shelter of his friends. This jewel among monkeys shall be able to change his form at will and go wherever he pleases at any speed he likes. No brahmin's curse will be able to kill him. His movements shall be unimpeded and he will become glorious. In war he will accomplish tremendous feats which make one's hair stand on end, thus causing the destruction of Ravana and the pleasure of Rama."

After this the gods departed and Vayu took Hanuman back to his mother. He began to grow up like a god. Overflowing with the exultation of his own power, and being possessed of the mischievous nature of monkeys, he started creating trouble for the rishis in the forest, knowing that they could not harm him. He would playfully throw about and break their sacrifical ladles and vessels, and tear to shreds the piles of soft bark they kept for making garments. Despite the efforts of his mother and father to check him, Hanuman continued with his pranks and went on harassing the ascetics.

Eventually the rishis, not wanting to harm the playful young Vanara, found a way to stop him. Touching sacred water, their leader uttered an imprecation. "As this one makes trouble for us depending upon his celestial strength, he shall forget his own power. Only when someone reminds him again by reciting his glories will he recall his strength."

Bewildered by that curse, Hanuman forgot about his might and began acting like an ordinary Vanara. He formed a strong friendship with Sugriva, going with him into exile when he was banished by Vali. He finally again remembered his power when Jambavan reminded him at the time of searching for Sita.

THE BENEFITS OF READING RAMAYANA

He who listens every day to this oldest epic, composed by the sage Valmiki, which is calculated to bestow religious merit, renown and longevity, and which lends support to the Vedas, is completely freed of sin. Kings will overcome their enemies and conquer the earth, men will overcome all difficulties and women will be blessed with excellent sons and grandsons. Those listening to this epic will receive from Sri Rama all the boons they desire. Through a hearing of this work all the gods are satisfied. One who keeps a copy in his house will find all his obstacles coming to an end. A man offering worship to and reading this historical work is completely rid of all sins and attains a long life; all the gods are thus pleased and one's ancestors are gratified forever. Those transcribing this work with devotion are guaranteed residence in heaven, while those hearing it will secure the growth of their family and wealth, supreme happiness and the accomplishment of all their objects on earth.

Yuddha Kanda

The gods, Gandharvas, Siddhas and rishis always listen with great pleasure to the Ramayana in heaven. This legend is the bestower of longevity, the enhancer of fortune and the dispeller of sins. It is the equal of the Vedas. A man reading even a quarter of it is freed from all sins; indeed, even if one sins daily he is released from the reactions if he recites just one verse of the Ramayana. A man gets the results of one thousand Ashvamedha sacrifices and ten thousand Vajpeya sacrifices merely by hearing this great work. He has visited all the holy shrines and bathed in all the sacred rivers. One who listens to the story of Sri Rama with full reverence roots out all sins and goes to the world of Vishnu. The Ramayana is the unsurpassed form of Gayatri. By hearing it with devotion one will undoubtedly achieve liberation, along with many generations of ancestors. The exploits of Sri Rama are the bestower of all four of life's objects—dharma, artha, kama and

moksha. Hearing even one line of this work with full devotion guarantees
one's attainment of the world of Brahma.

Uttara Kanda

GLOSSARY

Aditya Hridaya: Hymns in praise of the sun recited by Agastya Rishi to Rama just prior to the killing of Ravana.

Agastya: A powerful rishi who is a son of the god Varuna. said to have once swallowed the entire ocean and to have overpowered the terrible demons Ilvala and Vatapi. Rama recited many stories about this rishi to Lakshmana and Sita when they were in the forest.

Agni: The god of fire, thus also the Sanskrit word for fire.

Apsara: Celestial nymph. "One who, upon embracing a man, drives him insane." The beauty of the Apsaras is legendary and has made many great rishis fall down from their ascetic practice.

Arghya: A milk-based drink used as a respectful offering made to a guest.

Ashoka: A tree bearing beautiful red flowers. Sita was held in a grove of ashoka trees by Ravana.

Astra: A divine weapon, usually prefixed by the name of the particular god or force which presides over it; e.g. Brahmastra, a weapon presided over by Lord Brahma.

Asura: Class of celestial demons.

Brahma: The first of all the gods and the creator of the universe. He was directly manifested from Vishnu and is thus sometimes called "the unborn."

Brihaspati: The preceptor of the gods.

Chamara: Whisk made from yak-tail hairs and used for highly respectable persons.

Charana: A class of demigod noted for their poetic abilities.

Daitya: A class of powerful demonic beings.

Dandaka: The forest where Rama lived during his exile.

Danava: A class of powerful celestial demons and enemies of the gods.

Dhatri: Nurse.

Gandharva: A class of demigods noted for their martial and musical abilities.

Indra: King of the gods, also known as Purandara and Shakra.

Kinnara: A class of demigod, often having a half-human and half-animal form such as that of a centaur, and generally seen holding a lute.

Kusha: Darbha grass, considered sacred by the Vedas.

Kuvera: The god of wealth, who guards the northern quarter of the universe.

Lokapalas: Gods presiding over the four quarters of the universe.

Maya Danava: A celestial demon who possesses great skills at architecture and building.

Naga: A celestial serpent, often appearing in human form.

Narada: A celestial sage also known as Devarshi, or the rishi among the gods. He is famous as a devotee of Vishnu and frequently assists him in his pastimes on earth. The Vedas contain innumerable references to Narada's activities and teachings.

Nishadha: Tribal people living in the forest.

Parasurama: A rishi said to be an empowered incarnation of Vishnu. He is famous for having annihilated all the warrior kings of the world after his father, Jamadagni, had been killed by a king named Kartavirya.

Raghava: A name for Rama, meaning the descendant of Raghu, a great king in Rama's line.

Rahu: A powerful demon appearing as a planet. Said to be responsible for eclipses.

Rakshasa: Celestial demon, antagonistic to humankind.

Rama: The seventh of the *Dasavatara* incarnations of Vishnu, who appeared as a king in the solar dynasty (i.e. descending from the sun-god).

Ravana: A powerful leader of the Rakshasa race. His birth is described in Ramayana as follows:

Long ago on the slopes of Mount Meru there lived a sage named Pulastya, who was a mind-born son of Brahma. He was constantly engaged in the practice of severe asceticism. Many celestial maidens would come to sport in the beautiful region where he dwelt, and they would often disturb his meditations. Finally becoming impatient with them, he said, "If any maiden should again be seen by me, she will immediately become pregnant."

The maidens then carefully avoided Pulastya's ashrama. However, there was one girl, a daughter of another sage named Trinabindu, who had not heard about the curse. She ventured into the region where Pulastya sat and as soon as he saw her she found indications of pregnancy in her body. Astonished and fearful, she ran to her father and said, "Father, I cannot understand why I am suddenly appearing as if pregnant. No contact with any male has ever been had by me."

Trinabindu sat in meditation and by his mystic power he understood what had happened. He then went with his daughter to Pulastya and said to him, "O venerable sage, kindly accept my daughter as your wife. By your power she now carries a child. Please therefore take her hand in marriage. She will surely render you very pleasing service."

Pulastya agreed and he said to the girl, "O gentle one, you will give birth to a highly qualified son who shall be known as Visrava."

Like his father, Visrava became an ascetic and engaged himself in much penance and study of scripture. In due course he married a daughter of Bharadvaja and through her begot a son named Vaishravana, who by the grace of his father became the powerful Kuvera, the god of wealth.

At that time a great battle took place between the gods and the Rakshasas, who were finally put to flight by Vishnu. They sought shelter in the nether worlds, although one of them, Sumali, began to live on earth. As he wandered about he saw one day Kuvera flying overhead in the celestial Pushpaka chariot. The Rakshasa was astonished to see Kuvera's opulence. Knowing that the god was Visrava's son, and desiring to do good to the Rakshasas, he said to his young daughter Kaikasi, "It is high time you were wed, dear girl. Go quickly to Visrava's ashrama and ask that he accept you. That powerful sage will give you sons equal to the lord of riches; there is no doubt at all."

In obedience to her father, Kaikasi went to where Visrava was seated in meditation. She stood bashfully before him with folded palms, looking downward and scratching the earth with her toe. Seeing that girl, whose face resembled the full moon and who shone with a celestial beauty, the sage said, "Who are you and why are you here? Tell me the truth, O beautiful one"

The girl replied, "O sage, you should divine my purpose by your own mystic power, for I am too shy to tell you."

The sage meditated for some minutes and read her mind. He then said, "I have understood your purpose, O gentle one. You desire sons by me. Surely I am attracted to you and will accept your hand, but you have approached me at an inauspicious time. You will therefore have sons who will be cruel-minded, fierce-looking and given to evil deeds. O lady of shapely limbs, you will bring forth Rakshasas fond of drinking blood."

Kaikasi was upset. "O lordly sage, I do not desire such offspring. Kindly be merciful to me."

Feeling compassion, Visrava replied, "It cannot be any other way, dear girl, but I can bless you as follows. Although you will have such sons, your last son will be different. He will be virtuous and fully in accord with my family."

In due course Kaikasi gave birth to a hideous child with the form of a Rakshasa. He had ten heads, twenty hands, and was the color of coal. When he was born many inauspicious omens were seen. Vixens emitted flames from their mouths, blood fell from the sky, meteors dropped down and clouds thundered fiercely. The earth rocked with its load of mountains and the sea roared and sent up huge waves. Visrava named the child Dasagriva and he grew up frearful and cruel.

Next Kaikasi gave birth to Kumbhakarna, then Surpanakha, and finally Vibhishana. When this last son was born, flowers fell from the sky and the gods in heaven were heard to utter, "Good! Excellent!"

Some time after their birth Kuvera came on the Pushpaka to see his father. Seeing him blazing with glory and opulence, Kaikasi said to Dasagriva, "Son, you look here at your brother Vaisravana. Look at your self in comparison, so poor and lacking in power. Exert yourself so that you are the equal of your brother in every way."

Spurred on by his mother's words, Dasagriva said, "I swear to you that I shall rise equal to Vaisravana and even excel him in power. Do not grieve."

In a mood of envy for his brother and greed for power, Dasagriva engaged himself in severe austerities for a very long time. In the end he won his famous boons from Brahma, being blessed that he could not be slain by any creature other than a man or lesser animal, for whom he had no regard whatsoever.

Along with Dasagriva, both Kumbhakarna and Vibhishana also engaged themselves in asceticism. When Brahma appeared before them, Vibhishana asked for the boon that his mind would always remain fixed in righteousness, even when he was in the greatest difficulty. Brahma granted his request and then turned toward Kumbhakarna to accord him a boon.

At that time the gods became greatly fearful and they approached Brahma, saying, "O lord, no boon at all should be granted by you to this one. He has already wrought havoc in the heavens, devouring seven Apsaras, ten attendants of the mighty Indra, as well as numerous seers and human beings. What will he do if made powerful by a boon from yourself? On the pretext of granting a boon you should instead place him under a spell of delusion, thereby saving all the worlds from him."

Brahma smiled and said, "Be it so." He thought of the goddess of learning, Sarasvati, and when she appeared before him he said to her, "O goddess, become the speech in Kumbhakarna's mouth."

The goddess agreed and Brahma then asked Kumbhakarna, "What boon do you desire, O Rakshasa?"

Kumbhakarna, weary from his austerities, replied, "Let me sleep for many years."

"It shall be so. You will sleep for six months at a time and remain awake for one day."

Having made his reply, Brahma vanished along with all the gods.

After receiving his boon, Dasagriva, who became known as Ravana, considered himself invincible. He went to Lanka, where Kuvera lived, and challenged his brother. On the advice of Visrava, Kuvera left the city and it was taken over by Ravana and his hordes of Rakshasa followers.

Rishi: A spiritually advanced brahmin, usually inhabiting higher regions of the universe.

Rudra: A name for Lord Shiva.

Sagara: A king of the solar race who was Rama's ancestor. The ocean is also called "sagara" as it was the sons of this king who first excavated it.

Shabda: Literally "sound"—but generally used to refer to Vedic recitations; thus the "shabda-astra" has the power to destroy illusions.

Shiva: A partial expansion of Lord Vishnu who acts as the universal destroyer at the end of a cycle of ages.

Siddha: Literally, a perfected being. These are a class of gods possessed of great mystic powers.

Sita: The daughter of King Janaka who became Rama's wife. How she was born on earth is described in a Vedic literature known as the Devi Bhagavata as follows:

There was once a great rishi called Kushadvaja who had a daughter named Vedavati, who was said to be an incarnation of the goddess Lakshmi. Kushadvaja was petitioned by various celestials and demons for his daughter's hand, but she had set her mind on getting Vishnu as her husband.

One day a demon named Shambhu asked for Vedavati's hand in marriage, but he was refused. Becoming furious, he attacked and killed Kushadvaja. When Vedavati saw this she looked in anger at the demon and he was immediately burnt to ashes. She then went to the forest and began to meditate in order to propitiate Vishnu and get him as her husband. It was at that time that Ravana came there and insulted her, as described in the prologue of this book.

After she immolated her body, it is said that Ravana took her ashes with him back to Lanka. He kept them in a gold box in his palace. However, soon after this he saw many inauspicious omens in Lanka. The rishi Narada, on a visit to Lanka, informed Ravana that the cause of the ill omens was the presence of Vedavati's ashes. The demon then had them thrown into the ocean.

The box containing the ashes was carried by the ocean and deposited on the seashore near Mithila. It went into the earth and it was at that place that Janaka performed a sacrifice for getting a child. A part of his sacrifice was the furrowing of the earth and he thus found the box. Lakshmi had entered the ashes, and when Janaka unearthed the box he found a golden child inside. This child was named Sita.

Valmiki: The Ramayana's original author. The story of how he first came to compose the work is told in the Ramayana itself as follows:

One day Valmiki was visited in his ashrama by the celestial seer Narada. Valmiki asked him who was the most virtuous person in the world. Wanting to know if there was a perfect person anywhere, he asked, "Who is possessed of all power and knows what is right? Who is always truthful, firm of resolve and conscious of all services rendered? Who has subdued his self, conquered anger, is above fault-finding and, although being friendly to all beings, is nevertheless feared by even the gods when angry? O eminent sage, I have a great curiosity to know this and you are surely capable of telling me."

Actually, by his own spiritual practices and meditations Valmiki had been able to realise that the Supreme Lord, Vishnu, had appeared on the earth in a human form. He wanted Narada, whom he saw as a spiritual master, to tell him about the Lord's incarnation.

Narada replied, "There is one descended in the line of Iksvaku and known by men as Rama. He is powerful, radiant, resolute and has brought his senses under control. Intelligent, sagacious, eloquent, glorious and an exterminator of foes, he knows the secret of virtue, is true to his promise and is intent on the good of the people."

Narada went on at length describing Rama's many qualities. He then narrated in brief the whole story of Rama's pastimes. When he had finished he said, "This Rama is now ruling in Ayodhya. Indeed, you have already met him when he came to your ashrama. The remaining part of his pastimes are yet to be manifested. O sage, all this will soon be described by yourself. This sacred story of Rama, known as the Ramayana, should be heard by all men. It is on a par with the Vedas and capable of destroying all sins. Hearing or reading this narrative a man will, on departing from this world, be honored in heaven along with his sons, grandsons, followers and attendants."

Narada rose to leave and was worshipped by Valmiki. As the celestial seer rose into the sky by his mystic power, Valmiki stood thinking about Rama. He had already sensed his divinity when he met him some years back. Narada had confirmed his intuition. Feeling thrilled with transcendental ecstasy, Valmiki made his way toward the nearby river to take his midday bath, followed by his disciples.

As he went toward the riverbank, the rishi surveyed the beautiful forest scenery. He saw playing among the reeds by the river a pair of cranes. Those two birds were engaged in mating and they sported together making a delightful sound.

Suddenly, as Valmiki looked on, a Nishada huntsman fired an arrow and struck one of the birds. Mortally wounded and covered in blood, it thrashed about on the ground screaming in pain. Its mate also cried piteously and fell about in sorrow.

Seeing this, the soft-hearted Valmiki felt compassion. He saw the Nishada approaching with bow in hand. In grief, he said to that hunter, "As you have slain this poor bird while it was absorbed in pleasure, may you have no peace of mind for the rest of your life."

The curse came out in perfectly metered poetry. Astonished by this, Valmiki said, "What have I uttered? Tormented by grief I have composed a stanza filled with that emotion."

The sage, brooding over the incident, entered the river and took his bath. After coming out he went back to his hermitage still thinking on the rhyming couplet he had spoken to the hunter. When he reached his ashrama he took his seat and was about to commence his lessons to his disciples when Brahma suddenly appeared there. Seeing the great creator of the universe approaching on his swan carrier, Valmiki hastily rose and joined his palms in humility. He offered his prostrate obeisances and worshipped the deity with many prayers. Brahma then sat down on an exalted seat quickly brought for him by Valmiki's students.

Even though Brahma was present before him, Valmiki could not stop thinking about the incident with the hunter. He again recited the verse he had composed. Feeling sorry that he had lost control of himself, he appeared dejected and sighed.

Brahma laughed and said, "Let this poetic utterance of yours become the source of your glory. Do not brood any more, O sage. It was by my arrangement that this speech flowed from your lips. In that same meter you should now describe the pastimes on earth of the all-wise Rama. Tell the story of that hero as you have heard it from Narada. By my mercy you will be able to see every detail of that story, as clearly as a fruit held in the palm of your hand. Therefore, render this sacred and soul-ravishing tale into verse for the good of the world."

Brahma blessed the sage that his narrative would remain extant for as long as the mountains stood on the face of the earth. He also told him that he would be able to continue living anywhere he chose within the universe for the same length of time.

Having finished speaking, Brahma disappeared. Valmiki was filled with wonder. He and his disciples gazed in amazement at Brahma's seat for some time. Gradually regaining their presence of mind, the sage's students began reciting the verse he had uttered to the hunter. They were overjoyed at the honor bestowed upon Valmiki by Brahma. The sage then began to meditate on Rama's pastimes, gradually composing the Ramayana over the coming days.

Vanara: A type of celestial monkey.

Varuna: God of the waters and the nether worlds. He is one of the universal guardians. His famous weapon is the noose.

Vedas: Ancient Sanskrit scriptures.

Vidhyadhara: A class of demigod.

Vishnu: The Supreme Personality of Godhead.

Yaksha: A class of gods who are servants of Kuvera.

Yamaraja: The god who presides over death and destiny. He is empowered by Vishnu to award all beings the results of their actions. He guards over the southern quarter of the universe.

AUTHOR'S NOTE

My main aim in presenting the Ramayana was to share the book with others, having myself found it so uplifting and enjoyable. I am not a Sanskrit scholar and have worked from existing translations, simply trying to present the book in a way which is easy to read and understand. It is possible that students of the work will find the odd detail which is different from what they have read in other versions. There are in fact numerous versions of the original now extant and they all differ a little in some details here and there. But the main substance of the story is common to all of them.

I have not referred to Tulsidas's famous version, the Rama Carita Manasa as I did not want to confuse Valmiki's original telling of the story with later interpretations. I have included a few details from another Vedic literature known as the Adhyatma Ramayana, a text spoken by Lord Shiva to his wife Parvati. In that text, from the Brahmanda Purana, Shiva has elucidated some of the spiritual understandings of Valmiki's original work.

The book is written in the "omniscient narrator" style because this is how it was originally composed. The original text of the Ramayana itself explains how Valmiki was able to compose the work. He was personally visited by Lord Brahma, the creator of this universe, who told the sage that he should write Rama's history. Brahma promised Valmiki that by divine arrangement he would be able to understand everything about this history. Brahma said, "Whatever account there is of the all-wise Rama, as well as of Lakshmana and Sita, and indeed of all the Rakshasas and monkeys and any others, will all be known to you even if presently unknown."

Valmiki thus sat in meditation and composed the Ramayana, consisting of twenty-four thousand Sanskrit verses. These original verses have been more or less preserved up until the present day, although as I note above, one will find the odd variation in some minor details.

I pray I may not have given offense to any lovers of this work by my attempt to render it accessible to a modern reader. I have tried to remain as faithful as possible to the original, without adding any interpretations or interpolations of my own. I hope I may have succeeded in giving a little happiness to my readers, although the credit actually lies with Valmiki Muni, to whom I offer my most profound and humble respects.

Book Order Form

☎ Telephone orders: Call 1-888-TORCHLT (1-888-867-2458).
 Have your VISA, American Express, or MasterCard ready.
✳ Fax orders: 559-337-2354
✉ Postal orders: Torchlight Publishing, P. O. Box 52, Badger, CA 93641

▲ World Wide Web: www.torchlight.com

Please send the following:	Quantity	Amount

○ *Bhagavad-gita As It Is*
  Deluxe (1,068 pages) — $24.95   x_____ = $_____
  Standard (924 pages) — $12.95   x_____ = $_____
○ *Ramayana*
  Hardbound — $22.95   x_____ = $_____
○ *Mahabharata*
  Hardbound — $29.95   x_____ = $_____
  Shipping/handling (see below)................................. $_____
  Sales tax 7.25% (California only)........................ $_____
                                    TOTAL $_____

○ I understand that I may return any books for a full refund—no questions asked.

○ **Please send me your catalog and info on other books by Torchlight Publishing.**

Company_____
Name_____
Address_____
City _____ State_____ Zip_____

Payment:

○ Check / money order enclosed ○ VISA ○ MasterCard ○ American Express

Card number_____
Name on card_____ Exp. date_____
Signature_____

Shipping and handling: USA: $4.00 for first book and $3.00 for each additional book. Air mail per book (USA only)—$7.00. **CANADA:** $6.00 for first book and $3.50 for each additional book. (NOTE: Surface shippimg may take 3–4 weeks in North America.) **FOREIGN COUNTRIES:** $8.00 for first book and $5.00 for each additional book. Please allow 6–8 weeks for delivery.